M000117500

Organizational Behavior

People and Processes
in Management

The Irwin Series in Management and The Behavioral Sciences

L. L. Cummings and E. Kirby Warren *Consulting Editors*
John F. Mee *Advisory Editor*

Organizational Behavior

People and Processes in Management

Randall B. Dunham
University of Wisconsin–Madison

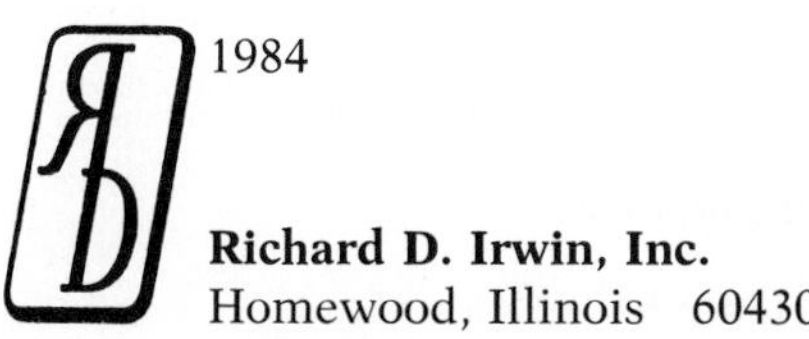

1984

Richard D. Irwin, Inc.
Homewood, Illinois 60430

ISBN 0-256-02627-0

Library of Congress Catalog Card No. 83–82966

Printed in the United States of America

1 2 3 4 5 6 7 8 9 0 V 1 0 9 8 7 6 5 4

Dedicated with Love to
my Children

Gregory James Dunham
and
Elizabeth Jean Dunham

Preface

I first began teaching organizational behavior (OB) at the University of Wisconsin–Madison in 1975. Since that time, over 4,000 students have enrolled in my OB classes. For the most part, these students have been very willing to share their reactions to the content of the course, and we have learned together. As a result, I understand organizational behavior more fully but realize that there is still much to learn. In this book I try to acknowledge the current limits of what OB has to offer and provide honest evaluations of the strengths and weaknesses of the issues covered. In writing this book, I am sharing with you a lot of me and a little of each of those 4,000 students.

Through interaction with my students, I have come to believe that a text that is conversational in nature has the best chance of communicating effectively. This book follows that belief. For you to gain from our conversation, the book must be much more than technically accurate and up to date. The content must also be relevant, concise, understandable, challenging, and enjoyable. The book must make clear *why* each issue is important and focus not only on the theoretical value of knowledge but the applied value as well. Although I am a firm believer in the value of basic knowledge, this book concentrates on knowledge that has clear and direct applications in organizations. I do not mean to imply that this book will tell you exactly what to do in any one particular organizational situation. You still must think, evaluate, and make your own decisions. However, application of this knowledge is possible and realistic if you are willing to work at it.

The material in this book is intended for anyone involved with organizations. Of the 4,000 students mentioned earlier, about half have been business majors in accounting, finance, management, marketing, and so forth. The rest have come from many different fields, including communication arts, economics, engineering, family resources, industrial relations, nursing, psychology, social work, and sociology. What these people all have in common is that they are now participating in, and will continue to participate in, organizations. The behaviors and attitudes of organizational members are influenced by a wide variety of factors—many of which are addressed in this book. It is my immediate goal to make your introduction to this material enjoyable and to get you excited about learning. My long-term goal is to have you *use* this material in your present and future organizations. I am excited about the field of organizational behavior and hope to share this with you through this book.

Throughout the book you will see materials and ideas provided by some of my previous students. If you have ideas for improvement, let me hear from you. When appropriate, this book will be revised and I would be happy to have your help in making it better. If you write, try to be as specific as possible about what you like or do not like. It would be interesting to know if you consider this the best or worst textbook you have ever seen, but it would be *useful* to know *why* you feel this way and to have your specific suggestions for change. Write to me through the publisher.

ACKNOWLEDGMENTS

Although I am the sole author of this book, its production involved many significant contributions from other people. To each of you, I extend my thanks.

My wife, Susanne, was extremely patient during the lengthy process of developing the book. Her support was tremendous.

Several colleagues from other institutions patiently and thoroughly reviewed earlier versions of the manuscript. Their comments were extremely helpful and provided much-needed guidance. In alphabetical order, these contributors were: Terry Cobb of Virginia Polytechnic Institute and State University, Chester C. Cotton of California State University, William Crampon of Sangamon State University, Howard Garland of the University of Texas–Arlington, David Greenberger of The Ohio State University, James McElroy of Iowa State University, and Ray Montagno of Ball State University.

E. Kirby Warren of Columbia University and L. L. Cummings of Northwestern University, Consulting Editors for the Management Series at Richard D. Irwin, Inc., provided valuable ongoing comments during the development of the manuscript. Larry's role dates back to the conception of the idea for creating this book. His thoughts and suggestions were many and greatly influenced the structure of what you see on these pages. Thank you, my friend, for the scholarly and social interactions of the past. I hope they continue well into the future.

Each chapter of this book contains one or more original interviews with scholars and/or practitioners in the field of organizational behavior. I would like to thank each of the interviewees for the significant amount of time and thought they put into these interviews. I learned from your comments and am convinced that students will do the same. I apologize for converting your in-depth interviews into one-page collections of excerpts, but I have attempted to retain their spirit. Once again, in alphabetical order I thank: J. Stacy Adams, Clayton P. Alderfer, L. L. Cummings, Fred E. Fiedler, John R. P. French, Jr., J. Richard Hackman, Bruce W. Hamstra, Frederick H. Herzberg, Irving L. Janis, Barbara M. Karmel, Steven Kerr, Ed Killeen, Bryan Lawton, John P. Kotter, Wayne H. Larson, Gary P. Latham, Edward E. Lawler, Edwin A. Locke, Greg R. Oldham, John Schienle, Leonard A. Schlesinger, Chester A. Schriesheim, Frank J. Smith, and James E. Ware.

Two students gave generously of their time in contributing to this book. Deb Hoelzel did extensive library research and related activities. Linda Bell volunteered to read the entire set of page proofs and thus contributed immensely to the quality control of the final product.

Randi K. Huntsman worked with me in Madison on the editing of the entire text. While writing, I have a tendency to get caught up in the spirit of the idea. Randi *constantly* reminded me that although the spirit moves, words communicate. For her help in producing, revising, and editing the manuscript, I am grateful.

In closing, I would like to extend my most heartfelt thanks to my friend and colleague from the University of Minnesota–Duluth, Jon L. Pierce. Jon participated in many discussions about the design and execution of the book. He listened to my ramblings about how good I wanted this book to be and provided a regular flow of ideas for how to accomplish this. He read every word of the manuscript and reacted in detail. In many other ways too difficult to describe, Jon has contributed to this book and to me personally. The first copy of this book is for you, Jon.

Randall B. Dunham

Contents

Part I **Organizational Behavior: Definition of Field and Standards for Evaluating Knowledge** **2**

1 Introduction and Overview **4**
Introduction. What Kinds of Questions Does OB Examine? What Is OB? Where Did It Come From? Where Is It Heading? *The Focus of OB. The Roots of OB. The Future of OB.* Organization of the Book. The Role of Theories and Research in Organizational Behavior: *The Use of Theory and Research. The Importance of Theories.* A Challenge to Use Organizational Behavior Knowledge.

2 Standards for Evaluating OB Knowledge **16**
Overview. Reliability: *Ways to Determine Reliability. Factors That Influence Reliability.* Validity: *Construct Validity. Internal Validity. External Validity.* The Relationship between Reliability and Validity. Summary.

Part II **Behaviors and Attitudes in Organizations: Their Definition and Impact** **30**

3 Behaviors and Attitudes in Organizations **32**
Overview. Attitudes: *Cognitive Component. Affective Component. Behavioral Tendency Component. Attitude Formation. Attitude Change. Job Satisfaction.* Job and Work Involvement: *Three Components of Work and Job Involvement.* Behaviors: *Participation. Effort. Performance. Productivity.* Summary.

4 Attitude → Behavior Relationships and Their Financial Impact **62**

Overview. Satisfaction → Turnover: *Empirical Findings. Models Explaining the Satisfaction → Turnover Relationship.* Satisfaction → Absenteeism: *Empirical Findings. A Satisfaction → Attendance Model.* Satisfaction → Performance: *Empirical Findings. A Satisfaction → Performance Model.* Satisfaction → Union Activity: *Empirical Findings. A Satisfaction → Union Model.* The Financial Impact of Attitudes in Organizations. A Procedure for Measuring the Financial Impact of Attitudes: *Step 1: Identification and Measurement of Relevant Attitudes. Step 2: Identification and Measurement of Relevant "Cost Items". Step 3: The Pricing of Behavioral "Cost Items". Step 4: Identification of Relationship between Attitudes and Behavioral "Cost Items". Step 5: Estimation of the Financial Impact of Attitude Changes.* Some Qualifying Remarks. Summary.

Part III Theories in Organizational Behavior **98**

5 Need Theories **102**

Overview. Maslow's Need Hierarchy Theory: *Maslow's Need Categories. A Different Perspective. Implications for Organizations. Research Support for Maslow's Theory.* Alderfer's ERG Theory. Manifest Need Theories. Herzberg's Motivation-Hygiene Theory: *Criticism and Controversy.* Summary.

6 Learning Theories and Behavior Modification **128**

Overview. Classical Conditioning. Operant Conditioning: *The Basic Operant Model. Techniques for Strengthening an S → R Link. Stimulus Discrimination and Generalization. Behavioral Shaping. Techniques for Weakening an S → R Link. Spontaneous Recovery. Schedules of Reinforcement.* Organizational Behavior Modification: *Outcomes. Behavioral Shaping in OBM. Examples of Organizational Behavior Modification. Recommendations for Effective Use of OBM. Ethical Issues Associated with OBM. A Note on Discipline Systems.* Summary.

7 Equity and Goal Theories **162**

Overview. EQUITY THEORY. Distributive Justice. J. Stacy Adams' Equity Theory: *Person's Perceived Outcomes. Perceived Outcomes for Others. Person's Perceived Inputs. Perceived Inputs for Others. Ratios. Perceived State of Equity. Perceived Under-Reward. Perceived Over-Reward. Alternatives for Reducing Perceived Inequity. Choice of Inequity-Reducing Action. Individual Differences in Equity Motivation.* Research on Equity Theory: *Research on Over-Reward. Research on Under-Reward. An Integrative Analysis.* GOAL THEORY. The Basic Model: *Goal Difficulty. Goal Specificity.* Expanded Model: *Goal-Directed Effort and Performance. Goal Acceptance and Goal Commitment. Satis-*

faction. Some Considerations for Application: *Does Goal Setting Work Equally Well for Everyone? How Should a Goal Be Set? Should Goals Be Assigned or Participatively Chosen? What Is the Role of Incentives in the Goal-Setting Process? What Is the Role of Competition?* Management by Objectives (MBO). Summary.

8 An Integrative Model: Expectancy Theory **200**
Overview. The Basic Model: *The Expectancy Perception. The Instrumentality Perception. The Valence Perception. Putting the Pieces Together. A Note on Intrinsic and Extrinsic Outcomes.* Research on Expectancy Theory. The Expanded Model. The Integrating Effect of the Expanded Model. Expectancy Theory Applications. Summary.

Part IV Personal Characteristics: Personality, Ability, and Perception **218**

9 Personality and Ability **220**
Overview. PERSONALITY. Locus of Control: *Internal versus External Locus of Control. Implications for Organizations.* Authoritarianism. Dogmatism. Machiavellianism. Type A and Type B Personalities: *Effects of A versus B Personality Types.* ABILITY. Intellective and Physical Abilities: *Intellective Abilities. Physical Abilities.* Interindividual versus Intraindividual Ability Differences. Techniques for Ability Management: *Selection. Placement. Training.* Summary.

10 Perception **240**
Overview. Major Components of Perception: *Sensation. Selection. Organization. Translation.* Reducing Perceptual Errors: *Self-Understanding. Self-Acceptance. Conscious Information Processing. Reality Testing.* Summary.

Part V Interpersonal Factors **268**

11 Communication in Organizations **272**
Overview. The Communication Process: *A Communication Model. Distortion in the Communication Process. The Functions of Communication.* Communication Networks, Patterns, and Channels: *Networks. Communication Patterns. Communication Channels.* Informal Communication (The Grapevine). Effective Communication Management. Summary.

12 Groups **298**
Overview. Types of Groups: *Formal and Informal Groups. Functional and Project Groups.* The Social Structure of Groups: *Group Representation. Closed/Open Groups. Group Roles.* Social Presence Effects. Factors Influencing Group Formation and Cohesion: *Safety and Security. Social Interaction and Affiliation. Esteem and Status. Power. Goal Achievement.*

Reward Systems. The Effects of Group Cohesion: *Communication. Conformance to Norms and Resistance to Change. Satisfaction. Performance.* Group Norms and Standards: *Characteristics of Norms. Factors which Influence Conformance to Norms.* Stages of Group Development: *Orientation. Conflict. Cohesion. Delusion. Disillusion. Acceptance. Regression.* Groupthink: *Symptoms. Consequences. Remedies.* Group Problem Solving: *Ordinary Groups. Brainstorming. Statistical Aggregation. The Delphi Technique. Nominal Group Technique.* Summary.

13 Power and Conflict **330**
Overview. POWER: *The Bases of Power in Organizations. Organizational Control over Power. The Acquisition of Power. Coalitions and Power. Power and Ethics.* CONFLICT: *The Causes of Conflict. The Conflict Process. The Selection of a Conflict Resolution Strategy.* Summary.

14 Leadership **360**
Overview. Leadership Defined. An Organizing Perspective. Universal Leadership Traits. Situation-Contingent Leadership Traits (Fiedler): *The Critical Leader Trait—LPC. Situational Favorableness. The Leader–Situation Match. Implications of Fiedler's Model.* Universal Leadership Behaviors: *Critical Leader Behaviors.* Situation-Contingent Leadership Behaviors: *Path-Goal Theory. Rational Decision-Making Theory.* Substitutes for Leadership. Summary.

Part VI Organizational Factors **388**

15 Job Design **390**
Overview. History of Job Design: *Scientific Management. Job Enlargement. Job Enrichment. The Job Characteristics Approach. Contemporary Job Characteristics Theory. Current Job Design Issues.* An Integrative Job Design Model: *Required Job Duties. Perceptions of Job Scope. Current Satisfaction. Future Attendance Motivation. Future Performance Motivation. Future Performance.* A Strategy for Job Redesign: *A Step-by-Step Guide for Job Redesign. Factors which May Go Wrong.* Summary.

16 Stress **426**
Overview. Stress. Stressors: *Job-Related Stressors. Organization Role Stressors. Career Stressors. Organization Structure/Climate Stressors. Interpersonal Relations Stressors. Extraorganizational Stressors.* Reactions to Stress: *Perceptions of Stress. Affective Reactions. Psychological Health Reactions. Physical Reactions. Behavioral Reactions.* The Role of Personal Characteristics: *Ability/Skill Levels. Psychological Condition. Physical Condition. Personality. Need States.* The Dynamic Nature of the Stress Model: *Changes in a Person Due to Reactions to Stress. Stressor*

Changes Due to Stress Reactions. Stress Management: *Changing the Stressor. Treating the Reaction. Changing the Person. An Integrative Strategy.* Summary.

Part VII The Management of Change and Ethics **458**

17 The Management of Change **462**

Overview. Forces to Change: *Why Change? Technological Forces. Human Needs and Values. The Social Environment. The Business and Economic Environment. The Organization.* Resistance to Change: *Fear of Loss of Something of Value. Misunderstanding and Lack of Trust. Disagreement on Advisability of Change. Low Personal Tolerance for Change.* Dealing with Resistance to Change: *Education and Communication. Participation and Involvement. Support. Incentives. Manipulation and Co-optation. Coercion.* Selecting a Change Strategy: *The Change Process. Selecting a General Change Strategy. Coordinating the Change Process. Identifying the Focus of the Change. Planning the Implementation Strategy. Implementation. Evaluation.* Summary.

Epilogue: Ethics **490**

Overview. Ethical Responsibilities. Influences on Unethical Behavior: *Personality. Rewards/Punishment. Competition. Organizational Statements/Policies.* Conclusion.

Appendix: The Sources of Knowledge **498**

Overview. Personal Experience: *Potential Advantages of Personal Experience. Potential Disadvantages of Personal Experience.* Case Studies: *Nonparticipant Case Studies. Participant Case Studies.* Field Surveys: Interviews and Questionnaires: *Some Potential Advantages of Surveys. Some Potential Disadvantages of Surveys.* Cross-Sectional Studies: *Some Potential Advantages of Cross-Sectional Studies. Some Potential Disadvantages of Cross-Sectional Studies.* Longitudinal Studies: *Some Potential Advantages of Longitudinal Studies. Some Potential Disadvantages of Longitudinal Studies.* Experimental Studies: *Laboratory Experiments. Simulation Experiments. Planned Field Experiments. Natural Field Experiments.* Summary.

Author Index **535**

Subject Index **539**

[illegible]

Part VII The Management of Change and Crisis [illegible]

The Management of Change [illegible]

[illegible]

Author Index [illegible]

Subject Index [illegible]

Organizational Behavior

People and Processes
in Management

Part

1 ■ Introduction and Overview

2 ■ Standards for Evaluating OB Knowledge

Organizational Behavior: Definition of Field and Standards for Evaluating Knowledge

The chapters in Part I introduce the field of organizational behavior (OB). Chapter 1 provides a sample of the types of questions addressed by organizational behavior and discusses the usefulness of OB knowledge. The past, present, and future of OB are explored briefly and an overview of the book is presented. Chapter 1 ends with a discussion of the role of theory and research in building usable OB knowledge and offers you a challenge to use the knowledge contained in this book.

Chapter 2 explains several significant standards used to evaluate the quality and usefulness of knowledge about attitudes and behaviors in organizations. In short, Chapter 2 will help you become a better consumer of knowledge. The ability to evaluate information critically will be useful in later parts of this book and whenever you need to examine information which might influence your decisions. At the heart of the evaluation of knowledge are the questions of reliability and validity. Chapter 2 addresses these through the use of examples of problems faced by managers in organizations.

1 Introduction and Overview

INTRODUCTION
WHAT KINDS OF QUESTIONS DOES OB EXAMINE?
WHAT IS OB? WHERE DID IT COME FROM? WHERE IS IT HEADING?
The Focus of OB
The Roots of OB
The Future of OB
ORGANIZATION OF THE BOOK
THE ROLE OF THEORIES AND RESEARCH IN ORGANIZATIONAL BEHAVIOR
The Use of Theory and Research
The Importance of Theories
A CHALLENGE TO USE ORGANIZATIONAL BEHAVIOR KNOWLEDGE

The physical sciences have now achieved such success that it is possible for all men to die together. Relatively little is being done to make it possible for us to live together.

Ross Stagner[1]

INTRODUCTION

This chapter is intended to provide you with your first formal exposure to the systematic study of behaviors and attitudes in organizations. After reading this chapter, you will have a basic understanding of what organizational behavior (OB) is, why it is important, and how it will be studied in this book.

WHAT KINDS OF QUESTIONS DOES OB EXAMINE?

Each chapter of this book examines important questions regarding the application of OB knowledge in organizations. Because human behaviors and attitudes cannot be predicted or explained with complete accuracy, the answers provided in this book are not absolutes. Rather than providing "the one perfect solution" to a problem, this book offers guidance from the OB field to help you learn how to find a good answer for each situation.

Although you will still be responsible for the decisions you make in managing behaviors and attitudes in organizations, this book will provide you with knowledge and perspectives to assist you in the decision-making process. If you expect this *book* to answer questions for you, you will be disappointed. If you expect it to help *you* answer questions, you should be pleased.

Here is a partial sample of some of the types of questions considered in this book:

1. Does job satisfaction influence performance?
2. What is the financial impact of satisfaction?

3. Can organizations motivate workers by making rewards contingent on performance?
4. Why do groups of competent individuals often make incompetent decisions? How can this be prevented?
5. How can workers have more power in organizations than management?
6. Are leaders "born," or can people be taught to lead?
7. What causes conflict in organizations? How can conflict be managed?
8. How can organizations manage stress?
9. How can communication systems contribute to the success or failure of organizational plans?
10. How can the introduction of new ideas in organizations be managed effectively?
11. What are the ethical implications of using organizational behavior knowledge?

WHAT IS OB? WHERE DID IT COME FROM? WHERE IS IT HEADING?

The Focus of OB

Organizational behavior focuses on the understanding of behaviors and attitudes within organizations. A primary purpose of the OB field is to understand *why* people in organizations feel and behave as they do. The study of OB attempts to document the organizational factors which influence workers (and therefore the organization itself). It also describes the processes by which these factors exert their influence. Thus, one major component of OB involves acquiring relatively pure knowledge (*why* things happen as they do). However, the power of our knowledge about organizational behavior comes from *applying* this knowledge. This book focuses both on understanding and applying OB information.

The Roots of OB[2]

Larry Greiner of the University of Southern California notes that archeological finds have demonstrated clearly that complex organizations have existed for centuries. He implies that the successful building of massive temples around 3500 B.C. is evidence that complex organizations not only existed but, to some significant degree, were managed successfully. We cannot know for sure how thoroughly our ancient predecessors understood behaviors and attitudes, nor how systematic they were in influencing the behaviors and attitudes of organizational members. The remains of their ac-

Ed Killeen is the vice president of employee relations of Wisconsin Power and Light.

Wayne H. Larson is South Central area director of Lutheran Social Services of Wisconsin and Upper Michigan.

John Schienle is the executive vice president of Foremost Guaranty Corporation.

A variety of managers and practitioners were invited to share their thoughts about the study of organizational behavior and the effective management of organizations. The following is a sampling of some of their comments.

Ed Killeen An effective leader accomplishes success through, or in concert with, other people. An effective leader is an educator and motivator of people. The leader must possess the skills to facilitate group dynamics and must be capable of bringing diverse positions into consensus. The leader also must be able to resolve conflict. The ultimate leader must: possess a sense of humor and be able to laugh at himself or herself; have survived several rounds of his/her decisions and mistakes; inspire excellence in others; serve others and their needs; and have a strong ethical underpinning.

Wayne H. Larson If there is one comment that I would most like to make to a student in organizational behavior, it is to keep systems simple in an organization. Average employees must be able to understand them in order to achieve their personal goals and contribute to organizational goals. The effectiveness of a leader is related not only to his/her ability to communicate and build a team, but also to the positive regard that the leader has for others, the sense of timing needed to know when the situation is correct for change, and the ability to achieve goals with average employees who are qualified (not just achieving goals through star performers).

John Schienle I have observed that some of the important skills frequently present among managers include drive, ambition, and technical skills. On the other hand, skills commonly missing include the patience to help others, empathy, listening, and the ability to pace oneself. Most training and schooling are technical in nature. This matches most entry-level jobs, which are technically oriented and usually involve working alone. Continued success as a manager, however, requires an understanding of organizational behavior obtained through a combination of observation, experience, and education.

complishments, however, make it clear that complex organizations were formed, managed, and achieved important organizational goals (the successful completion of massive temples, pyramids, etc.).

Unfortunately, the techniques used to manage organizational behavior were not well recorded until the 1800s, rendering massive amounts of information on OB unavailable for study. Scholars and practitioners from a number of fields began to record their acquired knowledge more thoroughly during the 19th century, but organizational behavior as a distinct field did not even exist until the 1940s or 1950s. Knowledge about the behaviors and attitudes of people in organizations came almost exclusively from psychology, sociology, political science, and related fields. Even today, substantial portions of OB knowledge come from outside the organizational behavior field. The OB field (and this book) draw from all possible sources of knowledge about behavior in organizations. This provides a distinct advantage in that a number of very different perspectives on the same organizational issues are available. This also provides an interesting challenge when integrating the knowledge from such diverse disciplines.

The Future of OB

In recent years, the field of OB has identified a number of significant issues for comprehensive examination. The majority of these are addressed in this book. It appears that the immediate future of OB will see scholars directing their efforts toward testing and refining current theories rather than developing radically new theories. Although it would not be surprising to see a few new theories emerge, most of these are likely to be hybrids developed through the integration of components of existing models. Perhaps most likely in the decade to come will be the development and refinement of techniques for *using* OB knowledge more effectively.

ORGANIZATION OF THE BOOK

This book is organized to provide a logical, systematic approach for studying organizational behavior, and is designed to help you use this knowledge. Part I provides the introduction and overview contained in this chapter. Chapter 2 introduces you to critical issues you must consider when evaluating the quality of information you obtain about behaviors and attitudes in organizations. These are expanded upon in the Appendix.

Part II identifies, defines, and discusses the behaviors and attitudes of major importance to organizations (Chapter 3). The relationships between attitudes and behaviors and the financial impact of attitudes in organizations also are explored in Part II (Chapter 4).

In Part III (Chapters 5–8), a variety of theories or frameworks are introduced which will help you understand *why* people behave and feel as they do in organizations. This will assist you in developing the ability to recognize and influence these behaviors and attitudes. These theories are not presented in a competitive light ("This one is *correct*, so the others must be *incorrect*"). Instead, the strengths of each theory are examined and cautions expressed about current limitations. Indeed, Chapter 8 utilizes one of the more recent theories to integrate major elements of each of the theories discussed in prior chapters. You also should be aware that the organizational implications of each theory are examined from an applied perspective. Therefore, you should have ideas on how to *use* the theories in organizations upon completing Part III.

Part IV focuses on the critical role of individual differences in the personal characteristics of organizational members. No two people react in an identical fashion to the same organizational experience. Personality characteristics and abilities each play important roles, for example, in the way you will react to events. Chapter 9 examines the specific manner in which personality and abilities contribute to differences in worker reactions to the organizational experience. Chapter 10 explores the importance of the perceptual process. Since people react to what they perceive is real whether or not their perceptions are accurate, it is absolutely essential that you have an understanding of factors which contribute to the formation of perceptions.

Part V looks at several interpersonal processes central to all organizations. The exchange of information in organizations occurs through communication (Chapter 11). Much of the work accomplished in organizations is performed by groups (Chapter 12). The relative influence of organizational members is determined by a collection of power sources (Chapter 13). Whenever two or more people interact, conflict is a distinct possibility (also Chapter 13). Finally, the role of leadership is explored as the process by which certain members guide the actions of others (Chapter 14).

Part VI deals with two issues typically affecting the entire organization: job design (Chapter 15) and stress (Chapter 16). The job design chapter investigates the manner in which the characteristics of jobs influence worker attitudes and effectiveness and provides a guide for the effective design of jobs. The chapter on stress not only identifies the determinants and consequences of stress in organizations but also provides suggestions for effective stress management.

In Part VII, the management of change is explored in detail (Chapter 17). Each of the preceding chapters contains ideas for change in organizations. Even the best of ideas, however, will not be particularly successful unless they are introduced properly. For this reason, Chapter 17 gives you tips on how to introduce change. First, common sources of resistance are examined and then techniques you can use both to prevent and to deal with it are described. This chapter also offers guidance in the planning, implementation, and overall management of change in organizations. This information is presented in such a way as to be useful whether the change is from an idea contained in this book, the introduction of a new technology, or from virtually any other source.

The Epilogue addresses a number of critical ethical issues. You may find it useful to read the Epilogue now and then read it again after you have completed the rest of the book. Your perspective on the importance of ethics in an OB course is likely to change substantially between these two points in time. One thing is very clear. If you study the material in your OB course diligently, you will acquire knowledge which can be used to influence the attitudes and behaviors of others in an organization. Before you use this knowledge, you must give very careful thought to the ethics of your behavior.

THE ROLE OF THEORIES AND RESEARCH IN ORGANIZATIONAL BEHAVIOR

The Use of Theory and Research

The material presented throughout this book is based on both theory and research. An attempt is made to provide a balanced treatment of the two. Indeed, theory and research are complementary in nature. Ideally, good theory is rooted in ideas shown to be true by research, and good research addresses issues of theoretical importance. The two should work together, with research leading to modification (i.e., improvement) of theory and theory guiding research by identifying important researchable issues.

A *theory* is a statement of the manner in which two or more concepts or variables are expected to be related. A theory could be relatively simple (involving as few as two variables) or extremely complex. The simplicity or complexity of a theory is not necessarily an indication of its adequacy. Robert Dubin tells us that a theory is an attempt to make sense out of observations which do not necessarily contain any inherent and obvious logic (until the theory is stated).[3] In 1980, John Miner made the following observations about what constitutes a "good" theory.

1. Theories "should aid understanding, permit prediction, and facilitate influence. The more they do these things, the better they are."
2. "The boundaries of application should be specified so that the theory is not utilized fruitlessly in situations for which it was never intended."
3. "A good theory should direct research efforts to important matters."
4. "Theories at their best yield a value added above the research efforts alone. If a number of hypotheses derived from a theory are confirmed by research, then the whole body of the theory becomes available for use . . . [and] thus has the potential not just for yielding a few isolated facts but for mobilizing the whole explanatory and predictive power of the theory."
5. Theories should be testable and "it should be clear exactly what must be done to either confirm or disconfirm them." If it is not possible to disprove a theory through research, it is not possible to prove it and we can never know for sure if the theory is "accurate."
6. "Theories should build on what is known . . . good theory . . . is logically consistent within itself and with other known facts."
7. All else being equal, "the best theory is one which is stated in the simplest terms. If a given set of phenomena can be explained tersely with only a few variables, that theory should be preferred over one that achieves the same level of explanation with a much more complex set of variables and relationships. Science does not value complexity for its own sake. There is enough of that in nature."[4]

As theories are presented in this book, the preceding seven characteristics of a "good" theory will be considered. No theory will satisfy all seven conditions perfectly, but each fulfills them to some substantial degree. The degree to which use of a theory is recommended will be, in part, a function of the degree to which these seven considerations are met and the degree to which research has supported the theory. In most cases, you will want to use only those parts of each theory best supported by research. Furthermore, a healthy use of multiple theories will help you obtain a well-balanced perspective. As you consider the relative importance of research and theory, remember that *research gives us our facts, but theory gives us our ideas*.

The Importance of Theories

The theories discussed in this book are presented to help you understand *why* people react to organizational events with particular attitudes and behaviors. It would be impossible to memorize every possible organizational situation, every possible action to take in each of these situations, and the possible responses to each of them. Theories help us understand the *processes* involved as people receive information and react to it. The frameworks that theories provide help you to understand new situations as they occur, based on the underlying processes involved. Thus, it is often possible to anticipate behaviors and attitudes in a new situation even though you never before have experienced that specific situation.

There is no answer to the question "What is the best OB theory?" None of the theories is best, and none of the theories is perfect. You must consider both the advantages and limitations of each theory. The idea, however, is not to present a theory, tear it apart, and then conclude that it is "no good." What is helpful is to take a theory, tear it apart, and determine which aspects of it are useful and which aspects are less useful (or better understood from the perspective of another theory). At the risk of presenting a "corny" analogy early in the book, consider the following:

> In your everyday life, you must make many decisions. To do this, you need information. Sometimes you have all of the information you need to make a particular decision. Sometimes you don't. If you feel that you do not have enough information to make a decision, you seek more information. After you obtain additional information, you still may not feel quite ready to make a decision because you are not quite sure what the information means. In a situation such as this, you might ask a friend or colleague to provide a different perspective on the issue at hand. Your friend's perspective may be somewhat different than your own, and you take this perspective into consideration. You don't have to follow your friend's advice to the letter, but it does get you to thinking. Quite often you may ask two or three friends—to get a variety of perspectives. After you have obtained these varied perspectives, you make a decision. Sometimes your friends' advice will be consistent with your original plan and makes you more confident about your decision. Other times your friends' perspectives will be different from yours, causing you to reconsider your original perspective.

Think of OB theories as friends. Theories provide new perspectives for you as you make important organizational decisions. Theories seldom tell you exactly what decision to make, but they do help you make a decision by providing guidance and by suggesting new ways of viewing the information you possess. Often, the best way to make a decision is to obtain a variety of perspectives (i.e., use diverse theories, or ask several different friends). Asking your friends or theories for advice does not relieve you of the responsibility of making decisions. You are responsible for the final integration and interpretation of information—and the ultimate decision. In short, treat your theories like friends. Respect their opinions, but don't make the mistake of assuming they are always right. This book will help you identify the strengths and weaknesses of your theories (you are on your own with your friends!).

A CHALLENGE TO USE ORGANIZATIONAL BEHAVIOR KNOWLEDGE

Past application of OB knowledge has been marked by a few stunning successes and a large number of adequate applications. Unfortunately, there also have been a disturbingly large number of "failures." Many of the failures of recent years can be attributed to the premature application of insufficiently developed ideas or to the application of poorly developed and untested ideas. A number of the other failures can be traced to overgeneralization (the inappropriate assumption that an idea which works in one organization will be sure to work in *any* other). All of these sources of difficulty have one thing in common—a failure to be adequately *systematic*. There is no room for sloppiness and carelessness in the study and practice of OB. The consequences can be too great to apply your knowledge in a haphazard fashion.

Although you do not want to apply ideas prematurely, you must be willing to take reasonable risks in managing organizations. The goal is to find and use the best information and ideas currently available when making decisions in organizations. You should not use this information unless there is reasonable evidence that it is basically sound. Nor should you use this information unless it is the best available. However, you cannot afford to wait until every shadow of a doubt is removed before deciding how to manage organizations. While you wait for the "ultimate truth," organizational effectiveness is left to chance. The ultimate truth will not be found. In OB, you will know more about the important issues tomorrow than you do today, due to research, theoretical exploration, and practice. But a significant amount of information (albeit imperfect) can be of great use right now. Use the best you have today, even though tomorrow you will have better. Consider the following observations of Jacoba Varela:

> Engineers and physical scientists cannot wait for theoretical perfection. If the Romans had waited for the elegance of the Verrazano-Narrows Bridge instead of fooling around with stone arches, the course of civilization would have changed. The Roman arches had their faults, but they have lasted nineteen centuries.
>
> Engineers do not build two Golden Gate Bridges to see which one will work best. They build the best bridge they can based on the principles they know.

> I am not making a case for the use of false findings, but I want to make clear that if we are to solve problems we must proceed on the assumption that the best research available is true. More often than not I find that it is. We must take risks if we are to progress.[5]

This book helps prepare you for building your organizational "bridges." Acquire knowledge, evaluate it, and use that knowledge to improve the odds as you take risks. You can take risks and have a reasonably good chance of "winning," or you can fail to take the risk and have a sure chance of losing.

A large portion of our lives is spent in organizational settings. OB knowledge can go a long way toward making it possible for us to live together within organizations. The goals of organizations and organizational members need not be in conflict. The satisfaction of employee needs does not have to mean the dissatisfaction of organization needs, or vice versa. The systematic application of OB knowledge can increase both satisfaction and performance. Indeed, there is considerable evidence that in well-managed organizations performance and satisfaction benefit both the employee and the organization. In the short run, it is often easier not to use OB knowledge, but you will make things harder for yourself in the long run if you don't use this knowledge. And remember, as you use your knowledge, be *systematic*.

STUDY QUESTIONS

1. Based on your personal experiences in organizations, answer the sample questions presented at the beginning of this chapter. Make a note of your answers.
2. Ask a friend or classmate to answer the sample questions. Compare his/her answers to your own. Discuss why your answers differ (if they do).
3. If your friend's answers were always "right," how would this influence the way you behave as a manager?
4. Most people possess their own theories about the causes and consequences of behaviors and attitudes. What do your theories say about the determinants of work-related attitudes? Motivation? Performance?
5. Ask your friend or classmate about his/her theories of attitudes, motivation, and performance. Compare those to yours and identify the differences and their implications.

NOTES

1. Quoted by **Varela, J.** (1978). Solving human problems with human science. *Human Nature, 1*, #10, 84–90.
2. A more thorough discussion of the "roots of OB" is contained in a chapter by **Greiner, Larry** (1979). A recent history of organizational behavior. In Steven Kerr (Ed.), *Organizational behavior* (pp. 3–14). Columbus, OH: Grid Publishing.
3. **Dubin, R.** (1976). Theory building in applied areas. In M. D. Dunnette (Ed.), *Handbook of industrial and organizational psychology* (pp. 17–39). Chicago: Rand McNally.
4. **Miner, J.** (1980). *Theories of organizational behavior* (pp. 7–9). Hinsdale, IL: Dryden Press.
5. **Varela,** 1978.

2

Standards for Evaluating OB Knowledge

OVERVIEW
RELIABILITY
Ways to Determine Reliability
Factors that Influence Reliability
VALIDITY
Construct Validity
Internal Validity
External Validity
THE RELATIONSHIP BETWEEN RELIABILITY AND VALIDITY
SUMMARY

There is only one good, knowledge, and one evil, ignorance.

Socrates

OVERVIEW

The focus of this chapter is on methods you can use to evaluate the quality of information about organizational behavior. As you make decisions in organizations, you anticipate the probable effects of each of the actions you are considering. Your expectations are, in large part, based on the "facts" you possess. Some of your facts will be based on personal experiences ("In situations like this which I have encountered in the past, being tough on my subordinates caused them to work harder."). Other facts are based on formal research conducted in your organization. Still other facts come from research done in other organizations.

With so many facts from which to choose, which should you use? Which can you trust? Which are most appropriate for use in your organization? The major purpose of this chapter is to help you answer these questions by evaluating the quality (and, therefore, usefulness) of each of the "facts" you possess. The most important measures of quality are reliability and validity.

Once you understand the concepts necessary for the evaluation of the quality of OB facts, you will have a better base from which to understand and evaluate the material presented later in this book, including both research and theory. You will be able to evaluate better the claims made by others concerning the value of new managerial procedures. This will protect you from "snake oil sellers." You may discover new procedures useful to you in your own situation. You also will be better prepared for evaluating the appropriateness of research findings from your own organization.

The Appendix explores a number of other "research methodol-

Chester A. Schriesheim of the University of Florida is noted for research in several areas, including leadership and attitude–behavior relationships.

What would you say is the most important and useful lesson a current or future manager can learn from the study of organizational behavior? Probably the most important lesson is that of reality testing. The lesson coming through time and time again is that you can't trust any single perspective as your only guide in an organizational setting.

What should a manager do to deal with this problem? Prior to making significant decisions in virtually any area, managers need to do research (broadly defined as gathering information pertinent to answering the question at hand). Those who gather data are much more likely to make good decisions than those who don't. Making the jump from symptoms to problem diagnosis to the development of solution alternatives, the assessment of alternatives, and so on, using a rational decision model is facilitated by the research process more than anything else.

If a manager is reasonably certain of the appropriate answer to a problem, why bother confirming this through research? For significant issues, managers would be well advised to go to the library and look up what's been written, go down the hall and talk to colleagues, go to meetings to find out what others have done and what sort of success they have had, or even conduct their own empirical research. In doing this, they often find that their initial perspective, no matter how intuitively correct, may need to be substantially altered. In summary, the most important and useful lesson a manager can learn from the study of OB is the need for research. Desirably, the more rigorous the better, but practically speaking, any form of research is preferable to the manager sitting alone in his or her office making decisions without seeing whether the bases, inferences, and facts being used are well based in reality.

ogy" issues. It is not the aim of this book to train you thoroughly in behavioral research methodology. However, this chapter, in conjunction with the Appendix, does provide a solid treatment of the major research-related issues which can enhance your capabilities as a manager. In the Appendix, each of the major techniques used to collect information is examined and evaluated relative to the issues discussed in this chapter. The combined information from this chapter and the Appendix not only will increase your ability to evaluate information provided by others but also will prepare you for basic fact gathering (research) of your own.

RELIABILITY

One of the first questions which should be asked about any "fact" is whether or not that fact is reliable. A behavior or attitude in an organization is reliable if you would get the same information when measuring it again. Perfect **reliability** would require that *exactly* the same information be obtained each time you measure. Total lack of reliability would be present if totally different information was obtained each time you repeated the measurement. Obviously, measures which totally lack reliability are of no use. On the other hand, it is extremely rare for measures used in OB to have perfect reliability. Therefore, you need: ways to determine if your "facts" are reliable enough to use, procedures for maximizing the reliability of facts, and a willingness to exercise caution in using facts which have relatively low reliability.

Ways to Determine Reliability

One way to obtain reliable information is to use measurement (fact-finding) procedures proven to provide consistently reliable

The Case of the Balance

Jeff was a chemist working for the Acme Oil Refinery. Jeff's job was to monitor the amount of sulfur particulates contained in the refinery's exhaust to determine whether the huge burners in the plant were being provided the proper fuel mixture. If the amount of sulfur particulate was too high or too low, the fuel was not being used efficiently and adjustments were necessary. Furthermore, if the amount of sulfur particulates exceeded a critical level, the plant could be found in violation of Environmental Protection Agency limits and fined, or possibly even shut down. For these reasons, it was important to have good information about the amount of sulfur particulate in the refinery's exhaust. To obtain this information, Jeff placed a collection filter in the exhaust stack of the refinery. Jeff removed the filter each day and used a balance to weigh the captured particles. He knew that the burners were tuned properly if between 12 and 13 ounces of particulate were collected each day. Jeff used a sensitive mechanical balance to weigh the amount of particulate collected.

Was Jeff obtaining reliable information about the amount of sulfur particulate contained in the refinery exhaust? To determine if his information was reliable, Jeff conducted a weekly reliability test. Every Wednesday, he measured each sample 10 separate times using the balance. If he obtained the same information each time he made the measurement, Jeff concluded his measurements were reliable. If the 10 measurements did not yield the same results, there was a reliability problem. Jeff felt that perfect reliability was not necessary, but it was important for reliability to be within one tenth of one ounce. Thus, he was willing to accept imperfect reliability as long as the degree of reliability present was within a reasonable range.

Once a month, Jeff conducted another test in addition to the preceding reliability test. In this test, three other employees also were asked to measure the sample collected. If Jeff's measure and the three additional measures agreed, Jeff gained even greater confidence in the reliability of his information.

Every three months, Jeff conducted a third type of reliability test. In this test, he not only used his regular balance but also measured each sample on two balances located in other company laboratories. Agreement of these measures also provided reliability information for Jeff.

For months, the reliability check involving two separate weighings produced results with acceptable agreement (these two measures were within one tenth of one ounce of each other). Toward the end of the first year, however, the two separate measures started to be farther and farther apart. Finally, they were always *more* than one tenth of an ounce apart. Because the two measures were still within one half of one ounce of each other, there was still some degree of reliability. The agreement was not close enough to provide what Jeff felt was acceptable reliability.

information. For most of the factors examined in this book, procedures have been developed which have been shown to provide acceptable (albeit imperfect) reliability. Careful choice of measurement procedures will increase the likelihood that your facts are reliable. In situations where measurement systems with documented reliability are not readily available, you may create your own procedures for measuring the issues of interest. You also may use a procedure developed by someone else which has unknown reliability. It thus becomes necessary to estimate just how reliable your facts are. Even when you use measurement procedures which have produced reliable results elsewhere, you can be more certain of the quality of your own information if *you* assess its reliability. An important point: the reliability of information is influenced not only by the technique you use to obtain information but also by the way you use that technique.

Three techniques commonly used to assess the reliability of OB knowledge are:

1. **Test/Retest Reliability.** Do two or more measurements of the same sample with the same technique provide the same information (assuming no real change occurred between the two measures)?
2. **Inter-Rater Agreement Reliability.** Do two or more different raters provide the same information when they measure the same sample?
3. **Alternate Forms Agreement Reliability.** Do two or more different forms of measurement (e.g., two different scales) provide the same information when they measure the same sample?

There are variations of the preceding techniques for assessing the reliability of information, but these are the primary techniques you will use when evaluating the reliability of information which you receive in organizations. Depending on the type of information you are investigating and its importance, you might choose to use one, two, or all three of the above methods. In short, choose a measurement technique which has provided reliable results when used by others. Then, conduct your own evaluation of reliability to confirm that the technique provides reliable information in *your* situation—the way you are using it.

Factors That Influence Reliability

There are two major ways to increase the reliability of information: improve the accuracy of the measuring device, and/or improve the manner of using the device. These steps help you to fine tune the tool you are using to obtain information and develop systematic procedures for using the tool. Other common approaches for solving this problem include:

The Case of the Job Satisfaction Measure

Susanne also worked for the Acme Oil Refinery. Susanne's job was to monitor the level of job satisfaction among the company's employees to determine how workers were reacting to various company policies and practices. If workers were dissatisfied with certain aspects of the organization, the company wanted to be made aware of this because top management felt that it was important to maintain good morale. Furthermore, the company felt that low satisfaction levels could impact the effectiveness of the company adversely by leading to high absenteeism and turnover levels. The company also believed that dissatisfied employees were more likely to join unions, and the company wished to remain nonunion. For these reasons, it was important to have good information about the levels of job satisfaction at the company. To measure satisfaction, Susanne used a job satisfaction questionnaire which had provided reliable information in a variety of other organizations.

Was Susanne obtaining reliable information about the levels of job satisfaction at the company? To determine if her information was reliable, Susanne considered each of the three types of reliability tests Jeff had used. She decided that multiple raters would not be appropriate in her situation, since job satisfaction was a very personal issue. She decided not to use the alternate forms agreement approach because she did not have a readily accessible alternative job satisfaction measure. Therefore, Susanne decided to use the *test/retest* procedure to determine if her information was reliable. She administered the job satisfaction questionnaire to a sample of 50 employees on March 1 and then again on March 15. Although she did not get exactly the same results on March 15 as on March 1, the results were similar enough so that Susanne could conclude that her measure of job satisfaction had reasonable reliability.

After Susanne was satisfied with the reliability of her information from the job satisfaction measure, she used it successfully throughout Acme Refinery for a period of years. The manager of Acme's Fruit Packaging Division, Kris, contacted Susanne one day to "borrow" the questionnaire. Kris then used it with the 5,000 fruit packers working for Acme. When Kris provided feedback to his managers based on the results of the job satisfaction questionnaire, many of them could not believe the results. Although Kris suspected that the managers just weren't aware of the actual satisfaction levels within the plant, he agreed to have Susanne conduct a reliability test similar to the one done at Acme Refinery. The results of the test-retest reliability check showed that, although there was some agreement between the two measures of job satisfaction, there were also wide differences. Susanne concluded that the reliability of the information was too low, and the results obtained from the job satisfaction questionnaire at Acme Fruit should not be used.

1. Repeating the measurement procedure several times and using the average measure as your best estimate of the "true" information.

2. Having two or more people obtain the same information and using the average measure.
3. Using two or more different measurement approaches (e.g., two balances or two satisfaction measures) and using the average measure.

Note that the latter approaches suggested not only increase the reliability of your information, but they also allow you to examine just how reliable that information is.

The Case of the Balance: A Second Look

What was adversely affecting the reliability of Jeff's measure? A wide range of factors had the potential to reduce the reliability of Jeff's measures. After a very careful investigation, he decided that the two major factors creating a problem were the measuring device itself and his use of it. His balance had become dirty and was sticking occasionally when weighing particulates. Furthermore, Jeff had become careless in the way he used the balance (working too quickly, not taking sufficient time to check the balance closely, etc.). The test/retest check alerted Jeff to the decreasing reliability of the information obtained.

How could Jeff increase the reliability of his measures? He had the scale cleaned and oiled, and he designed a specific systematic procedure to follow when using the scale. After taking these steps, the test/retest checks again demonstrated acceptable agreement and Jeff was once again confident of the reliability of his information.

The Case of the Job Satisfaction Measure: A Second Look

What was adversely affecting the reliability of Kris's measure? Again, although a wide range of factors could have been contributing to the low reliability of the job satisfaction measure at Acme Fruit, Susanne and Kris decided that there were two critical issues. The first problem was that Acme Fruit employees had lower education levels than did Acme Refinery employees. English was a second language for many. Results of Kris's and Susanne's investigation revealed that many of these employees were confused about the meaning of several questions in the satisfaction measure. Secondly, Kris was careless in the way he used the satisfaction measure. He had not provided adequate instructions and had rushed workers as they completed the questionnaire. The test/retest evaluation alerted Kris and Susanne to the low reliability of the information obtained.

How could Kris increase the reliability of the measure? Kris and Susanne worked with a sample of Acme Fruit employees to determine which questions were most confusing. They then rewrote those questions so that they were more understandable. Kris and Susanne also devised a systematic procedure to follow when using the job satisfaction measure (specific instructions, allowance of sufficient survey time, etc.). After taking these steps, the test/retest checks showed that Acme Fruit now had a way to make these measurements with adequate reliability.

The preceding examples show the importance of assessing (either formally or informally) the reliability of information before using it. You seldom need perfect reliability, but you never need totally unreliable information. Your goal should be to use the most reliable information available to you, determine how reliable that information is, and use it with appropriate caution based on its reliability level.

VALIDITY

Before you can assume that a piece of information is a "usable fact," you must determine how valid it is. There are several questions of **validity** that should be asked, three of which are of greatest importance as you acquire and use OB knowledge in the future.* All three aspects of validity relate to the following definition of validity: information which is sound, well-grounded in fact, and able to withstand objection.

Construct Validity

Construct validity is simply the degree to which it is appropriate for you to call the thing you are measuring by the name you are using. In other words, it addresses the question "Am I measuring what I think I am measuring?" This does not refer to the nature of relationships ("Does this thing I am measuring influence something else?"). Nor does it refer to the usefulness of the information in your situation ("Is it appropriate for me to use this information in this particular instance?").

Internal Validity

Internal validity addresses the question "In the information I am examining right now, is it appropriate for me to say A causes B?" Assume for the moment that A and B both have adequate construct validity (i.e., you really are measuring A and B, and A and B are statistically related to one another so that people who are high on A are also high on B). Internal validity asks if this relationship is present because A causes B, or if the relationship could be due to something else. For example, a third variable (C) may cause both A

*There is sometimes confusion regarding interpretation of the meaning of the three types of validity discussed here. Our discussion follows the widely accepted and very thorough treatment of these terms presented by T. D. Cook, & D. T. Campbell, (1976). The design and conduct of quasi-experiments and true experiments in field settings. In M. D. Dunnette (Ed.), *Handbook of industrial and organizational psychology* (pp. 224–246). Chicago: Rand McNally.

and B to be high, which makes it appear as though A might have caused B.

Leader Behavior and Satisfaction at Acme

Susanne at the Acme Oil Refinery has been using her job satisfaction questionnaire for several years. Results initially indicated that satisfaction with supervision was very low among nonsupervisory employees. Susanne designed a project to determine if satisfaction with supervision could be improved by training supervisors in interpersonal skills. Using her questionnaire with proven reliability, she measured satisfaction with supervision on March 1. At the same time, she asked each subordinate to rate the interpersonal skill level of his/her supervisor, using a measure that also was reliable. Susanne compared the interpersonal skill level of each supervisor to the average satisfaction with supervision level for the subordinates of that supervisor. She found that those supervisors with greater interpersonal skills had subordinates with higher levels of satisfaction with supervision. During April, each supervisor attended a four-day seminar designed to improve interpersonal skills.

In June, Susanne once again obtained measures of subordinate satisfaction with supervision and compared them to the interpersonal skill level of supervisors. Results showed that: supervisors now were rated as having greater interpersonal skills, subordinates were more satisfied with supervision, and those supervisors with the greatest interpersonal skills had subordinates who were most satisfied with supervision. Based on the information provided by this study, Susanne drew the following conclusions:

1. The greater the interpersonal skills of supervisors at the refinery, the more satisfied subordinates would be with supervision.
2. The four-day seminar increased the interpersonal skill levels of the refinery's supervisors.
3. The increases in interpersonal skill levels which resulted from the seminar led to increases in satisfaction with supervision.
4. The four-day seminar should also be held for the supervisors at the Acme Fruit Packaging Division. Holding the seminar at Acme Fruit will increase the interpersonal skill level of supervisors there and will lead to increases in satisfaction with supervision.

External Validity

External validity addresses the question "Is it appropriate for me to take the results from one study (or a series of studies) and assume that these results would also occur in another situation, with another group of people, or at a different point in time?" Assume for the moment that adequate construct validity and internal validity were present in a study done in an organization (A and B really were measured, and A was shown to "cause" B). You would be asking a question of external validity if you read this study and said, "I am convinced that A did in fact influence B in that organization, but I wonder if the same results would occur in my organization." In short, external validity (which is often called "generalizability" for obvious reasons) directly addresses the question of usability of accurate information in a particular setting.

Information which lacks construct validity has no value to anyone. Information which lacks internal validity has limited usefulness due to multiple possible interpretations of the meaning of the information. Information which satisfies construct and internal validity conditions might be of great use in some organizations but of little use in others. In other words, its usefulness depends on the degree to which it is appropriate to generalize from the situation(s) in which the information was obtained to the situation in which you wish to use it.

Let's return to Acme briefly to explore some examples of various combinations of the three types of validity.

Prior to drawing the preceding conclusions, Susanne should have asked three questions relating to the validity of her information:

1. *Do my measures have adequate construct validity*? Susanne needed to know if she really was measuring satisfaction with supervision and leader interpersonal skills. It might be that the measures used in the questionnaire to obtain information about these factors were "contaminated." For example, questions like "Is your supervisor helpful to you on the job?" may be answered based on more than the interpersonal skill level of supervisors. A supervisor who shares technical knowledge with subordinates might be rated high on this question, not only because of interpersonal skills but partially because of technical skills. This would produce information on interpersonal skill level with reduced construct validity (i.e., the measure of "interpersonal skill" is contaminated by a measure of technical skill).

Since it would be extremely difficult to obtain totally construct-valid information, your goal should be to use measures which are as construct valid as possible. You also must exercise appropriate caution when using the information, depending on the degree to which construct validity is present. To determine if her measures were construct valid, Susanne did three things. First, she asked a sample of employees from the refinery to look at the questions in her two measures and tell her what they thought the items measured. Next, she asked 25 managers from throughout the company to look at the questions and tell her what they thought the items measured. Finally, she asked a number of employees to fill out both her questionnaire and another questionnaire previously shown to have adequate construct validity. When all three of these tests indicated that her questionnaire did appear to measure supervision satisfaction and interpersonal skills, Susanne concluded that she really was measuring what she had intended to measure. Her measures were construct valid.

2. *Does the information from my study have adequate internal validity?* Susanne needed to ask if it was appropriate to say that the seminar caused the increases in interpersonal skill levels. She also questioned whether the skill increases were responsible for the subsequent increases in satisfaction with supervision. Internal validity raises the question of the nature of *cause→effect* relationships. Because the subject of cause→effect relationships will be explored in greater depth in the Appendix, the only point made here is that the demonstration of adequate internal validity involves primarily two factors:

a. Demonstrating that the direction of causality is A→B, as opposed to B→A. It is possible that being satisfied with a supervisor causes a subordinate to rate that supervisor as having good interpersonal skills, as opposed to good interpersonal skills causing subordinates to be satisfied.

b. Demonstrating that a third variable(s) does not explain the changes in B. If the supervisors at the refinery "handed out" pay raises on April 10, the subsequent increases in satisfaction with supervision might have been due at least in part to the pay increases, as opposed to increases in supervisory interpersonal skill levels. In short, Susanne has to rule out alternative reasonable explanations before she is safe in concluding that increases in interpersonal skill levels lead to increases in subordinate satisfaction. Some sources of knowledge are better equipped to rule out alternative explanations than are other sources (see Appendix).

3. *Does the information from my study have adequate external validity?* Susanne needed to ask whether it was appropriate for her to generalize and assume that the training seminar would have the same results for the the fruit packing division as was observed at the oil refinery division. Each source of knowledge and the degree to which each facilitates generalizations will be discussed in the Appendix. In general, however, it has been found that the appropriateness of generalizing from one situation to another increases as the similarity of the two situations increases. Therefore, Susanne should raise serious questions about the appropriateness of generalizing from the oil refinery to the fruit packing plant. Although both are owned by the same parent corporation, they differ greatly in location and types of jobs (highly technical versus manual). The employees differ in a number of potentially important ways (age, sex, education, native language, and culture).

In short, the fact that something "works" in one place does not necessarily mean that it will also work elsewhere. If research has shown that a particular effect occurs regardless of the situation, you can be relatively comfortable in generalizing. Under other circumstances, however, you must carefully evaluate the degree to which generalization is merited.

THE RELATIONSHIP BETWEEN RELIABILITY AND VALIDITY

The relationship between reliability and validity can be stated very simply. Good validity cannot exist without good reliability. Good reliability, on the other hand, does not guarantee good validity. Reliability is a necessary, but not sufficient, condition for validity. The use of a well-oiled, clean balance might provide reliable information (the same information each time something is measured). However, if the balance was calibrated incorrectly, it could reliably be providing information with low validity (it *consistently* overweighs or underweighs).

SUMMARY

It is important that the quality of information used in organizations possess both reliability and validity. Reliability is the degree to which the same information would be obtained if the "fact" were measured again. There are three techniques for assessing reliability: test/retest, inter-rater, and alternate forms. Reliability can be improved by improving the measuring device and/or by improving the manner of use of the device.

Before accepting information as usable fact, the information must have acceptable validity. Three types of validity are: construct, internal, and external. Without adequate validity, even a reliable piece of information is not usable.

You must remember that reliability is necessary for validity to exist but that reliability alone does not ensure validity. A rumor you hear 10 times, for example, is not necessarily valid just because the same information is provided repeatedly!

GLOSSARY

Reliability The degree to which the same information would be obtained if a measure were repeated.

Test/Retest Reliability Assessment The evaluation of reliability by comparing the results of two or more measurements using the same technique.

Inter-Rater Reliability Assessment The evaluation of reliability by comparing the results of measurements made by two or more different raters.

Alternate Forms Reliability Assessment The evaluation of reliability by comparing the results of measurements made by two or more different techniques.

Validity The degree to which a piece of information is sound, well-grounded in fact, and able to withstand objection.

Construct Validity The degree to which a piece of information is actually a measure of the fact it is believed to represent.

Internal Validity The degree to which an apparent cause→effect relationship between two variables actually exists.

External Validity The degree to which a fact that is true in one situation is also true in another situation.

STUDY QUESTIONS

1. Many organizations measure the performance level of organizational members. Usually, a person's supervisor rates his/her performance level using a "performance appraisal form." What problems could occur if you, as a manager, use performance information which has inadequate reliability?
2. What actions could you take to evaluate the reliability of the information produced by performance appraisals?
3. If your evaluation of performance information suggests inadequate reliability, what courses of action could you pursue?
4. What factors could reduce the construct validity of a supervisory measure of performance?
5. What problems could occur if you used performance information with inadequate construct validity?
6. Discuss the importance of internal validity to a manager as s/he introduces a new policy (e.g., a merit pay system) and evaluates worker reactions to the new policy.
7. Discuss the importance of external validity to a manager as s/he considers whether or not to adopt a new policy (e.g., a new benefit plan) after seeing the new plan work well in another organization.

Part

3 ■ Behaviors and Attitudes in Organizations

4 ■ Attitude→Behavior Relationships and Their Financial Impact

Behaviors and Attitudes in Organizations: Their Definition and Impact

Chapter 3 identifies and defines each of the major behaviors and attitudes examined by the field of organizational behavior. Of special importance are attitudes relating to the work (e.g., job satisfaction), and involvement in work and the job. Several critical behaviors are also explored, including participation (e.g., attendance, retention), effort, performance, and productivity. These behaviors and attitudes are introduced through the use of organizational examples. Techniques are presented for the measurement of each of these issues, and the importance of these factors to organizations is discussed.

In Chapter 4 various relationships between attitudes and behaviors are considered. In particular, the relationships between satisfaction and worker behaviors such as turnover, absenteeism, performance, and union activity are all examined. For each relationship, a model is presented to help you understand why such relationships may or may not exist. These models are useful for identifying techniques an organization can use to manage these behaviors. Examples of each type of relationship are presented from recent organizational studies. The last part of Chapter 4 presents a technique for documenting the financial impact of attitudes. Briefly, this technique documents employee attitudes and their relationship to behaviors. The organizational costs of variations in the behaviors are estimated. Projections based on these estimates assess the probable financial impact of changes in attitudes on a company's "bottom line." A complete step-by-step organizational example is provided to illustrate this technique.

3 Behaviors and Attitudes in Organization

OVERVIEW
ATTITUDES
- Cognitive Component
- Affective Component
- Behavioral Tendency Component
- Attitude Formation
- Attitude Change
- Job Satisfaction

JOB AND WORK INVOLVEMENT
- Three Components of Work and Job Involvement

BEHAVIORS
- Participation
- Effort
- Performance
- Productivity

SUMMARY

> The historian must have some conception of how men who are not historians behave.
>
> *Edward Morgan Forster*[1]

OVERVIEW

This chapter identifies, defines, and explores the major attitudinal and behavioral reactions of organizational members. You will learn to identify three distinct components of an attitude (cognitive, affective, and behavioral tendency) and explore concepts of work and job involvement. Important participation behaviors such as timeliness, attendance, and retention are examined. The differences and relationship between effort, performance, and productivity are noted. Although other attitudes and behaviors are dealt with in this book, obtaining a thorough understanding of these three is essential if you are to acquire and apply techniques for influencing them. Methods for measuring most of these responses are available, and this chapter provides examples of how to do so. After completing this chapter, you should have a good "feel" for the types of worker responses focused upon in the remainder of the book.

ATTITUDES

Co-Worker Attitudes at Boyer Instrument Company

Dave is an engineer for the Boyer Instrument Company. The following are some of his thoughts about his manager, Roxanne:

Roxanne has been my manager for four years, and I have never liked her. She uses people by putting the good of the department ahead of the good of the people who work for her. Roxanne is 54 years old, never went to college, and has been with the company for 25 years. This background makes her a poor manager. She has insufficient educational

(continued)

training; her experience from only one company is too narrow; she is unwilling to consider new ideas. I am unhappy that she makes over $60,000 a year when I make considerably less. Sure, she manages a department with a budget of over $3 million, but she only has been promoted to this position because she is a woman. I always have avoided Roxanne socially, and I intend to continue doing so. I do, however, plan to work closely with her to show her that I am qualified to be promoted to manager of another department. Once I get that promotion, I intend to beat her out for director of the division. To do this, I will take whatever steps I can to make her look bad to her manager. Once I am promoted above her and become her boss, I will restrict her responsibilities and slow her progress with the company.

Dave's "thoughts" about his manager actually define his **attitude** toward her. This complex attitude can be understood better by recognizing that every attitude has three distinct components (cognitive, affective, and behavioral tendency). They represent the beliefs, feelings and action plans you associate with another person and correspond roughly to the following three questions:

1. What beliefs do you hold about this person (or thing)?
2. What are your feelings toward this person (or thing)?
3. How do you intend to act toward this person (or thing)?

It is critical to differentiate between the three attitude components.

Cognitive Component

The **cognitive component** of an attitude consists of the information a person possesses about a person or thing (the "attitude object"). This is descriptive information and does not include the degree to which you like or dislike the attitude object. It also does not include the way you intend to behave toward the attitude object. The cognitive components of Dave's attitude toward Roxanne are:

Roxanne has been my manager for four years.
Roxanne manages a department with a budget of over $3 million.
Roxanne puts the good of the department before the good of people who work in the department.
Roxanne is 54 years old.
Roxanne has never worked for another company.
Roxanne has worked with this company 25 years.
Roxanne has no college education.
Roxanne makes over $60,000 a year.
Roxanne is a woman.
Roxanne has been promoted to manager because she is a woman.

All of the preceding are pieces of information Dave possesses about his manager. This information may or may not be true, but this is irrelevant. These beliefs will have the same effect on Dave whether or not they are true. The cognitive component of attitudes is based on what a person believes is true. This explains why so many racial, ethnic, and other biases are held so strongly despite facts to the contrary (see Chapter 10).

Each of Dave's co-workers also has attitudes toward Roxanne. The cognitive component of Gregory's attitudes include the beliefs that Roxanne is a 54-year-old woman, has a Harvard MBA, makes $50,000 a year, has 25 years of experience with the company, and was promoted to manager because she is competent. Specific parts of the cognitive component of an attitude frequently are included in the attitude of two different people (Roxanne is a 54-year-old woman who has worked for this company 25 years). Other components can be very different (Roxanne makes $60,000/$50,000; Roxanne was promoted because of sex/competence; Roxanne has no education/MBA).

Affective Component

The **affective component** of an attitude consists of the *feelings* a person has toward an attitude object. This involves evaluation and emotion and is often expressed as like or dislike for the attitude object. The following are parts of the affective component of Dave's attitude toward Roxanne:

Dave dislikes Roxanne personally.

Dave dislikes Roxanne because she puts the good of the department ahead of the good of employees.

Dave dislikes Roxanne because she makes more money than he does.

Dave feels that Roxanne is a poor manager because all of her experience is with one company, because she has no college training, and because this makes her unwilling to consider new ideas.

The affective component of an attitude can be treated as your reaction to the cognitive component. As such, the particular pattern of beliefs you hold about a person or thing exerts a major influence on your feelings toward that object. However, since people use different evaluative processes as they react to their beliefs, two people could have very different affective attitude components even if they possess similar cognitive components. Dave's co-worker James agrees that Roxanne has worked for this company for 25 years, puts the good of the department ahead of the good of its individual members, and makes $60,000. James, however, feels that the 25 years of experience make her a good manager and one who is helpful to him. He believes putting the good of the department first is proper, because he prefers that individuals take care of their own personal problems. He hopes Roxanne's high salary is a good sign for him since he too wants to be a good manager (and be rewarded).

Behavioral Tendency Component

The final element of an attitude concerns the way a person intends to behave toward an attitude object. The following are parts of Dave's **behavioral tendency component:**

I intend to avoid Roxanne socially.
I plan to work with Roxanne as much as I can to show her I am qualified and increase my chances of promotion.
I intend to make Roxanne look bad whenever I can.
Once I am promoted to Roxanne's level, I will try to beat her out for further promotions.
When I become Roxanne's boss, I will restrict her responsibilities and slow her progress with the company.

Both cognitive and affective components of an attitude influence the way you intend to behave toward an attitude object. Again, how-

ever, many different behavioral tendencies are possible, given a particular pattern of beliefs and feelings. Dave and James share both cognitive and affective components of their attitudes toward Roxanne. Nevertheless, Dave intends to undermine Roxanne because he feels she is incompetent, a threat to him, etc., whereas James intends to work with Roxanne so that he can learn some of her skills and become a good manager himself.

Most attitudes are quite complex, because each of the three components involved can be complicated. As you form attitudes in organizations, you often will have a wide range of beliefs, mixed feelings, and varied behavioral tendencies. It is important that you understand the distinction between the three components of attitudes. In knowing how your attitudes are formed and the variety of ways in which organizational events can influence them, you will learn how to manage attitudes.

Attitude Formation

The process of **attitude formation** is a gradual one. You are not born with specific attitudes but, rather, acquire them through the process of learning. This learning can occur because of your personal experiences with an attitude object, by associating an attitude object with something else for which you already have formed an attitude, or through social learning (i.e., information provided to you by others). Most attitudes are a mixture of each of the above.

Personal Experience. You gain *personal experience* in forming attitudes by coming in direct contact with an attitude object. You perceive certain characteristics or traits of the attitude object, and some of these are assimilated into your attitude about the object. Personal experiences usually have their first impact on the cognitive component of an attitude. A person who is hired at a corporation immediately after graduating from college could experience the following and incorporate these experiences into the cognitive component of his/her attitude toward the company:

1. There are a lot of employees at this company.
2. My job is very difficult.
3. My supervisor isn't as busy as I am.
4. Other workers complain a lot.

Remember, two new employees experiencing exactly the same situation may or may not form the same cognitive component. One may ignore certain factors which the other retains. The remaining attitude components, although based on personal experience, are somewhat removed from the events which were directly experienced. Thus, one worker's attitude includes "I like having lots of people around; I like the challenge of my duties; I'm grateful my supervisor has time to check my work; I don't understand why my co-workers aren't satisfied." Another employee, however, might form an attitude which includes "I feel paranoid around so many people; I didn't expect to work so hard at my first job; I think it is disgusting that I have more to do than my supervisor; I intend to seek employment elsewhere the moment something better turns up."

Association. When you "transfer" parts or all of your attitude about an old object to a new attitude object, *association* is forming your new attitude. Two attitude objects can be associated in a variety of ways. You might notice that a new employee is spending a lot of time with one of your co-workers who is competent and whom you like personally. To the degree that you associate these two people, you may begin to form an attitude about the new employee which includes competence and liking. Two attitude objects often are associated for any of a variety of reasons (similarity of appearance, location, etc.). Anything which causes you to associate two attitude objects creates the possibility that you will transfer your attitude from the first to the second. These transfers may be accurate; frequently, they are not. If your attitude toward one politician includes the belief that s/he is dishonest, you may feel the same way about the next politician you meet because of association (again, see Chapter 10).

Social Learning. A very common and powerful source of attitude formation comes from *social learning*. You often form attitudes toward objects you have not experienced directly. Sometimes, you do not even associate a new object with objects for which you already have formed attitudes. In this situation, your attitudes are influenced by information provided you by others who *have* formed attitudes toward the attitude object. In short, your beliefs are molded by others. Sometimes, but not always, the people you are learning from have experienced the attitude object directly. All too often, however, the cognitive components shared by others are not accurate. Since you have no direct experience with the attitude object, it is difficult to evaluate the accuracy of information given you.

Social learning influences not only beliefs but affective reactions and behavioral tendencies as well. Many non-Harvard students believe that Harvard students are rich, spoiled, pompous, self-centered individuals whose knowledge is not as great as they would like us to believe, who take advantage of the organizations which employ them, and who exploit co-workers. But, how many students who feel this way have formed their attitudes from direct contact with Harvard students? How many racial, sexist, and ethnic biases held today are attitudes which were learned socially? Many Americans share several factors in their attitudes toward Russia. How many of these Americans have experienced Russia directly? Finally, although these examples have stressed people (family, friends, coworkers) as sources for social learning, there are many other sources, including formal education, TV, and reading material.

Attitude Change

Attitudes are acquired through learning; **attitude change** occurs through learning. Just as they are formed through personal experience, association, or social learning, attitudes are changed in the same ways. Attitude change can involve addition, removal, or modification of one or more parts of any of the three components. Thus, it is possible for one or two components of an attitude to change while the other component(s) remains the same.

Although it sounds relatively easy to produce changes in attitudes, this usually is not true (see Chapter 17). Once an attitude is formed, it becomes an integral part of an individual. Changing an attitude changes a person. People often resist being changed because they don't want to admit that they were "wrong" in forming their original attitude. If new information conflicts with existing information, it has the potential to change attitudes. Typically, this type of information either is filtered out of a person's consciousness as unnecessary, or is very critically evaluated and treated as suspect. These actions reduce the likelihood of attitude change occurring.

If you wish to change attitudes in organizations, explore your possibilities:

1. Which of the attitude components do you wish to change?
   a. Cognitive component—You must add to, remove, and/or replace beliefs which a person holds about the attitude object.
   b. Affective component—Changing the cognitive component may lead to changes in the affective component. You also can attempt to influence the way a person reacts to beliefs s/he holds.
   c. Behavioral tendency—Changing the cognitive and/or affective components may lead to changes in the behavioral tendency component. You also can attempt to influence the way a person intends to react to the beliefs s/he holds.
2. What experiences can you provide for an individual to influence his/her attitude?
3. What associations can you encourage to influence an individual's attitude?
4. What social learning sources are available which might influence an individual's attitude?

Job Satisfaction

People in organizations form a wide range of attitudes about their work and work-related issues. Each of these attitudes contains cognitive, affective, and behavioral tendency components. The component of work-related attitudes which organizations can influence most directly is usually the cognitive component. This is accomplished by an organization influencing "objective reality" in the hopes that workers will base their beliefs on reality. The component of work-related attitudes which has the most direct impact on an organization is usually the behavioral tendency component. This is because the behavioral tendency has the most direct effect on actual behavior. The work-related attitude component receiving the most attention is the affective component. In fact, many organizations focus almost entirely on the affective component when measuring worker attitudes because they view this component as the most crucial reaction a worker has. After all, this involves the very personal feelings a worker has about his/her work experiences. **Job satisfaction** is the affective component of work and work-related attitudes.

Facets of Job Satisfaction. As is the case with most affective attitude components, job satisfaction is fairly complex. Job satisfaction consists of a variety of satisfaction facets involving workers' feelings toward separate dimensions of the work and work environment. Thus, your job satisfaction includes your feelings about the work itself, about pay, about co-workers, etc. Some of the most common and most important facets of job satisfaction are: the characteristics of the work itself, the amount of work, the physical conditions where the work is done, co-workers, supervision, compensation, promotional opportunities, and organizational policies and practices.

Each of these facets is involved to one degree or another in the job satisfaction of almost all workers in virtually any type of organization. Each of these facets is associated with a corresponding dimension of the work environment. Each is related to the corresponding cognitive component of your attitude toward work. For example, the primary impact of organizational pay is on the beliefs you hold about pay. This, in turn, exerts its primary influence on your pay facet of satisfaction. Keep in mind that two people might experience exactly the same pay system in an organization and still have different levels of pay satisfaction. These differences can be due to the formation of different cognitive components of their attitudes toward pay and/or differences in the way the two workers react to their beliefs about pay. Thus, one person who makes $30,000 per year might be very satisfied with the pay facet while another person making $30,000 could be very dissatisfied (see Part III for reasons why differences in reactions occur).

Your feelings about one facet can spill over and influence your feelings about other facets. Although this typically happens only to a moderate degree, it is very common. Your satisfaction with promotional opportunities, for example, is likely to have some impact on your satisfaction with pay. In spite of the spill-over effect, each facet involves a distinct feeling. For example, it is possible for you to have high satisfaction with pay but relatively low satisfaction with co-workers. Under these circumstances, satisfaction with pay may spill over and keep co-worker satisfaction from being as low as it would be otherwise. Similarly, low satisfaction with co-workers might spill over and prevent pay satisfaction from being as high as it could be. Nevertheless, you cannot fully understand a worker's affective reactions unless you consider each facet.

Overall Job Satisfaction. *Overall job satisfaction* (sometimes called "general job satisfaction") describes a person's overall affective reaction to the set of work and work-related factors. Your job satisfaction includes your overall job satisfaction as well as your facet satisfactions. Overall job satisfaction is a function of the set of facet satisfactions you have. This does not mean, however, you will feel each facet is equally important. Certain facets might be more important to you than others and, therefore, have a larger impact on your overall job satisfaction.

Exhibit 3–1 shows overall satisfaction and facet satisfactions for two employees named Carole and Marni.* Carole and Marni each have a moderate level of overall satisfaction. They both have relatively low satisfaction with facets of the work itself, supervision, and promotional opportunities. They each have moderate levels of satisfaction with facets of the amount of work and organizational policies. They both have high satisfaction with the physical conditions. Marni has a very high level of satisfaction with co-workers; Carole has a low level of satisfaction with this facet. Conversely, Carole has high satisfaction with the compensation facet, and Marni has low satisfaction. If you consider only the overall satisfaction level, you would not have a complete picture of the job satisfaction of either worker. Although the two workers have very similar overall levels of satisfaction, their facet satisfactions vary in two important aspects. The behavioral tendency components of Carole's and

---

*This information was obtained from two employees of a medium-sized multiline insurance company in the Midwest. These employees provided this information in response to a company attitude survey. The two workers held the same job and worked side by side in the same department.

Exhibit 3–1 Satisfaction Levels for Two Co-Workers

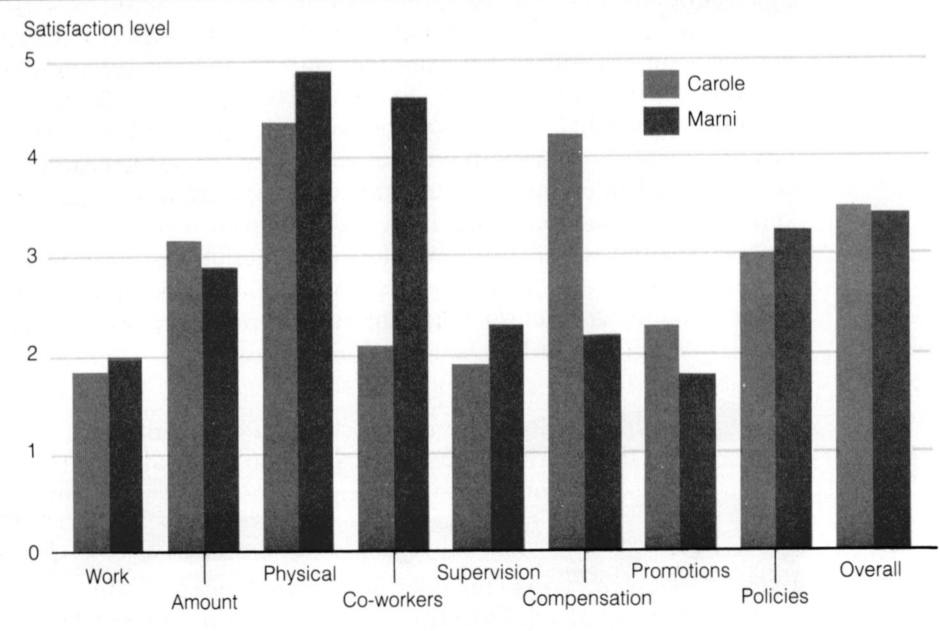

Source: Based on data collected by the author.

Marni's attitudes toward work could be very different due to the differences in facet satisfactions. Therefore, despite the fact that they share similar overall satisfaction levels, their subsequent work behavior also could be very different. Furthermore, any actions the organization could take to improve the satisfaction of these two workers should be influenced heavily by their individual patterns of facet satisfactions. To understand and apply techniques for improving worker satisfaction, you must be able to differentiate between the various facets.

Measurement of Job Satisfaction. Job satisfaction exists only inside a person's head. It cannot be measured directly, the way you can measure physical factors such as height, weight, or distance. Because satisfaction is so important to organizations, however, researchers have developed procedures for the *indirect* measurement of job satisfaction levels. These include: observation of worker behavior (which is very far removed from satisfaction), interviews with workers asking for reports of satisfaction levels, and "paper and pencil" questionnaires designed to obtain information systematically about satisfaction levels. Most measures of satisfaction in use today have poor reliability and validity. However, a tremendous amount of energy has been spent in demonstrating that a few good measures do indeed provide reasonable indirect measures of satisfaction. These measures have been used by practitioners and researchers alike to obtain reliable, valid measures of satisfaction facets and overall satisfaction.

One of the simplest approaches to measuring job satisfaction is shown in Exhibit 3–2, which presents an example of the use of the "Faces" technique.[2]

The Faces scale measures overall satisfaction. It also can measure any facet of satisfaction simply by reworking the directions to focus on the specific facet of interest. This measure of satisfaction is very straightforward, requires very low language skills, and only a small amount of respondent time. It has been shown to possess reasonable reliability and validity. Nevertheless, this technique does have some drawbacks. First, it does not measure satisfaction as precisely as some of the other approaches. Secondly, some workers are offended by what they consider to be its "juvenile" approach. Thirdly, many employees feel (and correctly so) that this approach does not allow them to express fully their feelings about their satisfaction level since it forces them to summarize these feelings into such a simple

Exhibit 3–2 Faces Technique for Measuring Job Satisfaction

Consider all aspects of your job. Circle the face which best describes your feelings about your job in general.

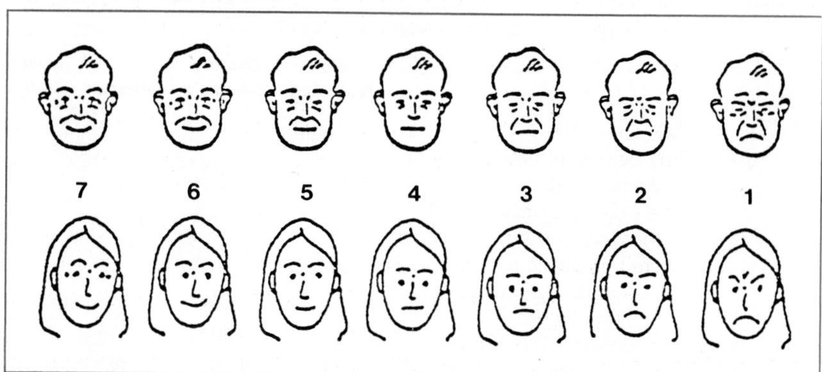

The male faces were originally developed by T. Kunin (1955) as reported in *Personnel Psychology, 8,* 65–78. The matching female faces were created by R. B. Dunham and J. B. Herman and published in the *Journal of Applied Psychology, 60,* 629–631, copyright 1975 by the American Psychological Association. Reprinted with permission of the publisher and authors.

type of response. Finally, because it is so obvious how satisfaction is being measured, respondents might distort their answers to demonstrate strongly their satisfaction or dissatisfaction. Despite these concerns, the Faces technique provides a reasonable overview of satisfaction levels. It is often used in conjunction with other, more thorough measures of satisfaction facets.

Exhibit 3–3 shows sample items from the Minnesota Satisfaction Questionnaire (MSQ).[3] This is another relatively straightforward measure. It asks workers to report how satisfied they are with issues relating to a variety of satisfaction facets. The MSQ also has been shown to provide reliable and valid information about satisfaction. It is more precise than the Faces approach, but it takes longer to answer the 100 items in the questionnaire. Also, as is true for the Faces technique, some respondents might distort their answers to demonstrate strongly their satisfaction or dissatisfaction.

Exhibit 3–4 presents sample items from the Job Descriptive Index (JDI) which is one of the most widely used job satisfaction questionnaires.[4] This measure of job satisfaction takes an interestingly different approach. A series of adjectives is presented to workers, and they are asked to indicate whether or not each adjective describes their own work situation. Thus, the JDI does not measure the affective component of the work attitude but, rather, addresses the cognitive component. Normally, this would not be acceptable, because different people may have different affective reactions to the same piece of information. However, developers of the JDI took very care-

Exhibit 3–3 Minnesota Satisfaction Questionnaire for Measuring Job Satisfaction

On my present job, this is how I feel about . . .

	Not Satisfied	Slightly Satisfied	Satisfied	Very Satisfied	Extremely Satisfied
My job security	1	2	3	4	5
The amount of pay for the work I do	1	2	3	4	5
The working conditions (heating, lighting, ventilation, etc.) on this job	1	2	3	4	5
The opportunities for advancement on this job	1	2	3	4	5
The technical "know-how" of my supervisor	1	2	3	4	5

Source: D. J. Weiss, R. V. Dawis, G. W. England, and L. H. Lofquist (1967). *Manual for the Minnesota Satisfaction Questionnaire* (Minnesota Studies in Vocational Rehabilitation No. 22). Minneapolis, MN: University of Minnesota Industrial Relations Center, Work Adjustment Project. Reproduced by permission. Copyright 1977 by Vocational Psychology Research, University of Minnesota.

Exhibit 3–4 Job Descriptive Index

DIRECTIONS: Think of your present work. What is it like most of the time?

Circle YES if it describes your work.
Circle NO if it does NOT describe it.
Circle ? if you cannot decide.

22a.	Fascinating	YES	NO	?	_____
b.	Routine	YES	NO	?	_____
c.	Satisfying	YES	NO	?	_____
d.	High-pressure job	YES	NO	?	_____
e.	Boring	YES	NO	?	_____

Source: P. C. Smith, L. M. Kendall, and C. L. Hulin. *The measurement of satisfaction in work and retirement.* Chicago, Rand McNally. Copyright 1975, Bowling Green State University, Bowling Green, Ohio, Department of Psychology.

ful steps to identify adjectives which led consistently to positive or negative affective reactions. In fact, over 85 percent of all workers agreed that an adjective was associated with a satisfying or dissatisfying job. In using this "descriptive" approach to measuring job satisfaction, the JDI avoids many problems associated with asking a person to "tell me how satisfied you are." In exchange, however, the JDI measures satisfaction somewhat less directly than do many other measures.

A questionnaire, known as the Index of Organizational Reactions (IOR), is illustrated in Exhibit 3–5.[5] As can be seen, measures of job satisfaction are obtained through a combination of descriptive, affective, and behavioral tendency questions. Both the descriptive and behavioral tendency items in the IOR have been shown to be tied closely to the satisfaction level of job incumbents. Again, however, satisfaction is measured less directly than with some other measures. The IOR has been shown to produce reliable and valid job satisfaction measures across a wide variety of jobs and organizations. In fact, Spanish and French versions of the IOR have been developed to allow cross-cultural comparisons.

The methods for measuring job satisfaction described here provide adequately reliable, valid, and efficient information. A group of 50 to 100 workers can complete one of these questionnaires during a 20-minute meeting. Each of these approaches can be used with a wide range of employees and organizations. The standardized format of the questionnaires allows comparison of results across jobs, departments, companies, etc. Nevertheless, you must realize that none of them is perfect.[6]

Satisfaction measures are used to assess worker reactions to the

Exhibit 3–5 Index of Organizational Reactions (IOR)

1. The people who supervise me have:
   1. Many more good traits than bad ones.
   2. More good traits than bad ones.
   3. About the same number of good traits as bad ones.
   4. More bad traits than good ones.
   5. Many more bad traits than good ones.

2. The supervision I receive is the kind that:
   1. Greatly discourages me from giving extra effort.
   2. Tends to discourage me from giving extra effort.
   3. Has little influence on me.
   4. Encourages me to give extra effort.
   5. Greatly encourages me to give extra effort.

3. How does the way you are treated by those who supervise you influence your *overall attitude* toward your job?
   1. It has a very unfavorable influence.
   2. It has a slightly unfavorable influence.
   3. It has no real effect.
   4. It has a favorable influence.
   5. It has a very favorable influence.

4. How much do the efforts of those who supervise you add to the success of your unit?
   1. A very great deal.
   2. Quite a bit.
   3. Only a little.
   4. Very little.
   5. Almost nothing.

Source: F. J. Smith. The index of organizational reactions. *JSAS Catalog of Selected Documents in Psychology*, 6, Ms. #1265. Copyright 1976 by Frank J. Smith.

work and work environment. An investigation by the American Society for Personnel Administration found that over 40 percent of employers conduct attitude surveys of their employees.[7] This was true across various types of industries, large and small alike. Most of these organizations measure overall satisfaction and one or more of the specific facets of satisfaction. The study also revealed that over 70 percent of organizations conducting surveys did so using questionnaires constructed by members of the organization. Unfortunately, only a small percentage of these questionnaires are adequately reliable and valid. This is not surprising since it took years of work to develop good measures such as the MSQ, JDI, and IOR. More organizations should take advantage of these reliable, valid measures of satisfaction.

Exhibit 3–6 Satisfaction Levels across Time for Sample of U.S. Workers

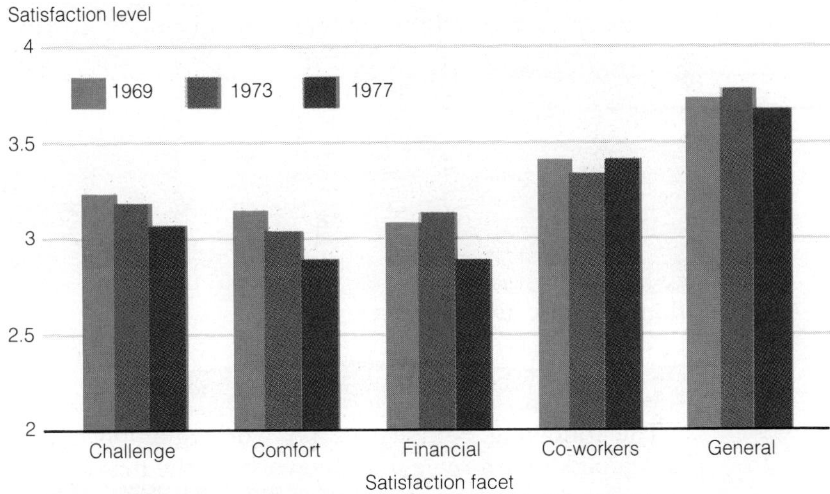

Source: Adapted from G. L. Staines (1979, May–June), Is worker dissatisfaction rising? *Challenge*, 38–45. Reprinted with the permission of the publisher, M. E. Sharpe, Inc., Armonk, New York.

Exhibit 3–6 presents evidence that worker satisfaction levels may be declining, at least for some facets of satisfaction.[8] These data are based on surveys conducted in 1969, 1973, and 1977 on representative samples of over 1,500 workers in the United States.

JOB AND WORK INVOLVEMENT

Job and work involvement are attitudes relating to specific jobs and to work in general. These attitudes deserve special attention because of their importance to both workers and organizations. The term *involvement* has been treated many different ways by both researchers and practitioners. Some refer to involvement as actual behaviors in which people engage (such as attendance, timeliness, and performance). Such a behavioral perspective is inappropriate. Involvement is an attitude and, as such, a variety of behaviors might be associated with a particular level of the involvement attitude. Therefore, involvement will be treated here as a psychological variable—an attitude.

It is important that you distinguish between work involvement and job involvement. **Work involvement** refers to your involvement with or alienation from *work in general.* **Job involvement**, on the other hand, refers to your involvement with or alienation from a *specific job*. The two could be quite different. An auto mechanic, for example, could be highly involved in repairing cars (high involvement in "work"). Her current job, however, requires her to work only on oil changes, something in which she has low involvement (low involvement in "job").

It has been argued that the work involvement attitude is primarily a characteristic attitude of a person which develops through his/her overall socialization.[9] Involvement in work may be influenced by the variety of job experiences you have had during your life, but work involvement at a particular point in time is not influenced heavily by the job you hold at that specific point in time. Job involvement, on the other hand, is an attitude which is influenced heavily by your current job situation. Job involvement is also influenced by previous work experiences (but to a much lesser extent than is work involvement).

Three Components of Work and Job Involvement

The following perspective on work and job involvement was developed after a review of the works of the major job involvement theorists and researchers.[10] *Three components of work and job involvement* can be identified.* The first of these involves a conscious desire and choice to participate in work or a job. The second component involves the degree to which an individual considers work or a job to be a central life interest. The final component is the degree to which a person considers work or a job to be central to his/her self-concept.

The first component of both work and job involvement is the degree to which you *decide* that you will participate in work or a job. This does not mean necessarily that you actually will engage in a higher level of physical involvement than a person who is low in this component. Your actual physical involvement might be restricted by other activities in which you are engaged, by health problems, etc. Conversely, a person who is low in this component might be forced to participate (or lose his/her job). The primary distinguishing factor here is that a person who is high in this involvement component wants to be physically and psychologically involved in work or the job. If you sign up for a class and say "I am really going to 'get into' this class," you are showing that you are high in this first component of involvement. Note that this component is loaded with behavioral tendencies.

The second component of work and job involvement is the degree

*It should be noted that the discussion here goes beyond that of Saleh and Hosek (see note 10). They focused on a general job involvement construct, while the present discussion utilizes their framework to treat work and job involvement as separate attitudes.

Frank J. Smith, currently president of Organizational Studies, Inc. in Chicago, was previously Director of Organizational Surveys for Sears.

What do you think is potentially the most valuable use of organizational surveys? Based on my experience, I would have to say there are several equally valuable and important uses of surveys: (1) They can provide a unique means by which management can evaluate the effectiveness of or reactions to many of the decisions and programs which management must devise or make from time to time. (2) When we have some demonstrated evidence of relationships between survey data and behavior, surveys can, of course, be extremely helpful to management in predicting the behavioral consequences of many of its decisions. (3) Surveys provide a measure of an organization's concern for its people. As such, they help establish an employee-relations discipline in the organization by which management and supervisors at all levels are held accountable for the attitudes of subordinates. (4) A survey can often serve as an "early warning system" for behavioral problems which have not yet emerged. This allows for action to prevent the problem from developing or, at the very least, preparation for dealing with the problem when it does emerge.

What is the most common misuse of organizational surveys? Although not the most common misuse, one of the most powerful abuses involves the violation of promised anonymity to employees. The most common misuse of surveys lies in the amateurish and often careless design of questionnaires and the resulting interpretation (frequently misinterpretation) of their results. In other words, nonobservance of psychometric standards in questionnaire design or the naive interpretation of results based on limited or nonexistent norms or standards would be my prime target for this question.

to which you consider work or the job to be a central life interest. This is simply the degree to which work or the job is an important part of your life. This does not imply any behavioral tendencies. The following statements might be made by a person who is high in the central life interest component of work/job involvement:[11]

The most important things that happen to me involve my work/job.

The major satisfaction in my life comes from my work/job.

I live, eat, and breathe my work/job.

The final component of involvement is the degree to which work or the job is central to your self-concept. A person who is high in this component of involvement makes frequent reference to work or the job in evaluating himself or herself as a person. If you ask "What kind of person am I?" and you answer by referring to work or job-related factors, you are high in this final component of involvement.

Note that none of the components of work/job involvement require that you do your work/job well, or that your work/job satisfy you. Even if you are psychologically committed to participating in your work/job, consider work/job to be an important factor in your life, and evaluate yourself as a person primarily through reference to work/job factors, you still may be a poor and/or dissatisfied worker. Involvement can influence your behavior and satisfaction levels, but involvement is neither performance nor satisfaction. Performance is a behavior. Satisfaction is an affective reaction to experiences. Involvement concerns attitude components which are neither behaviors nor affective reactions. One reason why work and job involvement is important to organizations is that the highly involved worker is likely to take work and the job more seriously and pay more attention to specific aspects of the organizational experience than the person who is less highly involved.

BEHAVIORS

There are many behaviors apparent in the work force, but some are more common than others. Although several of these behaviors are important to organizations, those behaviors related to organizational **participation, effort, performance,** and **productivity** are of special interest.

Participation

Participation is the degree to which a person actually participates in organizational events. This involves being physically present at the organization. Primary participation behaviors are: timeliness (do you arrive at the time you are expected), attendance (do you come to work at all on a particular day), and retention (do you "keep" your job). Negatively speaking, low levels of participation for **timeliness, attendance,** and **retention** are referred to as tardiness, absenteeism, and turnover.

Timeliness. Timeliness is simply the degree to which organizational members arrive at work when they are expected. Unfortunately, few statistics provide an indication of the frequency of on-time arrival. The organizational impact of timeliness depends on the degree to which organizational processes and other organizational members are dependent upon a "tardy" member.

Attendance. Attendance concerns whether or not an organizational member comes to work on a particular day. In most cases, organizational members are paid whether or not they are absent. Thus, the organization receives no work in exchange for its money. Furthermore, it has been estimated that each 1 percent of absenteeism reduces productivity by up to 2.5 percent, due to the necessity for rescheduling production or reshuffling employees.[12]

There are actually many types of absenteeism which can be grouped into two categories of importance to an organization: unavoidable and avoidable. Unavoidable absenteeism includes a variety of factors which are usually beyond a worker's control (physical and emotional illness, child care or other family responsibilities, transportation problems, or marital difficulties). Although organizations conceivably could force organizational members to come to work despite these problems, it would not be reasonable to do so. Avoidable absenteeism, on the other hand, involves a conscious decision on the part of an employee not to come to work on a day when it would be reasonable to do so. There is evidence that avoidable absenteeism accounts for a large amount of the total absenteeism experienced by organizations.

Although both avoidable and unavoidable absenteeism are important to organizations, it is avoidable absenteeism which is most frustrating to organizations and most heavily influenced by organizational events (see Chapter 4 regarding the relationship between job satisfaction and absenteeism). Although it is difficult for an organization to differentiate between unavoidable and avoidable (often called voluntary) absenteeism, it is important to do so. Very different factors influence the two categories.

Recent surveys conducted by the Bureau of National Affairs "Personnel Policies Forum" have revealed that almost all organizations collect and use absenteeism information on a regular basis. Survey results also indicate that most managers feel that it is "reasonable" for employees to miss five or six days of work per year. These same managers report that most of their blue collar workers missed more than a "reasonable" number of days per year, but office/clerical and supervisory/professional employees missed fewer days than would be reasonable.[13]

Exhibit 3–7 presents summary statistics for average absenteeism rates in U.S. organizations for 1976 through 1981.[14] What is not shown in Exhibit 3–7 is that absenteeism rates are considerably higher for larger organizations. Absenteeism also varies by industry, with manufacturing industries reporting the highest rates of absenteeism. Exhibit 3–7 shows that absenteeism rates have been at approximately 2 to 3 percent in the United States. This may not sound like much. Since, however, each 1 percent of absenteeism can lead to as much as a 2.5 percent loss in productivity, a 3 percent absenteeism level can account for as much as a 7.5 percent loss in productivity. Consider what this means to a company if it needs 100 employees to staff the organization. If the absenteeism rate is 3 percent, three extra employees are required just to get the work

Exhibit 3–7 U.S. Absenteeism Rates, 1976–1981

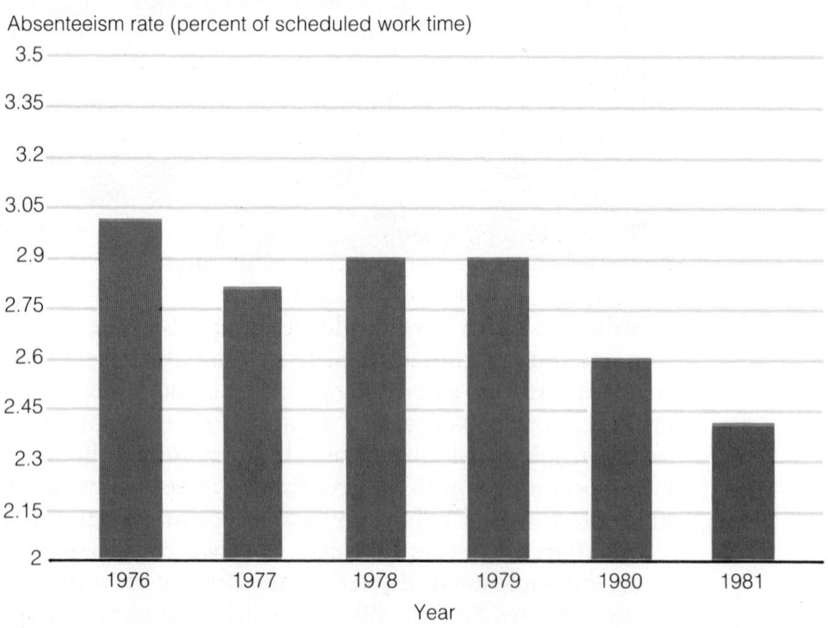

Source: *BNA job absence and turnover report* (1980, 1982).

done. To any company, the financial impact of absenteeism can be substantial. The information shown in Exhibit 3–7 is for all types of absenteeism, and it is not possible to know how much of this is due to avoidable causes. Even a small percentage of avoidable absenteeism, though, can have a major effect on an organization.

Retention. Retention occurs when an individual keeps a job with an organization. *Turnover* is the term used to describe the departure from an organization of one of its members. The costs associated with turnover are high. They include both direct costs (associated with replacement of a departed employee) and indirect costs (associated with training a new employee, lost productivity, organizational disruption, etc.).

There are several categories used to classify turnovers. The first of these is "involuntary" and applies to the termination of an employee by an organization. The only involuntary terminations considered here are those due to employee behavioral problems (low performance, high absenteeism, etc.). The second category of turnover is "voluntary" and applies to termination initiated by an employee. Voluntary turnover can be classified further as either avoidable or unavoidable. Unavoidable voluntary turnover occurs when an employee leaves because a spouse is transferred or for other reasons not centered on a desire to quit the company. Avoidable voluntary turnover occurs when an employee leaves an organization under conditions where s/he could have remained but chose to leave (often for another job).

Many organizations take great steps to reduce turnover levels. To be most effective, their efforts should be focused primarily on voluntary, avoidable turnovers. In addition, organizations should not assume all turnover is negative. Whereas the loss of a good employee is undesirable, the loss of a marginal or submarginal employee actually may be a gain for an organization. Organizations should classify carefully the types of turnover they are examining and attempting to influence.

Over 80 percent of organizations systematically collect and use turnover information on a regular basis.[15] Approximately 20 percent of managers responding to a recent survey report turnover problems costing thousands of dollars in direct costs alone. Exhibit 3–8 presents summary statistics for average turnover rates in U.S. organizations for 1976 through 1981.[16] These statistics show that turnover rates were averaging over 20 percent per year through the 1970s. Then, in the early 1980s, a recession occurred accompanied by record high unemployment rates. During this period, turnover rates dropped substantially (to near 15 percent). Even at a turnover rate of 15 percent per year, an organization is disrupted to a substantial degree.

Exhibit 3–8 U.S. Turnover Rates, 1976–1981

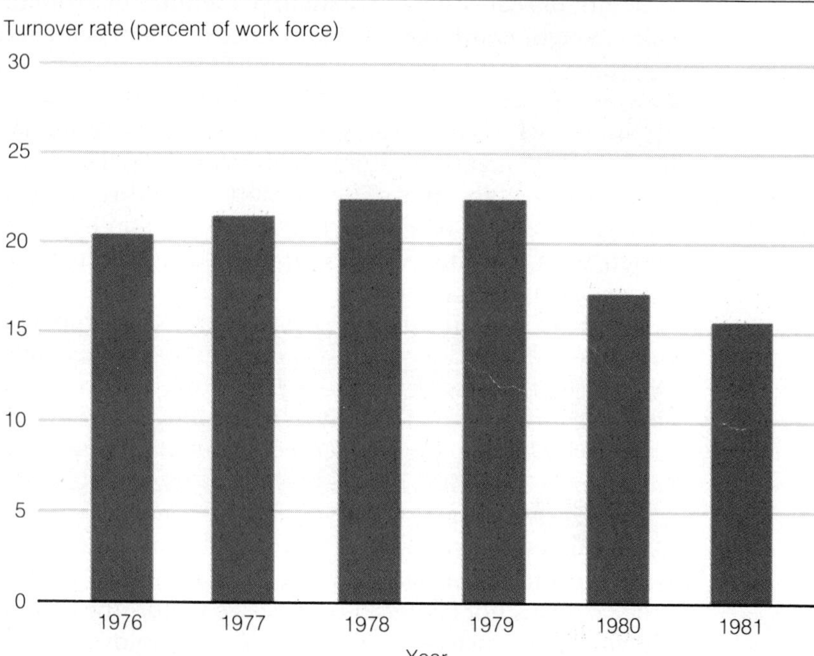

Source: *BNA job absence and turnover report* (1980, 1982).

Effort

Effort involves human behavior directed toward achieving performance. This does not mean effort necessarily will lead to performance. No matter how much effort you exert, little performance will result unless you have the abilities and other "tools" necessary to perform successfully. Despite these observations, however, an organization often has much more direct influence on workers' effort levels than on their performance levels. Your "best bet" is to attempt to increase and direct effort so that it is most likely to lead to performance. Succeeding chapters will address techniques for improving worker skills and providing "tools" needed to turn effort into performance.

Performance

Performance is treated in this book as the behaviors of organizational members which help meet organizational objectives. Effort is human behavior directed toward achieving an organizational objective. Performance is the degree to which that objective actually is met. Objectives vary as much as organizations. Performance can be assembling car parts; it can involve disassembling car parts (as in a recycling organization). Performance can involve concrete behaviors (building a product). It can involve abstract behaviors (supervision, planning, decision making, etc.). In short, performance involves the degree to which an organizational member accomplishes a task which contributes to organizational objectives. Note that performance includes both quantity and quality dimensions.

Performance is obviously a function of effort. Without effort, performance could not result. Effort alone, however, cannot cause performance; many other factors are necessary. Foremost among these is the degree to which an individual has the abilities required to accomplish the task (see Chapter 9). "S/he is a hard worker but just doesn't get the job done" describes a situation in which effort is high but performance is low. Other factors influencing the extent to which effort leads to performance include the degree to which task responsibilities are defined clearly (role clarity) and "tools" needed for successful performance are available (supplies, materials, support, etc.).

Productivity

Productivity is the output of individuals, groups, organizations, or countries and the economic value of the output. Many factors influence productivity levels. Certainly, human resources such as skills, health, training, and subsequent performance of organizational members impact on productivity. So do physical resources such as tools, machinery, and lighting. A high performer in a plant with worn-out machines will not be as productive as s/he would be in a plant with new, efficient equipment.

> Tom and Cindy worked side by side on identical punch press machines at ACME Tool and Die Works. Tom put a reasonable amount of effort into his work, but due to ability limitations, his performance was low in comparison to other workers at the plant (100 punches per hour). Cindy exerted considerably more effort than Tom, had higher abilities, and was the highest performer at the plant (150 punches per hour). On June 27, new punch press machines were put into operation at the plant. On the new machines, Tom made 170 punches per hour and Cindy made 250.

Tom was the lowest performer at the plant, whether he was working with old or new machines. Cindy was the highest performer either way. Tom is considered a poor performer, even though his productivity increased 70 percent after June 27. Tom's efforts did not account for his increases in productivity; new machines did. Productivity levels are influenced by both human and physical capital.

Productivity focuses heavily on quantity (i.e., the economic value of output). Productivity rates typically are figured on the basis of the value of output per hour of employee pay. As such, productivity is influenced not only by performance but also by absenteeism. The economic value of the output of a person who is paid but absent is zero. (Remember, 1 percent of absenteeism can reduce productivity by as much as 2.5 percent.) Productivity is also influenced by turnover. New workers typically produce less per hour until they learn their job more thoroughly. If 15 percent of a company's work force quits each year, a tremendous number of employees (those who were hired recently to replace those who left) are likely to be performing at relatively low proficiency levels at any given time.

Productivity figures can be calculated for individual workers, for organizations, and even for countries. The most frequent calculations involve organization-wide productivity and national productivity. The question "Is there a productivity problem in the United States?" was asked of 434 chief executive officers from organizations around the country.[17] Their replies were grouped to indicate their level of concern for productivity among different types of workers. Fifty-eight percent were concerned about the productivity of executives. Manager and sales productivity concerned 74 percent. Almost 90 percent expressed concern about the productivity levels of other salaried and all hourly employees.

These results clearly indicate that there is widespread concern about productivity levels in the United States. Is this concern justified by the facts? Exhibit 3–9 presents two sets of productivity statistics.[18] The first set of statistics shows the overall productivity level of each of nine industrialized countries. It is encouraging to see that the United States has the highest overall productivity of any of these countries as of 1981. The second set of statistics, however, does provide cause for concern. These figures show that the average annual productivity increase for the United States from 1973 to 1981 was only two tenths of 1 percent. During the same period, other countries were increasing at an annual rate of as much as 3.1 percent. The United States may not stay on top of the productivity ladder for long, given the relative rates of productivity change. The steep increases in productivity during the 1970s were related to technological advances and developments. The leveling and subsequent decreases of the trend in the 1980s indicates stagnating productivity in the United States.

Exhibit 3–9

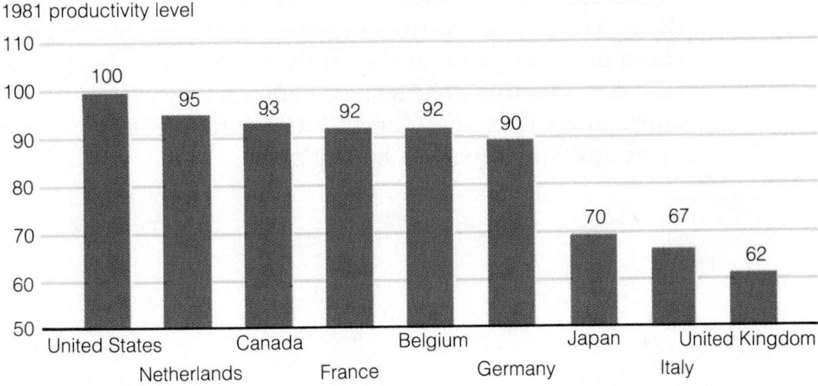

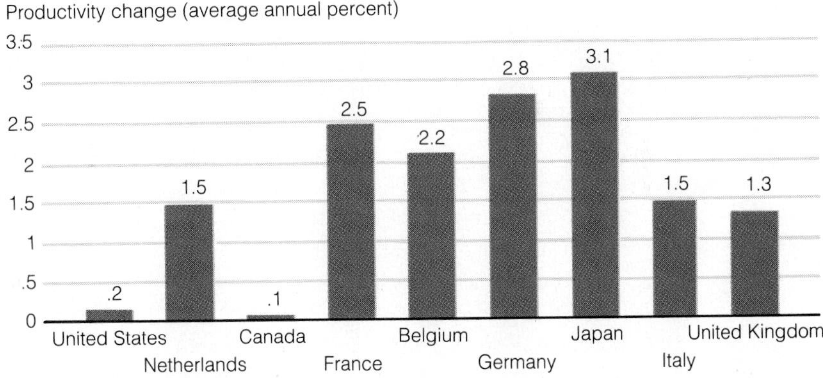

Source: U.S. still leads the productivity pack (1982, September). *Resource*, 8.

SUMMARY

There is a wide range of behaviors and attitudes you must study if you wish to manage effectively in organizations. These include work and work-related attitudes, job and work involvement, participation, effort, performance, and productivity. Each of these is developed and influenced in a somewhat different manner; thus, it is important to differentiate between them. Chapter 4 discusses the relationships between several of these behaviors and attitudes and examines the financial impact of these factors on organizations. In Part III, Chapters 5 through 8 explore the human processes by which behaviors and attitudes are formed and changed. The rest of this book investigates specific organizational determinants of these behaviors and attitudes and presents techniques for influencing them. The answer to the question "What factors do I need to understand and influence in the study of organizational behavior?" was contained in this chapter. The answers to "Why do people behave and feel as they do?" and "What influences these behaviors and attitudes?" are soon to be explored.

GLOSSARY

Attitude The beliefs, feelings, and behavioral tendencies held by a person about an object or person.

Cognitive Attitude Component The information a person possesses about an attitude object.

Affective Attitude Component The feelings a person has toward an attitude object.

Behavioral Tendency Attitude Component The way a person intends to behave toward an attitude object.

Attitude Formation The acquisition of an attitude through learning based on personal experience, association, or social learning.

Attitude Change The relearning of an attitude through personal experience, association, or social learning.

Job Satisfaction The affective component of work and work-related attitudes.

Work Involvement The degree to which a person: chooses to participate in a work experience, considers work to be a central life interest, and considers work central to his/her self-concept.

Job Involvement The degree to which a person: chooses to participate in a specific job experience, considers the job central to life interest, and considers the job central to his/her self-concept.

Participation The degree to which a person actually physically takes part in organizational events.

Timeliness The degree to which a person arrives at work on time (as opposed to tardiness).

Attendance The degree to which a person comes to work on the days s/he is expected (as opposed to absenteeism).

Retention The behavior of keeping a job within an organization (as opposed to turnover).

Effort Human behavior directed toward achieving performance.

Performance The degree to which organizational objectives are met by the behavior of an organizational member.

Productivity The economic value of the outputs of an individual, group, organization, or country.

STUDY QUESTIONS

1. Identify an attitude object (e.g., the organization you work for, a person you work with) and write a description of the three components of your attitude toward that "object."
2. Write a description of the three components of the attitude a friend or co-worker holds toward that same attitude object. Then ask that other person to describe his/her attitude. Were you accurate in your description of that person's attitude? Why or why not?
3. Why is it important to differentiate between the three components of an attitude?
4. Consider your own attitude described in Question 1. Describe the factors which contributed to the development of that attitude. What could cause you to change the attitude?
5. Why is it important to differentiate between job/work involvement and participation?
6. Distinguish between effort, performance, and productivity. Why is it important to make these distinctions?
7. If you were the manager of a large division of a company, how could you obtain information about the attitudes and behaviors in various parts of your division? Why would it be important to compare this information across divisions?

NOTES

1. **Forster, E. M.** (1936). *Abinger harvest.* Reprinted 1966, New York: Harcourt Brace Jovanovich.
2. The male faces were originally developed by **Kunin, T.** (1955) as reported in *Personnel Psychology, 8,* 65–78. The matching female faces were created by **Dunham, R. B., & Herman, J. B.** (1975) and published in the *Journal of Applied Psychology, 60,* 629–631.
3. **Weiss, D. J., Dawis, R. V., England, G. W., & Lofquist, L. H.** (1967). *Manual for the Minnesota Satisfaction Questionnaire* (Minnesota Studies in Vocational Rehabilitation No. 22). Minneapolis, MN: University of Minnesota Industrial Relations Center, Work Adjustment Project.
4. **Smith, P. C., Kendall, L. M., & Hulin, C. L.** (1969). *The measurement of satisfaction in work and retirement.* Chicago: Rand McNally.
5. **Smith, F. J.** (1976). The index of organizational reactions. *JSAS Catalog of Selected Documents in Psychology, 6,* Ms. #1265.

6. For detailed comparisons of these four approaches and their relative strengths and weaknesses, see **Dunham, R. B., Smith, F. J., & Blackburn, R. S.** (1977). Validation of the index of organizational reactions with the JDI, the MSQ, and the Faces scales. *Academy of Management Journal, 20*, 420–432.
7. *ASPA-BNA Survey No. 37*. (1979). Personnel policies: Research and evaluation. Washington, DC: Bureau of National Affairs.
8. **Staines, G. L.** (1979, May–June). Is worker dissatisfaction rising? *Challenge*, 38–45.
9. **Kanungo, R. N.** (1981). Work alienation and involvement: Problems and prospects. *International Review of Applied Psychology, 30*, 1–15; **Rabinowitz, S.** (1981). Towards a developmental model of job involvement. *International Review of Applied Psychology, 30*, 31–50.
10. **Saleh, S. D., & Hosek, J.** (1976). Job involvement: Concepts and measurements. *Academy of Management Journal, 19*, 213–224.
11. Adapted from **Lodahl, T. M., & Kejner, M.** (1965). The definition and measurement of job involvement. *Journal of Applied Psychology, 49*, 24–33.
12. Absenteeism policy guide. *BNA Policy and Practices Manual* (1981). #518, 214:101, p. 23.
13. *BNA Personnel Policies Forum Survey No. 132*. (1981, October). Job absence and turnover control. Washington, DC: Bureau of National Affairs; *BNA Personnel Policies Forum*. (1978, September). Personnel opinions: How much absence is acceptable. Washington, DC: Bureau of National Affairs.
14. *BNA job absence and turnover report*. (1980, December). Washington, DC: Bureau of National Affairs; *BNA job absence and turnover report*. (1982, September). Washington, DC: Bureau of National Affairs.
15. *BNA Personnel Policies Forum Survey No. 132*, 1981, October.
16. *BNA job absence and turnover report*, 1980, 1982.
17. Productivity strategies. *BNA Policy Guide* (1981). #505, 241:321.
18. U.S. still leads the productivity pack (1982, September). *Resource*, p. 8.

4 Attitude→Behavior Relationships and Their Financial Impact

OVERVIEW

SATISFACTION→TURNOVER

- Empirical Findings
- Models Explaining the Satisfaction→Turnover Relationship

SATISFACTION→ABSENTEEISM

- Empirical Findings
- A Satisfaction→Attendance Model

SATISFACTION→PERFORMANCE

- Empirical Findings
- A Satisfaction→Performance Model

SATISFACTION→UNION ACTIVITY

- Empirical Findings
- A Satisfaction→Union Model

THE FINANCIAL IMPACT OF ATTITUDES IN ORGANIZATIONS

A PROCEDURE FOR MEASURING THE FINANCIAL IMPACT OF ATTITUDES

- Step 1: Identification and Measurement of Relevant Attitudes
- Step 2: Identification and Measurement of Relevant "Cost Items"
- Step 3: The Pricing of Behavioral "Cost Items"
- Step 4: Identification of Relationship between Attitudes and Behavioral "Cost Items"
- Step 5: Estimation of the Financial Impact of Attitude Changes

SOME QUALIFYING REMARKS

SUMMARY

Once the heart selects a path the body soon will follow.

Burma Shave

OVERVIEW

The one topic most researched and written about in organizational behavior is the relationship between attitudes and behaviors, particularly the impact of job satisfaction on turnover, absenteeism, performance, and union activity. Until fairly recently, however, little of this attention was guided by any sort of theoretical framework. It was "intuitively obvious" that workers who were satisfied with their work would stay on the job, come to work on a regular basis, perform at a high level, be unlikely to engage in union activity, and would behave in other organizationally desirable ways. Research has shown that the "intuitively obvious" does not always exist, and this chapter presents what research has found to be true regarding these behavioral relationships.

One recent development has been the introduction of a way to estimate with reasonable accuracy the costs associated with employee turnover, absenteeism, and other relevant behaviors in organizations.[1] The behavioral science knowledge of attitude→behavior linkages has been combined with this technique for assessing the financial impact of attitudes. This chapter explores procedures necessary for applying this combined knowledge as a potential tool for your use as a manager.

The following information is a summary of the satisfaction→behavior relationships documented by research. The frequency with which satisfaction has been related to the behavior is reviewed as is the strength of the relationship (i.e., the degree to which satisfaction influences a behavior relative to other factors). A discussion of *why* satisfaction would or would not be expected to influence the behavior and the conditions under which the impact of satisfaction should be expected to be greatest follows the empirical findings.

SATISFACTION→TURNOVER

Empirical Findings

In the past 30 years there have been several comprehensive reviews of the relationship between **job satisfaction and turnover.**[2] These empirical findings indicate a fairly consistent inverse relationship between job satisfaction and turnover. Workers with low levels of job satisfaction are more likely to quit their jobs than are workers with high levels of job satisfaction. This is true for many different types of workers from a wide variety of organizations and jobs.

Satisfaction clearly influences a worker's decision to either stay with one employer or to leave voluntarily in favor of another. You must be very careful, however, to avoid overinterpreting the *strength* of this relationship. Although satisfaction usually has an effect on the turnover decision, the strength of the effect is typically only moderate.

At a large manufacturing company in Montreal, turnover among clerical workers had been averaging about 30 percent, compared to about 20 percent for other large companies in the Montreal area. Charles Hulin of the University of Illinois conducted a job satisfaction survey of the company's clerical workers, using the Job Descriptive Index (see Chapter 3 for a brief discussion of this measure of job satisfaction).[3]

During the six-month period following the survey, 26 of the employees surveyed quit their jobs voluntarily. The satisfaction levels of those who chose to quit were compared to those who chose to stay. As can be seen in Exhibit 4–1, those who quit had lower levels of job satisfaction for four of the five facets of satisfaction measured. During the next six-month period, another 17 of the previously surveyed workers quit. Again, this group had lower levels of satisfaction than those who did not terminate.

After the preceding study was conducted, the organization implemented several policy changes. Although the design of the following study did not allow proof of a cause→effect relationship (i.e., factors other than satisfaction also had an impact on the turnover decision), the policy changes were followed by increases in satisfaction and decreases in turnover.[4]

Exhibit 4–1 Job Satisfaction Levels for Terminators and Nonterminators

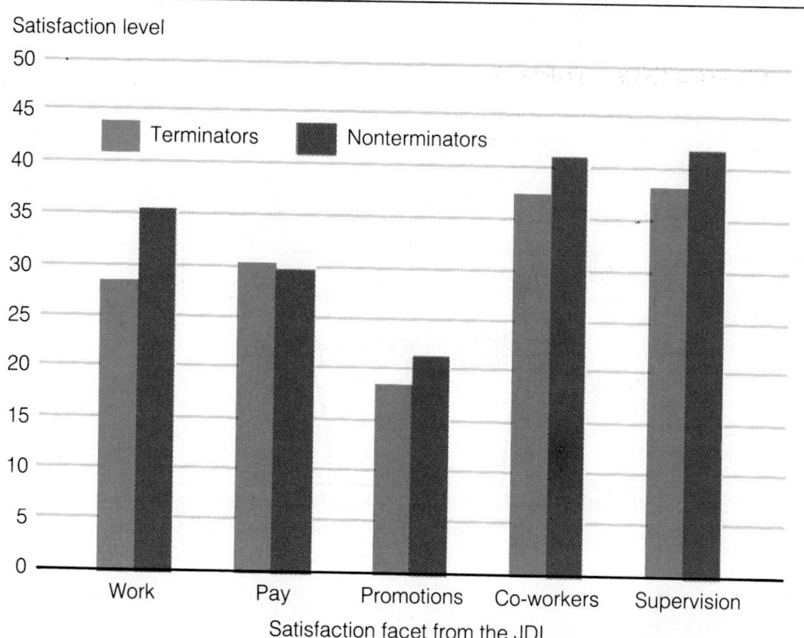

Source: Derived from C. L. Hulin, Job satisfaction and turnover in a female clerical population, *Journal of Applied Psychology, 50*, 280–285, copyright 1966 by the American Psychological Association. Adapted with permission of the publisher and author.

Models Explaining the Satisfaction→Turnover Relationship

Recently, a number of models have been developed to identify the conditions under which employees choose to terminate employment voluntarily.[5] Each of these models suggests that workers systematically examine and evaluate their situation and then make a conscious choice to quit or stay. The models also include other factors believed to influence the quit/stay decision: objective facts (e.g., the availability of employment alternatives), employee perceptions of job opportunities, and employee reactions to the current work experience. Furthermore, most of these models involve a decision to search (or to not search) for employment alternatives, followed by formation of an intent to stay or quit, followed by the actual quit/stay behavior. Even though job satisfaction is included as a determinant of turnover, many other factors also are included. It is not surprising, therefore, that research on the satisfaction→turnover

GUINDON by Guindon. © 1983 Field Enterprises, Inc.
Courtesy of Field Newspaper Syndicate

relationship has found only a moderate direct relationship between the two variables.

Exhibit 4–2 explains turnover by integrating most of the elements of the major turnover models.* A key factor in this model is "Intention to search for alternatives" located near its center. According to this hybrid model, the intention to search for alternatives is influenced primarily by the perceived desirability of movement (leaving) and the perceived ease of movement. The intention to search for alternatives is most likely to develop if movement is perceived to be very easy and desirability of movement is very high. Perceived desirability of movement is influenced both by satisfaction with the current job and by existing opportunities for other jobs within the current organization. Desirability of movement is greatest if you are very dissatisfied with your current job and see little opportunity to

*The right-hand side of the model is taken primarily from the work of Mobley, 1977. The left-hand side of the model originated in the work of March & Simon, 1958, and was modified by Heneman, G., III, & Schwab, D. P. (1975). Work and rewards theories. In D. Yoder & H. G. Heneman, Jr. (Eds.), *Motivation and commitment*. Washington, DC: Bureau of National Affairs, and is modified here to be consistent with the model of Arnold, H. J., & Feldman, D. C. (1982, June). A multivariate analysis of the determinants of job turnover. *Journal of Applied Psychology*, *67*, 350–360.

Exhibit 4–2 Turnover Model

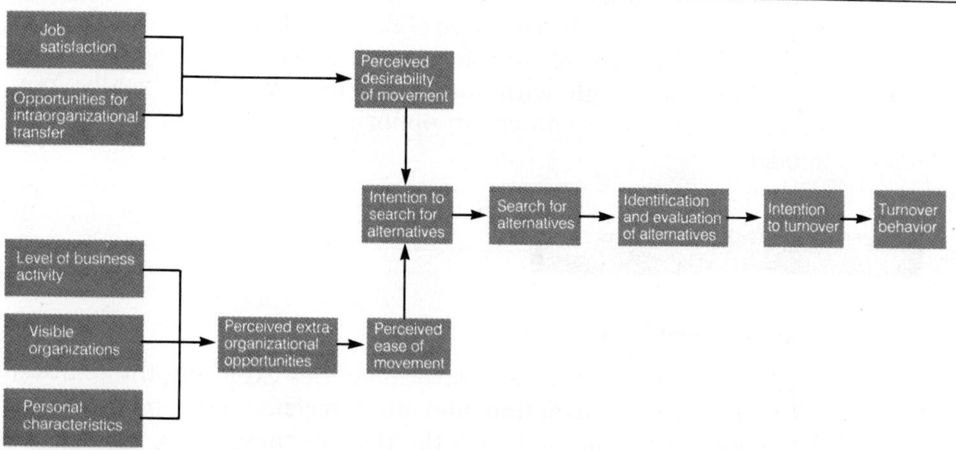

Portions of this model were derived from March and Simon, 1958; Heneman and Schwab, 1975; Mobley, 1977; and Arnold and Feldman, 1982. Adapted with permission of the publisher and authors.

escape it by taking another job within the same organization. Perceived ease of movement depends on perceptions of alternative job opportunities in other organizations. The perceived availability of opportunities outside of the organization is influenced by levels of business activity, how visible jobs at other organizations are to you, and your personal characteristics (skills, work history, etc.).

For those workers who do not develop the intention to search for alternatives, the rest of the model is more or less irrelevant (if you do not search for alternatives, you are unlikely to terminate voluntarily). For the worker who does intend to search for job alternatives, however, several additional processes are involved before engaging in actual turnover behavior. The first worker behavior involved in the decision-making process is to actually conduct the search for alternatives (although not all workers who intend to search follow through and actually engage in the search behavior). The next step is to identify and evaluate alternatives, followed by an intention to leave which directly impacts on the actual turnover behavior. Again, not all workers who intend to quit actually quit.

How well supported are turnover models such as the one shown in Exhibit 4–2? Do these models describe the actual decision-making process? Because Exhibit 4–2 is a hybrid prepared for this text, it has never been tested in its entirety. However, there is some evidence that such a model is appropriate. Heneman and Schwab, after evaluating research on what amounts to the left-hand side of the model, concluded: "By piecing together the evidence . . . there appears to be substantial support for many of these hypotheses."[6] In testing the right-hand side of the model, as well as several of the components of the left-hand side of the model, Michaels and Spector concluded that "The results of the . . . analyses were consistent with the model, although with some modifications. Specifically, perceived alternative employment opportunities added nothing to the model."[7]

SATISFACTION→ABSENTEEISM

Empirical Findings

Although there have been several studies exploring the relationships between **satisfaction and absenteeism**, these relationships have not been examined with the thoroughness of the satisfaction →turnover link.[8] Although there seems to be a fairly consistent inverse relationship between satisfaction and absenteeism (workers with low levels of satisfaction are more likely to be absent than are workers with high satisfaction levels), the strength of these relationships is best classified as moderate.

> It is not uncommon in review articles or in basic texts . . . to find a somewhat unrepresentative selection of empirical studies cited in support of the contention that absence and job satisfaction are causally related. . . . However, this confidence is not shared by all writers who have reviewed a portion of the relevant literature . . . [many] have felt it necessary to hedge generalizations . . . with caveats about the strength, reliability, and cause of the relationship. . . . Upon examination of the 29 studies addressing this question, it is outstandingly clear that inconsistencies abound in methods and measures used, populations sampled, and results reported and that few researchers have sought or achieved a sufficient degree of sophistication or comprehensiveness of approach. . . . At best it seems that job satisfaction and absence from work are tenuously related.[9]

One of the major problems hampering research on the satisfaction→absenteeism issue is the difficulty of differentiating avoidable from unavoidable absenteeism (see Chapter 3). Many of the studies conducted make no attempt to differentiate avoidable from unavoidable absenteeism. Those studies which do make the attempt still face the problem of accurately classifying each absenteeism occurrence. Since few organizational policies permit avoidable absenteeism (at least, without financial penalty), workers are not likely to admit that their absence was avoidable. Yet, it is these very occurrences which are most interesting. This dilemma and other methodological considerations make it impossible at this time to estimate confidently the true strength of the relationship between satisfaction and absenteeism.

There are several reasons why the actual relationship between satisfaction and absenteeism might be even stronger than that between satisfaction and turnover. These reasons center around a worker's relative freedom to be absent without severe consequence. Quitting your job can have rather major consequences. If you have no alternative job, a loss of income results. Even if you have an alternative job, changing jobs often leads to a loss of benefits (e.g., accumulated, but not yet "vested," pension amounts), loss of friendship opportunities with co-workers, disruption of established habits, and a wide variety of other potential problems. Choosing to be absent, on the other hand, seldom has any significant consequence

Satisfaction and Attendance: An Example

When Frank J. Smith was the Director of Organizational Surveys for Sears, Roebuck & Co., he surveyed groups of administrative, technical, and professional employees at the organization's headquarters in Chicago and New York.[11] These surveys used the Index of Organizational Reactions (see Chapter 3) to measure several satisfaction facets.

Under normal conditions, Sears did not permit employees to be absent from work for avoidable reasons without penalty. About four months after the satisfaction surveys were conducted, an unexpected major blizzard hit Chicago. On this day (April 2, 1975) in Chicago, it was both organizationally and socially acceptable to be absent from work. April 2, 1975, in New York was a pleasant weather day, so normal expectations and pressures existed for attendance.

In short, on April 2, 1975, at the New York Sears headquarters there was relatively little freedom for avoidable absenteeism. There were also moderate social and organizational sanctions against such behavior. In Chicago, there was almost complete freedom for avoidable absenteeism and very few social or organizational sanctions for being absent. Departmental attendance rates were measured at each of the two offices on this day, ranging from 89 to 100 percent in New York (median = 96 percent) and from 39 to 97 percent in Chicago (median = 70 percent).

Was there a relationship between departmental satisfaction levels and departmental attendance rates? Exhibit 4–3 answers this question as follows: in New York, absenteeism rates were just as high for satisfied groups of workers as for dissatisfied groups. In Chicago, however, those groups of workers with high satisfaction levels were much more likely to attend work than those with lower satisfaction levels.

Remember that, although there were quite strong satisfaction→absenteeism relationships in Chicago, this occurred under conditions of much greater freedom for voluntary absenteeism than typically is found in organizations. Nonetheless, the findings are significant.

Exhibit 4–3 Strength of the Satisfaction→Attendance Relationship

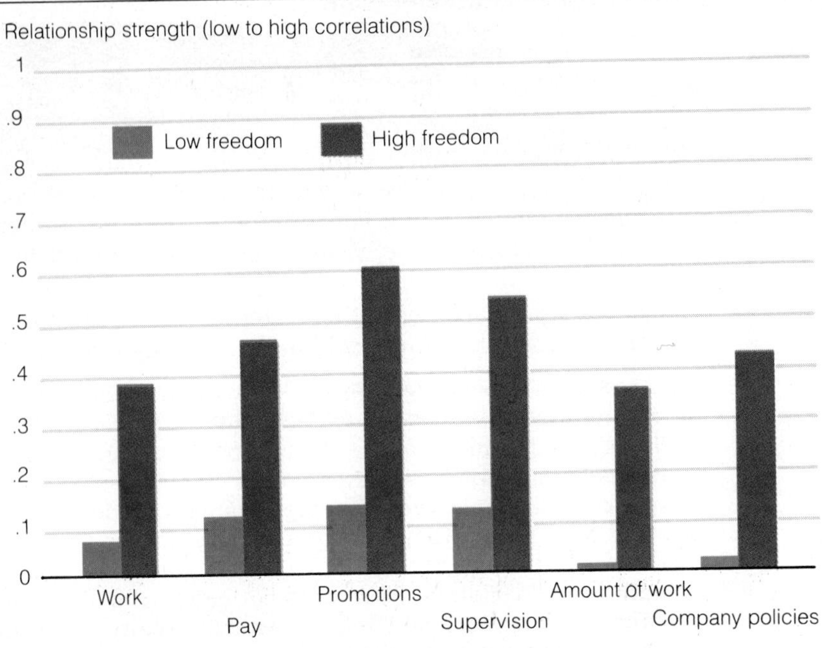

Source: Data for graph from F. J. Smith, Work attitudes as predictors of attendance on a specific day, *Journal of Applied Psychology, 62,* 16–19, copyright 1977 by the American Psychological Association. Adapted with permission of the publisher and author.

for a worker (unless absenteeism is very frequent). In most cases, workers are paid at their regular pay level when absent and benefit from a day of rest or recreation. Managerial censure for occasional absenteeism is unlikely. Most managers consider it reasonable for an employee to be absent five or six days during a year (see Chapter 3). Jeanne Brett of Northwestern University observes that the freedom of workers to be absent without penalty can vary substantially.[10] Therefore, satisfaction→absenteeism relationships should be expected only under circumstances in which the worker perceives a freedom to be absent without major penalty. Unfortunately, to date, few studies have considered directly the freedom/penalty issue when investigating the satisfaction→absenteeism relationship.

A Satisfaction→Attendance Model

Exhibit 4–4 presents portions of a popular model for identifying conditions under which employees would choose to attend or be

Exhibit 4–4 Attendance Model

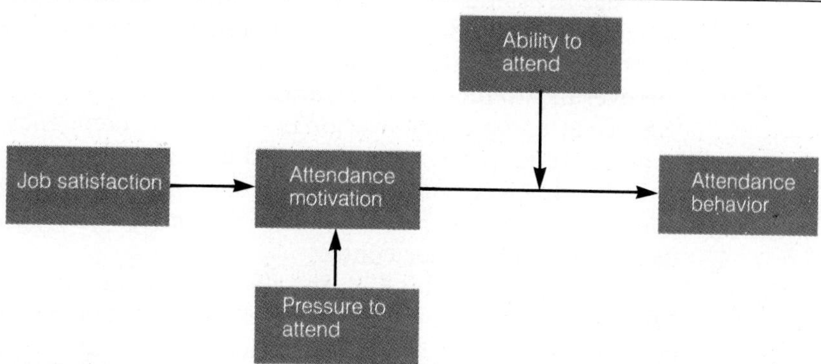

Source: Derived from Steers and Rhodes, Major influences on employee attendance: A process model, *Journal of Applied Psychology, 63,* 391–407, copyright 1978 by the American Psychological Association. Adapted with permission of the publisher and authors.

absent from work on a given day.[12] Note that this model places heavy emphasis on the role of satisfaction as a determinant of attendance/absenteeism behavior. It also considers a variety of other factors, including freedom to be absent without penalty. The model also attempts to differentiate between avoidable and unavoidable absenteeism.*

Exhibit 4–4 is a cognitive model (workers examine and evaluate their situation and make a conscious choice). A key factor in this model is the process of "Attendance motivation" located in its center. This represents a worker willingness to come to work. It appears that Steers and Rhodes intended for this to be treated as a behavioral tendency component of an attitude (see Chapter 3). Two factors are identified as primary determinants of the level of attendance motivation. The first of these is job satisfaction. Although Steers and Rhodes do not state explicitly *why* high satisfaction should increase attendance motivation, it is likely that if you have found previous work experiences to be enjoyable, you would expect future work experiences to be enjoyable (and choose to attend in the hopes of experiencing further enjoyment).

The second major determinant of attendance motivation is called "Pressure to attend." Pressure to attend is a function of economic

*The full model presented by Steers and Rhodes also identifies major determinants of job satisfaction, ability to attend, and pressure to attend. These portions of the model are not presented here since they will be addressed more thoroughly in later portions of this book.

and market conditions, organizational reward and penalty systems, and work-group norms. Steers and Rhodes also include personal work ethic and organizational commitment as factors influencing pressure to attend. Together, these considerations make it desirable for a worker to attend (and/or undesirable for a worker to be absent). Pressure to attend and job satisfaction combine to determine the overall attendance motivation level.

Since attendance motivation is a behavioral tendency component of an attitude, motivation to attend may or may not lead to actual attendance. An employee may plan to come to work but fail to do so due to laziness, car failure, family responsibilities, or a variety of factors beyond his/her control.

According to Exhibit 4–4, the effect of satisfaction on attendance behavior would depend on pressures to attend and ability to attend, neither of which has been systematically included in research on the satisfaction→attendance relationship. In fact, under many conditions (e.g., high pressure to attend or inability to attend) there is no reason to expect a direct satisfaction→attendance relationship. Under other circumstances (e.g., low pressure to attend and high ability to attend), strong satisfaction→attendance relationships should be expected. You can see why research results on this are ambiguous!

SATISFACTION→PERFORMANCE

Empirical Findings

The relationship between **satisfaction and performance** has been one of the most widely researched issues in organizational behavior. The results, however, have been among the most perplexing. For years it was assumed that there was a direct satisfaction→performance relationship, to wit: "A happy worker is a productive worker." If true, an organization which enhanced worker satisfaction would also enhance performance. Unfortunately, the research evidence is quite clear: there is no consistent direct effect of satisfaction on performance.[13] In fact, satisfaction seldom influences performance directly. When it does, the strength of the effect is usually quite small. Furthermore, almost without exception, studies which have shown a satisfaction→performance link were based on research designs incapable of proving the direction of cause→effect relationships or of eliminating reasonable alternative explanations (see Chapter 2). The most appropriate conclusion to draw is that a direct satisfaction→performance link does not exist.

Perhaps because a satisfaction→performance link was considered so desirable, a fair amount of attention was devoted to identifying the conditions under which satisfaction *would* influence performance directly. For example, although satisfaction does not always influence performance, might it do so under appropriate circumstances? Triandis suggested, and both Ewen and Bhagat demonstrated, that satisfaction could have a direct impact on performance if there were a low level of pressure to produce (under high levels of pressure to produce, all workers "have to produce").[14] Wood explored personality factors as possible determinants of whether or not satisfaction would impact performance.[15] Both Inkson and Lopez attempted to demonstrate that self-esteem levels determine whether a satisfaction→performance link exists.[16] Although these studies provide some potential, overall none of them has succeeded particularly well, primarily because they fail to provide an adequate impact on performance.

Brett provided a more reasonable and complete explanation by suggesting that situational factors may influence the impact of satisfaction on performance.[17] She suggested that lower limits are typically placed on acceptable performance levels by company policy. Upper limits, however, are often due to peer pressure, dependence on others, ability levels, and machine limitations. In effect, satisfaction may have little impact on performance because workers usually are not free to vary their performance levels to any significant extent. If there were no such constraints, a stronger satisfaction→performance relationship would be possible. Although this sounds reasonable, it has not been tested thoroughly. Neither does it provide the missing link: an explanation for *why* satisfaction should impact performance directly.

A Satisfaction→Performance Model

As you will discover later in this book (particularly in Chapter 8), it is really more appropriate to say that performance causes satisfaction, albeit indirectly. For now, Exhibit 4–5 shows the chain of events you should consider to understand the satisfaction→performance relationship.[18]

1. A worker performs at a particular level.
2. The worker perceives that his/her performance results in a set of consequences. These consequences include both intrinsic factors (related directly to the experience of performing the work) and extrinsic factors (administered "externally" by someone else).
3. The worker evaluates the consequences. Is each consequence positive or negative? How equitable is each consequence?
4. The worker forms a reaction to the consequences (the worker becomes more or less satisfied).

Exhibit 4–5 Model of Relationship between Satisfaction and Performance

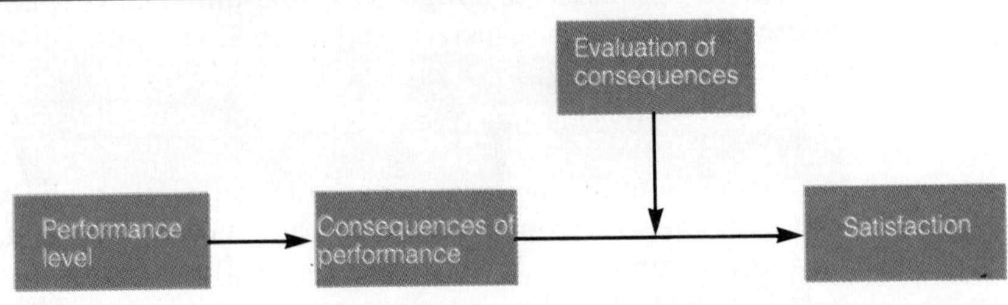

In summary, performance will lead to satisfaction if positive, equitable consequences follow performance (and dissatisfaction if they do not). If you believe that you will experience positive, equitable consequences from your performance, you will be motivated to perform. If you do not believe that performance will lead to positive, equitable consequences, or if you believe that performance will lead to negative and/or inequitable consequences, you will not be motivated to perform.

SATISFACTION→UNION ACTIVITY

Empirical Findings

There has been a long-standing belief that worker satisfaction has a major impact on the decision to join a union and the tendency to take action within a union setting (e.g., filing grievances or striking). Other than a pair of studies conducted 20 to 30 years ago, little adequate research was conducted on the **satisfaction→union** activity relationship until the mid-1970s.[19] This was not due to a lack of interest in the issue. More likely, it was that "everyone knew" satisfaction influenced union activity.[20] Furthermore, it was (and is) extremely difficult to obtain access to the information needed to conduct an adequately designed study of this relationship. Recently, however, several well-designed studies have been conducted exploring the satisfaction→union activity relationship.

In a series of studies involving 1,000 employees and 31 union elections, it was found that votes in union certification elections could be predicted with a high degree of accuracy using employee attitudes.[21] Both employee attitudes toward unions in general and overall job satisfaction contributed heavily to the decision to vote for or against a union in a certification election. In some of these studies, it was possible to predict union voting behavior with greater than 80 percent accuracy. These studies included some evidence that satisfaction with economic factors was a more important determinant of voting behavior than was satisfaction with noneconomic factors.

Over 60,000 employees participated in an attitude survey used to study the impact of job satisfaction on a wide variety of union activities.[22] Subsequent to the survey, employees from 94 participating organizational units experienced some level of union activity, while no union activity occurred in the remaining units. Results indicated that over 30 percent of the variance in union activity could be predicted, using measures of satisfaction. Satisfaction with supervision had the greatest single impact on union activity. Satisfaction with co-workers, career future, company policies, amount of work, physical work conditions, and the work itself contributed to union activity levels. Interestingly, in this study, satisfaction with pay had no significant impact on union activity level. The validity of these findings is supported by a cross-validation (a type of replication) conducted by Hamner and Smith which identified similar effects for a separate sample of workers.[23]

Another good example of the satisfaction→union activity relationship was conducted by Chester Schriesheim of the University of Florida, who explored the relative impact of several factors on voting behavior in union elections.[24] Included in the study were economic and noneconomic job satisfaction factors, attitudes toward unions in general, and attitudes toward the local union. As shown in Exhibit 4–6, union voting was more strongly associated with levels of economic satisfaction (security, pay, working conditions, and company policy) than with noneconomic elements (independence, variety, creativity, and achievement). Voting behavior was also influenced by worker attitudes toward the local union and unions in general. Overall, attitudes explained a very large portion of the variance in voting behavior.

A Satisfaction→Union Model

Exhibit 4–7 presents a basic model describing the probable relationship between satisfaction and union voting behavior. The central factor in this model is "Intention to vote for/against the union." This intention is influenced by satisfaction with both economic and noneconomic factors. A worker's intention to vote for a union will be enhanced if the worker is dissatisfied with economic factors relating to the job *and* s/he believes that the union can and will help improve economic conditions. Similarly, a worker's intention to vote for a

Exhibit 4–6 Relationship Strengths: Satisfaction→Union Activity

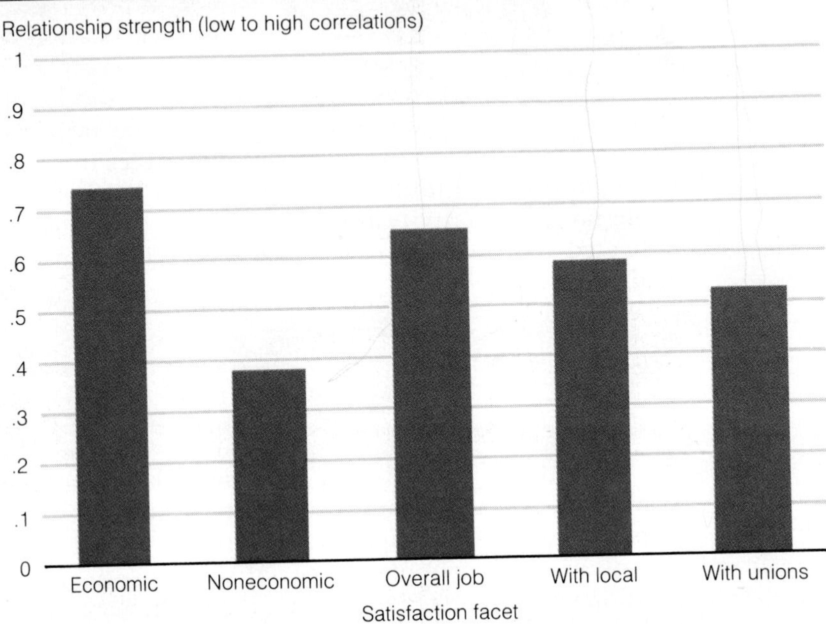

Source: Derived from C. A. Schriesheim, Job satisfaction, attitudes toward unions, and voting in a union representation election, *Journal of Applied Psychology, 63,* 548–552, copyright 1978 by the American Psychological Association. Adapted with permission of the publisher and author.

union will be enhanced if s/he is dissatisfied with noneconomic factors and the worker believes the union can and will help improve these noneconomic conditions.

Attitudes toward unions in general and toward the specific union involved in the election also play an important role in the intention to vote. If a worker has negative attitudes toward unions in general or the specific union involved in the election, the intention to vote for the union will be decreased (even if satisfaction is low and the worker believes the union could help). High satisfaction with the local union (and/or unions in general) should increase the degree of intention to vote for the union. Once the behavioral intention is formed, a worker will typically (but not always) vote consistently with the intention. (Factors such as peer pressure, fear of reprisal, etc., could cause a person who intended to vote one way actually to vote differently.)

Exhibit 4–7 Model of Relationship between Satisfaction and Union Voting

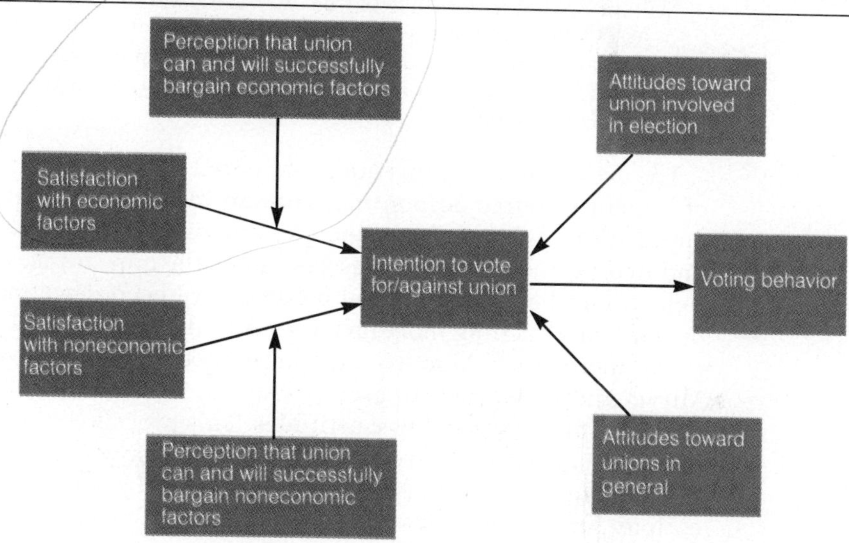

After reviewing Exhibit 4–7, reexamine findings reported in the recent literature by considering the following two factors: (1) union leaders frequently claim that unions cannot and should not deal with noneconomic issues;[25] and (2) research has indicated that satisfaction with economic factors usually has greater impact on voting behavior than does satisfaction with noneconomic factors. If unions state that they have little concern for noneconomic factors and workers agree, it is not surprising that satisfaction with noneconomic factors has little impact on voting behavior. According to the model in Exhibit 4–7, workers not only must be dissatisfied with noneconomic factors to develop the intention to vote for a union, they also must believe that the union can and *will* bargain such issues successfully. There is no substantial evidence to suggest that workers currently are more satisfied with noneconomic than with economic factors (indeed, the opposite may very well be true). It is possible, then, that intentions to vote for unions could be increased if unions convinced workers the union could and would bargain noneconomic issues.

THE FINANCIAL IMPACT OF ATTITUDES IN ORGANIZATIONS

A favorite cliché for the president's letter in corporate annual reports is "Our employees are our most important—our most valuable—

> asset." Turning from the president's letter and looking to the remainder of the report, one might ask, "where is this human asset on these statements which serve as reports on the firm's resources and earnings?" What is the value of this "most important" or "most valuable" asset? Is it increasing, decreasing, or remaining unchanged? What return, if any, is the firm earning on its human assets? Is the firm allocating its human assets in the most profitable way? No answers are to be found.[26]

The article in which this quote appeared marked the introduction of human resource accounting. **Human resource accounting** is the application of accounting principles and practices to the evaluation and management of *human* assets. Since the appearance of that article, a number of accounting models have been developed for the purpose of attaching monetary values to the behaviors of organizational members.[27] More recently, a methodology was developed by Mirvis and Lawler which greatly facilitates measurement of the financial impact of employee attitudes. This procedure, known as **behavioral accounting,** "treats attitudinal measures as indicators of subsequent employee behavior, which in turn have economic implications for the organizations that can be assessed using cost accounting procedures."[28]

Despite the promise of the approach, it has not yet "caught on." In fact, it is quite controversial among many accountants, management practitioners, and theorists. Perhaps this is because accountants are reluctant to work with less than precise information, and management theorists are reluctant to work with cost figures! At any rate, you will learn in later chapters of this book that there are specific actions which organizations can take to change attitudes. As a manager, it would be very useful to you to be able to estimate the potential benefits as well as costs of such actions. The behavioral accounting approach will enable you to estimate both the current financial impact of attitudes on organizations, as well as the probable financial effects of changes in attitudes.

Combining cost estimates with the predicted financial benefits of subsequent attitude changes will allow you to evaluate the potential cost-effectiveness of contemplated organizational programs aimed at enhancing worker attitudes.

This section presents a step-by-step outline of the procedures necessary to measure the financial impact of employee attitudes (this presentation is based primarily on the Mirvis and Lawler behavioral accounting approach). Remember, however, that behavioral accounting has not yet reached the level of precision usually associated with traditional cost accounting procedures. It is not possible, for example, to identify all cost factors associated with behaviors such as absenteeism and turnover. Secondly, current behavioral accounting practices are based primarily on sources of knowledge (cross-sectional and longitudinal studies) which are not capable of *proving* cause→effect relationships (see the Appendix). Therefore, exercise appropriate caution when using behavioral accounting information. Estimates of the financial impact of attitudes should be treated as exactly that—*estimates*. Use caution when generalizing findings over time and across locations until you have documentation that generalization is appropriate.

Remember that factors other than attitudes affect employee behaviors. It is also important to remember the nontangible impact of employee attitudes (e.g., quality of life) which have great (albeit not directly financial) value. Despite these qualifications, behavioral accounting promises to provide a valuable tool for your use as a manager.

A PROCEDURE FOR MEASURING THE FINANCIAL IMPACT OF ATTITUDES

Step 1: Identification and Measurement of Relevant Attitudes

The first step in the behavioral accounting process is to identify the attitudes you have reason to believe might be related to valued employee behaviors. Organizational behavior literature can help by identifying those attitudes which have been related to behaviors in other organizations. It is important to consider the issue of generalizing as you evaluate the experiences of other organizations (see Chapter 2). Evaluate reports of research contained in the literature which show attitudes related to behaviors in organizations similar to yours, with employees similar to yours, and with jobs like yours. Remember that the attitudes of greatest importance may vary somewhat from organization to organization. A good place to begin as you identify relevant attitudes would be the wide range of job satisfaction facets related to behaviors. Other attitudes may also be important. Mirvis and Lawler, for example found that organizational involvement and intrinsic motivation were important determinants of behaviors. At this stage of the process, you are playing an educated guessing game. Later, you will refine the set of attitudes of interest.

Once you have identified the relevant attitudes, you must measure them (usually using an attitude survey). This is not a particularly difficult or unusual task, since the majority of organizations measure employee attitudes. The critical consideration here is to be sure that your measures of worker attitudes are reliable and valid (see Chapter 2). There are a number of well-established surveys for measuring employee attitudes (see Chapter 3).[29] The behavioral accounting process will not function effectively unless attitudes are measured properly!

Step 2: Identification and Measurement of Relevant "Cost Items"

The second step in the behavioral accounting process is to identify and measure employee behaviors expected to have a relationship with the attitudes measured in Step 1. In practice, these first two steps usually are conducted concurrently. Again, organizational behavior literature can be helpful. Look for behaviors which have been related to attitudes in similar organizational situations. Since you now know that several behaviors are frequently influenced by attitudes (e.g., absenteeism, turnover, union activity), determine whether these exist in your situation and to what extent. Under certain circumstances, other behaviors also may be related to attitudes. For example, research has identified cases in which attitudes influenced learning speed, on-the-job accident rates, and industrial sabotage, each of which can have substantial financial impact.

Once you have identified the relevant behaviors, you must measure them. Sometimes this will be relatively easy, as would be the case in organizations which systematically collect good measures of absenteeism on a regular basis. Often, unfortunately, measurement will be more difficult, as in differentiating avoidable from unavoidable absenteeism. Behavioral measures should not be used unless there is evidence that they are both reliable and valid.[30]

Step 3: The Pricing of Behavioral "Cost Items"

The next step in the behavioral accounting process involves pricing each of the behavioral cost items. If, for example, absenteeism is selected as a relevant behavior, you must determine the cost of a day of absenteeism. Macy and Mirvis provide extensive suggestions for the pricing of behaviors, as does the Bureau of National Affairs *Policies and Practices Guide*.[31] Remember that pricing must be accurate for your organization and for the types of jobs being studied. Pricing procedures will be expanded upon during the presentation of the example later in this chapter.

Step 4: Identification of Relationship between Attitudes and Behavioral "Cost Items"

You already have examined typical relationships between attitudes and several relevant behaviors to give you some idea of the types of relationships you might expect to find in your organization. However, the application of behavioral accounting requires that you estimate the nature of the *actual* attitude→behavior relationships in your organization. The nature of these relationships can be determined, using a variety of techniques from straightforward visual inspection of data through very sophisticated statistical analyses. Regardless of the technique used, the questions remain the same: "Is there a relationship between this attitude and this behavior? How strong is the relationship?"

In the example presented at the end of this chapter, both a statistical and a graphical approach are described. Although moderate levels of statistical skills are necessary to use behavioral accounting techniques most effectively, the graphical approach is sufficient for making rough estimates of the impact of attitudes on behaviors. Some nonstatistically oriented managers might wish to use the graphical approach first. The rough results of that evaluation can be used to determine whether to obtain a statistically proficient individual to conduct a more precise analysis.

Step 5: Estimation of the Financial Impact of Attitude Changes

Once you have established the relationship between an attitude and a behavior, you can estimate the impact that an increase or decrease in attitude levels would be likely to have. If you estimate, for example, that an overall increase of "one unit" in satisfaction would lead to a decrease of two days of absenteeism per year per employee, and previous cost estimates indicated that the average cost of a day of absenteeism is $180 per day, an overall increase of "one unit" in satisfaction would be likely to lead to a savings of $360 per year per employee.

Example of Documentation of Financial Impact of Attitudes

This step-by-step example is based on the study conducted by Mirvis and Lawler introducing behavioral accounting to organizational behavior literature.[32] The study was conducted at the branch system of a midwestern banking organization. Participants were 160 tellers from 20 different bank branches. All of the information presented here is based on the actual relationships between attitudes and behaviors for the 160 tellers.

Step 1: Identification and Measurement of Relevant Attitudes. Based on a review of the empirical and theoretical literature, Mirvis and Lawler chose three employee attitudes they believed might exert an impact on employee behaviors:

1. *Intrinsic satisfaction*—level of satisfaction with work-related factors, such as achievement, learning, and skill development.

(continued)

Edward E. Lawler of the University of Southern California has contributed to many areas of OB, including the documentation of the financial impact of attitudes.

Do you believe most organizations can and/or should document the financial impact of worker attitudes? I think most organizations can document the financial impact of worker attitudes. I am not sure that it is important that they do it on a regular basis, but I do think it is useful for them to understand the relationship between behaviors such as absenteeism and turnover and their financial costs. In many cases I think they would treat employees differently if they realized how direct the connection was between attitudes, behaviors, and costs. In many cases, organizations liquidate their human resources in order to save costs in the short run. The long-term effects of this, however, are often disastrous for the organization.

Do many organizations actually use the techniques available for documenting the financial impact of worker attitudes? Why or why not? Very few organizations actually document the financial impact of attitudes. It's a complicated procedure and one that is not well accepted in industry. Indeed, I doubt if it ever will be widely practiced.

What cautions would you express to the manager who wishes to document the financial impact of worker attitudes? I am not sure that there are any cautions other than to point out that it is a bit of work and that any kind of documentation of this type makes some assumptions about costs that may not prove to be true in reality. Like any cost accounting exercise, there is a danger that some of the underlying assumptions may be wrong and that a change in attitudes may not actually result in the expected dollar return.

2. *Organizational involvement*—level of involvement with the bank branch.
3. *Intrinsic motivation*—level of motivation flowing from work-related factors, such as a sense of accomplishment.

These attitudes were measured through an attitude survey using items from the Michigan Assessment of Organizations (Survey Research Center, 1975). These are well-developed measures which have been shown to be both valid and reliable.

Step 2: Identification and Measurement of Relevant "Cost Items." Mirvis and Lawler chose these three behavioral measures ("cost items") because the literature suggested that they had a high probability of being related to employee attitudes. They were also available and convenient (i.e., the organization was keeping systematic records on each of these behaviors):

1. *Unauthorized absences*—absences of less than three days duration for short-term "illness" and "personal" reasons.
2. *Voluntary turnover*—all voluntary departures from the bank. This did *not* include involuntary terminations, maternity-related departures, or transfers within the bank system.
3. *Teller balancing shortages*—The number of teller shortages or overpayments to customers.

Step 3: Pricing of Behavioral "Cost Items." Mirvis and Lawler used the human resource accounting model to document the costs associated with each of the behaviors. The cost of cash shortages was estimated using the actual cash lost (shortages minus recovery). For absenteeism and turnover, however, two types of costs were identified. Direct costs were those directly expended in replacing an absent or terminating employee. Indirect costs were "opportunity lost" expenses (factors such as employee benefit payments, supervisor's time spent in replacing the missing employee, etc.). Mirvis and Lawler argue that this is a very important distinction, as the impact of direct costs will be felt immediately while indirect costs are realized only after subsequent reallocation of organizational resources. Both direct and total (direct + indirect) costs are examined in this example. Exhibit 4–8 identifies the costs associated with each of the three employee behaviors (adjusted for changes in the Consumer Price Index).

Step 4: Identification of Relationships between Attitudes and Behaviors. Mirvis and Lawler identified the relationships between attitudes and behaviors by conducting a longitudinal study (see Chapter 2). They measured the three employee attitudes using a survey. They then tracked worker behaviors over a subsequent three-month period to determine if employees with more positive attitudes were less likely in the future to: be absent, quit voluntarily, and have cash shortages than those employees with less positive attitudes.

Mirvis and Lawler examined these relationships by using a statistical technique known as regression analysis. Exhibit 4–9 shows the strength

(continued)

Exhibit 4–8 Cost per Incident of Absenteeism, Turnover, Shortages

Variable	Cost
Absenteeism:	
Absent employee	
Salary	$ 50.00
Benefits	13.89
Replacement employee	
Training and staff time	4.62
Unabsorbed burden	34.09
Lost profit contribution	41.60
Total direct cost	50.00
Total cost	144.20
Turnover:	
Replacement acquisition	
Direct hiring costs	637.87
Other hiring costs	402.64
Replacement training	
Preassignment	1,646.68
Learning curve	462.17
Unabsorbed burden	1,480.89
Lost profit contribution	842.55
Total direct cost	637.87
Total cost	5,472.80
Shortage	
Actual cash loss	17.86

Note: These figures have been adjusted to reflect an approximate increase in the Consumer Price Index of a factor of 2.17 since this study was conducted.

Source: Based on the work of Mirvis and Lawler in *Journal of Applied Psychology, 62,* pp. 1–8. Copyright 1977 by the American Psychological Association. Adapted with permission of the publisher and authors.

of the relationship between each of the attitudes and each of the behaviors expressed as correlations (the higher the correlation, the stronger the relationship). As you can see, six of the nine relationships are statistically significant (i.e., related more strongly than would be expected due to chance alone). With the exception of the very strong correlation between intrinsic satisfaction and absenteeism, these relationships tend to be relatively low but consistent with the types of satisfaction→ behavior relationships discussed earlier. Exhibit 4–10 presents an example of a "regression line" depicting the relationship between an attitude and a behavior. This example of the relationship between intrinsic satisfaction and absenteeism will also be helpful in Step 5, but for now notice that higher levels of intrinsic satisfaction are associated with lower levels of absenteeism.

(continued)

Exhibit 4–9 Attitude Behavior Relationships

Attitudes	Behaviors		
	Absenteeism	**Turnover**	**Shortages**
Intrinsic satisfaction	−.81†	−.20*	.10
Job involvement	.08	−.29†	−.12
Intrinsic motivation	−.26†	−.16*	−.23†

*Significant.
†Highly significant.
Source: Based on the work of Mirvis and Lawler in *Journal of Applied Psychology, 62,* pp. 1–8. Copyright 1977 by the American Psychological Association. Adapted with permission of the publisher and authors.

The relationships shown in Exhibits 4–9 and 4–10 are reasonably precise due to the statistical evaluation techniques used. These statistical techniques made it possible for Mirvis and Lawler to be accurate relatively quickly. They also illustrated which relationships were statistically significant (i.e., not due to chance). If you do not have good statistical skills, you can obtain rough estimates of the nature of these relationships graphically. Exhibit 4–11 presents a "scattergram" of the relationship between intrinsic satisfaction and absenteeism. To make such a graph, take the satisfaction score and subsequent absenteeism level of each of the 160 employees and place a dot on the graph to indicate the position of each employee. After all 160 dots have been placed on the graph, a pattern will emerge showing the relationship between intrinsic satisfaction and absenteeism. A visual "eyeball" examination of the pattern of dots allows you to draw a line which appears to express the relationship between the two variables. Comparison of this line to the regression line in Exhibit 4–10 shows that the two lines are about the same. Unfortunately, the scattergram approach usually does not provide as accurate an estimate of the nature of the relationship. Nor does it provide a statistical evaluation of the relationship (was the relationship significant?). Furthermore, nine such scattergrams would have to be prepared to examine the relationships between the three attitudes and each of the behaviors. Step 5 of this procedure is dependent on the accuracy of this information. Drawing a regression line based on an "eyeball" analysis is not as precise as that derived from statistical analysis. Nonetheless, this approach can be used for rough estimate purposes.

Step 5: Estimation of the Financial Impact of Attitude Changes. Once the nature of the relationships between attitudes has been determined, you can estimate the financial impact likely to result from a change in

(continued)

Exhibit 4–10 Relationship between Attitude and Behavioral "Cost Item" (Intrinsic Satisfaction→Absenteeism)

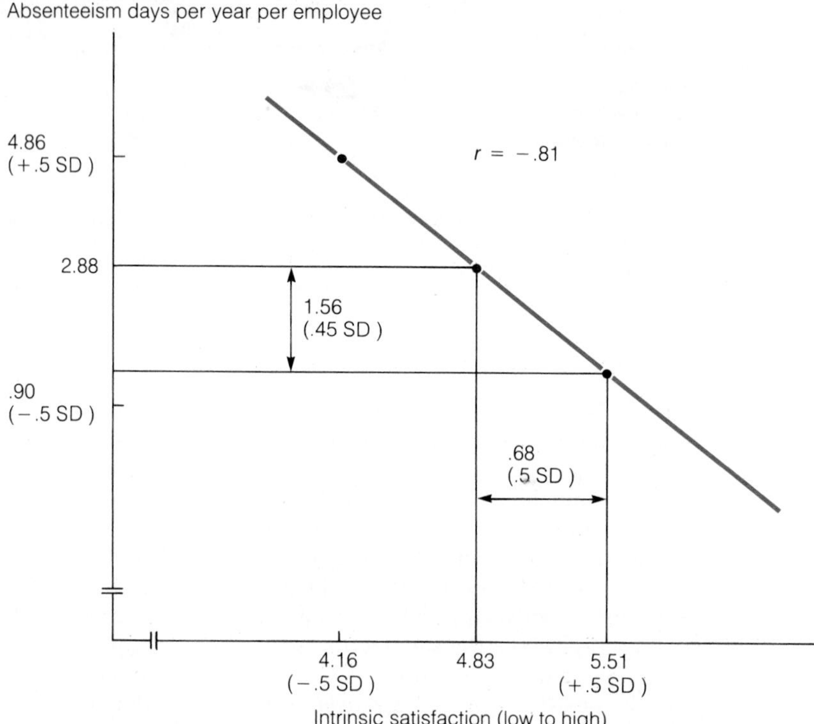

Source: Based on the work of Mirvis and Lawler in *Journal of Applied Psychology, 62,* pp. 1–8. Copyright 1977 by the American Psychological Association. Adapted with permission of the publisher and authors.

one or more of the attitudes. To do this, you must estimate the change in behavior which would follow a change in attitude. Then, place a financial value on the behavioral change. The regression line from Exhibit 4–10 (or Exhibit 4–11 if a scattergram is used) makes it possible to estimate the change in behavior likely. The cost information contained in Exhibit 4–8 allows you to assign an economic value to the change in behavior.

Mirvis and Lawler wanted to know how much behaviors would be likely to change if there were a moderately large improvement in attitudes. To find out, they examined the impact of an increase in intrinsic satisfaction of one half of a standard deviation (SD). The standard deviation is an indication of the range of behavioral scores across the 160 tellers. A change of one half of the SD for intrinsic satisfaction would increase it from the existing average of 4.83 to a new average of 5.51.

(continued)

Exhibit 4–11 Relationship between Attitude and Behavioral "Cost Item" (Intrinsic Satisfaction→Absenteeism Scattergram)

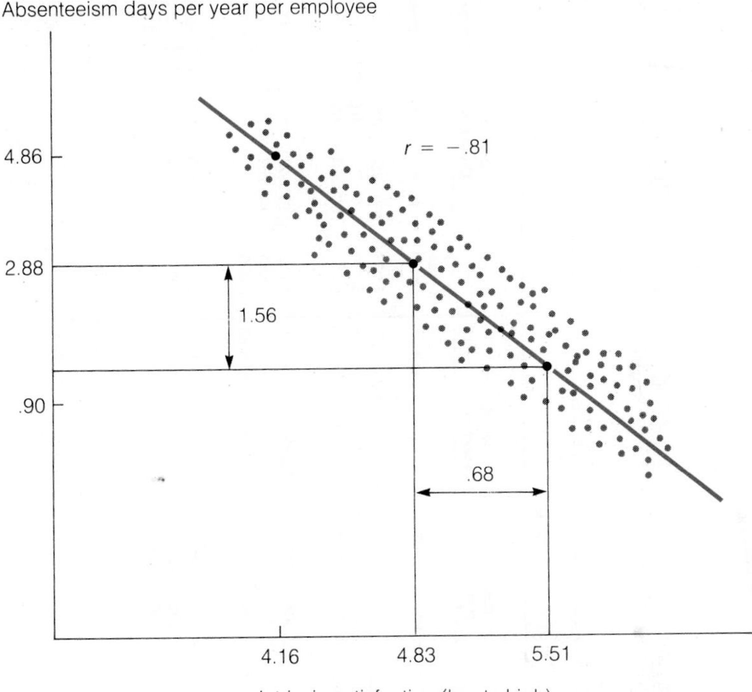

Source: Based on the work of Mirvis and Lawler in *Journal of Applied Psychology, 62,* pp. 1–8. Copyright 1977 by the American Psychological Association. Adapted with permission of the publisher and authors.

To obtain a statistical estimate of the impact of this change in attitude, Mirvis and Lawler used the equation:

$$\text{Estimated financial impact} = \text{(Amount of attitude change [in SDs])} \times \text{(SD of behavior) (Attitude}\rightarrow\text{behavior correlation)}$$

The same estimate of behavioral improvement could be obtained by constructing the regression line for each attitude→behavior relationship (as shown in Exhibits 4–10 or 4–11) and graphically estimating the impact of the attitude change as is shown in these figures. The vertical line drawn from 4.83 in Exhibit 4–10 represents the average intrinsic satisfaction score from the attitude survey. When this line intercepts the

(continued)

Exhibit 4–12 Annual Impact of Attitude for 160 Tellers

Attitude	Attitude Change		Absenteeism					Turnover					Shortages					Combined Cost Difference	
				Cost of Absenteeism		Cost Savings Compared to Current			Cost of Turnover		Cost Savings Compared to Current			Cost of Shortages		Cost Savings Compared to Current			
	SD	Score	Days Absent	Direct	Full	Direct	Full	Turnover Occur-rences	Direct	Full	Direct	Full	Shortage Occur-rences	Direct	Full	Direct	Full	Direct	Full
Intrinsic satisfaction	+.5	5.51	211	$10,550	$ 30,426	$ 12,500	$ 36,050	77	$ 49,116	$421,406	$ 24,239	$ 207,967	6,067	$108,357	$108,357	*	*	$ 36,739	$ 244,017
	0	4.83	461	23,050	66,476	—	—	115	73,355	629,373	—	—	5,894	105,267	105,267	—	—	—	—
	−.5	4.16	710	35,500	102,382	(12,500)	(36,050)	154	98,232	842,813	(24,239)	(207,967)	5,741	102,534	102,534	*	*	(36,739)	(244,017)
Job involvement	+.5	6.19	480	24,000	69,216	*	*	58	36,996	317,423	36,359	311,950	5,707	101,927	101,927	*	*	36,359	311,950
	0	5.81	461	23,050	66,476	—	—	115	73,355	629,373	—	—	5,894	105,267	105,267	—	—	—	—
	−.5	5.44	442	22,100	63,736	*	*	173	110,352	946,796	(36,359)	(311,950)	6,086			*	*	(36,359)	(311,950)
Intrinsic motivation	+.5	6.59	384	19,200	55,376	3,850	11,100	77	49,116	421,406	24,239	207,967	5,510	98,409	98,409	$ 6,858	$ 6,858	34,947	225,925
	0	6.11	461	23,050	66,476	—	—	115	73,355	629,373	—	—	5,894	105,267	105,267	—	—	—	—
	−.5	5.63	538	26,900	77,580	(3,850)	(11,100)	154	98,232	842,813	(24,239)	(207,967)	6,278	112,125	112,125	(6,858)	(6,858)	(34,947)	(225,925)
Combined effect	+.5	—	—	—	—	16,350	47,150	—	—	—	84,837	727,884	—	—	—	6,858	6,858	108,045	781,892
	0	—	—	—	—	—	—	—	—	—	—	—	—	—	—	—	—	—	—
	−.5	—	—	—	—	(16,350)	(47,150)	—	—	—	(84,837)	(727,884)	—	—	—	(6,858)	(6,858)	(108,045)	(781,892)

*Effect not significant and therefore not shown.

†Based on Table 4 from Mirvis and Lawler, 1977. Converted to annual basis for 160 employees. Adjusted (217 percent) for 10 year CPI change factor.

regression line, a horizontal line is drawn to the left. This horizontal line intercepts the absenteeism axis at 2.88 (which was the average absenteeism rate per year per employee). The vertical line drawn from 5.51 represents a "what if" line (What if average intrinsic satisfaction increased from 4.83 to 5.51?). The answer to this "what if" question is obtained by extending a line upward from 5.51 until it intercepts the regression line and then drawing a horizontal line to the left. This horizontal line intercepts the absenteeism axis at approximately 1.32. The answer to the question, therefore, is: "Average absenteeism would be likely to drop from 2.88 incidents per year per employee to 1.32."

With an average absenteeism rate per person of 2.88, the total number of absenteeism days per year for the 160 tellers was 2.88 × 160 = 461. With an average absenteeism rate per person of 1.32, the total number of absenteeism days per year for the 160 tellers would be 1.32 × 160 = 211. These figures are entered in Exhibit 4–12. This type of analysis was conducted for the impact of intrinsic satisfaction changes on turnover and cash shortages. It also was used to estimate the impact of the other two attitudes on each behavior. These figures were entered in Exhibit 4–12.

Information on the cost of each behavior was taken from Exhibit 4–8 and multiplied by the number of incidents of each behavior listed in Exhibit 4–12. The result was entered in Exhibit 4–12 to indicate the cost of each "level" of behavior. Through a simple subtraction process, it was possible to determine the financial impact of each change in behavior expected to follow the hypothetical change in each attitude. For example, Exhibit 4–12 shows the direct cost to the organization for 461 days of absenteeism would be $23,050 (461 × $50). The direct cost of 211 days of absenteeism would be only $10,550 (211 × $50). Thus, an increase of average intrinsic satisfaction from 4.83 to 5.51 would be likely to result in a financial savings of $12,500 ($23,050 − $10,550). Exhibit 4–12 shows the financial impact calculations for hypothetical increases and decreases in each of the attitudes (considering both direct costs and total costs).

What is the bottom line? If each of the attitudes were to increase by an average of .5 SD, it is likely that the subsequent changes in behaviors would result in a direct financial savings of $108,045 ($675.28 per employee). If full costs were considered, the impact would be $781,892 ($4,886.83 per employee).

SOME QUALIFYING REMARKS

The behavioral accounting technique is a good one, but it is not perfect and a number of cautions are necessary. Mirvis and Lawler point out that the time lag selected for examining the impact of attitudes on behaviors is critical, and no rule of thumb currently exists for identifying appropriate time lags. Mirvis and Lawler used a three-month lag, which they felt was consistent with the economic literature, but an organization would be well advised to consider a variety of intervals. It is also important for an organization to continue to study the relationship between attitudes and behaviors over time, since both the magnitude and nature of the relationships can change (particularly when you consider the nonattitude variables which influence behaviors).

A technical caution is also in order. If two or more attitudes included in the same financial analysis are strongly related to one another, overestimates of the behavioral impact of attitude change could occur. This was not a significant problem in the Mirvis and Lawler study, and it is a problem which can be easily solved by using a statistical technique (e.g., multiple regression analysis) to evaluate the joint impact of several attitudes on a behavior.

> There are a number of obvious advantages to the method. . . . It provides a practical approach to the problem of relating attitudes to costs . . . and it has the potential to increase significantly the impact and usefulness of attitudinal data. An attitude report to managers containing this information could serve to focus attention on the whole concept of employee satisfaction and motivation; and it could also stimulate them to introduce changes that would improve satisfaction and motivation. One useful feature of the model used in this paper is that it relates attitudes to future costs. Thus, organizations could use it as a way of diagnosing future costs and could initiate programs designed to reduce those costs. . . . Ultimately, the method could be used for undertaking a cost-benefit analysis of programs designed to improve employee satisfaction, motivation, group functioning, or supervision.[33]

An Estimate of the National Financial Impact of Attitudes

The following analysis was conducted to obtain a rough estimate of the direct financial impact which would occur if job satisfaction increased an average of .1 SD (a relatively modest increase) across all members of the American work force.

Data used:

1. The typical correlation between satisfaction and turnover was estimated at −.25 by Porter and Steers.[34]
2. The typical correlation between satisfaction→absenteeism would also be −.25.[35]
3. National turnover rates were estimated at about 15.6 percent on an annual basis, with a standard deviation of about 8.5 percent.[36]
4. Absenteeism rates are about six days per year per employee with a standard deviation of about 2.67.[37]

(continued)

5. The national work force was estimated at approximately 100 million.[38]
6. Average compensation (wages plus benefits) was estimated at $83.50/day or $20,850/year.[39]

Analysis:

1. Impact of increase of .1 SD in satisfaction on turnover using Mirvis and Lawler equation [(.1) (SD) (correlation)]:

   (.1) (8.5) (.25) = .213 percent turnover reduction
   (100,000,000 employees) (.00213) = 213,000 fewer turnovers
   If cost of turnover were only 10 percent of compensation . . .
   (213,000) (.10) ($20,850) = **$444,105,000** savings

2. Impact of increase of .1 SD in satisfaction on absenteeism:

   (.1) (2.67) (.25) = .067 days/year less absenteeism/worker
   (100,000,000 employees) (.067) = 6,700,000 fewer absences
   If cost of absenteeism is only average daily compensation . . .
   (6,700,000) ($83.50) = **$559,450,000** savings

3. $444,105,000 + $559,450,000 = *$1,003,555,000 total financial impact,* or ONE BILLION, THREE MILLION, FIVE HUNDRED FIFTY THOUSAND DOLLARS

SUMMARY

The relationship between attitudes (especially satisfaction) and a variety of behaviors has been given a great deal of attention in the organizational behavior literature and related literatures for decades. It has been only recently, however, that appropriate models has been developed to recognize the complexity of the existing satisfaction→behavior relationships. Although none of these models have yet been tested completely, preliminary findings generally support the basic structure of the models. Your knowledge of these models will guide you in understanding not only the relationships between satisfaction and behaviors, but *how* and *why* they exist.

Your knowledge of behavioral accounting estimates likewise will be valuable to you as a manager. Although this technique is not likely to be precise when first used by an organization, over time an organization will gain experience in using this method. In this way, both attitudes and behaviors can be identified and measured more accurately, and the financial impact of behaviors estimated more precisely. By using the steps outlined above, you will be able to refine the accuracy of your predictions of actual behavioral changes which will follow attitude changes. Behavioral accounting provides a useful tool for the manager and one which will grow in usefulness with time if used properly.

GLOSSARY

Job Satisfaction→Turnover Relationship A fairly consistent but moderate relationship; turnover is more likely when satisfaction is low.

Job Satisfaction→Absenteeism Relationship A fairly consistent, moderate relationship, with absenteeism more likely when low satisfaction exists.

Job Satisfaction→Performance Relationship A relationship which, in reality, does not exist in any consistent fashion. There is some evidence, however, that performance can lead to satisfaction.

Job Satisfaction→Union Activity Relationship An apparently consistent and strong relationship; union activity is more likely when satisfaction is low.

Human Resource Accounting The application of accounting principles and practices to the evaluation and management of human assets.

Behavioral Accounting The process of measuring the financial impact of employee attitudes.

STUDY QUESTIONS

1. Discuss steps an organization could take to manage turnover. Use the model shown in Exhibit 4–2 to guide this discussion.
2. Under what conditions would you expect the strongest impact of job satisfaction on turnover?
3. Discuss steps an organization could take to manage absenteeism. Use the model shown in Exhibit 4–4 to guide this discussion.
4. Under what conditions would job satisfaction have little or no impact on absenteeism?
5. Discuss the factors which prevent job satisfaction from having a direct impact on performance effectiveness.
6. How could a union use the model shown in Exhibit 4–7 to target organizations for union drives?
7. For an organization with which you are familiar, identify the potential benefits of documenting the financial impact of attitudes. Identify the difficulties you would encounter in trying to perform such a documentation.
8. Discuss reasons why very few organizations attempt to document the financial impact of attitudes.

NOTES

1. **Likert, R.** (1973). Human resource accounting: Building and assessing productive organizations. *Personnel, 50*, 8–24.
2. **Brayfield, A. H., & Crockett, W. H.** (1955). Employee attitudes and employee performance. *Psychological Bulletin, 52*, 396–424; **Herzberg, F., Mausner, B., Peterson, R. O., & Captwell, D. F.** (1957). *Job attitudes: Review of research opinion*. Pittsburgh: Psychological Series of Pittsburgh; **Vroom, V. A.** (1974). *Work and motivation*. New York: Wiley; **Porter, L. W., & Steers, R. M.** (1973). Organizational, work, and personal factors in employee turnover and absenteeism. *Psychological Bulletin, 80*, 151–176; **Price, J.** (1977). *The study of turnover*. Ames: Iowa State University Press; **Mobley, W. H., Griffeth, R. W., Hand, H. H., & Meglino, B. M.** (1979). Review and conceptual analysis of the employee turnover process. *Psychological Bulletin, 86*, 493–522.
3. **Hulin, C. L.** (1966). Job satisfaction and turnover in a female clerical population. *Journal of Applied Psychology, 50*, 280–285; **Smith, P. C., Kendall, L. M., & Hulin, C. L.** (1969). *The measurement of satisfaction in work and retirement*. Chicago: Rand McNally.
4. **Hulin, C. L.** (1968). Effects of changes in job satisfaction levels on employee turnover. *Journal of Applied Psychology, 52*, 122–126.
5. The most widely known of these models include those set forth by **Mobley, W. H.** (1977). Intermediate linkages in the relationship between job satisfaction and employee turnover. *Journal of Applied Psychology, 62*, 237–240 (later modified by **Mobley, W. H., Griffeth, R. W., Hand, H. H., & Meglino, B. M.**, 1979); **Price**, 1977; **March, J. G., & Simon, H. A.** (1958). *Organizations*. New York: Wiley (later modified by a number of theorists).
6. **Heneman, G., III, & Schwab, D. P.** (1975). Work and rewards theories. In *Motivation and Commitment*. Washington, DC: Bureau of National Affairs.
7. **Mobley et al.**, 1979; **Michaels, C. E., & Spector, P. E.** (1982). Causes of employee turnover: A test of the Mobley, Griffeth, Hand, and Meglino model. *Journal of Applied Psychology, 67*, 53–59.
8. **Vroom**, 1964; **Porter & Steers**, 1973; **Muchinsky, P. M.** (1977). Employee absenteeism: A review of the literature. *Journal of Vocational Behavior, 10*, 316–340; **Steers, R. M., & Rhodes, S. R.** (1978). Major influences on employee attendance: A process model. *Journal of Applied Psychology, 63*, 391–407.
9. **Nicholson, N., Brown, C. A., & Chadwick-Jones, J. K.** (1976). Absence from work and job satisfaction. *Journal of Applied Psychology, 61*, 728–737, pp. 728–729, 734. Copyright 1976 by the American Psychological Association. Reprinted by permission of the publisher.

10. Jeanne Brett in **Herman, J. B.** (1973). Are situational contingencies limiting job attitude-job performance relationships? *Organizational Behavior and Human Performance, 10,* 208–224.
11. **Smith, F. J.** (1977). Work attitudes as predictors of attendance on a specific day. *Journal of Applied Psychology, 62,* 16–19.
12. **Steers & Rhodes,** 1978.
13. **Brayfield & Crockett,** 1955; **Herzberg et al.,** 1957; **Vroom,** 1964, as well as a number of more recent reevaluations of the literature.
14. **Triandis, H. C.** (1959). A critique and experimental design for the study of the relationship between productivity and job satisfaction. *Psychological Bulletin, 56,* 309–316; **Ewen, R. B.** (1973). Pressure for production, task difficulty, and the correlation between job satisfaction and job performance. *Journal of Applied Psychology, 58,* 378–380; **Bhagat, R. S.** (1982). Conditions under which stronger job performance–job satisfaction relationships may be observed: A closer look at two situational contingencies. *Academy of Management Journal, 25,* 772–789.
15. **Wood, D. A.** (1974). Effect of work orientation differences on job attitude correlates. *Journal of Applied Psychology, 59,* 54–60.
16. **Inkson, J. H. K.** (1978). Self-esteem as a moderator of the relationship between job performance and job satisfaction. *Journal of Applied Psychology, 63,* 243–247; **Lopez, E. M.** (1982). A test of the self-consistency theory of the job performance–job satisfaction relationship. *Academy of Management Journal, 25,* 335–348.
17. Jeanne Brett in **Herman,** 1973.
18. This type of process has received reasonable support through recent research such as that by **Greene, C. N.** (1972). The satisfaction-performance controversy. *Business Horizons, 15,* 31–41.
19. **Fleishman, E. A., Harris, E. F., & Burtt, H. E.** (1955). *Leadership and supervision in individuals.* Columbus: Ohio State University, Personnel Research Board; **Fleishman, E. A., & Harris, E. F.** (1962). Patterns of leadership behavior related to employee grievances and turnover. *Personnel Psychology, 15,* 43–56.
20. **Dunnette, M. D., & Kirchner, W. K.** (1965). *Psychology applied to industry.* New York: Appleton-Century-Crofts; **Stagner, R., & Rosen, H.** (1965). *Psychology of union-management relations.* Monterey, CA: Brooks/Cole.
21. **Getman, J. G., Goldberg, S. B., & Herman, J. B.** (1972). The National Labor Relations Board voting study: A preliminary report. *Journal of Legal Studies, 1,* 233–258; **Getman, J. G., Goldberg, S. B., & Herman, J. B.** (1976). *Union representation elections: Law and reality.* New York: Russell Sage Foundation; **Herman,** 1973; **Getman, J. G., & Goldberg, S. B.** (1976). The behavioral assumptions underlying NLRB regulation of campaign misrepresentations: An empirical evaluation. *Stanford Law Review, 28,* 263–284.

22. **Hamner, W. C., & Smith, F. J.** (1978). Work attitudes as predictors of unionization activity. *Journal of Applied Psychology, 63,* 415–421.

23. Ibid.

24. **Schriesheim, C. A.** (1978). Job satisfaction, attitudes toward unions, and voting in a union representation election. *Journal of Applied Psychology, 63,* 548–552.

25. **Beer, M., & Driscoll, J. W.** (1977). Strategies for change. In J. R. Hackman & J. L. Suttle (Eds.), *Improving life at work: Behavioral science approaches to organizational change.* (pp. 364–453). Santa Monica, CA: Goodyear Publishing; **Kochan, T. A., Lipsky, D. B., & Dyer, L.** (1974, December). Collective bargaining and the quality of work: The views of local union activists. In *Proceedings of the Twenty-Seventh Annual Winter Meetings of the Industrial Relations Research Association.* San Francisco: Industrial Relations Research Association; **Piore, M.** (1974). Upward mobility, job monotony, and labor market structure. In J. O'Toole (Ed.), *Work and the quality of life: Resource papers for work in America.* Cambridge: MIT Press; **Strauss, G.** (1977). Managerial practices. In J. R. Hackman & J. L. Suttle (Eds.), *Improving life at work: Behavioral science approaches to organizational change.* Santa Monica, CA: Goodyear Publishing.

26. **Brummet, R., Flamholtz, E., & Pyle, W.** (1968). Human resource accounting—A challenge for accountants. *The Accounting Review,* 217–224.

27. **Likert,** 1973; **Likert, R., & Bowers, D. G.** (1973). Improving the accuracy of P/L reports by estimating the change in dollar value of the human organization. *Michigan Business Review, 25,* 15–24.

28. **Mirvis, P. H., & Lawler, E. E., III.** (1977). Measuring the financial impact of employee attitudes. *Journal of Applied Psychology, 62,* 1–8.

29. These are discussed more thoroughly, as is the entire attitude survey process, in a book by **Dunham, R. B., & Smith, F. J.** (1979). *Organizational surveys: An internal assessment of organizational health.* Glenview, IL: Scott, Foresman.

30. Guidance is available for the measurement of behaviors such as turnover and absenteeism. One source for such information is the Bureau of National Affairs *Policies and Practices Guide,* a publication updated biweekly to reflect current organizational practices.

31. **Macy, B. A., & Mirvis, P. H.** (1976). Measuring quality of work and organizational effectiveness in behavioral-economic terms. *Administrative Science Quarterly, 21,* 212–226.

32. Ibid, p. 2.

33. Ibid.

34. **Porter, L. W., & Steers, R. M.** (1973). Organizational, work, and personal factors in employee turnover and absenteeism. *Psychological Bulletin, 80,* 151–176.

35. **Vroom, V. H.** (1964). *Work and motivation*. New York: Wiley.
36. Information obtained from Bureau of National Affairs (BNA) reports on national turnover rates.
37. From BNA reports.
38. From BNA figures.
39. Economic figures from BNA.

Part

5 ■ Need Theories

6 ■ Learning Theories and Behavior Modification

7 ■ Equity and Goal Theories

8 ■ An Integrative Model: Expectancy Theory

Theories in Organizational Behavior

The chapters in Part III address the major theories in organizational behavior and provide a wide range of perspectives on behaviors and attitudes in organizations. Each has relative strengths and limitations. Together, these theories will help you understand *why* people react to organizational events with particular attitudes and behaviors. This understanding will assist you in predicting how organizational members will react to future events. More importantly, these theories are valuable if you are to make important organizational decisions. They will not tell you what decisions to make, but they will provide guidance and suggest new ways to view your organization.

The theories are presented in roughly the same order as the complexity of the human cognitive process assumed to be influencing attitudes and behaviors. The cognitive processes involve conscious thinking, understanding and inference. Need and operant theories (Chapters 5 and 6) make very few assumptions about the human cognitive process. In other words, it is not necessary for you to know what an individual is thinking to understand his/her reactions. Equity theories (Chapter 7) introduce a moderate level of cognitive processing by suggesting that people evaluate their situations by comparing them to the situations of others. Both goal theory (Chapter 7) and expectancy theory (Chapter 8) rely completely on understanding quite complex cognitive processes. According to these theories, organizational events will have little impact on organizational members unless the events are perceived, evaluated, and reacted to through complex cognitive processes.

A popular way of classifying theories is to define each as either "content," "reinforcement," or "process" based. A *content theory* concentrates on underlying needs which energize a person. Thus, the need theories discussed in Chapter 5 are all clearly content theories. A *reinforcement theory* focuses on environmental events which determine a person's behavior. The noncognitive learning theories discussed in Chapter 6 are reinforcement theories. A *process theory* explores the internal reasons why a person responds in a particular manner (i.e., the underlying *processes* are examined). There is general agreement that the theories discussed in Chapters 7 and 8 (equity, goal, and expectancy) are primarily process theories. The cognitive learning models discussed in Chapter 6 are also in part process theories due to the attention given to cognitive processes.

There is no way to identify the "best" theory. Indeed, the best perspective is obtained by combing the ideas of each. So that you may select the perspective most fitting in your situation, the best of each theory is explored (and its limitations noted). Your best bet is to follow the solid advice offered by Craig Pinder of the University of British Columbia:

> Students should be as impressed with basic guidelines for *evaluating* theories of motivation as they are familiar with the content of the theories themselves. They should develop the skill to evaluate and consume theories sensibly, both to forestall the likelihood of their growing obsolete once they leave the academic setting, and to avoid the human and organizational costs which can accompany a false sense of simplicity. They should be impressed that what we know about human motivation in organizations is much less than what many single, simplistic theories claim. Finally, they should be helped to develop the eclectic skills of approaching and understanding motivation or other organizational problems from any of several perspectives, simultaneously drawing on the strengths and weaknesses of various theories. Our combined knowledge, based on the theory and research of several different schools of thought on motivation, is substantial, although the contribution of no one theoretical approach justifies our complete faith.[1]

NOTE

1. **Pinder, C. C.** (1977) Concerning the application of human motivation theories in organizational settings. *Academy of Management Review, 2,* 393–394.

5 Need Theories

OVERVIEW
MASLOW'S NEED HIERARCHY THEORY
Maslow's Need Categories
A Different Perspective
Implications for Organizations
Research Support for Maslow's Theory
ALDERFER'S ERG THEORY
MANIFEST NEED THEORIES
HERZBERG'S MOTIVATION-HYGIENE THEORY
Criticism and Controversy
SUMMARY

When the stomach is full, it is easy to talk of fasting.

St. Jerome

OVERVIEW

All of the theories described in this chapter focus on the importance of human needs. Each states that people are motivated to satisfy their needs and that obtaining something you need can be satisfying to you. The theories differ in terms of the number and types of needs said to exist. Some theories propose a *hierarchy* of needs to determine the relative importance of needs. These theories, frequently referred to as "content theories," provide an understanding of what people will and will not value. They are relatively unconcerned, however, with the human cognitive processes involved. The most important of these theories are the need hierarchy theories, manifest need theories, and motivation-hygiene theory. You will have to understand how to recognize and satisfy human needs to be an effective manager.

MASLOW'S NEED HIERARCHY THEORY

Without question, the most widely known need hierarchy theory was developed by Abraham Maslow during the 1940s.[1] Maslow's early career as a psychologist focused heavily on primate behavior. His interests then turned to human personality theory and the understanding of human behavior through psychoanalysis. Maslow's clinical experiences as a psychologist influenced development of his five-level need hierarchy theory. Initially, Maslow's work generated much interest among other clinical and personality psychologists but had relatively little impact in organizations. Managers gained

HÄGAR The Horrible
by DIK BROWNE
WHAT IS IT THAT I REALLY WANT?
WHAT DOES ANY VIKING WANT?
MY NEEDS ARE FEW...
ONE FRIEND— MY SWORD
ONE BUGLE CALL — THE CHARGE!
ONE LOVE — THE SEA!
ONE GOAL — GLORY!
5-22
ANYTHING ELSE?
TWO BEERS

most of their exposure to Maslow's ideas in the 1960s, mostly because of the "popularized" writings of Douglas McGregor.[2]

Maslow's need hierarchy theory is based primarily on the following propositions:

a. People possess a common set of five universal needs (physiological/survival, safety/security, social, ego/self-esteem, and self-actualization).
b. If a need is not met, dissatisfaction is experienced. Furthermore, people are motivated to satisfy their needs and will behave accordingly.
c. When a need is met, satisfaction is experienced.
d. A need which is satisfied no longer motivates.
e. If satisfaction of a need is not maintained, the need regains its ability to motivate.
f. There is a particular order in which people will strive to satisfy their needs. This order follows a hierarchy from the lowest-level (most basic) needs through the highest-order needs.

Exhibit 5–1 illustrates Maslow's proposed hierarchy of needs. According to Maslow, you first direct your attention toward satisfying the lowest-level needs in this hierarchy (physiological and survival). Once you have fulfilled this set of needs reasonably well, you essentially lose interest in them. You then direct your attention toward satisfying needs at the next level of the hierarchy. When these have been met, you address needs at the next level of the hierarchy. This is repeated as you focus on satisfying needs at successively higher levels in the hierarchy. It should be noted (but seldom is) that Maslow identified this particular hierarchy as representative of the total set of humans. He never intended to suggest that *every* person will have needs arranged in exactly this hierarchical pattern.

> We have spoken so far as if this hierarchy were a fixed order but actually it is not nearly as rigid as we may have implied. It is true that most of the people with whom we have worked have seemed to have these basic needs in about the order that has been indicated. However there have been a number of exceptions. [For example] there are other, apparently innately creative people in whom the drive to creativeness seems to be more important than any other. . . . Their creativeness might appear not as self-actualization released by basic satisfaction, but in spite of lack of basic satisfaction.[3]

An overriding principle in this theory is that a person's attention and energy will be focused on satisfying the lowest-level need not currently satisfied. Thus, if you are starving, you will be motivated to find food to satisfy this basic physiological need. If the basic physiological needs are satisfied reasonably well, however, you are likely

Exhibit 5–1 Maslow's Need Hierarchy

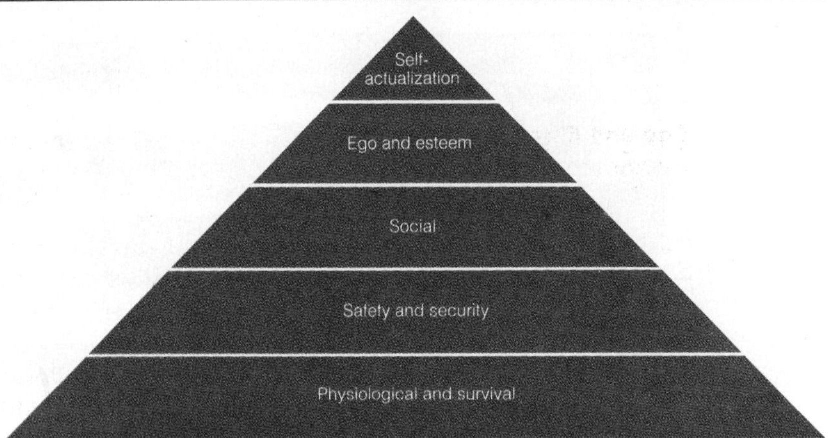

Source: Based on A. H. Maslow (1943). A theory of human motivation. *Psychological Bulletin, 50,* 370–396.

to devote attention to needs higher in the hierarchy. It is possible for a need to be satisfied at one point in time but become active (dissatisfied) again. You may not be motivated to eat immediately after a large meal, but you eventually can become hungry again. A need must be "maintained" (you must continue to eat occasionally), or it will become active again. According to Maslow, if a lower-level need is reactivated, a person once again concentrates on that need. In effect, you will lose interest in the higher-level needs whether or not they have been met adequately.

Maslow's Need Categories

Physiological Needs. **Physiological needs** constitute the most basic (lowest level) set of needs in Maslow's hierarchy. This extremely wide range of individual "chemical needs" includes the need for food, water, sex, sleep, activity, sensory satisfaction, and all other physiological requirements of the body.

Safety and Security Needs. **Safety and security needs** define the second level of the hierarchy. This set of needs involves meeting threats to the well-being of the individual such as extremes of temperature, wild animals, assault, murder, tyranny, or any of a wide range of causes for insecurity.

Social Needs. Originally referred to by Maslow as "love needs," **social needs** include the need for emotional love, friendship, and affectionate relationships with people in general. Thus, this set of needs includes the need for affiliation and a general sense of belonging. These needs could be addressed through friends, spouses, children, parents, and various types of group memberships.

Ego and Esteem. Needs relating to the desire for self-respect, self-esteem, and the esteem of others are referred to as **ego and esteem** needs. Internally focused needs in this category involve the need for achievement, confidence, independence, and freedom. Externally oriented needs include desire for prestige, recognition, reputation, attention, and appreciation.

Self-actualization. These needs are of the highest order in Maslow's hierarchy. **Self-actualization** is said to become dominant only after all lower-order needs have been satisfied reasonably well. Self-actualization involves a desire for self-fulfillment, "to become more and more what one is, to become everything that one is capable of becoming."[4] Since people are so different in their relative strengths and weaknesses, in capacities and limitations, the meaning of self-actualization varies greatly. For a musician, self-actualization could be making the best music possible. An artist might achieve self-actualization by creating the best art possible. For a student, self-actualization could involve learning as much as possible in his/her field of choice. If you are a student and have reached the top of the hierarchy, you *will* seek maximum learning. If you are a student not currently seeking maximum learning, you are not at the self-actualization stage. The need for self-actualization is different from all other need categories in one very important way—you can never satisfy this need fully. No matter what you become, you can always become more. Since this need can never be fully satisfied, it never loses its ability to motivate.

A Different Perspective

Maslow noted that it is possible to define a more basic hierarchy consisting of only two levels, deficiency needs and growth needs. This alternative was proposed, in part, to reflect differences in the way people order the five specific sets of needs. Presumably, the two-level hierarchy should exist more consistently across people. Lower-order needs (physiological, safety, and social) are classified as *deficiency* needs. Higher-order needs (esteem and self-actualization) are referred to as *growth* needs.

Implications for Organizations

Maslow's theory has been adopted widely by organizations and used frequently to guide important management decisions. The theory suggests that rewards or opportunities which satisfy currently active needs of employees will be motivating. It would seem reasonable, therefore, for organizations to assess need levels of their workers and identify which types of organizational rewards and opportunities would be most valuable. The model is an individual one, though, so organizations must realize there will be differences in need states across people. There also will be differences within one person over time. If an organization successfully helps an organizational member satisfy a need, the reward or experience will lose its motivating power to the next higher level in the hierarchy. Thus, different rewards and opportunities are needed as an individual grows within an organization. As organizational members move up in the organizational hierarchy, their needs move up the hierarchy. Maslow argues that this is desirable, particularly if a person reaches the self-actualization level. Once a person engages in self-actualizing behavior, s/he will be motivated to continue reaching higher levels of accomplishment. Exhibit 5–2 provides a summary of specific factors an organization could use to motivate employees at each of the five levels of Maslow's hierarchy.

Research Support for Maslow's Theory

Maslow's theory is accepted widely in its entirety. Research conducted on the model, however, does not merit such total acceptance. In spite of the tremendous amount of research generated by Maslow's theory, the theory has never been tested adequately as a complete theory, for a number of methodological reasons. Individual components have been tested with reasonably acceptable methods; results have been mixed.

Research indicates that:

1. There is a wide range of needs, and people are motivated to satisfy these needs.
2. Most needs can be addressed in organizational settings for the purpose of motivating organizational members.
3. For a given individual, some needs are more powerful than others at a particular point in time.
4. For a given individual, the importance of needs changes over time.
5. Different people have different needs.
6. Once a need is satisfied, it then becomes a less powerful motivator.
7. Some sort of hierarchy of needs exists.

Exhibit 5–2 Maslow's Need Hierarchy

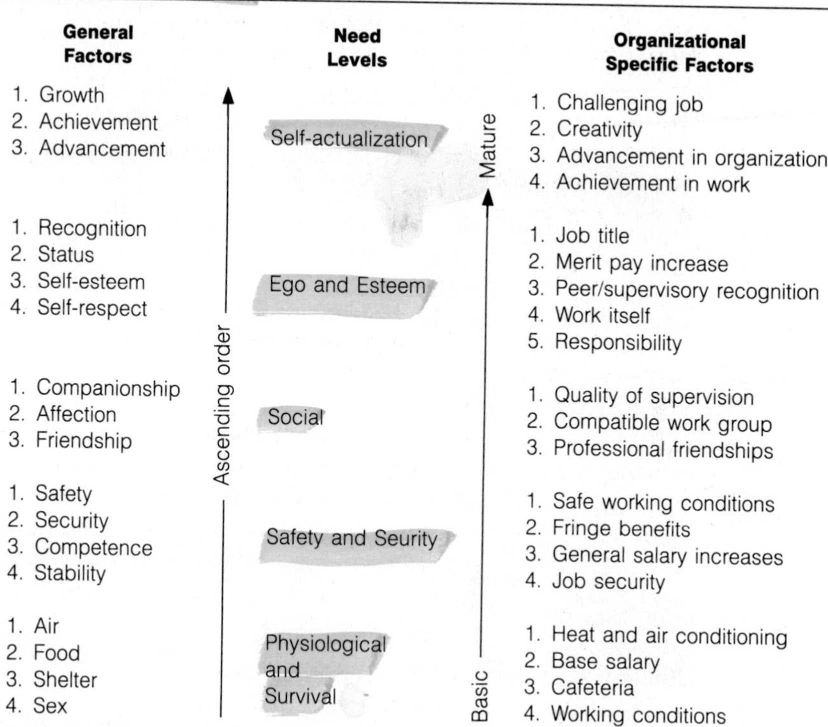

Source: A. D. Szilagyi, Jr. and M. J. Wallace, Jr. (1980). *Organizational behavior and performance,* 2nd ed., Santa Monica, CA: Goodyear Publishing. Data for "General Factors" and "Need Levels" from Hierarchy of Needs in "A theory of human motivation" in *Motivation and personality,* 2nd ed., by Abraham H. Maslow; copyright © 1970 by Abraham H. Maslow; reprinted by permission of Harper & Row, Inc. "Organizational specific factors" copyright © 1980 by Scott, Foresman & Co.

Each of the preceding was included in Maslow's theory, and the results conformed in most cases to the "spirit" of his ideas. In other words, they matched the *general* ideas Maslow proposed. They did not, however, conform to the "letter" of the theory (i.e., they did not match his ideas *exactly*). Several other findings appear even less supportive.

> There is no clear evidence that human needs are classified in five distinct categories, or that these categories are structured in a special hierarchy. There is some evidence for the existence of possibly two types of needs, deficiency and growth needs, although this categorization is not always operative.[5]

Although suffering from research design problems, a number of studies have questioned the hypothesis that the satisfaction of a need at one of the five levels will decrease its importance and increase the importance of the next higher need.[6] Interestingly, even though the five-level hierarchy is not well supported, Maslow's more general two-level concept does receive some support.

It is unfortunate that much of Maslow's theory has never received adequate empirical testing. It is disappointing that those components which have been tested have not always been supported fully. This does not mean, however, that the theory has no value. Maslow's theory has provided a number of valid ideas which continue to be developed by other theorists. Those parts of his theory not fully supported should not detract from the parts research has supported. The next section of this chapter addresses the best-known theory developed to capitalize on the strong aspects of Maslow's theory while dealing with the limitations.

ALDERFER'S ERG THEORY

Clayton Alderfer felt that modification of Maslow's theory was necessary in order to deal with some of its conceptual shortcomings and to be more consistent with the results of research. Consequently, he developed a reconfigured need hierarchy model known as the Existence, Relatedness, and Growth Theory (ERG).[7] ERG has only three levels in the need hierarchy (as opposed to Maslow's five). ERG also differs from Maslow's theory in the complexity of needs expected to influence an individual at a given point in time.

The three levels of Alderfer's model are:

1. *Existence Needs*. These are all forms of material and physiological factors necessary to sustain human existence. **Existence needs** include all of what Maslow referred to as physiological needs as well as needs relating to material safety.
2. *Relatedness Needs*. **Relatedness needs** incorporate all socially oriented needs. This includes Maslow's interpersonally related safety needs, social needs, and esteem needs related to others.
3. *Growth Needs*. Needs relating to the development of human potential are **growth needs.** Maslow's internally based self-esteem needs are located here, as is self-actualization.

Like Maslow, Alderfer suggested that individuals tend to "move up the hierarchy" as they satisfy needs. Whereas Maslow felt a person addresses primarily one set of needs at a time, however, Alderfer argues that two or more sets of needs can be active at one time. Furthermore, Alderfer specifies two ways you can shift your focus of attention from one set of needs to another. Similarly to Maslow, *satisfaction progression* can occur. In other words, as you satisfy one need, you will "move on" to another need. Alderfer,

Clayton P. Alderfer of Yale University is the developer of the ERG Theory.

What are the most significant similarities between your ERG Theory and Maslow's Need Hierarchy Theory? The first is a parallel in the overall structure of the need categories. The physiological, security, social, esteem, self-actualization hierarchy directly parallels the existence, relatedness, growth structure. The second similarity concerns *self-actualization,* which is Maslow's term, and *growth,* which is my term. There are minor differences between the meaning of the two, but mainly they are similar. The third major similarity is that both theories deal with movement upward in the hierarchy in the sense that satisfaction of lower-level needs predicts increasing importance of higher-level needs.

What are the most significant differences between your ERG Theory and Maslow's Need Hierarchy Theory? There are major differences in meaning between security, social, and esteem needs as used by Maslow and existence, relatedness, and growth needs as I use them. Second, ERG Theory specifies a mechanism for downward movement in the hierarchy, which Maslow does not provide. In addition, ERG Theory has a specified method, measures, and theory of method for testing the theory, but Maslow did not specify these. ERG Theory can be more thoroughly tested.

What would you identify as the weakest link in the ERG Theory? The proposition in ERG Theory for which there is least empirical support is the one that says growth frustration predicts increasing relatedness desires. I have almost no confirmation of this in my studies, although the literature review that I've done does provide some support for it. I do believe it's true, but to the extent that one defines the truth as what one can demonstrate by conventional social science methods, one would have to say that there is precious little support for that proposition at this point.

however, also proposes that *frustration regression* can occur. This means that if you attempt to satisfy needs at a certain level and fail, you will regress to the preceding level and direct your attention toward that level of need.

Another major distinction between Maslow and Alderfer concerns the basis for the hierarchy. Maslow argued that the hierarchy defines the level of importance you assign to needs and the order in which those needs will be addressed. Alderfer, on the other hand, distinguishes between the levels primarily on the basis of how abstract the actions are that you take to satisfy the needs. Existence needs, for example, are easy to identify in concrete form ("What do I need to satisfy my need for food or water?"). Relatedness needs can be addressed in only partially concrete terms. Interaction with other people (fairly concrete) is involved in satisfying these needs (but love and esteem are fairly abstract concepts). Growth needs are almost totally abstract.

ERG does deal with most of the major problems relating to Maslow's theory, but Alderfer's theory is too new for research to allow definitive statements about its accuracy or usefulness. Studies are under way to evaluate its merits and refine its content where necessary. Early research has provided some measure of support for the theory.[8]

MANIFEST NEED THEORIES

At about the same time as Maslow was developing his theory, Henry Murray set forth a model known as the Manifest Need Theory.[9] Murray identified a very wide range of needs which people supposedly acquired to one degree or another through interaction with their environment (see Exhibit 5–3). This differed from Maslow, who believed people are born with a particular set of needs. Murray's need theory also identified a different number of needs than did Maslow. Unlike Maslow, Murray felt that any need could have impact at any time, so his theory contained no hierarchy. Finally, whereas Maslow suggested that one need would be dominant at one point in time, Murray allowed for many concurrently "active" needs.

Because of the greater complexity of Murray's need categories, it was possible to focus on individual, relatively narrow need-related issues. The list is so long, however, that there is a separate need listed for almost every human behavior! A more parsimonious list would have been beneficial and easier to apply. Murray's theory drew significant attention from the nonapplied areas of psychology but had little direct impact on organizational psychology or organizational behavior. The theory was simply not manageable enough and did not provide sufficient guidance for organizational application.

Subsequent to the work of Murray, several researchers have pursued a few of these needs in greater depth. These include the need for achievement, the need for affiliation, and the need for power.

The Need for Achievement. One of Murray's needs caught the attention of David McClelland and associates (notably, John Atkinson). They initiated what was to become the most thorough series of investigations of the role of a particular need.[10] For a number of years, the study of the *need for achievement* dominated the work of these researchers/theorists. Results of the study led to a number of important findings for organizations and increased substantially the importance of acquired-need theories.

A person high in achievement need takes moderate risks by pursuing goals which are difficult, but not impossible. Essentially, this person chooses a reasonable challenge which will require some measure of accomplishment to succeed. A high need for achievement is associated with a desire for immediate feedback on progress toward a goal. Persons high in this need find task accomplishment to be intrinsically rewarding (whether or not financial or other economic gain occurs). Finally, persons high in need for achievement tend to become absorbed totally in a task until it is successfully completed.

McClelland has shown that need for achievement is an *acquired* need. The need is learned primarily during childhood, although training can enhance the motivation to achieve in adults. Your individual level of need for achievement has a significant impact on performance. Studies have shown that students in grade school, high school, and college who are high in the need for achievement perform better than do students with similar ability levels but lower levels of the need for achievement. Workers in a variety of jobs have been shown to have their performance influenced substantially by high levels of need for achievement. In fact, a tremendous volume of research has demonstrated that the achievement need can be a powerful motivator in many situations. Nevertheless, a high level of need for achievement is not sufficient to guarantee high performance. In addition, you also must perceive that the task you are facing (the job, the class, etc.) is challenging and provides immediate feedback. Thus, no matter how high your need is for achievement, you probably will not devote effort toward an easy or impossible task, nor toward a task which is boring (see Chapter 7).

McClelland argued that the need for achievement applies to entire societies as well as to individuals. He conducted a fascinating his-

Exhibit 5–3 Sample Items from Murray's List of Needs

Social Motive	Brief Definition
Abasement	To submit passively to external force. To accept injury, blame, criticism, punishment. To surrender. To become resigned to fate. To admit inferiority, error, wrongdoing, or defeat. To confess and atone. To blame, belittle, or mutilate the self. To seek and enjoy pain, punishment, illness, and misfortune.
Achievement	To accomplish something difficult. To master, manipulate, or organize physical objects, human beings, or ideas. To do this as rapidly and as independently as possible. To overcome obstacles and attain a high standard. To excel oneself. To rival and surpass others. To increase self-regard by the successful exercise of talent.
Affiliation	To draw near and enjoyably co-operate or reciprocate with an allied other (an other who resembles the subject or who likes the subject). To please and win affection of a cathected object. To adhere and remain loyal to a friend.
Aggression	To overcome opposition forcefully. To fight. To revenge an injury. To attack, injure, or kill another. To oppose forcefully or punish another.
Autonomy	To get free, shake off restraint, break out of confinement. To resist coercion and restriction. To avoid or quit activities prescribed by domineering authorities. To be independent and free to act according to impulse. To be unattached, irresponsible. To defy convention.
Counteraction	To master or make up for a failure by restriving. To obliterate a humiliation by resumed action. To overcome weaknesses, to repress fear. To efface a dishonor by action. To search for obstacles and difficulties to overcome. To maintain self-respect and pride on a high level.
Defendance	To defend the self against assault, criticism, and blame. To conceal or justify a misdeed, failure, or humiliation. To vindicate the ego.
Deference	To admire and support a superior. To praise, honor, or eulogize. To yield eagerly to the influence of an allied other. To emulate an exemplar. To conform to custom.
Dominance	To control one's human environment. To influence or direct the behavior of others by suggestion, seduction, persuasion, or command. To dissuade, restrain, or prohibit.
Exhibition	To make an impression. To be seen and heard. To excite, amaze, fascinate, entertain, shock, intrigue, amuse, or entice others.
Harmavoidance	To avoid pain, physical injury, illness, and death. To escape from a dangerous situation. To take precautionary measures.
Infavoidance	To avoid humiliation. To quit embarrassing situations or to avoid conditions which may lead to belittlement, the scorn, derision, or indifference of others. To refrain from action because of the fear of failure.

Exhibit 5–3 *(concluded)*

Social Motive	Brief Definition
Nurturance	To give sympathy and gratify the needs of a helpless object: an infant or any object that is weak, disabled, tired, inexperienced, infirm, defeated, humiliated, lonely, dejected, sick, mentally confused. To assist an object in danger. To feed, help, support, console, protect, comfort, nurse, heal.
Order	To put things in order. To achieve cleanliness, arrangement, organization, balance, neatness, tidiness, and precision.
Play	To act for "fun" without further purpose. To like to laugh and make jokes. To seek enjoyable relaxation from stress. To participate in games, sports, dancing, drinking parties, cards.
Rejection	To separate oneself from a negatively cathected object. To exclude, abandon, expel, or remain indifferent to an inferior object. To snub or jilt an object.
Sentience	To seek and enjoy sensuous impressions.
Sex	To form and further an erotic relationship. To have sexual intercourse.
Succorance	To have one's needs gratified by the sympathetic aid of an allied object. To be nursed, supported, sustained, surrounded, protected, loved, advised, guided, indulged, forgiven, consoled. To remain close to a devoted protector. To always have a supporter.
Understanding	To ask or answer general questions. To be interested in theory. To speculate, formulate, analyze, and generalize.

Source: C. S. Hall, and G. Lindzey, *Theories of Personality*. Copyright 1957 by John Wiley & Sons, New York.

torical evaluation by examining literature and other cultural artifacts of societies for evidence of achievement orientation.[11] These studies indicated that there were indeed differences across societies in the achievement need. In addition, high levels of need for achievement preceded economic growth. Lower levels of the need signaled subsequent economic decline of the entire society.

Current knowledge on the need for achievement indicates that organizations would be wise to:

1. Assess the level of need for achievement among job applicants as one basis for the selection decision.
2. Assess achievement orientation when making promotion decisions.
3. Assess the achievement-need level of organizational members and provide appropriately challenging tasks.
4. Provide training to influence and improve worker levels of need for achievement.

In addition to the massive amounts of research on the need for achievement, McClelland and his associates examined other needs in considerable detail (particularly affiliation and power).

The Need for Affiliation. Although the *need for affiliation* has not received the attention given the need for achievement, the implications of this need have been explored in some detail.[12] The need for affiliation is defined as the desire to establish and maintain friendly and warm relations with other persons. In many ways, this need is similar to Maslow's social needs. A person high in the need for affiliation seeks approval and reassurance from others, is easily influenced by the norms of others, and is genuinely concerned about the interests and feelings of others.

The need for affiliation is said to be acquired through learning and, thus, is influenced by experiences. Research has shown that people with high need for affiliation respond favorably to organizational experiences which provide opportunities to satisfy this need. Thus, situations in which there is social pressure for performance enhance the performance level of a person high in the need for affiliation. Persons high in this need will be more likely to have better work attendance records when the work provides opportunity for social interaction. Performance also can be enhanced if supportive feedback is provided contingent upon performance (to obtain the needed support, the individual must perform).

The implications of the affiliation need for organizations are fairly straightforward. It is important to assess the strength of the affiliation need in organizational members and place workers in jobs consistent with their affiliation needs. Thus, a person who is low in the need for affiliation might receive a position requiring that s/he work fairly independently. For individuals who are high in this need, an organization should provide: positions containing appropriate social opportunities, a general work environment which includes interaction, and organizational policies which tie the valued affiliation-satisfying experiences to performance.

The Need for Power. The *need for power* has received an unusual amount of attention from theorists and researchers. The need for power can be defined as the need to control other persons, to influence their behavior, and to be responsible for other people. Much of the relatively recent research on this topic also can be attributed to McClelland and associates. In fact, the focus of McClelland's work appeared to shift somewhat during the mid-1970s. This was due in part to his conclusion that the need for achievement had its primary impact on organizations only in entrepreneurial situations. These are cases where an individual is directly responsible for organizing and managing, and is involved personally in the risks of the business or enterprise. Therefore, McClelland focused on the need for power to explain much of the source of managerial success in general organizational situations.[13]

Persons who are high in the need for power may attempt to satisfy this need in either of two distinct ways.[14] *Personalized power* seekers attempt to dominate others for the sake of dominating. Conquering others provides satisfaction. Unfortunately, this method of satisfying the power need includes frequent rejection of organizational responsibilities in favor of personal concerns. Furthermore, these types of individuals have been shown to engage frequently in heavy alcohol use and derive satisfaction from fantasies of power (often induced by alcohol use). *Socialized power* seekers, however, satisfy power needs through concern for group goals, for finding goals which will motivate others, for working with a group to formulate and achieve goals. This method of satisfying power needs is not oriented toward the self but, rather, toward fulfilling important organizational responsibilities.

Of the needs for achievement, affiliation, and power, McClelland currently argues that the need for power (if satisfied through socialized power acquisition) is the most important determinant of general managerial success. Persons high in need for achievement tend to be overly oriented toward personal achievement. Persons high in the need for affiliation often show too little assertiveness to avoid offending the group. It is critical, however, that a managerial job provide opportunity for socialized power acquisition. Otherwise, a person high in the need for power may satisfy this need through acquisition of personal power to the detriment of an organization.

HERZBERG'S MOTIVATION-HYGIENE THEORY

The **Motivation-Hygiene Theory** was developed, researched, and widely publicized by Frederick Herzberg.[15] Herzberg argued that there are only two sets of needs. The first set of needs he called "motivators" (growth needs). Motivators relate to job content and the ability to achieve and, therefore, experience psychological growth. The second set of needs he termed "hygiene" (pain-avoidance). These needs relate to the job environment and stem from human nature and the "built-in drive to avoid pain" (plus learned drives developed to help avoid pain). According to Herzberg, growth needs motivate people and, when met, lead to the experience of satisfaction. Hygiene needs, on the other hand, must be met to avoid dissatisfaction (but do not necessarily provide satisfaction or motivation).

Frederick Herzberg of the University of Utah is the developer of the Motivation-Hygiene Theory.

What would you identify as the primary contribution of your theory to the practice of management? Calling management's attention to the motivational potential of the work itself. If you want people to do a good job, give them a good job to do—an enriched job.

Today's organization devotes much more attention to "motivators" than was the case 20 years ago. What impact do you think this has had on organizational effectiveness and on the meaning of work to organizational members? Much so-called attention to motivators is merely lip-service to words like *achievement, recognition,* and *growth,* while jobs remain fractionated and training is neglected. The result of such neglect has been declining motivation and productivity.

Your theory implies a person can be both satisfied and dissatisfied at the same time. Have you found this occurring frequently, or is it more common for a worker to have consistent feelings about motivator and hygiene factors? Virtually all the hundreds of replications of my original study, published in *Motivation to Work* (1959), have supported the independence of motivator and hygiene factors. That is, people tend to feel satisfied with motivator factors at the same time that they are dissatisfied with hygiene factors. Of course, there is always some slippage. People always have mixed feelings. Motivation-Hygiene Theory has been able to identify two separate dynamic directions of these feelings: long-term satisfaction that results from growth and short-term relief that results from avoidance of pain from the environment.

What advice would you offer the student and future manager concerning the use of your Motivation-Hygiene Theory? In managing people, you must always ask two questions: *Am I treating them well?* (the hygiene question) and *Am I using them well?* (the motivator question). . . . Merely treating people well will not motivate them to do a good job in the long run though, of course, changes in treatment result in short-term spurts. Using people well so that their talents can continue to grow on the job results in long-term quality productivity and job satisfaction.

Herzberg developed his theory in response to the results of 12 different studies he conducted. Over 1,600 workers from various types of jobs were asked to identify: (1) job events in their work experiences which had led to extreme satisfaction and (2) job events which had led to extreme dissatisfaction. Herzberg categorized and analyzed each response to these two questions. Exhibit 5–4 presents a summary of his findings.[16]

These studies allowed Herzberg to identify "critical incidents" (important work experiences) said to have caused either great satis-

Exhibit 5–4 Factors Affecting Job Attitudes

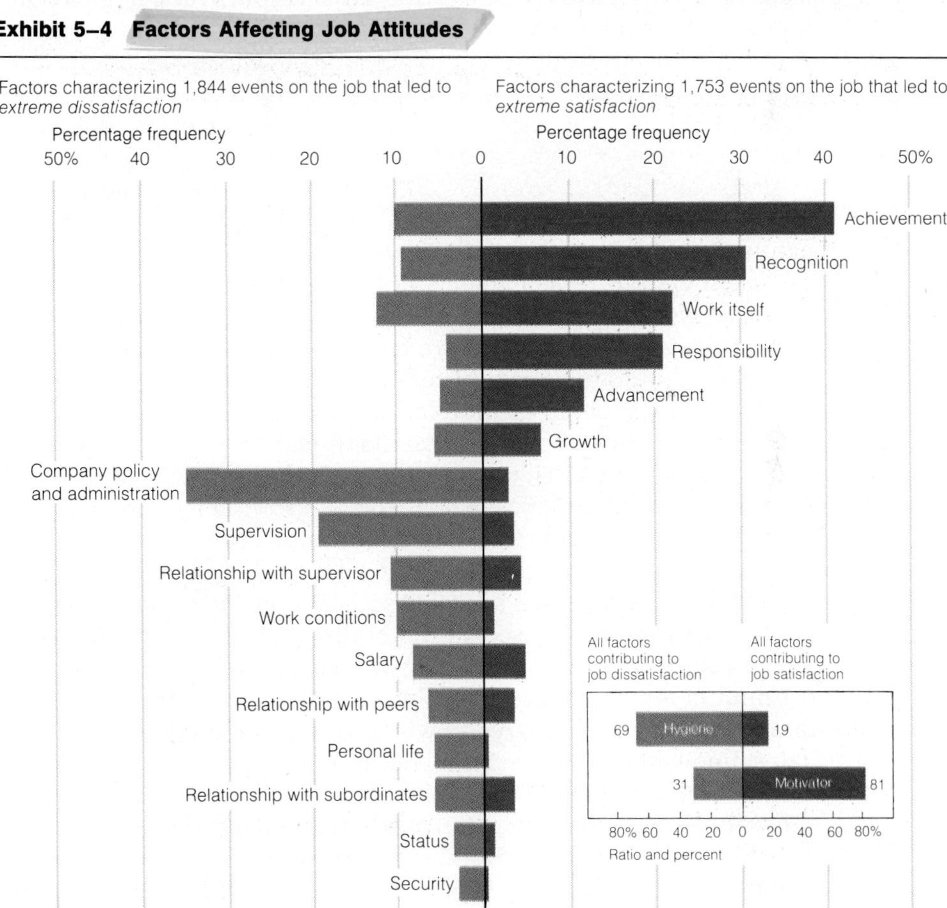

Reprinted by permission of the *Harvard Business Review*. One more time: How do you motivate employees? By F. Herzberg, faction or great dissatisfaction. Certain types of events seemed to cause primarily dissatisfying experiences. Other types of events were identified most frequently in relation to satisfying experiences. This led Herzberg to propose that there are two underlying sets of needs and associated experiences which influence people in organizations: motivator factors and hygiene factors.

Hygiene factors involve the need to avoid pain. These factors are not related directly to the work itself but rather to job context factors (pay, working conditions, supervision, and security). Herzberg also refers to these factors as "dissatisfiers" because of research results like those shown in Exhibit 5–4. These factors were associated so frequently with dissatisfying experiences that Herzberg claims they are unlikely to provide satisfaction. When hygiene factors are met, you avoid the dissatisfaction you would have experienced if the needs were not met. Meeting these needs, however, does not contribute to experiencing satisfaction. Furthermore, since these needs are not capable of providing satisfaction, Herzberg states that they are not capable of motivating workers.

Motivator factors involve the long-term need to pursue psychological growth. Motivators relate to job content (achievement, recognition, and the work itself). Herzberg also refers to these factors as "satisfiers" to reflect their ability to provide satisfying experiences for workers. When these needs are met, you experience satisfaction. Because these needs are capable of providing satisfaction, they also are said to be capable of motivating workers. More specifically, Herzberg believes motivating factors lead to performance (achievement), which leads to satisfaction.

One implication of Herzberg's theory is that satisfaction and dissatisfaction should not be considered as opposites. It is not possible, according to Herzberg, to use one continuum which contains both satisfaction and dissatisfaction. Instead, you should use one continuum to describe a person's level of satisfaction and a second continuum to describe the person's level of dissatisfaction. The degree to which your hygiene needs are met will determine where you lie on a continuum which ranges from "no dissatisfaction" through "high dissatisfaction." The degree to which motivator needs are met will determine where you are on a continuum which ranges from "no satisfaction" through "high satisfaction."

Exhibit 5–5(a) defines the range of satisfaction and dissatisfaction possibilities according to Herzberg, compares his view to the traditional continuum (Exhibit 5–5(b)), and identifies four types of workers:

A—This type of worker has both hygiene and motivator needs met. S/he is therefore is "not unhappy" (about hygiene needs) and is also "very happy" (about motivator needs).

Exhibit 5–5

(a) Herzberg's view of satisfaction and dissatisfaction

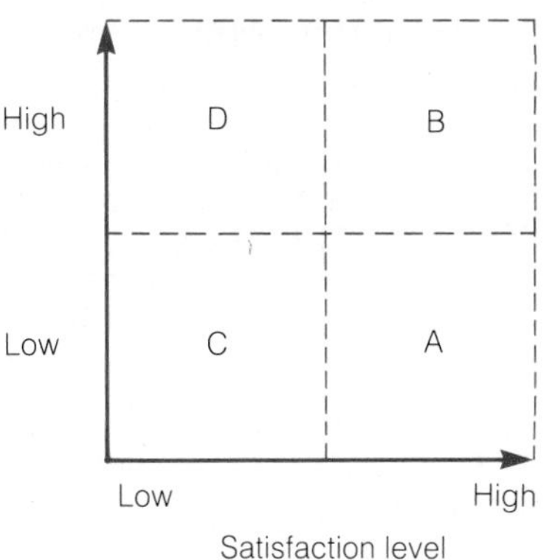

(b) Traditional view of satisfaction and dissatisfaction

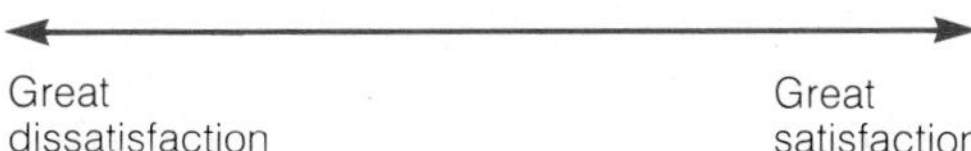

B—This worker has met the motivator needs but not the hygiene needs. S/he therefore is "happy" (about motivator needs) *and* "unhappy" (about hygiene needs).

C—A worker in this category has fulfilled the hygiene needs but not the motivator needs. S/he is thus "not unhappy" (about hygiene needs) but also "not happy" (about motivator needs).

D—Neither the hygiene nor the motivator needs have been met for this worker. S/he is both "unhappy" (about hygiene needs) and "not happy" (about motivator needs).

The organizational implications of Herzberg's theory are substantial. The theory specifies that hygiene factors (e.g., pay and working conditions) have low potential for motivating workers. The only potential organizational benefit of meeting employee hygiene needs is to avoid dissatisfaction. Thus, it is implied that hygiene factors should be given adequate but not excessive attention by organizations. An organization desiring to motivate employees must concentrate on motivator factors such as achievement, responsibility, recognition, and the characteristics of the work itself.

Criticism and Controversy

Herzberg's theory has been accepted widely and used by practitioners. Despite this, the theory has been the subject of widespread criticism and controversy regarding the presence of or lack of documentation for the theory. Herzberg, his associates, and students have conducted large amounts of research on the propositions contained in the theory. The results of this research appear to support the theory. Other researchers using the same methodologies as Herzberg also have found what appears to be supporting evidence. Outside of this circle, however, major aspects of Herzberg's theory are considered to be unproven and in part contradicted.[17]

A major point of contention concerns the critical incidents approach Herzberg used to evaluate his theory. It has been argued that the method used to collect information about satisfying and dissatisfying experiences biased Herzberg's research results.[18] Vroom believes that human defense processes lead people to identify dissatisfying events (Herzberg's hygiene factors) as being due to factors beyond their immediate control. Furthermore, since workers have both a conscious and subconscious desire to "look good," they tend to identify satisfying events (Herzberg's motivators) as due to their own actions. If true, the findings (such as those shown in Exhibit 5–4) do not reflect accurately the frequency with which the various types of incidents are actually associated with satisfying and dissatisfying experiences. Even if Herzberg's results are accurate, the fact that hygiene factors seldom have led to satisfaction does not mean they are incapable of doing so. It may be that hygiene needs simply have not been addressed well by organizations.

House and Wigdor argue that Herzberg oversimplified the complex sources of satisfaction and dissatisfaction and the relationship between satisfaction and motivation.[19] Their reanalysis of data from 17 samples led them to conclude that:

1. A particular type of event can cause job satisfaction for one person but dissatisfaction for another.
2. A given factor can cause both satisfaction and dissatisfaction in the same group of co-workers.
3. Intrinsic (motivator) factors actually produce greater impact on both satisfying and dissatisfying events than do extrinsic (hygiene) factors.

Reasonable rejoinders to criticisms of the motivation-hygiene theory have been offered.[20] Furthermore, not all recent research has contradicted Herzberg's findings. Indeed, even many of the highly critical researchers have confirmed parts of the theory. An illustration of the potential cross-cultural applicability of the theory, for example, was provided recently by a study in Zambia which produced results "consistent with the general notion underlying the two-factor theory* of motivation."[21]

The debate undoubtedly will continue. It would be beneficial, however, if researchers would direct their attention to constructively modifying the theory instead of trying to disprove it. Herzberg's theory and its contributions to later research, theory, and managerial practice cannot be denied. Whereas the theory as originally stated by Herzberg is not valid in its entirety, it has helped to identify the wide range of organizational factors capable of influencing worker reactions. Previously, most organizations attended primarily to hygiene factors. Because of Herzberg's contributions, organizations today realize the potential of motivators. Furthermore, his work has stimulated the development of job design programs in the United States (see Chapter 15). Applications of Herzberg's ideas in industry have involved a wide range of organizations, including Texas Instruments, AT&T, and Cummins Engine. Herzberg is living proof that a theory need not be perfect to make valuable contributions. As is the case with most theories, the motivation-hygiene theory will be modified or replaced by others which better describe reality, but the impact of Herzberg's work will be felt for decades.

SUMMARY

Each of the theories described in this chapter deals with the impact of human needs on attitudes and behaviors of organizational members. The theories differ in terms of the number and types of needs studied and in the proposed relationships between them. They are similar, however, in that each argues that people are motivated to fulfill needs. The theories also agree that the value people attach to experiences will be influenced by the degree to which needs have been met previously. The need theories explain when and why a person will be motivated by unmet needs. They provide only general information, however, about the specific types of behaviors a person probably will use to fulfill these needs. For the most part, the need theories only state that a person will behave so as to fulfill an existing need. Theories presented in later chapters deal with specific methods people try in order to satisfy their needs.

---

*Please note that Herzberg's theory has often been labeled the two-factor theory because it focuses on two continua. This name, however, implies that only two factors are involved, which is not correct. Herzberg prefers not to use the term because his two *sets* of needs identify a much larger *number* of needs.

GLOSSARY

Maslow's Need Hierarchy Theory A theory which specifies that people are motivated to satisfy needs arranged in a five-level hierarchy of primacy.

Physiological Needs Maslow's lowest-level needs ("chemical needs").

Safety and Security Needs Maslow's second-level needs, focusing on the well-being of a person.

Social Needs Needs which focus on affiliation and a sense of belonging (Maslow's third level).

Ego and Esteem Needs Needs relating to self-respect, self-esteem, and the esteem of others (Maslow's fourth level).

Self-Actualization Needs Maslow's highest-level needs, focusing on self-fulfillment.

Alderfer's ERG Theory A need theory based on three sets of needs: Existence, Relatedness, and Growth.

Existence Needs Alderfer's needs focusing on material and physiological factors.

Relatedness Needs Alderfer's socially-oriented needs.

Growth Needs Alderfer's needs relating to human potential and self-esteem development.

Manifest Need Theories Theories based on acquired needs such as achievement, power, and affiliation.

Herzberg's Motivation-Hygiene Theory A theory based on two *sets* of needs: motivation (involving growth needs) and hygiene (pain avoidance).

Motivator Factors Needs which focus on psychological growth.

Hygiene Factors Needs which focus on the avoidance of pain (pay, working conditions, etc.).

STUDY QUESTIONS

1. Discuss the organizational benefits possible when an organization has a good understanding of its employees' needs.
2. How might Maslow explain why organizational rewards which motivate workers today will not motivate the same workers 5 or 10 years from now?
3. Discuss techniques an organization could use to obtain information about employee needs.

4. Discuss the similarities and differences between Alderfer's ERG theory and Maslow's theory.
5. Evaluate your own level of existence, relatedness, and growth needs. Discuss how this knowledge can help you become a more effective manager.
6. If you were hiring workers to perform a very repetitive type of task, what pattern of needs would you want those workers to have to most benefit the organization?
7. Discuss how social needs can be met both inside and outside an organization.
8. Discuss the importance of Herzberg's motivators to an organization.

NOTES

1. **Maslow, A. H.** (1943). A theory of human motivation. *Psychological Bulletin, 50,* 370–396.
2. **McGregor, D.** (1960). *The human side of enterprise.* New York: McGraw-Hill.
3. **Maslow,** 1943.
4. Ibid, p. 382.
5. **Wahba, M. A., & Bridwell, L. G.** (1976). Maslow reconsidered: A review of research on the need hierarchy theory. *Organizational Behavior and Human Performance, 15,* 212–240.
6. **Lawler, E. E., III, & Suttle, J. L.** (1972). A causal correlational test of the need hierarchy concept. *Organizational Behavior and Human Performance, 7,* 265–287; **Wahba & Bridwell,** 1976.
7. **Alderfer, C. P.** (1972). *Existence, relatedness, and growth: Human needs in organizational settings.* New York: Free Press.
8. **Kaplan, R. E., & Smith, K. A.** (1974). The effect of variations in relatedness need satisfaction on relatedness desire. *Administrative Science Quarterly, 19,* 507–532; **Wanous, J. P., & Zwany, A. A.** (1977). A cross-sectional test of need hierarchy theory. *Organizational Behavior and Human Performance, 18,* 78–97.
9. **Murray, H. A.** (1938). *Exploration in personality.* New York: Oxford University Press.
10. **Atkinson, J. W., & McClelland, D. C.** (1948). The projective expression of needs. II. The effect of different intensities of the hunger drive on thematic apperception. *Journal of Experimental Psychology, 38,* 643–658; **McClelland, D. C., Atkinson, J. W., Clark, R. A., & Lowell, E. L.** (1953). *The achievement motive.* New York: Appleton-Century-Crofts.
11. **McClelland, D. C.** (1961). *The achieving society.* Princeton, NJ: Van Nostrand.

12. **Atkinson, J. W., & Raphelson, A. C.** (1956). Individual differences in motivation and behavior in particular situations. *Journal of Personality, 24,* 349–363; **DeCharms, R. C.** (1957). Affiliation motivation and productivity in small groups. *Journal of Abnormal Psychology, 55,* 222–276; **Birch, D., & Veroff, J.** (1966). Motivation: A study of action. Monterey, CA: Brooks/Cole; **Steers, R. M., & Braunstrin, D. N.** (1976). A behaviorally based measure of manifest needs in work settings. *Journal of Vocational Behavior, 9,* 251–266.
13. **McClelland, D. C.** (1975). *Power: The inner experience.* New York: Irvington.
14. **McClelland, D. C., Davis, W. N., Kalin, R., & Wanner, E.** (1972). *The drinking man: Alcohol and human motivation.* New York: Free Press.
15. **Herzberg, F., Mausner, B., & Snyderman, B.** (1959). *The motivation to work.* New York: Wiley.
16. **Herzberg, F.** (1968). One more time: How do you motivate employees? *Harvard Business Review, 46,* 54–62.
17. **Vroom, V. H.** (1964). *Work and motivation.* New York: Wiley; **House, R. J., & Wigdor, L. A.** (1967). Herzberg's dual-factor theory of job satisfaction and motivation: A review of the evidence and a criticism. *Personnel Psychology, 20,* 369–389; **King, N.** (1970). Clarification and evaluation of the two-factor theory of job satisfaction. *Psychological Bulletin, 74,* 18–31; **Waters, L. K., & Waters, C. W.** (1972). An empirical test of five versions of the two-factor theory of job satisfaction. *Organizational Behavior and Human Performance, 7,* 18–24.
18. **Vroom,** 1964.
19. **House & Wigdor,** 1967.
20. **Whitsett, D. A., & Winslow, E. K.** (1967). An analysis of studies critical of the motivator-hygiene theory. *Personnel Psychology, 20,* 391–415.
21. **Machungway, P. D., & Schmitt, N.** (1983). Successful motivation in a developing country. *Journal of Applied Psychology, 68,* 31–42.

6

Learning Theories and Behavior Modification

OVERVIEW
CLASSICAL CONDITIONING
OPERANT CONDITIONING
The Basic Operant Model
Techniques for Strengthening an S→R Link
Stimulus Discrimination and Generalization
Behavioral Shaping
Techniques for Weakening an S→R Link
Spontaneous Recovery
Schedules of Reinforcement
ORGANIZATIONAL BEHAVIOR MODIFICATION
Outcomes
Behavioral Shaping in OBM
Examples of Organizational Behavior Modification
Recommendations for Effective Use of OBM
Ethical Issues Associated with OBM
A Note on Discipline Systems
SUMMARY

> For the things we have to learn before we can do them, we learn by doing them.
>
> *Aristotle*

OVERVIEW

This chapter presents the two most widely known theories of human learning: classical conditioning and operant conditioning. These theories differ in the *types* of behaviors which can be conditioned (learned) and in the *processes* involved in learning. The two approaches are similar, however, in that both claim learning takes place through experiences with the environment. Both are noncognitive approaches; they do not examine conscious mental activity. This means you do not necessarily have to understand the thoughts of a person in order to understand his/her behavior.

This chapter also presents organizational behavior modification (OBM). OBM applies learning principles to organizations for the purpose of managing behavior. The OBM applications discussed here incorporate cognitive processes as central to the technique and argue that effective modification of behavior is not possible without consideration of the human thought process.*

CLASSICAL CONDITIONING

In **classical conditioning** a person learns to react to a particular event with a specific response. This learning occurs when the event is associated with some other event which produced that response

*Many purists would argue that OBM can be conducted without reference to cognitive processes. Research evidence, however, argues otherwise. OBM as treated here, therefore, deals not only with *how* people behave but also with *why* they behave this way.

Pavlov's Canine Example of Classical Conditioning

Pavlov observed that a dog, when presented a piece of meat began to salivate. He described this as the natural responsive relationship between an unconditioned stimulus (meat) and an unconditioned response (salivation at the sight and smell of the meat). This situation is described in Step 1 of Exhibit 6–1.

Over a period of time, Pavlov rang a bell each time he presented the dog with meat. Pavlov described this as the association of a conditioned stimulus (the bell) with an unconditioned stimulus (meat). As shown in Step 2 of Exhibit 6–1, the dog salivated when presented with this pair of stimuli because of the preexisting UCS→UCR linkage.

After several repetitions in which the CS and UCS were presented together, Pavlov rang the bell without presenting meat. The dog responded by salivating. Pavlov observed that learning had occurred since a new stimulus→response link now existed. Step 3 in Exhibit 6–1 describes this new link as a conditioned stimulus→conditioned response relationship.

in the past. If the sight of a hamburger makes your mouth water, you can be conditioned to respond that way to the appearance of a restaurant's logo. Classical conditioning has you learn to associate the company's logo with a hamburger. Eventually, you will salivate when you see the logo, whether or not a hamburger is present. Although the term "classical conditioning" is seldom used in the marketing field, its techniques frequently are used. Initial identification of the classical conditioning process was made by the Russian physiologist Ivan Pavlov (1902) through his famous experiments which conditioned a dog to salivate in response to a bell.[1]

Exhibit 6–1 diagrams the classical conditioning model. Before classical conditioning can occur, there must be some stimulus which already naturally elicits the desired response. Step 1 in Exhibit 6–1 illustrates this necessary preexisting relationship between a stimulus and a response. Because this initial relationship is reflexive rather than learned, the stimulus is referred to as an **unconditioned stimulus (UCS)** and the reflexive response is called an **unconditioned response (UCR).**

Through classical conditioning, you learn to respond to a new stimulus much like you responded to the original, unconditioned stimulus. The new stimulus is called a **conditioned stimulus (CS).** Learning occurs when the new stimulus is associated with the unconditioned stimulus as shown in Step 2. By being exposed repeatedly to the UCS and the CS at the same time, you learn to associate the UCS with the CS. This association teaches you to respond to the CS much the same as you reflexively respond to the UCS. Subse-

Exhibit 6–1 The Classical Conditioning Model

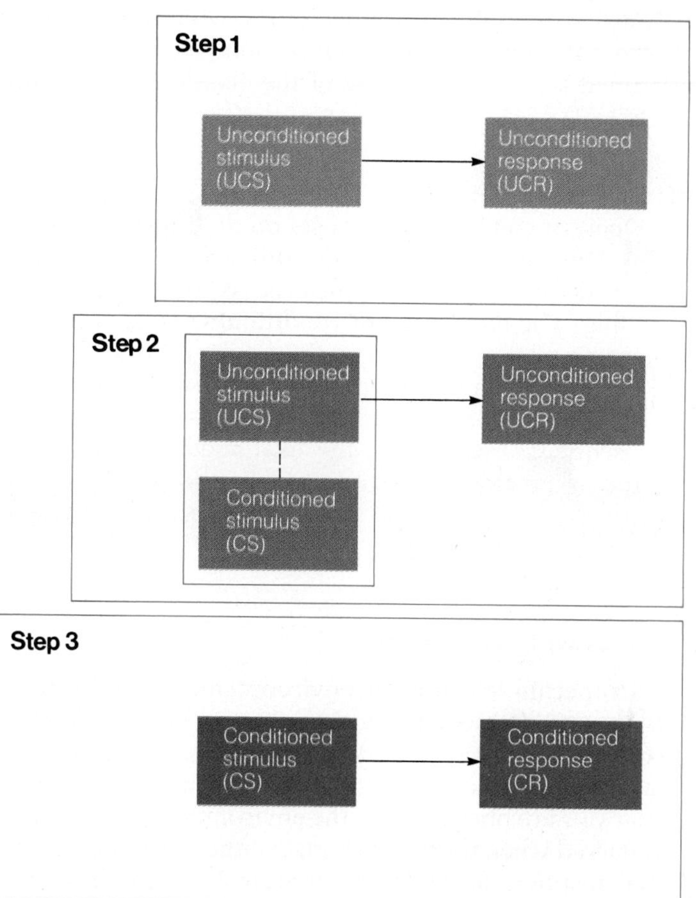

quently, as shown in Step 3, you respond to the CS even when the UCS is not present. Because the response is not a natural reflex but, rather, a *learned* response, it is called a **conditioned response (CR).** Although, technically, the CR is not identical to the UCR, it often appears to be very similar.

If an event can be paired with an unconditioned stimulus, it has the potential for becoming a conditioned stimulus which will elicit a response. Classical conditioning allows the use of almost any observable environmental event as a conditioned stimulus. Furthermore, a new CS can be developed through association with an existing CS. People are not dogs, however, and relatively few human responses can be conditioned this way. A response cannot be conditioned using classical learning unless that response (or a very similar response) already occurs naturally in reaction to some unconditioned stimulus. Thus, much of the wide range of complex human behavior important to organizations cannot be influenced or explained solely through use of the classical conditioning process.

OPERANT CONDITIONING

Operant conditioning focuses on the learning of voluntary behaviors. This means a much wider range of behavioral responses can be learned through the operant process than through classical conditioning. The term **operant conditioning** is used to indicate that the learning process is based on the results produced by a person "operating on" the environment. After you "operate on the environment" (i.e., behave in a certain fashion), consequences may occur. These consequences determine the likelihood of similar behavior in the future. Learning occurs because you do something to the environment, the environment reacts to this action, and your subsequent behavior is influenced by the way the environment reacts.

The Basic Operant Model

In operant learning, an environmental stimulus **(S)** is followed by a response **(R)** which is followed by an environmental consequence **(C)** (see Exhibit 6–2). The response to a stimulus is said to be "instrumental" in obtaining the consequence. This further emphasizes that you are operating on the environment. Learning is said to have occurred when there is a change in the future probability of a particular response following a stimulus. Learning has occurred because of the consequences which followed the behavior in the past.

Without question, the most well-known operant theorist/re-

Exhibit 6–2 General Operant Model: S→R→C

Ways to Strengthen S→R Link

1. S→R→C+	(Positive Reinforcement)
2. S→R⫽C−	(Negative Reinforcement)

Ways to Weaken S→R Link

1. S→R→(no C)	(Nonreinforcement)
2. S→R→C−	(Punishment)

searcher is B. F. Skinner.[2] Much of Skinner's work was performed with laboratory animals, although others have explored the same principles with humans.

The Skinner Box

A rat is placed in a small box which contains several features, including one or more lights, a press-bar, and a feeding dish. This type of device is now known as a Skinner Box. The rat initially wanders around the box exploring its new environment. During this exploration, the rat displays a variety of more or less random behaviors. When the rat presses the bar, a piece of rat chow drops into the feeding dish. When the rat engages in any other behavior, no noticeable consequence occurs. Over time, the frequency with which the rat presses the bar increases, and the frequency with which the rat engages in other behaviors decreases. Learning has occurred; the rat presses the bar more now than it did in the past.

For a full understanding of the operant learning process, the following definitions of stimulus, response, and consequence should be used.

Stimulus. An **operant stimulus (S)** is any environmental situation which can be detected by any of the human senses and which is followed by a behavioral response. A stimulus can be very simple or quite complex. It can be a person, an object, a spoken word, a sign, or anything else which is observable. A complex stimulus can be any combination of observables. An operant stimulus defines a situation in which a "voluntary" behavior follows. In the example of the rat in the Skinner Box, the stimulus was the bar in the box.

Response. An **operant response (R)** is any observable response which follows a stimulus. This response also can be very simple or very complex. An operant response can be a simple motion, a spoken word, or a complex combination of behaviors. Operant responses are voluntary, which makes them different from the reflexive behaviors involved in classical conditioning. The response of the rat in the Skinner Box was the pressing of the bar.

Consequence. An **operant consequence (C)** is any observable environmental event which follows an operant response. Depending on its nature, an operant consequence can strengthen or weaken the link between a stimulus and a response.

Techniques for Strengthening an S→R Link

You can strengthen an S→R link by providing a reinforcer after a response to a stimulus. A **reinforcer** is an operant consequence

HÄGAR THE HORRIBLE BY DIK BROWNE
I'VE HAD IT WITH THE PACK OF YOU!
I'LL BET ERIC THE RED DOESN'T HAVE PROBLEMS LIKE THIS!!
WHAT A DAY! I'VE GOT THE LAZIEST CREW IN THE WORLD!
THEY DON'T DO A THING UNLESS I'M THERE YELLING AT THEM EVERY MINUTE!!
THEY JUST DON'T CARE ABOUT THEIR WORK! NO PRIDE! NO DEDICATION!!
I CAN'T UNDERSTAND THEIR ATTITUDE!
MAYBE THEY DON'T HAVE ENOUGH INCENTIVE — WHAT DO YOU PAY THEM?
PAY?
DIK BROWNE 6-19
© 1983 King Features Syndicate, Inc. World rights reserved

which increases the likelihood that the same stimulus will be followed by the same response in the future. The rat chow placed in the feeding dish after the rat pushed the bar was a reinforcer. It increased the likelihood that, in the future, the rat again would push the bar when presented with the stimulus. The food would not have been a reinforcer if the future probability of the response following the stimulus had not changed.

Reinforcement is the operant term describing this process of strengthening the link between a stimulus and a response. The principle of reinforcement is based on Edward Thorndike's "Law of Effect," paraphrased as follows:

> Responses which are made to a stimulus situation and followed closely by satisfaction (reinforcement) are more likely to occur again in the future. Responses which are made to a stimulus situation and followed closely by discomfort (punishment) are less likely to occur again in the future.[3]

As shown in Exhibit 6–2, reinforcement can occur either through the introduction of something desirable (positive reinforcement) or through the removal of something undesirable (negative reinforcement). Positive reinforcement, negative reinforcement, and avoidance learning are three techniques for strengthening an S→R link.

Positive Reinforcement. A positive reinforcer is an outcome which, when *added* to the situation following a response, strengthens the S→R link. In short, it increases the probability that the response will follow the stimulus. The Skinner Box example involved **positive reinforcement,** since it was the introduction of an outcome (food) following the response which strengthened the S→R link.

Negative Reinforcement. A negative reinforcer is an outcome which, when *removed* from the situation following a response, strengthens the S→R link. Thus a rat in a Skinner Box can learn to press a bar if pressing the bar terminates an electrical shock. It is important to remember that both positive and negative reinforcement *strengthen* the S→R link. The difference between the two is in the method by which they operate. Positive reinforcement introduces an outcome; **negative reinforcement** removes an outcome.

A common example of negative reinforcement is the loud buzzer which sounds when a car is started without the seat belts being fastened. When you fasten the seat belts, the buzzer stops. The buzzer serves as part of the stimulus. The rest of the stimulus has to do with being in the car, etc. The response is to fasten the seat belt. The consequence is the termination of the buzzer. If, after experiencing this S→R→C sequence of events, you are more likely to respond to the stimulus by fastening the seat belt, learning has occurred. A negative reinforcer, therefore, can be a noxious event which defines the stimulus situation and also is involved in the reinforcement process (by being removed following the response).*

Avoidance Learning. **Avoidance learning** is a third technique for strengthening the S→R link. You now know that it is possible to learn to respond to a stimulus in order to terminate an undesired outcome (negative reinforcement). It is also possible to learn to respond to a stimulus to *avoid* an undesired outcome. A rat can be taught to avoid a shock in a Skinner Box by pressing a bar in response to a light which appears before the shock is introduced. A human can learn to fasten his/her seat belt before turning on the ignition to avoid hearing the buzzer. Responses which terminate an undesired outcome are often referred to as "escape" behaviors. Responses which prevent an undesired outcome from occurring are known as "avoidance" behaviors.

Reinforcers can be classified as primary or secondary. *Primary reinforcers* are innately rewarding (food, water, sex, and other biologically significant factors). These reinforcers are inborn as opposed to learned. *Secondary reinforcers*, on the other hand, have the potential for reinforcement because of value acquired through association with other reinforcers. Since secondary reinforcers are learned, their effectiveness varies across people. Primary reinforcers are innate and more universal.

Stimulus Discrimination and Generalization

Stimulus discrimination and generalization refer to the degree of specificity required for a stimulus to elicit a particular response. To obtain a particular response, do you have to use the *exact* same stimulus you used during learning? If so, extreme attention would have to be devoted to presenting an exact replica of the original stimulus when the response is desired. This would be time-consuming, difficult, and probably impossible. The more similar a stimulus is to the original stimulus, however, the more likely it is that the response will follow. *Stimulus generalization* can be encouraged by presenting somewhat similar, though not identical, stimuli during training and reinforcing responses to any of these similar stimuli. With high levels of stimulus generalization, you will respond to

---

*It is common for operant terminology to use the term "stimulus" to refer to consequences which follow behaviors, as well as to define a situation which elicits a response. Since it is confusing to use the same term to describe both the antecedent and consequence of a response, this practice is not used in this book.

stimuli which are "generally like" the initial stimulus. An employee's response to requests of *any* manager would indicate a fairly high degree of generalization. Responses to only one particular manager suggest specificity.

Many times it is desirable to increase the specificity of a stimulus through *stimulus discrimination*. This is the ability to differentiate between similar stimuli and respond only to a specific stimulus or a narrow set of stimuli. Stimulus discrimination can be learned by reinforcing responses only to stimuli which are identical to or *very* similar to a specific stimulus. Often, discriminating characteristics are added to a stimulus to identify the specific circumstances under which a response will be reinforced. For example, you can increase stimulus specificity in a Skinner Box by only reinforcing bar-pressing responses when the stimulus includes the bar *and* a particular color light *and* the ringing of a bell. A common childhood example of a discriminating characteristic of a stimulus is found in the game known as "Simon says." In this game, players should respond to a stimulus such as "raise your hand" only if the appropriate discriminating characteristic ("Simon says") is present. An organizational discriminating stimulus characteristic could be a safety light on a machine which flashes when the equipment is ready to begin operation.

Behavioral Shaping

To this point, you have been reading about the learning of relatively simple responses. Since most simple behaviors arise on a more or less random basis, you can wait for the appropriate response after presenting a stimulus and then reinforce the response. This works with rats in Skinner Boxes and for humans in many simple situations. When the desired behavior is a complex one, however, a potential problem arises. Specific complex responses seldom appear randomly. In many cases, the respondent currently is not even capable of performing the desired complex response. You probably cannot teach a person to fly an airplane by waiting until s/he successfully does so and then reinforcing that complex behavior!

Behavioral shaping is a procedure developed to deal with the need for learning complex behaviors. Shaping reinforces successive approximations of the desired complex behavior. For example, in the early learning stage of the behavior, you are presented with a stimulus. Any response you make which is even slightly related to the desired behavior would be reinforced. Over time, however, your responses would not be reinforced unless they became more similar to the final desired behavior. Thus, the desired behavior is gradually "shaped" until your final complex response is made. Shaping can be a time-consuming process for a very complex task if it takes many successive approximations to obtain the desired response. Compared to a nonshaping approach, however, this method is very useful for learning complex behaviors.

Techniques for Weakening an S→R link

Weakening an S→R link also constitutes learning. In short, a person is learning to behave differently in response to a stimulus. **Extinction** is the operant term used to identify the process by which the link between a stimulus and a response is weakened. Extinction is said to have occurred when the operant response no longer follows the operant stimulus. Operant conditioning theory identifies two ways extinction can occur: through nonreinforcement and through punishment (see Exhibit 6–2).

Nonreinforcement. **Nonreinforcement**-induced extinction occurs when the reinforcing consequence ceases to follow a response to a stimulus. When reinforcement is first withheld, the response typically continues to follow the stimulus for some period of time. Eventually, however, the response occurs less and less often. Finally, the response no longer occurs, regardless of how frequently the stimulus is presented.

Earlier, reinforcement taught a rat to press a bar in a Skinner Box in response to a light. During learning, the rat was reinforced for a bar-pressing response. For nonreinforcement to weaken this S→R link, you must terminate the reinforcement of this response. In other words, you stop providing rat chow when the rat presses the bar in response to the light being turned on. At first, the rat will continue to press the bar as before. Soon, however, the rat begins to respond to the light only occasionally. Eventually, the rat stops responding to the light entirely. The extinction process is said to have begun when the frequency of responses to the stimulus begins to decrease. Extinction has occurred when the frequency of response reaches zero.

Punishment. Punishment causes extinction to occur by providing an undesirable outcome following a response to a stimulus. Punishment also may involve removing a desirable outcome following the response. By definition, any consequence which follows a response to a stimulus and weakens the S→R link is **punishment.** Normally, extinction occurs much more rapidly through punishment than through nonreinforcement. The rat in the Skinner Box eventually will learn to quit pressing its bar if you use nonreinforcement. It will, however, stop pressing the bar much faster if it is shocked (punished) each time the response is shown. The worker who is "docked" when tardy is likely to change this behavior more rapidly than the worker who only suffers nonreinforcement.

Although punishment can extinguish a particular S→R link relatively quickly, it can produce some undesirable side effects. Frequently, an alternative response to the stimulus will replace the previous one. The alternative response may be even less desirable than the original (unless a more desired alternative response is reinforced). Another common drawback is that the person being punished often harbors a feeling of resentment toward the person who provides the punishment.

Spontaneous Recovery

The phenomenon of *spontaneous recovery* illustrates that extinction does not completely eliminate the S→R link but, rather, thoroughly suppresses it. After extinction has occurred, the S→R link will reappear spontaneously after a period of rest or separation from the stimulus environment. You can demonstrate this by removing the rat whose bar-pressing response was extinguished from the Skinner Box. When you place the rat back in the box after a few days, it usually will respond once again to the stimulus. Usually, however, the frequency of response produced by spontaneous recovery is not as great as was present prior to extinction.

What happens immediately after spontaneous recovery occurs has a magnified impact on subsequent behavior. Extinction will occur rapidly if nonreinforcement follows the reappearance of the S→R link (and particularly quickly if punishment follows). On the other hand, the S→R link will be strengthened substantially if reinforcement follows. Exhibit 6–3 illustrates typical S→R strengths during initial reinforcement, extinction, spontaneous recovery, and subsequent extinction or reinforcement.

Schedules of Reinforcement

There are two ways to reinforce appropriate responses to stimuli: continuously or intermittently. A **continuous reinforcement** schedule is one in which reinforcement *always* follows an appropriate response to a correct stimulus. An **intermittent reinforcement** schedule is being used if a reinforcer follows only *some* of the appropriate responses to a stimulus. The type of reinforcement schedule used influences four factors: *learning rate* (the speed with which an S→R link is established), *response rate* (the frequency of response per reinforcement), *response stability* (the degree to which responses are made on a regular basis), and *extinction rate* (the speed with which extinction occurs during nonreinforcement or punishment).

Exhibit 6–3 S→R Strength during Initial Reinforcement, Extinction, Spontaneous Recovery, and Subsequent Reinforcement or Extinction

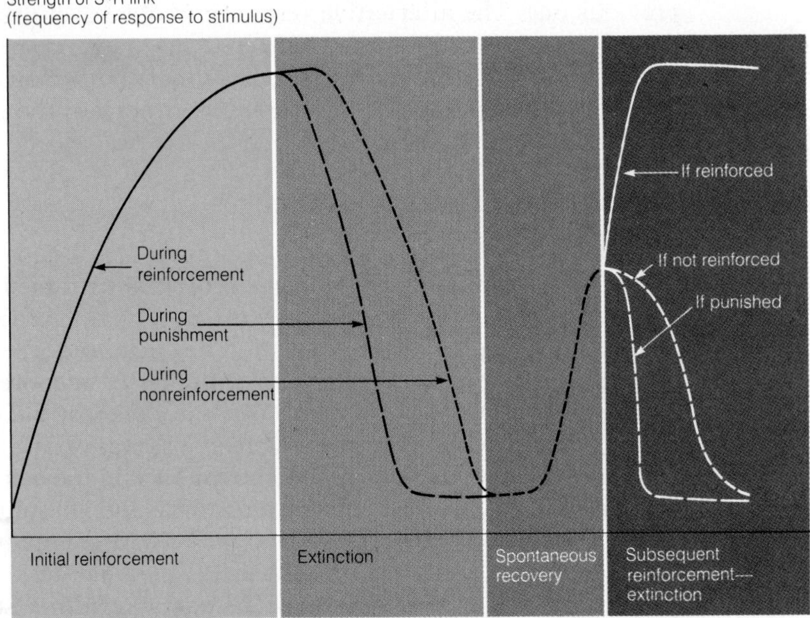

Continuous reinforcement occurs when every appropriate response to the stimulus is reinforced. Note that "continuous" does not imply that you are experiencing the reinforcing consequence constantly. Reinforcement is provided only after the appropriate response to the stimulus. Nor does it mean you are reinforced every time the behavior is shown. The behavior must be in response to the stimulus, not just randomly emitted. Continuous reinforcement schedules provide the fastest initial learning rate. Continuous schedules also provide the most stable rates of response. They do, however, require time and money when administered regularly. Continuous schedules have two additional drawbacks: a relatively low response rate (only one response is required for each reinforcement incident), and a relatively rapid extinction rate (it is very obvious when reinforcement ceases under a continuous schedule). Given this combination of strengths and weaknesses, organizations often use continuous schedules during early training to obtain relatively rapid learning and a regular rate of response. After the initial training period ends, however, continuous reinforcement is abandoned in favor of intermittent schedules.

Fixed Ratio. **Fixed ratio** reinforcement schedules provide reinforcement following every "*n*th" appropriate response to a stimulus. Thus, a fixed ratio schedule of 2:1 reinforces every second appropriate response to a stimulus. Fixed ratio schedules promote learning speeds almost as rapid as continuous schedules. In fact, a continuous schedule is actually a special case of the fixed ratio schedule (1:1). Fixed ratio schedules produce response rates which are among the highest and a stability of response rate surpassed only by continuous schedules. Unfortunately, fixed ratio schedules also are associated with an extinction rate exceeded only by continuous schedules. This is the type of reinforcement schedule used by most piece-rate pay plans.

Variable Ratio. **Variable ratio** reinforcement schedules are similar to fixed ratio schedules. The difference is the fixed ratio schedule reinforces *every* "*n*th" response; the variable ratio schedule *on the average* reinforces every "*n*th" response. With a variable ratio schedule of 2:1, reinforcement sometimes would occur more frequently and sometimes less frequently than every other time the appropriate response followed the stimulus. Use of a variable rather than a fixed ratio has very little effect on response rate or response stability. The variable ratio schedule does, however, tend to produce a very high level of resistance to extinction. Unfortunately, there is a trade-off in learning rate which makes the variable ratio schedule less desirable during early learning than most other schedules of reinforcement.

Fixed Interval. In a **fixed interval** schedule, a certain amount of time must have passed since the last reinforcement before another response to the stimulus will be reinforced. With a one-hour fixed interval schedule, for example, a supervisor visits a subordinate's work place, reinforces the first observed appropriate response, returns one hour later and reinforces the next observed appropriate response. This schedule does not imply that reinforcement will be received automatically after the passage of the time period. The time must pass *and* an appropriate response must be made. Fixed interval schedules produce response rates which are among the lowest and have relatively low resistance to extinction. They also provide the slowest learning rate and the least stable response rate of all the schedules. A typical response pattern produced by a fixed interval schedule has an individual responding frequently and vigorously near the end of the time interval. After reinforcement, however, the worker responds infrequently and sluggishly until the end of the next time interval approaches. Put simply, unless such an erratic pattern of responses is desired, the fixed interval reinforcement schedule is not very effective. It is, however, fairly widely used, due to a failure to recognize its drawbacks.

Variable Interval. **Variable interval** reinforcement schedules differ from fixed interval schedules in that the specified time interval passes *on the average* before another appropriate response is reinforced. Sometimes the time period is shorter than the average; sometimes it is longer. Variable interval schedules are superior to fixed interval schedules on each of the four key schedule-related factors (learning rate, response rate, response stability, and extinction rate). Nevertheless, variable interval schedules tend to produce only moderate learning rates, response rates, and response stability. They are, however, relatively resistant to extinction. A supervisor who visits a subordinate's work place, reinforces the first appropriate response to a stimulus, comes back every hour *on the average* and reinforces the first appropriate response to a stimulus is using a variable interval reinforcement schedule.

The characteristics produced by continuous reinforcement and each of the four most common types of intermittent reinforcement schedules are shown below in Exhibit 6–4 which compares these five schedules on each of the four major factors. Exhibit 6–5 presents a representative example of the learning process using each of the five schedules.

Exhibit 6–4 Key Characteristics of Various Schedules of Reinforcement

Learning Rate	Response Rate	Response Stability	Extinction Rate
FAST	HIGH	STABLE	SLOW
C	FR	C	VR
	VR		
FR		VR	VI
	VI	FR	
VI			FI
VR	FI	VI	FR
FI	C		C
		FI	
SLOW	LOW	UNSTABLE	FAST

C Continuous
FR Fixed Ratio
VR Variable Ratio
FI Fixed Interval
VI Variable Interval

Note: This table describes representative characteristics of each reinforcement schedule. Variations in ratios, intervals, etc., will influence the specific characteristics.

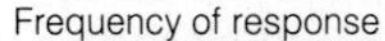

Exhibit 6–5 The Impact of Reinforcement Schedules

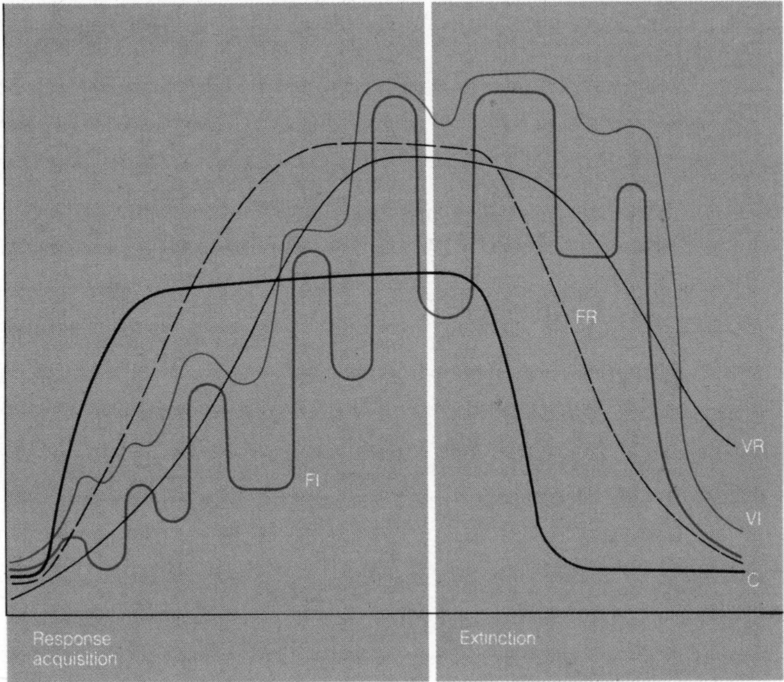

Note: These are characterizations of patterns. A number of factors would influence the nature of patterns found in specific situations.

It should be obvious by now that there is no one best reinforcement schedule. Each has specific strengths and weaknesses. The appropriateness of a particular schedule will depend on the objectives of the specific situation. In most cases, a combination of reinforcement schedules is needed to best accomplish organizational objectives.

ORGANIZATIONAL BEHAVIOR MODIFICATION

Organizational behavior modification (OBM) takes the learning theory principles (primarily operant) and systematically applies them to manage behavior within organizations. OBM theorists and practitioners frequently "go beyond" noncognitive operant principles when trying to understand and manage behavior. Organizational behavior modification as presented here differs from operant theory through the heavy use of cognitive learning processes. This allows discussion of *why* behavior changes by referring to the thoughts of the persons involved. Taking these cognitive processes into account can facilitate the effectiveness and efficiency of OBM.

Operant theory requires that a person directly experience S→R→C sequences over time before behavior will change. OBM argues that behavior can change in anticipation of future S→R→C sequences. If you have been hired by a company that says it will pay you if you come to work, you go to work anticipating they will do so—even though you have not yet received a paycheck. If your professor tells you that cheaters will be flunked out of the course, you believe it and refrain from cheating. This anticipation of future consequences makes it possible to influence behavior by specifying in writing or verbally the consequences which will follow responses to stimuli.

OBM recognizes the importance of social learning. It is possible, for example, for your behavior to change based on the S→R→C sequences you observe for someone else ("Jill got a pay raise for working extra hours; perhaps I will also get a pay raise if I work extra hours."). Social learning means it is not necessary for every individual to learn through personal "trial and error" experiences. If you observe (or are told about) what happened when your co-worker responded to a stimulus, it can change your intended response before you even receive the stimulus.

Outcomes

In using cognitive learning models, you will find it very useful to explore the value that organizational members attach to outcomes (see Chapter 5). If you fail to do this and try to use these outcomes as reinforcers or punishers, your plan may backfire. An intended positive reinforcer will produce the effects of punishment if a person values the outcome negatively. The need theory perspectives can aid you in selecting appropriately valued consequences. In doing so, you will improve the effectiveness of your organization's OBM programs.

Since OBM does pay attention to cognitive processes, both intrinsic and extrinsic outcomes can play an important role. *Intrinsic* consequences are "self-administered" outcomes and can function in any aspect of learning:

Positive reinforcement ("Completing this task gives me a real feeling of accomplishment").

Negative reinforcement ("Finishing this task removes the nagging guilt feelings I have been experiencing").

Punishment ("I'm sorry I did a poor job on this assignment").

Avoidance learning ("If I do a good job on this assignment, I will avoid bad feelings about myself").

Consequences considered from a pure operant theory perspective are all *extrinsic*, meaning that they came from outside of the individual (usually administered by someone else). For employees, for example, pay increases and promotions can be extrinsic outcomes. Extrinsic outcomes also can function in any aspect of learning.

In fact, intrinsic and extrinsic consequences often exert joint influences on learning. When intrinsic and extrinsic consequences are operating in a similar fashion, learning tends to occur rapidly. A worker who performs at a high level, for example, may feel a sense of accomplishment (intrinsic) and receive a cash bonus (extrinsic). When intrinsic and extrinsic factors operate in contradiction, conflict is created and learning slowed ("Cheating on the last exam has caused me a great deal of mental suffering but I got a high grade").

OBM in the Soviet Union

After months of warnings and harangues, the Soviet leadership . . . took the first concrete steps in its campaign to instill greater discipline in the inefficient, and often inebriated, Soviet work force.

In a 3,000-word decree that covered most of the front page of *Pravda*, the official party newspaper, the Communist Party Central Committee gave managers new authority to fire and demote bad workers, to dock workers' pay for producing faulty merchandise, and to punish absenteeism by taking away vacation time.

At the same time, the decree stressed good workers should receive rewards, such as extra vacation days, permits for the best vacation resorts, and higher priority for receiving new apartments.

A major problem with the [previous] discipline campaign, analysts had noted, was workers were rarely fired here. If they did get fired, they usually had little trouble landing new jobs.

"Who isn't familiar with this paradox?" the director of a brick plant wrote in December in the newspaper *Izvestia*. "Everyone knows that an employee is loafing and doing shoddy work, but there is no way to get rid of him."

The decree puts these other provisions at a manager's disposal:

1. Workers who frequently are drunk or absent can be demoted to lower-paying menial jobs, and they legally can be prevented from quitting that job for up to five months.
2. Workers who show up drunk or drink on the job—"the most severe violation," the decree said—can be summarily fired without trade union consent.
3. Workers who produce "faulty goods" can be docked up to one third of each month's pay for damages.[4]

You must consider both intrinsic and extrinsic consequences of behavior to prevent reduced effectiveness of OBM.

Intrinsic consequences are usually "self-administered" on a continuous reinforcement schedule ("I always feel like this when I behave this way"). This produces relatively rapid learning during early periods of the learning process, but also can result in relatively quick extinction if the intrinsic experiences cease to occur. Edward Deci and others have argued that, under certain circumstances, providing extrinsic reinforcement can reduce the impact of intrinsic reinforcement.[5] In an intrinsically motivating job, for example, extrinsic reinforcements can shift your focus away from you and onto the external source of reinforcement. If true, this would reduce the reinforcing impact of intrinsic factors.

Behavioral Shaping in OBM

OBM makes frequent use of *behavioral shaping* (learning a complex behavior through successive approximation of the desired behavior). Shaping is easier to accomplish if you can explain the desired behavior to the individual who is learning. Pure operant application of shaping requires you to reinforce a behavioral response which is remotely similar to the ultimate desired complex response. You must then wait until a more similar response is shown by the learner, reinforce that response, wait until an even more similar response is shown, etc. Learning can occur much more rapidly when the ultimate desired behavior and each desired step is explained to the learner.

Examples of Organizational Behavior Modification

Examples of the application of OBM principles abound in everyday life. Even if not identified formally as OBM, learning is occurring every bit as much as if OBM were being consciously used. If you are asked out on a date (the stimulus), you accept and go (the response), and you have a good time (a positively reinforcing consequence), you are more likely to say yes when asked out by this person in the future. If you go out and have a bad time (a punishing consequence) you are less likely to say yes to this person in the future. Furthermore, if punishment occurs for most dates, stimulus generalization will probably occur. As a result, you may respond by saying "no" to most date requests.

OBM is used within organizations on an everyday basis although it is not always referred to as such. Paying a person to take a job is positive reinforcement. "Docking" the pay of an employee who is late is punishment. Improving performance to get your boss "off

Steven Kerr of the University of Southern California has made a number of contributions to OB, particularly in the areas of leadership and reward systems, including a paper entitled "On the Folly of Rewarding *A* while Hoping for *B*."

Briefly, what is the "folly of rewarding *A* while hoping for *B*"? In short, this is the very common, almost universal, phenomenon in which an organization wants members to behave a certain way (*B*) but has reward systems which reward people for some other behavior (*A*).

Could you give us an example of this? I have talked to physicians who discuss the folly with regard to bed counts. With the surplus of hospital rooms in the country, they have sections of the hospital where they put the well patients. The hospital needs to have lots of people confined because hospital finances depend heavily on the bed count. The reward system encourages placing people in the hospital even when it is not totally medically necessary.

Why does the folly occur, and what can be done about it? You've asked a very complex question, so you are going to have to settle for a partial answer. One of the central problems is that people don't really attend to the reward system and recognize that they are rewarding the wrong behaviors. An awareness of the reward system is the first step. Examine what is being rewarded and punished. Performance is a very subtle, sensitive, subjective, sloppy concept, and organizations hate things that are sloppy and subjective. Organizations tend to measure things which are easily measured rather than what should be measured. That is why things like creativity, cooperation, and team building are routinely ignored in favor of observables like attendance. It is important that a reward system be improved first by developing healthy, robust, broad, multifaceted standards of performance. Only once these are explicated can an effective reward system be set up.

Absenteeism Reduction in a Hospital Using OBM

A study done by Stephens and Burroughs provides an interesting example of the degree to which a simple OBM program can impact absenteeism levels quickly and significantly.[7] The absenteeism level of 96 employees (registered nurses, licensed practical nurses, ward clerks, and nursing assistants) was measured at a large private hospital for a three-week period. This first measurement obtained an estimate of existing absenteeism levels (over 40 percent of the employees had at least one day of absenteeism during this period).

The employees were subsequently divided in half. The first group was to receive OBM Treatment A; the second group would receive OBM Treatment B. The employees receiving Treatment A were told that anyone who came to work every day for the next three weeks would be eligible for a lottery drawing. The group receiving Treatment B was told that there would be eight special days during the next three weeks. Everyone present on those eight days would be eligible for a lottery drawing, but they would not be told which days were the special ones. Each lottery would have a $20 prize for each 20 eligible persons.

your back" is negative reinforcement. Doing a good job to avoid getting in trouble with your boss is avoidance learning.

You can use OBM techniques for a wide range of organizational purposes. During job training, OBM principles can speed the rate at which learning occurs. As you now know, continuous schedules of reinforcement are common during initial training to speed learning. After this early learning period, you can switch to intermittent schedules for increased response rate and resistance to extinction. Try shaping for complex training by explaining the total desired behavior and each successive training step. Follow up with reinforcement practices to "bring the learner along" one step at a time as s/he masters each element of the final desired behavior.[6]

Most industrial safety programs incorporate OBM principles. Warning lights, bells, and whistles provide stimuli to warn of unsafe conditions. Punch presses can be rigged to warn you that your hand is in the way of the machine (a buzzer serves as a stimulus which elicits the response of moving your hand out of danger). Modern jetliners have ground proximity indicators which provide an automatic spoken stimulus ("Pull up . . . pull up . . . pull up") when an aircraft approaches the ground at an unsafe altitude or rate. The worker who has learned to respond to such a stimulus responds with the appropriate safe behavior. For obvious reasons, most safety applications of OBM do not have the trainee actually experience the specific S→R→C sequence during learning. Rather, learning usually is based on a combination of avoidance learning, social learning, and simulation.

Other examples of OBM use in organizations exist in several

Exhibit 6–6 Absenteeism and OBM

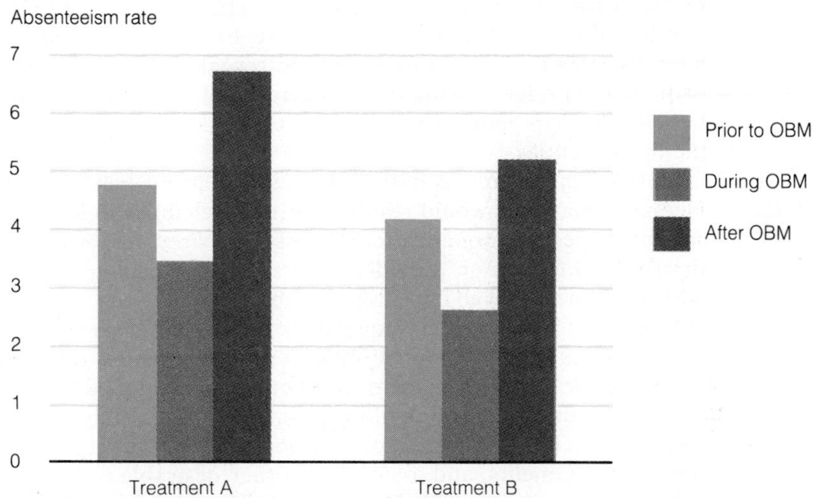

Source: Derived from T. A. Stephens, and W. A. Burroughs, An application of operant conditioning to absenteeism in a hospital setting, *Journal of Applied Psychology,* 518–521, copyright 1978 by the American Psychological Association. Adapted with permission of the publisher and authors.

areas, including turnover management, absenteeism control, performance motivation, and discipline. Examples presented in this chapter sample this wide range of OBM usage.

Both Treatment A and B in the hospital example involved a variable ratio reinforcement schedule of 20 : 1. This means, on the average, every 20th appropriate response would be reinforced. The responses required, however, differed. Under Treatment A, the response which would be reinforced was *no* absenteeism. Treatment B would reinforce no absenteeism during any of eight (unknown) days. Had this program continued indefinitely, the law of averages would have caused each person to be reinforced an average of every 20th time s/he responded appropriately.

Absenteeism was measured for the three-week period of the OBM program and again for two weeks after the OBM program. Exhibit 6–6 shows that absenteeism was significantly lower for both OBM groups than it had been prior to the OBM program. In addition, only 30 percent of the employees contributed any absenteeism during this period (compared to over 40 percent prior to the program). However, Exhibit 6–6 also shows that extinction of the low absenteeism response occurred after the OBM trials were canceled. Furthermore, absenteeism actually climbed to a higher level than was present prior to the OBM program. This illustrates one of the poten-

OBM Program to Enhance Airline Sales Performance

A much more complex example illustrates how OBM enhanced sales performance for reservations personnel at Scandinavian Airlines.[8] Prior to the beginning of this study, the only behavior measured was the number of calls taken per day per agent. Even this was not being reinforced systematically. An investigation revealed that agents were making firm booking offers during only 34 percent of potential sales opportunities. Round trip bookings were being made during only 17.5 percent of the opportunities.

An OBM program was designed to change agent behavior. Hopefully, increased bookings would result from these changes in behavior. A consultant helped the organization identify a desired response for agents. Briefly, agents were to provide specific offers to book and present supporting information to encourage the booking decision. A system was developed to measure the frequency of each desired response. Appropriate responses were reinforced; inappropriate responses received nonreinforcement or mild punishment. Reinforcement included a combination of extrinsic and intrinsic reinforcers (quantitative feedback, supervisory feedback, social recognition, recognition from top management, gifts, special assignments, and a variety of other desirable outcomes). Most reinforcement was provided using a combination of variable ratio and variable interval schedules.

tial drawbacks to OBM programs if they are not continued on a consistent basis.

This study provided fairly impressive results, even though it encompassed only a very short time period and had very rigid attendance requirements. A program which reinforced not only perfect attendance but also very good attendance (with a somewhat less valuable reinforcer) might have produced even more dramatic results.

Exhibit 6–7 shows the dramatic increase in the frequency of appropriate responses made after the OBM program Scandinavian Airlines was implemented. Specific and appropriate booking offers made during sales opportunities increased from 34 percent to over 80 percent. Other desired responses showed similar increases. Agent sales behavior was modified by the OBM program. So, too, were the number of successful round trip bookings (an increase from 17.5 percent to over 30 percent). The financial impact for the airline was substantial, even considering the cost of the training required. At the time of this writing, the program has been in effect for five years. According to Feeney et al., it "continues to produce useful feedback to the staff and productive training material for management."[9]

Exhibit 6–7 Sales and OBM

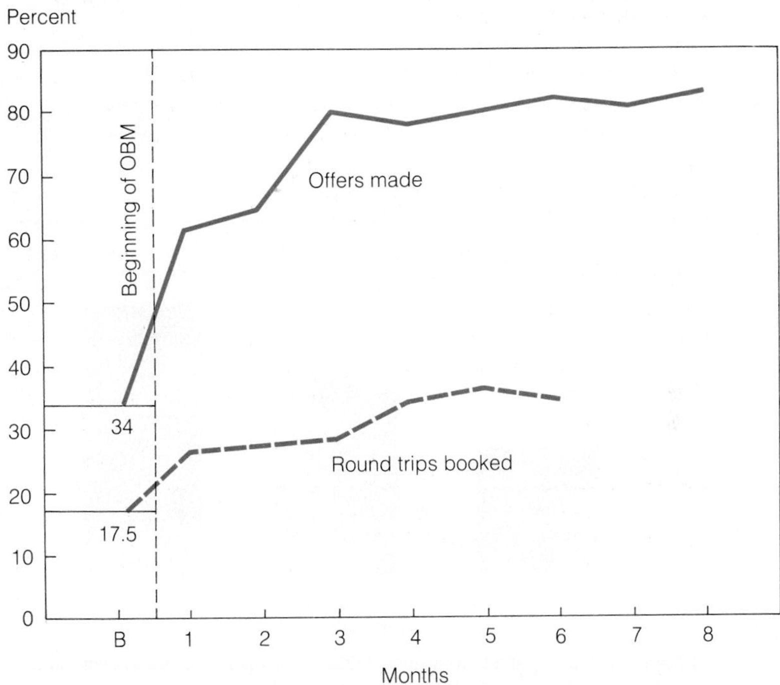

Source: Data from E. J. Feeney, J. R. Staelin, R. M. O'Brien, and A. M. Dickinson (1982). Increasing sales performance among airline reservation personnel. In R. M. O'Brien, A. M. Dickinson, and M. P. Rosow, Eds., *Industrial behavior modification: A management handbook,* 141–158. Maxwell House, NY: Pergamon Press.

Rodent Trapping Performance Improvements Using OBM

Latham and Dossett, and Saari and Latham twice studied the impact of two types of OBM programs on the effectiveness of 12 rodent trappers.[10] These trappers worked for a forest products company in the state of Washington. Their job was to capture rodents so they would not damage newly planted seedlings. Trapping performance measured for a four-week period indicated an average of .52 trappings per hour per worker.

After the initial four-week period, half of the trappers were placed on a continuous reinforcement schedule. This schedule provided $1 above and beyond the regular hourly compensation for each beaver trapped. The other half of the employees were placed on a variable ratio reinforcement schedule. On the average, every fourth trapping was reinforced (each reinforcement was $4, so that an average of $1 per trapping was provided to each group). Every week, the groups were alternated (the group receiving the continuous schedule was placed on the VR schedule, and vice-versa).

Exhibit 6–8 Rodent Trapping and OBM

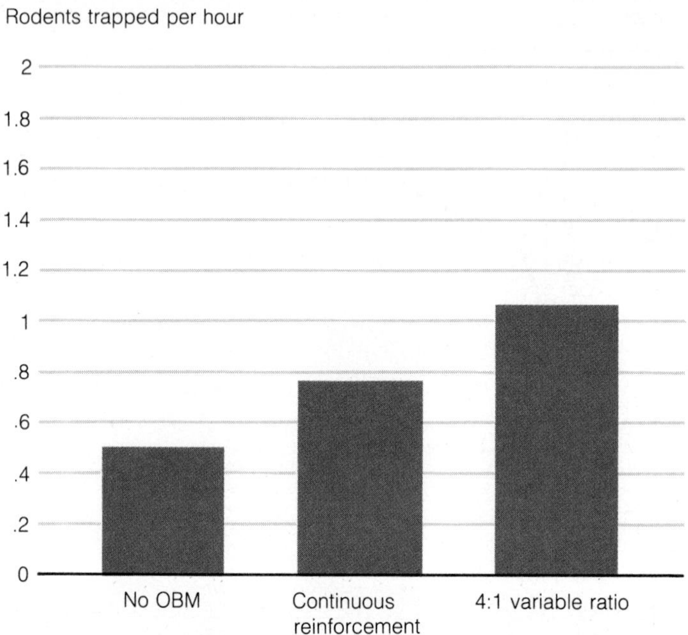

Source: L. M. Saari, and G. P. Latham (1982). Employee reactions to continuous and variable ratio reinforcement schedules involving a monetary incentive. *Journal of Applied Psychology, 62,* 506–508.

Exhibit 6–8 illustrates the results of these two OBM programs. Performance under the continuous reinforcement schedule increased 50 percent (from an average of .52 to .78). Performance under the variable ratio (VR) schedule was even higher (1.08, or a 108 percent increase). An additional interesting finding was obtained in the 1978 study which revealed that continuous schedules were more effective for inexperienced employees than VR schedules (as would be expected during early learning periods).

Saari and Latham also explored *why* the VR schedule was more effective when both programs had provided the same financial reinforcement. Interviews and surveys of the trappers revealed that they felt the VR schedule provided greater amounts of recognition and intrinsic reinforcement (e.g., a sense of task accomplishment and experienced meaningfulness of the work). After six years, the program is still operating with similar results.

Recommendations for Effective Use of OBM

How can you use OBM most effectively? Many authors have offered suggestions, and their general recommendations can help you decide what to do. All of these recommendations are consistent with other ideas in this chapter.[13]

1. Identify specific desired behaviors (responses).
2. Identify which consequences you can control.
3. Identify the values of those consequences you can control and use them appropriately. Be sure positive reinforcers are positively valued, for example, and punishers negatively valued.
4. Choose appropriate learning devices (e.g., positive reinforcement, punishment, etc.) carefully based on learning objectives and the resources available.
5. Use combinations of learning devices where possible.
6. Choose appropriate reinforcement schedules, depending on desired effects. For example, use continuous reinforcement during early learning and intermittent schedules later.
7. Specify R→C contingencies carefully. Be sure you tell a learner which behaviors will be reinforced, punished, etc.
8. Carefully measure behaviors (responses) and provide appropriate consequences.
9. Make both positive and negative consequences equal to the behavior (e.g., don't over- or under-reward or punish).
10. Consistently follow the R→C contingencies as planned and stated.
11. Make consequences follow responses as closely as possible so the learner will associate the two.
12. If you use punishment, explain to the learner what s/he is doing wrong.
13. If punishment is used, you also should provide reinforcement of desired behaviors.
14. Be careful if punishing in front of others. This can lead to "retaliation," misinterpretation by other work group members, and experienced punishment by the entire work group.
15. Remember that nonaction can modify behavior. For example, if you reward all workers equally, high performers may lower their performance.
16. Use shaping when a person must learn complex behaviors.

Ethical Issues Associated with OBM

Is the use of organizational behavior modification ethical? This question can be answered only by the individual using OBM. Some persons feel that any attempt to influence another person's behavior in any way is unethical. If you feel this way, OBM is clearly unethical for you. Others feel that OBM is ethical as long as behavior is not modified so as to compromise a person legally, morally, or emotionally. If you feel this way, whether or not OBM will be ethical for you depends on the types of behavior produced by its use. Still others believe that OBM is ethical so long as the person using it explains to the subject of OBM what behaviors are to be modified, why, and how. Even after taking all perspectives into consideration, you still may be left wondering "Who am I to decide that the things I am asking of this person are not 'illegal, immoral, or otherwise compromising?'" There is no easy answer to the ethical question of OBM use.

Howard Berthold of Lycoming College presents several questions frequently asked about the use of OBM:[14]

1. Isn't it unethical to modify another person's behavior?
2. Isn't behavior modification worse than some other methods because it is planned rather than unplanned, intentional rather than unintentional?
3. Aren't the techniques of behavior modification more objectionable than techniques associated with other methods?
4. Wouldn't a successful program of behavior modification cause people to lose their individuality?
5. Won't behavior modification be misused?

Berthold provides responses to each of these concerns. The basis of many of his responses rests on the fact that OBM does describe how behavior is influenced, whether or not it is ethical to use OBM. Furthermore, he observes:

> The preceding five questions typify the kinds of concerns many people express toward behavior modification. . . . The bottom line to most of these concerns is that the ethical questions directed at behavior modification turn out upon analysis not to be unique to this approach at all, but are issues that should be raised when any technique is applied to the sphere of management. There remains, therefore, only one real question, and that is how one ensures that any approach, regardless of its name or methods is ethical.[15]

Berthold then summarizes and discusses the appropriateness of six principles to consider before deciding whether OBM is being used ethically.[16] These will help you address the question of ethics, but they will not answer the question for you.

1. The use of behavior modification appears to be least controversial when it makes use of positive rather than negative tech-

niques, and when the techniques are applied to behaviors for which there is widespread agreement that behavioral management is justified.
2. Behavior modification appears to be least controversial when participants in a program have full knowledge of the methods and goals, and when they have the opportunity to accept or reject such techniques.
3. Behavior modification appears to be least controversial when there is a clearly established need or reason for using it.
4. Behavior modification appears to be least controversial when all reasonable alternatives have been specified, and there is general agreement that a given alternative is best.
5. Behavior modification appears to be least controversial when the people who practice it are well informed about the ethical issues involved, can discuss the issues in an intelligent way, and strive to follow the established guidelines of their profession.
6. Behavior modification appears to be least controversial when it advances and supports personal and social ideals held by people.

One other consideration may help you when deciding whether to use OBM in a specific situation. Ask yourself whether OBM is being used to "force" organizational members to do things against their wishes, or whether in fact OBM is helping these members behave in a way they desire. OBM can be used either way. The former is clearly manipulation; the latter is classified better as assistance. You may reject using OBM to manipulate. On the other hand, if your subordinates ask you to help them become better workers, learn to operate new equipment, or help them increase the safety of their behavior on the job, you may wish to use OBM in providing this assistance.

A Note on Discipline Systems

Discipline systems exist in most organizations. These systems are usually quite formalized, particularly in cases where a union contract specifies what types of organizational discipline are permissible. Although seldom described in these terms, discipline systems constitute a subset of the overall OBM program. According to Dallas Jones, discipline is either authoritarian or corrective.[11]

Authoritarian discipline focuses on retribution for an improper act. Little attention is given to changing the behavior of the person who behaved improperly. In fact, authoritarian discipline often involves expelling an offender from the organization. Authoritarian discipline attempts to modify the behavior of other potential offenders by serving as a deterrent. This type of discipline changes behavior through social avoidance learning. In short, others see the consequence which followed the improper response and behave in such a way as to avoid a similar negative consequence. In this way, authoritarian discipline hopes to modify the behavior of many people by "sacrificing" one person as an example.

Corrective discipline, on the other hand, focuses on changing the behavior of the person who behaved improperly so that s/he will not behave improperly again. This type of discipline changes behavior primarily through punishment, although some social avoidance learning may also accrue as others witness the punishment. Corrective discipline is thus concerned with modifying the behavior of the one "guilty party."

Hoyt Wheeler explored the two major types of discipline and analyzed over 300 industrial discipline cases subjected to legal arbitration.[12] His analysis of these cases revealed that authoritarian and corrective discipline were used about equally. This contradicted the popular expectation that corrective discipline was more frequent and more appropriate. There was little evidence, however, to indicate that the two disciplinary approaches were used systematically to accomplish the particular desired effect (i.e., to influence many nonoffenders through avoidance learning or to influence primarily one offender through punishment).

There are several limitations in using discipline, regardless of which form you select. First and foremost, discipline only tells an organizational member what *not* to do. Unless discipline is combined with reinforcement of desired behaviors, the offender probably will not behave automatically in the desired way. In fact, repressing a behavior through discipline often leads to a person engaging in some other undesired behavior. In addition, a person who is punished frequently resents the source of the punishment and has a lower level of motivation for meeting organizational objectives.

SUMMARY

Neither of the major learning theories discussed in this chapter (classical and operant) were developed in or for formal organizations. Despite this, application of these techniques and newer techniques based upon them (such as OBM) have shown much promise for managing behavior in organizations.

In classical conditioning, a "natural" (unconditioned) stimulus-response link exists prior to learning. By associating a new stimulus (conditioned) with the natural stimulus, the conditioned stimulus acquires the ability to elicit the response previously produced by the unconditioned stimulus. The focus, therefore, is on the acquisition of new stimuli.

In operant conditioning, learning occurs because of the environmental consequences which follow a response to a stimulus. In this approach, the focus is on the acquisition of new responses. Several options are available for both the strengthening and weakening of a stimulus-response link.

Organizational behavior modification capitalizes on the findings of both types of learning processes. OBM is distinguished by its focus on behavior occurring in organizations. It also incorporates a high level of cognitive involvement, which is in direct contrast to the noncognitive learning models.

Because of the potentially powerful effects of applying learning theories in organizations, ethical considerations are particularly important. Several key ethical considerations relevant to OBM were discussed, and you should consider them carefully before becoming involved in an OBM project.

GLOSSARY

Classical Conditioning The learning process through which a person learns to respond to a particular event (stimulus) because that event has been associated with some other event which previously produced a response.

Unconditioned Stimulus (UCS) A classical stimulus which naturally (reflexively) elicits a response.

Unconditioned Response (UCR) A classical response which naturally follows an unconditioned stimulus.

Conditioned Stimulus (CS) A classical stimulus which, through association with an unconditioned stimulus, acquires the ability to produce a (conditioned) response.

Conditioned Response (CR) A classical response which follows a conditioned stimulus.

Operant Conditioning The learning process through which a person learns to respond to a particular event (stimulus) because of the consequences which occur when the person reacts.

Operant Stimulus (S) Any environmental situation or event which is followed by a behavioral response.

Operant Response (R) Any observable response which follows a stimulus.

Operant Consequence (C) Any observable environmental event which follows an operant response.

Reinforcer An operant consequence which increases the likelihood that, in the future, the same stimulus will be followed by the same response.

Positive Reinforcement The strengthening of a stimulus→response link through the addition of an operant consequence following a response.

Negative Reinforcement The strengthening of a stimulus→response link through the removal of an operant consequence following a response.

Avoidance Learning The strengthening of a stimulus→response link which occurs when a person responds to a stimulus in order to avoid an undesirable consequence.

Behavioral Shaping The learning of a complex behavior through reinforcement of successive approximations of the desired complex behavior.

Extinction The process by which a stimulus→response link is weakened.

Nonreinforcement A technique for producing extinction which involves the nonpresentation of reinforcing consequences following a response.

Punishment A technique for producing extinction which involves the presentation of an undesired consequence following a response.

Continuous Reinforcement A reinforcement schedule in which each appropriate response to a stimulus is reinforced.

Intermittent Reinforcement Any reinforcement schedule in which some, but not all, appropriate responses to a stimulus are reinforced.

Fixed Ratio Schedule A reinforcement schedule which reinforces every "nth" appropriate response to a stimulus.

Variable Ratio Schedule A reinforcement schedule which, on the average, reinforces every "nth" appropriate response to a stimulus.

Fixed Interval Schedule A reinforcement schedule which consistently reinforces the first appropriate response to a stimulus following the passage of a specific interval of time.

Variable Interval Schedule A reinforcement schedule which reinforces the first appropriate response to a stimulus following the passage of a time period which, across time, averages to the specified interval.

Organizational Behavior Modification The systematic applied use of learning theory principles for the purpose of managing behavior within organizations.

STUDY QUESTIONS

1. What are some of the possible applications of classical conditioning in organizations?
2. What are some of the major limitations to the use of classical conditioning in organizations?
3. Should a cognitive component be included in operant theory to facilitate the use of the model?
4. Describe an organizational situation in which it would be appropriate to use a continuous reinforcement schedule. When would it be appropriate to use an intermittent reinforcement schedule?
5. Discuss the potential effectiveness and limitations of the use of punishment in organizations.
6. Discuss the merits of the following statement: "Organizational behavior modification is the systematic manipulation of organizational members and, therefore, should not be used."
7. Discuss the merits of the following statement: "Because organizational behavior modification focuses on the satisfaction of the needs of organizational members, it would be inappropriate not to use the technique."
8. Identify the major factors which determine the effectiveness of an organizational behavior modification program.

NOTES

1. **Pavlov, I. P.** (1902). *The work of the digestive glands.* London: Charles Griffin, (translated by W. H. Thompson).
2. **Skinner, B. F.** (1953). *Science and human behavior.* New York: Free Press; **Skinner, B. F.** (1969). *Contingencies of reinforcement.* East Norwalk, CT: Appleton-Century-Crofts; **Skinner, B. F.** (1971). *Beyond freedom and dignity.* New York: Bantam Books.
3. **Thorndike, E.** (1911). *Animal intelligence.* New York: Macmillan.
4. Soviets get tough with bad workers. (1983, August). *Wisconsin State Journal,* p. 1.
5. **Deci, E. L.** (1972). Intrinsic motivation, extrinsic reinforcement, and inequity. *Journal of Personality and Social Psychology, 22,* 113–120.
6. The interested reader might wish to explore these issues in **Duncan, P. K., & Lloyd, E. E.** (1982). Training format in industrial behavior modification. In R. M. O'Brien, A. M. Dickinson, & M. P. Rosow (Eds.), *Industrial behavior modification: A management handbook* (pp. 387–404). Maxwell House, NY: Pergamon Press.
7. **Stephens, T. A., & Burroughs, W. A.** (1978). An application of operant conditioning to absenteeism in a hospital setting. *Journal of Applied Psychology, 63,* 518–521.
8. **Feeney, E. J., Staelin, J. R., O'Brien, R. M., & Dickinson, A. M.** (1982). Increasing sales performance among airline reservation personnel. In R. M. O'Brien, A. M. Dickinson, & M. P. Rosow (Eds.), *Industrial behavior modification: A management handbook,* (pp. 141–158). Maxwell House, NY: Pergamon Press.
9. Ibid, p. 158.
10. **Latham, G. P., & Dossett, D. L.** (1978). Designing incentive plans for unionized employees: A comparison of continuous and variable ratio reinforcement schedules. *Personnel Psychology, 63,* 47–61; **Saari, L. M., & Latham, G. P.** (1982). Employee reactions to continuous and variable ratio reinforcement schedules involving a monetary incentive. *Journal of Applied Psychology, 62,* 506–508.
11. **Jones, D. L.** (1961). *Arbitration and industrial discipline.* Ann Arbor: Bureau of Industrial Relations, University of Michigan.
12. **Wheeler, H. N.** (1967, May). Punishment theory and industrial discipline. *Industrial Relations.* 235–243.
13. Three particularly well-presented sets of recommendations provided much of the inspiration for this section and can provide excellent resources for further reading in this area. See **Hamner, W. C., & Hamner, E. P.** (1976, Spring). Behavior modification on the bottom line. *Organizational Dynamics,* 3–21; **Kerr, S.** (1975). On the folly of rewarding A, while hoping for B. *Academy of Management Journal, 18,* 769–783; **O'Brien, R. M., & Dickinson, A. M.**

(1982). Introduction to industrial behavior modification. In O'Brien, R. M., Dickinson, A. M., & M. P. Rosow (Eds.), *Industrial behavior modification: A management handbook* (pp. 7–34). Maxwell House, NY: Pergamon Press.

14. **Berthold, H. C., Jr.** (1982). Behavior modification in the industrial/organizational environment: Assumptions and ethics. In R. M. O'Brien, A. M. Dickinson, & M. P. Rosow (Eds.), *Industrial behavior modification: A management handbook* (pp. 405–427). Maxwell House, NY: Pergamon Press.
15. Ibid, p. 415.
16. Ibid, pp. 415–424.

7 Equity and Goal Theories

OVERVIEW
EQUITY THEORY
DISTRIBUTIVE JUSTICE
J. STACY ADAMS' EQUITY THEORY
- Person's Perceived Outcomes
- Perceived Outcomes for Others
- Person's Perceived Inputs
- Perceived Inputs for Others
- Ratios
- Perceived State of Equity
- Perceived Under-Reward
- Perceived Over-Reward
- Alternatives for Reducing Perceived Inequity
- Choice of Inequity-Reducing Action
- Individual Differences in Equity Motivation

RESEARCH ON EQUITY THEORY
- Research on Over-Reward
- Research on Under-Reward
- An Integrative Analysis

GOAL THEORY
THE BASIC MODEL
- Goal Difficulty
- Goal Specificity

EXPANDED MODEL
- Goal-Directed Effort and Performance
- Goal Acceptance and Goal Commitment
- Satisfaction

SOME CONSIDERATIONS FOR APPLICATION
- Does Goal Setting Work Equally Well for Everyone?
- How Should a Goal Be Set?
- Should Goals Be Assigned or Participatively Chosen?
- What Is the Role of Incentives in the Goal-Setting Process?
- What Is the Role of Competition?

MANAGEMENT BY OBJECTIVES (MBO)
SUMMARY

Justice is not so much a question of how much one gives nor of how much one receives. The real question is the fairness of what one receives in return for that which is given.

Anonymous

Do not turn back when you are just at the goal.

Publilius Syrus

OVERVIEW

Equity theory is concerned with the affective and behavioral reactions people have to outcomes they receive as part of a "social exchange." According to equity theory, your reactions to the outcomes received from another person (or organization) depend both on how you value those outcomes in an absolute sense *and* also on the circumstances surrounding their receipt. Equity theory suggests that your reactions will be influenced by your perceptions of the "inputs" you provided in order to receive these outcomes ("Did I get as much out of this as I put into it?"). Even more important to you, according to equity theory, is your comparison of what you received for your inputs relative to what you believe others received for their inputs ("Did I get as much for my inputs as my co-worker got for his/hers?"). Equity theory argues, for example, that the way you feel about the pay you receive from an organization will be influenced by: how much pay you receive, how valuable that money is to you, how hard you believe you worked to earn the money, and whether you feel your "pay-to-work ratio" was fair in comparison to the "pay-to-work" ratio of others. If you perceive any of these factors to be unfair, you will experience dissatisfaction. This dissatisfaction will motivate you to make some kind of change to establish what you believe is a state of fairness (equity). Equity theory systematically identifies the factors influencing your perceived state of equity and explores actions you can take to reach a perceived state of equity if you feel it does not currently exist.

Goal theory is one of the simplest, most straightforward, logical, and best-supported theories examined in this book. Virtually all of its major elements have been tested and supported in both laboratory settings and in the "real world."

Goal theory states that if you are guided by specific, difficult goals, you will perform at higher levels than will a person who operates without goals. You will also perform better than someone guided by goals which are either too general or too easy. This higher level of performance is attributed primarily to direction, effort, and persistence. Specific goals *direct* your focus to relevant activities ("*This* is what I should be doing"). You devote more intense levels of *effort* toward difficult goals than easier ones ("I have to work *hard* to accomplish my goal"). Finally, specific, difficult goals encourage you to *persist* longer at a task than would be the case without such goals ("I have to *continue* working at this task if I am to reach my goal"). The goal theory perspectives and a separate treatment of management by objectives are presented in this chapter to give you an understanding of how organizational members are influenced by their perceptions (and how you, as a manager, can profit from this knowledge).

EQUITY THEORY

DISTRIBUTIVE JUSTICE

The concept of **distributive justice** was proposed by Homans to explain how people consider both inputs and outcomes when evaluating a social exchange.[1] Homans used the term *investment* to describe all inputs to a social exchange and the term *profit* for all outcomes from such an exchange. According to Homans, if you examine your investments and profits and find them to be more or less equal, you will experience distributive justice and be satisfied with the exchange. If you believe you have received distributive injustice, you will be dissatisfied. You then have two choices: either you will take action to restore a state of justice, or you will leave the situation ("I won't deal with you anymore").

Use of the terms *investment* and *profit* by Homans may confuse you, particularly if you have learned elsewhere that investments should produce a greater return than was invested, and that profit is the amount of return beyond the amount invested. To avoid this confusion, the terms *inputs* and *outcomes* will be used instead.

Inputs are any factors contributed by an individual to the social exchange which the person feels have value and are relevant to the exchange. Note that the value attached to an input is based on the person's perception of its relevance and value, whether or not anyone else agrees that the input is relevant or valuable. Common inputs in organizational exchanges include time, effort, performance level, education level, skill levels, and bypassed opportunities. Since *any* factor you consider relevant is included in your evaluation of distributive justice, it is not uncommon for factors to be included which an organization (or even the law) might argue are inappropriate (e.g., age, sex, ethnic background, social status).

Outcomes are any factors received by an individual from the social exchange which the person feels have value and are relevant to the exchange. Again, the value attached to an outcome is based on the person's perceptions and not necessarily "objective reality." Common outcomes from organizational social exchanges include pay, working conditions, job status, intrinsic experiences, and interpersonal relationships. Both positive and negative outcomes influence your evaluation of distributive justice. Thus stress, headaches, and fatigue are all potential outcomes. Since any outcome you consider relevant to the exchange influences your distributive justice evaluation, it is common for unintended factors to be included (peer disapproval, family reactions, etc.).

J. STACY ADAMS' EQUITY THEORY

Although a variety of "equity theories" exist, the most widely known, researched, and used has been that developed by J. Stacy Adams while he was a psychologist conducting research for the General Electric Company.[2] Adams agrees with Homans that evaluations of distributive justice play an important part in a person's reactions to a social exchange. Adams' theory goes further, however, and argues that you evaluate your experienced state of distributive justice through an extended social comparison. According to Adams, you will compare your own perceived level of distributive justice (expressed as a ratio of outcomes to inputs) to your perceptions of the distributive justice ratio for someone else (a "comparison other"). This allows you to determine whether you are being treated fairly (equitably) in comparison to others.

Adams states that you will be satisfied with your social exchange if your outcome-to-input ratio is similar to that perceived to exist for the comparison person or group. If the ratios are not perceived to be similar, a state of perceived inequity is said to exist. You will experience dissatisfaction and will be motivated to make a change which will lead to a state of perceived equity. The following four terms must be understood in order to develop Adams' equity theory more fully.

Person's Perceived Outcomes

O_p represents the combined value of all valued, relevant outcomes perceived by a person to be a result of the social exchange. This includes *anything* you perceive to be relevant and valuable, whether or not your organization intended for you to experience this outcome. For purposes of equity theory, the objective accuracy of these perceptions is not at issue since you will react to your *perceived* reality. Note also that outcomes might be provided by an organization which you will "ignore" when evaluating the social exchange (e.g., employee benefits which you are unaware of or don't care about, such as organizational contributions to social security, or unemployment compensation). Need theories provide a variety of useful perspectives for understanding the "absolute values" you attach to outcomes (see Chapter 5). These theories also emphasize that the values attached to a given outcome will vary across people and even across time for one person.

Perceived Outcomes for Others

O_o represents the combined value of all of the outcomes which a person believes a "comparison other" receives. It is very important to note that O_o is a perception in *your* mind, *not* in the mind of the comparison other. Thus, if you believe that your co-worker receives a $45,000 salary and immense intrinsic satisfaction from his/her work, your evaluation of the fairness (equity) of your own situation will be determined in comparison to these beliefs whether or not the comparison other actually receives these outcomes. A comparison other can be one person or a group of persons. Your reactions to the social exchange situation will be strongly influenced by your choice of a comparison other.

Person's Perceived Inputs

I_p represents the combined value of all of the relevant inputs which a person feels s/he is putting into the social exchange situation. As noted earlier, this can include *anything* you feel is a relevant input (whether or not anyone else agrees).

Perceived Inputs for Others

I_o represents the combined value of all of the relevant inputs which a person believes a comparison other puts into the social exchange situation. Once again, this is a perception in *your* mind (*not* in the mind of the comparison other).

Ratios

According to equity theory, a person will evaluate the following two ratios:

1. O_p/I_p The ratio of your perceived outcomes to perceived inputs. This is the distributive justice ratio considered by Homans.
2. O_o/I_o The ratio of your perceptions of the comparison other's outcomes to the comparison other's inputs. This is the distributive justice ratio perceived to exist for the comparison other.

The degree to which you believe a state of equity exists depends on your comparison of these two ratios. When the ratios are compared, one of three conditions will exist: (1) a perceived state of equity ($O_p/I_p = O_o/I_o$); (2) a state of "under-reward" ($O_p/I_p < O_o/I_o$); or (3) a state of "over-reward" ($O_p/I_p > O_o/I_o$).

Perceived State of Equity

When a **perceived state of equity** exists, you will be satisfied. Notice that a state of equity does not require that the two ratios be *identical,* only that they be *equal.* If you perceive that you have received less than the comparison other, but that you also had a proportionately lower level of inputs than did the other person, a perceived state of equity still exists.

A common misinterpretation of equity theory leads to the conclusion that a person who perceives a state of equity "is not motivated." This would suggest that it is in the organization's best interest to prevent organizational members from experiencing a state of perceived equity (it would be better to have members experience inequity and, thus, be motivated). This line of reasoning is clearly inappropriate. In fact, Adams predicted that workers who experience a perceived state of equity will be motivated to maintain that state of equity. This could be very beneficial to an organization if current member performance is at a desirably high level. To maintain this perceived state of equity, members will continue performing at a high level. A perceived state of equity could be undesirable to an organization, however, if current member performance is low. Maintenance of a perceived state of equity would be likely to involve continuation of low performance. Organizational objectives must be much more complex than to simply seek a state of perceived equity for members.

Perceived Under-Reward

When a perceived state of *under-reward* exists, a person will be dissatisfied, angered, and motivated to make some sort of change to produce a state of perceived equity (or to escape the situation). As will be discussed shortly, there are many actions you can take in dealing with under-reward.

Perceived Over-Reward

When a perceived state of *over-reward* exists, a person will be dissatisfied, guilty, and motivated to make some sort of change to produce a state of perceived equity (or escape the situation). The same types of actions are available for dealing with over-reward as for under-reward. Most people are less sensitive to over-reward than to under-reward.[3] Few employees go to their employers and complain they are overpaid!

Alternatives for Reducing Perceived Inequity

Adams identified a wide range of possibilities a person could pursue to reduce the tension produced by a perceived state of inequity. A perceived state of equity can be obtained through actual changes in the outcomes or inputs of the person or the comparison other, by distorting a person's perceptions of the outcomes or inputs of either party, by using a different comparison other, or by leaving the situation in which the social exchange is occurring.

Alter Inputs of the Person. The perceived state of equity can be altered through actual changes in the inputs of the person. If you perceive a state of under-reward, you could reduce any of your inputs. Common reductions include decreasing quantity or quality of performance. An over-rewarded individual, on the other hand, could produce a perceived state of equity by increasing inputs (e.g., quantity or quality).

Alter Outcomes of the Person. The person who perceives a state of under-reward could attempt to increase outcomes in an attempt to achieve a state of perceived equity. You could, for example, request a pay raise, a nicer office, a promotion, or other positively valued outcomes. Although it is less likely, a person experiencing over-reward could approach a state of equity through reduction in his/her outcomes.

Alter Inputs of the Comparison Other. When under-rewarded, you can try to achieve a state of perceived equity by encouraging the comparison other to increase his/her inputs. Demand, for example, that the comparison other "start pulling his weight," or perhaps help the comparison other become a better performer. Over-reward could be addressed by pressuring the comparison other to reduce inputs. A common example of this is peer pressure put on "rate-busters" (workers performing at such a high level that others look bad) to reduce their performance.

Alter Outcomes of the Comparison Other. A state of under-reward could be corrected by directly or indirectly reducing the values of the comparison other's outcomes. Making the comparison other look bad so s/he gets fewer raises or promotions is one possibility. Another possibility would be to provide negatively valued outcomes for the comparison other through social harassment. A state of over-reward could be altered by helping the comparison other increase outcomes. This could be done by telling a supervisor how valuable the comparison other's contributions are, by providing social praise (assuming the comparison other positively values this), etc.

Distort Perceptions of Inputs or Outcomes. It is possible to reduce a perceived state of inequity without making any changes in actual input or outcome levels. This can be accomplished by distorting a person's perceptions of the inputs or outcomes of the person or of the comparison other. This could involve any of the following types of perceptual changes:

"Jill does better work than I thought."
"Jill's work is not as good as I thought."
"I guess I'm doing better than I thought I was."
"I guess I haven't done as well as I thought I did."
"Jill gets paid more than I realized."
"Jill gets paid less than I realized."
"The value of my insurance benefits is more than I realized."
"The value of my insurance benefits is less than I realized."

Choose a Different Comparison Other. Both over- and under-reward can be dealt with by changing the comparison other ("Instead of comparing my situation to Beth's, it would be more appropriate for me to compare my situation to Allison's"). In many ways, this can be the simplest and most powerful change for dealing with perceived inequity. It is simple because it requires neither actual nor perceptual changes in inputs or outcomes for either the person or the comparison other. It can be the most powerful because it is possible to choose a comparison other with whom an equitable comparison is likely to exist. Despite the advantages of this technique, a number of factors reduce the likelihood that this option will be selected. Most comparison others (frequently they are co-workers or friends) are very visible to a person, making it difficult to ignore the appropriateness of the comparison. Furthermore, changing the comparison other is unlikely if you have been comparing yourself to that person for a long time.

A variation on "choosing a different comparison other" involves removing the comparison other from the situation. This could be accomplished, for example, by harassing the comparison other into quitting the job or requesting a transfer.

Leave the Situation. A final technique for dealing with a perceived state of inequity involves removing yourself from the situation in which the comparison is made. This could be accomplished through absenteeism, transfer, or termination. Usually, this approach is elected when perceived inequity is quite high or when other attempts at achieving equity are not readily available.

Choice of Inequity-Reducing Action

The particular action you select from the above choices is of great importance to an organization, since reduction of a perceived state of inequity could often be achieved through either functional or dysfunctional actions (from the organization's point of view). Although equity theory does not predict which specific actions are most likely to be chosen in a particular situation, Adams believes the following propositions influence this choice (remember, the overriding concern is to achieve or maintain a perceived state of equity):

1. Person will maximize positively valent [valued] outcomes.
2. Person will minimize increasing inputs that are effortful and costly to change.
3. Person will resist real and cognitive [perceptual] changes in inputs that are central to self-concept and to self-esteem. To the extent that any one person's outcomes are related to self-concept and to self-esteem, this proposition is extended to cover outcomes.
4. Person will be more resistant to changing cognitions about his/her own outcomes and inputs than to changing cognitions about other's outcomes and inputs.
5. Leaving the field will be resorted to only when the magnitude of inequity experienced is high and other means of reducing it are unavailable. Partial withdrawal, such as absenteeism, will occur more frequently and under conditions of lower inequity.
6. Person will be highly resistant to changing the object of comparisons. A comparison other, once it has stabilized over time . . . in effect has become an anchor.[4]

J. Stacy Adams of the University of North Carolina–Chapel Hill is a major contemporary behavioral theorist.

What would you identify as the major contribution of equity theory to organizational practice? I doubt that very many managers are acutely aware of equity theory in its academic robes, despite the exposure they may have had to it as business majors. More probable is that managers who make personnel decisions are defining what is equitable in terms that are influenced by equity theory. Specifically, "a fair day's pay for a fair day's work" is likely, nowadays, to be modified by the clause, "as perceived by the worker in relation to co-workers' pay and output." This revised usage of equity is far from universal, however, and even when followed, it is in a narrow context of pay, promotion, assignments, grievances, and similar personnel decisions.

What would you identify as the weakest area of equity theory from the perspective of the organizational user of the theory? Although easily understood, the theory is complex and difficult in application because the perceptions (and misperceptions) of employees are not easily assessed. Furthermore, the larger a manager's span of control, the greater the complexity. In part because of these complexities, equal systemwide rewards are preferred by many managers.

Equity theory suggests that a person who experiences over-reward will be dissatisfied, guilty, and motivated to produce a state of equity. How would you respond to the student who says, "It may sound nice in theory but I doubt that this really happens very often"? There is ample evidence that inequity impels people to behave in ways specified by the theory. It is true, however, that the association of guilt with over-reward is not strong. To the student who is impatient with theory, I would say, as Lewin did, that theory is a most practical thing—it is also very efficient—much more so than hunches. A good theory, in fact, instructs the practitioner and researcher what to observe.

Individual Differences in Equity Motivation

Miner reviewed much of the equity theory literature and concluded that people differ in the strength of their desire to reduce inequity.[5] He observed that persons who are high in achievement motivation (see Chapter 5) often have the strongest desire for perceived equity. Gamblers were said to accept inequity more readily.

RESEARCH ON EQUITY THEORY

Adams' equity theory has been subjected to a substantial amount of research. Although no single study has examined every aspect of the theory simultaneously, the body of research as a whole provides fairly strong support for many of the theory's components. The level of perceived equity or inequity *is* influenced by comparisons of inputs and outcomes. Perceived inequity *does* lead to dissatisfaction and tension. Most people have been found to have a drive to reduce this tension, and the drive becomes stronger as the magnitude of the perceived inequity increases. People are less sensitive to over-reward than to under-reward. Furthermore, there is evidence that inequity reduction can be achieved through the use of many of the alternatives proposed by Adams.

Research on Over-Reward

Early research on equity theory focused almost entirely on the impact of over-reward and was restricted primarily to the study of compensation outcomes. Five studies by Adams and his associates provided the earliest tests of the theory, leading to the following conclusions:[6]

1. Persons who experience overpayment for work performed at an hourly wage will produce a high quantity of work. Thus inequity is reduced by increasing the person's inputs (quantity) without increasing outcomes.
2. Persons who experience overpayment for work performed for piece-rate pay (pay based on the quantity of performance) will produce a relatively low quantity of high quality work. Thus, inequity is reduced by increasing inputs (quality) and keeping outcomes relatively low (if quantity is low, so are outcomes).

Most recent research using appropriate research designs to test the impact of over-reward has produced results consistent with the predictions of the theory.[7] A major limitation to these findings, however, should be noted. Because the great majority of these studies examined the impact of over-reward across a very short time period (usually only a few hours), the long-term effects of over-reward are not well understood.

Research on Under-Reward

More recently, research has also examined the effects of perceived under-reward. One prediction for perceived under-reward is that persons who experience under-reward on an hourly pay basis will provide a low level of work-related effort. In this way, they reduce inequity by reducing inputs, while keeping outcomes more or less constant. Most research has provided general support for this prediction.[8] Another prediction for perceived under-reward is that absenteeism and turnover should be relatively high. A study by Finn and Lee revealed that persons who were under-rewarded were not only dissatisfied but had a "higher propensity for separation."[9] Others have shown that under-reward is associated with actual turnover levels.[10]

An Integrative Analysis

Robert P. Vecchio of the University of Notre Dame has conducted an excellent integrative analysis of the impact of experienced over-reward, under-reward, and equity.[11] The studies chosen for examination by Vecchio involved four different geographic locations. Data were gathered at four points in time over a 13-year period. There were two limitations of the analysis: only piece-rate compensation situations were examined, and neither satisfaction nor perceived inequity was addressed directly. Nevertheless, the equity theory's performance predictions for over-reward (lower quantity/higher quality) and under-reward (greater quantity/lower quality) relative to perceived equity were thoroughly evaluated.

The findings were quite impressive. "The equity theory performance predictions . . . were supported in 11 of 12 comparisons."[12] In the overpayment conditions, quantity of performance decreased an average of 17 percent relative to equitable situations. Quality increased 26 percent (see Exhibit 7–1). Thus, inequity was reduced through both the reduction of outcomes (lower pay for lower quantity) and through an increase in inputs (higher quality). In the underpayment conditions, quantity increased 34 percent while quality decreased by 12 percent. Inequity was thus reduced through both increases in outcomes (higher pay for higher quantity) and through a decrease in inputs (lower quality).

Exhibit 7–1 Summary of Performance Results from Equity Research (on piece-rate compensation)

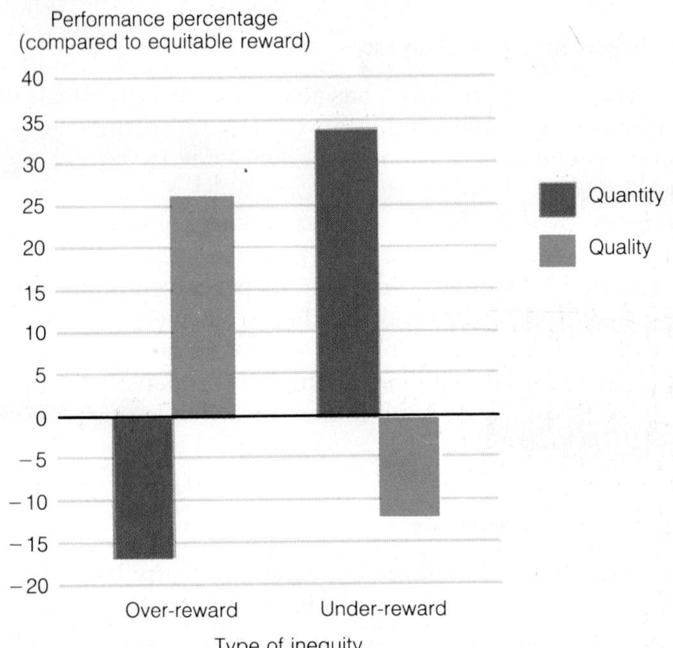

Source: From data summarized by R. P. Vecchio, 1982. Predicting worker performance in inequitable settings. *Academy of Management Review*, *7*, 103–110.

Perceptions of Inequity and Performance for Major League Baseball Players

Robert G. Lord and Jeffrey A. Hohenfeld of the University of Akron conducted a fascinating study of 23 major league baseball players.[13] These players chose to begin the 1976 season without contracts in order to become "free agents" during the 1977 season (so they could sign with any team they wished for 1977). The researchers felt that these players would perceive themselves as under-rewarded from an equity perspective since most had their pay reduced from the preceding year (as is permitted under these conditions), and since a number of potential "comparison others" had recently received widely publicized major pay increases.

(continued)

Exhibit 7–2 presents some of the results from this study. The "1975 equitable" period is from the 1975 season and represents a relatively equitably rewarded time period. The "1976 under-rewarded" period represents that period of time during the 1976 season when the same group of players played without contracts. The "1976 equitable" period comes from the latter part of the 1976 season after this group of players reached agreement, signed new contracts, and received pay increases. Consistent with equity theory, Lord and Hohenfeld predicted that performance should drop during "under-rewarded" conditions and increase once equity was reestablished through increases in outcomes. As can be seen in Exhibit 7–2, these predictions held for batting average, home runs, and runs batted in (but not for runs scored, a measure heavily dependent on the performance of other team members).

Exhibit 7–2 Performance Results from Equity Research on Major League Baseball Players

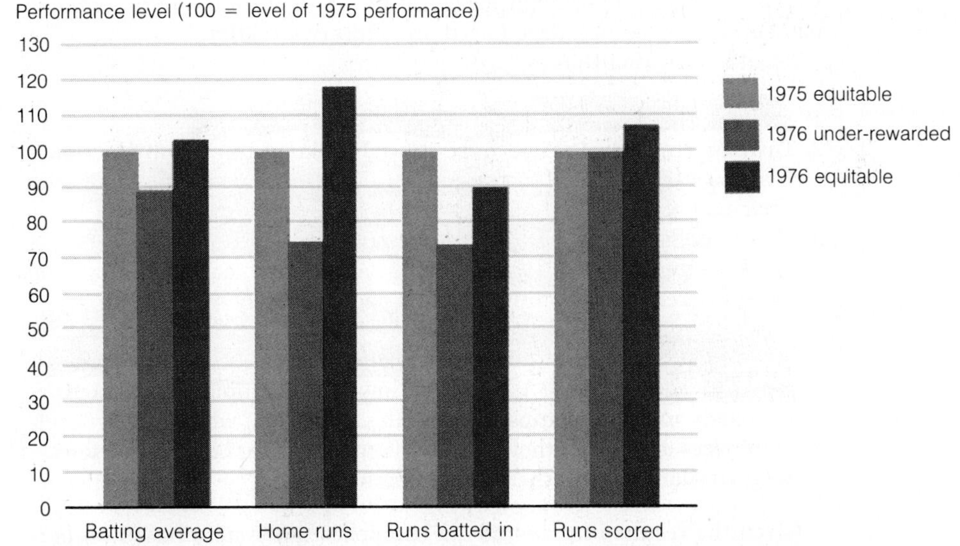

Source: Derived from R. G. Lord, and J. A. Hohenfeld, Longitudinal field assessment of equity effects on the performance of major league baseball players, *Journal of Applied Psychology, 1979,* 19–26, copyright 1979 by the American Psychological Association. Adapted with permission of the publisher and authors.

Distributive Justice, Equity, and Pay Satisfaction

Most studies of the effects of distributive justice and equity focused on performance but not satisfaction. At least one study, however, has examined the impact of these comparisons on satisfaction with pay for employees of a small insurance company.[14] Outcomes were defined as total compensation received from the company. Inputs were measured through a high level of employee participation in a "job evaluation" of each employee's position. This was a highly structured procedure which, in effect, quantified the total overall value of "relevant inputs." Pay satisfaction was measured by surveying each organizational member.

Distributive justice ratios were calculated for each person by dividing that person's total compensation by the value for that person's total inputs. Two types of social comparisons were made. The first was a comparison of each person's O_p/I_p ratio to a O_o/I_o ratio representing the "typical" outcome-to-input ratio for all employees in the organization. The second social comparison compared each person's O_p/I_p ratio to a O_o/I_o ratio representing the "typical" outcome-to-input for persons holding similar jobs in other organizations.

Limitations of this study included: (1) pay was the only outcome considered; (2) two comparison others were identified as "all employees in this organization" and "all workers holding similar jobs in other organizations" without asking workers if these actually were used as comparison others; and (3) although measures of inputs were based on employee perceptions, outcomes were based on "objective reality."

Results indicated that:

1. Level of pay had little relationship to pay satisfaction.
2. Distributive justice ratios were strongly related to pay satisfaction. Even workers with relatively low pay were reasonably satisfied with their pay if they felt it was related to the level of their inputs.
3. Equity comparisons within the organization produced moderately strong influences on pay satisfaction. Apparently, equity comparisons to co-workers were common and impacted on pay satisfaction.
4. Equity comparisons to others outside the organization had a significant influence on pay satisfaction only for managers at the highest levels of the company. Apparently, lower-level employees reacted primarily to social comparisons with co-workers, while higher-level employees compared their situations to co-workers *and* to persons with similar jobs in other organizations.

Given the results of this study, a compensation system based on performance was implemented (in response to the importance of distributive justice). The new compensation structure was based on the relative value of worker inputs (in response to the importance of equity comparisons with co-workers). Furthermore, particularly for higher-level employees, an attempt was made to provide compensation equitable in comparison to similar jobs in other organizations (in response to the importance of equity comparisons with workers in other organizations).

GOAL THEORY

It is difficult to identify the specific origins of goal theory as it exists today. Frederick W. Taylor, the "Father of Scientific Management," focused considerable attention on enhancing worker performance as early as 1911 by identifying appropriate goals for workers (although seldom using the term "goal"). Beginning in the 1930s, Kurt Lewin and his associates devoted considerable attention to determinants of aspiration levels (goals).[15] In the 1950s, Peter Drucker and Douglas McGregor utilized a number of goal theory principles while developing and applying "management by objectives" (MBO).[16] (Because of its unique characteristics, MBO will be discussed in a separate section at the end of this chapter.) According to Miner, current configurations of goal theory can be traced to a paper written by Thomas Ryan in 1964 (later published in 1970).[17] Without question, the theorizing and research of Edwin Locke of the University of Maryland has guided the field since the completion of his dissertation on the topic in 1966.

The two most common criticisms leveled at goal theory, according to Latham and Locke are described as follows:

> Some claimed it was so simple and self-evident that everyone, including themselves, already used it.
>
> Conversely, other managers have argued that the idea would not work, precisely *because* it is so simple [implying that something more radical and complex was needed]. (Parenthetical comment and emphasis added.)[18]

Latham and Locke's response to the first criticism is that, whereas it is true that people using the theory intuitively should be as effective as those following a formal theory, relatively few persons historically have followed the theory. Therefore, most could profit from it. Latham and Locke's response to the second criticism is to let the facts speak for themselves: if it works, it works! Indeed, the principle of parsimony discussed earlier (Chapter 1) argues that, all else being equal, the simplest explanation is the best.

Locke believes that the importance of goal setting "is recognized, explicitly or implicitly, by virtually every major theory of work motivation."[19] He observes that Taylor, in scientific management, focused on identifying appropriate goals (Taylor called them "tasks") for workers, providing feedback on whether goal progress was being made, and presenting incentives for reaching difficult goals. Locke argues that the positive effects attributed by Human Relations theorists to worker participation may, in fact, be due to goals set as a result of participation rather than from the participation per se. Regarding expectancy theory (discussed in Chapter 8), Locke states "it is possible to view values and expectancies as factors which influence the goals an individual chooses" and argues that it is the subsequently chosen goals which impact upon behavior.[20] Locke believes that theories such as Maslow's and Herzberg's have goal setting "smuggled into them" even though the concept was initially ignored or rejected by such theorists. He states that the concept of goals is necessary in order to explain the possibility of experienced accomplishment focused upon by both theories (i.e., how can you know if you have accomplished something unless there is a specific "goal" against which progress can be measured?). The importance of goals to organizational behavior modification is stressed by Locke in his claim that the terms "performance standards" or "desired behaviors" focused upon in OBM are "used as a synonym for goal."[21]

THE BASIC MODEL

Locke proposes a model like that shown in Exhibit 7–3(a) to identify the cognitive process by which goals are formulated and produce an effect on behavior. This model proposes that you perceive and evaluate an environmental occurrence. It thus becomes cognitive reality to you, and you react to it. Your reaction causes you consciously to adopt a goal for the future. That particular goal determines your subsequent behavior.

Exhibit 7–3(b) presents an example of this process for a student in organizational behavior. In this example, the environmental occurrence is receipt of a low grade on an OB exam. The student perceives this low grade and evaluates it as being below his/her standard. The student reacts to the grade with dissatisfaction. To deal with the situation, the student sets a specific, difficult goal (A−) for the next OB exam. The result of this goal is improved performance.

The basic goal theory model (Exhibit 7–4) identifies goal difficulty and goal specificity as the two most important goal attributes. A difficult goal is predicted to lead to higher performance than does an easy goal. A specific goal is expected to improve performance over the level produced by a general goal. To achieve maximum

Exhibit 7–3 Goal-Setting Process

(a) Cognitive model for goal theory

(b) Example

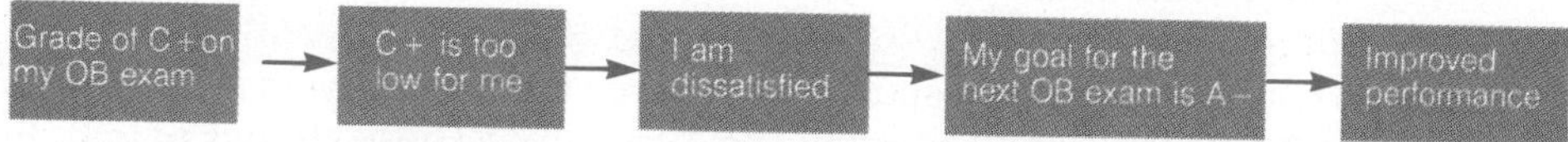

Source: Derived from *Theories of organizational behavior* by John B. Miner. Copyright © 1980 by The Dryden Press. Reprinted by permission of The Dryden Press, CBS College Publishing.

Exhibit 7–4 Basic Goal-Setting Model

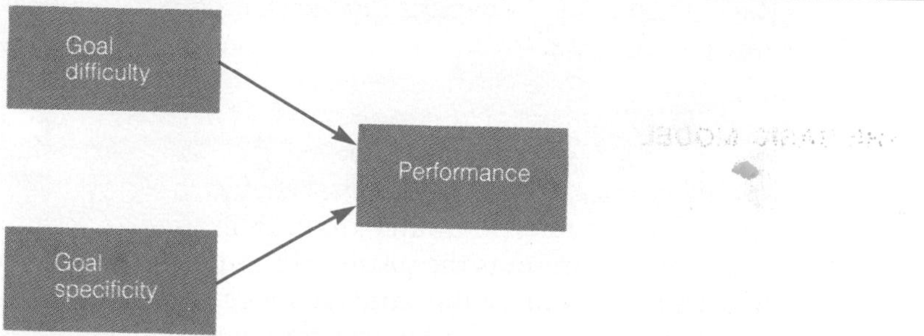

Source: E. A. Locke and J. F. Bryan, Goal-setting as a determinant of the effect of knowledge of score on performance, *American Journal of Psychology, 81,* 398–406, copyright 1968 by the University of Illinois Press.

performance, it is important that a goal be *both* difficult and specific. Thus, the commonly used goal, "I am going to do my best," usually is not very effective because it is too general. Note that goal difficulty and specificity are based on your perceptions of the goal (and not necessarily on objective reality).

Research on the basic goal theory model has produced broad support for the theory. A large number of studies which tested all or part of the basic goal-setting model were reviewed by Locke, Shaw, Saari, and Latham.[22] With few exceptions, these studies conformed to the predictions made by the basic model.

Goal Difficulty

A positive, linear relationship exists between **goal difficulty** and task performance (i.e., higher goals lead to higher performance). Of 57 studies which tested the impact of goal difficulty on performance in the Locke et al. review, 48 partly or wholly supported the proposed impact of goal difficulty.[23] Supporting results have been obtained for brief one-time tasks lasting as little as one minute and for ongoing tasks lasting as long as seven years.[24] The types of activities involved in these studies varied greatly, including clerical, typing, literary, mechanical, academic, technical, professional, physical, and forestry. Study participants ranged from four years of age to late adult. The bulk of these studies conformed well to the prediction that performance increases as goal difficulty increases. (For one example of such research, see the lab study on the impact of goal difficulty presented in the Appendix.) Those studies which did not provide the predicted results usually can be understood in light of the expanded goal-setting model presented later in this chapter. As you will see, the addition of a few qualifying considerations greatly enhances understanding of the circumstances under which difficult goals are most likely to increase performance. It should also be noted that there is some evidence that "dreaming the impossible dream" does not improve performance over use of the most difficult realistic goal.[25] In fact, Locke's results indicated that assignment of impossibly high goals produced no better results than did the assignment of less difficult but possible goals. It appears, then, that increased goal difficulty increases performance *only* if you believe there is some chance of reaching your goal. This is explored more fully in a later discussion of goal acceptance.

Exhibit 7–5 presents the results of a study which may be of particular interest to you. In this study, college students set goals ranging from A to C for a college history course at the beginning of a four-month semester. Students also rated the difficulty of the goals, indicating that a higher grade was perceived as a more difficult goal (less likely to be obtained). As can be seen in Exhibit 7–5, the more difficult a goal, the higher the actual performance in the course. (Although a no-goal condition was not included in this study, it is reasonable to assume that a student working without any goal probably would have performed at or below the level obtained by those who used an easy goal.) In 1983, Alberto Cabrero, then a student at the University of Wisconsin, conducted a creative replication of this study in an organizational behavior class.[26] His findings not only supported those of the study shown in Exhibit 7–5 but also indicated that goal difficulty was a better predictor of class performance than was previous grade point average, or ability as measured by an academic aptitude test.

Exhibit 7–5 Goal Difficulty and Academic Performance

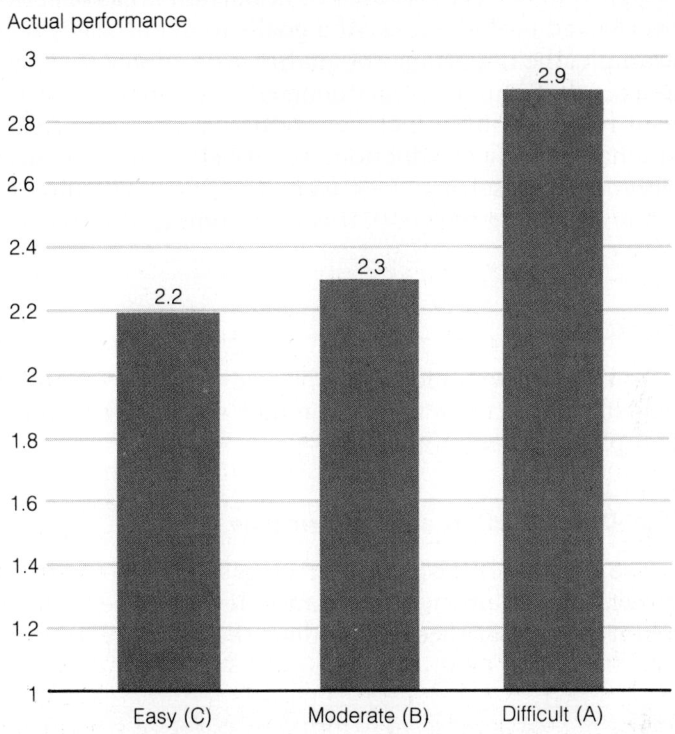

Source: E. A. Locke, and J. F. Bryan, 1968. Grade goals as determinants of academic achievement. *Journal of General Psychology, 79,* 225.

Goal Specificity

Specific goals have been found to lead to higher performance than general goals such as "do your best." In fact, of 53 studies reviewed by Locke et al. addressing this issue, 51 provided partial or complete support for the impact of **goal specificity.** Once again these studies covered a wide range of time periods, participants, and types of tasks. Note that a goal of "do your best" has approximately the same effect on performance as does a no-goal condition:

> We have not found any differences in the results obtained by studies in which no goals are assigned and those in which subjects are explicitly told to do their best. No goal subjects, it appears, typically try to do as well as they can on the assigned task.[27]

One important caution: Goal theory advocates the use of *specific* goals. But organizations must not lose sight of the fact that goals must be *appropriate* as well as specific. Often goals are very carefully designed to be very specific but important areas of performance are overlooked in the process. If a goal's total emphasis is quantity, for example, the importance of quality is deemphasized and may suffer as a result. Similarly, other nongoal areas are likely to be slighted. If your responsibilities include production and supervision, and goals emphasize only production, supervision may be deemphasized. Because goal setting does work (i.e., you will direct your effort toward meeting the goal), it is important that goals be constructed very carefully.

EXPANDED MODEL

You will understand better the role of goals by examining a model which expands upon the basic model shown in Exhibit 7–4. Exhibit 7–6 presents such a model.

Goal-Directed Effort and Performance

The basic goal theory model suggests that goal attributes have a direct impact upon performance level. Indeed, the majority of research on goal theory examines the direct relationship between

Exhibit 7–6 Revised Model

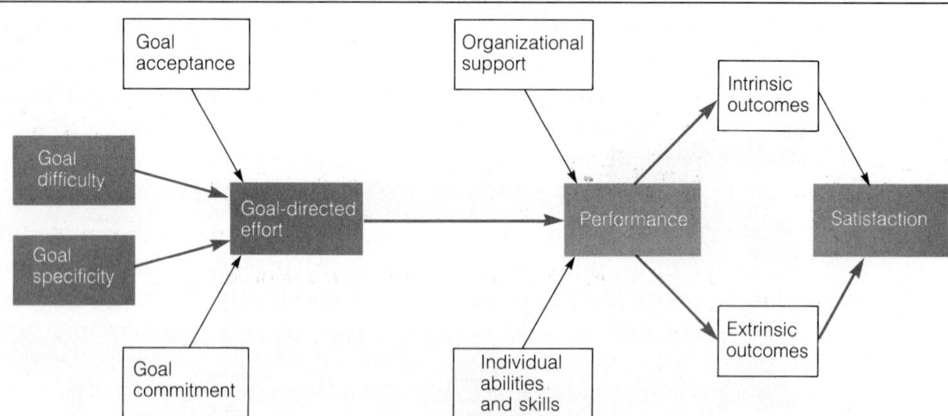

Source: Adapted from G. P. Latham, and E. A. Locke (1979). Goal setting—A motivational technique that works. *Organizational Dynamics*, 68–80, 77. A complete current description of the goal setting process is contained in Locke, E. A., & Latham, G. P. (1984). *Goal setting: A motivational technique that works!* Englewood Cliffs, N.J.: Prentice-Hall.

goal attributes and performance. In reality, goal attributes impact quite directly on *goal-directed effort* but only indirectly on *performance*. Difficult, specific goals lead you to direct high levels of effort toward your goal. The degree to which your effort actually results in high performance, however, is influenced by a number of other factors. These factors include organizational support and individual abilities.

Important *organizational support factors* include adequate resources (e.g., time, equipment, finances, and training). Without this type of support, you probably will not convert even high levels of goal-directed effort into successful performance. Organizational policies which support and allow performance at the level you seek, as well as the absence of unnecessary or inappropriate policies which impair your performance, are also necessary. Action plans which specify where your effort should be directed provide another important organizational support factor. Extremely important are the amount and nature of feedback you receive. In fairly typical findings, Strang et al. found that the impact of challenging goals decreased when no feedback was provided on the degree to which the goal was being met.[28] On the other hand, challenging goals in the presence of feedback greatly enhanced performance. Ivancevich and McMahon provided evidence that goal-accompanying feedback generated by the worker (i.e., you keep track of the degree to which the goal is or is not being met) is likely to be more effective than feedback provided by someone else. This suggests the desirability of designing tasks so that the worker can assess his/her own performance while working, rather than being dependent upon a supervisor for information concerning performance.

Individual ability levels also influence the degree to which goal-directed effort successfully produces performance. Despite high levels of goal-directed effort, you will not perform at a high level unless you also possess the necessary abilities for performing the task. Similarly, two individuals with equal levels of goal-directed effort will perform differently if they have different ability levels. After their thorough review of goal-setting literature, Locke et al. concluded that:

> Individuals must have the ability to attain or at least approach their goals. . . . Exerting more effort will not improve task performance if improvement is totally beyond the individual's capacity.[29]

More recent research has supported these findings. Howard Garland, for example, demonstrated that "Both assigned goals and ability had significant and independent effects on performance, as hypothesized."[30] Locke suggests that ability levels become even more important as goal difficulty increases (almost anyone has sufficient ability to attain extremely easy goals, while ability requirements increase as difficulty rises).[31]

It is clear that ability levels influence whether or not goal-directed effort will lead to performance. This emphasizes the need for organizations to select employees who possess acceptable abilities and/or train workers to develop the necessary abilities.

Goal Acceptance and Goal Commitment

The expanded model in Exhibit 7–6 identifies goal acceptance and goal commitment as two related factors. Together, they influence the degree to which the goal attributes of difficulty and specificity influence the amount of goal-directed effort you exert. Although much of the literature on goal theory fails to differentiate adequately between goal acceptance and commitment, there *is* an important distinction. **Goal acceptance** is the degree to which you accept a specific goal as your own (i.e., "This is *my* goal."). **Goal commitment** is the degree to which you are dedicated to trying to reach the goal you have adopted. Although these issues have not been researched adequately yet, it does appear clear that goal difficulty and specificity have little impact unless a worker accepts the goal as his/her own and has at least some personal commitment to achieving it.

Goal acceptance, according to Latham and Locke, most commonly is resisted because you believe that the goal is not reachable or because you perceive no personal benefit if the goal is reached.[32] If you believe yourself incapable of reaching the goal (due to lack of confidence, ability, or knowledge), organizational support factors such as training can help. If personal benefits such as compensation, promotion, or recognition are missing, organizational policies can be developed which reward you for goal acceptance and, particularly, for goal performance. Goal acceptance is also enhanced through the use of fair and reasonable goals which do not appear exploitive, by a state of trust in management, and by the absence of threats related to goal behavior.

It should be noted that, although you are more likely to accept a specific goal if you perceive that it is reachable, this does not mean that you will never accept an unreachable goal.[33] Indeed, Garland has noted that unreachable goals are often accepted by workers (although a more likely behavior is for you to reject the unreachable goal and select another somewhat less difficult goal).[34] Garland points out that it may be very misleading to treat goal acceptance as a dichotomous (all or nothing) variable. For example, if you have been producing 15 widgets a day and are assigned an unreachable goal of 90 widgets per day, you will reject this unreachable goal.

Rather than operate without any goal, however, you accept a "compromise" goal of 60 widgets per day and show substantial performance improvement. It is the goal you accept (choose) which drives your behavior and not necessarily the goal which is assigned (unless you accept the assigned goal).

Goal commitment is influenced by many of the same factors which impact upon goal acceptance. You probably will have greater personal commitment and dedication to reaching a goal if you perceive the goal to be reachable and likely to lead to your personal benefit. The thing to remember is that goal acceptance is determined *prior* to beginning work on a goal-related task, while goal commitment can continue to increase or decrease substantially *after* goal-directed behavior is begun. This means that continued attention must be paid to the factors which influence commitment. Furthermore, goal commitment must be at a maximum to produce the greatest effect on goal-directed effort and subsequent performance, while only the minimum requirements are necessary to produce goal acceptance.

Satisfaction

The expanded goal-setting model identifies two sources of satisfaction (intrinsic and extrinsic) related to goal-seeking behavior. Put simply, you will experience satisfaction if positively valued outcomes are experienced. If negatively valued outcomes are experienced, you will be dissatisfied. (The degree of satisfaction or dissatisfaction can be expected to be influenced by equity comparisons.)

Intrinsic outcomes are related to personal feelings of accomplishment and achievement. If you reach your goal, you probably will experience intrinsic satisfaction (particularly if you perceived that goal as being difficult). If you fail to achieve your goal, you likely will experience intrinsic dissatisfaction. This pattern of results has been documented by studies such as that conducted by Jackson and Zedeck.[35] *Important*: Even though the use of difficult goals will probably increase performance, dissatisfaction may result if the difficult goal is not attained. Furthermore, it becomes less likely you will accept such a difficult goal in the future.

Extrinsic outcomes are the results of actions administered by an organization subsequent to performance. If your performance is followed by positively valued outcomes (e.g., pay or promotion), extrinsic satisfaction will be enhanced. A major consideration here is whether extrinsic outcomes are provided on the basis of performance or on the basis of whether or not the goal is met. If you do not quite meet a very difficult goal, you will not be rewarded—even for relatively high performance—if reward is based on goal attainment. Once again, dissatisfaction results and future acceptance of similar goals is reduced. On the other hand, if pay is performance-based whether or not the goal is actually reached, goal commitment may be reduced and your performance may suffer. This exact pattern of results was documented in a study conducted by Mowen, Middlemist, and Luther of Oklahoma State University.[36] Such findings led Jackson and Zedeck to conclude:

> The implication of these results for applying goal-setting theory is clear: Supervisors will need to learn how to strike a balance in order to set goal levels high enough to result in improved performance without setting them so high that they are unrealistic and likely to cause dissatisfaction.[37]

SOME CONSIDERATIONS FOR APPLICATION

Does Goal Setting Work Equally Well for Everyone?

As previously noted, goal setting has proved successful for a very wide variety of jobs. Not every attempt at goal setting, however, has led to improved performance. This should not be surprising, given the necessary conditions presented in the expanded model. In fact, most cases in which goal setting did not "work" can be fully explained through consideration of the entire model. Some of the failures, for example, involved the assignment of specific difficult goals to workers without the steps necessary to encourage acceptance of and commitment to the goal. Other "failures" involved cases where workers did not have abilities sufficient to accomplish the desired high performance or were not provided adequate organizational support for meeting the goals.

Although not yet thoroughly researched, there is little reason to believe that factors such as age, education level, race, tenure length, or sex will influence the appropriateness or effectiveness of goal setting. There is some evidence that certain personality characteristics may be important. Persons with high self-esteem, for example, are more likely to respond to goal setting (this could be due to increases in acceptance and commitment because they believe a goal is reachable). Your need-for-achievement level may influence the effectiveness of goal setting in an interesting way. Persons who are high in achievement motivation will strive to meet an internal standard of excellence (see Chapter 5). Presumably, an accepted goal defines this standard. Thus, if you are a high-achievement motivation person, you probably are more highly committed to a goal (and devote greater amounts of goal-directed effort). An interesting twist on this issue is the well-established finding that high-achievement motivation persons are most likely to accept goals of moderate difficulty (with perhaps a 50 percent chance of success).

Edwin A. Locke of the University of Maryland is the leading contemporary goal-setting theorist. **Gary P. Latham** of the University of Washington is a leading practitioner of goal-setting principles.

Goal setting appears to be an extremely effective practice. Given this, why doesn't every organization have a formal goal-setting program? LOCKE: First, goal setting isn't self-evident, so even though it works it doesn't mean everyone will know what it is or how to use it effectively. Second, some managers think it is too simpleminded to work, so they think you have to have something more esoteric if you want to be effective. The third reason that sometimes comes up is the belief that unions would oppose it and, therefore, it is not worth trying. This turns out not to be true if you implement it correctly.

Under what conditions might a goal-setting program fail? LATHAM: First, the goal may be too vague rather than specific, and it may be far too easy (which is likely to occur if goal attainment rather than actual performance is measured). Putting primary emphasis on goal attainment is the second reason why goal-setting programs fail. If Pat sets a goal of 80 for a final grade in the class and earns an 83, and Sam sets a goal of 95 and earns an 89, who did better in the class? The answer depends on what is used as a criterion. If salary increases are contingent upon goal attainment, would you set specific hard goals? A third reason for failure is that goals are set too high. Accomplishments often are perceived as disappointing if there is a wide disparity between one's performance and one's goal. As a result, one loses interest in pursuing the goal, and a decrease in self-assurance occurs. A goal-setting program may fail if the boss or peer group is not supportive. Failure to reinforce working toward a goal can lead to failure. Lack of feedback can cause failure. A goal-setting program based on quantity as opposed to quality, cost reduction, market share, etc., will fail if it is likely to result in people being laid off.

Goals which are so high as to be unreachable are unlikely to be accepted and lead to low levels of goal-directed effort. Thus, for you, the most appropriate goals are those which you perceive as having a moderate chance of being reached.

How Should a Goal Be Set?

It is clear that a goal should be perceived as specific and difficult but how does a person or an organization identify such a goal? Latham and Locke discuss several options.[38] First, consider the ability levels and self-confidence of the individual (you are unlikely to perceive a goal as difficult unless it pushes your ability levels). Furthermore, the self-confident individual probably will accept and be committed to more difficult goals than a less self-confident person with similar abilities. Another, very structured approach to objectively identifying challenging tasks involves the use of time and motion studies to determine how much work can be performed by an individual in a given period of time. This approach is very scientific (it was developed during the Scientific Management era), but the process often decreases acceptance even though the goals identified may be "objectively appropriate." Furthermore, this approach only works with relatively simple, straightforward, observable tasks (e.g., assembly lines). Sometimes goals are set based on average past performance levels of job incumbents. Although these goals frequently are accepted, they often are too easy—particularly if past performance has been considerably below attainable difficulty levels. There are external constraints to consider (e.g., actions of competitors, market limitations, machine limits, legal restrictions) as well as overriding organizational goals with which individual goals must be consistent. It should be clear that there is no one best way to set goals. A healthy combination of two or more of the preceding suggestions may be useful.

Should Goals Be Assigned or Participatively Chosen?

The lack of guidance for setting appropriate goals has led many organizations to involve workers in planning their own goals. This approach has been stimulated by a philosophical belief in the appropriateness (humanness) of participation. There is a significant amount of research which demonstrates that the process of participation can increase your satisfaction if you positively value participation. Whether or not participation impacts upon your performance, however, is a very different issue. Your participation in goal setting will increase your performance if, and only if, participation leads to increased goal difficulty, goal specificity, goal acceptance, and/or goal commitment. There is no reason to believe that participation in and of itself will enhance satisfaction. Unfortunately, these issues have not been documented thoroughly through research. There is a fair amount of research on decision-making processes which shows that participation often increases acceptance and commitment. There is also some evidence that participation in goal setting will increase performance if goal difficulty is increased by the process.[39] More research is needed, however, to obtain a full understanding of the role of participation in goal setting.

What Is the Role of Incentives in the Goal-Setting Process?

Incentives can serve several purposes relevant to the goal-setting process. You can be rewarded for setting goals which are both specific and difficult, as is frequently the case in organizations which have formal goal-setting programs. Although such incentives can be direct and immediate, it is more common to have incentives for appropriate goal setting tied into a general performance appraisal review for compensation and promotion purposes. Incentives can also encourage your acceptance and commitment to a goal. The option here is whether to provide the incentive upon acceptance of the goal or upon achievement of the goal. The former approach is effective for encouraging your acceptance while the latter is effective in encouraging your continued commitment. Incentives, if received, also enhance satisfaction due to the receipt of valued outcomes. Incentives which you receive due to successful goal behavior not only enhance your satisfaction but also encourage goal-setting activity in the future. What should be used as an incentive? Any positively valued outcome. This includes money, promotion, recognition, travel awards, or any other outcome you appreciate.

There is some evidence that the method by which incentives are administered can have a major impact on worker performance. The two most common ways of providing incentives are on a piece-rate basis (you are rewarded for each unit produced regardless of goal level) and the bonus basis (you are rewarded if you meet or exceed the stated goal). Exhibit 7–7 shows the results of an interesting study conducted by Mowen, Middlemist, and Luther. In this study, one group of participants was provided piece-rate incentives while the other was provided a bonus if they met or exceeded the assigned goal. Three different goal levels were assigned: low (which virtually everyone could achieve), medium (which about half the participants could achieve), and high (which few, if any, participants could reach). Because participants perceived both the low and medium

Exhibit 7–7 Goal Setting and the Role of Incentives: Two Approaches

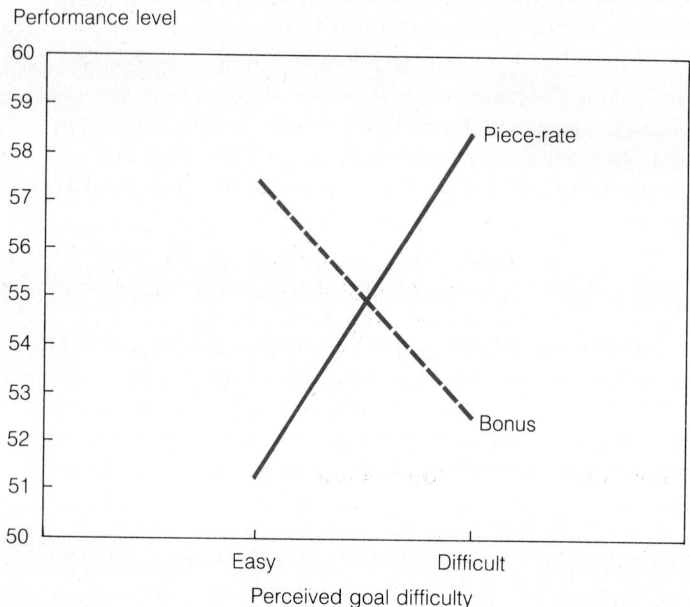

Source: Derived from J. C. Mowen; R. D. Middlemist; and D. Luther, Joint effects of assigned goal level and incentive structure of task performance: A laboratory study, *Journal of Applied Psychology, 66,* 598–603, copyright 1981 by the American Psychological Association. Adapted by permission of the publisher and author.

goals to be equally easy, the results shown in Exhibit 7–7 combine these two conditions (remember that it is the *perceived* difficulty, not actual difficulty, which influences behavior). As can be seen from Exhibit 7–7, the bonus incentive plan was considerably more effective (i.e., led to higher performance) for easy goals, while the piece-rate plan was more effective for difficult goals.

> Individuals will tend to reject goals that are set too high when a goal-contingent bonus is employed because the effort expended will be unrewarded when the goal is not reached. In contrast, when the effort expended is fully rewarded even though the goal is not reached, as in performance-contingent compensation, it seems likely that the goal will not be rejected but will be utilized as a reference point. Incentives exist for the subject to keep striving because increased performance will result in increased benefits regardless of whether the goal is reached.[40]

Piece-rate paid participants in the study performed at a higher level with difficult goals than with easy goals. This was with full knowledge that they probably would fail to meet the assigned goal. It is not clear whether these people adopted substitute goals which provided some of the drive for their behavior. If they did, and met the lower (but accepted) personal goal, they probably received not only the extrinsic financial reward but also the intrinsic reward of accomplishment. Participants who neither accepted the assigned goal nor adopted an alternative goal probably performed at a lower level than they would have if both financial incentive and the drive to meet a goal had been provided. Furthermore, the model in Exhibit 7–6 made clear that overall satisfaction is influenced by both extrinsic (financial) and intrinsic (accomplishment) outcomes. Working toward a goal which is not reached does not deliver the potentially powerful intrinsic rewards—even if extrinsic rewards are received through use of a piece-rate incentive structure.

What Is the Role of Competition?

Goals can be set for individual workers or for a group of individuals (a work team, department, etc.). Competition can occur between individuals who are working toward individual goals, between individuals from the same group who are working toward a group goal, between individuals from different groups, and between groups of individuals. Goals must be set at the appropriate level. If workers are interdependent, as is the case on the assembly line or in a work team, at least part of the goals set should be based on group performance. This encourages within-group cooperation but, unfortunately, removes control over performance away from the individual (thus reducing the motivating power of the goal[s] for the individual). If workers are independent of one another, usually goals should be geared toward individual performance. This maximizes individual control over goal attainment and increases the motivating power of the goal, but discourages cooperation between workers.

Latham and Locke encouraged informal competition:

> This further reinforces commitment and may lead employees to raise goals spontaneously. A word of caution here, however: We do not recommend setting up formal competition, as this may lead employees to place individual goals ahead of company goals. The emphasis should be on accomplishing the task, getting the job done, not "beating" the other person.[41]

The suggestion by Latham and Locke is good, but one which must be qualified. If goals are individual goals, competition between workers should be encouraged. On the other hand, if goals are group goals, intergroup competition should be encouraged and competition between workers should be discouraged. Maximum motivating power is often obtained through a combination of individual and group goals.

MANAGEMENT BY OBJECTIVES (MBO)

> MBO can properly be defined as: A managerial process whereby organizational purposes are diagnosed and met by joining superior and subordinates in the pursuit of mutually agreed-upon goals and objectives, which are specific, measurable, time-bounded, and joined to an action plan; progress and goal attainment are measured and monitored in appraisal sessions which center on mutually determined objective standards of performance.[42]

It is clear from this definition that goal setting lies at the heart of MBO, a management practice first introduced by the well-known management author Peter Drucker.[43] Since the introduction by Drucker, MBO has become an extremely popular (albeit not always effective) tool used by a wide variety of organizations. One proponent has even gone so far as to suggest that MBO is *the* dominant form of management in the United States.[44] Although this claim may be a bit ambitious, there is no question but that MBO is extremely popular.

Hodgson has noted that "MBO, like ice cream, comes in 29 flavors."[45] Indeed, MBO has become a generic term used to describe virtually any type of program which contains at least the following elements:

1. Joint setting of objectives (goals) by supervisor and subordinate.
2. Working toward the objectives.
3. Review of performance and the degree to which objectives are met.

Although all MBO programs appear to have at least the above three features, a wide variety of specific approaches exists. The different approaches add a variety of other features in an attempt to enhance the effectiveness of the program.

The difference between MBO programs and more general goal-setting applications as discussed earlier in this chapter is not always clear. One distinction is the driving force behind the two ideas. Goal setting, as discussed earlier, has been directed heavily by empirical research aimed at determining the specific techniques and conditions under which goal setting will work. MBO, on the other hand, has been guided more by theory and an intuitive belief that MBO should work. The effectiveness of MBO programs has been researched inadequately despite the hundreds of articles discussing the practice. Particularly lacking have been serious attempts to examine individual elements of the MBO approach to refine the approach based on fact. One distinction which can be drawn concerns MBO as a *philosophy* versus MBO as a *technology*. After reviewing the MBO literature, Covaleski and Dirsmith stated:

> Our conclusion is that, as a goal-directed form of management technology, MBO may lead to dysfunctional decision making at the institutional level within organizations, especially those facing complex, dynamic environments. However, if viewed as a philosophy of management administered at the sub-unit level, MBO may serve as a catalytic agent for encouraging decentralized decision making and performance evaluation.[46]

There is little question but that MBO is effective more often than it is not. A review by Kondrasuk suggests that successes appear to dominate failures by a ratio of at least 5:1 (and perhaps as much as 10:1).[47] Success as classified by Kondrasuk is any statistically significant improvement in performance. What is not addressed is whether the improvements found realize the full potential of goal-setting techniques. A review of this literature suggests that most do not. It is likely that a combination of empirical knowledge arising from goal-setting research and the conceptual and theoretical strength of MBO approaches would be very beneficial.

Currently, most MBO programs require participative goal setting, despite the fact that research has shown participation enhances goal-directed effort only if it leads to increases in goal specificity, difficulty, acceptance, and/or commitment. MBO is used almost exclusively with management and professional employees despite research which shows the technique to be appropriate with a wide range of employees. MBO uses almost exclusively long-term goals, but research shows that short-term goals can also be effective. Furthermore, MBO applications often devote insufficient attention to the critical goal attribute of goal difficulty.

SUMMARY

Values attached to outcomes are important, but other considerations must be taken into account if you are to understand fully how organizational members react to exchanges between themselves and the organization. Specifically, people compare the value of outcomes received to the level of inputs provided. This evaluation of "distributive justice" influences feelings and subsequent behavior. It is clear that organizational members make social comparisons to determine whether their own level of distributive justice is "fair" in comparison to what they perceive to exist for others. These social comparisons also influence feelings and behaviors.

Equity theory argues in a convincing fashion that people who perceive inequity will be motivated to make changes which reduce the amount of inequity experienced. The theory identifies various actions a person can take to reduce inequity. It offers some suggestions about the conditions under which one particular type of action is more or less likely to be chosen to reduce inequity. Unfortunately, the theory is not precise enough to predict which specific actions are most probable (see Chapter 8 for an expanded treatment of this problem).

Goal theory states that goals guide a great deal of human behavior in organizations. In particular, the theory states that goal-directed effort will be greatest if you accept and become committed to a specific and difficult goal. If you have adequate abilities and appropriate organizational support, your effort will be translated into performance. If positively valued outcomes follow, satisfaction will result.

Goal theory is thus a very straightforward, usable model which has benefited a wide range of individuals and organizations. The applied implications of equity theory for organizations, however, have not been explored fully (except for compensation systems). It is clear, however, that organizations must consider the value of outcomes and inputs as well as the role of social comparison if they are to meet the demands of their workers.

GLOSSARY

Distributive Justice The degree to which a person perceives his/her outcomes match the level of his/her inputs into a social exchange.

Perceived Equity The degree to which a person perceives that his/her ratio of outcomes to inputs matches his/her perceptions of the outcome-to-input ratio of a comparison other.

O_p A person's perception of the level of outcomes s/he receives from a social exchange.

I_p A person's perception of the level of inputs s/he provides in a social exchange.

O_o A person's perception of the level of outcomes received by a comparison other.

I_o A person's perception of the level of inputs provided by a comparison other.

Goal Difficulty The probability that a goal will be achieved.

Goal Specificity The degree to which a particular (specific) goal is identified.

Goal-Directed Effort The amount of energy directed toward goal accomplishment.

Goal Acceptance The degree to which a person accepts a specific goal as his/her own.

Goal Commitment The degree to which a person is dedicated to reaching an accepted goal.

Management by Objectives The application of goal-setting principles in organizations. Usually involves joint setting of goals by superior and subordinate, monitoring of goal progress, and feedback on progress.

STUDY QUESTIONS

1. How can equity theory explain why a person who receives a high salary might be dissatisfied with his/her pay?
2. What steps could an organization take to influence a person's perceptions of O_p, I_p, O_o, I_o?
3. How could an organization influence a person's selection of a comparison other?
4. Equity theory identifies a number of possible alternatives for the reduction of perceived inequity. How could an organization influence which of these alternatives a person will pursue?

5. Under what conditions would it be appropriate for an organization to encourage perceptions of equity? Inequity?
6. What type of goals would be most likely to enhance your performance in your organizational behavior course? What other conditions should be present for your performance to be enhanced?
7. How could an organization decide whether it would be more appropriate to assign goals to organizational members or to allow members to set their own goals?
8. Identify two reasons why a formal goal-setting program might be dysfunctional for an organization.
9. Discuss the importance of feedback in the use of goal setting.
10. Using the model shown in Exhibit 7–6, identify five reasons why a management by objectives (MBO) program might fail to enhance performance.

NOTES

1. **Homans, G. C.** (1961). *Social behavior: Its elementary forms*. New York: Harcourt, Brace, and World.
2. **Adams, J. S.** (1965). Inequity in social exchange. In L. Berkowitz (Ed.), *Advances in experimental social psychology*. (Vol. 2). New York: Academic Press.
3. **Andrews, I. R.** (1967). Wage inequity and job performance: An experimental study. *Journal of Applied Psychology, 51,* 39–45; **Adams, J. S.** (1963a). Towards an understanding of inequity. *Journal of Abnormal Social Psychology, 67,* 422–436; **Adams, J. S.** (1963b). Wage inequities, productivity and work quality. *Industrial Relations, 3,* 9–16.
4. **Adams,** 1965, pp. 295–296.
5. **Miner, J. B.** (1980). *Theories of organizational behavior*. Hinsdale, IL: Dryden Press.
6. **Adams, J. S. & Rosenbaum, W. B.** (1962). The relationship of worker productivity to cognitive dissonance about wage inequities. *Journal of Applied Psychology, 467,* 161–164; **Adams, J. S., & Jacobsen, P. R.** (1964). Effects of wage inequities on work quality. *Journal of Abnormal and Social Psychology, 69,* 19–25; **Adams,** 1963a; **Adams,** 1963b.
7. See **Goodman, P. S., & Friedman, A.** (1971). An examination of Adams' theory of inequity. *Administrative Science Quarterly, 16,* 271–288; **Miner** (1980) for reviews of this literature.
8. **Goodman & Friedman,** (1971); **Kessler, J. J., & Wiener, Y.** (1972). Self-consistency and inequity dissonance as factors in undercompensation. *Organizational Behavior and Human Performance, 7,* 456–466.

9. **Finn, R. H., & Lee, S. M.** (1972). Salary equity: Its determination, analysis, and correlates. *Journal of Applied Psychology, 56,* 283–292.

10. **Telly, C. S., French, W. L., & Scott, W. G.** (1971). The relationship of equity to turnover among hourly workers. *Administrative Science Quarterly, 16,* 164–172.

11. **Vecchio, R. P.** (1982). Predicting worker performance in inequitable settings. *Academy of Management Review, 7,* 103–110.

12. Ibid, p. 106.

13. **Lord, R. G., & Hohenfeld, J. A.** (1979). Longitudinal field assessment of equity effects on the performance of major league baseball players. *Journal of Applied Psychology, 64,* 19–26.

14. **Dunham, R. B.** (1978). *Two job evaluation techniques and determinants of pay satisfaction.* Paper presented at the convention of the American Psychological Association, Toronto, Ontario, Canada.

15. **Lewin, K.** (1935). *A dynamic theory of personality.* New York: McGraw-Hill; **Lewin, K.** (1938). *The conceptual representation and the measurement of psychological forces.* Durham, NC: Duke University Press; **Lewin, K., Dembo, T., Festinger, L., & Sears, P. S.** (1944). Level of aspiration. In J. McVicker Hunt (Ed.), *Personality and behavior disorders* (pp. 333–378). New York: Ronald Press.

16. **Drucker, P.** (1954). *The practice of management.* New York: Wiley; **McGregor, D.** (1957). An uneasy look at performance appraisal. *Harvard Business Review, 35,* 89–94.

17. **Miner, J. B.** (1980). *Theories of organizational behavior.* Hinsdale, IL: Dryden Press; **Ryan, T.** (1964, published 1970). *Intentional behavior: An approach to human motivation.* New York: Ronald Press.

18. **Latham, G. P., & Locke, E. A.** (1979). Goal setting—A motivational technique that works. *Organizational Dynamics,* 68–80, p. 77. A complete current description of the goal setting process is contained in **Locke, E. A., & Latham, G. P.** (1984) *Goal setting: A motivational technique that works!* Englewood Cliffs, N.J.: Prentice-Hall.

19. **Locke, E. A.** (1978) The ubiquity of the technique of goal setting in theories of and approaches to employee motivation. *Academy of Management Review, 5,* 594–601.

20. Ibid.

21. Ibid.

22. **Locke, E. A., Shaw, K. N., Saari, L. M., & Latham, G. P.** (1981). Goal setting and task performance: 1969–1980. *Psychological Bulletin, 90,* 125–152, p. 129.

23. Ibid.

24. **Locke, E. A.** (1982). Relation of goal performance with a short work period and multiple goal levels. *Journal of Applied Psychology, 67,* 512–514; **Latham, G. P. & Baldes, J. J.** (1975). The practical significance of Locke's theory of goal setting. *Journal of Applied Psychology, 60,* 187–191; **Latham & Locke,** 1979.

25. **Locke,** 1982.

26. **Cabrero, A.** (1982). Goal theory and expectancy predictions of effort and performance. Unpublished student paper, University of Wisconsin, Madison.
27. **Locke et al.,** 1981.
28. **Strang, J. R., Lawrence, E. C., & Fowler, P. C.** (1978). Effects assigned goal level and knowledge of results on arithmetic computation: A laboratory study. *Journal of Applied Psychology, 63,* 446–450; **Ivancevich, J. M., & McMahon, J. T.** (1982). The effects of goal setting, external feedback, and self generated feedback of outcome variables: A field experiment. *Academy of Management Journal, 25,* 359–372.
29. **Locke et al.,** 1981.
30. **Garland, H.** (1983). Influence of ability-assigned goals, and normative information of personal goals and performance: A challenge to the goal attainability assumption. *Journal of Applied Psychology, 68,* 20–30.
31. **Locke,** 1982.
32. **Latham & Locke,** 1979.
33. **Locke,** 1982.
34. **Garland,** 1983.
35. **Jackson, S. E., & Zedeck, S.** (1982). Explaining performance variability: Contributions of goal setting, task characteristics, and evaluative contexts. *Journal of Applied Psychology, 67,* 759–768.
36. **Mowen, J. C., Middlemist, R. D., Luther, D.** (1981). Joint effects of assigned goal level and incentive structure of task performance: A laboratory study. *Journal of Applied Psychology, 66,* 598–603.
37. **Jackson & Zedeck,** 1982.
38. **Latham & Locke,** 1979.
39. Ibid.; **Locke et al.,** 1981.
40. **Mowen et al.,** 1981.
41. **Latham & Locke,** 1979.
42. **McConkie, M. L.** (1979). A clarification of the goal setting and appraisal processes in MBO. *Academy of Management Review, 4,* 29–40, p. 37.
43. **Drucker,** 1954.
44. **Odiorne, G. S.** (1979). *M. B. O. II.* Belmont, CA: Fearon.
45. **Hodgson, J. S.** (1973). Management of objectives: The experience of a federal government department. *Canadian Public Administration, 16,* 422–431.
46. **Covaleski, M. A., & Dirsmith, M. W.** (1981). MBO and goal directedness in a hospital context. *Academy of Management Review, 6,* 409–418.
47. **Kondrasuk, J. N.** (1981). Studies in MBO effectiveness. *Academy of Management Review, 6,* 419–430.

8 An Integrative Model: Expectancy Theory

OVERVIEW
THE BASIC MODEL
The Expectancy Perception
The Instrumentality Perception
The Valence Perception
Putting the Pieces Together
A Note on Intrinsic and Extrinsic Outcomes
RESEARCH ON EXPECTANCY THEORY
THE EXPANDED MODEL
THE INTEGRATING EFFECT OF THE EXPANDED MODEL
EXPECTANCY THEORY APPLICATIONS
SUMMARY

The direction of the body is guided by the soul. The soul is the slave of the mind. The mind is a slave to logic.

Anonymous

OVERVIEW

Expectancy theory is one of the most complex, intricate, and logical theories examined in this book. In its fully expanded form, however, it is one of the most complete theories for detailing not only *how* people feel and behave but also *why* they react as they do. Furthermore, expectancy theory provides a useful framework for integrating the elements of most of the other theories discussed in this book. Unfortunately, in spite of its usefulness, the apparent complexity of expectancy theory discourages many would-be users. Nonetheless, you will not find expectancy theory difficult to use if you approach it properly.

Several different versions (as well as several different names) of expectancy theory exist. Its popularity has caused it to become a dominant theory, driving the work of scholars and becoming increasingly important to practitioners. The version of expectancy theory presented here conforms most closely to an expanded concept described by Porter and Lawler, although numerous theorists have made important contributions to the concept.[1]

Expectancy theory is sufficiently general so as to be useful in a wide variety of situations. Choices between job offers, between working hard or easy, between going to work or being absent, between majoring in organizational behavior or accounting, or virtually any other set of possibilities can be addressed by expectancy theory. Basically, the theory focuses on two related issues:

1. When faced with two or more alternatives, which will you select?

2. Once you choose an alternative, how motivated will you be to pursue that choice?

The attractiveness of an alternative is determined by your "expectations" of what is likely to happen if you choose that alternative. The more you believe that the alternative chosen will lead to positively valued outcomes, the greater the attractiveness of that alternative. Expectancy theory states that, when faced with two or more alternatives, a person will select that alternative which appears most attractive. And, the greater the attractiveness of the chosen alternative, the more motivated the person will be to pursue it.

A useful analogy for understanding expectancy theory is that of magnetic force. Exhibit 8–1 presents three alternatives as three magnetic forces. Each force exerts an influence on the direction you will choose. The positive forces of Magnet 1 and Magnet 2 draw you toward them, while the negative force of Magnet 3 drives you away. In accordance with the laws of physics, you gravitate to Magnet 2 because of its superior positive force.

There is little difference between the basic tenets of magnetic theory and those of expectancy theory. In each case, the attractiveness of alternatives determines the direction chosen and the vigor with which the most positive alternative is approached. Expectancy theorists even use the term **Force** to describe the overall attractiveness of an alternative. The primary distinction between the two theories is that magnetic theory is based on objective physical characteristics of objects while expectancy theory is based on the perceived characteristics of alternatives. In Exhibit 8–1, therefore, you did not need to know that the magnets were present or what their relative forces were in order to react. In expectancy theory, however, a person reacts to *perceived reality.* Before you can react to an alternative, you must be aware of its existence and must form an impression about the alternative. You react to your beliefs about the alternative, whether or not they are accurate.

THE BASIC MODEL

Expectancy theory is a cognitive model (i.e., it is based on conscious thoughts about the situation). According to the theory, you will evaluate the attractiveness of alternatives by asking three sets of questions about each. Together, these specific questions ask the general question: "If I choose this alternative, what is likely to happen to me?"

1. If I choose this alternative, will I succeed? (Expectancy Perception)
2. If I succeed, what outcomes will I receive? (Instrumentality Perception)
3. How much do I value these outcomes? (Valence Perception)

Exhibit 8–1 The Effect of Magnetic Force

(a) The conditions

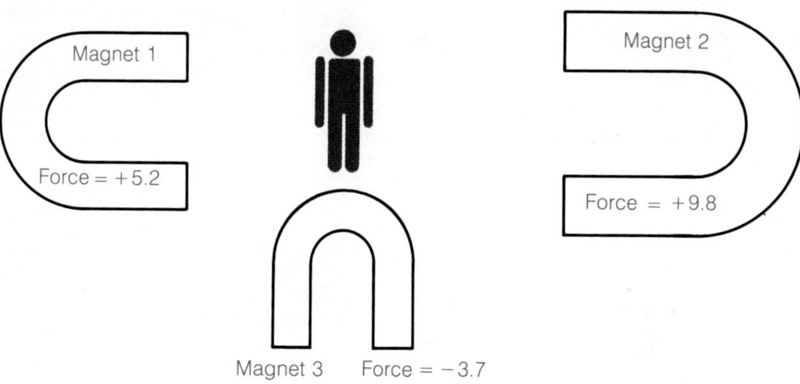

(b) The results

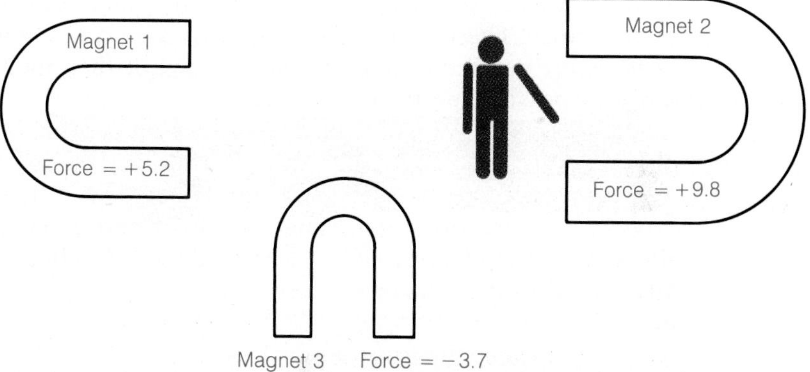

The Expectancy Perception

The first question relates to **expectancy perception.** Because this often involves the perceived likelihood that effort will lead to performance, the most common abbreviation used for this perception is **E→P.** Exhibit 8–2 illustrates the possibilities which might be perceived if you were deciding whether to attempt high performance or moderate performance at work. As illustrated in Exhibit 8–2, you perceive that attempted high performance has an 80 percent chance of leading to moderate performance but only a 20 percent chance of leading to high performance. You perceive that at-

Exhibit 8–2 Expectancy Perceptions

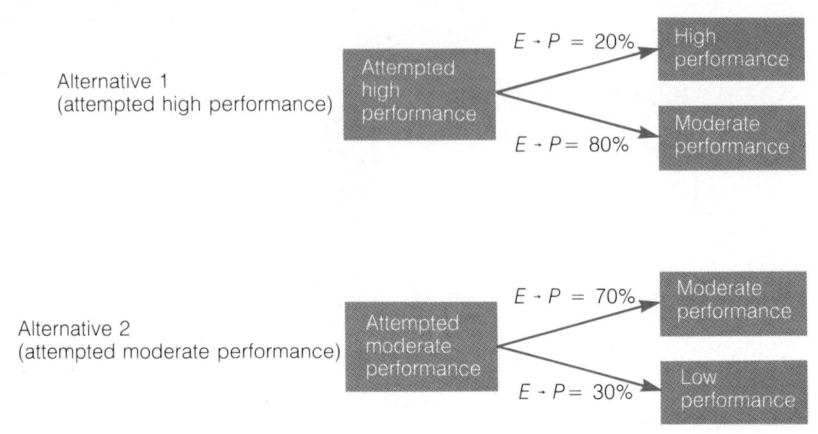

tempted moderate performance has a 70 percent chance of leading to moderate performance and a 30 percent chance of leading to low performance. These perceptions will influence your choice, whether or not they are accurate and whether or not they include the full range of possible performance levels.

Factors which influence the expectancy perception often include past experiences of success or failure, training, self-confidence, perceived level of ability, perceived role clarity, etc. The value of the expectancy perception can range from 0 (there is no chance that effort would lead to performance) through 1.0 (effort would definitely lead to performance).

The Instrumentality Perception

The second question focuses on the **instrumentality perception.** The abbreviation **P→O** is used for this perception since it involves the perceived likelihood that performance (if it occurs) will lead to the receipt of outcomes. Instrumentality is illustrated in Exhibit 8–3. In this example, you are deciding whether to attempt high or moderate performance in a situation where you perceive that high, moderate, or low performance are all possible. You perceive that high performance, if achieved, would have a 60 percent chance of leading to a pay raise, a 50 percent chance of leading to special recognition, and a 70 percent chance of producing stress. You perceive that moderate performance, if achieved, would have a 40 per-

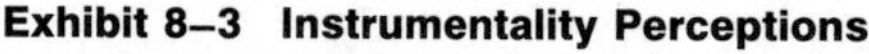

Exhibit 8–3 Instrumentality Perceptions

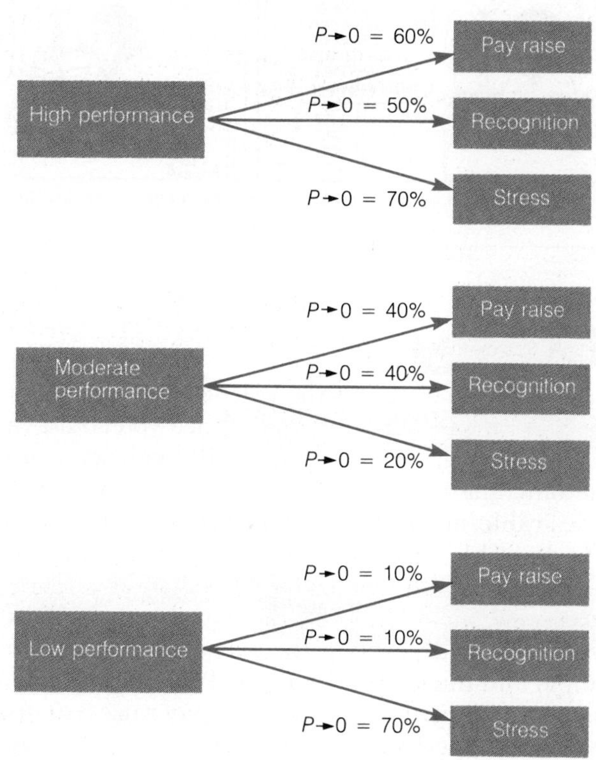

cent chance of leading to a pay raise, a 40 percent chance of obtaining special recognition, and a 20 percent chance of leading to stress. Finally, you perceive that low performance would have a 10 percent chance of leading to a pay raise, a 10 percent chance of special recognition, and a 70 percent probability of producing stress. These perceptions will influence your choice to pursue high or moderate performance whether or not they are accurate and whether or not all possible outcomes were considered.

Some of the factors influencing instrumentality perceptions include reward and penalty systems (e.g., pay system), organizational policies, and prior experiences (e.g., "In the past, did this type of performance lead to a pay raise? To recognition? To stress?"). The value of the instrumentality perception can range from 0 (this performance level definitely would not lead to this outcome) through 1.0 (this performance level definitely would lead to this outcome).

SALLY FORTH by Greg Howard. © 1983 Field Enterprises, Inc. Courtesy of Field Newspaper Syndicate

The Valence Perception

The final question concerns the **valence perception (V).** Valence is the value you attach to an outcome. Since you could value an outcome positively, negatively, or neutrally, valence can range from −1.0 (the outcome is extremely undesirable) to 0 (the outcome is neither desirable nor undesirable), through +1.0 (the outcome is extremely desirable). As discussed by the need theories (see Chapter 5) the value attached to outcomes varies widely across people and even within one person across time. Exhibit 8–4 identifies the valences associated with each of the expected outcomes in the previous example and integrates the E→P, P→O, and V perceptions. As can be seen in Exhibit 8–4, you value a pay raise +.6, special recognition +.4, and experienced stress −.5.

Putting the Pieces Together

The information contained in Exhibit 8–4 describes your thoughts when choosing between attempting high performance or moderate performance. This information can be described qualitatively or quantitatively. The qualitative description probably best captures your actual thoughts when making this decision (few people actually think in terms of statistical perceived probabilities!), but the quantitative description best predicts the choice you will make when faced with these two alternatives. Both descriptions are useful.

Qualitative Description. I have to decide what performance level I am going to try to obtain on my job. The only two levels I would consider seriously are high performance and moderate performance.

If I attempt high performance, I have only a mild chance of succeeding. If I were to reach high performance, I would have a strong chance

Exhibit 8–4 The Complete Expectancy Theory Process

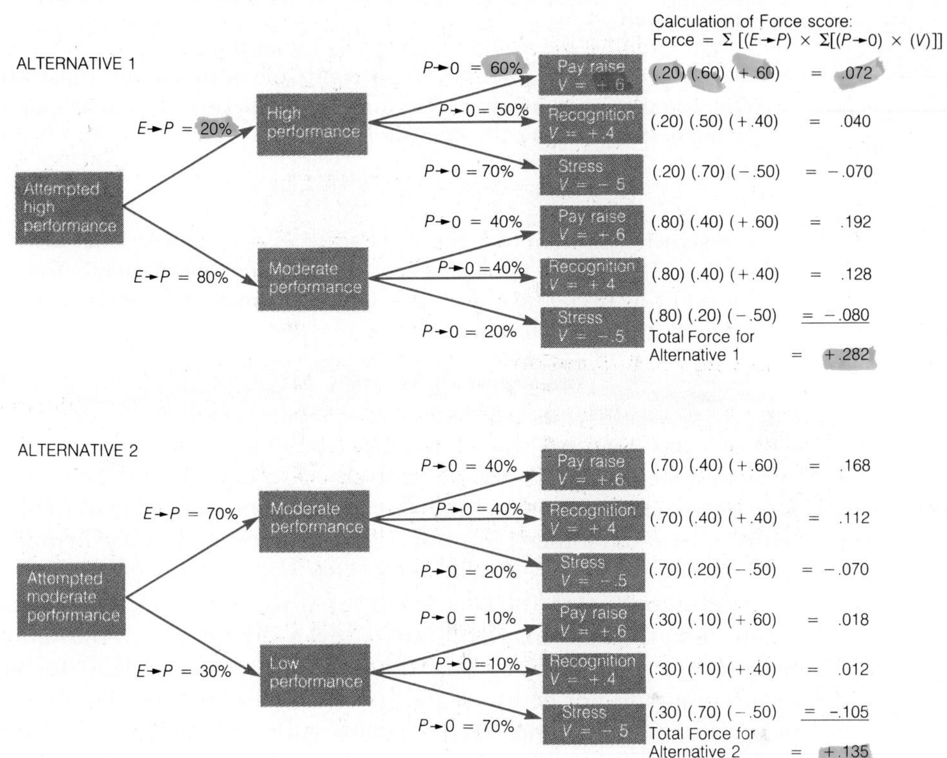

of obtaining a pay raise and a 50-50 chance of receiving special recognition from my supervisor for my work. Also, most likely I would experience stress. I honestly believe that attempting high performance would almost certainly not produce high performance but, rather, a moderate level of performance. Moderate performance would provide a moderate chance of a pay raise, a moderate chance of special recognition, and only a slight chance of stress. I would feel quite positive about receiving a pay raise, moderately positive about special recognition, and quite negative about experiencing stress.

If I attempt moderate performance, I almost certainly would actually reach a moderate performance level. This would probably lead to a moderate chance of a pay raise, a moderate chance of special recognition, and a slight chance of stress. There is a mild chance that attempting moderate performance might actually lead to low performance. If this were to happen, there is only a remote chance of obtaining either a pay raise or special recognition, and I would almost certainly experience stress. My feelings about a pay raise are quite positive, moderately positive about special recognition, and quite negative about stress.

All things considered, I will attempt to achieve high performance. Even if I only obtain moderate performance, things will work out pretty well.

Quantitative Description. Exhibit 8–4 quantifies each of your E→P, P→O, and V perceptions. The far right side of this figure illustrates the calculation of a Force score for each of the two alternatives under consideration, using the equation:

$$\text{Force} = \Sigma[(E \rightarrow P) \times \Sigma[(P \rightarrow O) \times (V)]]$$

As shown in Exhibit 8–4, the Force score associated with Alternative 1 is +.282 compared to a Force score of +.135 for Alternative 2. You are most likely to choose Alternative 1, given its more positive Force score (i.e., attractiveness).

Note that the Force equation is based on a multiplicative function (i.e., if any of the three elements is zero, the product will be zero). Thus, if you perceive that your effort has no chance of leading to performance, you will not be motivated to choose and pursue an alternative (even if it is certain that performance would lead to positively valued outcomes). Similarly, if you perceive that performance will not lead to valued outcomes, you will not be motivated to choose and pursue the alternative (even if you are certain that effort would lead to performance). Finally, even if you believe that effort will lead to performance and that performance will lead to outcomes, you will not be motivated to choose and pursue the alternative unless the outcomes are positively valued. Thus, all three components of the model must be positive to encourage choice of a particular alternative and to increase the amount of energy devoted to the alternative after it is chosen.

Although it may look complicated, the example presented in Exhibit 8–4 is relatively simple. It deals with only two alternatives. Each alternative is associated with only two possible performance levels, each of which is associated with just three possible outcomes. In theory, there is no limit to the number of alternatives which could be included in the decision process, nor is there a theoretical limit to the number of possible performance levels or outcomes. In reality, most people choose to deal with a relatively small number of alternatives. Furthermore, most people consider only a small set of possible consequences (performance levels, outcomes, etc.) when evaluating the merits of alternatives under consideration. In effect, people regularly ignore a number of "objectively important" factors when making choices. The key is that the only factors which influence choices are those of which you are cognitively aware and choose to include in your evaluative scheme. This simplification

L. L. Cummings of Northwestern University has contributed to many areas of OB, including the development and application of theory.

Do you see an advantage in studying theory in an OB course in addition to material which has direct application value? The major advantage I see is that the sole study of direct applications quickly becomes dated. The kinds of changing and complex environments that most managers face mean that they need something other than a cookbook of applications in dealing with human problems and human opportunities in organizations. They need a diagnostic framework, and it is exactly that diagnostic framework that can be provided by good theory in OB. Theory tells us what are the likely causes, what are the likely constraints, what are the likely influencing factors when a change or intervention occurs in an organization. The diagnostic framework is particularly useful in predicting the effects of these changes rather than being caught by surprise.

Specifically, how can theory help in the application of OB knowledge? Theory helps us recognize innovative and perhaps unnoticed opportunities for the application of current knowledge. Many times current solutions are developed to current problems and those solutions are not transferred from one organization to another or from one group or one individual to another. Theory provides a tool for helping us see that applications developed in one context may be appropriate in another context.

Are theories really important, however, once the student is out of school? Studying OB theory will become increasingly important the longer the student is away from the course. That is, the theory can provide a framework or frameworks for integrating continuing developments of knowledge which students will be exposed to through their business and professional reading after they graduate. The theoretical models can become a structuring or organizing mechanism for helping individuals absorb important knowledge and new developments in OB.

eases the decision-making burden substantially. Failure to simplify sufficiently leads to statements like: "This decision is difficult because there are too many choices"; "There are so many factors which influence my decision, I just don't know where to start"; and "I can't even remember all of the issues, much less make the decision."

A Note on Intrinsic and Extrinsic Outcomes

The distinction between *intrinsic outcomes* (outcomes which stem directly from the work itself, such as a sense of accomplishment and interest in the work) and *extrinsic outcomes* (outcomes which are administered by other people, such as pay increases and promotions) becomes very important in expectancy theory. At the very least, it is important for organizations to recognize that there are two major sets of outcomes influencing your choices (and influencing the Force driving you *after* the choice is made). Since intrinsic outcomes stem directly from your work experience, instrumentality values (P→O) associated with intrinsic outcomes are often quite high ("If I reach a high performance level, I experience a sense of accomplishment whether or not my boss notices"; "If I enjoy doing my work, I experience pleasure whether or not anyone else notices"). An intrinsic outcome with a valence of +.5 and an instrumentality value of 1.0 would have a more powerful effect on a worker ($1.0 \times +.5 = +.5$) than would a more highly valued extrinsic outcome with a valence of +.8 but an instrumentality value of only .5 ($.5 \times +.8 = +.4$). This relatively strong impact of intrinsic outcomes is often overlooked by organizations which focus on formal extrinsic outcomes. (Chapter 15, on job design, addresses the role of intrinsic outcomes.)

RESEARCH ON EXPECTANCY THEORY

Research on the principles of expectancy theory has been plagued by a wide variety of technical methodological problems. In fact, there never has been a totally acceptable concurrent test of all aspects of the theory. Because of these limitations, empirical evaluation of the theory must be based on a careful assessment of bits and pieces of a wide range of individual research studies (each of which adequately tests part but not all of the theory). After reviewing this collection of research, Miner concluded:

> These research tests have now yielded sufficient theoretical support so that it seems safe to conclude that expectancy theories are on the right track. They certainly do not explain all motivated behavior in all types of work organizations, but they do explain enough to be worth pursuing further.[2]

THE EXPANDED MODEL

Exhibit 8–5 presents an expanded expectancy model. This model deals primarily with events which occur *after* you have made a choice from among available alternatives. Moving from left to right in the model, it can be seen that (as was previously discussed) E→P, P→O, and V values combine to determine the Force (effort) you devote to the chosen alternative.

Effort alone is not sufficient to obtain good performance. You also must have the necessary human tools, such as abilities and skills. Furthermore, proper perceptions of role requirements (i.e., "This is how to do the job") must be present to direct the use of these abilities and skills. The chances of high performance are greatest when effort, abilities and skills, and appropriate role perceptions are all present.

Performance may or may not lead to outcomes. The probability of performance leading to intrinsic outcomes depends heavily on the design of the job ("Does the job provide me with feedback about how well I am doing the work? Is the work challenging? Interesting?"). The probability of performance leading to extrinsic outcomes will be influenced heavily by organizational policies and

Exhibit 8–5 Expanded Expectancy Model

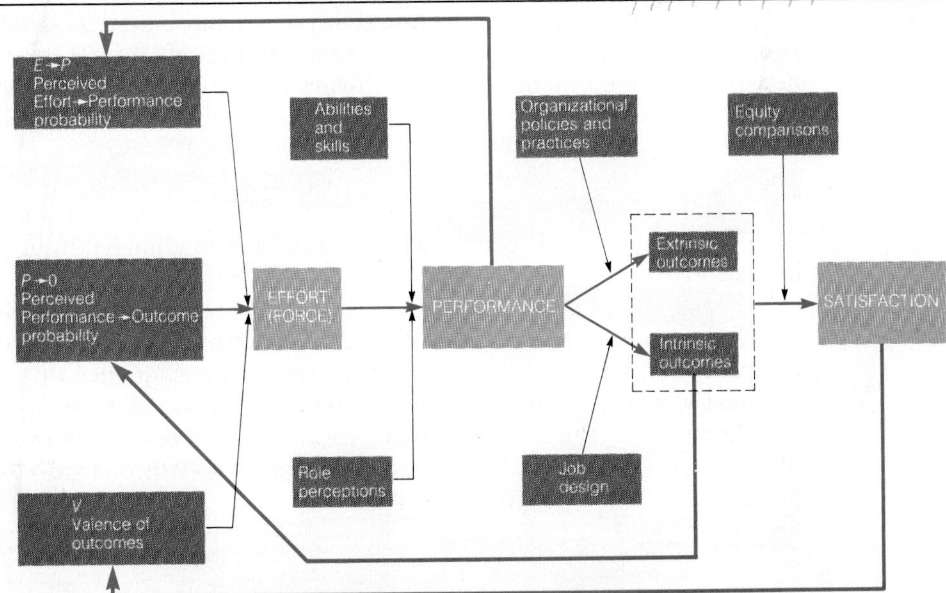

Source: Based on a model presented by L. W. Porter, and E. E. Lawler (1968). *Managerial attitudes and performance*. Homewood, IL: Irwin.

practices. Performance is most likely to lead to the receipt of a pay increase, for example, if the organization has a system for the assessment of performance, a policy of rewarding high performance with pay, and managers who follow through on these policies.

Once you have received outcomes, satisfaction may or may not follow. Naturally, the valence of the outcomes received exerts a major influence on the degree to which these outcomes lead to satisfaction. In addition, however, you make equity comparisons concerning these outcomes and react accordingly (see Chapter 7).

The three arrows "feeding back" from right to left in the model emphasize the fact that this model is dynamic. Future values of expectancy perceptions (E→P) are influenced by the degree to which effort actually has led to performance. Future values of instrumentality perceptions (P→O) are influenced by the degree to which performance actually has produced outcomes. Future valences are influenced by experienced levels of satisfaction. Changes in these perceptions will influence the overall Force score (and effort level) which, in turn, influences performance, etc. (thus producing a *very* dynamic model!).

THE INTEGRATING EFFECT OF THE EXPANDED MODEL

The expanded model shown in Exhibit 8–5 effectively integrates major elements of the other theories discussed in this book. Consider the following examples:

1. *Need theories* (Chapter 5) state that you are motivated to satisfy your needs. You positively value outcomes that satisfy unmet needs, negatively value outcomes which thwart the satisfaction of unmet needs, and assign a neutral value to outcomes which do neither. In effect, the need theories help to explain how valences are formed. The need theories also point out how the valence of outcomes can differ from person to person (due to different need levels) and even within any given person across time (due to changes in need levels).

2. *Learning theories* (Chapter 6) state that you probably will repeat a response (behavior) in the future which was reinforced in the past (i.e., followed by a positively valued consequence or the removal of a negatively valued consequence). This is the basic process involved in the formation of perceptions of instrumentality (P→O). Learning theories and expectancy theory both argue that interactions between you and your environment influence your future behavior. The primary difference is that expectancy theory explains this process in very cognitive terms through discussion of perceptions of expected future events, while most learning theories focus on observable past events. Learning theorists might state:

> A behavior which is followed by a positively valued consequence is more likely to occur in the future *because the positively valued consequence occurred in the past.*

Expectancy theorists would be more likely to state:

> A behavior which was followed by a positively valued consequence in the past is more likely to occur in the future *because the person perceives that the positively valued consequence is likely to occur in the future.*

3. *Equity theories* (Chapter 7) state that your level of satisfaction with a set of outcomes depends not only on how positively or negatively you value them but also on the circumstances surrounding their receipt. According to equity theory, satisfaction is influenced by your comparison of outcomes received to the level of inputs you made to obtain them, and by comparing what you received for your inputs relative to what you believe others have received in exchange for their inputs. A person who perceives a state of equity is more likely to be satisfied than a person who perceives inequity. Equity theory, therefore, explains the process shown in the expanded expectancy model by which a person reacts to outcomes received. Because of the "feedback loop" in the model from satisfaction to valence, perceptions of inequity not only can reduce satisfaction, but also are capable of reducing future valences associated with the outcomes. If this occurs, it is likely that future effort will be reduced due to a lower Force score. Conversely, if equity is perceived, satisfaction will increase, future valences will increase, and subsequent effort will be increased due to a higher Force score.

4. *Goal theory* (Chapter 7) can be integrated with the expanded expectancy model in several ways. Locke has noted that expectancy theory can explain how an individual goes about choosing a particular goal (presumably, you will choose a goal which has the highest associated Force score).[3] A reexamination of the revised goal-setting model from Chapter 7 reveals other similarities between that model and the expanded expectancy model. Locke's use of the term "goal acceptance" to identify the personal adoption of a goal is very similar to the "choice of an alternative" in the expectancy model. Locke's "goal commitment," the degree to which you are committed to reaching your accepted (chosen) goal, is very much like the expectancy description of Force as your level of motivation to pursue the chosen alternative. Locke argues that the difficulty and specificity of a goal are major determinants of the level of performance attempted (goal-directed effort), and expectancy theory appears to be consistent with this argument (even though expectancy theory is not so explicit on this point). The following is a list of

additional observations implied by goal theorists followed (in parentheses) by a corresponding statement from expectancy theory.

1. A goal should be viewed as attainable. (Expectancy perceptions should be positive.)
2. Goal attainment should be rewarded. (Instrumentality perceptions should be positive.)
3. Rewards should be valued. (Outcomes should be positively valent.)

Other similarities can be observed through comparison of the goal and expectancy models. It reasonably can be concluded that the major underlying processes explored by the two models are very similar and seldom would lead to inconsistent recommendations.

EXPECTANCY THEORY APPLICATIONS

Traditionally, expectancy theory has been:

> primarily a theory for the scholar and the scientist rather than for the practitioner. . . . It is becoming increasingly evident, though, that applications are possible and that they might well prove very fruitful."[4]

Organizations can exert tremendous influence over Force scores, thus influencing not only the alternative chosen but also the amount of energy likely to be committed to that choice. Practical applications of expectancy theory by organizations include:

1. Increasing the E→P perceptions associated with organizationally desirable alternatives by: selecting organizational members who have the necessary abilities, providing proper training, providing experiences of success, clarifying job responsibilities, etc.

2. Increasing the P→O perceptions associated with desirable alternatives by policies which specify that desirable behavior will lead to desirable outcomes, and that undesirable behavior will lead either to no outcomes or to undesirable outcomes. These policies must be enforced so that workers believe such contingencies actually exist. Jobs must be designed to increase the chances of receiving intrinsic outcomes. Organizational members should be given the opportunity to perform and to be rewarded.

3. Systematically evaluating which specific outcomes members value. The greater the valence of outcomes offered for a behavior, the more likely a person will choose and be committed to that alternative. By recognizing that different organizational members may have different values and that values may change over time, organizations can provide the most highly valued outcomes.

4. Ensuring that a worker is capable of performing a behavior

once s/he has chosen a particular alternative so effort actually translates into performance. This includes clarifying the actions leading to performance as well as appropriate training.

5. Ensuring that the worker experiences appropriate outcomes once performance has occurred by providing extrinsic outcomes and appropriate job design (so the work experience itself provides intrinsic outcomes).

6. Examining the level of outcomes provided the worker. Are they equitable, given the level of inputs provided by the worker? Are they equitable in comparison to the way other workers are treated?

7. Monitoring satisfaction levels to determine if the entire sequence of events experienced by the worker has produced positive or negative reactions.

SUMMARY

Expectancy theory states that human behavior and attitudes are guided by rational, conscious thoughts which usually follow a logical, predictable pattern of seeking valued outcomes. By combining all of the theories discussed in this and previous chapters, the expanded expectancy model identifies a major set of conditions necessary for organizational effectiveness. The model provides a very useful tool for understanding, predicting, and influencing behavior and attitudes in organizations. To utilize this information, an organization must recognize the primacy of worker perceptions of the environment and deal with perceived reality as well as objective reality (see Chapter 10).

GLOSSARY

Force The overall attractiveness of an alternative and the relative amount of energy likely to be devoted to the alternative if it is selected.

Expectancy Perception (E→P) The perceived probability that effort will lead to performance.

Instrumentality Perception (P→O) The perceived probability that performance will lead to one or more outcomes.

Valence Perception (V) The value attached to outcomes by a person.

STUDY QUESTIONS

1. How does the expanded expectancy model presented in Exhibit 8–5 integrate the previous theories (need theories, learning theories, equity theory, goal theory)?
2. Discuss why an alternative might not be attractive to an individual, even if the outcomes associated with the alternative are very attractive.
3. What steps can an organization take to increase the Force score associated with the alternative it hopes an organizational member will pursue?
4. Discuss reasons why a high level of effort could lead to low performance.
5. How could high performance lead to low satisfaction?
6. Is the expanded expectancy theory model so complicated that it is rendered unusable for organizations?
7. Can an organization use the expectancy model effectively even if it does not wish to calculate Force scores mathematically?
8. How could the instructor of your organizational behavior course use expectancy theory to motivate you to exert a high level of effort in the course?
9. How could a manager use expectancy theory to motivate subordinates to decrease their absenteeism rates?

NOTES

1. **Porter, L. W., & Lawler, E. E.** (1968). *Managerial attitudes and performance*. Homewood, IL: Irwin; **Vroom, V. H.** (1960). *Some personality determinants of the effects of participation*. Englewood Cliffs,

NJ: Prentice-Hall; **Vroom, V. H.** (1964). *Work and motivation.* New York: Wiley; **Galbraith, J., & Cummings, L. L.** (1967). An empirical investigation of the motivational determinants of task performance: Interactive effects between instrumentality-valence and motivation-ability. *Organizational Behavior and Human Performance, 2,* 237–257.

2. **Miner, J. B.** (1980). *Theories of organizational behavior.* Hinsdale, IL: Dryden Press.
3. **Locke, E. A.** (1978). The ubiquity of the technique of goal setting in theories of and approaches to employee motivation. *Academy of Management Review, 5,* 549–601.
4. **Miner,** 1980, pp. 160–161.

Part

9 ■ Personality and Ability

10 ■ Perception

Personal Characteristics: Personality, Ability, and Perception

This would be a very short book if all individuals had the same reactions to a particular set of organizational events. Much of the book to this point has focused on differences in how and why people feel and behave as they do. The need theories, for example, explored why you value the same outcome differently than your co-worker does. The learning theories dealt with why you two respond differently to the same organizational event. Equity theory identified reasons why you might be satisfied with a set of organizational outcomes while your colleague is not. Goal theory focused on the differences you and another worker experience in goal-setting behavior. Finally, expectancy theory explored why you choose a particular alternative, and how intensely you pursue it. In short, a major purpose of the theories described in this book has been to identify a systematic method for predicting and understanding the differences between people in the ways they react to organizational events. Part IV expands on the factors covered by these theories by examining personal characteristics which influence these reactions.

Three characteristics of people which significantly influence reactions to organizational events are personality, ability, and perception. *Personality* factors influence your personal preferences and the development of your personal style of behavior. *Ability* levels determine your capacity to behave in specific ways. The *perceptual* process determines which organizational events you will notice and the meaning you give to them. Indeed, perception is critical to virtually every issue discussed in this book because attitudes and behaviors are based on reactions to perceptions (whether or not your perceptions are based on a complete or accurate picture of the organization). Thus, an organization must pay significant attention not only to what is "real," but also to what organizational members perceive to be real.

Personality and Ability

OVERVIEW

PERSONALITY

LOCUS OF CONTROL

- Internal versus External Locus of Control
- Implications for Organizations

AUTHORITARIANISM

DOGMATISM

MACHIAVELLIANISM

TYPE A AND TYPE B PERSONALITIES

- Effects of A versus B Personality Types

ABILITY

INTELLECTIVE AND PHYSICAL ABILITIES

- Intellective Abilities
- Physical Abilities

INTERINDIVIDUAL VERSUS INTRAINDIVIDUAL ABILITY DIFFERENCES

TECHNIQUES FOR ABILITY MANAGEMENT

- Selection
- Placement
- Training

SUMMARY

By nature, men are nearly alike; by practice, they get to be wide apart.

Confucius

OVERVIEW

Personality distinguishes you from other people and defines your general nature. Your overall personality is composed of a collection of psychological characteristics or traits which determines your personal preferences and individual style of behavior. Your performance will depend to a great deal upon the amount and type of ability you possess. Ability is the degree to which you are capable of performing. Any task requires one or more abilities in order to perform that task. The more of these required abilities you possess, the greater your capability to perform the task. The following discussion is devoted to normal personality differences and abilities affecting organizational behavior. This should enhance your knowledge of why people react to organizational events as they do and provide guidance to organizations in the management of their human resources.

PERSONALITY

Although personality factors can change over an extended period of time, they do so slowly and tend to be relatively stable from one situation to another. Thus, if you are a good-natured person, you probably are likely to be good natured in a wide variety of situations. You should also be better natured in any one particular situation than a person with a less agreeable personality.

The study of personality has produced a wide range of theories. Each presents a unique formulation of the factors which determine personality and the impact of personality on attitudes and behaviors. No attempt is made here to explore the full range of personality theories or the complete set of personality characteristics. Instead, this section focuses on a set of personality traits particularly interesting within organizations.

LOCUS OF CONTROL

The **locus of control** personality trait determines the degree to which you believe that your actions influence the outcomes you experience in life. Even though this personality trait can be found anywhere on that continuum, it is possible to characterize people as having primarily either an internal or external locus of control.

Internal versus External Locus of Control

If you have an *internal* locus of control, you believe you control your own fate. The *external* person, on the other hand, believes that other factors (e.g., luck, other people, organizations) are the primary determinants of his/her destiny. Locus of control beliefs can range anywhere from totally external ("My behavior has absolutely no impact on what happens to me") through totally internal ("Everything that happens to me is a direct result of my own behavior"). Exhibit 9–1 presents some of the questions frequently used to measure locus of control. This scale was developed by Julian B. Rotter, who has made major contributions to the identification and

Exhibit 9–1 Measurement of Locus of Control

Internal Control I more strongly believe that:	External Control OR
Promotions are earned through hard work and persistence.	Making a lot of money is largely a matter of getting the right breaks.
In my experience I have noticed that there is usually a direct connection between how hard I study and the grades I get.	Many times the reactions of teachers seem haphazard to me.
The number of divorces indicates that more and more people are not trying to make their marriages work.	Marriage is largely a gamble.
When I am right I can convince others.	It is silly to think that one can really change another person's basic attitudes.

Source: Julian B. Rotter, © 1971, *Psychology Today*, American Psychological Association. Derived from Rotter's I-E test.

measurement of locus of control and has helped to determine its impact on behavior.[1]

If you are an internal locus of control individual, you do not necessarily receive more outcomes than an external; you simply believe that the outcomes were received because of factors within your control. The external individual receiving a promotion probably would conclude "I got lucky." You likely would feel "I earned this promotion." The key distinguishing factor is whether or not a person perceives that outcomes are contingent upon his/her behavior.

Implications for Organizations

Locus of control has a number of significant implications for organizations.[2] Management techniques such as organizational behavior modification (Chapter 6) and goal setting (Chapter 7) are more likely to work for internal locus of control individuals. An external person, on the other hand, is not likely to believe that particular patterns of behavior influence the outcomes received and, thus, is less motivated by such a program. From an expectancy theory perspective (Chapter 8), it is not surprising that external individuals usually have lower expectancy perceptions (E→P) and lower instrumentality perceptions (P→O) than internal persons. This does not suggest that an external person always will have low E→P and P→O perceptions and that an internal person always will have high perceptions. Rather, when faced with identical organizational situations, an internal person probably will form higher E→P and P→O perceptions than will an external person. This will lead to a higher motivational level for internals and the development of a more effective organizational member. This is particularly true in situations which allow expression of individual control.

AUTHORITARIANISM

An *authoritarian* person believes that there should be clearly defined status and power levels in organizations. If you are this type of person, you believe that an effective organization must assign power to a small number of individuals; all other organizational members should obey willingly those who possess the power. Indeed, you readily will obey such authority and conform closely to rules. If placed in a leadership role, you will expect similar respect for your authority. Thus, you have a good chance of being an effective leader if followers are also high in this type of personality trait, but will have severe difficulties attempting to lead nonauthoritarian individuals.[3]

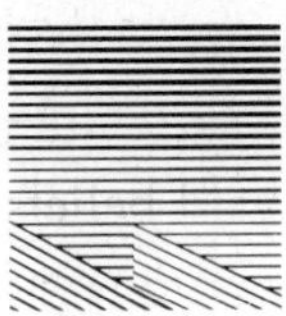

Barbara M. Karmel is president of the Reed Company, which is a specialized management consulting firm in Portland, Oregon.

You have focused much of your attention on the organizational impact of a person's willingness to take risks. What types of roles does risk taking play in organizations? One important impact is that a lower-level manager is much more likely to progress into the executive ranks if s/he has shown a propensity to take appropriate risks. This is due to two factors: the quality of the risky decisions and the simple fact that the person was willing to take the risks. In most organizations, top management must be willing to take risks.

What differentiates a good risk taker from a poor risk taker? Obviously, irresponsible and capricious risk taking seldom benefits an organization. The good risk taker knows when to take the right risk. This person engages in a lot of searching behavior, carefully researching the factors surrounding the risk. When a risky route is chosen, contingency plans are made to protect against the downside risk. The good risk taker is willing to acknowledge and accept the fact that not all decisions will work, to accept responsibility when the risk fails, and to continue with appropriate risky decisions in the future.

What can be done to develop a good risk taker into an effective employee? The basic approach is to provide opportunities for risky behavior. Give the person a chance to fail so s/he can learn to function with uncertainty. The risk taker's manager can help reduce anxiety by letting the subordinate know the boss's support is present and that the boss will back up the risk taker's action. It is also important to match the risk taker with a job in which risk taking is appropriate. For example, if an organization has an accountant it wishes to develop as a risk taker, it would be a poor idea to place this person in the controller's office (where standard operating procedure is carefully followed). Placing this person in the auditor's office, on the other hand, would take advantage of the risk taker's less conventional searching behavior and could contribute substantially to the effectiveness of the auditing function.

DOGMATISM

A highly *dogmatic* person is closed-minded, while a low dogmatic individual is open-minded. If you are a highly dogmatic person, you possess a very rigid belief system and have difficulty considering ideas which are not consistent with these tightly held beliefs. You feel threatened by the environment and use your rigid views as a type of defense to specify the rules of acceptable operation. You tend to accept readily the authority position of others, perhaps because this helps define the structure of the world for you to follow. If the rules are not clear, you are uncomfortable and ineffective. In solving problems, you tend to consider only a small set of alternatives which fit your preexisting views of the world, make decisions quickly, and are highly confident about the appropriateness of these decisions. Because of your narrow view of the world, however, creative or innovative alternatives are unlikely to be considered—much less chosen. In short, a highly dogmatic person is good at following a rule book. When there is no rule book and decisions must be made without the guidance of a highly developed belief system which specifies how to behave, a highly dogmatic person functions poorly.

MACHIAVELLIANISM

If you have a *Machiavellian* personality, you believe that it is appropriate to behave in any manner which will meet your needs. Your primary focus is on obtaining and using power to further your own ends regardless of the impact on others. In short, you are not a team player. You contribute to the needs of organizations or individuals only to the extent that "There is something in it for me." This personality characteristic can be present to any degree, although moderate levels of Machiavellianism are more common than extreme levels.

Machiavellianism is named after Niccolo Machiavelli, who wrote *The Prince* over 450 years ago.[4] The concept has not died, however, as is witnessed by recent research and writing on the topic.[5] High Machiavellian personalities tend to operate with psychological detachment and little emotion. They are not easily influenced by others but effectively manipulate others through convincing lying and use of false praise, and by using any other tools available to meet their personal objectives.

Exhibit 9–2 presents some of the questions developed by Christie and Geis for Machiavellian-level measurement. Surprisingly, research has shown that a significant number of people score relatively high (Machiavellian) on this scale.

Exhibit 9–2 Measurement of Machiavellianism

	Strongly Disagree	Disagree	Neutral	Agree	Strongly Agree
1. The best way to handle people is to tell them what they want to hear.	1	2	3	4	5
2. One should take action only when sure it is morally right.*	1	2	3	4	5
3. There is no excuse for lying to someone else.*	1	2	3	4	5
4. It is safest to assume that all people have a vicious streak which will come out when given a chance.	1	2	3	4	5

*Reverse scored.
Source: Sample items based on Christie & Geis's Scale, R. Christie, and F. L. Geis, (Eds.) (1970). *Studies in Machiavellianism*, New York: Academic Press.

TYPE A AND TYPE B PERSONALITIES

A frequently used distinction in personality characteristics is Type A versus Type B.* A **Type A personality** works aggressively under pressure at an intense level with an impatient and competitive approach to others. In short, Type As choose to live high-pressure lives. The **Type B personality,** on the other hand, chooses and prefers a low-pressure life and is a more relaxed, easy-going, sociable person. Exhibit 9–3 illustrates some of the questions used to determine whether a person has a predominately Type A or Type B personality.

Effects of A versus B Personality Types

There are a number of well-documented effects of A versus B personality types.[6] Type A personalities usually work better alone. When working with others, they tend to be impatient and aggressive and often react strongly when intentionally or unintentionally provoked. They are better performers than Type Bs in work situations with time pressures. They work rapidly, producing a greater quantity of output. They are unlikely to be bothered by high demands,

*As is the case with the other personality traits, this characteristic varies along a continuum. In practice, however, this continuum is almost always used to classify persons as either Type A or Type B.

Exhibit 9–3 Measurement of Type A versus Type B Personalities

To find out which type you are, circle the number on the scale below that best characterizes your behavior for each trait.

1. Casual about appointments	1	2	3	4	5	6	7	8	Never late
2. Not competitive	1	2	3	4	5	6	7	8	Very competitive
3. Never feel rushed even under pressure	1	2	3	4	5	6	7	8	Always rushed
4. Take things one at a time	1	2	3	4	5	6	7	8	Try to do many things at once, think about what I am going to do next
5. Slow doing things	1	2	3	4	5	6	7	8	Fast (eating, walking, etc.)
6. Express feelings	1	2	3	4	5	6	7	8	"Sit" on feelings
7. Many interests	1	2	3	4	5	6	7	8	Few interests outside work

Total your score: ________________ Multiply it by 3: ________________

The interpretation is as follows:

Number of Points	**Type of Personality**
Less than 90	B
90 to 99	B +
100 to 105	A −
106 to 119	A
120 or more	A +

Source: Derived from A. P. Brief, R. S. Schuler, and M. Van Sell, *Managing job stress* (Boston: Little, Brown, 1981), p. 87; and from R. W. Bortner, A short rating scale as a potential measure of Pattern A behavior, *Journal of Chronic Diseases*, 1966, 87–91, copyright 1966 by Pergamon Press, Ltd.

since this matches their personality style. A significant area where Type Bs tend to excel is in situations involving long-term, problem-solving types of tasks. The Type B person is willing to take the time necessary to weigh the issues carefully, explore a wide range of alternatives, and make well-thought-out decisions. Type As are uncomfortable with this type of task, preferring instead to push on at a rapid pace and make quick decisions. For this reason, they may be less effective performers in policy-making top management positions which have long-term planning as a major component.

A major and well-documented difference between Type A and Type B personalities concerns physical health. Type As react more strongly to both physical and psychological stress and experience a much higher incidence of serious heart disease. They are like machines running at high rates of speed for a long period of time without sufficient rest. These machines are very effective while operating, but they are much more likely to suffer a catastrophic failure than machines operated at more reasonable rates.

ABILITY

The preceding chapters (5–8) have repeated that "Motivation alone is insufficient for obtaining performance. Appropriate ability also must be present." Performance motivation is the degree to which you *attempt* to perform, while **ability** is the degree to which you are *capable* of performing. For a given level of motivation, the more required abilities you have, the greater your level of performance.

INTELLECTIVE AND PHYSICAL ABILITIES

It is difficult to identify exactly how many distinct human abilities exist. Theorists and researchers have addressed this question

"I agree, Wimple. You do have a lot of drive, ambition and self-confidence. . . .But you haven't a spark of ability."

From *The Wall Street Journal*, with permission of Cartoon Features Syndicate from several different perspectives, thus producing several different "answers." Two representative and widely used approaches to classifying intellective and physical abilities follow. Together, they identify many of the wide range of human abilities.

Intellective Abilities

L. L. Thurstone, J. P. Guilford, and others contributed to the development of a cubical model like that of Exhibit 9–4 to identify the set of known **intellective abilities.**[7] This "structure of intellect" defines the unique abilities you need for performing well in certain mental activities. Three classification "facets" combine to define 90 specific abilities: *operations* (cognition, memory, divergent thinking, convergent thinking, and evaluation), *products* (units, classes, relations, systems, transformations, and implications), and *contents* (figural, symbolic, and semantic). It is possible to identify the set of intellective abilities most important to a particular job or task. It is

Exhibit 9–4 Structure of Intellect

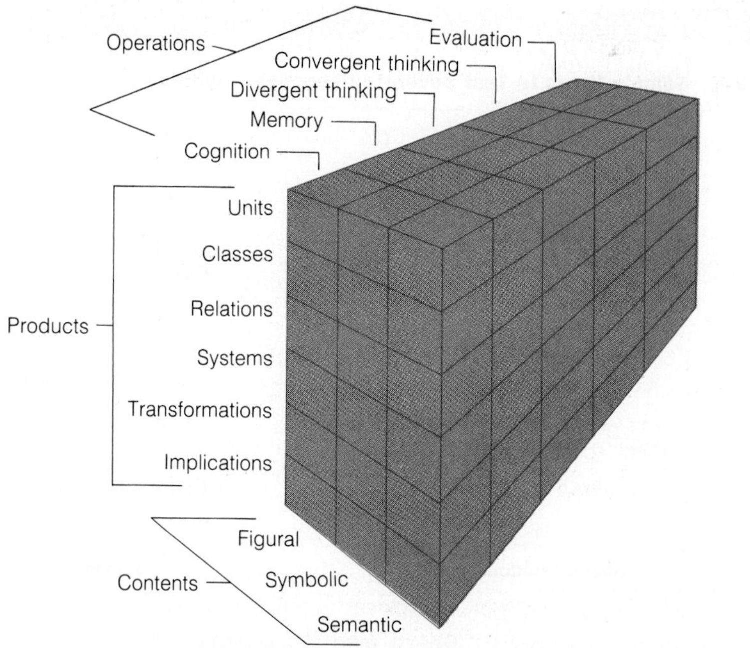

Source: J. P. Guilford, Three faces of intellect, *American Psychologist, 14,* 470, copyright 1959 by the American Psychological Association. Reprinted by permission of the author.

also possible to develop tests for each of these ability areas. In fact, tests currently exist for most, if not all, of these abilities. Exhibit 9–5 provides examples of items which can be used to test ability levels for several of the abilities included in the structure of intellect.

Physical Abilities

Edwin Fleishman of the Advanced Research Resources Organization in Washington, D.C., has been the most productive theorist/researcher in the area of **physical abilities.**[8] After examining the ability requirements of hundreds of jobs, Fleishman and his associates concluded that a general physical ability does not exist, but it is possible to identify nine basic physical abilities involved in the performance of any physical task (see Exhibit 9–6). You can determine the extent to which a job requires each of these by using a technique described by Fleishman as the "physical abilities analysis." Fleishman also developed a series of ability tests known as the "basic fitness tests" to identify the amount of each of these abilities possessed by a person.[9] Fleishman identified nine additional abilities required for the performance of such motor activities as machine operation: control precision, multilimb coordination,

Exhibit 9–5 Sample Items to Test Several Intellective Abilities

Symbolic Cognition	Semantic Cognition
Put vowels in the following blanks to make real words:	
P_W_R M_RV_L C_RT_N	Gravity means ______ Circus means ______ Virtue means ______
Symbolic Classes	**Semantic Classes**
Which letter group does not belong?	Which object does not belong?
XECM PVAA QXIN VTRO	Clam tree oven rose
Symbolic Relationships	**Semantic Relationships**
JIRE : KIRE : : FORA : ____	poetry : prose : : dance : ____

Source: Derived from J. P. Guilford, Three faces of intellect, *American Psychologist, 14,* 469–479, copyright 1959 by the American Psychological Association. Adapted by permission of the author.

Exhibit 9–6 Nine Basic Physical Abilities

Strength Factors	
1. Dynamic strength	Ability to exert muscular force repeatedly or continuously over time
2. Trunk strength	Ability to exert muscular strength using the trunk (particularly abdominal) muscles
3. Static strength	Ability to exert force against external objects
4. Explosive strength	Ability to expend a maximum of energy in one or a series of explosive acts
Flexibility Factors	
5. Extent flexibility	Ability to move the trunk and back muscles as far as possible
6. Dynamic flexibility	Ability to make rapid, repeated flexing movements
Other Factors	
7. Gross body coordination	Ability to coordinate the simultaneous actions of different parts of the body
8. Balance	Ability to maintain equilibrium despite forces pulling off balance
9. Stamina	Ability to continue maximum effort requiring prolonged effort over time

Source: Derived from E. A. Fleishman, Evaluating physical abilities required by jobs, *Personnel Administrator,* 1979, 82–92, copyright 1979 by The American Society for Personnel Administration, Berea, OH.

response orientation, timing, manual dexterity, finger dexterity, arm-hand steadiness, reaction time, and aiming.

INTERINDIVIDUAL VERSUS INTRAINDIVIDUAL ABILITY DIFFERENCES

Interindividual differences in abilities are differences across people regarding a particular ability. Your fellow students, for example, have different levels of verbal ability, quantitative ability, motor ability, etc. If the entire population were tested for ability level, the resulting pattern for most abilities would appear very much like that shown in Exhibit 9–7. As can be seen in Exhibit 9–7, a relatively small number of people have very low ability levels; the

Exhibit 9–7 Interindividual Differences in Ability

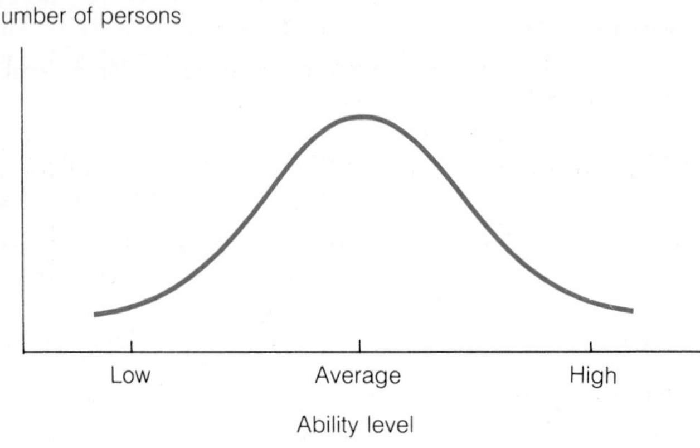

majority have ability levels which are about "average"; and a few individuals have very high levels of ability. This wide range of ability levels contributes heavily to differences in performance levels across people, even for people with similar motivation levels. Given two equally motivated persons (e.g., students, engineers, football players, politicians), the individual with the greater ability level will perform at a higher level. Ability and motivation are partially compensatory; a high level of motivation can "compensate for" a relatively low level of ability and vice versa (although at least a minimal amount of ability must be present or motivation will not help, no matter how high it is).

Intraindividual differences in abilities are differences within one person. There are two types, the first of which is a difference in ability level from one ability to another. For example, you may have a high verbal ability but a low quantitative ability. An individual tends to perform better on tasks which utilize his/her stronger abilities. The second type of intraindividual difference is a difference in the level of one ability within one person over time. Your current level of verbal ability, for example, is probably higher than it was 10 years ago. An individual tends to perform better on a particular task if s/he obtains increases in the required abilities.

TECHNIQUES FOR ABILITY MANAGEMENT

This discussion of abilities and performance is intended to increase your understanding of the role that ability plays in translating motivation into performance. If you utilize the motivation theories discussed in this book without regard for ability levels, you may be very disappointed in performance results. There is, however, a more important purpose for this discussion than the lowering of your expectations about using OB knowledge to enhance performance in organizations. You now have a general idea of the process involved in managing human abilities in organizations. The greatest potential for enhancing performance lies in the combined management of motivation and ability.

There are three major *techniques for ability management*: selection, placement, and training. Each of these takes advantage of one of the previously discussed differences in abilities. At times, two or more of these activities are performed concurrently. Selection and placement, for example, frequently are done at the same time.

Selection

Selection is the process of deciding which individuals to choose for membership in the organization. The first step in the selection process is for you to identify the abilities required for performance. Next you must assess candidates for selection (either formally or informally) to determine the degree to which they possess the necessary abilities. Finally, you choose those candidates with the appropriate ability levels for organizational membership. A full discussion of the selection process is beyond the scope of this book, but many techniques are used to carry out the selection process.[10] Some sort of job analysis usually is used to identify abilities required for job performance. Abilities of individual candidates are assessed through a variety of techniques including interviews, formal ability tests, and "assessment centers" which simulate a work-like situation.

Placement

Placement involves matching individuals with specific jobs. Taking advantage of intraindividual differences, you identify a person's strong points (high ability areas) and match that person to a job which requires similar abilities. Thus, you will place a given person into a job at which s/he is most likely to succeed.

Training

Training addresses the development of abilities for individuals who are already in the organization. Intraindividual differences also recognize that a particular person's ability level can change over time. In the training process, the organization compares the ability levels required by the job to the ability levels possessed by *current* job incumbents. Where improvement in abilities would enhance performance, training is provided to increase the level of required abilities and, thus, improve subsequent performance.

An Example of Ability Management

This example is based on a "real-life" experience with a group of statistical clerks in a moderate-sized insurance company. It illustrates the potential utility of ability management. Prior to the beginning of this study, the company used only informal techniques for selecting statistical clerks (e.g., interviews of a very general nature). Training was limited to a brief introduction to the work by a supervisor followed by assistance from co-workers when requested. Performance of the clerks averaged about 4.2 on a 7-point scale (4 was considered to be "acceptable," 5 was "good," 6 was "very good," etc.).

A procedure known as job analysis identified quantitative ability as one of the most important abilities for job performance. When existing employees took a brief test to assess their levels of quantitative ability, the results revealed a distribution very much like that shown in Exhibit 9–7 (with an average ability score of about 5 on a 10-point scale). This indicated that the organization apparently had been hiring employees without discriminating much on the basis of quantitative ability. Since both ability and performance scores were available for all employees, it was possible to examine the actual relationship between the two. This revealed a moderately strong relationship between the two (as expected). The diagonal line in Exhibit 9–8 shows that employees with higher ability levels tended also to have higher performance levels.

The organization immediately began to administer the ability test to all job applicants (at a cost of about $10 per applicant) and use the results of the test as one factor in the selection of employees. At the end of one year, the average quantitative ability of job incumbents had increased from about 5 to almost 6.7. At the same time, performance increased from 4.2 to 4.8 (almost a 15 percent increase; see Exhibit 9–8).

Encouraged by the program's results during the first year, the organization initiated a training program for all job incumbents (at a cost of about $200 per employee). The purpose of the training was to increase quantitative ability levels. Training consisted of a series of mathematical drills. Feedback was given to trainees and instructive suggestions provided. At the end of the training program, average ability had increased to 8.2, and performance had risen to an average of 5.3 (see Exhibit 9–8).

The company concluded that the selection and training programs had realized most of the performance improvement potential possible through ability increases (an overall performance increase of 26 percent). The next set of performance improvement programs focused on increasing motivation to encourage more effective use of existing high ability levels.

Exhibit 9–8 The Results of Ability Management

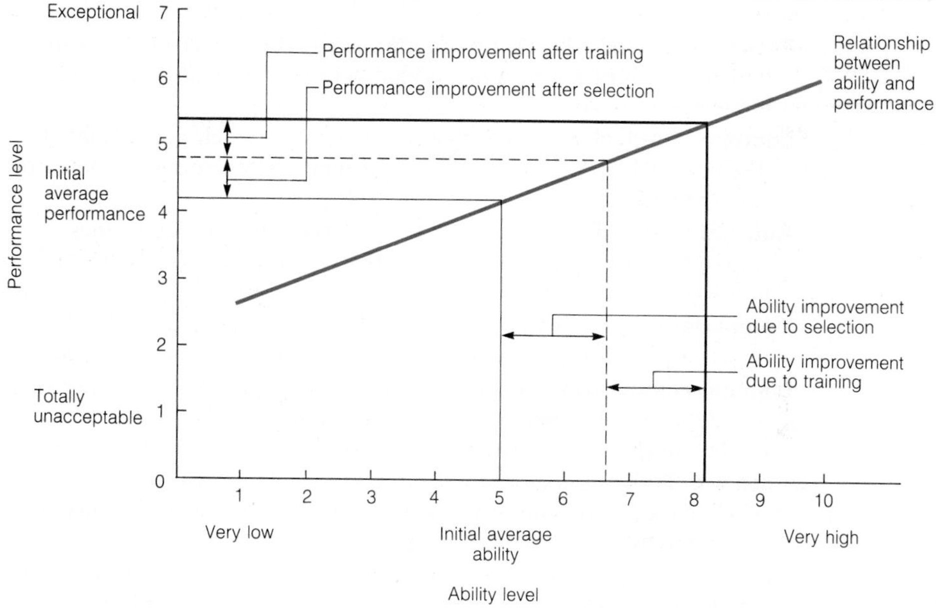

Source: Based on an unpublished study by Randall B. Dunham.

SUMMARY

From your personal experiences, you know that people vary widely in personality characteristics. You also know that people with different personalities often (but not always) behave differently when faced with the same situation. Although the brief and incomplete discussion of personality characteristics presented here cannot do justice to the tremendous volumes of theorizing and research on personality, you at least are aware of some of the personality factors important in organizational behavior. Knowing how these factors qualify organizational members' reactions to events can prove useful in choosing and utilizing management strategies.

Performance in an organization can be enhanced best by the joint management of motivation and abilities. The three basic ability management techniques identified briefly in this section, when combined, have the potential for effective management of abilities. Together, these techniques capitalize on ability differences existing across people and ability differences which exist within persons. This knowledge will be most useful to you if you remember that

Performance is a function of the interaction of motivation and ability:

$$\mathbf{P = f(M \times A)}.$$

GLOSSARY

Personality The collection of psychological characteristics or traits which determines a person's preferences and individual style of behavior.

Locus of Control A personality characteristic which determines the degree to which a person believes his/her actions influence outcomes experienced.

Authoritarianism A personality characteristic which determines the degree to which a person believes there should be clearly defined and followed status and power levels in organizations.

Dogmatism A personality characteristic which determines the degree to which a person is closed-minded, with a very rigid belief system.

Machiavellianism A personality characteristic which determines the degree to which a person focuses on obtaining and using power to further his/her own ends, regardless of the impact on others.

Type A/B Trait A personality characteristic which determines the degree to which a person chooses to work aggressively under pressure with an impatient and competitive approach to others.

Ability The degree to which a person is capable of performing a task.

Intellective Abilities Those abilities needed to perform mental activities.

Physical Abilities Those abilities needed to perform physical activities.

Interindividual Ability Differences Differences which exist across people on a particular ability.

Intraindividual Ability Differences Differences which exist within one person across time and/or from one ability to another.

Selection The process of deciding which individuals to choose for membership in the organization.

Placement The process of matching individuals with jobs.

Training The process of developing the abilities and skills of organizational members.

STUDY QUESTIONS

1. Many organizations utilize performance-based pay systems in hopes of motivating high performance. For what type of person would these systems work best, an individual with an internal locus of control or an external locus of control? Why?

2. In what type of organization would a highly dogmatic person be most likely to function effectively? Ineffectively?
3. Why would it be important for you as a manager to understand whether each of your subordinates has a Type A or Type B personality?
4. Discuss whether it would be appropriate for an organization to measure the personality characteristics of job candidates and use this information when making selection decisions.
5. Discuss why it is important to recognize that there exists a wide range of specific abilities as opposed to simply a general ability factor.
6. Discuss steps which an organization could take to coordinate and integrate the selection, placement, and training processes.
7. Would the relative importance of selection, placement, and training programs be the same in a young, rapidly growing organization as in an older, stable organization?
8. How can an individual member of an organization take advantage of interindividual and/or intraindividual differences in abilities to enhance his/her effectiveness in the organization?

NOTES

1. **Rotter, J. B.** (1966). Generalized expectancies for internal versus external control of reinforcement. *Psychological Monographs, 80,* 1–28.
2. Interesting papers include: **Anderson, C., Hellriegel, D., & Slocum, J.** (1977). Managerial response to environmentally induced stress. *Academy of Management Journal, 19,* 260–272; and **Mitchell, T., Smyser, C., & Weed, S.** (1975). Locus of control: Supervision and work satisfaction. *Academy of Management Journal, 17,* 623–631.
3. A classic description of the authoritarian personality is contained in book by **Adorno, T. W., Frenkel-Brunswich, E., Levinson, D. J., & Sanford, R. N.** (1950). *The authoritarian personality.* New York: Harper & Row.
4. **Machiavelli, N.** (1513). *The Prince.* (Written, but not published, in 1513.) English translations include: Adams, R. M. (1977). *The prince,* New York: W. W. Norton.
5. Recent work on Machiavellianism includes **Christie, R., & Geis, F. L.** (Eds.). (1970). *Studies in Machiavellianism,* New York: Academic Press; **Geis, F. L., & Moon, T. H.** (1981). Machiavellianism and deception. *Journal of Personality and Social Psychology, 41,* 766–775.
6. Examples of research on this issue include **Jenkins, C. D.** (1976). Recent evidence supporting psychological and social risk factors for coronary disease. *New England Journal of Medicine, 294,* 987–

994, 1033–1038; **Pittner, M. S., & Houston, B. K.** (1980). Response to stress, cognitive coping strategies, and the Type A behavior pattern. *Journal of Personality and Social Psychology, 39,* 147–157; **Burnam, M. A., Pennebaker, J. W., & Glass, D. C.** (1975). Time consciousness, achievement-striving, and the Type A coronary-prone behavior pattern. *Journal of Abnormal Psychology, 84,* 76–79; and **Glass, D. C., Snyder, M. L., & Hollis, J.** (1974). Time urgency and the Type A coronary-prone behavior pattern. *Journal of Applied Social Psychology, 4,* 125–140.

7. **Thurstone, L. L.** (1938). *Primary mental abilities.* Chicago: University of Chicago Press; **Guilford, J. P.** (1956). The structure of intellect. *Psychological Bulletin, 53,* 267–293; **Guilford, J. P.** (1967). Three faces of intellect. In D. N. Jackson & S. Messick (Eds.), *Problems in human assessment.* New York: McGraw-Hill, pp. 421–433.
8. **Fleishman, E. A.** (1979, June). Evaluating physical abilities required by jobs. *Personnel Administrator, 24,* 82–92; **Fleishman, E. A.** (1972). Structure and measurement of psychomotor abilities. In R. Singer (Ed.), *Psychomotor domain: Movement behaviors.* Philadelphia: Lea and Febiger; **Fleishman, E. A., & Hogan, J. C.** (1978, June). *A taxonomic method for assessing the physical requirements of jobs: The physical abilities analysis approach.* (Technical Report). Washington, DC: Advanced Research Resources Organization.
9. **Fleishman, E. A.** (1964). *Structure and measurement of physical fitness.* Englewood Cliffs, NJ: Prentice-Hall.
10. A good introduction to selection, placement, training, and other personnel issues is contained in a book by **Heneman, H. G., III., Schwab, D. P., Fossum, J. A., & Dyer, L. D.** (1983). *Personnel/Human resource management.* Homewood, IL: Irwin.

10 Perception

OVERVIEW
MAJOR COMPONENTS OF PERCEPTION
Sensation
Selection
Organization
Translation
REDUCING PERCEPTUAL ERRORS
Self-Understanding
Self-Acceptance
Conscious Information Processing
Reality Testing
SUMMARY

What is perceived as real is, in fact, real in its consequences.

W. I. Thomas

3 var
Phys char
Environ

OVERVIEW

Persons in organizations are bombarded constantly by thousands of visual, auditory, tactile, gustatory, and olfactory stimuli. You may, for example, be subjected to written messages, spoken questions, pats on the back, food and drink, and machine odors. By far, the most common response to sensory stimuli is to ignore the stimulus. Yet, somehow, you will choose a relatively small set of these stimuli to process. You will organize and interpret this subset of stimuli and react to the messages you receive.

Perception is the process by which you access information from the environment, organize it, and obtain meaning from it. Since it is *perceived* reality which people react to in organizations (and not necessarily an accurate representation of objective reality), it is essential that you fully comprehend the perceptual process if you wish to understand and influence attitudes and behaviors in organizations.

MAJOR COMPONENTS OF PERCEPTION

The perceptual process has four major components (see Exhibit 10–1): sensation, selection, organization, and translation. As you learn about each of these components, you soon will discover that three general categories of variables influence the overall perceptual process. Naturally, the actual *physical characteristics* of an object or event (the stimulus) influence your perception. Secondly, the *environment* in which the stimulus occurs has an influence (two objectively identical stimuli can produce very different results, de-

Exhibit 10–1 The Perceptual Process

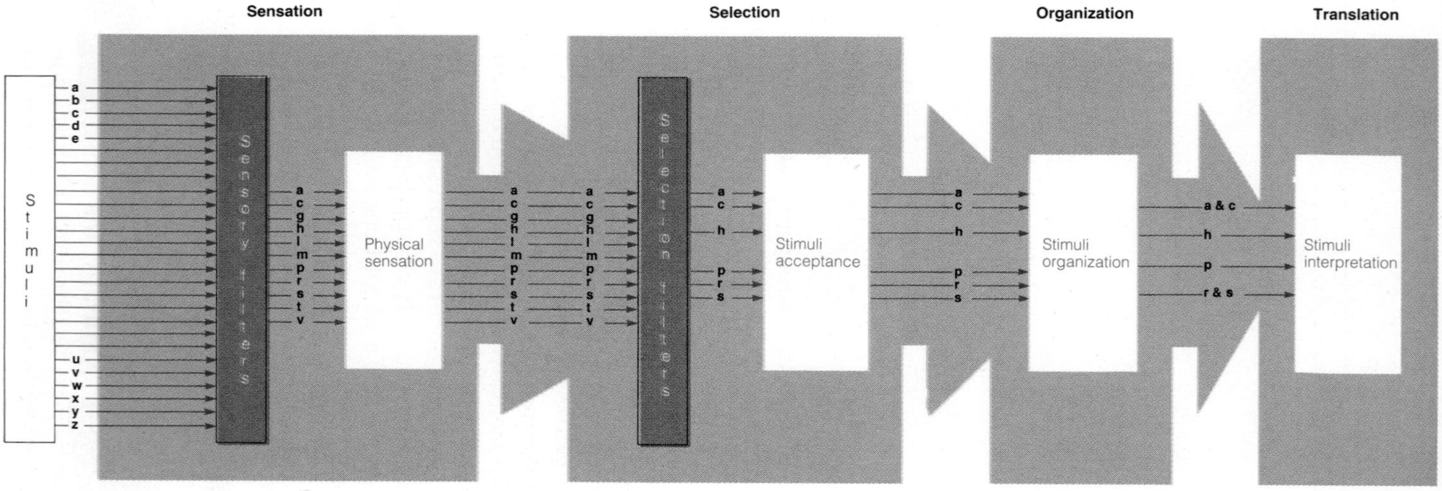

Sensation

Selection

Organization

Translation

Stimuli

a b c d e

u v w x y z

Sensory filters

a c g h l m p r s t v

Physical sensation

a c g h l m p r s t v

a c g h l m p r s t v

Selection filters

a c h p r s

Stimuli acceptance

a c h p r s

Stimuli organization

a & c h p r & s

Stimuli interpretation

pending on the circumstances surrounding their presentation). Finally, a variety of *your characteristics as the perceiver* are important. Two different people frequently perceive an identical object or event quite differently. Each of these factors will exert an influence at one or more stages of the perceptual process.

Sensation

A few of the many sensory stimuli you receive produce a physiological reaction of recognition. This reaction is known as **sensation.** Before you sense a stimulus, it must pass through a collection of sensory filters (see Exhibit 10–1). Stimuli which make it through all of your filters are sensed, while you have absolutely no reaction to those which are filtered out.

A variety of factors are involved in the filtering of stimuli. A stimulus will be filtered out, for example, if its intensity is below the threshold of the sensory organ involved. To be detected by the normal human eye, for example, a visual stimulus must be sufficiently intense to activate the rods and/or cones of the eye. Also, the sensory filters only allow stimuli within a certain range to pass. Thus, light will be filtered out and not sensed unless it falls within a frequency range from about 400 millimicrons (purple) through about 700 millimicrons (red). In addition, a stimulus can be masked by another stimulus, as is the case when bright sunlight makes it impossible to determine whether a small dim light is on or off. Finally, physical objects can act as sensory filters, as is the case with sunglasses and earplugs. Not everyone has identical sensory filters, as is witnessed by differences in visual acuity, hearing ability, etc. Furthermore, filters change somewhat even for a particular person (e.g., with age, fatigue). Thus, the sensation process is very personalized!

Once sensation has occurred, your *body* acknowledges the presence of the stimulus. The conscious (cognitive) portion of your *mind*, however, does not acknowledge the stimulus until the **selection** stage of the perceptual process.

Selection

After you sense a stimulus (and *only* if it has been sensed), it becomes a candidate for further processing. Of the many stimuli which succeed in being sensed, you choose only a few as worthy of conscious attention. This process of choosing certain stimuli for further processing is known as *selection*. The selection process involves the use of a collection of psychological filters (see Exhibit 10–1) to determine which stimuli you will accept and which you will reject.

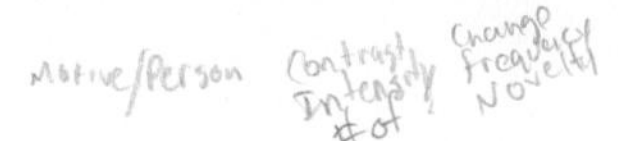

You become aware of those stimuli which are selected but remain consciously unaware of those which you reject.*

There are a number of factors influencing the selection process. Some of these are characteristics of the perceiver (e.g., your motives and personality).† Other influences stem from characteristics of the stimulus, such as contrast, frequency, intensity, change, number of stimuli, and novelty (see Exhibit 10–2 for an illustration of the influence of many of these factors). Together, these factors influence a major portion of the selection process.

Motives and Personality. Human **motives** and **personality** factors influence selection filters to make you more (or less) sensitive to certain types of stimuli. The probability of noticing stimuli such as food odors or pictures of food, for example, is influenced by your hunger level. If you are sexually deprived, you probably will notice many stimuli with sexual connotations. There is a strong likelihood of attending to job-threatening comments if you feel insecure about your job. Power seekers are more likely to notice power-related stimuli. Socially-oriented individuals pay attention to interpersonal stimuli. In short, you likely will notice stimuli relevant to current active motives and compatible with major personality characteristics.

Contrast. Stimuli which **contrast** with the surrounding environment are more likely to be selected for attention than stimuli which blend in. When you initially looked at this page, one of the first things you probably noticed was the word "contrast" boldly printed in a different color. You noticed this colored word primarily because it contrasted with the other words on the page. A contrasting effect can be caused by color, size, or any other factor which distinguishes one stimulus from others present. Your attention is drawn, not so much because of the characteristics of the stimulus per se, but because you are comparing these characteristics to those of surrounding stimuli. For example, the word "contrast" appears several times on this page, but only the contrasting appearance of the word jumped out at you. The contrast effect also explains why a person in

* Note that selection determines whether or not you become consciously aware of a stimulus. This is not the same as a noticing a stimulus but then consciously choosing to pay no attention to it. Such phenomena will be addressed at the translation stage of perception.

†Other characteristics of the perceiver which influence selection include stereotypes, perceptual halo, projection, perceptual readiness, selective perception, primacy/recency, and perceptual defense. Since these factors usually exert their major influence upon translation, they are discussed in a later section on translation.

Exhibit 10–2

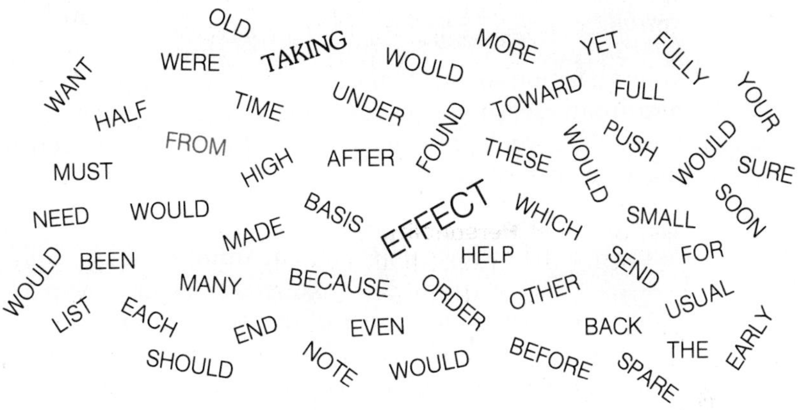

jeans stands out in a crowd of people wearing suits. There is nothing unusual about jeans but, when surrounded by suits, they stand out. This is why key terms are printed in boldface print throughout this text.

Frequency. The greater the **frequency** with which a sensory stimulus is presented, the greater the chances you will select it for attention. This should not be surprising, since repetition is one of the most common ways of getting your attention. Listen to some radio or TV commercials tonight, and you will discover what a popular advertising technique this is. There is one exception to the frequency rule which leads to a curvilinear relationship between frequency and the probability of attending. If a stimulus is presented an excessive number of times, you may choose to filter it out completely to avoid becoming irritated. This is what happened to the shepherd's boy in *Aesop's Fables* who cried wolf too often.

Intensity. The greater the **intensity** of a stimulus, the more likely you will notice it. In effect, an intense stimulus has more power to push itself through your selection filters than does a weaker stimulus. Thus, a shout is more attention-getting than a normal speaking voice, and you notice a bright light more than a dim one. A common advertising practice to get your attention (although the Federal Communications Commission disallows it, and broadcasters swear they never use it) is to raise the volume level during commercial messages.*

Change. You are more likely to notice a stimulus which shows **change** than one which remains constant. An animated sign gets your attention sooner than a fixed billboard does. A warning light at a railroad crossing is more effective when flashing. A professor who alters her speech patterns increases her chances of getting and keeping your attention.

Number of Stimuli. The greater the **number of stimuli** presented at one time, the less likely it is you will notice any one particular stimulus. Only a certain number of messages can make it through your selection filters at one time. This is in large part due to your information processing capacity. This filtering is also used as a coping mechanism to reduce the number of messages to a reasonable, comfortable level. The manager who gives a subordinate 20 instructions at once reduces the chances that the subordinate will pay attention to each. If a message is particularly important, you should present it in a situation where it will compete with few other stimuli for attention.

Novelty. You likely will notice a stimulus with **novelty** sooner than one you see on a fairly regular basis. Advertisers take advantage of the impact of novelty by creating a unique or original method for communicating information about a product or service. The contrast effect discussed earlier operates because of the *difference* between the characteristics of the stimulus object and the characteristics of surrounding objects. Thus, our person in jeans stood out in a crowd of people wearing suits (even though there is nothing particularly unique or unusual about wearing jeans). The novel stimulus, on the other hand, will get your attention regardless of the surrounding environment. A person with purple hair tends to stand out no matter what is being worn by others in the room (unless, of course, you are used to seeing people with purple hair). Frequently, a unique stimulus will produce both a novelty and contrast effect, but a stimulus which contrasts with other stimuli will not necessarily also produce a novelty effect. In a sense, a novelty effect is like a

---

*Students often ask "If intensity is so important, why is a whisper effective in getting my attention?" The answer lies in the fact that a whisper often contrasts with the rest of the noisy environment. This emphasizes the point that the selection factors discussed here often combine in a very complex fashion.

© King Features Syndicate, Inc., 1977. World rights reserved

macro-contrast: it contrasts with everything else in your perceptual experiences.

Other Considerations. The various factors influencing selection do not operate in a vacuum. It is common for more than one to be present at the same time (as is the case with frequently repeated, loud demands from a supervisor). Furthermore, there are no hard and fast rules about whether contrast is more powerful than repetition, or if intensity overpowers novelty, etc. Just be aware of the variety of techniques which can be used to influence the selection process and note that they may also influence other parts of the perceptual process (particularly translation). Getting people to pay attention to your message is one half of the problem; making sure they derive its desired meaning is the other.

Organization

After you have chosen a set of stimuli for further processing (selection), **perceptual organization** must occur to position them within a framework which will facilitate interpretation of their meaning. Although there are great individual differences in organizational strategies, several factors frequently influence the way stimuli are organized. These include similarity, proximity in space, proximity in time, figure-ground differentiation, closure, and continuity. The pattern of organization used can be very important, since stimuli which are grouped together tend to be recalled together. The meaning you attach to one stimulus tends to spill over and influence the meaning of stimuli stored nearby in your psychological filing cabinet.

Similarity. As you organize stimuli, you are more likely to group two stimuli together if they have physical **similarities.** What will happen, for example, if you receive three red memos, four green memos, and three blue memos? The chances are that, as you psychologically organize the 10 memos, you will mentally group them by color (whether or not the messages of the memos are related). In fact, color coding of memos is a common practice in organizations for this very reason. You also tend to group stimuli by size, intensity, and any other physically distinguishing characteristics.

Proximity in Space. Stimulus objects are often perceived to be related and grouped together because of **proximity in space.** Professors tend to associate two students who sit next to each other because of their physical closeness (be sure to sit next to a good student!). Several workers in an organization may be grouped together perceptually because they are located in nearby offices. In fact, objects which are physically grouped together often are perceived as being parts of a whole (e.g., a team, a department). Physical grouping of objects can be a useful technique for facilitating the recall of materials you wish to associate. Unintentional proximity will have a similar, but less desirable, effect.

Proximity in Time. Stimulus objects are frequently grouped together perceptually due to **proximity in time.** When you observe two objects or two events which occur at about the same point in time, you are more likely to group them together than if they occurred at very different points in time. It is hoped your organizational behavior lectures take advantage of this effect by presenting all information on one topic before presenting information about another. Imagine how difficult it would be to organize information if your professor randomly presented material from every topic covered by this course. Or, what if your supervisor said:

> I would like to give you some feedback about your performance during the last six months. The amount of work you have been completing is very impressive and places you as one of the most productive workers we have. The quality of your work is also good, although I would prefer that you slow down a bit and improve the quality of your

work even more. Overall, with only a few exceptions, I am very pleased with your work.

By the way, I saw you at the Club the other night. I didn't realize you were such a flashy dresser. You know, it is really interesting how differently people behave at a bar than they do at work. Hey, that reminds me. Is that person you were with the one you're married to?

Listen, I've got to run now. I just wanted to take a minute to give you some feedback about your performance. If you have any questions, let me know.

Did the information in the second paragraph above have any relationship to the information contained in the first paragraph? Was the boss trying to tell you something about your off-the-job behavior and its relevance to your work? Whether the boss was trying subtly to make a point or clumsily confusing performance feedback with casual conversation, it is likely that you will organize these two pieces of information together perceptually because they were presented to you at the same time. You probably would not do this if your boss had made the two sets of comments on two different days.

Figure-Ground Differentiation. Your psychological storage and subsequent interpretation of information will be affected by whether you classify the information as *figure* or background (*ground*). Typically, information you classify as figure is assigned more importance than that which you view simply as background. The overall meaning you assign to a stimulus also will be influenced by your treatment of figure and ground relationships. Exhibit 10–3 presents a classic example of the importance of **figure-ground differentiation**. The organization (and interpretation) of this ambiguous figure changes substantially, depending on whether the white portion of the figure is organized as the figure or as the ground. To see this effect, first concentrate on the white portion of the figure and then on the colored portion.

People differ in the degree to which they perceive stimuli (figures) independent of the background. This is known as your level of field (ground) independence and can have a major impact on the way you perceive organizational factors. Gene Stone of New York University, for example, showed that workers who are "field independent" are more sensitive to job characteristics.[1] Field independents, therefore, may react more strongly to job design (see Chapter 15).

Closure. The tendency to organize perceptual stimuli so that, together, they form a complete message is known as **closure.** Although you probably are most familiar with *visual* examples of closure (see Exhibit 10–4), such effects can occur with verbal stimuli ("You

Exhibit 10–3 Figure-Ground Illustration

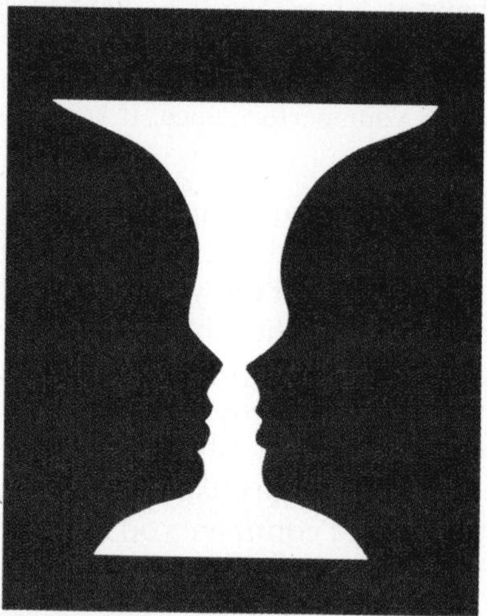

make me so mad, I could just ____________!") or any other type of stimulus.

The organization phase of the perceptual process is the first point at which you begin to manipulate perceptual information. Although interpretation per se is not performed at this stage of the perceptual process, the organization you do here has a major influence on your subsequent interpretation of stimuli. Since people learn and use very different organizational strategies, they organize the same information in very different ways. Look at the ways you organize your class notes, your clothes, etc. Compare your methods with those of your roommate or a friend. Your perceptual organizational patterns undoubtedly vary just as much as your strategies for arranging these physical items.

Translation

At the **translation** stage of the perceptual process, you interpret and gain meaning from stimuli. A reexamination of Exhibit 10–1 reveals that relatively few of the sensory stimuli presented to you progress to the stage where you interpret them. Furthermore, you organize the stimuli you interpret into a particular pattern prior to

Exhibit 10–4 Closure Illustration

Source: Reprinted with permission from *Introduction to psychology: Explorations and applications* by Dennis Coon, Copyright © 1977 by West Publishing Company. All rights reserved.

the beginning of interpretation. The total perceptual process is influenced by: the objective characteristics of the stimulus object (e.g., intensity), the environment in which the object exists (e.g., contrast), and your characteristics as the perceiver (e.g., personality). Translation also is influenced by each of these factors.

Of particular interest to organizations are several phenomena which frequently influence the translation part of the perceptual process (stereotypes, halo effects, projection, perceptual readiness, primacy/recency, perceptual defense, and attribution). Each of these phenomena impacts on the meaning you attach to stimulus objects. Frequently, these phenomena cause your interpretation of a stimulus to depart from objective reality much as optical illusions can distort your evaluation of visual stimuli (see Exhibit 10–5). Since you can react only to your perceived reality, and the only avenue of communication in organizations involves the perceptual process, it is critical that organizations pay significant attention to the entire perceptual process.

Stereotype. Frequently, you receive information about a person (or any other stimulus object) which causes you to believe that the person is a member of an identifiable group (e.g., social, racial, ethnic). When your perceptions of that person are influenced by your gen-

Exhibit 10–5 Common Optical Illusions

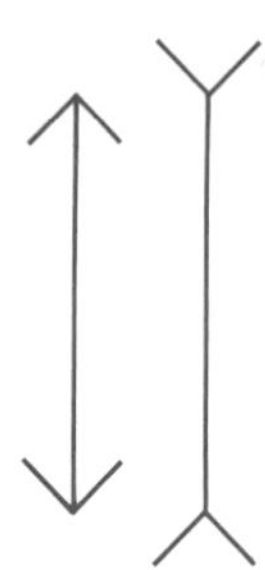

Which vertical line is longer? Measure them.

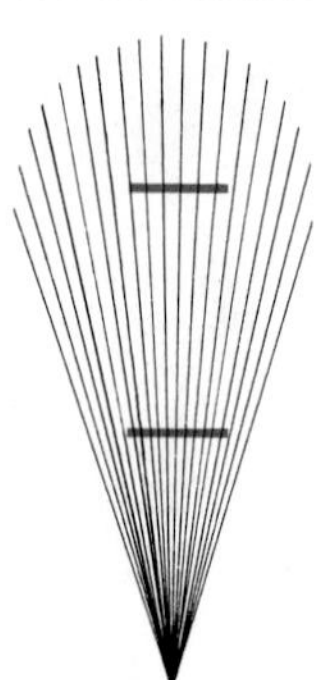

Which horizontal line is longer? Measure them.

eral beliefs about members of that group, a **stereotype** effect has occurred.* Stereotypes frequently are based on sex, race, age, religious group, nationality, occupation, etc. When a stereotype operates, you draw conclusions concerning certain characteristics of a person, even though you have no direct information to support these conclusions.

An interesting example of the impact of a stereotype was documented by Mason Haire.[2] In this study, two groups of people were presented a description about an individual. The descriptions provided of this person differed in only one way: one group was told that the person was a manager while the other was told he was a union representative. Despite the fact that every other piece of information about the person was identical, over 70 percent of the group told that the person was a manager described him as honest. Only 50 percent described the union representative as honest. Whether or not union representatives are less honest than managers, perceptions of honesty were influenced by the stereotype.

Everyone forms stereotypes even though they seldom are aware of it. Think about the people described in the following sketches:

After Jane received her MBA degree in finance, she accepted a job with IBM.

---

*Although a stereotype can influence both perceptual selection and organization, its major effect is at the translation stage.

Sarah attended a private school in upstate New York starting in the sixth grade and is now a senior at a very expensive private college.

Bill has been a member of the Teamster's Union since 1943. Since 1969 he has been an elected official of the local union.

John was the captain of his high school football and basketball teams and is currently a starter on the Texas A & M football team.

Craig is 80 pounds overweight.

Form an overall impression about each of the people described above. Then reread the *facts* about each person and determine just how much of your overall impression of each is based on actual information about the person as opposed to stereotypes which you hold.

Stereotypes are shortcuts for classifying people. It takes much less time to stereotype a person than to obtain all of the information needed to form a judgment based on facts. All stereotypes are learned, some through direct experience with members of the stereotype group. Many more are acquired through social learning (see Chapter 6) and are particularly vulnerable to inaccuracies. Stereotypes are not always inaccurate or negative, however. Most jocks really are in good physical condition; many engineers do have very good quantitative skills; most corporate executives really are highly motivated.

Halo Effect. Sometimes, when you form a general impression of an individual, it inordinately influences your perceptions about specific characteristics for which you have little, if any, direct information. Frequently, this general impression, or **halo effect,** is based on information about a single characteristic of that person. The halo effect, which can be positive or negative (a reverse halo), is another shortcut for making judgments quickly. Halo effects are not always inaccurate, although they probably are more often wrong than right.[3] Common examples of halo effects include: the worker who is always 10 minutes early and perceived by the boss to be competent, the attentive student who is perceived by the professor to be learning a lot, the employee with poor personal hygiene whom co-workers believe to be a poor performer.

Barry Nathan and Robert Lord of the University of Akron recently conducted an interesting study on the impact halo effects have on college students as they rate the performance of lecturers.[4] In this study, the authors created a halo by showing students videotaped lectures which reflected either favorable or unfavorable overall performance. Students were then asked to rate a variety of specific performance dimensions (some of which were consistent with the halo and some of which were inconsistent). The results indicated that both the halo effect and actual behavior on the specific dimensions influenced the ratings of performance:

> behavioral manipulation within dimensions was inconsistent with an overall impression of the lecturer, true behavioral differences between tapes were suppressed by (halo).[5]

Projection. The process which causes you to see your own characteristics in other people is known as **projection.** The most common use of this phenomenon is to project your negative traits onto others. The projection of negative traits often serves as a defense mechanism against admitting to yourself that *you* possess such negative traits. Thus, cheaters perceive others to be cheaters; liars perceive others as liars; irresponsible individuals see others as irresponsible. Not everyone, however, projects only negative traits. It is not uncommon for happy people to see others as happy, motivated individuals to perceive motivation in others, etc.

Perceptual Readiness. A common phenomenon in perception is **perceptual readiness** (sometimes called "expectancy"). This process causes you to perceive a stimulus object consistent with your expectations. If you expected your OB class to be boring, you are more likely to perceive it as boring than if you had expected it to be interesting and exciting. Perceptual readiness is based on learned expectations. You may have taken a behavioral course in the past and found it to be boring, or perhaps other students who have taken OB told you it would be boring. As is the case with the other factors discussed in this section, perceptual readiness causes you to interpret a stimulus based on factors other than the observed characteristics of that stimulus.

The best-known research on perceptual readiness (and perhaps most controversial for ethical reasons) was conducted by Robert Rosenthal and his associates.[6] In this research, teachers of grade school students were told that certain students possessed greater intellectual capacity than other students (even though no real differences existed). In subsequent interaction with the "bright" students, teachers perceived signs of greater intelligence and higher performance. The teachers saw what they expected. Such effects also have been documented with negative expectations (persons expected to be troublemakers are often perceived as such, whether or not this is justified by the facts).

It is interesting to note that perceptual readiness often leads to a self-fulfilling prophecy in which a person actually begins to develop the characteristics perceived. Follow-up research in the Rosenthal studies revealed that, over time, the "bright" students showed actual increases in intellectual capacity while the other students remained unchanged. The explanation for this self-fulfilling prophecy apparently lies in the fact that teachers behaved differently toward the students who were perceived as more intelligent. In doing so, they sparked additional intellectual development. Similar effects can be expected in organizations: an employee reported to have "outstanding promise" develops into a superior employee compared to employees for whom no such expectations are present.

Robert Dipboye of Rice University has developed a model which deals with perceptual readiness and the self-fulfilling prophecy in the selection interview.[7] This model (see Exhibit 10–6) identifies a variety of ways in which preinterview expectations can influence significantly: the way an interviewer conducts the interview, an interviewee's perceptions of the interviewer's expectations, an interviewee's behavior in the interview, and an interviewer's perceptual selection, organization, and translation processes. For example, if you interview two job candidates with comparable qualifications, you probably will form a more positive impression of the candidate for whom you had higher expectations prior to the interview.

You probably will be interviewing for a job in the not-too-distant future. How will your interviewer react to you during the interview? Naturally, your behavior during the interview will influence the evaluation made of you and your qualifications. Beyond this, however, the expectation which your interviewer brings into the interview probably will play an important role. If a particularly well-prepared résumé or a complimentary call from one of your references creates a positive impression of you prior to the interview, you may be evaluated more positively than if the interviewer has a less positive level of expectation.

Primacy/Recency Effects. In the translation stage of perception, you form impressions of stimulus objects based on information obtained at various points in time. The point in time at which you collect a particular piece of information influences the relative impact which that information has on your overall impression. The most common time-related effect of this type is **primacy.** The primacy effect causes you to weight first impressions very highly. Thus, your reaction to the first day of class, a first date, or the first week on the job will have a strong and lasting effect on your overall reactions. You are likely to see subsequent information about the stimulus object con-

Exhibit 10–6 A Model of the Self-Fulfilling Prophecy in the Interview

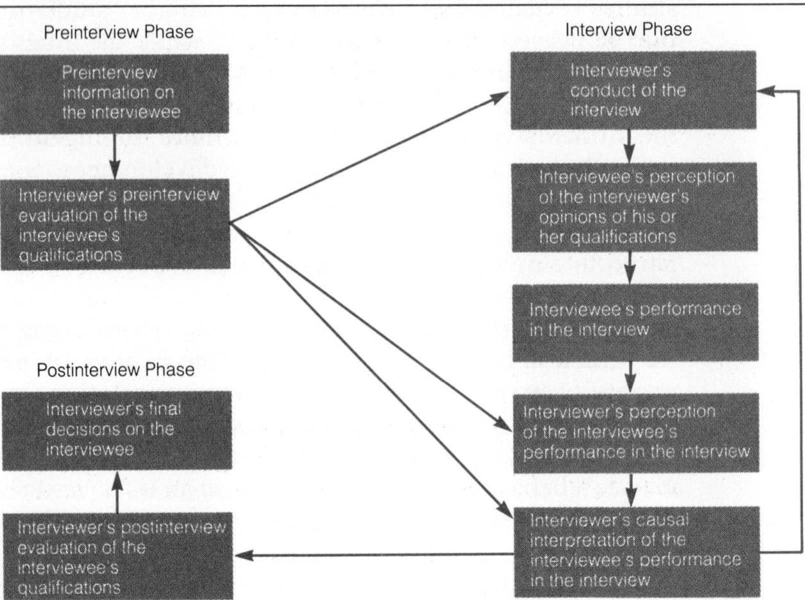

Source: Robert L. Dipboye (1982). Self-fulfilling prophecies in the selection-recruitment interview. *Academy of Management Review, 7,* 579–586.

sistent with your first impression, and if inconsistency is observed, you will tend to favor your first impression. The second most common time-related effect on perception is a **recency** effect (or last impression). Although the importance assigned to last impressions seldom approaches that of first impressions, you weight most heavily the most recent information you receive. Try the following:

If you have been dating one person for some time, try to recall your first date. Your most recent date. Your 12th date.

If you currently hold a job, recall your first day on the job. Your most recent day. Your 83rd day.

So far, this section of the book has described five factors which influence perceptual translation. What was the first factor discussed? The most recent? The third?

Primacy and recency effects can produce nonrepresentative overall perceptual impressions. This is often the case with performance appraisals and job interviews.

Perceptual Defense. Once you have developed reactions to a stimulus object, you are likely to defend these reactions against new information which would conflict with your existing impressions. This process of **perceptual defense** is performed by: denying the existence or importance of conflicting information, distorting the new information to match the old, or acknowledging the existence of the new information but treating it as a nonrepresentative exception.[8] The manager who says "Women don't make good managers. Yes, I know Paula is a good manager but she is an exception. I still don't think women make good managers." is using perceptual defense to protect a stereotype. Thus, even in the face of facts to the contrary, the existing perception is defended.

Attribution. You receive many perceptual stimuli from your observations of a person's behavior. The **attribution** process plays a particularly important role in the way you interpret these stimuli.[9] Your perception of a person will depend to a large extent on whether you attribute the observed behavior to internal causes (e.g., abilities, motives, or traits) or to external causes (e.g., luck or situational factors). If you attribute the cause of a person's behavior to external causes, that behavior will have relatively little impact on the perception you form about that person. After all, if the observed behavior was due to external factors beyond the person's control, the behavior tells you more about the external factors than about the person. On the other hand, if you attribute the cause of the observed behavior to the person (and his/her abilities, motivation, etc.), this information will influence your perceptions of the person.

Suppose, for example, you notice one of your subordinates performing at a low level. Will this cause you to conclude that this person is a poor employee? It will, if you attribute the cause of poor performance to internal factors such as insufficient effort or inadequate ability. If, on the other hand, you attribute the cause of the poor performance to external factors such as equipment malfunctions or inadequate materials, you are less likely to conclude that this is a poor employee. Thus, a particular piece of information (poor performance) could be interpreted as information about a person or about a situation, depending on the causal attribution you make.

Recently a distinction has been drawn for internal attributions which suggests that it is important to consider whether internal attributions focus on ability or effort (both internal factors). William Knowlton, Jr., of the U.S. Military Academy and Terence Mitchell of the University of Washington hypothesized that supervisor evaluations of subordinate performance will be more

Exhibit 10–7 Predicted Performance Evaluations

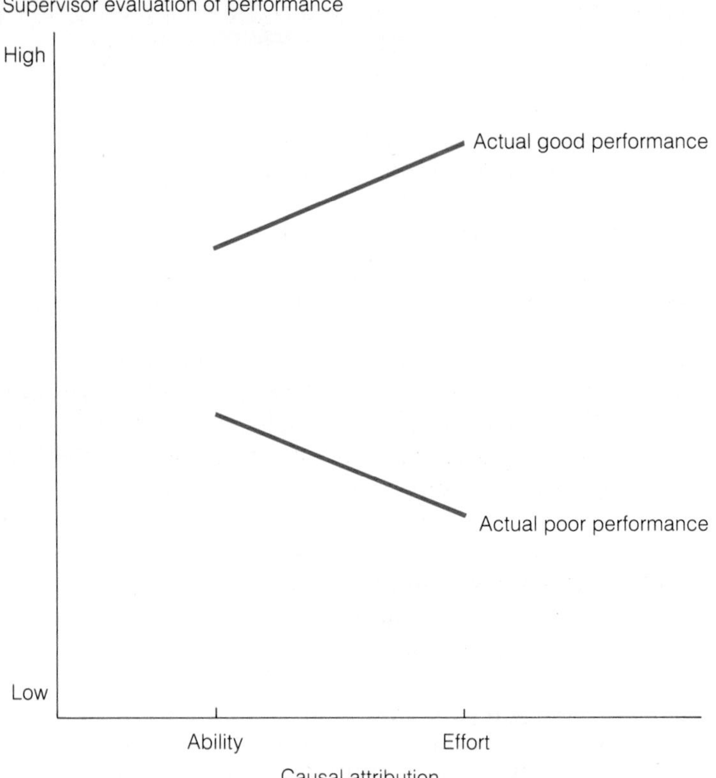

Source: Derived from W. A. Knowlton, Jr., and T. R. Mitchell, Effects of causal attributions on a supervisor's evaluation of subordinate performance, *Journal of Applied Psychology, 65,* 460, copyright 1980 by the American Psychological Association. Adapted by permission of the publisher and author.

extreme if the supervisor attributes performance to effort rather than ability (see Exhibit 10–7).[10] This probably is due to the fact that supervisors feel a subordinate has relatively little direct control over his/her ability level but has very direct control over effort level. The results of a study designed to test their hypothesis supported these predictions. Workers with identical high performance levels were evaluated more positively by supervisors when the high performance was attributed to effort rather than ability. Likewise, poor performers were evaluated more negatively when low performance was attributed to effort.

Almost 30 years ago, Heider argued that most observers tend to attribute the behavior of others to internal causes (even in cases where this is not appropriate).[11] Recent research has supported this.[12] Excessive attributions to internal causes will distort your overall impressions of others. To enhance the accuracy of your perceptual translations, you should make an attempt to determine whether the behavior you observe in others is internally or externally caused.

REDUCING PERCEPTUAL ERRORS

When you react to organizational policies, practices, and events, you are actually reacting to your perceptions of these factors. For reasons just discussed, your perceptions may be incomplete, nonrepresentative, or inaccurate when compared to reality. The majority of this book deals with techniques for managing policies, practices, and events to enhance worker reactions to the organizational experience. Because of the fact that the perceptual process may distort your reactions to organizational reality, organizations must manage perceptions as well as policies, practices, and events. Failure to do so will result in a loss of predictability of the probable impact of these organizational actions. Reexamine Exhibit 10–1 to review the many transformations which take place between objective reality and perceived reality.

What steps can you take to reduce perceptual errors? Although there is no simple answer to this question, you can try the following:[13]

Self-Understanding

Self-understanding means you acknowledge your susceptibility to perceptual errors caused by stereotypes, halo effects, etc. Because these perceptual shortcuts tend to function subconsciously, simply being aware of their dangers is the first major step toward defeating them. Careful attention to the perceptual process and a conscious awareness of the role of factors such as stereotypes increases the match between reality and your perceptions.

Self-Acceptance

Self-acceptance means you understand that you are not perfect (yet!), and that even you possess some undesirable traits and characteristics. If you are able to do this, your need for the use of projection will be greatly reduced.

Conscious Information Processing

You must carefully and consciously examine the "facts" during the perceptual process. Thus, at the selection stage of perception,

Bruce W. Hamstra is managing director in the Educational Services Department of the Life Insurance Marketing and Research Association (LIMRA). LIMRA, located in Hartford, Connecticut, is a trade association in the insurance industry.

How much impact does the perceptual process have on the accuracy of interviews? Potentially, a great deal. A wide range of factors, such as halo effects, stereotypes, primacy and recency effects, all play a role. To be an effective interviewer, a person must be able to spot and confront these problems.

What can an organization do to help an interviewer deal with perceptual problems during the interview? LIMRA has developed a programmatic approach to training interviewers. One of the keys of this program is to separate the task of collecting information from that of evaluating the meaning of the information. We stress that the purpose of the interview is to collect facts about the candidate. Furthermore, we strongly emphasize the need for a structured interview guide to be followed during the interview to ensure that the same questions are asked of each candidate. Only after the interview is completed should the facts and the candidate be evaluated.

Do you have a specific training program for interviewers? Yes, we offer a one-day program which follows what we refer to as the **PESOS** plan. First, we **P**repare the student by discussing the need for this training and offering an overview of the issues to be covered, including the perceptual biases of typical interviewers. Next, we **E**xplain through readings and "lectures" the relevant issues and describe appropriate interviewing techniques. Then, we **S**how the student examples of interviews using audio and videotapes, after which the students evaluate the strengths and weaknesses of these interviews. Following this, we provide students with information on a "job candidate" and have each student conduct an interview with that person. During the interview, the trainer and other students **O**bserve and evaluate the strengths and weaknesses of the interview, providing feedback on interviewing skills. After a final wrap-up, the students return to their respective insurance companies where they conduct interviews using their new skills. To follow up on their interviewing effectiveness, we continue to **S**upervise them. Typically, a member of their own insurance company who is highly skilled at interviewing will observe the former student during actual on-the-job interviews and evaluate his/her effectiveness. Ideally, this follow-up would be conducted immediately after completion of our program and then again after 6 to 12 months.

you document and systematically select the specific pieces of information you need. At the organization stage, you examine the selected information and arrange it for future recall according to its meaning (rather than on the basis of physical similarity, temporal proximity, etc.). At the translation stage you focus on information directly relevant to the issue at hand as opposed to irrelevant factors such as the sex or race of a person involved. In short, the use of **conscious information processing** makes the subconscious perceptual process a more cognitive and precise activity.

Reality Testing

Reality testing can be a very effective technique for determining whether your perceptions are accurate by comparing your perceptions about a stimulus object to some other measure of that object. One of the most common methods is to compare your perceptions to those formed by a different person with a different perspective on the same issue. You could, however, compare your perceptions to those of another person, find they match, conclude that your perceptions are accurate, and still be wrong. The obvious limitation is that the other person may share some of your perceptual problems (such as stereotypes). So, comparison of your perceptions to those of another is useful, but more of a measure of reliability than of validity (see Chapter 2 for a discussion of reliability and validity). Reality testing also can be performed by comparing your perceptions to one or more objective measures of the object being perceived. For example, you could count how many widgets an employee produces per day, the number of those widgets returned for repair within 30 days, and compare your perception of his/her performance to these actual numbers. Comparison of your perceptions to an objective measure such as this is one form of validity assessment.

Reality testing is most useful for determining whether your perceptions *may* be in error or *may* be accurate. Unless the stimulus object under consideration has measurable physical characteristics (such as weight, color, or size), a reality test cannot *prove* accuracy or inaccuracy. Reality testing does, however, make you more aware of the perceptual process and helps to focus your attention on potential perceptual problems.

SUMMARY

The total perceptual process has four distinct stages: sensation, selection, organization, and translation. Each stage is influenced by: the actual objective characteristics of the stimulus object, the environment in which the object exists, and the characteristics of the perceiver. It is unlikely your perceptions will be exactly "correct," but you can take definite steps to increase the accuracy of your perceptions and the perceptions of others within the organization. Because of the pervasive impact of perception on attitudes and behaviors, it is imperative that both individuals and organizations recognize and deal with the issues involved in the perceptual process.

GLOSSARY

Perception The process by which a person organizes and obtains meaning from the sensory stimuli s/he receives from the environment.

Sensation The physiological recognition of a sensory stimulus.

Selection The process a person uses to eliminate some of the sensory stimuli which have been sensed and retain others for further processing.

Motives/Personality and Selection Stimuli which are relevant to current motives and compatible with personality characteristics are more likely to be selected for perceptual processing.

Contrast The difference between one stimulus and surrounding stimuli which makes that stimulus more likely to be selected for perceptual processing.

Frequency The repetition which makes a stimulus more likely to be selected for perceptual processing.

Intensity The forcefulness which enhances the likelihood that a stimulus will be selected for perceptual processing.

Change The variety causing a stimulus to be selected for perceptual processing.

Number of Stimuli The amount of stimuli present (the fewer the number, the more likely a particular stimulus will be selected for perceptual processing).

Novelty The uniqueness of a stimulus.

Perceptual Organization The process of placing selected perceptual stimuli into a framework for "storage."

Similarity The physical resemblance of some stimuli which causes them to be associated during perceptual organization.

Proximity in Space The physical nearness of stimuli to one another during perceptual organization.

Proximity in Time When one stimulus is observed at about the same point in time as another.

Figure-Ground Differentiation The tendency to distinguish and focus on a stimulus which is classified as figure as opposed to background (ground).

Closure The tendency to organize perceptual stimuli so that, together, they form a complete message.

Translation The stage of the perceptual process at which stimuli are interpreted and given meaning.

Stereotype The impact on perception caused by the perceiver's belief that a person is a member of an identifiable group (e.g., social, racial, ethnic).

Halo Effect The way a favorable (or unfavorable) perception of one characteristic influences perception of other characteristics.

Projection The process which causes a person to perceive his/her own characteristics in other people.

Perceptual Readiness The process which causes a person to perceive a stimulus object consistent with his/her expectations.

Primacy/Recency Effect The disproportionately high weight given to the first (primacy) or last (recent) information obtained about a stimulus object.

Perceptual Defense The way a person retains existing perceptions in spite of new information which would conflict with existing perceptions.

Attribution The degree to which a perceiver's overall perception of a person is influenced by his/her evaluation as to the cause of the observed person's behavior (i.e., external or internal).

Self-Understanding Acknowledgement by a person that s/he is susceptible to perceptual errors.

Self-Acceptance An understanding by a perceiver that s/he possesses some undesirable traits and characteristics.

Conscious Information Processing A deliberate examination of stimulus objects during the perceptual process.

Reality Testing A comparison of perceptions of a stimulus object to other information about the object (e.g., another person's perceptions, objective "facts," etc.).

STUDY QUESTIONS

1. Discuss some of the differences across people in sensitivity to sensation of perceptual stimuli. Why are these differences important to an organization?
2. Discuss examples of factors in organizations which encourage members to select appropriate stimuli for further processing. Discuss factors which unintentionally discourage appropriate selection.
3. What undesirable consequences could result if an organization focuses too much on influencing perceptual attendance without considering the effects on translation?
4. Discuss techniques an organization (or individual) could use to facilitate effective perceptual organization.
5. Discuss organizational practices which often interfere with effective perceptual organization.
6. Describe an organizational situation in which the accuracy of perceptions is distorted by each of the following: stereotypes, halo effect, projection.

7. Discuss the steps which you could take as a manager to reduce perceptual errors as you appraise the performance of your subordinates.
8. If you wish to manage effectively the perceptual process, why is it necessary to distinguish between sensation, selection, organization and translation?

NOTES

1. **Stone, E. F.** (1979). Field independence and perceptions of task characteristics: A laboratory investigation. *Journal of Applied Psychology, 64,* 305–310.
2. **Haire, M.** (1965). Role-perception in labor-management relations: An experimental approach. *Industrial and Labor Relations Review, 8,* 204–211, p. 208.
3. A comprehensive evaluation of the differences between valid and invalid halo effects is contained in a recent paper by C. J. Bartlett. (1983) of the University of Maryland: What's the difference between valid and invalid halo? Forced-choice measurement without forcing a choice. *Journal of Applied Psychology, 68,* 218–226.
4. This study was the the first author's master's thesis: **Nathan, B. R., & Lord, R. G.** (1983). Cognitive categorization and dimensional schemata: A process approach to the study of halo in performance ratings. *Journal of Applied Psychology, 68,* 102–114. The results discussed here are but one part of a sophisticated paper which explored the processes involved in performance rating in some detail.
5. **Nathan & Lord,** (1983) p. 108.
6. **Rosenthal, R., & Jacobsen, L.** (1968). *Pygmalion in the classroom.* New York: Holt, Rinehart & Winston.
7. **Dipboye, R. L.** (1982). Self-fulfilling prophecies in the selection-recruitment interview. *Academy of Management Review, 7,* 579–586.
8. **Bruner, J. S., & Postman, L.** (1947). Emotional selectivity in perception and reaction. *Journal of Personality, 16,* 69–77; **Haire, M., & Grunes, W. F.** (1950). Perceptual defenses: Processes protecting an organized perception of another personality. *Human Relations, 3,* 403–412.
9. Some of the earliest work on attribution theory was conducted by **Heider, F.** as reported in Social perception and phenomenal causality. *Psychological Review,* 1944, *51,* 358–374, and *The psychology of interpersonal relations,* New York: Wiley (1958). One of the most popular papers on the topic was authored by **Kelley, H. H.** (1967).

Attribution theory in social psychology. In D. Levine (Ed.), *Nebraska symposium on motivation,* Lincoln: University of Nebraska Press. A thorough review of the issue is contained in **Kelly, H. H., & Michela, J. L.** (1980). Attribution theory and research. *Annual Review of Psychology, 31,* 457–501.

10. **Knowlton, W. A., Jr., & Mitchell, T. R.** (1980). Effects of causal attributions on a supervisor's evaluation of subordinate performance. *Journal of Applied Psychology, 65,* 459–466.
11. **Heider,** 1958.
12. See, for example, **Jones, E. E., & Nisbett, R. E.** (1972). The actor and the observer: Divergent perceptions of the causes of behavior. In E. E. Jones, D. E. Kanouse, H. H. Kelley, R. E. Nisbett, S. Valins, & B. Weiner (Eds.), *Attribution: Perceiving the causes of behavior.* Morristown, NJ: General Learning Press.
13. See **Zalkind, S. S., & Costello, T. W.** (1962). Perception: Some recent research and implications for administration. *Administrative Science Quarterly, 7,* 227–229.

Part

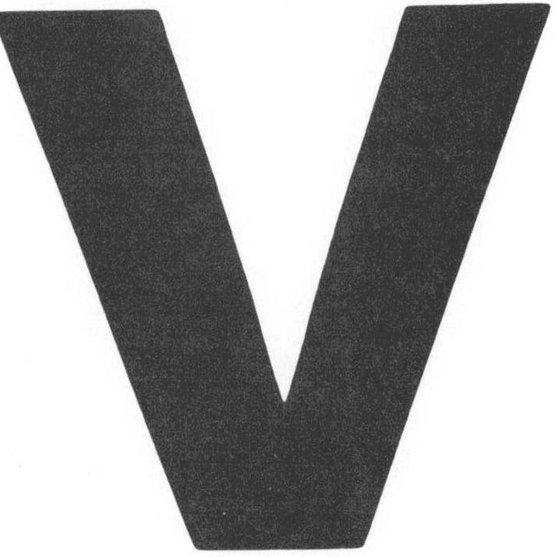

11 ■ Communication in Organizations

12 ■ Groups

13 ■ Power and Conflict

14 ■ Leadership

Interpersonal Factors

Part V explores a variety of primarily interpersonal issues, particularly communication, groups (their formation, structure, processes, and decision making), power, conflict, and leadership.

The functions and processes of communication in organizations are examined in Chapter 11. A model explaining the various stages of communication is developed and used to help you understand a number of potential problems with communication. A wide range of communication options is explored and a step-by-step guide provided to help you approach systematically the task of communicating effectively.

Chapter 12 examines a variety of issues related to small groups in organizations. The most common types of groups, the way in which they are formed, and their purposes are explored, as are group structure and methods of interaction in groups. Factors which contribute to and detract from group cohesion are identified, and the impact of cohesion on group effectiveness is studied. Typical stages of group development are documented and suggestions made for facilitating group effectiveness at each stage. The strengths and weaknesses of several group problem-solving techniques are discussed. The overriding objective of Chapter 12 is to help you better understand the nature of groups in organizations so that you can enhance group effectiveness. Such skills can distinguish you as a manager and leader.

Two issues examined in Chapter 13 often go hand-in-hand: power and conflict. Various sources of power can be combined to define your total power base. Identifying these sources and the reasons why power can be acquired from them are discussed. A step-by-step guide for the acquisition of power is presented, and a brief discussion of the ethics of power building and use is included. Conflict often occurs in organizations when two persons or groups have incompatible goals. This chapter explores the causes of conflict and five distinct stages in the conflict process. Various strategies for managing conflict are identified and information provided on how to select one most appropriate for a particular situation.

Chapter 14 addresses the critical organizational issue of leadership. A historical perspective outlines the development of strategies to identify and/or develop effective leaders. Although there is still more to learn, a great deal currently is known about the basis of effective leadership. This knowledge is used to provide you with specific guidance for improving your effectiveness as a leader and for managing other leaders in your organization.

---

11 Communication in Organizations

OVERVIEW
THE COMMUNICATION PROCESS
- A Communication Model
- Distortion in the Communication Process
- The Functions of Communication

COMMUNICATION NETWORKS, PATTERNS, AND CHANNELS
- Networks
- Communication Patterns
- Communication Channels

INFORMAL COMMUNICATION (THE GRAPEVINE)
EFFECTIVE COMMUNICATION MANAGEMENT
SUMMARY

I have often regretted my speech, never my silence.

Publilius Syrus

OVERVIEW

Communication is the meaningful transfer of information from one person (or group) to another. Given this definition, communication does not occur unless: one person transmits a piece of information; another person receives the piece of information; and the received information has meaning to the receiver. All three of these conditions must be met for communication to have occurred. If you write a letter to a friend, put it in a mailbox, and the Post Office loses it, communication has not occurred (your friend did not receive the information). If your friend receives the letter but can't read it because it got wet and the ink ran, communication has not occurred (the information had no meaning to your friend). If your friend receives the letter, reads it, and it has meaning to her, communication has occurred (whether or not your friend interprets the letter the way you intended).

These three conditions of communication hold true for both the formal and informal communication within organizations. Any one of the links in the specific sequence can enhance or detract from the overall efficiency and accuracy of the communication process. This chapter focuses on the common functions of communication and the major issues critical for effective communication: common barriers to communication, the physical channels required to transmit messages, and the impact of communication on satisfaction.

How important is communication in organizations? Without communication, it would be impossible to manage behaviors and attitudes in organization. Indeed, there could be no organization at all without some form of communication. None of the issues addressed in this book could be used by organizations without communication. Managers devote most of their time to the communication process; many top executives typically spend over 75 percent of their working hours engaged in communication.[1]

THE COMMUNICATION PROCESS

A Communication Model

Communication between persons or groups can occur in a wide variety of ways (face to face, over the phone, in writing). All have in common the communication process shown in Exhibit 11–1. A sender in the communication process is responsible for two actions: selection of an intended message and encoding of the message. The **intended message** is simply a piece of information which you intend to transmit to a receiver. **Encoding** is the process by which you convert the idea of the message into some transmittable form (written words, spoken words, computer codes, gestures, etc.). You send the encoded message in the receiver's direction by placing it into a **communication channel** (a phone line, computer system, etc.) which serves as the physical medium for transmission of the message. The receiver is then responsible for two actions: decoding of the message and receipt of the message. **Decoding** is the process by which the receiver retranslates the message to give it meaning (by reading, listening, seeing, feeling, etc.). Once the message is decoded, it is accepted (*received*) by the receiver. The communication process is complete (Exhibit 11–2).

It should be obvious that the perceptual and communication processes cannot be separated. Chapter 10 presented a general model of the perceptual process for dealing with the processing of *any* environmental sensory stimulus. This chapter is heavily de-

Exhibit 11–1 The Communication Process

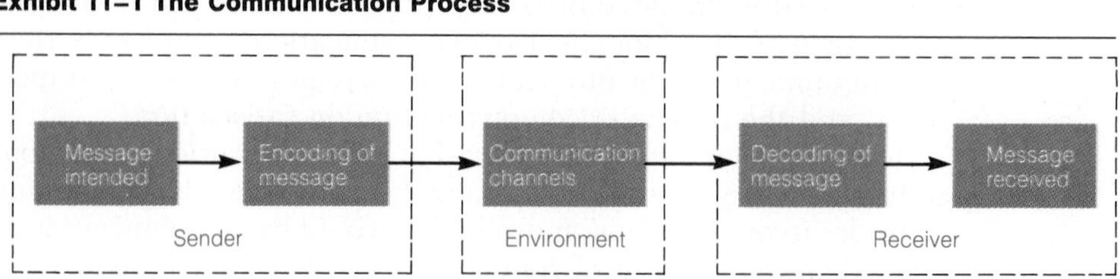

Exhibit 11–2 The Communication Process in Action

pendent on that information but differs in two ways: (1) communication is concerned only with a subset of stimuli (those created to exchange a message); and (2) communication focuses on how to prepare a communication message and how that message is processed once it has been sent. Exhibit 11–3 gives you a general idea of the overlap of the perceptual and communication processes. As you can see from this exhibit, the sensation, selection, organization, and translation of information (from Chapter 10) is particularly relevant after a communication message has been encoded. You will not decode a message unless it is first sensed and selected. Once you select a message, decoding is influenced by the way you perceptually organize various aspects of it. Finally, the various perceptual factors which influenced translation (e.g., halo effects, perceptual readiness, and perceptual defense) impact on your decoding of any message.

Exhibit 11–3 Integration of the Communication and Perceptual Processes

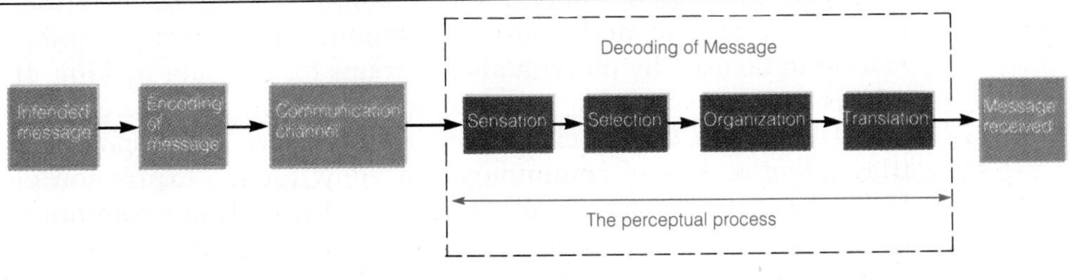

Distortion in the Communication Process

The communication process contains a number of points at which distortion can occur. Because of this, the message received is seldom the exact message intended by the sender (see Exhibit 11–2). Distortion can occur for a variety of reasons.

Encoding. If a sender is careless or unskillful in encoding the message, the receiver may not perceive it properly. For example, is this book written skillfully enough so that you are understanding the intended messages?

Inadequate Communication Channels. If the physical media are improper or insufficient, the receiving process may be impaired. Is this book printed clearly and with large enough print to transmit the message effectively? Is there sufficient lighting present to read the book?

Perceptual Difficulties. Distortion also can be caused by the receiver and his/her carelessness, lack of decoding skill, or personality. Do you, for example, have reading skills adequate for this book? Are you well rested enough to understand the concepts in it? Do you have biases which influence your perception of the message?

Noise. Distortion also can be created by distractions in the environment. If you are distracted by loud music, bright lights, loud co-workers, etc., you may not encode a message well. The communication channel also can be affected by environmental noise, a literal example of which is the static sometimes experienced during a long-distance phone call (distorting transmission of the spoken message). Finally, environmental noise can influence a receiver's decoding of the message (again, by loud music, lights, etc.).

The Functions of Communication

Communication serves several distinct purposes in organizations. William Scott and Terence Mitchell of the University of Washington identified four major functions of communication: information, motivation, control, and emotive.[2] Communication provides *information* to be used by individuals or groups for decision making. It addresses *motivation* by encouraging commitment to organizational objectives. *Control* clarifies duties, authority, and responsibilities. *Emotive* uses of communication allow for the expression of feelings and the satisfaction of social needs. Virtually any communication incident involves at least one of these four functions, and most involve more than one.

HÄGAR The Horrible
by DIK BROWNE
I WONDER WHAT MAMA'S YELLING ABOUT?
STUPID!
DUMB!
UGH!
OH... DADDY MUST BE HOME...
YOU CAN'T DO ANYTHING RIGHT!!
WHY ARE YOU YELLING AT DADDY?
HE CAUGHT A MAGIC TROLL
IS THAT BAD?
NO! IT'S GREAT! A TROLL WILL GIVE ANYTHING TO BE FREED! MONEY! JEWELS! POWER!
ALL HE HAD TO DO WAS ASK FOR THREE WISHES!
I DID! WHAT MORE DO YOU WANT?!
YOU COULD LEARN TO SPEAK CLEARLY!!
6-4 DIK BROWNE
© King Features Syndicate, Inc. 1978 World rights reserved

COMMUNICATION NETWORKS, PATTERNS, AND CHANNELS

Networks

Communication *networks* (patterns of communication channels) are formed in organizations to facilitate the flow of information from one person or group to another. A wide variety of network patterns have been used and evaluated. Six of the most frequently used networks are illustrated in Exhibit 11–4. As you can see, the structure of these networks varies substantially.

The *chain* is a simple hierarchical network. The greatest power typically is located at the top of the chain and the least power at the bottom. The *Y* is a slight modification of the chain; there are two equal top-level members. The Y also can be inverted to produce a network with two equal low-level members. The *wheel* is structured with a leader at the center; all communication must flow through the leader. The *circle* allows members to communicate with either of two adjacent members but no others. Such a network could consist of equal power members or be hierarchical (with greater power at the upper end of the wheel). The *star* is a democratic type of network and frequently is found in voluntary or informal groups. In this network, any member can communicate with any other member. Finally, the *com-con* network is a variation of the wheel and star. As in the star, any member may interact with any other. The difference, however, is that one member is located in the center of the network (as in the wheel) and is considered the leader.

A great deal of research has been conducted on the impact of the various communication networks.[3] Exhibit 11–5 provides an overview of many of the findings of this research. There is no one best communication network. The effectiveness of the various networks varies, depending on which criteria are considered. As shown in Exhibit 11–5, at least six potential criteria exist: decision quality, decision speed, message distortion, satisfaction, network centralization, and information overload. As you choose a communication network, you will need first to identify the most critical criteria, and then to explore the alternatives for one which best meets these needs.

Communication Patterns

Communication networks typically use *patterns* to channel their messages. These patterns involve channels for downward communication (Exhibit 11–6A), upward communication (Exhibit 11–6B), and horizontal communication (Exhibit 11–6C). A network may allow for one or more directions of communication, depending on

Exhibit 11–4 Common Communication Networks

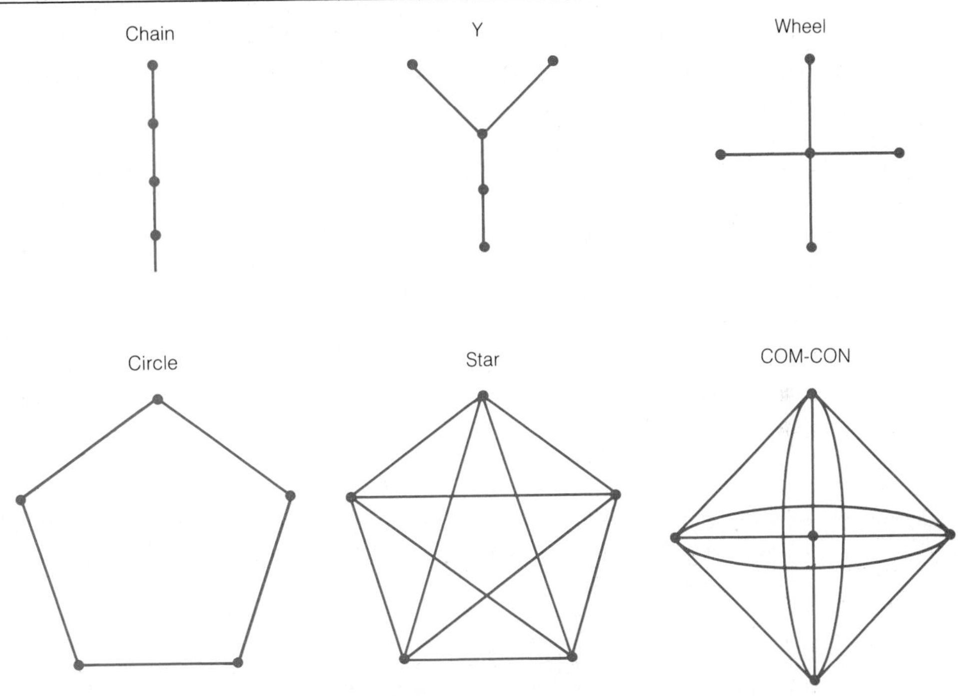

the objectives of the network. The com-con network, for example, allows downward, upward, and horizontal communication. Each direction of communication serves particular purposes and is unique in nature, content, and limitations. The relative frequency of **upward, downward,** and **horizontal communication** are suggested by Exhibit 11–7.

Downward Communication. Downward communication flows from one level of an organization or group to a lower level. Classic organizational structures typically specify the chain of command for communicating downward as illustrated in the organizational chart for a small film laboratory in Exhibit 11–8. Brian Hawkins and Paul Preston of the University of Texas–San Antonio identified the following as five major types of information flowing through downward communication channels:[4]

1. Specific task directives; job instructions.
2. Information designed to produce understanding of the task and its relation to other organizational tasks: job rationale.

Exhibit 11–5 Evaluation of Communication Networks

Criterion	Chain	Y	Wheel	Circle	Star	Com-Con
	Type of Network					
Decision quality	Dependent on leader	Dependent on leader	Dependent on leader	Moderate	High	High
Decision speed	Slow	Moderate	Fast	Moderate	Slow	Depends on situation
Distortion	High	Moderate	Moderate	Moderate/ high	Low	Low/ moderate
Satisfaction	• High at top • Low at bottom	• High at center • Low at ends	• High inside • Low outside	Moderate	High	High
Centralization	Moderate	High	Very high	Low	Very low	Moderate
Overload	Moderate	• High at center • Moderate at ends	• Very high at center • Moderate outside	Moderate	Moderate	Moderate

Source: Based on an analysis of the communication literature, from Brian L. Hawkins, and Paul Preston, *Managerial communication,* copyright © 1981 by Scott, Foresman and Co., reprinted by permission; and D. Hellriegel, J. W. Slocum, Jr., and R. W. Woodman. (1983). *Organizational behavior.* St. Paul, MN: West Publishing.

Exhibit 11–6 Directions of Communication

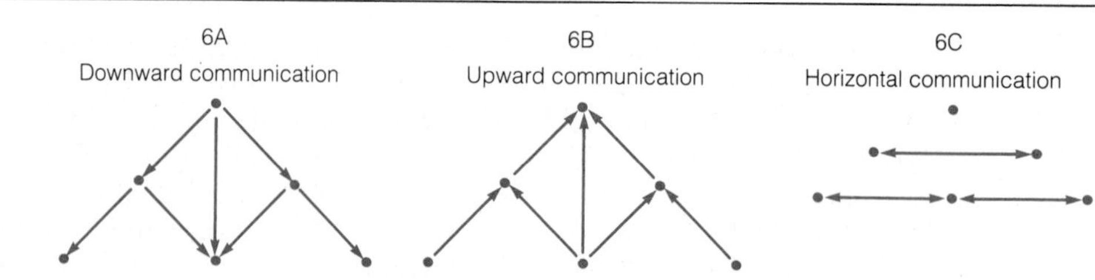

Exhibit 11–7 Downward, Upward and Horizontal Communication

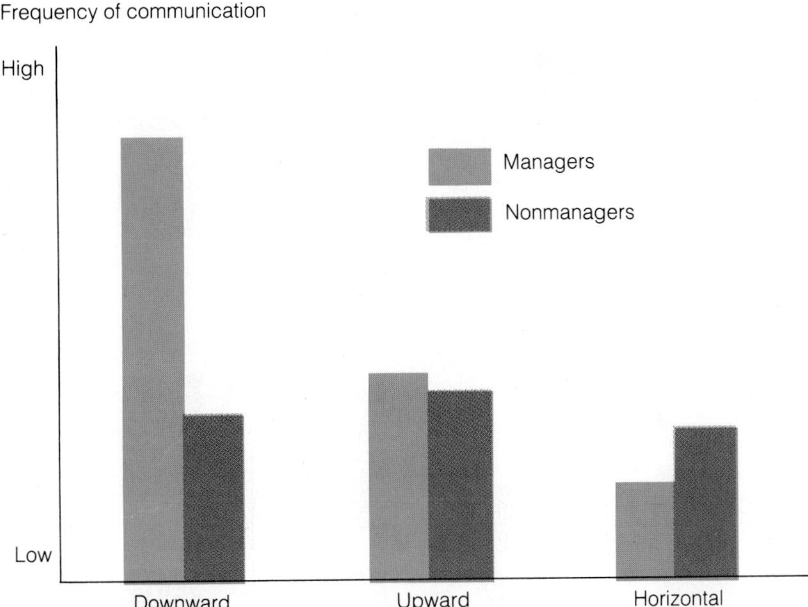

Source: Data from Table 1 of S. B. Bacarach, and M. Aiken (1977). Communication in administrative bureaucracies. *Academy of Management Journal, 20,* 374.

3. Information about company policies and orders: organizational procedures and practices.
4. Feedback to the subordinates about performance.
5. Information of an ideological character to inculcate* a sense of mission: indoctrination of goals.

Often, it is assumed that downward communication channels function effectively. Such an assumption frequently is not merited, however. It has been estimated, for example, that by the time a message is sent downward from top management to rank-and-file workers, over 80 percent of the original information is lost.[5] Thus, an inspector in the production department of Acme Film Laboratory (Exhibit 11–8) usually receives only a small portion of a message sent by the general manager through existing downward communication channels. Information sent through downward

* *Inculcate*: To teach and impress by frequent repetitions or admonitions.

Exhibit 11–8 Acme Film Laboratory

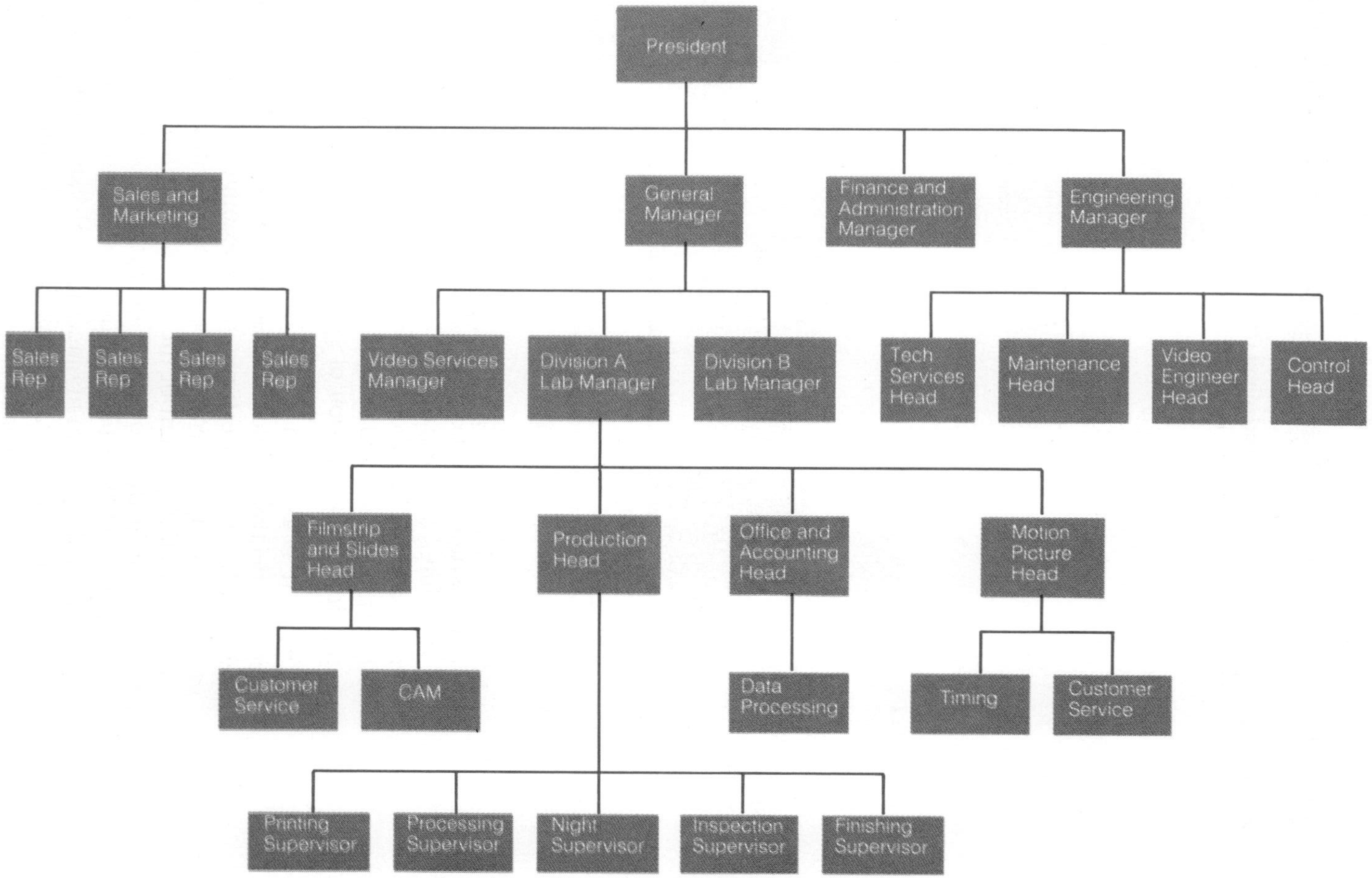

President

Sales and Marketing

Sales Rep

Sales Rep

Sales Rep

Sales Rep

General Manager

Video Services Manager

Division A Lab Manager

Division B Lab Manager

Filmstrip and Slides Head

Customer Service

CAM

Production Head

Printing Supervisor

Processing Supervisor

Night Supervisor

Inspection Supervisor

Finishing Supervisor

Office and Accounting Head

Data Processing

Motion Picture Head

Timing

Customer Service

Finance and Administration Manager

Engineering Manager

Tech Services Head

Maintenance Head

Video Engineer Head

Control Head

channels not only is lost, it also is distorted frequently and/or not understood by the receiver.[6]

Upward Communication. Upward communication flows from one level of an organization or group to a higher level. Organizational structures typically also provide for the use of upward channels. Leslie Rue and Lloyd Byars of Georgia State University identified four major types of information which often flow through upward communication channels:[7]

1. Information on subordinate achievement, progress, and future plans.
2. Information about work problems which require assistance from higher up in the organization.
3. Ideas for improvement in work-related activities and functions.
4. Information on subordinate feelings about work and work-related issues.

There is usually distortion in the upward communication process. Low-level members of the organization with aspirations for "moving up" send fewer critical messages upward than similar persons with lower mobility desires.[8] Individuals who distrust the organization (or the person immediately above them in the communication network) may conceal critical information.[9] In short, upward communication is subject to filtering as information passes from person to person because subordinates tend to summarize information selectively prior to passing it upward.[10]

Horizontal Communication. Horizontal communication flows between same-level individuals or groups. Frequently, an organization will not identify formal horizontal channels of communication. They can have great importance, however, in determining organizational effectiveness. Horizontal channels appear to be important and common, particularly at lower organizational levels where they can reduce the need for upward/downward coordinating communication.[11] Major functions of horizontal communication include:

1. Coordination of activities across multiple parts of the organization.
2. Information about work activities in same-level parts of the organization.
3. Persuasion of others at similar levels in the organization.
4. Information about colleagues' feelings on work and work-related issues.

Information is less filtered in horizontal than in vertical communications. This has both advantages and disadvantages. An obvious advantage is that information you obtain from horizontal communication probably is more complete, allowing you to interpret the meaning of the information on your own. Since the information is less filtered, however, you must sort through a greater amount of data. This can lead to overload, which inhibits your ability to process all of the information you receive.

One-Way and Two-Way Communication.[12] A communication channel can flow in one direction, or in two. **One-way communication** allows information to flow from Point A to Point B, but not from B to A. Radio or television transmissions, or a boss who sends information to you but who does not allow you to send information back, are examples of one-way communication. **Two-way communication** allows A-to-B and B-to-A communication. Face-to-face discussions and phone conversations are usually two-way. One of the most common ways you use two-way communication is providing *feedback* to the sender of a message. Through your use of feedback, a sender can determine whether or not you received his/her message and your interpretation of its meaning.

Two-way communication may increase the total volume of messages, but it does not have to. Your feedback, for example, may help the sender tailor messages to your needs, avoid unnecessary communication, and modify the communication while it is being sent. Even when communication time is increased by the use of two-way communication, its quality and your satisfaction with the process are usually increased.[13]

Communication Channels

Earlier, a communication channel was defined as the physical medium for transmission of a message. Both human and mechanical communication channels are available for your use. **Human channels** utilize the natural senses and, therefore, include transmission devices such as speech, sight, and body movements. **Mechanical channels** assist in the transmission of messages beyond the capability of the human body and can involve a wide range of devices such as letters, newspapers, telephones, television, and computer networks.

Appropriate channels communicate information in a timely, complete, accurate, and understandable manner. The channel or combination of channels which best meets these objectives depends on the nature of the message you are sending and the characteristics of the receiver. In evaluating alternative channels for use in a particular communication application, you must consider several characteristics of the channel.

One-Way versus Two-Way Communication

For a simple illustration of one-way versus two-way communication, try the following. Refer back to Exhibit 11–1, which appears earlier in this chapter. Ask one of your friends, roommates, or fellow students who has not taken an organizational behavior course to give you a few minutes of his/her time. Explain the model of the communication process shown in Exhibit 11–1 to this person until you are reasonably certain s/he understands the model. Use one-way communication only. Separate yourselves so you cannot see each other (to avoid nonverbal feedback) and don't allow the receiver to give you verbal feedback. Keep track of the following factors:

1. How long the communication process takes.
2. How satisfied you are with the communication process.
3. How satisfied the receiver is with the communication process.
4. How well the receiver understands the message you attempted to transmit (after you are completely finished communicating, ask him/her to explain the model to you and compare this explanation to the model shown in Exhibit 11–1).

Next, get a second volunteer and repeat the communication exercise, using two-way communication. This time, let the person sit facing you and engage in any two-way communication s/he wishes, including verbal or nonverbal feedback. Again, keep track of the four factors described above.

Channel Capacity. **Channel capacity** is the amount of information which can be sent through a channel in a given period of time without significant distortion. A memo is a relatively low-capacity channel because it depends on your reading speed. The telephone, on the other hand, has greater capacity. Television has a very high capacity. One factor you must consider when choosing a communication channel is the amount of information you need to send and the amount of time available for transmission. As the amount of information contained in a message increases and/or the amount of time available decreases, your need for capacity in a communication channel rises.

Channel Modifiability. The degree to which the rate of transmission can be altered is **channel modifiability.** Modifiability is high for written communication channels, since you can read at whatever speed you choose. Verbal channels are also relatively modifiable in two-way communication, since you can request a sender to "hurry up" or "slow down." A television channel, on the other hand, is not modifiable unless you have a video recorder which allows replay and/or fast/slow motion. The need for modifiability increases as the complexity of the message increases.

Duplication. A communication channel can involve the use of subchannels for reiteration or elaboration of the message. Television, for example, has both visual and auditory subchannels. The next time you turn on the TV, pay close attention to commercials and note how these subchannels are used in conjunction with one another to expand upon and reinforce the central message. A similar commercial played over the radio contains less **duplication** since the visual subchannel is lost. Duplication is important when a message is very critical. Commercial airplanes, for example, have ground proximity indicators with a great deal of duplication. If an airplane approaches an unsafe altitude, a visual indication appears on a dial, a light flashes, a warning buzzer sounds, and a synthetic voice demands that the pilot "pull up! pull up!" Duplication is also important when a message is complex and requires elaboration, which is why figures and charts accompany the written text in this book.

Immediacy. Immediacy is the speed at which a message can be transmitted through a channel. Suppose you work in Cincinnati and want to send a business report to a client in San Francisco. One of the factors you want to know is the amount of time it will take to get the report to your client. Using the regular U.S. Postal Service will take about three days. If you use the United Parcel Service "blue label" service, two days are required. Federal Express overnight service delivers the report by 11 A.M. the next day. Or, you can transmit the report by telecopier or computer network in less than an hour. If your client is out of the office for a week, it is not critical which communication channel you use, since any would meet the immediacy requirement of one week or less. On the other hand, if your client is leaving the office tomorrow after lunch for a two-week trip, the importance of delivery before noon is very great.

Bilateral Channels. Although you already know about two-way communication, the importance of **bilateral channels** and simultaneous feedback should be emphasized. For many communication tasks, a bilateral channel is not necessary. You have little need for bilateral capability, for example, when you are using a channel solely for the purpose of providing easy-to-understand, descriptive information. But, a bilateral channel can be of critical importance when you need a reaction to your message in order to modify it during transmission. This is frequently the case in instructive or persuasive communications.

Minimum Linkages. Although the **number of linkages** can influence some other channel characteristics (e.g., immediacy), the primary reason for using the *minimum* number of linkages is to reduce the noise and distortion which tend to be added with each additional linkage. This occurs whether the channel is physical (such as a phone line with many connections across a long distance) or human (as is the case when a message is passed by word of mouth from one person to another).

Nonverbal-Verbal Communication

Body language (or **nonverbal**) communication channels have been singled out for special attention recently.[14] These channels are used in face-to-face communication, alone or as a supplement to the use of verbal channels. Some people are very skilled in the use of body language to improve the effectiveness of intentional communication. Others, however, communicate a great deal of information nonverbally without realizing it. Frequently, a nonverbal channel sends a message which contradicts the verbal message, as is the case when a shaking, sweating, anxious co-worker tells you he will definitely have his portion of a project completed on schedule.

When you finish reading this chapter, take a few minutes to strike up a conversation with a friend. Raise a few issues which you think may involve rather sensitive points for your friend (e.g., "Do you remember the $20 I loaned you?" "What are your feelings about herpes?" "Have you ever cheated on an exam?"). As you conduct the conversation, pay close attention to the following types of nonverbal factors and see what information you receive beyond the spoken words:

Eye contact	Posture	Physical contact
Eye movement	Facial expressions	Gestures
Distance	Nervous activity	Orientation

There is reason to believe that a large percentage of face-to-face communication occurs nonverbally and subconsciously.[15] Furthermore, nonverbal communication tends to be more honest and accurate than the spoken word.[16] For these reasons, you may find it useful to pay special attention to nonverbal cues sent by others while carefully monitoring your own transmission of such messages.

Appropriateness. You should consider the **appropriateness** of a channel for your message. It would be entirely appropriate, for example, if you placed an advertisement in a local newspaper to sell your car. It would be rather tacky, however, to place an ad in that same paper informing a subordinate that s/he is being fired. The channel chosen should match your personal style as well. Otherwise, you may distract the receiver and, thus, distort the message.

Unfortunately, most of us give relatively little thought to the characteristics of available communication channels prior to selecting one for use. More often, we tend to choose from a small subset of available channels and use them on a fairly regular basis without attending sufficiently to the requirements of the specific message to be communicated. A small amount of thought and evaluation prior to the selection of communication channels can go a long way toward improving your communication effectiveness.

INFORMAL COMMUNICATION (THE GRAPEVINE)

To this point, you have read about formal communication networks and channels officially created and recognized by organizations. All of the issues discussed, however, apply equally to informal communication. An informal communication network is typically referred to as the **grapevine.** The grapevine consists of communication channels existing outside of official channels and evolves through the interaction of friends and co-workers within organizations. Often, the grapevine includes connections which do not exist in formal networks, thus allowing the exchange of information between a variety of sources within the organization.

Many organizations wish the grapevine did not exist, since it reduces the amount of control possessed by an organization over information flow. The grapevine also may detract from regular job duties. When a major focus of the grapevine is on the exchange of social information, "time on the vine" is nonproductive time. Furthermore, the grapevine often transmits information contradictory to formally transmitted information. Such is the case when rumors passed through the grapevine suggest that layoffs are imminent in spite of formal statements to the contrary.

Despite possible undesirable effects of the grapevine, it often serves valuable organizational purposes. The grapevine can enhance organizational effectiveness by opening job-related communication channels which an organization has overlooked. The grapevine grows new branches quickly, so the need for speed often favors the grapevine (even when formal channels do exist). Despite popular belief to the contrary, grapevines frequently are very accurate conveyers of information.[17] In general, the accuracy of the grapevine is influenced by the very same factors which influence the accuracy of formal communication.

You can see the potential effectiveness of informal communication channels by re-examining the formal channels of communication shown in Exhibit 11–8. If the night supervisor at Acme Labs has a technical engineering problem with a machine, s/he needs to communicate with the Engineering Technical Services Head. This can be accomplished by following formal channels of communica-

James E. Ware is director of personnel at Intermountain Gas Company and has served as treasurer and chairman of the American Society for Personnel Administration.

What do you feel are some of the most critical barriers to effective communication in organizations? The most major barrier to effective communication is, in my estimation, a lack of acquired understanding in the communication process. Most of us feel that communication consists solely of the issuing forth of verbiage and memoranda of various and sundry sorts. You have to realize, however, that actual communication involves the creation of understanding—not just the issuance of information.

What recommendations do you have for the creation of understanding in the communication process? You can create understanding in a variety of ways. Sometimes this requires changing your style based upon your audience. I don't believe you talk in our business to a group of field welders the same way you talk to a group of junior accountants. You talk differently and you use different words. This is not to say that one group of workers is more important or less effective than the other. I'm merely saying you should know your audience as you start to communicate. Flexibility is required to communicate effectively in different situations.

Do you have any other comments on the communication process in organizations? Yes. It is common for management to try to take total responsibility for communication in organizations without realizing that the people who work for the organization should also be involved in the communication process. These people also need to communicate, and we should communicate with them in a manner in which they are willing to listen and speak.

tion (Night Supervisor to Production Head to Division Lab Manager to General Manager to Engineering Manager to Technical Services Head and back the same route). Or, it can be accomplished by an informal telephone call directly to the Technical Services Head. Obviously, the informal channel would be quicker; it probably also would be more accurate.

EFFECTIVE COMMUNICATION MANAGEMENT

Effective communication is not an easy goal. Indeed, no matter how hard you try, you will never be a totally effective communicator. It is possible, however, to enhance greatly your communication effectiveness through the systematic use of ideas covered in this chapter and in Chapter 10. Because communication needs vary substantially from situation to situation, there is *no one best way* to communicate. Instead, your communication strategy should be tailored to the nature of your message, your primary communication objectives, your receiver, and the communication channels available to you. Exhibit 11–9 provides a guide to help you systematically approach the task of effective communication.

Exhibit 11–9 A Guide to Effective Communication Management

1. *Clearly establish intended message and communication objective(s)* (e.g., informational, motivational, controlling, emotive).
2. *Establish primary communication needs* of the message (e.g., amount of information in messages, need for modifiability, need for duplication, need for speed, need for feedback).
3. *Identify characteristics of the receiver(s)* (e.g., communication strengths and weaknesses, perceptual problems and biases).
4. *Identify all available channels.*
5. *Evaluate each available channel* along the criteria in Item 2, relative to characteristics of the receiver(s), based on susceptibility to distortion, and cost.
6. *Select channel(s) for use.* Is there one channel which meets all your needs? Can two or three channels together meet your needs?
7. *Carefully encode the message* to match the channels used and the receiver(s) involved. Consider factors which influence perceptual sensation, selection, organization, and translation.
8. *Place the message in the channel* (i.e., send it).
9. *Obtain feedback.* Was the message received? What meaning did the message have to the receiver(s)? Did the message accomplish its objective(s)?
10. *If necessary, follow up* with repeat or elaboration of message over the same or additional channels.

The following paragraphs elaborate on the suggestions in Exhibit 11–9:

1. You begin by establishing clearly the message you intend to send and your reasons for sending it. Do you wish to tell your employee that s/he has done a good job on a *specific* project, that his/her *overall* performance has been good? Why do you wish to send this message? Simply to provide information? To motivate? To control? To satisfy? All of the above?

2. You should establish the primary communication characteristics and needs of the message. How much information is to be transmitted, a general statement of performance level or an in-depth description detailing performance? How quickly does the message need to be sent?

3. Carefully consider your intended receiver's strengths and weaknesses. Is s/he a good listener? A slow reader? Hearing impaired? Busy? Defensive? What types of communication are likely to be most effective with this person?

4. Identify all available communication channels. Could your message be sent by memo? In person? Over the phone? By telegram? All reasonable alternatives should be put on your list of channels to consider.

5. Evaluate each available channel. This evaluation should take into account the primary communication needs of the message. If it needs to be sent quickly, interdepartmental mail may be inappropriate. If you need quick feedback, don't send a letter. The channel should also be evaluated to determine the degree to which it matches the characteristics of your intended receiver. If the receiver is hearing-impaired, for example, use of the phone may be inappropriate. Evaluate the channel in terms of the amount of distortion likely to occur. Finally, consider the cost (financial and time) of the channel to see if it fits your budget and matches the importance of your message.

6. Exercise great caution as you actually choose a channel(s) for use. If there is one channel which meets all of your criteria well, your choice will be easy. Usually, however, it is a question of compromise. A phone call may be quick and allow feedback, but it is rather impersonal compared to a face-to-face discussion. A face-to-face meeting may be very personal, but it can take a lot of time. In considering such compromises, take care to favor your primary objectives. Frequently, a combination of two or more channels may be required to meet all of your communication needs. Perhaps you can follow up a quick phone call containing the main elements of your message with a more extensive memo. One more comment: don't do more than you really need to. If a short memo can accomplish your objectives, don't send a long one. If a black-and-white photograph will suffice, don't send a color videotape.

7. Once you have selected a channel, carefully encode your message to match both the channel and the receiver. Complete sentences, for example, need not be used in a telegram. Use appropriate language levels which will match the receiver's language skill level. To be certain that the message is sensed and selected for attention, use the ideas discussed in Chapter 10 (intensity, contrast, etc.). Recognize the factors which will influence your receiver's organization of material, and pay close attention to perceptual phenomena such as perceptual readiness (again, see Chapter 10).

8. This may sound obvious, but be certain that you place the encoded message in the appropriate communication channel. A surprising number of letters are never sent, ads never placed, phone calls not made.

9. After you send the message, get feedback. Find out if the message was received. If possible, determine what meaning the message had to the receiver (i.e., how the message was translated). Evaluate whether or not the message accomplished all of its objectives. If the message was not received, if the message received did not match the message sent, or if all of your communication objectives were not met, follow up. If your receiver did not get the message, repeat it over the same channel (send another memo) and/or send it through an additional channel (make a follow-up phone call). If you need to expand the message, elaborate, using the most appropriate available channel.

10. One final note: learn from your communication experiences. With experience, you will identify a variety of available communication channels and learn about their strengths and weaknesses. You will discover more about the characteristics of your receiver(s) as you remember what has or has not worked in the past. You will acquire better encoding techniques, become more effective at obtaining and interpreting feedback, and fine-tune your follow-up skills. Communication is extremely vital to the management of organizations, yet few managers have well-developed communication skills. Development of these skills not only will make you more effective, but also is likely to create a positive halo about your overall capabilities.

SUMMARY

Communication is the meaningful exchange of information and serves many purposes, including information, motivation, control, and emotive. The communication process consists of developing a message, encoding and transmitting it, decoding of the message, and its subsequent acceptance or receipt. Many factors affect this process, including perceptual phenomena and distortion. A variety of communication networks exist, each of which has strengths and weaknesses. The communication channels which hold these networks vary in capacity, modifiability, duplication, speed, and feedback. Although perfect communication is impossible, guidelines are available for effective management of communication systems. These guidelines identify the importance of precommunication planning, implementation of communication, and follow-up after a message is sent.

GLOSSARY

Communication The meaningful transfer of information from one person to another.

Intended Message The piece of information which a sender intends to transmit to a receiver.

Encoding The process by which the idea of a message is converted into transmittable form.

Communication Channel The physical medium for the transmission of a message.

Decoding The process by which a receiver retranslates a message to give it meaning.

Communication Network A pattern of communication channels.

Downward Communication Information flow from one level of an organization to a lower level.

Upward Communication Information flow from one level of an organization to a higher level.

Horizontal Communication Information flow from one level of an organization to the same level.

One-Way Communication Information flow which goes in only one direction between two points.

Two-Way Communication Information flow which goes in both directions between two points.

Human Communication Channels Channels which utilize the natural human senses.

Mechanical Communication Channels Channels which are beyond the natural human capabilities.

Channel Capacity The amount of information which can be sent through a channel in a given period of time without significant distortion.

Channel Modifiability The degree to which the rate of communication through a channel can be altered.

Channel Duplication The degree to which a channel has subchannels for reiteration or elaboration of a message.

Channel Immediacy The speed at which a message can be transmitted through a channel.

Bilateral Channel A channel which allows the flow of information in two directions.

Number of Linkages The number of "connections" necessary to transmit a message through a channel (minimizing linkages reduces distortion).

Channel Appropriateness The degree to which the channel chosen for communication matches the type of message being sent.

Nonverbal Communication Channels Communication channels which do not involve the use of words ("body language").

Communication Grapevine The informal communication network which exists in an organization.

STUDY QUESTIONS

1. Discuss the role of the perceptual process in communication.
2. Discuss factors which often introduce distortion into the communication process in organizations (during encoding, while information is in a communication channel, during decoding).
3. Discuss reasons why there is no "one best communication network" for all organizational communication needs.
4. Discuss organizational situations in which two-way communication is desirable. Undesirable?
5. Identify the types of communication channels which would be appropriate for use by a supervisor who is providing a subordinate with information about his/her performance.
6. Ask a friend or fellow student to describe an awkward situation which s/he experienced at work. Watch carefully for nonverbal information. What did the nonverbal information tell you that the verbal information did not?
7. Discuss the useful functions served by the "grapevine" in an organization.
8. Discuss steps which could be taken to increase the effectiveness of communication between members of a student study group.
9. Discuss steps which could be taken to increase the effectiveness of communication between members of a project team in an organization. Are these different from the steps to be taken with a student study group?

NOTES

1. **Mintzberg, H.** (1973). *The nature of managerial work*. New York: Harper & Row.
2. **Scott, W. G., & Mitchell, T. R.** (1976). *Organization theory: A structural and behavioral analysis*. Homewood, IL: Irwin.
3. See, for example, **Shaw, M. E.** (1964). Communication networks. In L. Berkowitz (Ed.), *Advances in experimental social psychology*. New York: Academic Press, pp. 111–147; **Guetzkow, H., & Simon, H.**

(1955). The impact of certain communication nets upon organization and performance in task-oriented groups. *Management Science, 1*, 233–250. A good summary is provided by **Hawkins, B. L., & Preston, P.** (1981). *Managerial communication.* Santa Monica, CA: Goodyear Publishing.

4. **Hawkins & Preston,** 1981, p. 201.
5. **Hawkins & Preston,** 1981, p. 202. See also **Davis, K.** (1968). Success of chain-of-command oral communication in a manufacturing management group. *Academy of Management Journal, 11*, 379–387.
6. **Davis, K.** (1968). Readability changes in employee handbooks of identical companies during a 15-year period. *Personnel Psychology, 21*, 413–420.
7. **Rue, L. W., & Byars, L.** (1980). *Communication in organizations.* Homewood, IL: Irwin.
8. **Hawkins & Preston,** 1981.
9. **Read, W. H.** (1962). Upward communication in industrial hierarchies. *Human Relations, 15*, 3–15.
10. **March, J. G., & Simon, H. A.** (1958). *Organizations.* New York: Wiley.
11. **Simpson, R.** (1959). Vertical and horizontal communication in formal organizations. *Administrative Science Quarterly, 4*, 188–196; **Wickesberg, A.** (1968). Communications networks in the business organization structure. *Academy of Management Journal, 11*, 253–262.
12. See **Leavitt, H. J., & Mueller, R. A. H.** (1951). Some effects of feedback on communications. *Human Relations, 4*, 401–410.
13. Although this discussion has focused on the degree to which two-way communication increases the accuracy of information exchanged, a large body of literature also addresses the impact additional information obtained through feedback can have on organizational members. For example, performance can be increased as shown by **Migliore, R. H.** (1970). Improving worker productivity through communicating knowledge of work results. *Management of Personnel Quarterly, 9*, 26–32; worker satisfaction can also be increased, as suggested by **Dodd, W. E., & Pesei, M. L.** (1977). Managing morale through survey feedback. *Business Horizons, 20*, 36–45.
14. **Mehrabian, A.** (1972). *Nonverbal communication.* Chicago: Aldine-Atherton; **Harper, R. G., Wiens, A. N., & Matarzzo, J. D.** (1978). *Nonverbal communication: The state of the art.* New York: Wiley.
15. **Harrison, R.** (1970). Nonverbal communication. In J. H. Campbell & P. W. Harper (Eds.), *Dimensions in communication.* Belmont, CA: Wadsworth.
16. **Ekman, P., & Friesen, W. V.** (1969). Nonverbal leadage and clues to deception. *Psychiatry, 32*, 88–105.

17. Some of the most complete and interesting commentary on organizational grapevines is provided by **Davis, K.** (1972). *Human behavior at work.* New York: McGraw-Hill; **Davis, K.** (1969). Grapevine communication among lower and middle managers. *Personnel Journal, 48*, 269–272.

12 Groups

OVERVIEW
TYPES OF GROUPS
- Formal and Informal Groups
- Functional and Project Groups

THE SOCIAL STRUCTURE OF GROUPS
- Group Representation
- Closed/Open Groups
- Group Roles

SOCIAL PRESENCE EFFECTS
FACTORS INFLUENCING GROUP FORMATION AND COHESION
- Safety and Security
- Social Interaction and Affiliation
- Esteem and Status
- Power
- Goal Achievement
- Reward Systems

THE EFFECTS OF GROUP COHESION
- Communication
- Conformance to Norms and Resistance to Change
- Satisfaction
- Performance

GROUP NORMS AND STANDARDS
- Characteristics of Norms
- Factors Which Influence Conformance to Norms

STAGES OF GROUP DEVELOPMENT
- Orientation
- Conflict
- Cohesion
- Delusion
- Disillusion
- Acceptance
- Regression

GROUPTHINK
- Symptoms
- Consequences
- Remedies

GROUP PROBLEM SOLVING
- Ordinary Groups
- Brainstorming
- Statistical Aggregation
- The Delphi Technique
- Nominal Group Technique

SUMMARY

Unity makes strength, and, since we must be strong, we must also be one.

Gross Herzog Friedrich Von Baden

OVERVIEW

A **group** is a collection of two or more people sharing a common goal or interest who interact with one another and who perceive themselves to be a group. *Interaction* can occur face to face, in writing, over the phone, across a computer network, or in any other fashion which allows communication between group members. It is not necessary for all members of a group to interact simultaneously, but each member must interact at least occasionally with one or more members of the group. The *shared goal or interest* identifies a common concern of group members and provides a psychological definition of the purpose of the group. If a group has a variety of goals or interests, each group member must share at least one of the group's concerns (but not necessarily all of them). Shared concerns can be almost anything, including performance objectives, political concerns, or social interests. *Perception of group membership* is the recognition that the group is not merely a collection of individuals but, rather, a separate entity. Typically, the perception that a group exists results directly from the recognition that group members are interacting with one another for the purpose of facilitating their common goal or interest.

This chapter explores types of groups, the way they are formed, their purposes for existing, their social structure, and their methods of interaction. Factors which contribute to the formation, cohesion, and effectiveness of groups are examined, as are the effects of group membership on individual members. Typical stages of group development are documented, along with suggestions for facilitating group effectiveness at each stage. Finally, several popular techniques for enhancing group problem solving are described and evaluated.

TYPES OF GROUPS

Formal and Informal Groups

Formal groups are created by organizations for the specific purpose of accomplishing one or more organizational objectives. Usually, management appoints members to formal groups (as when a committee is formed). Organizational structure often results in the formation of a department or work team. On occasion, however, group membership is determined by vote, assignment, or volunteerism.

An organization *should* attempt to isolate all four components of a formal group: (1) identify two or more members, (2) define interaction patterns, (3) state the purpose(s) for group existence, and (4) make individuals aware of the group's existence and their membership in it.

Even though an organization may define all components necessary for group formation, a group does not exist unless all four distinguishing characteristics of a group actually are present. Thus, before a "formal collection of people" becomes a "formal group," members not only must be identified but must engage in interaction (although not necessarily the way the organization specified). They also truly must share a common goal or interest (although it need not be the one assigned by the organization). Finally, members must perceive themselves to be a group. Unless all of these conditions are met, a collection of people may exist but there is no group. Indeed, many "ineffective groups" are not actually groups at all but merely an ineffective collection of people. In many cases, had the collection of people become a group, effectiveness might have resulted.

Informal groups are not created by organizations but by the group members themselves. These groups develop naturally out of the interactions of members who join voluntarily. Informal groups can be as simple as a luncheon group meeting once a week for the sole purpose of social interaction, or as complex as a coalition of organizational members formed to gain control of the organization. Informal groups also must be two or more interacting people sharing a goal or interest who perceive themselves to be a group.

The membership, interaction, and goals of formal and informal groups may or may not overlap. Membership of an informal group often is contained entirely within one formal group. A departmental softball team is an informal group composed only of people who also belong to the formal group (the department). Cliques are informal groups which often develop within a formal group to serve a particular social, political, or economic interest. Equally common, however, are informal groups with membership spanning a wide range of formal groups (political parties or social clubs).

You should not assume that the goals of informal groups in organizations are always inconsistent with organizational goals. Although it is true that such goals are often inconsistent, this sweeping assumption is unwarranted. Indeed, many informal groups are formed for the specific purpose of facilitating organizational objectives, such as an ad hoc committee to develop ideas for problem-solving techniques or ideas for improving organizational effectiveness. If you form an informal study group to improve your knowledge of organizational behavior, your primary goal is totally consistent with the primary goal of the formal group (the class). Even though you may not choose the same pattern of interactions and methods for goal attainment as those used in the formal group (you are unlikely to lecture to each other, for example), the primary goal is still the same. The existence of the informal group should help meet the objectives of the formal group. Similar task-oriented informal groups are not uncommon in other organizations.

Functional and Project Groups

Both formal and informal groups tend to be primarily either functional or project-oriented. The **functional group** has goals or interests which focus on current activities within a particular area. Most departments in organizations are functional groups. An accounting department, for example, is responsible for the ongoing coordination and administration of an organization's financial records. A quality control department is responsible for the continuing quality of an organization's products. Thus, a functional group concentrates on a general and continuing area of responsibility.

A **project group** has the specific purpose of accomplishing a defined task (or closely related set of tasks). Most organizational committees and special task forces are project groups. For example, an organization may form a group to develop a new set of accounting procedures, or a committee to solve a particular quality control problem. Once such groups accomplish their major objective, they normally cease to exist (they no longer have a goal).

THE SOCIAL STRUCTURE OF GROUPS

Group Representation

A group can be classified by the degree to which its total membership represents horizontal and/or vertical slices of the organization.

Melville Dalton used this classification scheme to identify types of informal cliques, but such a strategy can be used to characterize any group.[1] A **horizontal group** has members of similar rank from the same work area. A **vertical group** contains members from multiple levels within one work area. A **complex group** contains members from both multiple areas and multiple levels.* You may want simply to classify groups based on the number of levels and work areas represented. Exhibit 12–1 illustrates such a strategy and provides several examples.

Closed/Open Groups

A **closed group** has a fixed, unchanging membership. An **open group** has frequent movement of individuals both in and out of membership.[2] Open groups spend more time socializing new members than do closed groups. Open groups also provide greater power and status opportunities for new members who broaden the group's frame of reference by introducing new ideas. Open groups tend to be less stable and typically are less concerned with long-term issues than are closed groups.

Exhibit 12–1 Group Representation

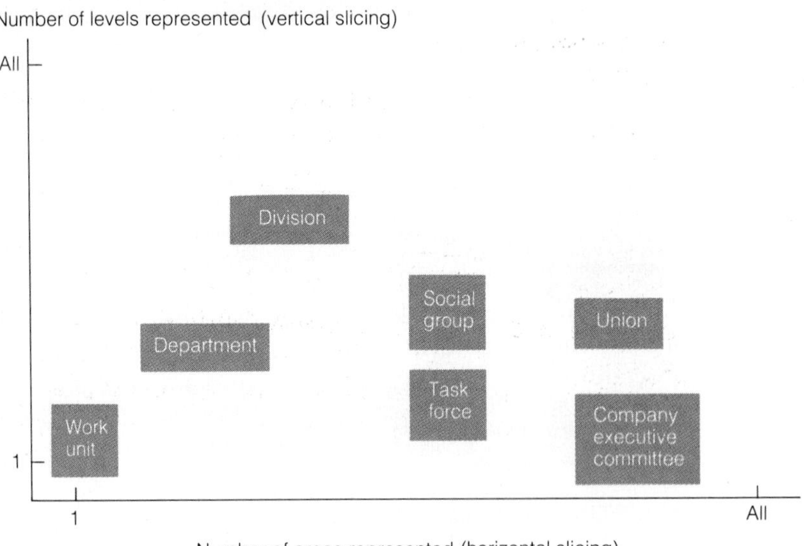

*H. J. Reitz referred to this as a "random group" (see Note 2).

Whether an open group will be more effective than a closed group depends on the objectives of the group. A group designed to develop new product ideas probably will function best with at least a moderate degree of openness (to encourage rapid development of creative new ideas). A group established for long-range planning, on the other hand, will benefit from the stability and longer-term perspective of a relatively closed group. As you structure a group, carefully consider its objectives prior to establishing the group as open or closed.*

Group Roles

Role Definition. A **role** is a set of expectations for an individual group member. In most groups, a set of roles is developed or assigned to coordinate and facilitate the behavior of group members. If a role is clearly defined, all members understand how each is expected to behave. The term **role set** is used to describe the people who interact with you in a role and who expect you to fill certain role expectations. Frequently, a group assigns two or more roles to the same individual. A supervisor, for example, may be expected to establish a positive working relationship with her subordinates, yet terminate employees who are performing inadequately. It is also common for one individual to have roles from two or more different groups (e.g., a worker who is also a union member).

Role Ambiguity. When a role is incompletely or inadequately described, **role ambiguity** (an uncertainty about role expectations) is likely to result. Role ambiguity can lead to stress, dissatisfaction, and poor performance because of inadequate job guidance. Exhibit 12–2 presents some of the questions frequently used to assess role ambiguity level. For example, which should you emphasize, quantity or quality? Should you spend more time as a leader developing interpersonal relationships or structuring tasks for subordinates?

Intraperson Conflict. Intraperson conflict occurs when there is a conflict between the specified role expectations and the personal values, beliefs, or preferences of the person holding the role. If you personally believe that only the very best products should be provided to your company's customers, but your role definition tells you to cut costs wherever possible, you will experience intraperson conflict. Intraperson conflict also creates dissatisfaction and stress. It also frequently delays or prevents role accomplishment.

---

*In reality, groups vary along a continuum from very open to very closed.

Exhibit 12–2 Role Ambiguity Items*

	Strongly Agree	Agree	Neither Agree Nor Disagree	Disagree	Strongly Disagree
1. I know exactly what is expected of me.	1	2	3	4	5
2. I feel certain about how much authority I have.	1	2	3	4	5
3. I have clear, planned goals and objectives for my job.	1	2	3	4	5
4. I know that I have divided my time properly.	1	2	3	4	5

*High scores equal high ambiguity.
Source: Adapted from J. R. Rizzo, R. J. House, and S. I. Lirtzman (1970). Role conflict and ambiguity in complex organizations. *Administrative Science Quarterly, 15,* 150–163.

Intrarole Conflict. **Intrarole conflict** occurs when two members of a role set provide conflicting expectations. If you are marketing a product, your role set includes both the customer and a superior representing your company. Your boss expects you to sell at the highest possible price; your customer expects the lowest possible price. Although intrarole conflict of this type does not necessarily damage performance, it too creates dissatisfaction and stress.

Interrole Conflict. When expectations from two or more roles held by one person are inconsistent, **interrole conflict** results. You probably will have a job soon with roles demanding large amounts of time and energy. You also may have a family making demands for that same time and energy. Interrole conflicts such as this are very common and difficult to resolve. Thus, they serve as continuing sources of stress and dissatisfaction. People often deal with this type of conflict by dividing their time between the two roles (often failing to meet either set of role expectations well).

SOCIAL PRESENCE EFFECTS

The social environment significantly influences behavior due to a psychological and physical arousal caused by having other people present. In fact, both your learning rate and performance level are influenced whether or not those present are members of a group to which you belong. If you have ever had a part in a play, given a speech, or performed in an athletic event, you have experienced this "audience effect." Your heart raced; your palms were sweaty; your mental alertness spiked. What impact does this arousal have on performance (see Chapter 16)? If you are learning a new task while extremely aroused, your learning performance will be impaired due to overarousal. On the other hand, if you are performing a task you already know well, arousal will facilitate performance (at least until you reach the point where arousal is so great you "fall apart"). Exhibit 12–3 presents the pattern of results expected under conditions of high and low arousal when learning and performing.[3]

The implications are obvious: learning new tasks is performed best in situations where few, if any, other people are present. This is one of the reasons why many organizations conduct training in isolated training rooms. On the other hand, the performance of well-learned tasks improves in the presence of others. For this reason, many organizations design work layouts such that large numbers of workers are present in the same room.

Exhibit 12–3 The Effects of the Presence of Others While Learning and While Performing

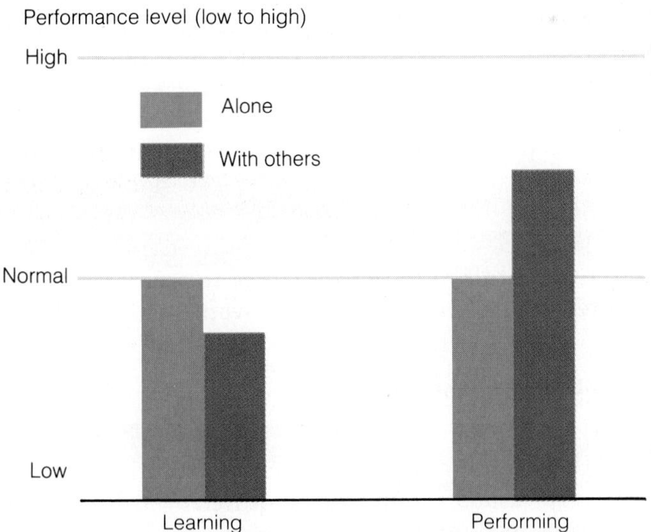

Source: Adapted from R. B. Zajonc, Social facilitation, *Science, 149*, 269–274, copyright 1965 by the American Association for the Advancement of Science.

FACTORS INFLUENCING GROUP FORMATION AND COHESION

Several significant factors contribute to both *group formation* and *group cohesion*. Group cohesiveness can be thought of as the strength of the "glue" which holds the group together.

> A group which is important to its members, which elicits strong loyalty and support, whose members identify with each other and work for group goals is referred to as a highly cohesive group. A group whose members are generally indifferent toward each other or the group, whose loyalty and support are mediocre or variable, and which has little influence over its members' behavior is low in cohesiveness.[4]

Most factors discussed below contribute to both group formation and cohesion, although some contribute more heavily to one effect than to the other. Almost all of the factors contributing to group formation and cohesion can be traced to whether the group is perceived to be instrumental in satisfying the needs of its members (see Chapter 5). In general, people join a group because they expect it to satisfy their needs. Cohesion develops if these hopes are realized.[5] The strength of needs varies across people and across time (again, see Chapter 5). Therefore, the relative impact of each of the following factors for encouraging group membership and cohesion will also vary.

Safety and Security

Historically, one of the first functions of groups was to provide physical safety for its members, since a group could defend itself better against predators. Today, *safety and security* needs still motivate group membership and contribute to cohesion when realized. Indeed, this was one of the reasons for the formation and strength of unions. Threats to the existence or safety of a group provide one of the strongest contributions to cohesiveness, and attempts to dissolve a group often strengthen it significantly instead. Union busters discovered this in the early part of the century, as did those who attempted to dissolve the peace movement of the 1960s.

Social Interaction and Affiliation

Group membership can satisfy the need for *social interaction* and *affiliation* with others. Friendship opportunities and acceptance by a positively valued group can be quite rewarding. These are common reasons for joining and becoming attached to informal groups (primarily social groups) but are frequently important for formal groups as well. Social needs usually are met when members share physical, political, or attitudinal similarities, when they are located physically close to one another, when frequent interaction opportunities are available, and when groups are relatively small.[6]

Esteem and Status

It is possible to meet your needs for *esteem and status* by being a "big fish in a little pond," a "little fish in a big pond," or, if you are very special, a "big fish in a big pond." Joining a high status group can help you acquire esteem in the eyes of persons outside the group whether or not you are a distinguished member of the group. Joining a relatively low status group, on the other hand, provides you with an opportunity to distinguish yourself within the group. The most powerful effect on group formation and cohesion can be expected if you distinguish yourself within a high status group. This gives you esteem from other group members, as well as very special recognition from persons outside the group who recognize you as the best of the best.

Power

The need for **power** is one of the most important influences on the organizational behavior of managers (see Chapter 5). Power encourages group membership and cohesion in two curiously different ways. First, groups can provide collective power (see Chapter 13) by combining the power of individual members. This produces a higher level of power for the group than was possessed by any individual member, and people will join in order to share in the resulting high collective power. On the other hand, many individuals are motivated to obtain personal power within a group. If this is your primary concern, you will join groups with members possessing less power than you have so that you can influence others within the group. Thus, groups meet power needs either by providing sufficient collective power to influence persons outside of the group, or by providing opportunity for influence within the group.

Goal Achievement

Groups can facilitate individual *goal achievement* in two ways. A group which combines the resources of individual members is capable of accomplishing objectives which would be difficult for members to reach individually. A medical team consisting of individuals with nursing, surgical, and anesthesiology skills completes a surgical procedure more effectively than could any one of the individuals alone. This provides an incentive for group membership and rewards, thus enhancing cohesion. Notice that homogeneity within the group enhances the socially rewarding aspects of group membership, but heterogeneity is more likely to increase group achievement reward aspects. Many people are attracted to groups in which they are able to distinguish themselves as high achievers relative to other members of the group. Put simply, if you want to be the best in a group, you join a group which contains only members who are not as good as you. If you are driven by the need for individual achievement within a group, you are less likely to join or experience cohesion with a group composed of extremely high individual performers.

Reward Systems

A powerful factor influencing cohesiveness is the type of *reward system* used with a group. A reward system which is based neither on intragroup nor intergroup competition has little effect on group cohesiveness. Reward systems based on intragroup cooperation and/or intergroup competition (e.g., group bonuses) enhance cohesiveness. On the other hand, systems based on intragroup competition (e.g., individual bonuses for top performers) tend to decrease group cohesion.

THE EFFECTS OF GROUP COHESION

Group cohesion level has been shown to affect communication within the group, conformance to group norms and resistance to change, member satisfaction with the group, and performance.[8]

Communication

Highly cohesive groups engage in greater amounts of *communication* than do less cohesive groups.[9] There is also evidence that more communication time is spent exchanging facts in cohesive groups than in less cohesive groups. When cohesion is influenced heavily by social factors, however, a large amount of time is devoted to prolonged, socially-oriented discussions.[10]

Conformance to Norms and Resistance to Change

Group cohesion level heavily influences the degree to which group members will conform to *norms*. Furthermore, because norms define "the way the world should be," attempts to change often are *resisted*. For this reason, the introduction of organizational change usually is resisted most vigorously by the most cohesive groups (see Chapter 17).

Group Formation among Students

A group of OB students at the University of Wisconsin recently conducted a study exploring factors contributing to group formation. Ninety-five students in two OB classes were required to form groups, each of which would conduct a major class project. The only constraint on group membership was that members had to come from within one of the two classes.

As shown in Exhibit 12–4, the results of this study identified six important factors influencing group membership choices: accomplishment of shared goal, amount of previous interaction with group members, physical proximity of members, personal similarities which would enhance social factors, personal differences which would enhance performance, and physical attractiveness of members.[7]

Exhibit 12–4 Factors Influencing Group Formation among OB Students for a Class Project

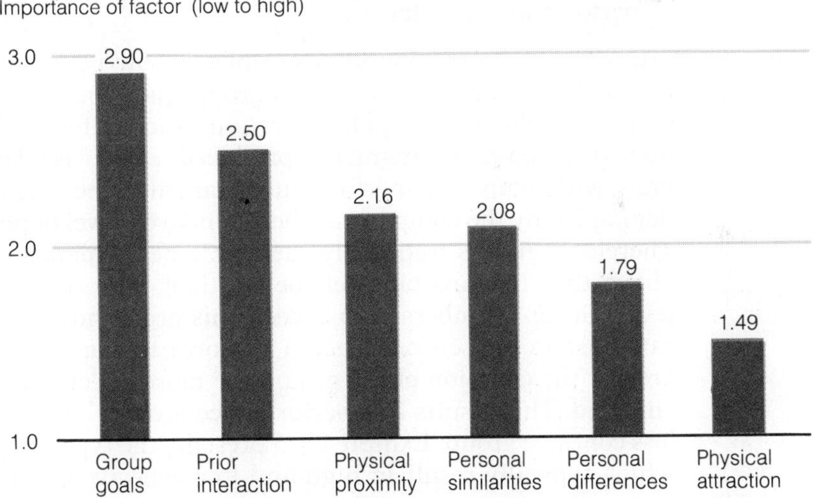

Source: S. Armstrong, J. Burdick, S. Johnson, M. Mastenbrook, and B. Sweeney. An investigation of small group behavior. Unpublished paper, University of Wisconsin, 1982.

Satisfaction

Members of highly cohesive groups are more *satisfied* with their groups than are members of low cohesive groups because group members see their group as instrumental in satisfying needs.[11] In addition, through repeated pairings of the group with need satisfaction, the group itself takes on satisfying characteristics.

Performance

One of the most widely held management beliefs is that cohesive groups are also high performing groups. Although this belief sounds intuitively appealing, reality suggests a more qualified conclusion. Indeed, research on the relationship between cohesion and *performance* reveals that cohesion may increase *or* decrease performance levels.[12] This can be explained by the following observations consistent with goal theory (see Chapter 7):

1. Highly cohesive groups are more likely to accomplish their goals than low cohesive groups.
2. Groups can choose high or low performance goals.
3. A highly cohesive group which chooses a high performance goal will perform at a high level.
4. A highly cohesive group which chooses a low performance goal will perform at a low level.
5. A low cohesive group which chooses a high performance goal will perform at a moderate level.
6. A low cohesive group which chooses a low performance goal will perform at a low level.

One of the most common examples of low performance among high cohesion groups is found in groups paid on a piece-rate basis (where employees are paid a certain amount for each item produced). If too many items are produced, employees fear the company will change the performance standard (the number of items demanded by the company as the "standard" level of performance). Therefore, groups frequently identify a performance goal slightly above the standard but well below their performance capability level. Group members who exceed this group goal are considered rate-busters and encouraged to conform to the group norm. The greater the cohesion of the group, the more effectively the norm is enforced. This results in a performance level below that found in a less cohesive group. Exhibit 12–5 presents the types of performance which typically result in high and low cohesive groups with high and low performance goals.

GROUP NORMS AND STANDARDS

Group norms are standards of expected behavior specified by the group (e.g., the piece-rate performance standards discussed in the preceding section). Norms provide a common understanding for members by saying "This is the way we look at the world, and this is the way you are expected to behave."

Exhibit 12–5 Performance as a Function of Group Cohesion and Group Goals

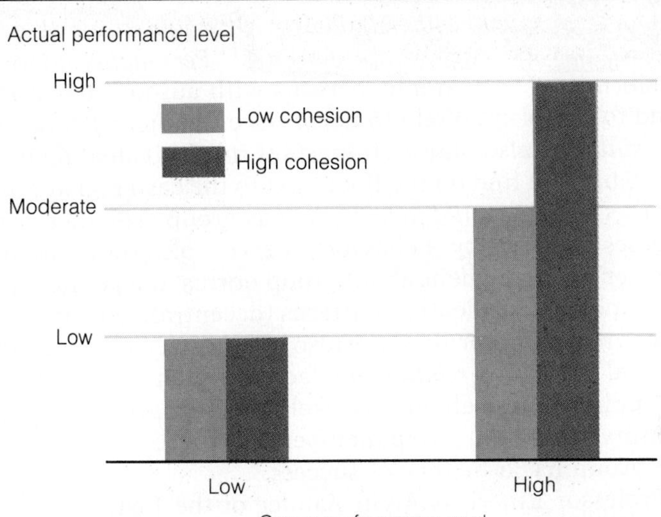

Characteristics of Norms

Richard Hackman of Yale University identified five major *characteristics of norms* which provide a good understanding of their development, purpose, and scope:

1. Norms summarize and simplify the group influence process. This shortcut reduces the need for the leader (or other members) to monitor and control constantly member behavior.
2. Norms apply to group behavior rather than group thoughts and feelings. Thus, it is not necessary for a member to agree with or psychologically accept group norms as long as s/he follows behavioral requirements of the norms.
3. Norms usually are developed only for those behaviors considered important and which occur often.
4. Norms develop and change slowly. Although it is possible for a group to decide to make a radical change in norms, this seldom occurs.
5. Some group members have the freedom to deviate from group norms. Typically, this privilege is reserved for high level or high status members.[13]

Factors which Influence Conformance to Norms

As previously shown, high cohesion leads to high conformity to norms. In addition, Shaw has identified four *factors which influence conformance to norms*: personality, situational characteristics, situational factors, intragroup relations.[14] *Personality* factors influence conformity. For example, persons with authoritarian personalities tend to conform closely to norms (see Chapter 9). *Characteristics* of the *situation* also play an important role (is it stealing if you pick up a $10 bill you find on the floor next to the cash register at the supermarket?). *Situational factors* such as group size (increasing size increases conformity behavior), degree of group unanimity (the greater the agreement about group norms, the greater the conformity), and communication patterns (decentralized patterns may produce greater conformity) are also important. Finally, Shaw observes several *intragroup relationship* factors which contribute to conformity. Conforming behavior is likely if direct group pressure for conformity is applied, group members are perceived as competent, and the group has a history of success.

Professor Emeritus Alvin Zander of the Institute for Social Research at the University of Michigan carefully reviewed the role of norms and standards and concluded that:

> Standards are necessary if a group is to be a viable unit. Most members support and follow these standards. Persons whose behavior deviates from the standards are pressed by colleagues to keep in line and, in the extreme case, removed from the group if they will not do so. Standards stating how group members should behave are created to ensure that valued qualities will be achieved in those units. Responsible members exert social pressures to support these standards and do a number of things to increase the influence of their pressures. Yet not all members need to conform; they can, if they are able, resist their group's pressures or even change group standards in ways the members come to see as desirable.[15]

You may find yourself wanting to encourage adherence to group standards at some times, but discourage it at other times. For this reason, Exhibits 12–6 and 12–7 provide guidelines for enforcing and opposing group standards. These guides are based on research which suggests that they can be effective if followed carefully.

STAGES OF GROUP DEVELOPMENT

Groups vary in effectiveness according to their level of maturity. In a fully mature group, members recognize and accept without prejudice the relative strengths and weaknesses of individual group members. Conflicts may arise relating to the group's tasks, but these

Exhibit 12–6 A Guide for Enforcing Group Standards

Arouse a desire in members to remain in the group because the power of a group over its members is greater when the group is more cohesive.

Show participants how the group's standards contribute to the achievement of important qualities in the group and how adherence to the group's standards facilitates movement toward its goal, maintains the body's unity, lets members develop clear opinions on issues, and helps the group maintain good relations with other units.

Increase each member's involvement in the group's work by asking the target person to give up individual gains in favor of the group's success.

Show a member, where possible, that the difference between what the group asks and what the member prefers is not large and that there is thus little need to resist group pressures.

Help all members see how their contributions help the group accomplish its purposes.

Give participants a say in establishing standards because standards are more closely followed by those who make them.

If conformity of members cannot be detected directly, develop a means for determining whether members have done what the group's standards require.

Develop a means for rewarding and approving persons who conform to the group's standards, such as a bonus payment, a place on the honor roll, a gold medal, a membership in an honorary society, or a public recognition day.

Demand of a member goals s/he can attain so that s/he derives a sense of pride in his/her work for the group.

Encourage members to come up with new ideas (even if these do not suit established standards) when creativeness is needed to develop new aspects of the group's life.

Make it known that any groupmate who does not conform to the group's standards will be removed from the unit.

Do not reject a deviant from the group if s/he has a history of helping the body, a high-status position, deviates on noncritical matters for the fate of the group, or the group has a tradition of helping rather than shunning deviants.

Help a deviant deal with the strain, guilt, and loss of self-esteem that accompanies his/her removal from the unit.

Source: Based on A. Zander (1982). *Making groups effective.* San Francisco: Jossey-Bass, 55–56.

are resolved through rational discussion of the issues to find the best solution for the group. There is a recognition in a mature group of the roles of individual members as well as of the total group process.

Linda Jewell of the University of South Florida and Joseph Reitz of the University of Florida integrated a wide range of theories and research on group processes.[16] They identified six stages of *group development* through which most groups pass on the way from their immature beginnings to a realization of their potential as mature

Exhibit 12–7 A Guide for Opposing Group Standards

Decide which of your beliefs are important, what goals you propose to achieve as an individual, and what goals you want the group to achieve.

Identify the rewards or coercions offered by colleagues and decide whether you will accept or ignore their appeal.

Recognize the extra weight associates place on their urgings as they claim their expectations need immediate attention.

Do not give up legitimate personal preferences merely to prevent disharmony in the group.

Recognize when you have lost interest in a group because this reduces the threat of being rejected by that body. If you do not wish to remain, you have no need to defend the group's standards. Hold out against social pressures by concealing from others what you do or think. (People yield less to pressures to think differently than they do to pressure to change their actions.)

Recognize like-minded members and join forces with them, to feel support from hearing their views and to develop with them plans for joint opposition to the standards.

Source: A Zander, *Making groups effective.* San Francisco: Jossey-Bass (1982), p. 56.

groups. The first three stages are concerned primarily with the development of power and authority structures. The last three stages focus on the development of interpersonal relationships. Unfortunately, because few groups progress to full maturity, most fail to become fully effective. Exhibit 12–8 depicts the six stages of group development and corresponding levels of group maturity (and, therefore, effectiveness). Specific steps can be taken by an organization and/or group members to facilitate group development.

Orientation

A newly created group starts at the *orientation* stage. The first meeting of a new group begins with a great deal of uncertainty about the group's purpose, structure, leadership, procedures, and the roles of individual members. At this stage, most groups spend a lot of time exchanging information about member backgrounds and attempting to clarify the group's specific goals. There is also a high level of dependence on the leader.

Although orientation is important and necessary for further group development, a group at this stage is not very effective in accomplishing group objectives. An organization dealing with such a group (or individual members of the group) should try to move the group forward quickly to a stage where it will be more productive by:

Exhibit 12–8 Stages of Group Development

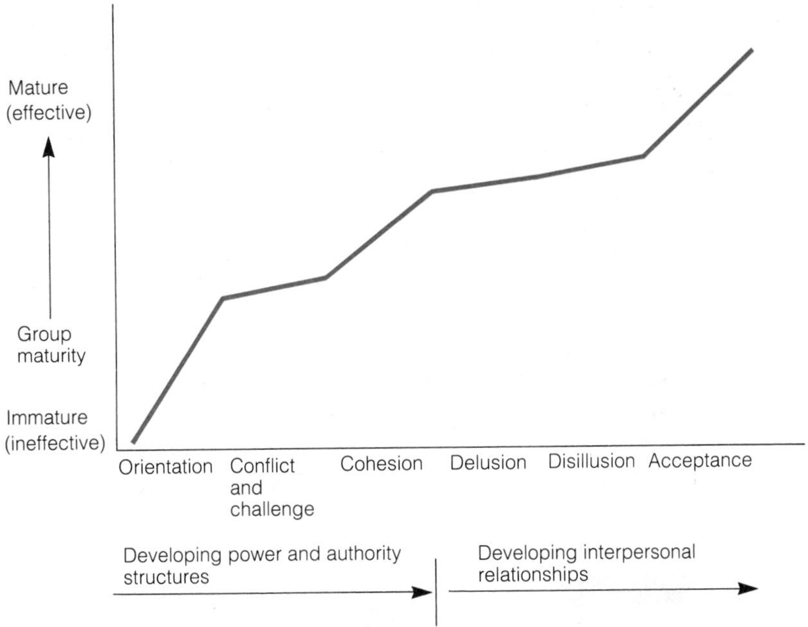

Source: Adapted from *Group effectiveness in organizations* by Linda N. Jewell and H. Joseph Reitz, p. 20. Copyright © 1981 by Scott, Foresman and Co. Reprinted by permission.

1. Providing a strong leader who is willing and able to structure and guide the rest of the group.
2. Encouraging the exchange of information about individual members.
3. Assigning or having the group develop specific group goals.
4. Assigning or having the group develop specific member roles (e.g., committee memberships and assignments).
5. Answering members' questions about the group (e.g., why it was created, how long it will exist, who the group reports to).

Conflict

After accomplishing the major functions of the orientation stage to a reasonable extent, most group members experience an early sense of comfortableness with the group and its reasons for existence. Once this occurs, most groups quickly and spontaneously enter the *conflict* stage of development. This stage of group development is marked by interpersonal conflict, including serious questioning of the leader's ideas and authority, and even rebellion against the leader. Members may test the limits of the group by violating group norms. Sometimes, the group splits into subgroups with different interests or opposing ideas about group direction.

Although some work does get done during this stage of development, effectiveness is quite low when conflict exists. Unfortunately, many groups never advance beyond the conflict stage. In spite of this, the conflict stage is a normal part of group development. To avoid it might increase the chances of regression to conflict at later stages of development. Therefore, an organization should allow the conflict stage to occur, but shorten its duration by:

1. Allowing conflict to emerge unsuppressed.
2. Allowing members to test, but not exceed, the limits of group norms.
3. Allowing the formation of subgroups but maintaining interactions (e.g., meetings or communications) between the entire group to preserve its identity.
4. Above all, recognizing that the conflict stage is a painful requirement for further group development (sort of an initiation rite).

Cohesion

Clear, decisive action is required to move a group out of the conflict stage and into the important *cohesion* stage. During this stage, members work through their differences and agree upon a continuing structure for the group. This is also the point at which a strong sense of group identity develops and is projected in a unified fashion to persons outside the group for the first time. A leader (formal or informal) is required at this stage who can facilitate problem solving within the group without becoming emotionally involved and without attempting to acquire personal power.

The cohesion stage of group development is marked by rapid increases in group effectiveness. Productivity improvements of similar magnitude are unlikely to occur again unless the group reaches full maturity. Although substantial energy is required to facilitate development of the cohesion stage, it usually pays off handsomely. Whatever steps are necessary should be taken to support this stage, including:

1. Providing a fair, well-balanced, nonpower-seeking leader who is willing to work for the good of the group (as opposed to personal gain).
2. Developing a mechanism which encourages members to address and resolve their disagreements (see Chapter 13).

3. Developing a sense of group identity and broadcasting it outside the group through public statements from the group.
4. Formalizing an operating structure.

Delusion

Few groups at the cohesion stage recognize that further group development can produce major improvements. For this reason, efforts at advancing group development often end when a group reaches the cohesion stage. If group development does continue, the cohesion stage usually evolves into the *delusion* stage. The most noticeable characteristic of this stage is the delusion that significant problems no longer exist despite the fact that they do. To avoid disrupting this delusion, interpersonal conflicts are either totally ignored or glossed over, and differences between members are covered up.

Because of the euphoria created by the delusion stage, there is little natural incentive for continued group development, and improvements occur at a very slow pace. Put simply, this is a very pleasant stage of group development which members attempt to preserve at virtually any cost. It is at this stage that a group is most likely to fall victim to the problems of Groupthink discussed later in this chapter. Since the onset of the delusion stage is a natural progression from the cohesion stage, usually no conscious effort is necessary to stimulate its occurrence. The only way an organization (or group members) can deal with the delusion stage is to:

1. Accept that the delusion stage is normal and allow it to occur.
2. Take steps to prevent the onset of Groupthink.
3. Avoid prolonged continuation of delusion so that further development is possible.

Disillusion

A group must be forced to leave the delusion stage if the group is to continue to mature. The *disillusion* stage is one in which "the bubble bursts." Suddenly, members realize that serious problems do exist and that they have lost valuable time for dealing with these problems. Some members will try to force the lost intimacy to redevelop, while others intentionally avoid it. Special interest subgroups may form. A new dependence on the leader may evolve, and s/he is frequently asked to resolve conflicts between subgroups or individual members. Group cohesiveness decreases; absenteeism and tardiness increase. If you are ever a member of a group which enters the disillusion stage, you undoubtedly will experience a severe sense of disappointment.

Effectiveness during the disillusion stage shows little improvement due to interference of interpersonal problems. It is not unusual for groups to permanently divide into subgroups or even dissolve at this stage. Most members are very pessimistic about improvement of group relations and effectiveness. This stage of development should not be discouraged, despite its generally negative nature, since it is the necessarily painful stage of "group puberty" which must occur prior to full maturation of the group. An organization (and group members), therefore, should:

1. Not try to prevent the onset of disillusionment as it occurs. Allow it to come into the open.
2. If necessary, force development of the stage by identifying problems and presenting them to the group.
3. Allow the formation of subgroups, but do not allow them to divide the group permanently. Develop some task or activity which brings the entire group together at least occasionally.
4. Provide a directive leader who is capable of and willing to resolve conflicts between subgroups and individual members.
5. Recognize and emphasize to group members that the disillusion stage is a normal but difficult part of the group maturation process. Emphasize that things can get much better.

Acceptance

It is very unlikely that a group will remain at the disillusion stage for any extended period of time. The group either will regress to an earlier stage of development or advance to the *acceptance* stage. Unless specific action is taken, regression is more likely than advancement. The same type of unselfish leader skilled in interpersonal relations who earlier helped move the group from conflict to cohesion is needed for advancement to occur. At the acceptance stage of development, members openly discuss their differences to resolve problems for the good of the group. Subgroups dissolve, and relationships focus on the needs of the total group once again. The unique qualities of each member are recognized and valued. Communication between members occurs on a regular and realistic basis. An analogy to human stages of development would classify this stage of group development as the "self-actualization" stage (see Chapter 5).

The acceptance stage produces one of the most rapid increases in group effectiveness and the highest levels of productivity realized under any stage of development. Very few groups ever reach this stage of maturity, although virtually any group could if managed properly. Those reaching this stage become fully mature and are the only groups which function with full effectiveness. A lot of work is required to facilitate development of the acceptance stage and to maintain the level of maturity reached when this is accomplished. The return on this investment, however, can be great. The development and maintenance of the acceptance stage can be encouraged by:

1. Providing a leader with interpersonal skills who is dedicated to the good of the group.
2. Encouraging open discussion of differences which focus on the issue, *not* on personalities.
3. Taking steps to dissolve subgroups by making commitment to the group more rewarding.
4. Identifying the unique qualities and contributions of each member and making all members aware of these.
5. Structuring regular channels of communication for the exchange of accurate, necessary, realistic information.
6. Using decision-making techniques which avoid unnecessary interpersonal conflict, and which are issue- and group-oriented.

Regression

Groups are capable of *regressing* from one stage of development to a prior, less mature level. This frequently occurs when a group is rushed through developmental stages too quickly. Regression also can occur if steps are not taken to maintain a given level of maturity. A group at the acceptance stage, for example, may well regress if: individual members begin to focus on their own issues to the exclusion of the group, conflicts irrelevant to the group's purpose are allowed to develop, or members lose sight of the value of each individual member. Obviously, care should be taken to avoid regression. If regression does occur, the group must be led through the subsequent developmental stages once again by following the same suggestions provided for initial development. Usually, a substantial effort to "break the ice" after a regression is followed by rapid redevelopment.

GROUPTHINK

Irving Janis of Yale University has documented a powerful group phenomenon which can lead to disastrous group decisions even when individual members of a group are extremely capable.[17] This phenomenon, known as **Groupthink,** provides a group drive for consensus which is so strong that dissent is (unintentionally) almost completely suppressed. When dissent is suppressed, effectiveness declines. Janis's documentation of the types of groups most likely to

"Good, we're all agreed. I like it when we're all agreed."
Drawing by C. Barsotti; © 1979 The New Yorker Magazine, Inc.

suffer from Groupthink corresponds very closely to groups at the delusion stage of group development. It is important to take steps to prevent the onset of Groupthink or to reduce its effects if it does begin to occur. For this reason, the symptoms, consequences, and remedies of Groupthink are identified here.

Symptoms

1. *Illusions of invulnerability* which cause the group to ignore danger signs and take excessive risks.
2. *Rationalization* as to why warnings or any information inconsistent with past decisions should be ignored.
3. The *morality* of the group goes unquestioned. ("Since we can do no wrong, we need not concern ourselves with ethical issues.")
4. Persons or groups with opinions which differ from those of the group are *stereotyped* as evil, weak, or stupid.
5. *Conformity pressure* is applied very strongly by the group to any member who deviates or even expresses doubts about group norms.
6. *Self-censorship* occurs as individual group members apply pressure to themselves to avoid deviating from group norms.
7. *Illusions of unanimity* occur as each member believes that all other members agree with group norms (even if they are silent).
8. *Mindguards* are developed by members who protect leaders and fellow members from outside information which might be disturbing.

Consequences

1. *Few alternatives* are considered for problem solutions.
2. Once a decision is made, *reexamination is unlikely* even in the face of new information.
3. Once an alternative is rejected *reconsideration is unlikely*.

Irving L. Janis of Yale University is the developer of the Groupthink concept.

Do you have any idea how frequently Groupthink occurs among groups in business organizations? Colleagues who have extensive experience with policymaking groups in business organizations have given me estimates ranging from about 10 percent to 33 percent of the major (strategic) policy decisions made by the average organization. These are impressionistic judgments. I do not know of any careful, more systematic investigation of this question.

In your 1971 article on Groupthink, you identified some of the major causes of the phenomenon. Have you discovered any additional factors which contribute to the onset of Groupthink? Yes. Some of the factors identified more recently are discussed in my 1982 book, *Groupthink*. Some of these include structural faults of the organization, such as: insulation of the group, lack of impartial leadership, lack of norms requiring methodical procedures, and homogeneity of members' social background and ideology. Provocative situational context factors are also important, including: high stress from external threats and low self-esteem induced by recent failures, excessive difficulties in decision making, and moral dilemmas.

What are some of the best-known examples of Groupthink? Other psychologists have noted Groupthink symptoms in the way Nixon handled the Watergate cover-up. I have done a detailed analysis of the unedited Nixon tapes and have used it to elaborate on the theory of concurrence seeking (see the 1982 book on Groupthink). In that book I discuss results from a study which examined the discussions of Nixon and his White House advisors both before and after disintegration of the in-group. Prior to disintegration, a large number of Groupthink symptoms were present and a coordinated cover-up policy was followed. After the group began to disintegrate, Groupthink symptoms decreased substantially.

4. *Experts are used very little* as a source of accurate information.
5. *Facts are ignored* unless they are supportive of the group.
6. *Risks are ignored* or inadequately considered for the group's preferred plans of action.

Remedies

1. Each member should be encouraged to do *critical evaluation* of group ideas openly.
2. Key members should adopt an initial *neutral stance* on solutions.
3. *Outside evaluation groups* should be used to address group problems.
4. *Discussions with outsiders* should be held to obtain reactions.
5. *Expert advisors* should be used to challenge group views.
6. A *devil's advocate* role should be played by at least one member to challenge the ideas of other group members.
7. *Alternative scenarios* should be developed to consider possible reactions of other groups.
8. *Subgroups* should be used to develop alternative solutions and compare conclusions.
9. *Second-chance meetings* should be held to reconsider decisions prior to implementation.

The Role of Groupthink at the Bay of Pigs

"'How could we have been so stupid?' President John F. Kennedy asked after he and a close group of advisers had blundered into the Bay of Pigs invasion."[18]

The answer is not that they were stupid but that they took stupid action. Janis's examination of the records concerning the ill-fated U.S. invasion of Cuba in 1961 reveals that almost all of the symptoms and consequences of Groupthink were involved in the decision to invade Cuba.

They ignored the opinions of experts. They failed to consider adequately the risks involved. They overlooked facts which did not support their plan. They failed to reconsider their plan even after evidence emerged that it would probably fail. They gave inadequate consideration to alternative invasion plans or to alternatives to invasion. Individual members suppressed opinions which were inconsistent with the plan. They considered their plan invulnerable even though objective evaluation gave it little chance of succeeding. They perceived their plan as just because of higher principles even though it violated U.S. law and would cause many deaths. They formed an inaccurate stereotype of Castro and his forces as incompetent, bungling, ill-prepared fools. And the list goes on.

The end result was that a very cohesive collection of very competent individuals, motivated by an overriding drive for consensus, made a very incompetent decision because of Groupthink.

— GROUP PROBLEM SOLVING

It is rare that major organizational problems or decisions are resolved by one individual acting alone. Instead, groups are called upon with the hope that better, more widely accepted solutions will result. How do groups go about making decisions and solving problems? Most groups have a particular, favored problem-solving strategy which has evolved within the group over time. This strategy is used more or less automatically whenever a decision must be made. Usually, this strategy involves some variation of the *ordinary group procedure* (also known as the interacting group procedure).

Despite the fact that this is the most common approach for group problem solving, it is not always the best. A variety of alternative problem-solving strategies, each of which has its own strengths and limitations, is available. A group would be wise to consider the nature of the problem it is facing and choose an appropriate decision strategy which has the greatest potential for that type of problem.

Keith Murnighan of the University of Illinois reviewed the five most popular decision strategies and evaluated each against nine important criteria (see Exhibit 12–9).* This comparative evaluation should prove useful as you select group decision strategies for use in particular situations. As you do so, recognize that it is usually ineffective to use one particular strategy for all problems. Tailor the strategy to the situation. Furthermore, keep in mind Murnighan's conclusion that:

> There are a variety of strategies that an individual can select when a group decision is indicated. Portions of different techniques can be combined and/or modified to fine-tune the problem-solving procedure.[19]

Ordinary Groups

Relatively unstructured **ordinary group interaction** is the most common of group decision strategies. A chairperson calls the meeting to order, states the problem, controls who speaks and when, and identifies a consensus if reached (or controls a vote if one is taken). Because of the lack of structure, relatively few alternatives are considered, discussion is lengthy, social pressure has a major impact, and suboptimal decisions are often reached just to end the meeting. The major role of the leader makes the success of the group highly dependent upon that one person. Ordinary groups have the advantage of providing extensive personal contact between group mem-

---

*An excellent paper by J. K. Murnighan, Group decision making: What strategies should you use? *Management Review* (February, 1981), pp. 55–62 is used as the basis for most of this section.

Exhibit 12–9 An Evaluation of Five Popular Decision Strategies

Criteria	Ordinary	Brainstorming	Aggregation	NGT	Delphi
Number of ideas	Low	Moderate	n.a.*	High	High
Quality of ideas	Low	Moderate	n.a.*	High	High
Social pressure	High	Low	None	Moderate	Low
Time/money costs	Moderate	Low	Low	Low	High
Task orientation	Low	High	High	High	High
Potential for interpersonal conflict	High	Low	Low	Moderate	Low
Feelings of accomplishment	High to low	High	Low	High	Moderate
Commitment to solution	High	n.a.*	Low	Moderate	Low
Builds group cohesiveness	High	High	Low	Moderate	Low

*n.a. = Not applicable.

Source: J. K. Murnighan, Group decision making: What strategies should you use? *Management Review*, February 1981, p. 61. © 1981 by AMACOM, a division of American Management Associations, New York. Reprinted by permission of the publisher. All rights reserved.

bers, and groups which develop good working relationships can perform quite well despite all of the potential problems.

Brainstorming

Brainstorming is a group process designed to generate a wide range of possible solutions to a problem. This is attempted by encouraging as many ideas as possible in an unstructured situation while prohibiting evaluation or criticism. "Piggy-backing" (one person expanding upon the ideas already presented by others in the group) is common. Brainstorming succeeds to the extent that members enjoy the experience and obtain a sense of accomplishment from the process. The ideas generated, however, are usually no better than those which would be developed by group members working alone. Furthermore, since the technique prohibits evaluation of ideas, this process generates *potential* solutions but does not lead to the selection of an actual solution. This must be accomplished through the use of some other technique.

Statistical Aggregation

The **statistical aggregation** technique is used when the problem is quantitative in nature (e.g., how many widgets should be produced, how much should be charged for a widget). With this technique, several people make independent judgments of the best answer to the question. These individual results are then statistically aggregated (usually using a mean or median) to identify the final solution.* This technique can be quick, efficient, and virtually eliminates any effects due to social pressure. Advantages of social interaction are lost, however.

The Delphi Technique

The **Delphi technique** (developed by Norman Dalkey and his coworkers at the Rand Corporation) is a highly structured approach to problem solving which expands upon the aggregation method. In this process, members do not meet face to face. Communication occurs through the mail or through similar communication channels. At the first stage of the Delphi technique, a statement of the problem is sent to each group member. Each member records potential solutions and returns these to the chairperson. The chairperson summarizes the suggestions of all members and sends this summary to each member for reactions and generation of additional suggestions. These are summarized and sent to each member. This process continues until a clear solution emerges (or until a vote is taken). This technique has the advantage of allowing participation of a large number of group members from wide geographical areas. Social pressures are reduced, although not eliminated, by the technique. In exchange, however, a number of logistical problems are created (not the least of which is the time required for exchange of information back and forth). The potential advantages of direct social interaction are lost due to the impersonality of the technique. The leader's role is pivotal since s/he interprets, translates, and summarizes input from members at each stage of the process.

Nominal Group Technique

The **nominal group technique** (NGT) was developed by Andre Delbecq and Andrew Van de Ven to take advantage of the strengths of a variety of other problem-solving techniques. Careful use was made of research on groups and group processes. The nominal group process begins by identifying the problem. This is followed by a brief period during which members independently record in writing ideas for possible problem solution. (The name "nominal group" arises from this beginning, since this is a group only in the nominal

---

* Note how this process increases the reliability of the final answer through the use of "multiple raters" (see Chapter 2).

sense that all members are physically present and addressing the same problem.) A round-robin session follows during which all ideas are listed on a master recording sheet. Next, a discussion is held to clarify and evaluate each idea (but not to make decisions). Each member then privately rank-orders the best several ideas. Finally, member votes are secretly recorded and statistically aggregated to produce an overall evaluation of the ideas. The structured nature of this technique balances the participation and influence of all members. It produces a high number of creative ideas and high member satisfaction while reducing social influences. Issues are confronted, but on a problem-solving basis, not a personal assault basis. Finally, this technique produces a strong sense of closure and accomplishment (and is fun!). A major constraint of this technique is that it addresses only one specific, well-defined problem at a time. It works best where relatively creative solutions are needed and is quite efficient in generating such solutions.

SUMMARY

Groups are critical to organizations. Indeed, organizations *are* groups. Many types of groups exist. Group formation and cohesion are influenced by a number of factors which enhance or inhibit the satisfaction of member needs. Organizations can encourage or discourage the development of groups by managing these need satisfaction factors. The physical presence of other people can detract from performance (during learning) or enhance performance (after a task is well learned). The group cohesion level affects the nature of group communication, conformance to group norms, satisfaction with the group, and performance. Groups develop norms which provide standards for group behavior. As groups develop toward maturity (and effectiveness) they pass through a number of stages. Specific actions at each stage of development can facilitate or slow the group development process. Inappropriate actions can sometimes lead to disastrous results, as when Groupthink occurs. When faced with the need to solve a problem or make a decision, a group has a variety of solution-generating processes from which to choose. Each has strengths and weaknesses, and careful thought must be given to the selection of a technique. Groups are a complex component of organizations and must be carefully formed, monitored, and managed to produce effective results.

GLOSSARY

Group A collection of two or more people sharing a common goal or interest who interact with one another and who perceive themselves to be a group.

Formal Group A group created by an organization for the purpose of accomplishing organizational objectives.

Informal Group A group created not by the organization but by group members themselves.

Functional Group A group with goals or interests which focus on current activities within a particular organizational area.

Project Group A group formed for the purpose of accomplishing a specific defined task.

Horizontal Group A group composed of members of similar rank from the same organizational level.

Vertical Group A group composed of members from multiple organizational levels.

Complex Group A group composed of members from multiple areas and multiple levels of an organization.

Closed Group A group with fixed, unchanging membership.

Open Group A group with frequent movement (in and out) of membership.

Role A set of expectations for an individual group member.

Role Set The people who interact with you in a role and who expect you to fulfill certain expectations.

Role Ambiguity When a role is incompletely or inadequately described.

Intraperson Conflict A conflict between role expectations and the values, beliefs, or preferences of the person holding the role.

Intrarole Conflict When two members of a role set provide conflicting role expectations.

Interrole Conflict When the expectations of two roles held by one person are inconsistent.

Group Cohesion The degree to which a group is important to its members, elicits loyalty and support, has members who identify with one another, and work toward group goals.

Group Norms Standards of expected behavior specified by the group.

Groupthink A group drive for consensus which is so strong that dissent is almost completely suppressed.

Ordinary Group Interaction A relatively unstructured, very common mode of group interaction.

Brainstorming A wide-open group process designed to generate a great number of possible solutions to a problem in a relatively short period of time.

Statistical Aggregation The determination of a final solution to a quantifiable problem through statistical combination of independent solutions.

Delphi Technique A highly structured problem-solving technique which expands on the statistical aggregation approach without meeting face to face.

Nominal Group Technique (NGT) A highly structured problem-solving technique which combines individual and group contributions in an attempt to obtain representative insightful solutions to a problem.

STUDY QUESTIONS

1. Discuss reasons why an organization might discourage the existence of informal groups. Why an organization might encourage the existence of informal groups?
2. Discuss the advantages and disadvantages of having a closed group work on the development of a new product. The advantages and disadvantages of having an open group work on the development of a new product.
3. If an organization is forming a new task force to be composed of members from several different parts of the organization, what steps could be taken to enhance group cohesion?
4. How could knowledge of the six stages of group development help a group to become more effective more quickly?
5. Is it necessary for every group to attempt to reach full group maturity? Why or why not?
6. If you created a group in your organization (but were not a member of the group), what steps could you take to avoid the onset of "Groupthink"?
7. There is a group which has as its primary purpose the identification of new marketing strategies for an existing product. The product is beginning to lose a major part of its market share. Discuss the type of group problem-solving approach you feel would be best for this group.
8. Discuss steps which could be taken by a college student to prepare him/herself to be an effective group member in the future. How can s/he become an effective group leader?

NOTES

1. **Dalton, M.** (1959). *Men who manage*. New York: Wiley.
2. See **Ziller, R. C.** (1965). Toward a theory of open and closed groups,

Psychological Bulletin, 64, 164–182; **Reitz, H. J.** (1981). *Behavior in organizations,* Homewood, IL: Richard D. Irwin.

3. The original contemporary discussion of these effects is presented in **Zajonc, R. B.** (1965). Social facilitation. *Science, 149,* 269–274.
4. **Jewell, L. N., & Reitz, H. J.** (1981). *Group effectiveness in organizations* (pp. 5–6). Glenview, IL: Scott, Foresman.
5. One of the most comprehensive reviews of these factors is provided by **Shaw, M. E.** (1976). An overview of small group behavior. In J. Thibant et al. (Eds.), *Contemporary topics in social psychology.* Morristown, NJ: General Learning Press.
6. See **Jewell & Reitz,** 1981.
7. **Armstrong, S., Burdick, J., Johnson, S., Mastenbrook, M., & Sweeney, B.,** An investigation of small group behavior. Unpublished paper, University of Wisconsin, 1982.
8. Good discussions of these issues are contained in **Shaw**, 1976, and **Jewell & Reitz,** 1981.
9. **Moran, G.** (1962). Dyadic attraction and orientational consensus. *Journal of Abnormal and Social Psychology, 64,* 190–196; **Lott, A. J., & Lott, B. E.** (1965). Group cohesiveness as interpersonal attraction: A review of relationships with antecedent and consequent variables. *Psychological Bulletin, 64,* 259-302.
10. **Back, K. W.** (1951). Influence through social communication. *Journal of Abnormal and Social Psychology, 46,* 9–23; **Shaw, M. E., & Shaw, L. M.** (1962). Some effects of sociometric grouping upon learning in a second grade classroom. *Journal of Social Psychology, 57,* 453–458.
11. **Shaw**, 1976.
12. **Seashore, S. E.** (1954). *Group cohesiveness in the industrial work group.* Ann Arbor: University of Michigan Press; **Stogdill, R. M.** (1972). Group productivity, drive, and cohesiveness, *Organizational Behavior and Human Performance, 8,* 26–43.
13. **Hackman, J. R.** (1976). Group influence on individuals. In M. P. Dunnette (Ed.) *Handbook of industrial and organizational psychology.* Chicago: Rand McNally.
14. **Shaw**, 1976.
15. **Zander, A.** (1982). *Making groups effective.* San Francisco: Jossey-Bass, p. 54.
16. **Jewell & Reitz**, 1981.
17. **Janis, I. L.** (1971). Groupthink. *Psychology Today, 5,* p. 43ff.
18. **Janis,** 1971, p. 43.
19. **Murnighan**, 1981, p. 62.

13 Power and Conflict

OVERVIEW

POWER

The Bases of Power in Organizations

Organizational Control over Power

The Acquisition of Power

Coalitions and Power

Power and Ethics

CONFLICT

The Causes of Conflict

The Conflict Process

The Selection of a Conflict Resolution Strategy

SUMMARY

> Power tends to corrupt and absolute power corrupts absolutely.
>
> *Lord Acton*

OVERVIEW

As individuals in organizations interact, two often-related processes are inevitable: power and conflict. When one individual attempts to influence the behavior of another, a power relationship is involved. Power is not totally independent of ideas covered elsewhere in this book. Indeed, you already have read about techniques for influencing the behavior of others. Here, however, you will assemble those techniques with new ones into an integrated framework for demonstrating the ability of one individual (or group) to acquire and use power. Conflict arises when two people have apparently inconsistent interests. A discussion of conflict also contains concepts familiar to you (see Chapter 12). However, since mid- and top-level managers spend about 20 percent of their time dealing with some form of conflict, this chapter explores in depth some of the causes of conflict and strategies for dealing with it.[1]

POWER

Most definitions of power agree in general with Weber's classic definition: **power** *is the probability that a person can carry out his or her own will despite resistance.*[2] Beyond this general agreement, however, some theorists attempt to draw a fine line between power and *influence, authority,* and *control.*[3] For purposes of this chapter, Weber's definition will be adopted and used to imply that power involves a person's (or group's) ability to influence the fate of others and to maintain control over his/her own fate.

This chapter identifies the major sources of power available to individuals and/or groups in organizations. It explores the importance of perception to the acquisition of power. It identifies several characteristics of the "target" of power which influence the amount of power possessed. It also considers briefly why some organizational members seek power more than others. Finally, the formation of interpersonal coalitions for the building of a power base are examined.

As you read this section, keep three issues in mind. First, power is the *ability* to influence others or to maintain control over your own fate. You possess a certain amount of power regardless of whether or not you ever use it. Secondly, remember that power is "in the eye of the beholder." You possess power only to the extent that others perceive you to possess it. Finally, remember that power in organizations is acquired. Because of this, everyone has the potential to increase or decrease his/her total power base.

The Bases of Power in Organizations

The total power you possess in an organization is a collective function of power acquired from all sources. Thus, a power weakness in one area potentially can be compensated for by a power strength in another. The classic work on the *bases of power in organizations* was performed by John R. P. French, Jr., and Bertram Raven.[4]

French and Raven originally identified five common bases of power (see Exhibit 13–1): reward power, coercive power, legitimate power, referent power, and expert power.* As noted in the interview in this chapter, a sixth base of power (information power) was later added.

Reward Power. For you to have **reward power** over another individual, that person must perceive *all* of the following:

1. That you have the *ability* to provide a positively valued outcome (i.e., a reward).
2. That you *control* the reward (i.e., you can decide whether or not the reward will be provided).
3. That you are *willing* to provide or withhold the reward at your discretion.

---

*It should be noted that the French and Raven taxonomy of power bases is not without dispute. S. B. Bacharach and E. J. Lawler, for example, state that this model fails to provide a "cogent theoretical framework." They argue that the *bases* of power (what a person controls to have power) and *sources* of power (the source from which the base of power is acquired) should be differentiated. See Bacharach & Lawler, 1981, p. 34.

Exhibit 13–1 Total Power Base

Reward power	Coercive power	Legitimate power
Referent power	Expert power	Information power

Source: Based on the work of J. R. French, and B. Raven (1959), The bases of social power. In D. Cartwright (Ed.), *Studies in social power*, pp. 150–167, Ann Arbor, MI: Institute for Social Research, The University of Michigan.

The first condition is very similar to the concept of instrumentality from expectancy theory (Chapter 8). Simply, you are perceived as the potential source of a reward. Since reward power is based on the perception of ability to reward, in the short run it is irrelevant whether or not you actually have the ability to reward. The person merely must perceive you have the ability. In the long run, however, the target of your power is likely to change his/her perception about your ability to reward if you are not observed providing the reward. The reward could be an organizationally related reward such as pay or promotion or any other kind of reward, including social rewards. There are often considerable differences across persons in the value attached to an outcome (see Chapter 5). Thus, it is important to understand the value attached to outcomes by the target of the power. The greater the perceived value of the reward, the greater your potential power.

The second condition of reward power concerns the perception that you actually control provision of the reward. Thus, you must not only have the ability to provide the reward, but you must also have the discretion to not provide the reward if you so choose. A supervisor who has the ability to provide a paycheck every Friday but who is perceived simply as a messenger in providing the paycheck does not have reward power over the receiver of the check. For the paycheck to provide reward power, the target of the power must perceive that the supervisor could choose not to provide the check. It is not relevant whether or not the supervisor actually has this discretion so long as the perception exists. It is still likely, though, that this perception may not persist unless the supervisor is observed actually withholding the paycheck upon occasion.

Finally, even if it is perceived that you have the ability to provide a reward and that you can choose to provide it or not, you will not have reward power unless it is perceived that you are willing to provide or withhold the reward. Over time, if you always provide a reward or never provide a reward, it probably will be perceived that you are not using discretion and therefore do not have reward power. A supervisor who is perceived always to provide a bonus will have no more reward power than the supervisor who is perceived never to provide a bonus.

Coercive Power. For you to have **coercive power,** the target of the power must perceive *all* of the following:

1. That you have the *ability* to provide a negatively valued outcome or remove a positively valued outcome.
2. That you *control* the outcome.
3. That you are *willing* to provide or remove the outcome at your discretion.

Coercive power is very similar to reward power in that it is based both on your manipulation of outcomes and on the perceptions of the target person. Again, the outcomes involved may relate to formal organizational outcomes or social outcomes. The amount of coercive power increases as the value of the outcomes involved increases.

Two interesting phenomena relating to coercive power often occur in organizations. The first of these is the "bluff." In this situation, the three conditions above are met perceptually, but the first two are not backed by reality (the power holder does not have the ability to provide the outcome and/or lacks the discretion to control the reward personally). A supervisor who threatens to terminate an employee unless performance improves acquires coercive power if the employee believes the bluff to be true. In reality, however, the supervisor may not have the ability or discretion actually to fire the employee. Bluffs of this sort are often quite effective and potentially can be maintained for a long time. If the bluff works and performance improves, the worker will never know for sure whether or not the supervisor actually could and would have terminated him/her. If the threat is not particularly convincing, often the target of power will "call the bluff" by saying something to the effect of "So fire me!" If the person who made the threat does not follow through, coercive power in the future probably will be weakened substantially (not only with this target person but with others who observed the failure to follow through).

The second phenomenon is the "empty threat." In this situation, the power holder does in fact have the ability and discretion to control the outcome but is not willing to follow through and act on the threat. Failure to act also weakens coercive power (again, not only with the target person but with others as well).

Death by Contract

For months, Golden West Airlines, the nation's sixth-largest commuter carrier, had urged its employees to accept 10 percent pay cuts or face unemployment. The Teamsters, which represents most Golden West employees, and ALPA, the pilots' union, were invited to audit the company's books to see for themselves the seriousness of the situation. Both unions, however, chose instead to call the carrier's bluff. At midnight on April 22, Golden West closed its doors, saying it was unable to meet the week's payroll. As a result of the bankruptcy, some 400 Golden West employees are now out of work.[5]

Legitimate Power. You have **legitimate power** over a person if that person perceives you have a right to influence him/her. This is what Bacharach and Lawler refer to as *authority*: "power based on rights of control and concomitant obligations to obey."[6] Legitimate power can be based on a formal organizational position (your boss has the right to tell you what to do), an organizational assignment (the chairperson of a committee has the right to control a meeting), or a social norm (an elder has the right to make certain demands of younger members). It is possible to acquire legitimate power through assignment, election, or informal recognition.

Legitimate power is often accompanied by other sources of power (the boss often has reward and coercive power as well as legitimate power). Nevertheless, if two individuals have equivalent levels of power from other sources, the person who also has legitimate power will have the greater amount of total power. On the other hand, legitimate power alone is often insufficient as a total power base. Organizations frequently fail to provide an intended leader with a complete set of power bases, relying instead almost solely on legitimate power. That power may be less than expected, though, if the authority (legitimate power) of the leader is questioned by the target persons.

Legitimate power usually is limited to the "right" to influence a certain subset of individuals. A supervisor only has legitimate power over subordinates, for example. Furthermore, the domain of influence usually is restricted to certain areas of behavior. For organizational subordinates, for example, legitimate power usually is limited to job-related factors plus a small set of off-the-job behaviors. A supervisor usually is not perceived to have the legitimate right to influence personal activities away from the work place. Indeed, current laws restrict the use of legitimate power away from the work place.

Notice that legitimate power is not limited to persons assigned formal positions by the organization. A union leader often has sig-

John R. P. French, Jr., of The University of Michigan's Institute of Social Research is a major theorist concerned with the development and use of interpersonal power.

In your classic article, "The Bases of Social Power," you identified five major sources of power. Twenty-five years later, would you still classify these as the primary sources of power? Yes. Subsequent research has confirmed the importance of these five bases of interpersonal power. However, we cannot generalize these findings to intergroup power (e.g., power relations between labor and management) nor to interorganizational relations.

Do you see signs of any other major sources of power evolving? Now I would hasten to add a sixth type of power, i.e., informational power. A person with no special expertise can influence your behavior if that person has information you need. This influence is independent of any continuing relation with the stranger and it does not depend on his surveillance to monitor your compliance with his directions. Many other sources of power will likely evolve when there is more research on power relations between groups and between organizations.

Typically, what are the most and least effectively used sources of power in organizations? It all depends on who is influencing whom. When one worker tries to influence another, referent power is the most effective because it is strongest, because it requires no surveillance of compliance, and because it does not reduce other bases of power. In relations among co-workers, the least effective basis of power is legitimate power because workers hold equal roles where one has no legitimate right to prescribe behavior for another. When we consider superior-subordinate relations, the effectiveness of various power bases is quite different. Within any hierarchy the asymmetry of legitimate power is generally recognized: a superior has a right to prescribe behavior for a subordinate. Under these conditions legitimate power is the most effective. The least effective is coercive power because coercion reduces other bases of power.

nificant legitimate power at work. Similarly, a worker with many years of work experience often is perceived to have the legitimate right to influence others. Social leaders can possess a great deal of legitimate power both in and out of the organization. If persons possessing these various forms of legitimate power make conflicting demands on a target of power, other sources of power may determine who will successfully exert the greatest influence.

Referent Power. Persons who are attractive to others because of their personal characteristics possess **referent power.** If others like to interact with you for the pleasure of the interaction, you have referent power. At first glance, referent power appears very different from the other sources of power. In fact, many view referent power as an almost mystical characteristic possessed by some but not by others. Upon closer inspection, however, the degree of distinction becomes less clear. One possible interpretation is that referent power is based simply on reward and coercive power relating specifically to interpersonal outcomes. Viewed this way, you allow yourself to be influenced by the holder of referent power in hopes of receiving the positively valued outcome of association with this person. If you are already associated with the person, you allow yourself to be influenced to avoid the negative consequence of disassociation. The key factor distinguishing referent power from reward/coercive power is that referent power does not involve the active control of outcomes by the power holder.

> If a member is attracted to a group and he conforms to its norms only because he fears ridicule or expulsion from the group for nonconformity, we would call this coercive power. . . . if he conforms in order to obtain praise for conformity, it is a case of reward power. . . . to the extent that [a person] avoids discomfort or gains satisfaction by conformity based on identification, regardless of [the power holder's] responses, we are dealing with referent power.[7]

Referent power increases the chances that the power target will behave as desired by the power holder. In addition, however, referent power frequently produces other changes in behavior. Most of these changes can be classified loosely as *imitative* or *conforming*. In short, people try to "be like" the holder of referent power.

The base of referent power is tied frequently to physical attractiveness, interpersonal attractiveness, fame, prestige, and/or status. A major element of referent power is a sense of identification with the power holder ("I want to be like this person; I would like to be a part of this person's life"). The stronger these factors, the greater the referent power. It also has been hypothesized that increases in attraction increase not only the total amount of referent power, but also the range of situations in which referent power can exert its influence.[8]

Expert Power. For you to have **expert power** over another, *all* of the following conditions must exist:

1. The target must perceive that you possess expert knowledge which s/he does not have.
2. The target must want the expert knowledge you possess.
3. The target must perceive that you are (or will be) willing to share your expert knowledge.

Expert power can be increased by increasing the amount of desirable expert knowledge. Increases of expert power in areas of no concern to the target, however, have no impact on expert power. Thus, a person who has tremendous computer skills may be viewed as an expert but unless you want computer knowledge, the computer jock will not gain expert power. Likewise, even a limited amount of expert knowledge can provide a lot of power if that knowledge is wanted badly enough.

Alternative sources of expert knowledge also influence your expert power. Even if the target desperately needs expert knowledge which you possess, your expert power is limited if the knowledge is also available from others. If you are the sole source of expert knowledge, however, your expert power may be substantial.

The scope of expert power can be limited by the range of situations in which the expert knowledge is useful. A person who has tremendous expert power in situations involving computer systems will have little expert power in situations requiring conflict resolution skills (unless the computer jock also has conflict resolution skills).

An interesting point concerning expert power is that "as you use it, you lose it." The more you share your expert knowledge with others, the less you have to offer. Consequently, unless your total base of desired expert knowledge continues to grow, your expert power will decline.

Information Power. If you possess (nonexpert) information desired by others, you have **information power**. This source of power is similar to expert power in that you must possess information the target does not have; the target must want the information; the target must believe you are willing to share the information. Information power differs from expert power, however, in that special skills or abilities are not involved. Rather, information power is based on desired information collected through experience. Low-level staff members in organizations frequently accumulate extensive information power due to the massive amount of information to which they are exposed. A secretary who "knows where everything is" possesses information power whether or not s/he even understands what the information means. It is not unusual for the amount of information power possessed by an organizational member to be disproportionate to the employee's formal organizational level.

Interaction of the Sources of Power. Although your total power is a combination of the six major sources of power, the combination is seldom a simple additive combination of the individual elements. In some cases, the combination of two sources of power provides greater power than the sum of the two individual sources. For example, referent and expert power can combine to produce an extreme power effect, or reward power actually may increase referent power. At times, two sources of power can provide a combined power base which is less than the sum of the two effects. If coercive power is used excessively, it can lead to a decrease in referent power (as the target decides "I don't want to be like this person").

Organizational Control over Power

Most organizations attempt to define which members will have power by developing a formal organizational chart. In doing this, an organization is attempting to use legitimate power to differentiate power positions. Since legitimate power alone may not be sufficient, most organizations also try to use other sources of power to reinforce the intended authority structure. Reward and coercive power are particularly popular for this purpose; organizational policies specify who controls rewards and punishments.

In reality, the actual power structure typically deviates substantially from that charted. This realization is often quite a surprise to an organization. The difference between intended and actual power structures, however, is quite understandable when you consider the principles of power acquisition:

1. An organization can define legitimate positions of power to influence actual legitimate power. However, legitimate power only exists to the extent that the target perceives the power holder to have the legitimate right to influence him/her. If the target does not accept the organization's "assignment" of power, it does not exist.
2. Few organizations have well-developed and -administered reward and penalty systems. Without these, the potential power

The Use of Power by Industrial Supervisors

A. S. Tannenbaum conducted a study to determine why organizational members comply with the requests of supervisors. Workers were asked "When you do what your immediate superior requests you to do on the job, why do you do it?" The importance of six reasons for compliance were explored. Five of these corresponded to reward, coercive, legitimate, referent, and expert power.

Exhibit 13–2 shows the results of this study in both small and large plants in the United States. As can be seen, legitimate and expert power were rated as the most important and coercive power was rated as least important.

Exhibit 13–2 Supervisory Use of Power

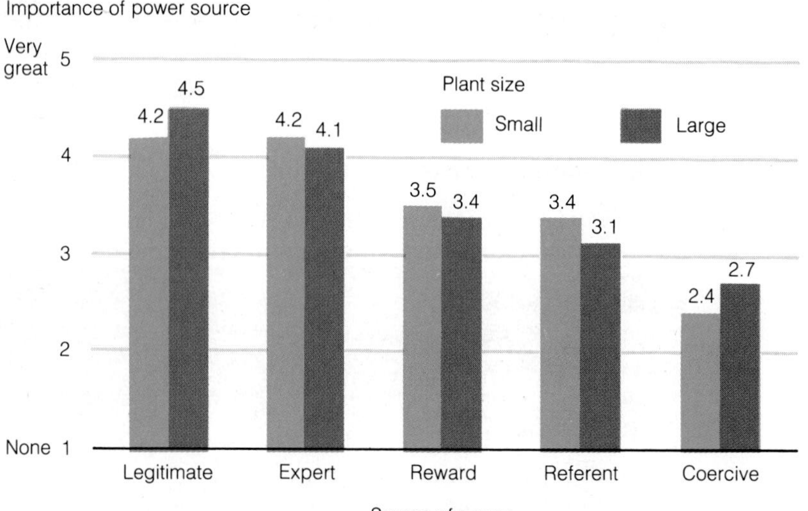

Source: Based on the results of a study done by A. S. Tannenbaum (1974). *Hierarchy in Organizations.* San Francisco, CA: Jossey-Bass.

holder will not have positively and negatively valued outcomes powerful enough to obtain reward and coercive power.

3. Even when adequate reward and penalty systems are in place, targets often fail to perceive that the power holder actually controls the outcomes and is willing to use them in a discretionary fashion. This results in a loss of power.
4. Many power sources exist beyond those controlled by the organization. If these contribute to the building of power bases which

do not match the official organizational authority structure, the actual power structure will vary from that expected by the organization.

The Acquisition of Power

Power from any of the six major potential sources is available to almost everyone in an organization. Some of the major factors you should consider when developing a strong power base are listed below. These suggestions also can be used by an organization to develop a desired power structure.

1. Reward power—Identify a set of outcomes which are positively valued by the target. Determine which of these you have the ability to control. Identify which others you could acquire the ability to control. Make the target aware that you are both willing and able to control these outcomes.
2. Coercive power—Identify a set of outcomes which are negatively valued by the target and a set of positively valued outcomes already being experienced by the target. Determine which of these you have the ability to control and which you could acquire the ability to control. Make the target aware that you are both willing and able to provide negatively valued outcomes and/or to remove positively valued outcomes.
3. Legitimate power—Identify the existing information which specifies your "right" to influence the target. Identify other definitions which could add to this (e.g., organizational policies, verbal pronouncements by a higher-up in the organization). Make the target aware of these legitimate definitions of power. Use reward and coercive power to reinforce this position of legitimate power.
4. Referent power—This is a very difficult power base to develop. However, altering your behavior to emphasize attributes viewed favorably by the target and gaining interpersonal skills training can enhance this power base. If the target is attracted to you, provide opportunities for interaction. If the target perceives you negatively, avoid forced interactions.
5. Expert power—Identify the target's existing expert knowledge needs. Identify how much of this knowledge you possess and which portions of this knowledge you can acquire (through reading, training, etc.). Make the target aware that you possess this expert knowledge and are willing to share it.
6. Information power—Identify the target's existing information needs. Identify how much of this information you possess and which portions you could acquire. Make the target aware that you possess this information, or have access to it, and that you are willing to share it.

Keep in mind that power is perceptually based and use the information from Chapters 10 (Perception) and 11 (Communication) to increase the effectiveness of your communications concerning power. Since power is a *relative* issue, your power base must be stronger than that of the target. You can increase your ability to influence a target person by increasing your own overall power base and/or by decreasing the power base of the target.

Coalitions and Power

There are times when you desire the ability to influence another, have an insufficient total power base to do so, and cannot easily develop sufficient personal power. When this occurs, you either can give up, or you can consider forming a coalition. A **coalition** is an association of two or more individuals formed for the purpose of developing a stronger collective power base than any possessed by the individual coalition members.

Coalitions are very common and can be very effective. An individual employee with a complaint about his/her supervisor usually has relatively little power to influence the supervisor. If all workers supervised by that person combine forces and complain to the supervisor's boss, however, they can exert a very powerful influence. Probably the best-known examples of coalitions are collective bargaining groups. Imagine how far you would get if you alone marched into your employer's office and demanded a shorter work week, higher pay, and better health insurance. All of these demands have been met, however, by unions using the collective power acquired through a coalition.

Much research has been conducted on coalition formation and structure.[9] Unfortunately, most of this research was in environments not representative of typical organizational settings. Despite this, several important aspects of coalitions emerged. Coalitions are formed specifically to increase the power of coalition members so personal gains can be realized. Individuals prefer to participate in coalitions which contain the smallest number of people necessary to acquire the total amount of desired power. Coalitions tend to form at lower levels of an organization to deal with the hierarchy of authority at top management. Centralized organizations with power concentrated at the top are less vulnerable to coalitions than decentralized organizations.

Power and Ethics

The techniques discussed here have coldly and matter-of-factly addressed the effective acquisition and use of power. If you have

sufficient power, it is possible to exert major influences over another person, or even force that person to behave against his/her will. Is it, therefore, unethical to acquire and use power? This is not an easy question to answer. Most would agree that it is unethical to force a person to the point of inflicting serious physical or psychological damage. But what about the use of power to prevent a person from hurting him/herself or injuring another? Should power be used to encourage a person to perform the routine organizational duties agreed to when he/she joined the organization? The judgment of ethics and the use of power is personal; only you can decide if your use of power is unethical (see the Epilogue of this book for a more complete discussion of these issues). What is clear is that power per se is not bad. It is how you use it which determines whether you are behaving ethically.

One final note. Remember that the power of one person over another is a function of the relative power bases of the two persons. Because of this, you can increase your ability to influence the behavior of others *and* reduce the ability of others to influence you. This can be accomplished either by increasing your own power base or by defusing the power base of the person who influences you.

CONFLICT

Conflict occurs when two parties possess incompatible goals and interact in such a way that the behavior of one (or both) of them threatens the other's goal attainment. There are many causes of conflict and many reasons why people choose different strategies for dealing with a conflict situation.

One important point should be made before proceeding: conflict is *not* always bad for people and organizations. It is true that conflict often is associated with many negative outcomes, including decreased performance, decreased cohesion, decreased satisfaction,

In the following situation, Tanya and Eric have incompatible goals but are not in a state of conflict. In fact, both of them are cooperating to facilitate the goal-seeking behavior of the other.

Tanya and Eric both work in the Research and Development Department of American Solar Energies Corporation. Tanya has an idea for a solar-powered home air conditioning unit. Tanya wishes to convince American Solar to develop and market her idea. Eric has an idea for a solar-powered energy supply for long-distance telephone communications. Eric hopes to convince American Solar to develop and market his idea.

Tanya and Eric believe that development of either product alone would cost about $10 million. However, if done at the same time, development of both products would cost only about $15 million. Tanya and Eric decide to combine forces to convince the corporation to invest the $15 million necessary for developing both products.

Six months later, Tanya and Eric still have incompatible goals. Now, however, they are behaving in ways which threaten to frustrate each other's goal attainment. They are engaged in conflict.

Based on the arguments made by Tanya and Eric, American Solar agrees that it would be a wise move to enter new solar markets. The company also agrees that both projects address a potentially large market and that the first company to enter that market would be very likely to earn a large profit.

Upon examining its financial resources, American Solar realizes that it can afford to invest no more than $12 million in new solar products at the present time. Because of this, the decision is made to put the full $12 million into the development of one of the products during the current fiscal year. The second product will be reconsidered during the next fiscal year.

The Board of Directors asks Tanya and Eric to help them decide which product to pursue. Each is given two weeks to prepare a presentation to the board in defense of his/her idea. During the two-week period, Tanya refuses to share technical knowledge with Eric and Eric declines to assist Tanya with cost analyses. At the board meeting two weeks later, both Eric and Tanya make presentations which focus on the strengths of their own ideas and the weaknesses of the other's.

In the above situation, Tanya and Eric clearly are engaged in conflict.

sabotage, physical aggression, and other organizationally dysfunctional consequences. Despite this, however, conflict can produce positive effects. Conflict, for example, can provide needed change in organizations, increase group cohesion and cooperation, and generate creative new ideas.[10] Furthermore, conflict can serve important group functions (see Chapter 12). Basically, conflict almost always is painful, but it need not always produce solely negative effects.

The Causes of Conflict

Conflict does not arise merely because of the presence of incompatible goals. One person's behavior must interfere with the goal-seeking behavior of the other party.

Obviously, the primary underlying condition necessary for the development of conflict is the existence of incompatible goals. Incompatible goals evolve for many reasons. Organizational structure and job assignment often create incompatible goals. A quality control department of an organization is assigned responsibility for making sure that every item manufactured is produced properly; a production department is responsible for rapid, high-quantity production; a cost assessment office must minimize the cost of production. (Yet, a high-quality item may not be produced rapidly or cheaply.) The competitive nature of reward systems often creates incompatible goals. This is the case when only the "best" worker is to receive a bonus or promotion. The needs, values, and personalities of employees also contribute to the incompatibility of goals. A worker with a very strong achievement need, for example, is likely to have very different goals than a person with a strong social need. Competition for limited resources frequently contributes to incompatible goals. Indeed, Tanya and Eric were cooperating with one another until they had to compete for the same limited resources.

Nevertheless, the existence of incompatible goals does not necessarily lead to conflict. Other factors contribute to an atmosphere conducive to conflict. Interdependency increases the probability of conflict.[11] For example, the publisher of this book was dependent upon the author to write a manuscript; the author was dependent upon the publisher to produce and market the text. Neither could meet their primary objectives unless the other performed as required. Time pressure on one or both parties increases the chances of conflict.[12] Unequal distributions of power and status encourage conflict. Finally, one party's perceived intent of another party's behavior can influence conflict behavior.[13] If you perceive that someone's behavior is (or will be) a threat to your own interests, you are more likely to engage in conflict behavior yourself.

The Conflict Process

Exhibit 13–3 presents a model of the **conflict process.** This model, developed by Kenneth Thomas, identifies five major events which typically occur as conflict evolves: frustration, conceptualization, behavior, reactions from the other party, and the aftermath of the conflict episode.[14]

Exhibit 13–3 The Conflict Process

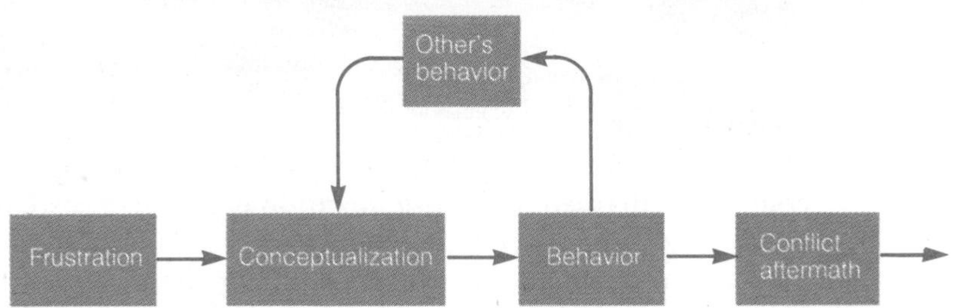

Source: Adapted from K. W. Thomas (1976). Conflict and conflict management. In M. D. Dunnette (Ed.), *Handbook of industrial and organizational psychology*. Chicago: Rand McNally, p. 889.

Frustration. The conflict process begins when you experience or anticipate *frustration* of a personal concern. According to Thomas, your frustration could center on anything you care about (a performance goal, a promotion, personal power, economic resources, values, beliefs, status, or any personal need). In short, if there is something of value you hope to acquire or accomplish and you are (or expect to be) prevented from doing so, you become frustrated.

Frustration is also the measure by which you determine whether or not a conflict has been resolved. When frustration is totally gone, the conflict is totally resolved. Unfortunately, most conflicts are never thoroughly resolved, thus leaving a residual frustration as part of the conflict aftermath. Remaining frustration tends to lead to dissatisfaction, anxiety, anger, depression, and aggression. Furthermore, this frustration can feed a future conflict. In the American Solar example, both Tanya and Eric are likely to experience some residual frustration after the decision over which project to fund is made. In future interactions, these two are more likely to experience conflict because of the residual frustration from the earlier conflict.

Conceptualization. The *conceptualization* stage of conflict is very critical and very subjective. This is when you evaluate the situation and ask the following types of questions:

1. Why am I experiencing frustration?
2. What issue(s) underlies this conflict?
3. What would I like to obtain in resolving this conflict?
4. What do I think the other party would like to obtain in resolving this conflict?
5. How do I expect the other party to behave during this conflict?
6. How do I intend to behave during this conflict?

In short, during the conceptualization stage you formulate perceptions about the nature of the conflict. All of the perceptual phenomena discussed in Chapter 10 impact upon your evaluation of the conflict situation. Because of this, many conflicts are based at least in part on distorted or nonexistent issues. The conceptualization stage is also the point at which you develop behavioral intentions for dealing with the other party engaged in the conflict. Factors which contribute to the selection of behavioral strategies will be discussed later, together with ways for choosing strategies that best match each type of behavior.

Behavior. A popular and useful strategy for classifying conflict *behaviors* is shown in Exhibit 13–4.[15] According to this model, you can deal with any conflict on the basis of **cooperativeness** (the

Exhibit 13–4 Conflict Strategies

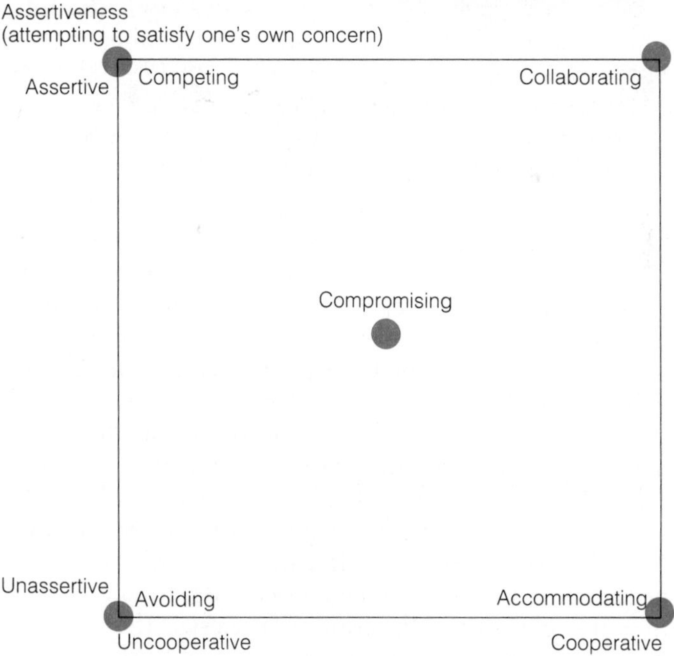

Source: Thomas Rubie and Kenneth Thomas, Support for a two-dimensional model of conflict behavior, *Organizational Behavior and Human Performance, 16,* Fig. 1, p. 145 (1976).

degree to which you attempt to satisfy the other party's concerns) and/or **assertiveness** (the degree to which you attempt to satisfy your own concerns). The combination of these two dimensions produces five distinct types of conflict strategies:

1. *Competing*—an attempt to satisfy your own concerns at the other party's expense. This is an aggressive strategy, usually combative in nature, in which you try to overpower the other party (typically through use of the six sources of power discussed earlier in this chapter).
2. *Accommodating*—an attempt to satisfy the concerns of the other party at your own expense. This is a very passive, even submissive, strategy that tries to determine what the other party wants and how you can meet those needs.
3. *Avoiding*—an attempt to withdraw from the conflict by ignoring both your concerns and those of the other party. With this strategy, no attempt is made to resolve the strategy in one direction or the other.
4. *Collaborating*—an attempt to satisfy the concerns of both parties by solving the problems that are preventing both parties from satisfying their needs. With this strategy, attempts are made to identify the underlying problems and collectively resolve them.
5. *Compromising*—an attempt to satisfy partially the concerns of both parties through mutual sacrifice. With this strategy, attempts are made to identify mutually acceptable but suboptimal solutions for both parties.

Reactions from the Other Party. Remember, you are not alone in a conflict situation; you must take the *reactions from the other party* into account. The other party in a conflict relationship engages in both proactive and reactive behavior. *Proactive behavior* of the other party is initiated prior to or at the same time as you initiate your behavior and is determined by the same conceptualization process which led to your initial choice of conflict strategy. (The other party also chooses from one of the five conflict strategies shown in Exhibit 13–4.) In addition, the other party adjusts his/her behavior in reaction to yours (*reactive behavior*). As you observe the other party's behavior, you reconceptualize the nature of the conflict and behave accordingly (i.e., you make tactical adjustments). The result of this dynamic element in the conflict process is that the behavior of each party changes often during the course of the conflict. Depending on the nature of the conflict and the types of conflict strategies used by the two parties, this dynamic loop (shown in Exhibit 13–3) may be followed many times prior to resolution of the conflict.

Examples of Conflict Handling Strategies

As a part of his dissertation research, James Riggs conducted a series of studies designed to identify specific examples for each of the five conflict handling strategies.[16] The following are examples of behaviors frequently used in each approach.*

Competing

1. Pursue your own goals with determination, regardless of the other person's concerns.
2. Make the first move in the conflict to gain control of the situation and maximize chances of obtaining your demands.
3. Prolong the discussion of the issues until the other person tires and gives in to your approach for handling the problem.

Accommodating

1. Offer to handle the problem any way the other person wants.
2. Go along with whatever the other person requests, rather than get into the difficulties of direct confrontation.

Avoiding

1. Downplay the seriousness of the problem and suggest the two of you not waste time with the matter.
2. Tell the other person that the problem does not concern you.
3. Explain that there is no point in trying to resolve a conflict between two people with such basically different personalities.

Collaborating

1. Try to sort out where each of you stands and identify options available to meet both parties' needs.
2. Suggest that you take your ideas and the other person's ideas and put them together to make an even more workable idea.
3. Express your concern for the differences between you and let the other person know you want a resolution which satisfies both of you.

Compromising

1. Point out to the other person that if you both will make a few concessions, the conflict can be resolved quickly.
2. Point out that if the disagreement is to be resolved, some sacrifices must be made by both of you.

*My apologies to Jim Riggs for focusing on a small number of issues from a very sophisticated dissertation.

Conflict Aftermath. The **conflict aftermath** involves a variety of outcomes. Four types of these are particularly important in evaluating the consequences of conflict.[17]

The first outcome is the degree of *goal attainment* by each party upon resolution of the conflict. Conflicts can produce win/lose solutions (one party attains most or all of its goals, while the other party accomplishes few, if any). This often occurs in competing resolutions in which one party wins. In lose/lose resolutions, neither party achieves all of its goals. This typically results in compromising resolutions or in competing resolutions in which neither party wins (as would be the case in a bilateral nuclear war). Win/win resolutions lead to the attainment of most or all of the goals of both parties. This is most likely to occur with collaborating resolutions.

A second important outcome involves changes in *human resources*. The nature of conflict resolution can influence satisfaction, motivation, cohesiveness, levels of interpersonal trust, openness of communication, and other relevant attitudes and behaviors. Although the level of goal attainment obviously has a major impact on these factors, the conflict experience itself exerts a major impact independent of goal attainment levels.

The third important outcome involves *resource consumption*. A wide variety of organizational and personal resources can be exhausted during the conflict process. Always present is the time and energy which the parties involved devote directly to the conflict. Indirect time and energy spent thinking and worrying about the conflict also can be significant. Of particular relevance here is the work which would have been performed had this time and energy not been spent in conflict. Frequently a conflict also will disrupt the work activities of those not directly involved, but who are dependent upon those involved in the conflict. They cannot function well while the conflict continues. Another significant cost of conflict is the time and energy devoted by others to resolve the conflict. This may involve a co-worker, supervisor, or third-party interventionist.

The final important outcome concerns the *positive effects* of the conflict. In evaluating the aftermath of a conflict, it is important to consider positive results as well as negative ones. Positive results can include needed organizational change, increased cohesion among those who cooperated to resolve a conflict, new ideas which resulted from the conflict, increased maturity on the part of the conflict parties, the avoidance of Groupthink, etc.

The Selection of a Conflict Resolution Strategy

There are two ways to examine the *selection* of a **conflict resolution strategy**. The first of these is to examine factors typically used as persons select conflict strategies. This approach can help you anticipate probable behaviors in conflict situations. It also can help you understand why people choose the conflict strategies they do. The second perspective used to examine strategy choice focuses on the most appropriate strategies for particular situations. This approach can help you select a conflict strategy which best matches the conflict situation. It is interesting to note that the most commonly chosen conflict strategies are not always the most desirable strategies.

Factors which Typically Influence Strategy Choice. Despite the importance of understanding the determinants of conflict-handling strategies, literature has not provided a well-integrated answer to the question: "What influences an individual's choice from among the five types of conflict strategies?" In an attempt to rectify this situation, Jim Riggs conducted a thorough review of organizational behavior, social psychology, and communication literatures.[18] In doing so, he developed a model which uses three major factors for predicting choice of conflict-handling strategy: an individual's general orientation to conflict, the nature of interdependence between the two parties involved in the conflict, and the expected behavior of the other party involved in the conflict (see Exhibit 13–5).

Your *general orientation to conflict* tends to favor one of the five conflict strategies shown in Exhibit 13–4. It is possible to measure your general orientation using items such as those shown in Exhibit 13–6. All things being equal, you will be more likely to choose a conflict strategy consistent with your general orientation. Another strategy might be chosen by a person with a different orientation.

Exhibit 13–5 A Model of Conflict Strategy Choice

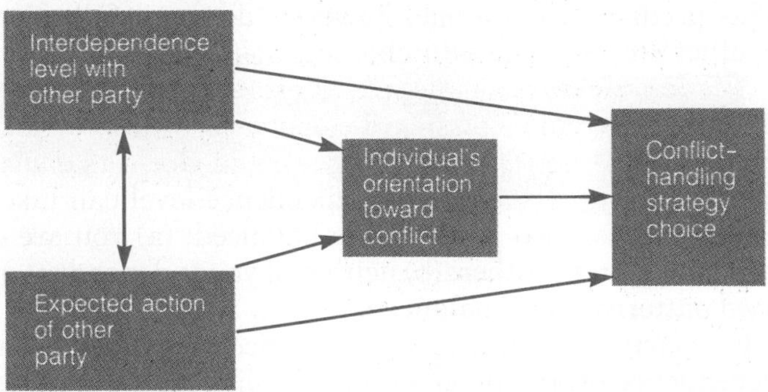

Source: Adapted from C. J. Riggs, Communication, coordination and conflict in work organizations: interpersonal contingencies of conflict interaction among co-workers (Ph.D. diss., University of Wisconsin, Madison, 1983).

Exhibit 13–6 Conflict Mode Instrument

Directions: From each pair of statements, please select the one (A or B) that most accurately describes how *you* handle conflicts with co-workers.

1. A. I try to find a compromise solution.
B. I attempt to deal with all the other person's concerns as well as my own.

2. A. I try to find a compromise solution.
B. I sometimes sacrifice my own wishes for the wishes of the other person.

3. A. I sometimes avoid taking positions which would create controversy.
B. I will let the other person have some points if s/he lets me have some of mine.

4. A. I propose a middle ground.
B. I press to get my points made.

5. A. I try not to hurt the other person's feelings.
B. I try to convince the other person of the merits of my position.

6. A. I am usually firm in pursuing my goals.
B. I try to do what is necessary to avoid tensions.

7. A. I attempt to get all concerns and issues immediately out in the open.
B. I try to postpone the issue until I have had some time to think it over.

8. A. I propose a middle ground.
B. I feel that differences are not always worth worrying about.

Source: K. W. Thomas and R. H. Kilmann (1974). *Thomas-Kilmann conflict mode instrument.* Tuxedo, NY: Zicom.

This predisposition alone, however, does not fully determine the conflict strategy you will choose.

The *interdependence level* which exists between you and the other party involved in a conflict (the degree to which you are dependent on the other for attaining your goals and vice versa) also influences your choice of strategy. Interdependence level can take any one of four patterns. Two patterns are balanced: (a) you are each highly dependent on the other; (b) neither of you is dependent on the other. Two patterns are unbalanced: (a) you are highly dependent on the other party, who has low dependence on you; (b) you have low dependence on the other party, who has high dependence on you. The proposed impact of interdependence on conflict strategy choice is somewhat complex. It is likely, however, that you will become more cooperative as your dependence on the other party increases. As the balance of interdependence favors you, you are likely to become more assertive.

The *expected behavior of the other party* involved in the conflict has a direct impact on your choice of conflict strategy. You will select a conflict strategy which matches the strategy you expect from the other party. Given the importance of the expected behavior of the other party, it is interesting to note that perceptions of the other party's strategy tend to be extremely biased. For example, managers are 10 times more likely to perceive collaboration behavior from themselves than from the other party in a conflict, and almost 4 times as likely to perceive conflict behavior from the other party (in situations where equal amounts of the two types of behaviors actually exist).[19]

The combined effects of the above three determinants may be quite complex and have not yet been thoroughly researched. Riggs attempted to test all possible combinations, but the full impact of each of the three determinants will not be known for some time.

Factors which Should Influence Strategy Choice. There is no one best conflict strategy. Just as there are multiple criteria for evaluating the outcomes of conflict, there are many factors which influence the choice of appropriate strategies. Indeed, it can be argued that any of the five conflict strategies can be appropriate, depending on the circumstances surrounding the conflict. Exhibit 13–7 presents a list of appropriate situations for using each conflict strategy (a group of chief executive officers provided the input for this list).

SUMMARY

Power is the ability of a person (or group) to influence the fate of others and maintain control over his/her own fate. Six major sources of power are: reward, coercive, legitimate, referent, expert, and information. Each source of power is dependent upon the perceptions of the target and the target's belief that you will treat him/her according to whether or not his/her behavior matches your desires. The use of power in organizations should not be taken lightly. You should give careful consideration to the ethical issues involved before exercising your power.

Conflict is the interaction of two parties with incompatible goals such that the behavior of one (or both) threatens the goal attainment of the other (or both). There are five stages in the conflict process: frustration, conceptualization, behavior, reactions from

Exhibit 13–7 Uses of the Five Conflict Modes as Reported by a Group of Chief Executive Officers

Conflict-Handling Modes	Appropriate Situations
Competing	1. When quick, decisive action is vital—e.g., emergencies. 2. On important issues where unpopular actions need implementing—e.g., cost cutting, enforcing unpopular rules, discipline. 3. On issues vital to company welfare when you know you're right. 4. Against people who take advantage of noncompetitive behavior.
Collaborating	1. To find an integrative solution when both sets of concerns are too important to be compromised. 2. When your objective is to learn. 3. To merge insights from people with different perspectives. 4. To gain commitment by incorporating concerns into a consensus. 5. To work through feelings which have interfered with a relationship.
Compromising	1. When goals are important, but not worth the effort or potential disruption of more assertive modes. 2. When opponents with equal power are committed to mutually exclusive goals. 3. To achieve temporary settlements to complex issues. 4. To arrive at expedient solutions under time pressure. 5. As a backup when collaboration or competition is unsuccessful.
Avoiding	1. When an issue is trivial, or more important issues are pressing. 2. When you perceive no chance of satisfying your concerns. 3. When potential disruption outweighs the benefits of resolution. 4. To let people cool down and regain perspective. 5. When gathering information supersedes immediate decision. 6. When others can resolve the conflict more effectively. 7. When issues seem tangential or symptomatic of other issues.
Accommodating	1. When you find you are wrong—to allow a better position to be heard, to learn, and to show your reasonableness. 2. When issues are more important to others than yourself—to satisfy others and maintain cooperation. 3. To build social credits for later issues. 4. To minimize loss when you are outmatched and losing. 5. When harmony and stability are especially important. 6. To allow subordinates to develop by learning from mistakes.

Source: Based on Table 1 of K. W. Thomas (1977). Toward multidimensional values in teaching: The example of conflict behaviors. *Academy of Management Review, 2,* 487.

the other party, and conflict aftermath. Five common conflict strategies are: competing, accommodating, avoiding, collaborating, and compromising. The major determinants involved in selecting a conflict strategy are: interdependence level with the other party, expected action of the other party, and an individual's orientation toward conflict. Finally, you should attempt to select for each conflict situation the most useful one of the five types of strategies. Although there is still much to learn about conflict management, you can improve your handling of such situations through careful consideration of the factors which influence the conflict process.

GLOSSARY

Power The ability to influence others or to maintain control over your own fate.

Reward Power Power derived from the belief that a person is able and willing to provide rewards.

Coercive Power Power derived from the belief that a person is able and willing to provide punishment.

Legitimate Power Power derived from the belief that a person has the right to exert influence.

Referent Power Power derived from the attractiveness of the power holder.

Expert Power Power derived from the belief that a person has and is willing to share desirable expert knowledge.

Information Power Power derived from the belief that a person has and is willing to share desirable information.

Coalition An association of two or more individuals formed for the purpose of developing a stronger collective power base than that possessed by any of the individuals alone.

Conflict A situation in which two parties possess incompatible goals and interact in such a way that the behavior of one threatens the other's goal attainment.

Conflict Process The sequence of events involved in a conflict (frustration, conceptualization, behavior, reactions from the other party, and the aftermath of the conflict episode).

Cooperativeness The degree to which one party of a conflict attempts to satisfy the other party's concerns.

Assertiveness The degree to which one party of a conflict attempts to satisfy his/her own concerns.

Conflict Aftermath The degree to which, following a conflict, the parties involved have attained goals, changed human resources, consumed resources, and obtained any other positive results.

Conflict Resolution Strategy The approach selected in dealing with a conflict in hopes of resolving the conflict.

STUDY QUESTIONS

1. Discuss the degree to which an organization can *assign* power to an individual as opposed to an individual *acquiring* power.

2. What steps can an individual take to increase his/her overall power base?
3. Discuss the circumstances under which an organizational member could possess more overall power than his/her boss.
4. Discuss the importance of perception in power acquisition.
5. Discuss the ethics of the use of power in an organization.
6. Discuss conditions under which conflict would be beneficial to an organization; conditions under which conflict would be harmful.
7. Why would it be useful to be able to anticipate the type of conflict resolution strategy likely to be chosen by another person with whom you have a conflict?
8. What steps could be taken by an organization to reduce the likelihood of conflict developing between organizational members?

NOTES

1. **Thomas, K. W., & Schmidt, W. H.** (1976). A survey of managerial interests with respect to conflict. *Academy of Management Journal, 19*, 315–318.
2. **Weber, M.** (1947). *The theory of social and economic organization.* (A. M. Henderson & T. Parsons trans. and eds.). New York: Oxford University Press.
3. See **Bacharach, S. B., & Lawler, E. J.** (1981). *Power and politics in organizations*. San Francisco, CA: Jossey-Bass; **Pfeffer, J.** (1981). *Power in organizations*. Marshfield, MA: Pitman Publishing.
4. **French, J. R., Jr., & Raven, B. H.** (1959). The bases of social power. In D. Cartwright (Ed.), *Studies in social power*. Ann Arbor, MI: University of Michigan Press; **Raven, B. H.** (1974). A comparative analysis of power and power preference. In J. T. Tedeschi (Ed.), *Perspectives on social power*. Chicago: Aldine; **Raven, B. H., & Kruglanski, A. W.** (1970). Conflict and power. In P. Swingle (Ed.), *The structure of conflict*. New York: Academic Press.
5. Official Airline Guide/Frequent Flyer, August 1983, p. 39.
6. **Bacharach & Lawler,** 1981, p. 33.
7. **French & Raven,** 1959, p. 161.
8. Ibid.
9. Five major coalition theories are explored in the following: **Caplow, T.** (1968). *Two against one*. Englewood Cliffs, NJ: Prentice-Hall; **DeSwann, A.** (1973). *Coalition theories and cabinet formation*. San Francisco: Jossey-Bass; **Gamson, W. A.** (1961). A theory of coalition formation. *American Sociological Review, 26*, 373–382; **Komorita, S. S., & Chertkoff, J.** (1973). A bargaining theory of coalition formation. *Psychological Review, 80*, 149–162.

10. **Robbins, S. P.** (1974). *Managing organizational conflict: A nontraditional approach*. Englewood Cliffs, NJ: Prentice-Hall; **Simmel, G.** (1965). *Conflict*. New York: Free Press; **Deutsch, M.** (1973). *The resolution of conflict*. New Haven: Yale University Press.

11. **Filley, A. C.** (1975). *Interpersonal conflict resolution*. Glenview, IL: Scott, Foresman.

12. **Tedeschi, J. T., & Lindskold, S.** (1976). *Social psychology: Interdependence, interaction and influence*. New York: Wiley.

13. **Thomas, K. W., & Pondy, L.** (1977). Toward an "intent" model of conflict management among principal parties. *Human Relations, 30*, 1089–1102.

14. **Thomas, K.** (1976). Conflict and conflict management. In M. D. Dunnette (Ed.), *Handbook of industrial and organizational psychology*. Chicago: Rand McNally.

15. Development of this model was contributed to by several theorists/researchers. This particular configuration was described by **Ruble, T., & Thomas, K.** Support for a two-dimensional model of conflict behavior. *Organizational Behavior and Human Performance, 16*, 143–155.

16. **Riggs, C. J.** (1983a). *Communication, coordination, and conflict in work organizations: Interpersonal contingencies of conflictive interaction among co-workers*. Unpublished doctoral dissertation, University of Wisconsin, Madison. Riggs, C. J. (1983b). Dimensions of organizational conflict: A functional analysis of communication tactics. In R. N. Bostrom, ed., *Communication Yearbook* 7 (Beverly Hills, Calif.: Sage, 1983).

17. This discussion is based in part on **Thomas, K. W.** (1979). Organizational Conflict. In S. Kerr (Ed.), *Organizational behavior*. Columbus, OH: Grid.

18. **Riggs,** 1983a.

19. **Thomas & Pondy,** 1977.

14 Leadership

OVERVIEW
LEADERSHIP DEFINED
AN ORGANIZING PERSPECTIVE
UNIVERSAL LEADERSHIP TRAITS
SITUATION-CONTINGENT LEADERSHIP TRAITS (FIEDLER)
The Critical Leader Trait—LPC
Situational Favorableness
The Leader–Situation Match
Implications of Fiedler's Model
UNIVERSAL LEADERSHIP BEHAVIORS
Critical Leader Behaviors
SITUATION-CONTINGENT LEADERSHIP BEHAVIORS
Path-Goal Theory
Rational Decision-Making Theory
SUBSTITUTES FOR LEADERSHIP
SUMMARY

This chapter is dedicated to the memory of Ralph M. Stogdill, a leader in the theory and research of leadership. His contributions to this field will be neither forgotten nor surpassed.

OVERVIEW

A lot is known about **leadership** in organizations. At least as much is still to be learned. The central question regarding leadership is (depending on your preference):

WHAT MAKES A GOOD LEADER?
or
WHAT MAKES A LEADER GOOD?

Despite general agreement on the importance of the above question, there is little agreement on *the* answer. Indeed, it is unrealistic to expect to find a single simple answer to this question. There are thousands of research studies on the various leadership theories, most presented in a competitive tone (if one is "right," the others must be "wrong"). This chapter focuses on both the good and bad points of several leadership perspectives so that you may take advantage of the strengths and avoid the weaknesses of each. Despite the fact that many organizations adopt a single leadership theory, *there is no adequately comprehensive single leadership theory*. To act as though there were one is a mistake.[1]

LEADERSHIP DEFINED

It is not surprising that there are many different theories to explain leadership; there are over a hundred different definitions of leadership. The definition used here was proposed by Arthur Jago of the University of Houston:

> Leadership is both a process and a property. The *process* of leadership is the use of noncoercive influence to direct and coordinate the activities of the members of an organized group toward the accomplishment of group objectives. As a *property,* leadership is the set of qualities or characteristics attributed to those who are perceived to successfully employ such influence.[2]

Although leaders may use force or coercion to alter the behavior of followers, leadership as discussed in this chapter deals with influence of the leader on the voluntary behavior of followers. This definition also allows anyone in an organization to be a leader, whether or not that person is formally identified as such. Indeed, informal leaders are often extremely important to organizational effectiveness.

It is possible to draw a distinction between leadership and supervision.[3] As described above, leadership focuses on voluntary influences on followers. Supervision influences followers through the use of rewards, punishments, and other formal tools. George Graen of the University of Cincinnati has even provided evidence that a person holding a formal position of authority tends to "lead" some subordinates and "supervise" others.[4] Presumably, the same subordinate could be both led and supervised. Although this distinction between leadership and supervision is important, some leadership theories fail to include it. This does not necessarily make them bad theories—it simply makes them theories which cover both leadership and supervision.

AN ORGANIZING PERSPECTIVE

The majority of leadership theories fall into one of four categories (see Exhibit 14–1). These four categories are created through a combination of: (*a*) trait approaches (the focus of the theory is on leader traits) versus behavioral approaches (the theory concentrates on leader behaviors), and (*b*) the belief that the traits/behaviors producing effective leadership are universal versus contingent.

Trait approaches specify that leaders with the appropriate characteristics (physical, skill, personality, or social) are more effective than leaders without these characteristics. **Behavioral approaches** focus on observable behaviors (consideration, structuring) of the leader as the determinants of leader effectiveness. **Universal theories** state that there is "one best kind of leader" who will be effective regardless of the leadership situation. **Contingency theories** claim that the most effective traits/behaviors depend on the nature of the situation.

Exhibit 14–1 Leadership Theories: An Organizing Perspective

Focal Construct	Theoretical Approach: Universal	Theoretical Approach: Contingent
Traits	Type I Universal leadership traits	Type II Situational contingent leadership traits
Behaviors	Type III Universal leadership behaviors	Type IV Situational contingent leadership behaviors

Source: Reprinted by permission of A. G. Jago, Leadership perspectives in theory and research, *Management Science 28,* 316. Copyright 1982 by The Institute of Management Sciences.

UNIVERSAL LEADERSHIP TRAITS

Theory and research on leadership during the first half of this century focused almost exclusively on identifying the profile of traits which characterize the successful leader. It was hoped that a relatively small number of factors could be identified which, when combined, would determine the degree to which a person would become an effective leader. The implications of finding such a set of traits were great. Identifying and selecting people for leadership roles could be performed mechanically by comparing the characteristics of a person to the list of necessary traits. Since this approach assumed that a person with these traits would be effective in *any* leadership situation, only one set of traits would be needed, regardless of whether the leader was to function as President of the United States or as head of a student study group.

The results of the thousands of studies exploring leadership traits were mildly successful.[5] A series of traits exist which distinguish leaders from followers, effective leaders from ineffective leaders, and higher-level from lower-level leaders. As can be seen in Exhibit 14–2, the traits involved include a wide range of physical, ability, personality, social, and related characteristics. Exhibit 14–2 also identifies energy level, intelligence, knowledge, dominance, and self-confidence as traits which show the most consistently high associations with leadership.[6]

Exhibit 14–2 Leadership Traits

Physical and Constitutional Factors	Skill and Ability	Personality Characteristics	Social Characteristics
Activity, energy	Administrative ability	Achievement drive, ambition	Cooperativeness
Appearance, grooming	**Intelligence**	Adaptability	Interpersonal skills, sensitivity
Height	Judgment	Adjustment, normality	Popularity, prestige
Weight	**Knowledge**	Aggressiveness	Sociability
	Technical competence	Alertness	Socioeconomic position
	Verbal fluency	Antiauthoritarianism	Talkativeness
		Dominance	Tact
		Emotional balance, control	
		Enthusiasm	
		Extraversion	
		Independence, nonconformity	
		Initiative	
		Insightfulness	
		Integrity	
		Objectivity	
		Originality	
		Persistence	
		Responsibility	
		Self-confidence	
		Sense of humor	
		Tolerance of stress	

Note: Traits shown in boldface have the greatest association with leadership.
Source: Reprinted by permission of A. G. Jago, "Leadership perspectives in theory and research," *Management Science 28,* 317. Copyright 1982 by The Institute of Management Sciences.

Unfortunately, although the traits just discussed have *statistically significant* relationships to leadership effectiveness, their practical utility is greatly limited. For several reasons, these traits are not powerful enough predictors of leadership to make them useful as the basis for choosing leaders. The limitation is that the relationships between traits and leadership are too weak and have too many exceptions for practical use. Compounding this problem is the frequent finding that the most appropriate traits are dependent on the situation. For these reasons, most leadership theorists, researchers, and practitioners have abandoned the use of traits for identifying a universally effective leader.

SITUATION-CONTINGENT LEADERSHIP TRAITS (FIEDLER)

The dominant trait-oriented, situation-contingent leadership theory is that developed by Fred Fiedler of the University of

Washington.[7] Although controversial, this is a well-developed and thought-provoking perspective on leadership. According to Fiedler, the effectiveness of a leader is determined by the degree of match between a dominant trait of the leader and the favorableness of the situation for the leader.

The Critical Leader Trait—LPC

The dominant trait is a personality factor causing the leader to be either **relationship-oriented** or **task-oriented:**

> The relationship oriented leader (note that this is a goal orientation, not an observed behavior) "looks at the individual not only as a co-worker but also as a person who might otherwise have some acceptable, if not admirable, traits. . . . [This] leader sees close interpersonal relations as a requirement for task accomplishment."[8]
>
> The task-oriented leader "shows a strong emotional reaction to people with whom he or she cannot work. . . . This is the typical pattern of a person who, when forced to make the choice, opts first for getting on with the task and worries about his interpersonal relations later."[9]

To assess the critical leader trait, Fiedler developed the LPC (Least Preferred Co-worker) scale (see Exhibit 14–3).[10] This scale asks you to evaluate your least preferred co-worker along 16 dimensions. Leaders who describe their least preferred co-worker in positive personal terms (pleasant, friendly, accepting, etc.) are given high LPC scores and considered by Fiedler to be relationship-oriented. Leaders with low LPC scores are considered to be task-oriented. The idea behind the LPC scale is that you learn about the *leader* by obtaining his/her view of poor co-workers.

One of the major controversies surrounding **Fiedler's model** concerns the true meaning of an LPC score. This is a question of "construct validity" (see Chapter 2). It simply is not clear exactly what the LPC measures. Show Exhibit 14–3 to friends who have not taken OB and ask what it appears to measure. If they say it appears to measure a leader's underlying psychological orientation to relationships versus tasks, they agree with Fiedler. There is some evidence that high LPC leaders are interpersonally oriented, but the evidence is less clear about the nature of low LPC leaders.[11]

Situational Favorableness

The key situational factor identified by Fiedler concerns **situational favorableness:**

> the degree to which the leader has control and influence and, therefore, feels that (s/)he can determine the outcomes of the group interaction.[12]

Exhibit 14–3 Fiedler's LPC Scale

Think of the person with whom you can work least well. This may be someone you work with now, or someone you knew in the past. It does not have to be the person you like least well, but should be the person with whom you had the most difficulty in getting a job done. Describe this person as s/he appears to you.

Pleasant	8	7	6	5	4	3	2	1	Unpleasant
Friendly	8	7	6	5	4	3	2	1	Unfriendly
Rejecting	1	2	3	4	5	6	7	8	Accepting
Helpful	8	7	6	5	4	3	2	1	Frustrating
Unenthusiastic	1	2	3	4	5	6	7	8	Enthusiastic
Tense	1	2	3	4	5	6	7	8	Relaxed
Distant	1	2	3	4	5	6	7	8	Close
Cold	1	2	3	4	5	6	7	8	Warm
Cooperative	8	7	6	5	4	3	2	1	Uncooperative
Supportive	8	7	6	5	4	3	2	1	Hostile
Boring	1	2	3	4	5	6	7	8	Interesting
Quarrelsome	1	2	3	4	5	6	7	8	Harmonious
Self-assured	8	7	6	5	4	3	2	1	Hesitant
Efficient	8	7	6	5	4	3	2	1	Inefficient
Gloomy	1	2	3	4	5	6	7	8	Cheerful
Open	8	7	6	5	4	3	2	1	Guarded

Note: LPC score is the sum of the answers to these 16 questions. High scores indicate a relationship orientation; low scores, a task orientation.

Source: From *Leadership and effective management* by Fred E. Fiedler and Martin M. Chemers. Copyright © 1974 by Scott, Foresman & Co. Reprinted by permission.

Situation favorableness is determined through a combination of leader-member relations, task structure, and position power. The favorableness of the situation increases for the leader as: *leader-member relations* are such that group members trust and like the leader and are willing to follow the leader's guidance; *task structure* clarifies for subordinates what to do and how to do it; and, *position power* of the leader is high. As shown at the bottom of Exhibit 14–4, the most favorable situation exists with good leader-member relations, high task structure, and strong position power. The least favorable situation consists of poor leader-member relations, low task structure, and weak position power. Intermediate favorableness levels lie in between.[13]

The Leader–Situation Match

After examining the results of various combinations of leader LPC- and situation-favorableness, Fiedler concluded that task-motivated (low LPC) leaders would be more effective than relationship-motivated (high LPC) leaders in situations which are either very favorable or very unfavorable.* Relationship-oriented leaders, on

Exhibit 14–4 Fiedler's Contingency Model Leader–Situation Matches

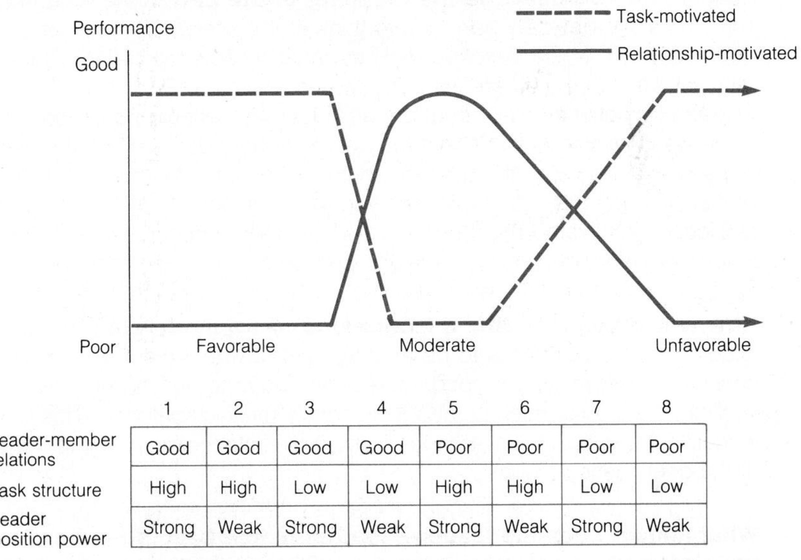

	1	2	3	4	5	6	7	8
Leader-member relations	Good	Good	Good	Good	Poor	Poor	Poor	Poor
Task structure	High	High	Low	Low	High	High	Low	Low
Leader position power	Strong	Weak	Strong	Weak	Strong	Weak	Strong	Weak

Source: From *Leadership and effective management* by Fred E. Fiedler and Martin M. Chemers. Copyright © 1974 by Scott, Foresman & Co. Reprinted by permission.

*Fiedler's index of leader effectiveness is the performance level of subordinates. Satisfaction is not directly addressed by this model.

Fred E. Fiedler of the University of Washington is the developer of the well-known Contingency Theory of Leadership.

What advice can you offer the student reading this book who hopes to become an effective leader? The leadership program which we developed involves three basic steps. The first is to determine your leadership style, usually by taking the LPC scale. The second is to diagnose the leadership situation, i.e., how much control you have by virtue of your leader/member relations, task structure, and position power. The third part of this task is to engineer the situation so it fits your particular leadership style.

How would you describe the meaning of the LPC scale to a manager? The LPC scale basically asks you to think of the one person with whom you can work least well. If you describe this individual by saying in effect, "I can't work with you, therefore, you are just no good as a person," this implies a high degree of emotional rejection of an individual with whom one cannot work. This is the way in which low LPC people describe their least preferred co-worker. Higher LPC people on the other hand say, in effect, "You may be a poor co-worker and you may be stupid, but you are pleasant." In other words, the relationship-motivated (high LPC) individual is more concerned with the person that he or she is describing than with the task.

How would you describe a leader who has a moderate LPC score? The middle LPC leader comes to be independent of what others think of him/her, less concerned with making a good impression, tends to benefit more from intelligence and experience, and is generally more dispatched. This type of leader tends to be effective under many circumstances in many of the quadrants of the contingency model.

What impact does the leader-situation match have on subordinate satisfaction? We have found that high LPC leaders who are dull and low LPC leaders who are bright tend to have the most satisfied groups. Low LPC bosses with low LPC leaders tend to have a very tense situation. High LPC with high LPC and low LPC with high LPC tend to work out better.

the other hand, should excel in situations of intermediate favorableness. It is not clear what types of situations best match the leader with an intermediate LPC score.

Another major controversy regarding Fiedler's model concerns the underlying reasons *why* the pattern shown at the top of Exhibit 14–4 occurs. Fiedler has not specified fully the theoretical reasons for the expected effects nor has the underlying process ever been subjected to adequate evaluation. As a result, the model is *predictive* but not *explanatory*.

Implications of Fiedler's Model

Fiedler's theory has some very interesting implications for the management of leaders in organizations:

1. The favorableness of leadership situations should be assessed using the instruments developed by Fiedler (or, at the very least, by a subjective evaluation).
2. Candidates for leadership positions should be evaluated using the LPC scale.
3. If a leader is being sought for a particular leadership position, a leader with the appropriate LPC profile should be chosen (task-oriented for very favorable or very unfavorable situations and relationship-oriented for intermediate favorableness).
4. If a leadership situation is being chosen for a particular candidate, a situation (work team, department, etc.) should be chosen which matches his/her LPC profile (very favorable or unfavorable for task-oriented leaders and intermediate favorableness for a relationship-oriented leader).

The preceding recommendations sound very straightforward, but what do you do if the leader and the situation are mismatched? One obvious solution is to remove the leader and replace him/her with a person whose LPC trait matches the situation. A second choice for dealing with a mismatch is to change the situation to match the leader.

Fiedler and his associates have developed a self-paced leadership education program known as *Leader Match* for exactly this purpose.[14] This program deals systematically with techniques for altering the favorableness of a situation by: altering leader-member relations (increasing or decreasing the amount of informal time spent with subordinates); changing the task structure (simplifying or expanding the scope of the job); or changing position power (exercising one or more bases of power or decreasing use of power). Although there is some evidence that the *Leader Match* program can succeed, you should think twice before intentionally decreasing the favorableness of a situation.[15] The potential side effects of such changes should also be considered (see, for example, Chapter 15).

Fiedler recommends against trying to change the characteristic trait of a leader. He suggests that this usually is ineffective, partially because the LPC is thought to be an underlying stable personality characteristic. In any event, since no one seems to know exactly what the LPC score measures, it would be difficult to design a training program to change an unknown underlying trait.

Fiedler's theory remains quite controversial among leadership scholars. Studies examining individual parts of Fiedler's model have provided partial support for its merits. Very few complete tests have been conducted, though, and those that have contain mixed and often contradictory findings.[16] Furthermore, since the central concept (LPC) is somewhat mysterious, the underlying theory is difficult to accept. It might be best if future research were to identify specific leader *behaviors* associated with the various leader LPC levels. Until then, you may conclude that, although not all details of the theory are supported, it does explain a lot of the variation in leader effectiveness (as measured by subordinate performance). Because the evidence is not clear on *why* the theory works, however, its use at the present time is not without risk.

UNIVERSAL LEADERSHIP BEHAVIORS

In the late 1940s, a series of research projects began which focused on observable leader *behaviors* rather than underlying leadership traits.[17] Much of the significant work on the impact of leader behavior was conducted by the Leadership Group at Ohio State University under the direction of Ralph Stogdill, Edwin Fleishman, and John Hemphill.* This research succeeded in identifying critical dimensions of leader behavior. Attempts to define a "one best style" of leader behavior were less successful, but laid the groundwork for the behaviorally-based contingency theories discussed in the next section.

Critical Leader Behaviors

Two *critical leader* behaviors were identified: initiating structure, and consideration. **Initiating structure** is observable leader behav-

*A thorough review of the Ohio State research and other leadership research is contained in an incredible volume: B. M. Bass (1978). *Stogdill's handbook of leadership*. New York: Free Press. This book is a major revision of the late Ralph Stogdill's original 1974 version of the book. Containing over 5,000 references and 600 pages, it is an indispensable reference book for the serious student of leadership.

ior which focuses on the degree to which a leader clarifies and defines roles and responsibilities for subordinates. This behavior tells subordinates the *what, when, and where* of their jobs. **Consideration** is observable leader behavior concentrating on the comfort, well-being, status, needs, and satisfaction of followers.

Together, these dimensions of behavior appear to define the majority of observable leader behaviors in interactions with subordinates. A well-established and reliable questionnaire is available for measuring the degree to which a leader shows each of these behaviors (see Exhibit 14–5).[18] Initiating structure and consideration are not two ends of a continuum. They define two relatively independent dimensions of leader behavior. Thus, a leader may show any combination of these two behaviors. This is illustrated in Exhibit 14–6, which presents a popularized version of the two-dimension leader behavior classification known as the *Managerial Grid®*.[19]

Much of the research on consideration and initiating structure has tried to identify the consequences of the two leader behaviors on subordinate satisfaction and performance. Unfortunately, although the two behaviors frequently were related to worker responses, a universal pattern failed to emerge. Initiating structure at times has positive effects on satisfaction; at other times it produces negative effects. Performance sometimes is positively influenced by initiating structure; sometimes it is not. The impact of consideration on performance also was inconsistent: sometimes a positive relationship was found; at other times no effect was apparent. Since no universal pattern has been identified, it is not possible to specify the "one best style" of leader behavior which will be equally successful in all situations. Attention to situational contingencies is required.

It is worth noting that one widely utilized leadership training program is based on the concept of a universally effective leadership style. This is Blake and Mouton's *Managerial Grid®* which is purported to lead to "productivity, satisfaction, creativity, and health."[20] The *Managerial Grid®* is an intuitively appealing, well-structured, comprehensive leadership program which appears to do a good job of classifying leaders along the two dimensions of initiating structure, and consideration (referred to as "concern for production" and "concern for people"). According to Blake and Mouton, *the* effective leader style is the "9,9" style which has high concern for both production and people. Because the *Managerial Grid®* is based on a questionable research base, it has been referred to as the "great hi-hi leader behavior myth."[21] Blake and Mouton counter with conceptual arguments of why the "9,9" style *should* work.[22]

Exhibit 14–5 The Leader Behavior Description Questionnaire—Form XII

How frequently does your leader do each of the following:

Code	Behavior	Never	Seldom	Occasion-ally	Often	Always
IS	Lets work unit members know what is expected of them.	1	2	3	4	5
C	Is friendly and approachable.	1	2	3	4	5
IS	Encourages the use of uniform procedures.	1	2	3	4	5
C	Does little things to make it pleasant to be a member of the work unit.	1	2	3	4	5
IS	Tries out his/her ideas in the work unit.	1	2	3	4	5
C	Puts suggestions made by the work unit into operation.	1	2	3	4	5
IS	Makes his/her attitudes clear to the work unit.	1	2	3	4	5
C	Treats all work unit members as his/her equals.	1	2	3	4	5
IS	Decides what shall be done and how it should be done.	1	2	3	4	5
C	Gives advance notice of change.	1	2	3	4	5
IS	Assigns work unit members to particular tasks.	1	2	3	4	5
C	Keeps to himself/herself.*	1	2	3	4	5
IS	Makes sure that his/her part in the work unit is understood by the work unit members.	1	2	3	4	5
C	Looks out for personal welfare of work unit members.	1	2	3	4	5
IS	Schedules the work to be done.	1	2	3	4	5
C	Is willing to make changes.	1	2	3	4	5
IS	Maintains definite standards of performance.	1	2	3	4	5
C	Refuses to explain his/her actions.*	1	2	3	4	5
IS	Asks that work unit members follow standard rules and regulations.	1	2	3	4	5
C	Acts without consulting the work unit.*	1	2	3	4	5

Codes: C = Consideration item.
IS = Initiating Structure item.
* = Reverse scored item.

Source: Derived from R. M. Stogdill (1963). *Manual for leader behavior description questionnaire—form XII*. Columbus, OH: Ohio State University Bureau of Business Research.

Exhibit 14–6 The Managerial Grid®

Concern for people
High 9
8
7
6
5
4
3
2
Low 1
1,9
Country club management
Thoughtful attention to needs of people for satisfying relationships leads to a comfortable, friendly organization atmosphere and work tempo.
9,9
Team management
Work accomplishment is from committed people; interdependence through a "common stake" in organization purpose leads to relationships of trust and respect.
5,5
Organization man management
Adequate organization performance is possible through balancing the necessity to get out work with maintaining morale of people at a satisfactory level.
1,1
Impoverished management
Exertion of minimum effort to get required work done is appropriate to sustain organization membership.
9,1
Authority-obedience
Efficiency in operations results from arranging conditions of work in such a way that human elements interfere to a minimum degree.
1 2 3 4 5 6 7 8 9
Low
Concern for production
High

Source: R. R. Blake and J. S. Mouton (1978). *The New Managerial Grid.®* Houston: Gulf Publishing Company, p. 11. Reproduced by permission.

Since research indicates that the effectiveness of specific leader patterns is influenced by the nature of the leadership situation, most leadership theorists, researchers, and practitioners have abandoned the search for a universally effective pattern of leader behaviors. The schemes for classifying leader behaviors have been retained, as researchers look for situational factors which dictate the most appropriate pattern of leader behaviors.

SITUATION-CONTINGENT LEADERSHIP BEHAVIORS

The "in" theory of leadership today argues that leader effectiveness is determined by matching the *behavior* of the leader to the leadership situation. Two of the most prominent of these theories (path-goal theory and the rational decision-making theory) are discussed here. Both of these models attempt to resolve the apparently contradictory findings generated by research on universal leadership behaviors.

Path-Goal Theory

Path-goal theory, initially formulated by Martin Evans and extended by Robert House and associates of the University of Toronto, is the most complete of the situation-contingent leadership theories.[23] The leader is said to be effective to the extent that s/he provides or clarifies for the subordinate a **path** to work and personal **goal** attainment. The theory adds the following two propositions to clarify the conditions under which a particular type of leader behavior will enhance the satisfaction and performance of subordinates:

1. Subordinates will be satisfied with their leader's behavior if they perceive that the leader's behavior: (*a*) provides immediate satis-

faction of subordinate needs, or (*b*) is instrumental in obtaining future satisfaction of subordinate needs.

2. Subordinates will increase work-related effort (and, subsequently, performance) if the leader behavior: (*a*) makes satisfaction of subordinate needs contingent upon effective performance, or (*b*) provides needed coaching, guidance, support (e.g., supplying resources and removing barriers to performance), rewards, or other structure which otherwise would be lacking in the worker's environment.

The leader's primary job, according to path-goal theory, is to make certain that subordinate goals are consistent with organizational goals and help the subordinate achieve these goals.* The specific leader behavior required to accomplish this will depend upon the subordinate involved (need states, ability, etc.) and environmental conditions (task structure, role ambiguity, etc.).

The Leader-Situation Match. The path-goal theory allows for the incorporation of many subordinate and environmental factors in establishing a leader-situation match. As the theory continues to be developed, however, the primary situational focus has been on the degree to which the work environment provides structured, unambiguous work expectations for the subordinate. The leader behaviors examined most carefully are the initiating structure and consideration behaviors identified by the universal leadership behavior research.†

The "contradictory" findings uncovered by that research concerning *initiating structure* can be resolved as follows:

1. The impact of initiating structure on subordinate satisfaction will be: (*a*) positive, if structure is needed by the subordinate because the environment is unstructured and ambiguous; (*b*) negative, if the subordinate already has a structured, unambiguous environment.
2. The impact of initiating structure on subordinate effort/performance will be: (*a*) positive, if structure is needed by the subordinate because the environment is unstructured and ambiguous;

---

*Note the similarities between the basic principles of path-goal theory and the more general expectancy theory of motivation (see Chapter 8.)

†Rather than use the terms *initiating structure* and *consideration*, path-goal theorists often use the terms *instrumental* and *supportive*. The two sets of terms are treated equally here. Recent revisions of the model also incorporate discussion of *participative* and *achievement-oriented* leadership behavior. Since these behaviors have not yet been as well integrated or researched, they are not addressed at this point.

(*b*) neutral, if the subordinate already has a structured, unambiguous environment.

The findings concerning *consideration* disclosed the following:

1. The impact of consideration on employee satisfaction will be positive.
2. The impact of consideration on employee effort/performance will be: (*a*) positive, if consideration is provided contingent upon subordinate performance; (*b*) neutral, if consideration is provided regardless of subordinate performance level.
3. If consideration is provided, a subordinate accepts initiating structure more readily.

The bases for the preceding expectations are described by Arthur Jago of the University of Houston:

> When task demands are unclear, or when formal procedures, regulations and policies are ambiguous, structuring behavior complements the task by providing the required guidance and instruction likely to clarify expectations and the paths to goal accomplishment. On the other hand, when task demands are self-evident, as in the case of highly routine or formalized work roles, followers may resent a leader's attempt to initiate further structure. Such behavior may do little to further clarify path-goal relationships and may be viewed as excessively directive and unnecessarily restrictive. Instead, the effective leader in a structured situation engages in personally supportive behavior which provides a source of extrinsic rewards for followers. Such extrinsic rewards reduce the frustration and stress that presumably accompany a highly structured task having little challenge and few sources of intrinsic satisfaction.[24]

To date, research on path-goal theory is promising but not unqualified. Further research is needed before a final judgment can be made on the appropriateness of the model. It is also likely that development of the model will incorporate a wider range of situational factors, subordinate characteristics, and leader behaviors.[25]

Implications of Path-Goal Theory. Path-goal theory has a number of management implications. Because the theory suggests that a leader's behavior can be altered to match the requirements of the situation, these implications are quite different from those of the other leadership approaches. The most significant implications are:

1. The degree of structure and ambiguity present in the leadership situation should be assessed, either through a subjective evaluation or by using one or more of the reliable, valid instruments available for this purpose.[26]

2. If the leadership situation is ambiguous and unstructured, the leader should use a significant amount of both initiating structure and consideration behavior.
3. If the leadership situation is unambiguous and structured, the leader should use a substantial amount of consideration behavior but only enough initiating structure behavior to maintain sufficient structure.
4. Instead of changing leader behavior to match the situation, you may increase or decrease the amount of structure present to match the typical behavior of the leader. If the leader shows a lot of initiating structure and the situation is already structured, structure could be decreased (through job redesign, for example). If the leader shows little initiating structure and the situation is unstructured, additional structure could be built into the situation (through job redesign, creation of manuals, policies, etc.).

Often, a leader must operate in multiple environments with varying degrees of structure. This creates a problem if a leader cannot alter his/her behavior from situation to situation. Typically, this leader will be effective in some situations, but not in others. Otherwise, the structure present in some of the situations will have to be changed to match the leader's behavior (which is difficult and unlikely). The path-goal model argues that it is possible (although not easy) for a leader to alter his/her behavior to match each situation. This would allow effectiveness in each situation. Indeed, behavioral contingency theories of leadership stress the need for leader flexibility.

Rational Decision-Making Theory

A useful, concise, but somewhat narrow, situation-contingent leadership behavior theory has been proposed by Vroom and Yetton.[27] The **rational decision-making theory** (known also as "the normative theory of leadership" or the "Vroom and Yetton model") attempts to systematically specify the conditions under which a leader should make decisions using various behavioral styles.

The Leader Behavior Styles. According to the theory, there are five distinct styles of decision making available to a leader (see Exhibit 14–7). The importance of group participation increases as you move from AI (totally autocratic) through GII (high group involvement).

Choice of Styles. Each of these styles is appropriate in some situations but not in others. For any particular situation, you can choose from among the five alternative styles by using a highly structured

Exhibit 14–7 Rational Decision Making Behavioral Strategies

Strategy	Symbol	Definition
Autocratic I	AI	You solve the problem or make the decision yourself, using the information available to you at the present time.
Autocratic II	AII	You obtain any necessary information from subordinates, then decide on a solution to the problem yourself. You may or may not tell subordinates the purpose of your questions or give information about the problem or decision you are working on. The input provided by them is clearly in response to your request for specific information. They do not play a role in the definition of the problem or in generating or evaluating alternative solutions.
Consultative I	CI	You share the problem with the relevant subordinates individually, getting their ideas and suggestions without bringing them together as a group. Then *you* make the decision. This decision may or may not reflect your subordinates' influence.
Consultative II	CII	You share the problem with your subordinates in a group meeting. In this meeting you obtain their ideas and suggestions. Then *you* make the decision which may or may not reflect your subordinates' influence.
Group	GII	You share the problem with your subordinates as a group. Together you generate and evaluate alternatives and attempt to reach agreement (consensus) on a solution. Your role is much like that of chairperson, coordinating the discussion, keeping it focused on the problem, and making sure that the critical issues are discussed. You can provide the group with information or ideas that you have but you do not try to "press" them to adopt "your" solution and are willing to accept and implement any solution which has the support of the entire group.

Source: Adapted from V. H. Vroom and P. H. Yetton, *Leadership and decision making,* by permission of the University of Pittsburgh Press. © 1973 by the University of Pittsburgh Press.

"decision tree" (see Exhibit 14–8). This tree requires you to answer seven yes-no questions about the situation. As you answer questions and follow the branches of the tree from left to right, you identify feasible decision strategies for that situation. The set of acceptable strategies could be as few as one or as many as five.

When more than one alternative is feasible for a situation, look for

Exhibit 14–8 Rational Decision-Making Decision Tree

A. Does the problem possess a quality requirement (i.e., is one solution better than another)?

B. Do I have sufficient information to make a high quality decision (without help from subordinates)?

C. Is the problem structured (i.e., is it clear what problem needs to be solved)?

D. Is acceptance of decision by subordinates important for effective implementation?

E. If I were to make the decision by myself, is it reasonably certain that it would be accepted by my subordinates?

F. Do subordinates share the organizational goals to be attained in solving this problem?

G. Is it likely subordinates will disagree about the best solution?

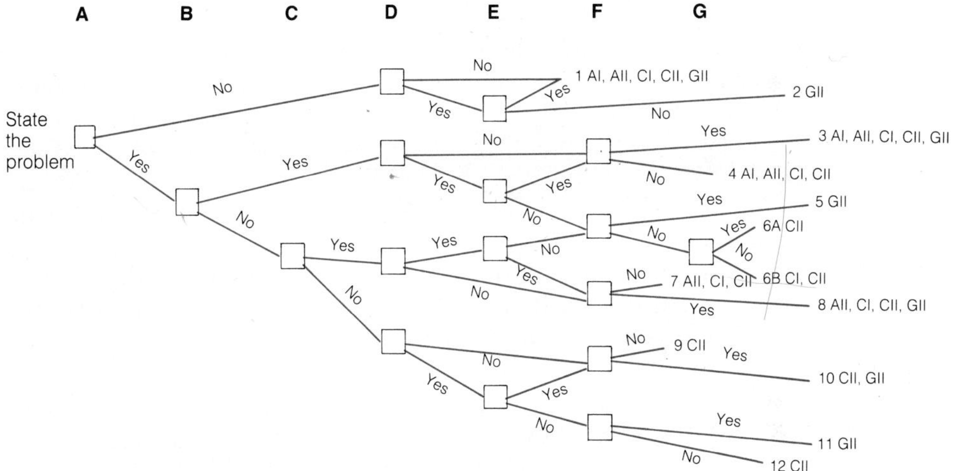

Source: Adapted from V. H. Vroom and P. H. Yetton, *Leadership and decision making,* by permission of the University of Pittsburgh Press. © 1973 by the University of Pittsburgh Press.

reasons to choose one feasible alternative over another. When considering whether to use group participation, for example, remember that the amount of time required to reach a solution increases as group participation increases. Yet, acceptance of and commitment to a solution also increase as group participation increases. Furthermore, subordinate learning increases with increased group participation. These and similar considerations will help you select from among the acceptable alternatives.

Implications of the Rational Decision-Making Theory. Because of the implications of the rational decision-making theory, you may wish to follow these specific recommendations for managing leadership behavior:

1. Assess the nature of the situation, paying close attention to each of the seven critical factors shown in Exhibit 14–8 (quality requirement, information possessed, problem structure, importance of acceptance for implementation, likelihood of acceptance of autocratic decision, congruence of subordinate and organizational goals, and likelihood of subordinate disagreement over solution).
2. Use the decision tree to identify a set of feasible decision strategies.
3. Select the strategy to be used from among those in the feasible set, taking into consideration time constraints, the importance of subordinate acceptance and commitment, and the desirability of subordinate learning.

There appears to be reasonable evidence that this model can improve the effectiveness of leader decision making.[28] It is not a total leadership model, however, because it is concerned solely with leader decision making and not other leader-subordinate interactions. Furthermore, there may be several limitations to its use.[29] The very systematic nature of the model gives it strength; it also consumes a large amount of time. Furthermore, the more you use the model, the greater the amount of time you consume (a leader faced with several different types of situations would spend a lot of time with the model). A final concern is that many leaders are not willing to use it since it "tells them what to do" rather than "letting them decide on their own how to lead."

SUBSTITUTES FOR LEADERSHIP

Traits and/or behaviors of a leader are assumed to impact on subordinate attitudes and behaviors. Recently, though, considerable attention has been given to the idea that certain subordinate, task, or organizational factors may act as **substitutes for leadership** and decrease the importance of leader traits and behaviors.[30] If so, it is possible to identify three roles which might be played by the subordinate, task, and organizational factors:[31]

Substitutes for leadership make leader behavior unnecessary and redundant. Substitutes could include any subordinate, task, or organizational factor which clarifies role expectations, motivates employees, or satisfies employees (making it unnecessary for the leader to do so).

Neutralizers of leadership prevent the leader from behaving in a particular way. Neutralizers could include any factors which make it impossible for a leader to impact on subordinate attitudes or behaviors (e.g., a pay system based on seniority which prevents a leader from rewarding good performers).

Supplements to leadership coexist with leader behavior and "fill in" for leadership behavior as the situation dictates. Supplements could include any of the factors capable of substituting for leadership. Sometimes, these factors can act as substitutes; at other times they do not.

Exhibit 14–9 identifies some of the most likely substitutes and neutralizers of leadership behavior. For example, subordinates with extensive experience, ability, and training already know how to perform the job (they do not need to have structure provided by the leader). Jobs containing a lot of structure guide the worker through his/her tasks (eliminating the need for a leader to provide structure).

Exhibit 14–9 Substitutes and Neutralizers of Leader Behavior

	Leader Behavior Influenced	
Substitute or Neutralizer	**Supportive Leadership**	**Instrumental Leadership**
A. *Subordinate Characteristics:*		
1. Experience, ability, training		Substitute
2. "Professional" orientation	Substitute	Substitute
3. Indifference toward rewards offered by organization	Neutralizer	Neutralizer
B. *Task Characteristics:*		
1. Structured, routine, unambiguous task		Substitute
2. Feedback provided by task		Substitute
3. Intrinsically satisfying task	Substitute	
C. *Organization Characteristics:*		
1. Cohesive work group	Substitute	Substitute
2. Low position power (leader lacks control over organizational rewards)	Neutralizer	Neutralizer
3. Formalization (explicit plans, goals, areas of responsibility)		Substitute
4. Inflexibility (rigid, unyielding rules and procedures)		Neutralizer
5. Leader located apart from subordinates with only limited communication possible	Neutralizer	Neutralizer

Source: Based on G. A. Yukl (1981). *Leadership in organizations.* Englewood Cliffs, NJ: Prentice-Hall, p. 163.

Members of cohesive work groups obtain needed interpersonal support from co-workers (reducing the need for supportive leadership behavior). A leader who is physically removed from subordinates, making communication difficult, is unable to interact (thus is neutralized).

The concept of substitutes for leadership is somewhat new and not yet thoroughly researched. Early studies, however, indicate preliminary support for some of the proposed substitutes, neutralizers, or supplements. Two studies, for example, have shown that formal structure provided by job design, work units, or organizational design, can serve as very strong neutralizers of leader structuring behavior.[32]

The primary implication of the idea of substitutes, neutralizers, and supplements of leadership is that the leader does not exist in an environmental vacuum. The importance and impact of the leader can be influenced substantially by the circumstances in which the leader operates.* Organizations would be well advised to evaluate the characteristics of subordinates, the structure provided by the task, and the broader organizational characteristics when developing and managing leadership.

SUMMARY

It has been argued that both leader traits and leader behaviors are important determinants of leader effectiveness. Whereas a single type of leader trait or pattern of leader behavior was thought to be effective in any leadership situation, we now know a leader's effectiveness is contingent upon the conditions of the leadership situation.

The leader trait and behavior theories of leadership appear to conflict. This is due at least in part to the failure of each perspective to consider adequately the potential impact of the other. Exhibit 14–10 illustrates the potential integration of trait and behavioral models. This model is not an attempt to provide a new theory; it describes how the various factors involved in the leadership situation may interact.

The model shown in Exhibit 14–10 suggests that leader traits influence leader behaviors which, in turn, are influenced by situational factors and previous subordinate reactions. Leader behaviors then impact on subordinate reactions, depending upon the situation involved. These worker reactions, in turn, alter future leadership situations and leader behaviors. Although little has been done to

---

* The substitute for leadership concept, therefore, involves a situation-contingent leadership model.

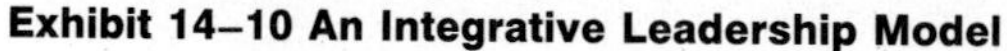

Exhibit 14–10 An Integrative Leadership Model

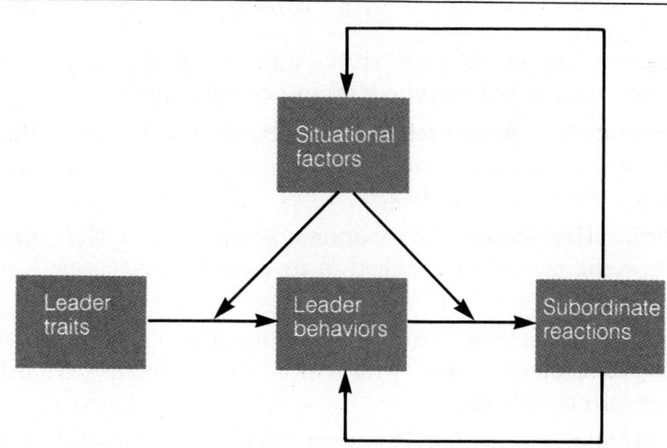

date to fully integrate the various leadership perspectives, the ideas presented in this chapter should allow you to take major steps toward such integration. Do not make the mistake of believing there is *one* adequately comprehensive single leadership theory!

GLOSSARY

Leadership The use of noncoercive influence to direct and coordinate the activities of the members of an organized group.

Leadership Trait Approaches Perspectives which specify that leaders with the appropriate characteristics are more effective than leaders without these characteristics.

Leadership Behavioral Approaches Perspectives which specify that the specific behaviors engaged in by a leader determine leadership effectiveness.

Universal Leadership Theories Theories which specify that there is "one best kind of leader" who will be most effective, regardless of the leadership situation.

Contingency Leadership Theories Theories which specify that the most effective type of leader depends upon the nature of the leadership situation.

Fiedler's Contingency Theory A trait-oriented, situation-contingent leadership theory which states that leadership effectiveness is determined by the match of the leader's personality (LPC) to the favorableness of the situation.

Relationship-Oriented Leader [High LPC] A leader who, according to Fiedler, sees desirable characteristics even in poor co-workers.

Task-Oriented Leader [Low LPC]—A leader who, according to Fiedler, shows a strong emotional reaction to poor co-workers.

Situational Favorableness The critical situational factor in Fiedler's theory which is based on leader/member relations, task structure, and position power of the leader.

Initiating Structure Leader behavior which focuses on clarifying and defining roles and responsibilities for subordinates.

Consideration Leader behavior which focuses on the comfort, well-being, status, needs, and satisfaction of subordinates.

Path-Goal Theory A situation-contingent, behavior-based leadership theory which states that leader effectiveness is a function of the degree to which the leader provides or clarifies for subordinates a path to work and personal goal attainment.

Rational Decision-Making Theory A situation-contingent, behavior-based leadership theory which specifies the conditions under which a leader should make decisions using various behavioral styles.

Substitutes for Leadership Subordinate, task, or organizational factors which decrease the importance of leader traits and behaviors.

STUDY QUESTIONS

1. Discuss the task faced by an organization as it attempts to have effective leaders if the organization assumes that leader traits determine leader effectiveness.
2. If an organization assumes that leader behaviors determine leader effectiveness, how would its strategy differ from that taken in Question 1?
3. Would it be possible to utilize the ideas contained in the path-goal leadership theory without conducting formal evaluations of leader behaviors and the leadership situation? How?
4. Would it be possible to utilize the ideas contained in Fiedler's contingency leadership model without conducting formal evaluations of leader traits and the leadership situation? How?
5. How could you use the knowledge contained in the leadership theories discussed in the chapter to prepare yourself for a position of leadership in an organization?
6. How could an individual leader use the theories discussed in this chapter to evaluate his/her own leadership effectiveness and develop a plan for improvement?
7. Is it possible to use the knowledge from both trait- and behavior-based leadership theories, or must you make a choice to use one or the other?

NOTES

1. Chapter 14 draws heavily on: **Jago, A. G.** (1979, June). *Leadership: Perspectives in theory and research*. Presented at the TIMS XXIV International Meeting, Honolulu, HI; **Jago, A. G.** (1982). Leadership: Perspectives in theory and research. *Management Science, 28,* 315–336; and **House, R. J., & Baetz, M. L.** (1979). Leadership: Some empirical generalizations and new research directions. In B. M. Staw (Ed.), *Research in organizational behavior,* Vol. 1. Greenwich, CT: JAI Press, pp. 341–423.
2. **Jago,** 1982, p. 315.
3. **Jacobs, T. O.** (1971). *Leadership and exchange in formal organizations.* Alexandria, VA: Human Resources Research Organization.
4. **Graen, G., & Cashman, J. F.** (1975). A role-making model of leadership in formal organizations: A developmental approach. In J. G. Hunt, & L. L. Larson (Eds.), *Leadership frontiers*. Kent, OH: Kent State University Press, 143–165.
5. **Stogdill, R. M.** (1948). Personal factors associated with leadership: A

survey of the literature. *Journal of Psychology, 25,* 35–71; **Stogdill, R. M.** (1974). *Handbook of leadership: A survey of theory and research.* New York: Free Press.

6. **House & Baetz,** 1979, p. 349.
7. **Fiedler, F. E.** (1967). *A theory of leadership effectiveness.* New York: McGraw-Hill; **Fiedler, F. E.** (1976). The leadership game: Matching the man to the situation. *Organizational Dynamics, 4,* 6–16.
8. **Fiedler,** 1976, p. 9.
9. Ibid.
10. **Fiedler, F. E., & Chemers, M. M.** (1974). *Leadership and effective management.* Glenview, IL: Scott, Foresman.
11. **Schmidt, E. E.** (1976). The least preferred co-worker (LPC) measure: A review and reinterpretation of the research. Unpublished manuscript, Department of Psychology, University of Washington, Seattle.
12. **Fiedler,** 1976, p. 9.
13. **Fiedler, F. E., Chemers, M. M., & Mahar, L.** (1977). *Improving leadership effectiveness: The leader match concept* (Rev. ed., New York: Wiley) provides a description of the *leader match* program for assessing situational favorableness, leader characteristics, and developing matches between the two.
14. **Fiedler et al.,** 1977.
15. **Fiedler, F. E., & Mahar, L.** (1979). A field experiment validating contingency model leadership training. *Journal of Applied Psychology, 64,* 247–254; **Jago,** 1982, p. 323.
16. See, for example, the supporting results of **Chemers, M. M., & Skrzypek, G. J.** (1972). Experimental test of the contingency model of leadership effectiveness. *Journal of Personality and Social Psychology, 24,* 172–177, and the contradictory results of **Vecchio, R. P.** (1977). An empirical examination of the validity of Fiedler's model of leadership effectiveness. *Organizational Behavior and Human Performance, 19,* 180–206.
17. Although the Ohio State leadership studies are focused on here, other similar studies were conducted at about the same time producing similar results. A relatively recent review discusses some of the findings of many of these studies: **Locke, E. A., & Schweiger, D. M.** (1978). Participation in decision-making: One more look. In B. M. Staw (Ed.), *Research in organizational behavior, Vol. 1.* Greenwich, CN: JAI Press, 265–339. Also see: **Likert, R.** (1967). *The human organization: Its management and value.* New York: McGraw-Hill.
18. **Stogdill, R. M.** (1963). *Manual for the leader behavior description questionnaire—form XII.* Columbus, OH: Ohio State University Bureau of Business Research.
19. **Blake, R. R., & Mouton, J. S.** (1982, Spring). A comparative analysis of situationalism and 9,9 management by principle. *Organizational Dynamics,* p. 21.

20. **Blake & Mouton,** 1982, p. 21.

21. **Larson, L. L., Hunt, J. G., & Osborn, R. N.** (1976). The great hi-hi leader behavior myth: A lesson from Occam's razor. *Academy of Management Journal, 19,* 628–641.

22. **Blake & Mouton,** 1982.

23. **Evans, M. G.** (1968). *The effects of supervisory behavior upon worker perceptions of their path-goal relationships.* Unpublished doctoral dissertation. New Haven, CT: Yale University; **House, R. J.** (1971). A path-goal theory of leader effectiveness. *Administrative Science Quarterly, 16,* 321–338; **House, R. J., & Mitchell, T. R.** (1974). Path-goal theory of leadership. *Journal of Contemporary Business, 5,* 81–97.

24. **Jago,** 1982, p. 325.

25. See **House & Baetz,** 1979.

26. For examples of the use of such instruments see: **Pierce, J. L., Dunham, R. B., & Cummings, L. L.** (1984). Alternate sources of environmental structure. In press, *Organizational Behavior and Human Performance.*

27. **Vroom, V. H., & Yetton, P. W.** (1973) *Leadership and decision-making.* Pittsburgh, PA: University of Pittsburgh Press.

28. **Jago.** 1982; **House & Baetz,** 1979.

29. **Filley, A. C., House, R. J., & Kerr, S.** (1976). *Managerial process and organizational behavior.* Glenview, IL: Scott, Foresman.

30. **Kerr, S., & Jermier, J. M.** (1978). Substitutes for leadership: Their meaning and measurement. *Organizational Behavior and Human Performance, 22,* 375–403.

31. This is based on **Kerr, S., & Jermier, J. M.** (1978) and **Howell, J. P., & Dorfman, P. W.** (1981). Substitutes for leadership: Test of a construct. *Academy of Management Journal, 24,* 714–728.

32. **Howell & Dorfman,** 1981; and **Pierce et al.** (in press).

Part

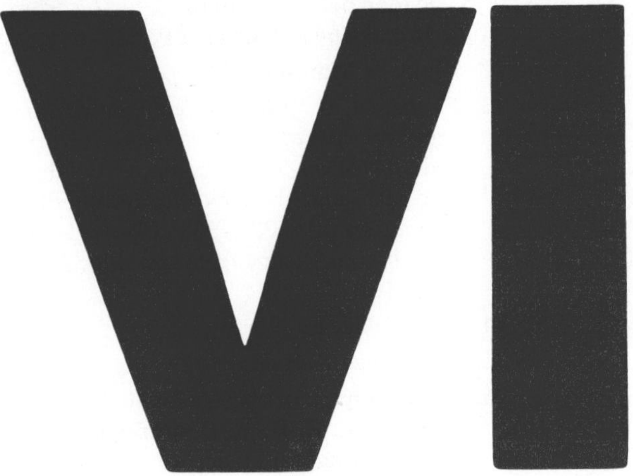

15 ■ Job Design

16 ■ Stress

Organizational Factors

Part VI explores two issues important to an entire organization: job design and stress. Job design is a critical concern because it actually defines the central reason why a person is in an organization. Stress and stress management are of growing concern to organizations and individual organizational members alike.

In Chapter 15, job design and redesign are given substantial attention. A brief historical perspective reveals why jobs are designed as they are in today's organizations. Organizational examples of various job design strategies and their impact on job incumbents are presented. A complete model is provided to help you understand the somewhat complex nature of job design and related issues. This understanding can be applied to your organization through use of the step-by-step guide for the design and redesign of jobs. An illustration of the application of this guide is included to demonstrate its potential effectiveness. The seven most common reasons why job design often fails to achieve its potential are described so that you may avoid common pitfalls.

Chapter 16 discusses widespread misunderstandings about the nature and impact of stress. Through the use of a model which documents the determinants, nature, and consequences of stress, you will receive an overview of this important issue. After describing the primary organizational determinants and consequences of stress, the chapter moves on to identifying strategies for stress management. Three different strategies which can be implemented by any of three agents are discussed. Each can be useful for stress management, but each has strengths and weaknesses. For this reason, you will be provided an integrative strategy for the timely, lasting and effective management of stress.

15 Job Design

OVERVIEW
HISTORY OF JOB DESIGN
Scientific Management
Job Enlargement
Job Enrichment
The Job Characteristics Approach
Contemporary Job Characteristics Theory
Current Job Design Issues
AN INTEGRATIVE JOB DESIGN MODEL
Required Job Duties
Perceptions of Job Scope
Current Satisfaction
Future Attendance Motivation
Future Performance Motivation
Future Performance
A STRATEGY FOR JOB REDESIGN
A Step-by-Step Guide for Job Redesign
Factors which May Go Wrong
SUMMARY

Without work all life goes rotten. But when work is soulless, life stifles and dies.

Albert Camus

OVERVIEW

Job design is concerned with the specific tasks you perform, the techniques or processes used to perform these tasks, and the meaning of these tasks and processes. Every job has a job design, whether that design has been carefully crafted or has emerged without systematic planning. You need to know systematic approaches for managing job design, whether you are creating a job "from scratch" or changing a previous job design. Specific objectives of job design include the enhancement of satisfaction, motivation, attendance, and performance.

To accomplish these objectives, a short history of the job design field is presented. Issues critical to effective job design management are explored, together with a wide variety of job design and job redesign techniques. Finally, a step-by-step strategy for job redesign is presented.

The following job design examples are from one specific organization, but there is nothing particularly unique about the organization, jobs, or people involved. You will discover evidence that a job design problem exists and acquire knowledge to help you understand the situation described in this example. More importantly, you will learn techniques for improving job designs and people's subsequent reactions. There cannot be one "best job design" for all jobs and all people. There are, however, strategies you can use to identify desirable job design for a wide range of jobs and people. By the end of this chapter, you will have developed tools useful in a wide range of situations.

Job Design Examples from the United General Insurance Co.*

United General Insurance Company is a multiline insurance organization. Some of the major functions of an insurance company are to accept policy applications (or policy change orders) from agents, rate (price) the policy, and prepare and issue the policy. Exhibit 15–1 illustrates the basic work flow for these functions at one of the regional offices of the company in late 1981.

Most of the people holding these jobs were bright, dynamic, competent individuals. However, the design of clerical jobs at this time was very specialized, routine, and repetitive. Satisfaction with the work was low in comparison to that of clerical workers throughout the country. Turnover was relatively high, and performance was adequate but management felt productivity was below desirable levels.

Policy applications received were routed to rating and change departments. The clerks in each of these departments dealt exclusively with one type of policy (auto, homeowner, special). Within each department, the work was then batched and given to a clerk for processing without regard to the geographical region or agent who had sent in the application. When the batch of applications had been processed, they were sent to a department of typing clerks for preparation of the policies, and a new batch of applications was given to a rating and change clerk. If the rating and change clerk had a question about a policy, s/he sent it to an underwriter who provided a response. The rating and change clerk then completed the work and sent it on for typing.

Typists received their work in a similar fashion (work batched without regard to agent, geographical region, or rating and change clerk who had processed the policies). When a typist completed a batch of work, another batch was provided. Although a typist might work on two or three different variations of an auto policy, for example, the job involved basically typing very similar policies over and over again.

These workers tended to be isolated in their own part of the organization without a good understanding of the work done by others. Few channels existed for feedback about performance from supervisors, other clerical workers, underwriters, or agents. Individual workers had relatively little decision-making authority. The work and work flow were highly structured. Most of these people appeared to be underchallenged.

* The name of the company has been changed to preserve the anonymity of the company.

Exhibit 15–1 Job Design at United General Insurance Company

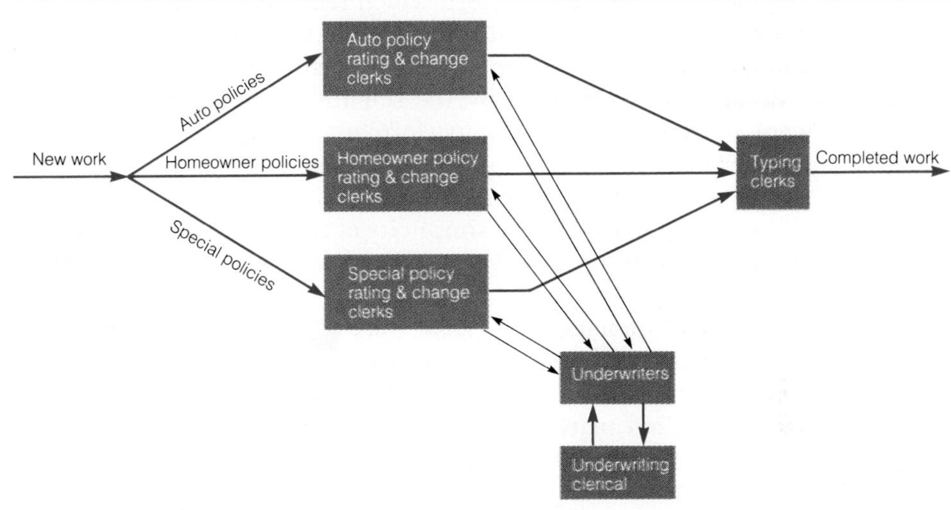

HISTORY OF JOB DESIGN

The design of jobs received a tremendous amount of attention from scholars and practitioners from a variety of fields, resulting in a wide range of perspectives for job design. All of these perspectives share a concern for the motivation and performance of job incumbents. They differ substantially, however, in identifying techniques to achieve these objectives. They also differ in the degree to which satisfaction with the work experience is treated as a central issue. The following brief historical perspective of major job design approaches of the 20th century provides an understanding of the evolution of critical issues. You also can draw ideas for job design from the information it contains.

Scientific Management

The first systematic approach to designing jobs to increase worker effectiveness was set forth by Frederick W. Taylor.[1] This approach, known as **scientific management**, attempted to identify "the one best way" of doing a job. Management would then require each worker to perform the job in this specific manner.

At the heart of scientific management was work simplification and specialization. An organization examined the total work to be performed and divided it into the smallest possible pieces. The organization then conducted a time-and-motion study to determine the one best way of performing each narrow task. (Time-and-motion studies examine the movements required to perform a task and time each movement.) Alternative movement patterns were then explored and timed. The pattern which required the least amount of movement and time was used to define the job. The result of this approach was the development of very simple, repetitive jobs.

Because jobs designed by the scientific management approach were so simple, successful performance required only a limited number of skills. This greatly reduced the ability and skill requirements necessary for a job incumbent, thus increasing the potential job pool. Furthermore, the simplicity of the task greatly reduced the amount of training time required to reach adequate performance levels.

Scientific management jobs were very highly structured. A worker was told exactly how to perform the job and exactly how much time it should take. To motivate employees, scientific management relied primarily on financial incentives: "Whenever the workman succeeds in doing his task right, and within the time limit specified, he receives an addition of from 30 percent to 100 percent to his ordinary wages."[2]

Taylor and the scientific management approach have been much maligned in the latter part of the 20th century. It is often stated, for example, that Taylor cared about productivity but not about employee needs. Taylor's writings and the practice of scientific management do not merit such treatment, however. Taylor's practices were consistent with many of today's contemporary theories of motivation. By simplifying, defining, and teaching the task, management provided support for performance. By including financial incentives, management offered positively valued outcomes to workers. Furthermore, there is some evidence that, in the early part of the century, financial needs were among the most powerful for members of the work force. The belief that Taylor did not care about the welfare of workers is inconsistent with his philosophy that:

> It should be distinctly understood that in no case is the workman called upon to work at a pace which would be injurious to his health. The task is always so regulated that the man who is well suited to his job will thrive while working at this rate during a long term of years and grow happier and more prosperous instead of being overworked.[3]

According to Locke (see Chapter 7), the principles of scientific management are quite consistent with many of the principles of goal-setting theory. Goal theory, one of the most popular contemporary motivation theories, advocates the establishment of a difficult, specific, but reachable goal. These were also at the core of scientific management. Goal theory recommends providing feedback to a worker regarding progress made toward goal accomplishment. So did scientific management. Goal theory argues for the provision of valued incentives for goal attainment. Scientific management did likewise.

There is little question but that scientific management met its objectives of improving worker effectiveness. A worker could conserve time and energy (and increase his/her earnings). An organization could enjoy decreased training costs and increased productivity (and thus conserve money).

Although scientific management did improve productivity, there were significant drawbacks. Whereas, according to Gilbreth, "It is the aim of scientific management to induce men to act as nearly like machines as possible,"[4] most workers don't like to "act like machines" for long periods of time. Many workers in "scientific management jobs" experienced a sense of lost control. Broad skill development was slowed because few skills were used on the job which, in turn, limited promotional opportunities. Employees perceived work to be depersonalized, meaningless, and monotonous. These experiences caused workers to become dissatisfied, leading to absenteeism, turnover, and general discontent.[5]

The jobs described earlier at the United General Insurance Company were quite consistent in design with the propositions of scientific management. Work to be accomplished was broken down into small pieces. A worker performed the same job many times in the course of a day. The motivational component of the scientific management approach (incentive pay for performance above a "standard") was not utilized, however, as workers were paid on a straight hourly basis.

Job Enlargement

The first widespread attempts to counteract negative side effects of the scientific management approach to job design evolved from the job enlargement movement. **Job enlargement** focused primarily on increasing the number of activities engaged in by the worker.* Instead of performing one simplified task, the worker was assigned multiple tasks. Usually these tasks were of similar difficulty to one another, so the primary effect was on "horizontal loading" of the job (a greater number of similar level tasks).

Job enlargement was very popular from the late 1940s through the early 1960s. Among the many organizations to use job enlargement programs were IBM, AT&T, the U.S. Civil Service, the U.S.

---

*Although job enlargement theorists often proposed increasing discretion over work methods, most applications of job enlargement focused most directly on providing a wider range of activities.

Social Security Administration, and The Maytag Co. Research used to document the effectiveness of these programs was often inadequately designed, but cumulative evidence suggests that satisfaction and quality of performance increased. On the other hand, both training costs and job ability requirements increased. Quantity of performance appears to have been relatively unaffected.[6]

Job Enlargement at Maytag

A series of studies was conducted at The Maytag Co. to examine the effectiveness of several different job design strategies for building washing machine water pumps.[7] Exhibit 15–2 is an approximation of the job design when the studies began. At that time, pumps were assembled in a highly structured, paced, and specialized assembly line. In fact, the design of these jobs was very consistent with the scientific management principles.

Through a series of job enlargement changes, jobs were designed as shown in Exhibit 15–3. At this point, each worker's job had been enlarged so that approximately six times as many tasks were performed as with the original assembly line design. Now each worker sat at a work bench and completely constructed a water pump by him/herself. The six tasks were not necessarily more difficult or challenging, but they did provide greater variety.

The enlarged jobs were preferred by most workers and appeared to increase job satisfaction. Furthermore, assembly time per pump dropped by about 18 percent and production costs dropped by about 13 percent.

Job Enrichment

The job design focus which has provided probably the greatest impetus for job design as it is known today evolved in the 1960s.

Exhibit 15–2 Assembly Line Jobs at Maytag

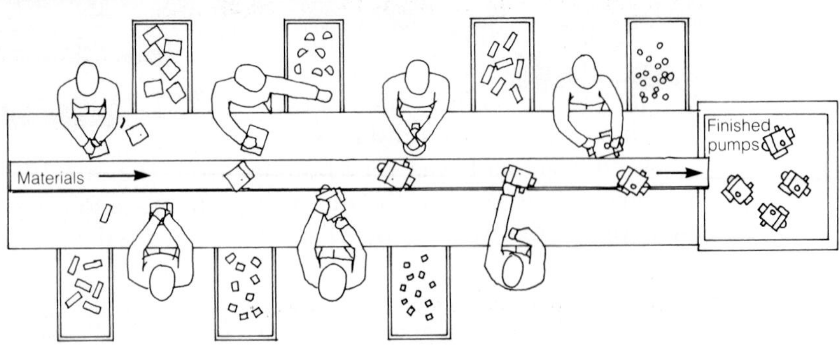

Exhibit 15–3 Individual Work Benches at Maytag

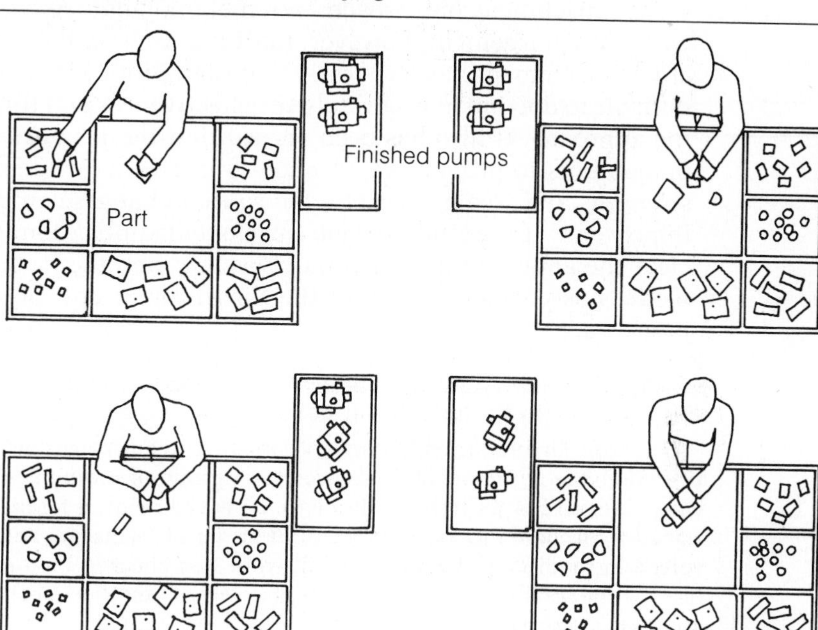

This approach, **job enrichment**, focused on providing opportunity for employee growth through "vertical job loading." Vertical job loading introduces a greater depth of responsibility as opposed to simply a wider range of similar level responsibilities (as was the case with job enlargement).

The driving force behind the job enrichment movement was Frederick Herzberg, developer of the Motivation-Hygiene theory (see Chapter 5).[8] According to Herzberg, ideas which address "motivator" factors and enrich a job's design are:

1. *Accountability*—The worker should be given responsibility for his/her own performance.
2. *Achievement*—The job should provide the opportunity for the worker to accomplish something worthwhile.
3. *Control*—The worker should have control over how the work is done.
4. *Feedback*—Information should be provided to inform the worker about task effectiveness.
5. *Personal growth and development*—The opportunity should be provided for the worker to learn new skills.

6. *Work pace*—The worker should have control over the work pace.[9]

Job enrichment has proven extremely popular. As was the case with job enlargement, however, most research on the effectiveness of job enrichment has had research design problems. This makes it difficult to document accurately the effectiveness and limitations of the approach. It also has been argued that the job enrichment approach fails to provide an adequate framework for identifying the strengths and weaknesses of a job so that changes can be made to improve it.[10] Case studies of job enrichment applications have made clear the approach has potential, however, and the job enrichment model has provided much of the thrust for recent job design approaches.

Job Enrichment in the U.S. Air Force

Herzberg directed a wide range of job enrichment programs for the U.S. Air Force.[11] In one of these projects a group of mechanics installed wing slats on F-4 jet fighters. Prior to job enrichment, a foreperson assigned a mechanic to work on a subset of the 217 separate activities involved in modifying the airplane. All work was checked by a quality officer or the foreperson. If an error was detected, another mechanic was assigned to correct it.

After job enrichment, the total installation on an aircraft was assigned to a work crew. The crew scheduled and inspected most of its own work. The foreperson or quality officer conducted only spot checks. When these checks were conducted, the inspector worked with the mechanic involved rather than the foreperson. If an error was found, the mechanic who made the error was responsible for correcting it. These changes together enriched the job substantially.

Exhibit 15–4 illustrates the financial effectiveness of 29 of the projects directed by Herzberg. Exhibit 15–5 compares attitudes of the employees involved in the job enrichment to those employees performing similar work without job enrichment. As these figures show, both satisfaction and financial benefits resulted from the job enrichment programs.

The Job Characteristics Approach

Early Development. Arthur Turner and Paul Lawrence of Harvard University published results of the first large-scale job characteristics study in 1965.[12] Although some have classified this approach as a radical departure from earlier job design perspectives, it is actually a logical progression. One of the major factors which distinguished the work of Turner and Lawrence was the development of a technique for identifying and measuring job attributes believed to influence worker attitudes and behaviors. Six attributes related to

Exhibit 15–4 Cost–Benefit Analysis of 29 Job Enrichment Projects for the U.S. Air Force

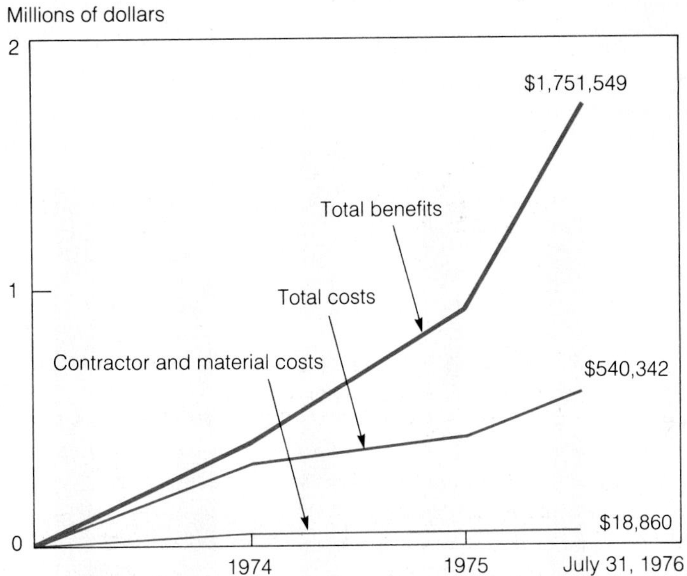

Source: F. Herzberg (1977). Orthodox job enrichment. *Defense Management Journal, 13,* 21–27.

worker attitudes and, to a lesser extent, to worker attendance were: variety, autonomy, required interaction, optional interaction, knowledge and skill required, and responsibility. These six characteristics are fairly consistent with the combined set of job factors used by the job enlargement and job enrichment perspectives. It was now possible, however, to measure the levels of each of these characteristics. This would prove very useful later for the planning of job design strategies.

The Importance of Worker Values. Turner and Lawrence also discovered that not all workers responded equally strongly to high levels of task attributes. Workers from small towns appeared to respond quite positively to high levels of the attributes. Workers from urban settings did not. Later, it was proposed that the reason for this finding might relate to the degree of alienation from the middle-class work norm. Workers who value achievement and responsibility and believe in the intrinsic value of hard work respond positively to jobs high on task attributes. Workers who are alienated from these values do not.[13]

Exhibit 15–5 Attitudinal Analysis of 29 Job Enrichment Projects for the U.S. Air Force

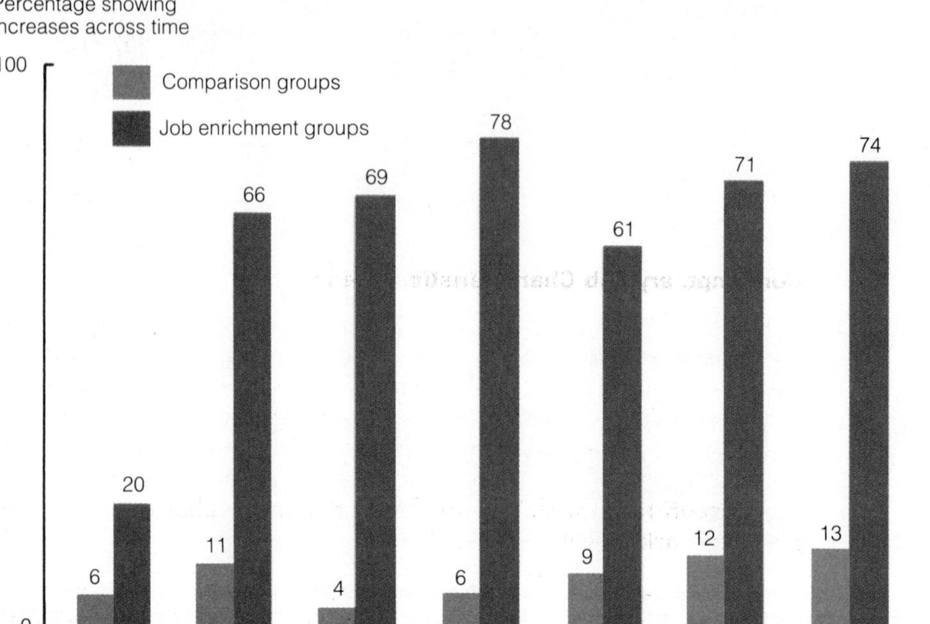

Source: Data obtained from F. Herzberg (1977). Orthodox job enrichment. *Defense Management Journal, 13,* 21–27.

The Hackman and Lawler Contributions. Two major contributions were made by Hackman and Lawler in a study reported in 1971.[14] They modified the questionnaire developed by Turner and Lawrence to identify four "core job characteristics" (variety, autonomy, task identity, and feedback) and two less critical characteristics (dealing with others, and friendship opportunities). A measure of "higher-order need strength" (a desire for higher-order outcomes such as personal growth and accomplishment) was also developed in an attempt to identify why some workers respond more positively to job characteristics than do others. The results of this study indicated that greater amounts of job characteristics were associated with more positive worker reactions. Perhaps even more important was the finding that workers with strong higher-order need strength responded most strongly to the job characteristics.

GOOSEMYER by Parker and Wilder. © 1982 Field Enterprises, Inc. Courtesy of Field Newspaper Syndicate

Contemporary Job Characteristics Theory

The work of Richard Hackman of Yale University and Greg Oldham of the University of Illinois has produced the greatest impact in the job design area in recent years.[15] These theorists/researchers have developed measures of job characteristics (The Job Diagnostic Survey) and individual characteristics (The Growth Need Strength Scale). More importantly, however, they have provided a more complete theoretical model for explaining *how* job characteristics impact on worker reactions (see Exhibit 15–6).

Exhibit 15–6 The Job Characteristics Theory

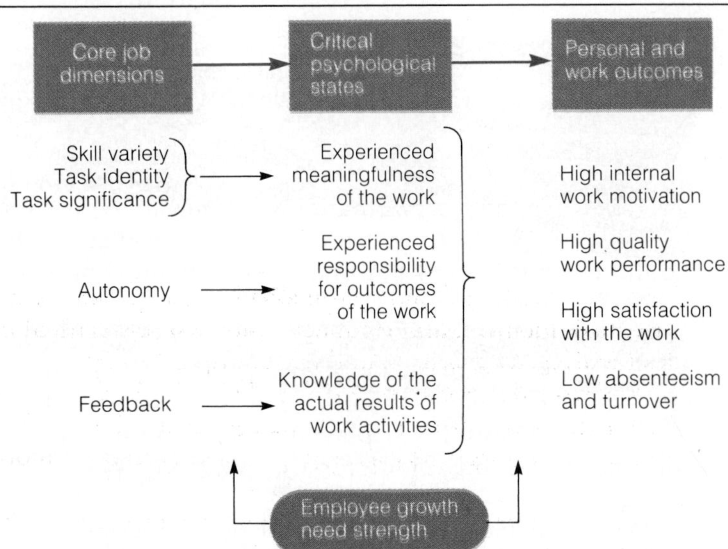

Source: J. R. Hackman and G. R. Oldham (1976). Motivation through the design of work: Test of a theory, *Organizational Behavior and Human Performance, 16,* 250–279.

Core Job Characteristics. According to the model shown in Exhibit 15–6, five core job characteristics (each of which is measured by the Job Diagnostic Survey) are of primary importance to the design of a job:*

1. *Skill variety*—The degree to which a job requires a variety of different activities using a number of different skills and talents.
2. *Task identity*—The degree to which the job requires completion of a "whole" and identifiable piece of work; that is, doing a job from beginning to end with a visible outcome.
3. *Task significance*—The degree to which the job has a substantial impact on the lives or work of other people, whether in the immediate organization or in the external environment.
4. *Autonomy*—The degree to which the job provides substantial freedom, independence, and discretion to an individual, both in scheduling the work and in determining the procedures used in completing it.
5. *Feedback*—The degree to which carrying out work activities required by the job results in an individual obtaining direct and clear information about the effectiveness of his/her performance.[16]

Portions of the Job Diagnostic Survey and the Job Characteristics Inventory (an instrument derived from the Job Diagnostic Survey) are shown in Exhibit 15–7. The Job Characteristics Inventory appears to be a somewhat more reliable and valid measure of the underlying job characteristics.[17]

Critical Psychological States. The five core job characteristics combine to influence three *critical psychological states*. Together, skill variety, task identity, and task significance determine the *degree to which you will perceive a meaningful work experience*. Autonomy influences the *level of responsibility you experience for work outcomes*. Feedback determines *how much you know about the results of your work activities*. The three critical psychological states then combine to influence the set of personal and work outcomes.

Growth-Need Strength. Growth-need strength is the *degree to which a person desires complex, challenging work*. The level of employees' growth-need strength (measured by the scale of the same name shown in Exhibit 15–8) plays two important roles in the model shown in Exhibit 15–6. First, persons with high growth-need

---

*Note that a fifth job characteristic (task significance) has been added by Hackman and Oldham to the four identified by Hackman and Lawler.

Exhibit 15–7 Sample Items from Measures of Job Characteristics

	Very Little	Little	A Moderate Amount	Much	Very Much
Variety					
1. How much variety is there in your job?	1	2	3	4	5
2. How repetitious is your job?	1	2	3	4	5
Autonomy					
3. How much are you left on your own to do your own work?	1	2	3	4	5
4. To what extent are you able to act independently of your supervisor in performing your job function?	1	2	3	4	5
Identity					
5. How often do you see projects or jobs through to completion?	1	2	3	4	5
6. To what extent are you involved in a job from the beginning to end?	1	2	3	4	5
Feedback					
7. To what extent do you find out how well you are doing on the job as you are working?	1	2	3	4	5
8. To what extent does doing the work required by the job provide chances for you to figure out how well you are doing?	1	2	3	4	5
Significance					
9. To what extent can other people be affected by how well you do your job?	1	2	3	4	5
10. How significant or important is your job in the broader scheme of things?	1	2	3	4	5

Sources: Items 1, 2, 3, 4, 5, 6, and 7 are from H. P. Sims, A. D. Szilagyi, and R. T. Keller (1976), The measurement of job characteristics, *Academy of Management Journal, 19,* 195–212 (Item 6 is revised); Items 8, 9, and 10 are revised from J. R. Hackman, and G. R. Oldham, Development of the job diagnostic survey, *Journal of Applied Psychology, 69,* 159–170. Copyright 1975 by the American Psychological Association and adapted by permission of the publisher and authors.

strength theoretically will be more sensitive to the level of the core job dimensions. They likely will experience high levels of the critical psychological states if the core job dimensions are high, and experience low levels of these states if the job dimensions are low. The second impact of growth-need strength is said to determine the kinds of reactions a person is likely to have after experiencing the critical psychological states. High-growth-need-strength persons should react more favorably to high levels of the psychological states.

Exhibit 15–8 A Measure of Growth-Need Strength

INSTRUCTIONS

People differ in what they like and dislike in their jobs. Listed below are twelve pairs of jobs. For each pair, you are to indicate which job you would prefer. Assume that everything else about the jobs is the same—pay attention only to the characteristics actually listed for each pair of jobs.

If you would prefer the job in the left-hand column (Column A), indicate *how much* you prefer it by putting a check mark in a blank to the left of the "neutral" point. If you prefer the job in the right-hand column (Column B), check one of the blanks to the right of "neutral." Check the "neutral" blank *only* if you find the two jobs equally attractive or unattractive. Try to use the "neutral" blank rarely.

Column A		Column B
1. A job which offers little or no challenge.	Strongly prefer A — Neutral — Strongly prefer B	A job which requires you to be completely isolated from co-workers.
2. A job where the pay is very good.	Strongly prefer A — Neutral — Strongly prefer B	A job where there is considerable opportunity to be creative and innovative.
3. A job where you are often required to make important decisions.	Strongly prefer A — Neutral — Strongly prefer B	A job with many pleasant people to work with.
4. A job with little security in a somewhat unstable organization.	Strongly prefer A — Neutral — Strongly prefer B	A job in which you have little or no opportunity to participate in decisions which affect your work.
5. A job in which greater responsibility is given to those who do the best work.	Strongly prefer A — Neutral — Strongly prefer B	A job in which greater responsibility is given to loyal employees who have the most *seniority*.
6. A job with a supervisor who sometimes is highly critical.	Strongly prefer A — Neutral — Strongly prefer B	A job which does not require you to use much of your talent.
7. A very routine job.	Strongly prefer A — Neutral — Strongly prefer B	A job where your co-workers are not very friendly.
8. A job with a supervisor who respects you and treats you fairly.	Strongly prefer A — Neutral — Strongly prefer B	A job which provides constant opportunities for you to learn new and interesting things.
9. A job where you have a real chance to develop yourself personally.	Strongly prefer A — Neutral — Strongly prefer B	A job with excellent vacations and fringe benefits.
10. A job where there is a real chance you could be laid off.	Strongly prefer A — Neutral — Strongly prefer B	A job with very little chance to do challenging work.
11. A job with little freedom and independence to do your work in the way you think best.	Strongly prefer A — Neutral — Strongly prefer B	A job where the working conditions are poor.
12. A job with very satisfying team-work.	Strongly prefer A — Neutral — Strongly prefer B	A job which allows you to use your skills and abilities to the fullest extent.

Source: J. R. Hackman and G. R. Oldham (1974). *The job diagnostic survey: An instrument for the diagnosis of jobs and the evaluation of job redesign projects* (Tech. Rep. No. 4). Cambridge, MA: Yale University, Department of Administrative Sciences.

Research on the Model. The job characteristics theory has generated a tremendous amount of research, resulting in support for many of the critical elements of the model (although other aspects appear less valid).[18] There is little question but that differences in job characteristics impact heavily on satisfaction. The strength of the effect on workers' behavioral responses, however, is considerably less clear.

Although there is some evidence that the critical psychological states may intervene between job characteristics and worker responses, this has not been tested adequately. Perhaps the biggest controversy concerns the role of growth-need strength. Although the results can be interpreted in different ways, it appears that most workers in the United States respond positively to higher levels of the core job characteristics. Persons with high levels of growth-need strength respond most strongly.

After reviewing the literature, Ricky Griffin of Texas A & M University concluded:

> A common folk-saying heard quite frequently is that you must learn to walk before you can run. Scientific management was our first attempt at crawling. During the job rotation and job enlargement era, we tried to struggle to our feet. Job enrichment found us standing on our feet and moving forward, although we frequently stumbled and fell. Finally, we learned to walk confidently and steadily with the job characteristics theory. Now, we must learn to run.[19]

Current Job Design Issues

A number of "new" issues related to the job design model have emerged during recent years, most of which lead to constructive modification and expansion of the model. These issues include: the exploration of a wider range of individual characteristics influencing reactions to job characteristics, examination of the role of organizational design factors, the impact of technology factors, the importance of leader behavior in combination with job design, the relevance of the job context (nontask organizational factors), and the importance of objective measures of job characteristics. You will note that all but the last of these issues are perceptual measures.

Individual Characteristics. In addition to a person's growth-need strength level, a number of other personal characteristics may influence the impact of job design on worker reactions. Since people often perceive the same sensory stimulus in very different ways (see Chapter 10), your perception of the objective characteristics of a particular job may be influenced by several factors. The perception

J. Richard Hackman of Yale University and **Greg R. Oldham** of the University of Illinois are widely known for their development of the Job Characteristics Theory.

How well matched are people and jobs in most organizations today? OLDHAM: Some commentators would estimate that there are 20 to 30 million people in the U.S. labor force who are inappropriately matched to their jobs. In most cases, this is due to the fact that jobs are too simplified and too routinized for the needs and skills of the people who are doing them. The result of this is a lot of frustrated, angry, and dissatisfied employees in our work organizations.

Why are there so many mismatches of people and jobs? HACKMAN: Work design has taken two routes. The first route attempts to fit jobs to people by designing work to provide a meaningful work experience. This leads to matches of worker needs and the job. The second approach (which is traditional), however, allows engineering expertise and technological advances to dictate the way jobs and work systems will be designed. Then attempts are made to somehow match the people to the needs of the job. This often produces mismatches of the needs of people and the realities of the job.

Does this mean that technological advances such as the computer revolution will always lead to mismatches? HACKMAN: No. This is still very much in a state of flux. In fact, some organizations are using the microprocessor revolution to provide better jobs, which provide people with opportunities to learn, to contribute more on the job, and place more power on the desk of the individual worker. Other organizations are using the same technological advances to provide even more centralized control in making people even more like robots or puppets at the end of a string than they were before.

What are some of the most important emerging issues in the job design area? OLDHAM: First, I think we will look much more carefully at appropriate ways to design work for groups of individuals. Secondly, I think that more attention will be given to the way the job design interacts with the physical environment of the organization. Finally, more attention will be given to the importance of referent jobs that employees use as standards of comparison against which to evaluate their own jobs.

of identical tasks varies significantly from one person to the next as a function of age, education, job tenure, worker cognitive structure, dominance, and field independence (a perceptual phenomenon discussed in Chapter 10).[20] Given these findings, it is clear that organizations must manage not only the actual design of jobs but also the processes by which jobs are perceived.

Organizational Design. It now appears reasonably certain that the nature of the organization in which a job exists influences the results produced by the design of the job. Consider the classic organization design continuum proposed by Burns and Stalker over 20 years ago.[21] According to this framework, the design of an organization can lie anywhere from "organic" to "mechanistic." In a mechanistic organization, for example, tasks and relationships are highly specialized, structured, and spelled out in detail. In an organic organization, on the other hand, structure is much more flexible and adaptive, and a degree of dynamic evolution of structure exists. Exhibit 15–9 specifies other characteristics of the two approaches. A great deal of research has focused on the relative effectiveness of the two approaches and the conditions under which one or the other would be most appropriate. It has been argued, for example, that an organic design is more appropriate for a relatively unstable, rapidly changing environment, while a mechanistic design is preferable for a stable environment.

Porter, Lawler, and Hackman developed a model to predict the effects of various combinations of organization design, job design, and employee growth-need strength.[22] This model was subsequently modified and tested by Pierce, Dunham, and Blackburn, with results as shown in Exhibit 15–10.[23] The best combination was predicted to exist when a strong-growth-need-strength person experienced both a complex job and an organic organization. The worst combination combined a strong-growth-need-strength person with a simple job in a mechanistic organization. These and the remaining predictions made in Exhibit 15–10 were based on the following propositions:

1. Most workers will react more favorably to jobs high on the core dimensions than jobs which are low.
2. Most workers will react more favorably to jobs high in organic design than those which are mechanistic.
3. The relative importance of job design is greater than that of organization design due to the "closeness" of the job to the person's everyday work experiences.
4. Workers with high growth-need strength will react more strongly to job and organization design factors than persons low in growth-need strength.

Exhibit 15–9 Mechanistic and Organic Organizations

Mechanistic	Organic
1. Tasks are highly fractionated and specialized; little regard paid to clarifying relationship between tasks and organizational objectives.	1. Tasks are more interdependent; emphasis on relevance of tasks and organizational objectives.
2. Tasks tend to remain rigidly defined unless altered formally by top management.	2. Tasks are continually adjusted and redefined through interaction of organizational members.
3. Specific role definition (rights, obligations, and technical methods prescribed for each member).	3. Generalized role definition (members accept general responsibility for task accomplishment beyond individual role definition).
4. Hierarchic structure of control, authority, and communication. Sanctions derive from employment contract between employee and organization.	4. Network structure of control authority and communication. Sanctions derive more from community of interest than from contractual relationship.
5. Information relevant to situation and operations of the organization formally assumed to rest with chief executive.	5. Leader not assumed to be omniscient; knowledge centers identified where located throughout organization.
6. Communication is primarily vertical between superior and subordinate.	6. Communication is both vertical and horizontal, depending upon where needed information resides.
7. Communications primarily take form of instructions and decisions issued by superiors, of information and requests for decisions supplied by inferiors.	7. Communications primarily take form of information and advice.
8. Insistence on loyalty to organization and obedience to superiors.	8. Commitment to organization's tasks and goals more highly valued than loyalty or obedience.
9. Importance and prestige attached to identification with organization and its members.	9. Importance and prestige attached to affiliations and expertise in external environment.

Source: Adapted from T. Burns, and G. M. Stalker (1961). *The management of innovations*. London: Tavistock, pp. 119–122.

As can be seen in Exhibit 15–10, job design, organization design, and growth-need strength clearly interact. You cannot understand fully the impact of one of these factors without also considering the others (i.e., the effect of a particular job design varies as a function of the existing organization design). The accuracy of the predictions

Exhibit 15–10 The Interaction Effects of Organization Design, Job Design, and Growth-Need Strength

Job Design*	Organization Design	Growth Need	Predicted Favorableness	Actual Favorableness†	
				Work Satisfaction	Overall
Complex	Organic	High	1	**1**	**1**
Complex	Mechanistic	High	2	**2**	**3**
Complex	Organic	Low	3	**3**	**2**
Complex	Mechanistic	Low	4	**4**	**4**
Simple	Organic	High	5	7	7
Simple	Organic	Low	6	**6**	**5**
Simple	Mechanistic	Low	7	5	**6**
Simple	Mechanistic	High	8	**8**	**8**

*Complex jobs are high in the "core" job characteristics.
†Results within one rank of predictions are highlighted.
Source: Based on data from J. L. Pierce, R. B. Dunham, and R. S. Blackburn (1979). Social systems structure, job design, and growth-need strength: A test of a congruency model. *Academy of Management Journal, 22,* 223–240.

tested was quite good, particularly for satisfaction with the kind of work (the worker response usually most strongly affected by job design). The few deviations from predictions appear to be related to an overemphasis on the importance of growth-need strength.

Technology. The technology of an organization is defined by the way the organization transforms materials and other inputs (information, ideas, etc.) into outputs (products, services, etc.). Technologies may be "long-linked" (assembly lines where tasks are performed in a predefined serial order), "mediating" (choosing one from a set of standardized processes, as is often the case with banks and insurance companies), and "intensive or custom" (nonstandardized techniques are used and tasks performed in part through reaction to the emerging demands of the task).[24]

Denise Rousseau of Northwestern University conducted an interesting study of the relationship between technology and job design.[25] Her results indicated that perceived levels of job variety, identity, significance, and autonomy were all associated with the dominant technology of the organization. This and other findings lead to the following two conclusions. First, when planning a major change in technology, you should evaluate the effects of the change on job design and consider the subsequent effects on worker reactions. Second, when planning a major change in job design, take into account the degree to which the existing technology will inhibit or facilitate the change.

Leader Behavior. Griffin has developed and tested (part of) a conceptual framework which argues for the concurrent consideration of job design and leader behavior.[26] First, a leader should examine the degree to which a subordinate's needs are matched by his/her job design. If the match is consistent, the leader should support it. If not, the leader should supplement it. Another component of this concept is that the design of a job can influence leader behavior. Changes in job design likely would lead to changes in leader behavior (for example, if a subordinate was assigned decision-making responsibilities previously held by the leader). A third argument is that leader behavior can influence job design (for example, when a leader uses his/her discretion to redesign the job for a subordinate). This would be particularly important when the leader has a large amount of freedom in work assignments and/or techniques.

AN INTEGRATIVE JOB DESIGN MODEL

The job design model presented in Exhibit 15–11 combines past theories and much research to integrate the numerous and complicated issues involved in the study of job design (see Chapter 8, Exhibit 8–5). The major concepts and processes included in the model are: *required job duties, perceptions of job scope, worker satisfaction, future attendance motivation,* and *future performance.*

Required Job Duties

The actual objective responsibilities assigned to a job incumbent are required job duties, whether these involve the construction of a

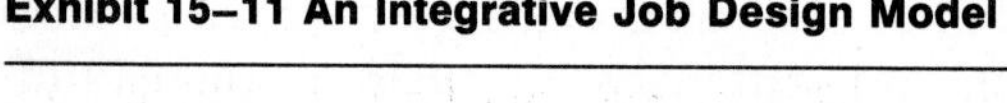

Exhibit 15–11 An Integrative Job Design Model

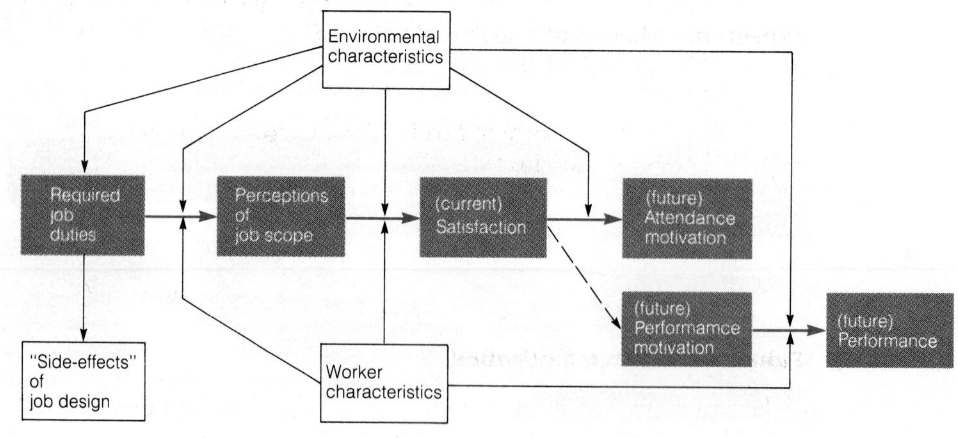

product or the development of an idea. Just as job duties are influenced by organizational factors such as organizational design, technology, and leadership, job duties produce several significant side effects. Job duties influence, for example, the ability and compensation requirements of jobs.[27]

Although it has been very popular in job design literature to call for objective measures of job characteristics, only a few examples of such measurements exist. There is, however, a wide range of very good techniques for assessing and categorizing job duties through job analysis.[28] Although most of the job design literature has focused on *perceived* job characteristics, it is the *objective* job characteristics which are manipulated during job design and redesign.

Perceptions of Job Scope

Required job duties are translated into perceptions of job scope (the degree to which you perceive a job to possess variety, autonomy, etc.) through the perceptual process (see Chapter 10). In addition to previously discussed factors such as age, education, job tenure, cognitive structure, dominance, and field independence, there is some evidence that social cues (such as information provided by co-workers) can impact on perceptions of job scope.[29] It is perceptions of the job which drive the remainder of the job design model. Although a number of important job scope dimensions have been identified by researchers, it is likely that other important dimensions exist.

Current Satisfaction

Perceptions of job scope are treated as intrinsic outcomes in this model (see Chapter 8). The valence attached to these outcomes has a major impact on current satisfaction (as soon as you receive these outcomes, you react to them). Consistent with the principles of expectancy theory, the greater the positive value of outcomes, the greater the potential for satisfaction. Without question, the most consistent and strongest evidence from the thousands of job design studies reveals that higher levels of job scope are associated with higher levels of satisfaction. As was shown earlier, both worker characteristics (e.g., growth-need strength) and organizational characteristics (e.g., organizational design, technology, leadership) interact with perceptions of job scope as determinants of satisfaction.

Future Attendance Motivation

To the degree that you experience satisfaction in your job, future attendance motivation will be enhanced. This is consistent with the results of research on satisfaction→attendance relationships (see Chapter 4). The focus here is on future attendance motivation (the worker comes to work in anticipation of the satisfying experience it provides). The arrow in Exhibit 15–11 from current satisfaction to future attendance motivation implies a direct link. This is because, unless there are major job design changes, current intrinsic experiences should be indicative of future ones. Attendance motivation as defined here is consistent with the expectancy theory definition of "Force" to pursue an alternative (see Chapter 8). The Force associated with an alternative (attendance) will be high when a worker perceives that the job will provide valued outcomes. Consistent with the attendance models, environmental characteristics such as organizational constraints against nonattendance and the availability of alternative jobs will also influence attendance motivation (see Chapter 4).

Future Performance Motivation

The arrow in the model between current satisfaction and future performance motivation implies a less certain link. This is due to the fact that you must perceive that satisfaction is contingent upon high performance before you will be motivated to high performance. The satisfaction in this model is heavily dependent upon intrinsic factors, many of which are obtained whether or not performance is high. This may be one reason for the frequent findings that job design and performance have only a marginal relationship. The alternative of "acceptable performance" may be more attractive overall than "high performance" if both provide similar intrinsic outcomes but high performance also provides negatively valued outcomes (such as fatigue). This pattern of results may be apparent particularly in the absence of extrinsic outcomes contingent on high performance (as might be the case for a salaried worker with few promotional opportunities). In short, the force driving high performance will be increased by job design only if you perceive that the intrinsic outcomes from the job design are contingent upon high performance.

Future Performance

The final link in the model ties future performance motivation to future performance. In a fashion identical to that proposed by expectancy and other theories, performance motivation will lead to performance only to the degree that you possess the necessary skills and abilities *and* the organization provides support for performance (e.g., policies and practices consistent with performance efforts).

This is a second reason why extremely strong simple relationships between job scope and performance should not be expected.

The model provided here is not intended to be totally exhaustive (even if you do feel totally exhausted after reading about it!). It is, however, consistent with the majority of job design research and is useful for understanding the role of job design in organizations.

A STRATEGY FOR JOB REDESIGN

Job redesign involves a significant organizational change and is subject to all of the considerations explored in Chapter 17 (Managing Change). Although that chapter provides a "generic change management" strategy useful for almost any type of change in an organization, there are several issues which it would be profitable to discuss briefly at this point: how to determine whether job design change is merited, what specific types of changes should be made, several common types of job changes, and some of the factors which frequently go wrong in job design. As an example, the description of a major job redesign effort (of the insurance company jobs described at the beginning of this chapter) is included later in this chapter to illustrate the points discussed here.

A Step-by-Step Guide for Job Redesign

A step-by-step guide for job redesign presented in Exhibit 15–12 takes into account the special integrative job design requirements shown in Exhibit 15–11.* (Exhibit 15–12 expands on the general change model in Chapter 17, Exhibit 17–9.)

Step 1: Recognizing the Need for Change. The need for job design changes may arise from many sources, such as worker reactions or worker desires (see Chapter 17). These produce *reactive change*; an organization with a problem reacts to it by looking for a cure (e.g., job design). The need for change can also be recognized on a *proactive* basis. In this case, a specific problem may not have occurred yet, but the organization recognizes the opportunity to avoid problems and/or improve upon an existing situation.

Step 2: Diagnosis of Work System and the Context. This is the stage at which you assess the key determinants of worker reactions, using work system, context factors, and measurement techniques discussed earlier in this chapter (see Chapter 17 for identification of potential resistance to job changes). Although this assessment can

---

* This guide draws heavily on the well-prepared guidance of Griffin, 1982, pp. 207–223.

Exhibit 15–12 A Step-by-Step Guide to Job Redesign

Step 1. Recognition of need for change

Step 2. Diagnosis of work system and context
- *a.* Required job duties
- *b.* Job scope perceptions
- *c.* Worker characteristics
- *d.* Environmental characteristics
- *e.* Potential resistance

Step 3. Assessment of existing worker reactions
- *a.* Satisfaction
- *b.* Attendance motivation and attendance
- *c.* Performance motivation and performance

Step 4. Identification of potential job changes

Step 5. Cost/benefit analysis of proposed changes

Step 6. Go/no-go decision

Step 7. Selection of specific change strategy

Step 8. Implementation of the change

Step 9. Evaluation of the effectiveness of the change

be done through personal observation techniques, more formal systematic techniques usually provide more reliable and valid diagnoses (see the Appendix). Required job duties, for example, can be assessed through the use of job analysis techniques; you can measure the perceived job with instruments such as the Job Diagnostic Survey or the Job Characteristics Inventory.

Step 3: Assessment of Existing Worker Reactions. It is useful to systematically assess existing levels of worker reactions such as satisfaction, attendance motivation, attendance, performance motivation, and performance. Techniques for measuring these and other job design factors are explored in some detail in Chapter 3.

Step 4: Identification of Potential Job Changes. You can identify potential job changes based on your diagnosis of the existing job design and its consequences. The literature provides considerable guidance in this area. Potential job enlargement, enrichment, and related strategies abound. Hackman, Oldham, Janson, and Purdy, for example, identify five "implementing concepts": form natural work units, combine tasks, establish client relationships, provide vertical loading, and open feedback channels.[30] Examine your own specific situation, identify strengths and weaknesses, and explore potential job changes which would enhance job scope perceptions and subsequent worker reactions. Seek opinions; job incumbents are often very effective at identifying promising job changes.

Step 5: Cost/Benefit Analysis. Once you have assessed the work system, its context, and worker reactions, project the probable benefits of job redesign. This can be done two ways. The first approach is to rely on existing theory and research to draw conclusions about the likely impact of job changes. Theory (supported by research) argues, for example, that the low satisfaction of high-growth-need-strength workers could be caused in part by existing jobs which are simple and located in an organization with a mechanistic design. This same theory suggests that increasing job scope has the potential to increase satisfaction and that a concurrent change to an organic organizational design could produce very powerful results.

In the second approach, the actual relationships between the various parts of the job design model in your organization are statistically established. Although a complete discussion of these techniques is beyond the scope of this book, the Appendix addresses this issue in some detail. Note that the benefits of job redesign in the satisfaction area are relatively straightforward (assuming the job is redesigned to provide valued work experiences). Obtaining attendance motivation requires additional attention to environmental characteristics. Obtaining performance motivation and attendance requires attention not only to the design of the job but to instrumentality perceptions, to environmental characteristics, and to worker characteristics.

You should also consider the potential costs associated with job redesign. It was mentioned earlier, for example, that even a successful job redesign effort could increase worker ability requirements, selection and training needs, and the compensation value of jobs. Beyond this, there are costs associated with the acquisition and installation of new equipment and procedures (e.g., equipment costs, downtime during installation). Short-term costs may be incurred as workers experience role ambiguity, uncertainty, and role overload. Conflict and alienation may result from resistance to change. Potential costs also include the failure of parts of the redesign effort (a new procedure or machine does not work well), unplanned delays, additional changes which become necessary, and conflicts with other parts of the organization (communication channels may change, structural changes in other parts of the organization may be necessary, etc.).

Step 6: Go/No-Go Decision. Once the primary potential benefits and costs are identified and compared, a go/no-go decision must be made. This can be difficult, particularly since most cost/benefit analyses are not totally quantifiable. This decision will also depend on your objectives for job redesign. Some organizations are willing to redesign jobs to increase satisfaction as long as no performance or attendance decreases occur. Others are willing to make changes only if performance is likely to increase. Groups are often used in this decision process (see Chapter 12).

Steps 7–9: Selection of Change, Implementation, and Evaluation Strategies. Once you have decided to go with a promising set of job changes, you must develop a careful strategy for introducing change (see Chapter 17). Many a good job design idea has failed because inadequate attention has been given to this vital first stage. After selecting the appropriate strategy, follow each of the three implementation stages discussed in Chapter 17 (unfreezing, changing, and refreezing). Finally, do not overlook the importance of a systematic evaluation of the effectiveness of the change. This evaluation aids discovery of which elements of the change did and did not work, identifies areas where constructive change should be made, and provides guidance for further job redesign efforts. Your evaluation typically will require the reassessment of all components of the job design model (Exhibit 15–11) which may have been influenced by the process. Again, this can be done informally or through the use of more systematic techniques (see the Appendix).

Factors which May Go Wrong

The following is a list of the most common reasons why job redesign efforts may fail to achieve their potential.*

1. Inadequate diagnoses of the work system are conducted.
2. Planned job changes are implemented in name only without being fully integrated and used.
3. There are negative side effects for the surrounding work system (other departments have conflicting requirements, supervisors are adversely affected, etc.).

---

*This list uses the six reasons identified by J. R. Hackman (1975, September–October). Is job enrichment just a fad? *Harvard Business Review*, 129–138. The seventh is added here to make the list more complete.

Job Redesign at the United General Insurance Co.

Because of attendance and turnover problems, the management of United General Insurance recognized that a job design problem existed. In addition, the personal experiences of managers showed that their workers felt that "There must be a better way!" Management's interest in job design was motivated by these observations and an awareness of the potential of job redesign based on the experiences of other companies.

A complete diagnosis of the work system and context was conducted with reliable, valid, well-established procedures. Worker reactions were also thoroughly assessed. Statistical analyses revealed that worker reactions were related to job duty requirements and job scope perceptions. Therefore, job changes should have the potential to improve worker responses.

To identify potential job changes, 6- to 10-person "Job Improvement Teams" (JITs) were formed. Members included workers from three nonsupervisory job levels and two supervisory levels. Each team contained representatives from a major work area. In addition, a resource person from the corporate office of the company was included, as was an outside consultant who served as a group facilitator. The results of the work system diagnosis and worker reaction assessment were presented to the JITs in nonstatistical form. Ideas for potential job changes from the job design literature were also shared with the group. The JITs used their extensive and varied job experiences to interpret the meaning of the diagnosis and assessment results.

After several group meetings, the JITs identified a number of potential job changes. These suggestions were evaluated two ways. First, the proposed job change was placed in the context of the job design model. Predictions were made of the probable impact of these changes on worker reactions. These predictions were based on theory, empirical literature, and data collected at the company. Next, those changes which appeared to be good candidates for improving worker reactions were presented to management for a feasibility evaluation. A very small number of potential changes was eliminated from further consideration due to organizational constraints. The outside consultant prepared a report outlining the nature of suggested changes, the probable effects of the changes, and the recommendations of the JITs. The report also estimated potential costs and risks of the changes.

Together, corporate and local management selected a subset of the proposed changes for implementation. The changes were well representative of the total set proposed by the JITs and received favorable cost/benefit analysis. Management decided to implement the job changes for a three-month trial period for a trial group of employees. Evaluation of the impact of the changes at the end of three months would determine future job redesign action.

(continued)

Some of the job redesign changes were quite major. The original job and organizational design for these jobs was shown in Exhibit 15–1. The new design is shown in Exhibit 15–13. Work groups of about 12 employees were formed, consisting of a combination of employees from all of the previously separate work areas shown in Exhibit 15–1. The team was given total responsibility for all work performed for a defined geographic area of the country. The group made decisions about how to process the work involved. Programs were created for cross-training (employees training each other in skills they each possess), and the involvement of employees in a wider range of tasks was encouraged. The team was physically located together and encouraged to interact with one another. The supervisor's job was elevated to more of a management and resource position than that of a worker who also supervised. Regular group meetings were scheduled, and a formal performance effectiveness feedback program was created.

Planning the implementation of the change involved the workers themselves, and management provided excellent support. Extensive information on the nature of the changes, and the logic underlying them was provided to all employees. Personal meetings were held to discuss the changes. Furniture and equipment were moved over a weekend, the computer system was modified to facilitate the new work design, and the new job design took effect the following Monday morning. Each work group was permitted to implement job changes, such as the learning and sharing in new tasks, at their own pace.

At the conclusion of the three-month period, work system diagnosis and worker reaction assessment procedures were repeated. Changes which occurred for the trial groups (the work groups) were compared to changes which occurred in "control groups" (similar departments which had continued working under the old job design). Although not all of the anticipated effects of the job redesign had taken place, most changes were in the direction expected. Perceptions of job scope increased, as did satisfaction with the work itself, the amount of work, and with supervision. Internal work motivation increased. Individual performance changes could not be assessed, but the total amount of work processed was greater under the group approach than it had been under the old design. The speed of processing policy information increased substantially. One part of the job redesign which involved a quality measure of the work performed received negative reactions (the measure used did not work well). For all other changes, slight modifications were suggested by group members, who stated a desire to continue with the new job design.

The new job design was retained for all trial groups and a plan was developed for the gradual introduction of the new design into other areas of the organization (including those groups which had served as the comparison groups during this study).

One year has elapsed since the conclusion of the initial trial period. All groups still exist, and informal evidence suggests that members are still quite pleased with the new design. Other groups of employees have now converted to the new job design and report initial positive reactions.

Exhibit 15–13 Job Redesign at United General Insurance Company

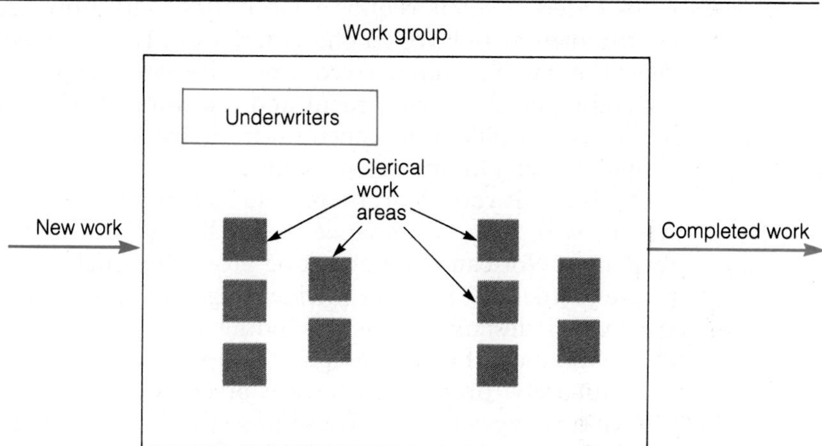

4. Inadequate evaluations are conducted, preventing effective "fine-tuning" and guidance for future job redesign.
5. Managers and staff obtain inadequate education in job redesign and become overwhelmed by its demands, since they don't have the knowledge required to deal with the redesign.
6. Traditional bureaucratic practices creep into job design activities and interfere with their planning and/or implementation.
7. Organizational members resist the introduction of the job redesign intervention.

Job redesign has gotten much "bad press" as a technique which often does not work. It is true that many job redesign projects have failed to produce positive results; some have even produced negative effects. Most of the failures, however, probably could have been avoided through the use of a comprehensive systematic approach. Critical steps are often overlooked, changes are rushed into without adequate consideration. You cannot guarantee your organization that job redesign will produce positive effects, but you can increase the odds greatly by managing the process carefully.

SUMMARY

It is very clear that the specific design of your job (the tasks you perform and the techniques you use) can have a major impact on your attitudes and behaviors. A variety of systematic approaches have evolved over the last 75 years for the purpose of designing jobs effectively. These approaches have explored many philosophies of job design; when combined, they provide a great deal of guidance.

It appears that workers form perceptions of critical job characteristics based on their required job duties (and influenced by both environmental and worker characteristics). These perceptions influence the satisfaction derived from the work experience (again, depending on the environment and the worker). Their satisfaction has the potential to influence future behaviors if the appropriate supporting conditions are present.

One factor is very clear: there is no "one right way" to design a job which will always enhance both behavioral and attitudinal responses. Nor can a handbook be provided which specifies appropriate job design. Because a wide range of factors must be considered when designing jobs (including environmental and worker characteristics) this task is quite complex.

Fortunately, procedures have evolved which can be used with almost any types of jobs. These procedures focus on the processes involved in worker reactions to the characteristics of a job. If you follow these procedures carefully, they can help you produce an effective job design. In short, this chapter described a procedure for designing jobs, but not a specification of the end results. That will depend on the people involved and the environment in which the jobs exist.

GLOSSARY

Job Design The specific tasks performed on the job, the techniques or processes used to perform these tasks, and the meaning of these tasks and processes.

Scientific Management The job design approach set forth by Frederick W. Taylor to identify the "one best way" of doing a job through work simplification and specialization.

Job Enlargement A job redesign strategy which focuses on increasing the number of activities engaged in by a worker.

Job Enrichment A job redesign strategy which focuses on providing employee growth through the introduction of a greater depth of job responsibility.

The Job Characteristics Approach to Job Design A job design/redesign strategy which focuses on enhancing the degree to which the job possesses skill variety, task identity, task significance, autonomy, and feedback.

STUDY QUESTIONS

1. Discuss the logical reasons why the scientific management approach to job design is appealing to a profit-oriented organization.
2. Would it be possible to use job enlargement jointly with job enrichment? Is this advisable? Why or why not?
3. Describe a job with which you are familiar which could benefit from job enlargement and/or job enrichment.
4. Is it possible to design a job effectively without knowing anything about the needs and values of the people who will hold the job?
5. The job characteristics approach described in this chapter frequently uses formal techniques for designing jobs. Systematic approaches are used for measuring job characteristics, personal characteristics of job incumbents, etc. Would it be possible for a manager to use the knowledge from this approach without having to use the formal "tools"?
6. Discuss the importance of considering organizational design factors when designing or redesigning jobs.
7. What problems might be expected when redesigning a job which workers have held for a long period of time?

NOTES

1. **Taylor, F. W.** (1911). *The principles of scientific management*. New York: Harper. Also see **Gilbreth, F. B.** (1914). *Primer of scientific management*. New York: Van Nostrand.
2. **Taylor,** 1911, p. 59.
3. Ibid., 1911, p. 59.
4. **Gilbreth,** 1914, p. 50.
5. **Golembiewski, R. T.** (1965). *Men, management, and morality: Toward a new organizational ethic*. New York: McGraw-Hill.
6. **Griffin, R. W.** (1982). *Task design: An integrative approach*. Glenview, IL: Scott, Foresman.
7. **Kilbridge, M. D.** (1960). Reduced costs through job enrichment: A case. *The Journal of Business, 33,* 357–362.
8. **Herzberg, F., Mausner, B., & Snyderman, B.** (1959). *The motivation to work*. New York: Wiley; **Herzberg, F.** (1968). One more time: How do you motivate employees? *Harvard Business Review, 46,* 53–62.
9. **Herzberg, F.** (1974, September–October). The wise old Turk. *Harvard Business Review,* 70–80.
10. **Aldag, R. J., & Brief, A. P.** (1979). *Task design and employee motivation*. Glenview, IL: Scott, Foresman.
11. **Herzberg, F.** (1977). Orthodox job enrichment. *Defense Management Journal, 13,* 21–27; **Herzberg, F., & Rafalko, E. A.** (1975). Efficiency in the military: Cutting costs with orthodox job enrichment. *Personnel, 52,* 38–48.
12. **Turner, A. N., & Lawrence, P. R.** (1965). *Industrial jobs and the worker*. Cambridge, MA: Harvard University, Graduate School of Business Administration.
13. **Blood, M. R., & Hulin, C. L.** (1967). Alienation, environmental characteristics, and worker responses. *Journal of Applied Psychology, 51,* 284–290; **Hulin, C. L., & Blood, M. R.** (1968). Job enlargement, individual differences, and worker responses. *Psychological Bulletin, 69,* 41–55; **Hulin, C. L.** (1971). Individual differences and job enrichment—the case against general treatments. In J. Mahler (Ed.), *New perspectives in job enrichment*. New York: Van Nostrand-Reinhold.
14. **Hackman, J. R., & Lawler, E. E., III.** (1971). Employee reactions to job characteristics. *Journal of Applied Psychology Monograph, 55,* 259–286.
15. **Hackman, J. R., & Oldham, G. R.** (1975). Development of the job diagnostic survey. *Journal of Applied Psychology, 60,* 159–170;

Hackman, J. R., & Oldham, G. R. (1976). Motivation through the design of work: Test of a theory. *Organizational Behavior and Human Performance, 16,* 250–279; **Hackman, J. R., & Oldham, G. R.** (1980). *Work redesign.* Reading, MA: Addison-Wesley Publishing.

16. **Hackman & Oldham,** 1976, pp. 257–258.
17. See **Griffen,** 1982, pp. 79–88 for a review of the two instruments.
18. **Pierce, J. L., & Dunham, R. B.** (1976). Task design: A literature review. *Academy of Management Review, 1,* 83–97; **Aldag & Brief,** 1979; **Griffin,** 1982; **Roberts, K. H., & Glick, W.** (1981). The job characteristics approach to task design: A critical review. *Journal of Applied Psychology, 66,* 193–217.
19. **Griffin,** 1982, p. 43.
20. **Stone, E. F.** (1977). Some personality correlates of perceptions of and reactions to task characteristics. Working paper, Purdue University; **Aldag, R. J., & Brief, A. P.** (1977). Moderators of relationships of job behaviors to perceptions of core task dimensions. *Proceedings of the 8th annual Midwest conference of the Midwest division of the American institute for decision sciences,* 327–329; **Stone, E. F.** (1979). Field independence and perceptions of task characteristics: A laboratory investigation. *Journal of Applied Psychology, 64,* 305–310.
21. **Burns, T., & Stalker, G. M.** (1961). *The management of innovation.* London: Tavistock.
22. **Porter, L. W., Lawler, E. E., III, & Hackman, J. R.** (1979). *Behavior in organizations.* New York: McGraw-Hill.
23. **Pierce, J. L., Dunham, R. B., & Blackburn, R. S.** (1979). Social systems structure, job design, and growth-need strength: A test of a congruency model. *Academy of Management Journal, 22,* 223–240.
24. **Thompson, J. D.** (1967). *Organizations in action.* New York: McGraw-Hill; **Rousseau, D. M.** (1977). Technological differences in job characteristics, employee satisfaction, and motivation: A synthesis of job design research and sociotechnical systems theory. *Organizational Behavior and Human Performance, 19,* 18–42.
25. **Rousseau,** 1977.
26. **Griffin, R. W.** (1980). Relationships among individual, task design, and leader behavior variables. *Academy of Management Journal, 65,* 665–683; **Griffin,** 1982.
27. For studies addressing job design and ability/compensation requirements, see **Dunham, R. B.** (1977). Relationship of perceived job design characteristics to job ability requirements and job values. *Journal of Applied Psychology, 62,* 760–763; **Schneider, B., Reichers, A. E., & Mitchell, T. M.** (1982). A note on some relationships between the aptitude requirements and reward attributes of tasks. *Academy of Management Journal, 25,* 567–574.

28. For a discussion of a wide range of such approaches, see **Levine, E. L.** (1983). *Everything you wanted to know about job analysis and more! . . . A job analysis primer.* Tampa, FL: Mariner Publishing.
29. See **Salancik, G., & Pfeffer, J.** (1978). A social information processing approach to job attitudes and task design. *Administrative Science Quarterly, 23,* 224–253.
30. **Hackman, J. R., Oldham, G. R., Janson, R. & Purdy, K.** (1975). A new strategy for job enrichment. *California Management Review, 17,* 57–71.

16 Stress

OVERVIEW
STRESS
STRESSORS
- Job-Related Stressors
- Organization Role Stressors
- Career Stressors
- Organization Structure/Climate Stressors
- Interpersonal Relations Stressors
- Extraorganizational Stressors

REACTIONS TO STRESS
- Perceptions of Stress
- Affective Reactions
- Psychological Health Reactions
- Physical Reactions
- Behavioral Reactions

THE ROLE OF PERSONAL CHARACTERISTICS
- Ability/Skill Levels
- Psychological Condition
- Physical Condition
- Personality
- Need States

THE DYNAMIC NATURE OF THE STRESS MODEL
- Changes in a Person Due to Reactions to Stress
- Stressor Changes Due to Stress Reactions

STRESS MANAGEMENT
- Changing the Stressor
- Treating the Reaction
- Changing the Person
- An Integrative Strategy

SUMMARY

. . . each of us, whether boss or co-worker, has a great responsibility for providing a decent, humane work environment—one that does not literally kill people.

Industrial/Organizational Psychologist upon learning of his father's stress-related death

OVERVIEW

Although stress is an important concern in organizations, there is widespread misunderstanding about what it is, what causes it, its impact on organizational members, and how to deal with stress. This makes stress management in organizations very difficult! Since you should understand a problem in order to manage it effectively, this chapter presents an integrated stress model.

The general model used in this chapter is shown in Exhibit 16–1. In this model, **stressors** are environmental factors influencing your stress level. **Stress** is a physiological state. **Stress reactions** are various responses your body and mind make due to your stress level. Your own **personal characteristics** determine both the specific impact a stressor has on your stress level and your subsequent reactions to stress. The model is dynamic, primarily because your current reactions to stress make you a different person in the future and because your reactions may themselves serve as future stressors. A more detailed explanation of this model follows, together with a discussion of the three basic stress management strategies: changing stressors, treating reactions to stress, and changing the person.

STRESS

Both the popular press and behavioral journals frequently fail to distinguish stress from its determinants (stressors) and consequences (reactions). This is unfortunate, not only because it is

Exhibit 16–1 The Stress Model

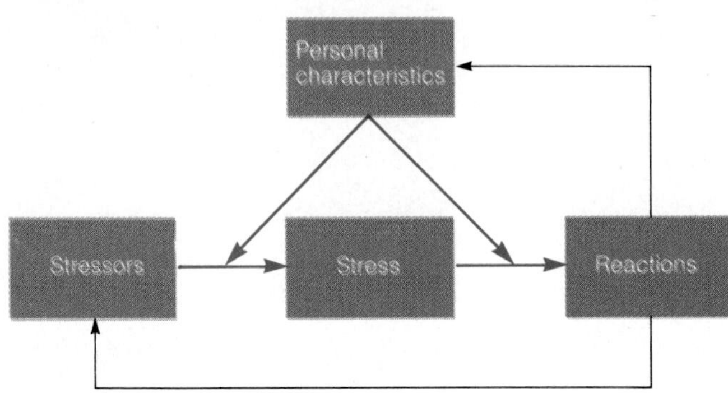

sloppy, but because it has hampered the understanding and management of stress.

Although the nature of stress is not fully understood or completely agreed upon, it is clear that stress involves a *physiological* state of the individual. Several specific aspects of your physiology are involved in determining your stress level, regardless of the types of factors which influence them (and certainly independent of any subsequent reactions you may have.)[1]

Although it is possible to treat stress as the "black box" shown in Exhibit 16–1, you can obtain a more complete understanding of stress by examining the physiological model shown in Exhibit 16–2.[2]

When a stressor is presented to the body, it first impacts on the brain (the cerebral cortex recognizes its presence). The cerebral cortex passes this information along to the hypothalamus. Among other things, this activates the autonomic nervous system and the pituitary gland. The pituitary produces a hormone known as adrenocorticotrophic (ACTH) which, along with arousal provided by the autonomic nervous system, activates the adrenal glands. The adrenals produce critical hormones (catecholamines), including adrenaline, noradrenaline, and corticoids. These hormones are placed into the bloodstream, which carries them to the rest of the body.

It is possible to measure ACTH levels in the blood. More commonly, however, physiological stress level is assessed by testing for catecholamine levels (adrenaline and noradrenaline) in the bloodstream or in urine. Because most noradrenaline is absorbed by

A Day in the Life of Clark Browne

Personal Characteristics

Clark is a well-trained, highly competent 29-year-old staff accountant in a national accounting firm. Although in reasonably good physical condition, during the last week Clark has not eaten well, has had trouble sleeping, and has been suffering from hay fever.

Stressors

Today, Clark is trying to reconcile what may be a major error in an audit he directed at a local firm. Clark's boss has just reminded him he needs to have a proposal ready for a new client by the end of the day. One of Clark's assistants in the audit went home sick at noon. On the way to work, his car had a flat tire, making Clark late for the monthly staff meeting. He has just canceled his opening match in the annual racquetball tournament at his club so he can work late.

Stress

Although he is not fully aware of it, Clark's physiological state has changed dramatically during the last few hours. His adrenaline level, for example, has risen considerably above normal.

Reactions to Stress

Today, Clark feels extremely anxious, has a headache, and is suffering from diarrhea. He is impatient with his co-workers and has provoked an argument with his boss. His coffee intake has increased dramatically, and he is smoking more. Despite these negative reactions, Clark has been performing at a sustained high level all day. Tonight, he plans to have three or four stiff drinks to help him "unwind" and fall asleep at a reasonable hour.

nerve endings or bound to tissues, adrenaline is probably the most reliable direct measure of stress level currently available. Blood samples reflect changes in stress levels more immediately than do urine samples. Although both urine and blood sampling are somewhat obtrusive, both techniques have been used in a variety of situations.[3]

Due in part to the awkwardness and difficulty of using blood and urine samples to measure stress levels, many researchers and practitioners have turned to other measures. These indirect techniques usually either measure the existence of stressors or measure reactions to stress. Although these methods are useful, they are *not* direct measures of stress. The former are preconditions of stress (which may or may not have a particular impact on stress). The

Exhibit 16–2 Stress: The Physiological State

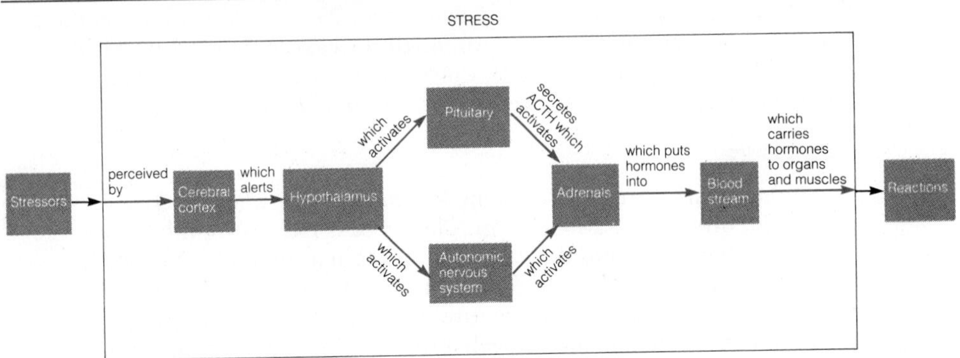

Source: Adapted from *Stress and work: A managerial perspective* by John M. Ivancevich and Michael T. Matteson, p. 81. Copyright © 1980 by Scott, Foresman and Co. Reprinted by permission.

latter are consequences of stress (which may be influenced by factors other than stress). A very popular indirect measure of "stress" involves psychological perceptions of stress which do not measure stress itself but, rather, a psychological reaction to stress. One major problem of this technique is that many people are not consciously aware of their physiological stress level. On the other hand, others are overly sensitive to minor changes in stress level. Therefore, indirect measures of stress are less valid and provide less accurate indications of a person's underlying stress level.

Do not confuse the physiological factors constituting stress with other physiological factors which are *reactions* to stress. A primary difference between the two is that stress factors are tied to any stressor, regardless of its nature, and constitute a first-level direct reaction to stressors. When stress increases, the process shown in Exhibit 16–2 *will* occur. Other physiological reactions may or may not occur, and when they do, they do so in reaction to the stress factors.

One final comment: stress per se is not negative. After all, based on the definition of stress just presented, the *only* time you could have a zero stress level would be when the portions of your brain and critical glands discussed here were not functioning (you're dead!).

STRESSORS

A stressor is any environmental factor which influences (raises, lowers, or maintains) your stress level. This definition is so broad that any observable environmental stimulus *potentially* could serve

Exhibit 16–3 The Facets of Stressors in Organizations

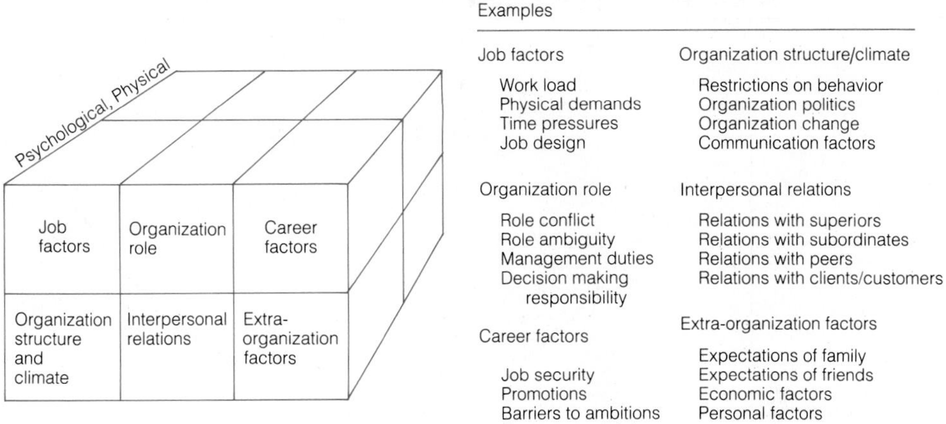

Source: Based loosely on C. L. Cooper and J. Marshall. Sources of managerial and white-collar stress. In C. L. Cooper and R. Payne (Eds.), *Stress at work*. Copyright 1978, John Wiley & Sons, Ltd., London. Reprinted by permission.

as a stressor. Indeed, over 150 individual stressors important to organizations can be identified.[4] Exhibit 16–3 shows examples of the six major categories of stressors of particular interest to organizations: job factors, organization roles, career factors, organization structures and climates, interpersonal relations, and extraorganizational factors.

Although some stressors impact on stress primarily because of either a physical or a psychological component, many stressors possess both psychological and physical components. A materials handler in a steel mill, for example, may be required to guide multiton rolls of steel as a crane places them onto a truck. This activity acts as a stressor with both physical (the pushing and pulling of rolls of steel) and psychological (concern about effects of mishandling the roll) components. Both psychological and physical components activate the same stress response (as illustrated in Exhibit 16–3). It is important to distinguish between the two, however, since their management may require different tactics.

More of a stressor does not always increase stress level, and less does not always decrease it. For most stressors, a curvilinear relationship exists such that understimulation and overstimulation both produce high stress, while moderate levels of the stressor tend to create lower levels of stress. Exhibit 16–4 is based on the relationship between task stimulation level and stress level (as measured by catecholamine excretions).[5]

Exhibit 16–4 The Stressor→Stress Relationship

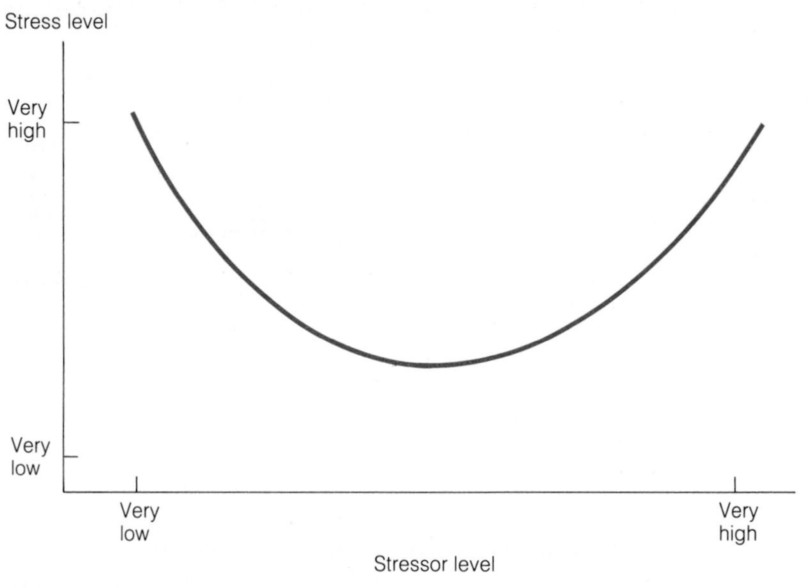

Job-Related Stressors

Many job-related stressors influence stress level (e.g., the amount of light, noise, vibration, ambient temperature, and air pollutants).[6] Time pressures as well as physical and intellectual demands can increase stress.

A study which illustrates the degree to which the job can act as a stressor was conducted recently by James Shaw and John Riskind of Texas A & M University.[7] Their research included an extremely wide range of jobs (executive, architect, college professor, pulp mill worker, secretary, and sewer worker). Each job was described by multiple persons using a well-developed, valid job analysis questionnaire. Job profiles were then compared to existing data on typical stress levels for each of the job types studied. The results indicated a fairly strong relationship between job characteristics and indirect measures of stress.

The levels of many job-related stressors can be measured using existing instruments. John McNeill and William Snavely of Miami University of Ohio modified several existing instruments for assessing job-related stressors, used them to assess stressor/stress rela-

Exhibit 16–5 Sample Items for Measuring Job-Related Stressors

How frequently is each of the following a source of stress?	Never	Rarely	Occa-sionally	Some-times	Often	Usually	Always
Quantitative Role Overload							
1. I have to take work home in the evenings or on weekends to complete it.	1	2	3	4	5	6	7
2. I am responsible for an almost unmanageable number of projects or assignments at the same time.	1	2	3	4	5	6	7
3. I simply have more work than can be done in an ordinary day.	1	2	3	4	5	6	7
Qualitative Role Overload							
1. My assigned tasks are sometimes too difficult and/or complex.	1	2	3	4	5	6	7
2. This organization expects more of me than my skills and/or abilities can provide.	1	2	3	4	5	6	7
3. I have insufficient training and/or experience to discharge my duties properly.	1	2	3	4	5	6	7

Source: J. McNeill and W. Snavely (1983). *Job-related stressors: A scale analysis.* Paper presented at the Midwest Academy of Management Convention. Adapted from J. M. Ivancevich, and M. T. Matteson (1980). *Stress and work: A managerial perspective.* Glenview, IL: Scott, Foresman, pp. 118–119.

tionships in organizations, and provided reliability and validity evidence for the measures.[8] Exhibit 16–5 provides excerpts from that research.

Organization Role Stressors

A variety of organizational role stressors also have been related to stress.[9] Probably most thoroughly explored has been the impact of role conflict, role ambiguity, and decision-making responsibility. There are also measures available for many of the organizational role factors which influence stress. Exhibit 16–6 provides examples of two of these scales.

Exhibit 16–6 Sample Items for Measuring Organizational Role Stressors

How frequently is each of the following a source of stress?	Never	Rarely	Occasionally	Sometimes	Often	Usually	Always
Role Conflict							
1. I have to do things that should be done differently.	1	2	3	4	5	6	7
2. I work under incompatible policies and guidelines.	1	2	3	4	5	6	7
3. I have to do things that are against my personal principles.	1	2	3	4	5	6	7
Role Ambiguity							
1. I am uncertain about the limits of my authority on my present job.	1	2	3	4	5	6	7
2. My job lacks clear, planned goals and objectives.	1	2	3	4	5	6	7
3. I am uncertain about my job responsibilities.	1	2	3	4	5	6	7

Source: Revised from McNeill and Snavely (1983). Original source: J. R. Rizzo, R. J. House and S. I. Listzman (1970). Role conflict and ambiguity in complex organizations, *Administrative Science Quarterly, 15,* 150–163.

Career Stressors

Career stressors influencing stress level include job security, promotions, demotions, lack of promotions, barriers to ambitions, career uncertainty, and transfers.[10] Career changes inconsistent with worker expectations may be particularly stressful. Exhibit 16–7 presents one measure of career stressor levels.

Organization Structure/Climate Stressors

Organization structure/climate stressors which influence stress include behavioral restrictions, organization politics, communication processes, and organization change. One example of the type of impact possible is shown in an Italian study of the impact of piece-rate pay (pay based on performance quantity) and assembly line work arrangements.[11] This study showed that stress levels (as measured by adrenaline, noradrenaline, and 11-hydroxycorticosteroid levels) were higher when workers were paid on a piece-rate (as opposed to salaried) basis. Stress levels were also higher under assem-

Exhibit 16–7 Sample Items for Measuring Major Career Stressors

How frequently is each of the following a source of stress?	Never	Rarely	Occasionally	Sometimes	Often	Usually	Always
Career Development							
1. I lack the proper opportunities to advance in this organization.	1	2	3	4	5	6	7
2. If I want to get promoted I have to look for a job with another organization.	1	2	3	4	5	6	7
3. I am hurting my career progress by staying with this organization.	1	2	3	4	5	6	7
4. I have few opportunities to grow and learn new knowledge and skills in my job.	1	2	3	4	5	6	7
5. I feel that I am at a standstill in my career.	1	2	3	4	5	6	7

Source: Adapted from *Stress and work: A managerial perspective* by John M. Ivancevich and Michael T. Matteson. Copyright © 1980 by Scott, Foresman and Co. Reprinted by permission.

Exhibit 16–8 Sample Items for Measuring Organization Structure/Climate Stressors

How frequently is each of the following a source of stress?	Never	Rarely	Occasionally	Sometimes	Often	Usually	Always
Structure							
1. A person at my level has little control over the job.	1	2	3	4	5	6	7
2. The formal structure has too much red tape.	1	2	3	4	5	6	7
3. The chain of command is not followed.	1	2	3	4	5	6	7
Communication Apprehension							
1. I often feel intimidated by my supervisor.	1	2	3	4	5	6	7
2. I am afraid of what my supervisor may think of me.	1	2	3	4	5	6	7
3. I feel shy around my supervisor.	1	2	3	4	5	6	7

Source: Structure items are from Ivancevich and Matteson (1980). Communication apprehension items are from J. McNeill and W. Snavely (1983). *Job-related stressors: A scale analysis*. Paper presented at the Midwest Academy of Management Convention.

bly line conditions than under nonassembly line conditions. Exhibit 16–8 provides examples of measures of two of these stressors.

Interpersonal Relations Stressors

A lot of interpersonal activity takes place in organizations. All of it has the potential to act as stressors. The most common interpersonal stressors involve relations with superiors, subordinates, peers, and clients/customers. Relationships involving low trust, low supportiveness, low interpersonal interest, functional dependence, and power imbalances increase stress.[12] A primary source of interpersonal stressors is conflict (see Chapter 13). Exhibit 16–9 identifies some of the common interpersonal stressors.

Exhibit 16–9 Sample Items for Measuring Interpersonal Stressors

How frequently is each of the following a source of stress?	**Never**	**Rarely**	**Occasionally**	**Sometimes**	**Often**	**Usually**	**Always**
Co-worker Stressors							
1. I cannot trust my co-workers.	1	2	3	4	5	6	7
2. I cannot count on my co-workers for support.	1	2	3	4	5	6	7
3. My goals and those of my co-workers are not compatible.	1	2	3	4	5	6	7
Subordinate Stressors							
1. Dealing with my subordinates is a power struggle.	1	2	3	4	5	6	7
2. I cannot trust my subordinates.	1	2	3	4	5	6	7
3. My subordinates try to make me look bad.	1	2	3	4	5	6	7
Customer Stressors							
1. My customers are not honest with me.	1	2	3	4	5	6	7
2. My customers and I have an adversarial relationship.	1	2	3	4	5	6	7
3. My interests and those of my customers are not compatible.	1	2	3	4	5	6	7

Source: Prepared by the author for illustration purposes.

Extraorganizational Stressors

There are a tremendous number of stressors outside the workplace which can influence your stress level. Most of these center around family, friend, economic, and personal factors. Although these are extraorganizational factors, they should be of interest to organizations because of their impact on organizational members. Exhibit 16–10 identifies a few of the many extraorganizational factors which act as stressors. These are arranged in order from the most to least stress producing. (Note that even *positive* events can act as powerful stressors.)

REACTIONS TO STRESS

Stress literature reveals a wide range of human reactions influenced by stress level. Unfortunately, much of the research on this issue has been clouded by research designs using indirect measures of stress (usually measures of stressor levels) instead of direct physiological measures of stress. Because many of these studies treat stress as a "black box" between stressors and reactions to stress,

Exhibit 16–10 Sample Items for Measuring Extraorganizational Stressors

Which of the following events have you experienced in the last 12 months?

Stressor	Stress Produced
Death of spouse	100
Divorce	73
Jail term	63
Death of close family member	63
Marriage	50
Sex difficulties	39
Change in financial state	38
Death of a friend	37
Change in living conditions	25
Revision of personal habits	24
Change in residence	20
Change in social activities	18
Change in sleeping habits	16
Vacation	13
Minor violation of the law	11

Note: The number next to each stressor is an indicator of the relative amount of stress usually produced by that stressor.

Source: Adapted from T. H. Holmes and R. H. Rahe. The social readjustment rating scale, *Journal of Psychosomatic Medicine, 11,* 213–218. Copyright 1967, Pergamon Press, Ltd.

you cannot be certain whether a specific stress→reaction relationship actually is due to the impact of stress. Nevertheless, you can use the accumulated evidence to identify a number of factors which appear to be related to stress level.

Exhibit 16–11 identifies six of the major reactions to stress. Although more are being discovered on a regular basis, virtually all of the stress reactions discussed here can be measured by valid, reliable instruments.

It was noted earlier that stressors often have a curvilinear relationship with stress level so that both high and low levels of a stressor can produce high levels of stress (see Exhibit 16–4). There is also some evidence that the relationship between stress level and reactions to stress may be curvilinear (see Exhibit 16–12). This means that the most positive reactions to stress occur with moderate levels of stress, while both very low and very high stress levels may be associated with negative reactions. Being "understressed," for example, may be both boring and dissatisfying. A special variation on this relationship between stress level and performance will be discussed later in this chapter.

Perceptions of Stress

Many studies which measure "stress" actually measure perceptions of stress which are *reactions* to stress. The physiological stress state is linked to perceptions of stress, but the link is not perfect.[13] Many people do not perceive how high their stress levels have risen. Others "feel" stressed at the slightest increase in stress level. For these reasons, perceptions of stress are treated here as reactions to stress, *not* as a measure of stress.

Affective Reactions

Stress is capable of producing powerful and rapid effects on your affective reactions (such as job satisfaction).[14] Stress can influence all eight facets of satisfaction discussed in Chapter 3. Although stress usually has its greatest impact on the particular facet of satisfaction most directly related to existing stressors (conflict with your supervisor will influence supervision satisfaction more than it will co-worker satisfaction), stress effects often spill over and affect a wide range of job satisfaction areas.

Psychological Health Reactions

Psychological health is often threatened by stress. Factors commonly identified in this category include anxiety, low self-esteem, alienation, neuroses, depression, suicide, and several psychoso-

Exhibit 16–11 Examples of Reactions to Stress

Affective (Satisfaction with . . .)	Psychological	Physical	Behavioral: Personal	Behavioral: Nonperformance	Behavioral: Performance (Change in . . .)
Kind of work	Anxiety	Headaches	Nicotine use	Absenteeism	Quantity
Amount of work	Alienation	Sleep loss	Alcohol use	Tardiness	Quality
Physical work conditions	Low self-esteem	Skin disorders	Caffeine use	Turnover	Timeliness
Co-workers	Neuroses	Ulcers	"Soft" drug use	Early retirement	Efficiency
Supervision	Depression	High cholesterol level	"Hard" drug use	Sabotage	Decision making
Career	Psychosomatic symptoms	High blood pressure	Conflict	Theft	Coordination with others
Compensation	Boredom	Heart disease	Aggression	Job actions	Materials waste
Company	Mental fatigue	Perspiration	Suicide	Grievance filing	Safety practices
Leisure activities	Lost concentration	Diarrhea	Legal violations	Participation	Record-keeping
Life	Anger	Physical fatigue	Poor sexual relations	Complaining	Organization effectiveness

Exhibit 16–12 Proposed Relationship between Stress and Reactions

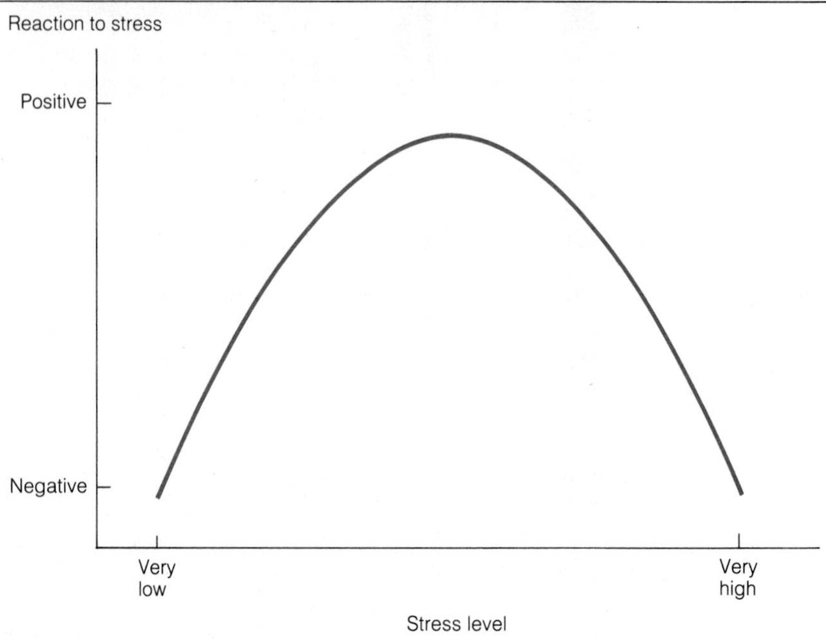

matic reactions (physical symptoms with psychological causes).[15] Psychological reactions often escalate rapidly if not treated. This is particularly true if continued presence of critical stressors maintains a high stress level.

Physical Reactions

Physical reactions to stress span virtually every human malady. These include gastrointestinal-intestinal distress, diarrhea, headaches, skin disorders, and ulcers.[16] Stress appears to affect cholesterol levels, blood pressure, and heart rate.[17] Stress has even been linked to cancer.[18]

The potential link between stress and heart disease is particularly interesting. Although the research evidence still appears to be very circumstantial, convincing theoretical arguments have been made for the link.[19] In terms of both human suffering and loss and financial cost, the magnitude of the heart disease issue is illustrated by the following:

> In an organization with 4,000 employees, approximately 1,000 can be classified as high coronary risks (males between the ages of 45 and 65). In a typical year, six of these persons will die from heart-related illnesses and another three will be forced to retire prematurely. The cost to the organization for paid time off the job and for treating these persons prior to death is over $15,000 each. The cost of replacing the lost employees will be about $6,000 each. Therefore, direct annual costs related to the heart-disease-related loss of employees will be over $189,000. The eventual cause of death for 2,000 of the employees of this organization will be heart disease.*

Behavioral Reactions

Stress impacts on three general categories of behaviors: personal behaviors, organizational nonperformance behaviors, and performance behaviors. The three behavioral reactions often interact with one another, as is the case when alcohol abuse impacts on attendance and performance.

Personal Behaviors. Thorough research has addressed the impact of stress on a variety of personal behaviors. It has been shown, for example, that the consumption of nicotine, caffeine, alcohol, and other drugs can all be related to stress level.[20] A well-known pattern at colleges and universities is for alcohol and marijuana use to increase at exam time in reaction to stress. Stress can also influence interpersonal relations both inside and outside an organization, with conflict and aggression often increasing in response to stress.

Nonperformance Behaviors. Absenteeism, tardiness, and turnover can all be influenced by stress level.[21] Grievance filings and collective actions (e.g., strikes) are also susceptible to the effects of stress.

Performance Behaviors. It is often assumed that performance decreases as stress increases. This assumption clearly is not merited; the relationship between the two is much more complex. Research on the relationship between stress and performance indicates that increases in stress can produce increases in performance—up to a certain point. After that point, excessive stress appears to interfere with successful performance. These findings lead to a preliminary conclusion that the stress→performance relationship could be represented by the graph shown in Exhibit 16–12. These types of findings suggest that increasing stress raises your arousal level, causing you to be more attentive to job demands and perform more ef-

* These are revised estimates based on an analysis by Ivancevich & Matteson, 1980, p. 92.

fectively.[22] At a critical point, however, further increases in stress make you incapable of coping, and performance drops.

One qualification of the "inverted-U" relationship shown in Exhibit 16–12 focuses on the importance of the difficulty of the task involved.[23] Exhibit 16–13 illustrates that, for simple tasks, even extremely high levels of stress can improve performance. As task complexity increases, however, the optimal level of stress decreases. Because of this, even moderate levels of stress can impair performance on extremely complex tasks.

The same pattern of results is likely if you consider the degree to which the task is learned. For well-learned tasks, performance continues to increase until a relatively high level of stress is encountered. During learning, on the other hand, low levels of stress are usually best. This is an interesting dilemma since the learning experience itself can be a stressor, increasing stress levels to nonoptimal points.[24]

Exhibit 16–13 Relationship between Stress and Performance

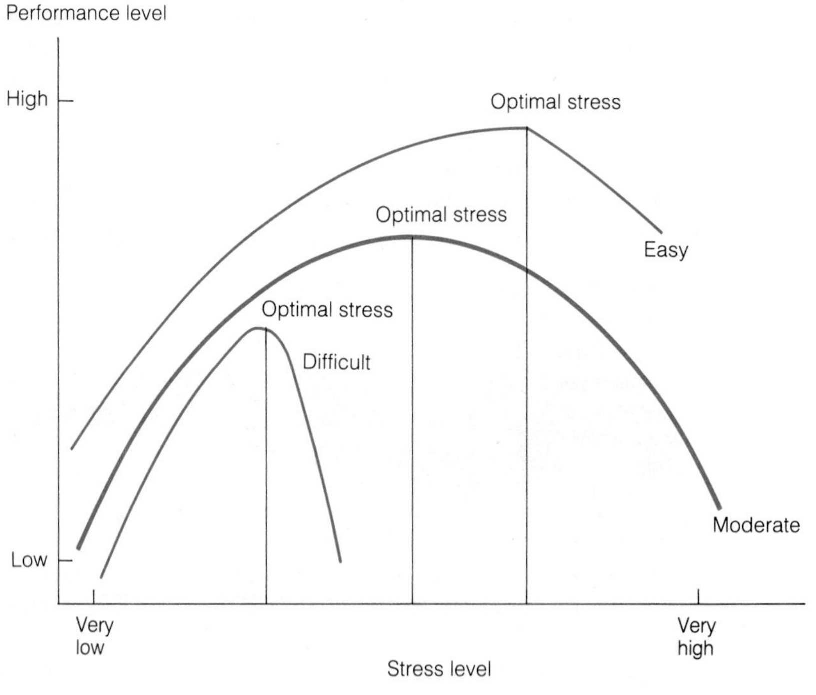

THE ROLE OF PERSONAL CHARACTERISTICS

A person involved in a potentially stress-producing situation has several characteristics which impact the stress process. As shown in Exhibit 16–1, these "moderating effects" occur in two ways. First, your personal characteristics determine the degree of stress you experience in reaction to a particular stressor. A young, healthy, physically fit person probably will not experience much of a stress reaction when climbing a flight of stairs. An older, out-of-shape, unhealthy individual may experience a very high stress level in response to the exact same stressor. These differences can also occur across time for one person. If you come to your annual job performance appraisal well rested and prepared to discuss job performance, whether goals were met, etc., your stress reaction will be very different than if you are unprepared and tired. This second effect involves your reaction to a particular stress level. A well-conditioned athlete, for example, is less likely to have a heart attack in reaction to a high stress level than is an out-of-shape sedentary individual.

Five major categories of individual characteristics have the potential to influence stressor→stress and stress→reaction relationships: *ability/skill levels, physical condition, psychological condition, personality,* and *need states* (see Exhibit 16–14 for examples of each).

Exhibit 16–14 Examples of Personal Characteristics Which Influence the Stress Process

Psychological Condition	Physical Condition	Abilities/Skills
Anxiety	Muscular condition	Job skills
Mental fatigue	Stamina	Perception skills
Intelligence	Rest	Coping skills
Security	Diet	Problem-solving skills
Self-esteem	Disease	
Confidence	Physical fatigue	
Personality	**Need States**	
Type A/B	Safety	
Introversion/extroversion	Security	
Dogmatism	Social	
Authoritarianism	Ego	
Locus of control	Achievement	
Tolerance for ambiguity	Self-actualization	

Ability/Skill Levels

Your ability/skill levels impact on your reactions to stress. Perceptual skills influence your translation of a stressor and its effect (see Chapter 10). Job skills and abilities (see Chapter 9) determine the degree to which many stressors are easy or difficult for you. This, in turn, determines the impact on stress of many stressors (a highly skilled individual will not react with high stress to moderate demands for production). Job skills also determine the nature of response to stress. As previously noted, high levels of stress can enhance performance for well-learned tasks but decrease performance for poorly learned tasks. Thus, the greater your mastery of a job, the less the potential for a negative impact of stress on performance. Abilities related to job tasks will also influence other reactions to stress ("I'm under the gun but I can handle it" versus "I'm under the gun and don't know if I can handle it"). Problem-solving and coping skills affect both stress reactions to stressors and subsequent reactions to stress.[25] A person who is capable of "rolling with the punches" will respond less dramatically to stressors and to stress.

Psychological Condition

Your psychological condition influences the impact of stressors on stress and the impact of stress on reactions. If you are mentally fatigued, for example, you have more extreme reactions to both stressors and stress. It has been shown that depression reduces resistance to stressors.[26] Persons lacking self-esteem and confidence will react more negatively to a challenging stressor. These, and many other elements of your psychological fitness, play an important role in determining the specific nature of your responses to stressors and stress.

Physical Condition

> Healthy people seem to be able to cope better with stressors than not-so-healthy people. . . . If, as Selye and others maintain, there is a finite amount of adaptive energy available, then directing some toward a physical problem leaves less for dealing with a . . . stressor. . . . Put another way, the employee with even mild chronic health problems is much more likely to experience negative stress reactions than a colleague.[27]

For the above reasons, your physical condition is a critical element in the stress process. Good physical condition has two advantages: it makes it less likely you will have an extreme stress reaction and, for a particular stress level, it is less likely you will have dysfunctional reactions.

Personality

A number of personality factors influence the stress process. Introverts usually respond more negatively to high levels of stressors due to their sensitivity to the environment.[28] Closed-minded, dogmatic persons tend to avoid stressors by gravitating toward stress-free working conditions. More flexible persons tend to meet the stressor "head-on" and may react more strongly to stressors because they don't "give in."[29] Internal-locus-of-control individuals react strongly to stressors over which they *do not* have control (because this violates their belief that they are in control), while external-locus-of-control persons react strongly to stressors over which they *do* have control.[30] The greater your tolerance for ambiguity, the more resistant you are to stressors involving uncertainty.[31]

Without doubt, the personality factor receiving the most attention in stress literature has been the Type A versus Type B personality. Chapter 9 described the Type A person as impatient and competitive with others. The Type A person tends to react strongly when provoked or thwarted, and works aggressively under pressure. For these reasons, the Type A person reacts strongly to stressors which interfere with the rapid, aggressive, successful completion of work. The Type B person, on the other hand, takes time to deal with stressors and, thus, has less extreme stress reactions to stressors. There is little evidence to suggest that a given stress level produces more extreme reactions for Type A persons. On the other hand, Type A persons tend to develop higher stress levels when presented with stressors. This means that reactions of Type A persons are often more negative than for Type B persons. It has been shown, for example, that Type A persons experience twice the amount of heart disease as Type B persons.[32] Although part of these differences probably are due to the fact that Type As tend to expose themselves to more extreme stressors, much of the effect undoubtedly is due to the type of reactions made by Type As to these stressors.

Need States

Your need state will influence your reactions to stressors and, to a lessor extent, to stress. If you have a strong safety or security need, for example, you experience more stress when threatened by a stressor than if your safety and security needs have been satisfied fairly well (the threat presented by the stressor is simply not as critical). If you have a strong social need, interpersonal stressors have a powerful impact on your stress level. If you possess a high need for achievement, you probably will not give in to a stressor which threatens accomplishment (and, if you fail to succeed, you probably will react strongly). These and other need characteristics influence your stressor→stress relationships. In short, a stressor which threatens an active need substantially influences your stress level.

THE DYNAMIC NATURE OF THE STRESS MODEL

The stress model discussed in this chapter is dynamic due to its two feedback loops. Because of the *dynamic nature of the model,* your reaction to stressors and to stress will vary across time.

Changes in a Person Due to Reactions to Stress

The majority of stress reactions produce one or more changes in your future makeup. Since these changes make you a "different" person, you will react differently to stressors (and to stress itself) in the future than the way you reacted today. These changes can occur in any of the five areas summarized in Exhibit 16–14 and may make you more or less sensitive to the effects of stressors and stress.

If you are given a difficult work assignment and fail, your future self-confidence will be lowered. This, in turn, increases your stress reactions to similar stressors in the future. If you begin jogging, you probably will have strong physical reactions to the stress produced. These reactions, however, normally improve your physical condition. In the future, your reactions to jogging will be less extreme. If you respond to jogging with a heart attack, your physical condition is weakened. Future stressors will have greater impact on your stress level, and a given stress level may produce another heart attack. These are but a few examples of the way you are changed by reactions to stress and respond differently in the future to stressors and stress.

Stressor Changes Due to Stress Reactions

The second feedback loop in the stress model recognizes that a reaction to stress can itself become a stressor in the future. The experience of suffering a heart attack can itself become a stressor as you worry about your future health. Sexual failures in response to stress often become stressors producing further negative reactions, including more sexual failures. Poor performance due to stress can act as a stressor.

The circular nature of this feedback loop has the potential to become catastrophic if not treated. Without intervention, a closed loop can occur (your reactions provide a new stressor, which add to existing stressors, which produce stronger reactions, which create more powerful stressors, which elicit stronger reactions . . .).

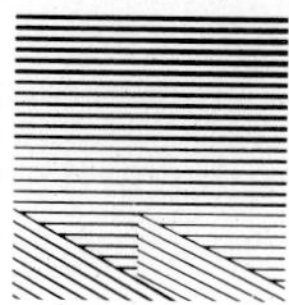

Bryan Lawton, trained as a clinical psychologist, is vice president and director of Employee Assistance Services at Wells Fargo Bank. He is coordinator of that company's health promotion task force and has been central in the development and implementation of Wells Fargo's successful stress management training program.

What are some of the arguments for and against an organization developing a stress management program? One argument against such a plan is that stress management is the individual's responsibility, and management should not interfere with one's privacy and personal life. It has been shown, however, that health promotion efforts sponsored by an organization are more effective than individual efforts (due to greater access to help, broader participation in stress management, better social support from managers and co-workers, and the availability of communication vehicles for ongoing reinforcement). Another concern is that a stress management program might increase awareness of stress-related problems. This is really an unnecessary concern, since most employees are already well aware of the problems associated with stress. Some of the best arguments in favor of an organizational stress management program focus on spiraling health costs and the fact that many health problems are stress related. It is now more critical than ever to take a proactive posture to control health and workers' compensation costs and to improve morale, interpersonal relations, and productivity.

Would you comment briefly on your philosophy of stress management? An effective program must be easily disseminated with a minimum of organizational disruption. The training must be spaced over time and supported through ongoing reinforcement. Our goals are to: help our employees become more aware of stress, its causes, and its consequences; alter attitudes related to stress; identify stress-related problems; incorporate behavioral self-management techniques to change emotions and behaviors; and, when that is not possible, seek help in changing the situation. Our program should be available to all 17,000 of our employees. It is not just weak people who feel stress—it is part of every person's everyday life. We all can do something about it.

What are some of the features of the Wells Fargo stress management program? We have a "train the trainer" program which teaches personnel officers and some other managers to become experts in the subject of stress and organizational practices to reduce stress. They are also trained in providing stress management sessions for employee groups. These trainers are taught to use a modular component 2½-day stress management program which is built upon a video/workbook approach developed by Time-Life and a trainer's manual we developed and tailored to our work place. Our trainers tailor the program further to the needs of individual employee groups. This program provides the instruments necessary for participants to confidentially self-evaluate existing or potential stress problems and their sources. Guidance is then provided for changing attitudes and behaviors to deal with these. Our primary focus is to provide the tools needed for the employee to self-manage stress problems and self-monitor progress. We also look at the organizational setting and attempt to modify it (when needed) through changes in factors such as physical working conditions, job design, and work demands.

STRESS MANAGEMENT

Most attempts at stress management have been haphazard and/or faddish and, consequently, not very effective. A few efforts have been well organized and effective. The distinguishing characteristic of the more effective attempts has been the systematic approach taken with regard to both action strategies and action initiators (agents).

There are three **action strategies** (changing the stressor, treating reactions to stress, changing the person) and three **action initiators** (the individual, the organization, and society). Together these provide a wide range of options for the management of stress.[33] Since each of three action strategies can be taken by any of the three action initiators, there are nine general strategies available for the management of stress. When combined with the six types of stressors, six types of reactions, and five types of individual characteristics, 51 specific approaches are possible. For each specific approach, many subsets of action exist (see Exhibit 16–15).*

Depending on how you view Exhibit 16–15, it either provides a framework rich with possibilities or a staggering commentary on the vast number of actions potentially involved in managing stress. Because some of the action/initiator combinations have more promise than others, Exhibit 16–15 also provides a general idea of the potential for success of each specific approach.†

Changing the Stressor

Changing the stressor is managing stress through prevention. In other words, you must alter or remove a stressor so that dysfunctional stress levels and reactions are not produced. Keep in mind, however, that a stressor level which is too low can be almost as stress producing as one which is too high. For this reason, changes in the stressor should attempt to produce optimal stress levels. Sometimes, individuals can change stressors directly. Frequently, however, an organization must initiate these changes. If role ambiguity is a stressor, either you can ask for clarification of job responsibilities or the organization can initiate a program for defining responsibilities. Although less frequently, society sometimes attempts to change stressors, as is the case when legislation limits work hours or requires pollution control devices.

---

*Although not all ideas discussed here have been researched thoroughly, there are strong theoretical and conceptual arguments for their appropriateness.

†In Exhibit 16–15, "success" is defined as prevention or reduction of negative reactions to stress, regardless of technique or reason.

Exhibit 16–15 Strategies for the Management of Stress

Type of Action	Initiator of Action: Individual	Organization	Society
Change Stressor	*Job Role *Career Structure *Interpersonal †Extra-organization	†Job †Role *Career †Structure *Interpersonal Extra-organization	*Job Role Career Structure Interpersonal *Extra-organization
Treat Reaction	*Affective †Psychological †Physical †Personal behavior *Nonperformance behavior *Performance	Affective *Psychological *Physical *Personal behavior *Nonperformance behavior †Performance	Affective *Psychological *Physical *Personal behavior Nonperformance behavior Performance
Change Person	†Psychological †Physical Personality *Needs †Abilities	*Psychological *Physical Personality *Needs †Abilities	*Psychological *Physical Personality *Needs *Abilities

* Moderate potential for success.
† High potential for success.

Strengths. Changing the stressor is the most thorough and permanent technique for managing stress. You can avoid many adverse reactions by changing an individual stressor. If role overload is producing a high stress level with headaches, nausea, and anxiety, you may be able to decrease or eliminate all three reactions by reducing the amount of role overload.

Limits. Unfortunately, you cannot always change a stressor. A deadline which cannot be changed, for example, remains a stressor. Furthermore, you can address only one stressor at a time. If negative reactions are being caused by stress emanating from several stressors, changing one stressor may not be particularly effective.

Treating the Reaction

Treating the reaction means you treat a symptom directly, rather than treating the cause of the symptom. This is why sleeping pills

are prescribed for insomnia, counseling is provided to help cope with anxiety, and medication is used to control high blood pressure. Individuals can initiate treatment by seeking a physician or psychologist to provide actual treatment. Organizations can facilitate treatment of reactions through health insurance plans or counseling programs. Society often assists by providing health clinics, by funding hospitals, etc.

Strengths. Because this approach devotes full energy to a specific problem, it can be very effective for treatment and prompt relief of a specific, critical reaction. Thus, you can treat a headache effectively without determining its specific cause(s). This approach is effective in treating reactions which are functions of multiple stressors. It is simpler to treat a headache than to change job designs, career factors, etc.

Limits. Treating a symptom does not remove the source of the problem. The stressor continues to produce stress, possibly leading to negative reactions other than the one effectively being treated ("My headache is gone but now I am nauseous"). If multiple symptoms exist, complete treatment might be quite complex compared to the removal of the stressor which is the source of the problem.

Changing the Person

Changing the person involves managing stress by changing your sensitivity to stressors and/or stress. If you are prepared physically, psychologically, and so forth, the magnitude of your reaction to a stressor can be lowered. You also can reduce subsequent reactions to stress. An individual usually initiates this type of change. However, both the organization and society can be supportive or even effective initiators of action under certain conditions. A person can improve his/her physical condition through exercise. Organizations today frequently support this by providing exercise facilities, health club memberships, etc. Society is supportive through public recreation facilities and programs. A person can also change through counseling, medical treatment, education and training, meditation, etc.

Strengths. Changing the person has broad potential impact on the stress process. This is due in part to the fact that changes in the person intervene between stressors and stress, as well as between stress and reactions. This approach is further strengthened because many changes in a person influence the impact of a wide variety of stressors. This approach can be very useful when dominant stressors cannot be easily altered.

Limits. Changing the person does not remove the source of the problem; thus, pressures persist. In addition, changing a person usually takes time. An exercise program, for example, does not provide full results overnight. When symptoms are severe, it is often difficult to change the person (i.e., it may be "too late" for this approach).

An Integrative Strategy

A good combination strategy exists for managing stress. As a package, this strategy has the potential to produce timely, lasting, and powerful effects by:

1. Identifying existing critical reactions and providing treatment to give relief (see Exhibit 16–11).
2. Identifying the most critical stressors and developing and implementing changes to alter them (see Exhibit 16–3).
3. Diagnosing the primary weaknesses of an individual and developing and implementing a program to change that person (see Exhibit 16–14).

Although the preceding may sound simple, the application of this strategy actually takes a lot of work. The possible actions in Exhibit

Another Day in the Life of Clark Browne

The day in the life of Clark Browne discussed earlier presented a pretty sad picture. However, the next day . . .

Thanks to his decision to skip the drinks last night, and aided by 30 minutes of meditation prior to bed, Clark got a full eight hours of sleep. His diarrhea is controlled by a prescription from his physician and by the well-balanced meal he ate the night before. He still has some hay fever, but this is not as troublesome when not compounded by other maladies.

Upon rising at 6 A.M., Clark runs two miles, showers, and has a healthy breakfast. He has only one cigarette and limits his coffee to one cup. He dresses and takes a cab to work to avoid traffic hassles.

Upon arriving at work, Clark begins preparing the proposal for the new client. Yesterday, his boss contacted the new client and arranged a lunch meeting for the day after tomorrow to present the proposal. Therefore, the proposal need not be finished until the end of the day tomorrow. Yesterday, before leaving work, Clark organized the materials from the questioned audit and assigned the review work to an assistant. When the work is finished, Clark and the assistant will review the findings.

During the course of the day, Clark feels good and works effectively. He has a pleasant lunch with two co-workers. He limits his smoking, skips the martini, and has just one cup of coffee. At the end of the day, he feels the situation is well under control. He looks forward to a relaxing evening with a friend and finishing his proposal in the morning. As he leaves work, he realizes he has not had a headache all day, grabs a cab, and reads the newspaper on the way home.

16–15, together with techniques explored earlier in this book, should be useful in planning stress management strategies.

SUMMARY

Stress is a measurable physiological state of an individual. Stressors are environmental conditions which influence the stress level. There are many different stress reactions, and several characteristics of an individual impact on those reactions. These same characteristics also influence the level of stress produced by a stressor. A dynamic model (Exhibit 16–1) summarizes the relationships of these variables, and the chapter text explores them in more detail. Based on this model, you can identify three types of stress management actions (changing the stressor, treating the reaction, changing the person). Each of these actions can be initiated by either individuals, organizations, or society. Remember, effective stress management *is* feasible if you take a systematic approach to capitalize on the strengths of the various approaches.

GLOSSARY

Stress A physiological state of the individual which is influenced by stressors and which is indicated by several chemical levels which can be directly measured.

Stressor An environmental factor which influences an individual's stress level.

Stress Reactions Human responses to the stress level, including affective, psychological, physical, and behavioral reactions.

Personal Characteristics and Stress Characteristics of a person which influence reactions to stressors and experienced stress. These include psychological, physical, personality, need, and ability/skill factors.

Stress Management Action Strategies Three major action strategies for stress management include changing the stressor, treating the reaction, and changing the person.

Stress Management Action Initiators Three major action initiators can be involved in stress management, including the individual, the organization, and society.

STUDY QUESTIONS

1. Ask three friends or fellow students to give you their definition of stress. How similar are these definitions to one another? How similar are they to the definition used in this book?
2. What impact would you expect from the different definitions of stress obtained from your friends or fellow students when approaching stress management?
3. Discuss why it is important to treat stressors, stress, and stress reactions as distinct factors.
4. Discuss steps which could be taken by an individual to prevent a dysfunctional stress level from developing. What could an individual do to reduce an undesirable stress level once it occurs?
5. Consider the organization for which you work (or, if you have no job, consider some organization with which you are familiar). What arguments could you make for the development of a stress management program for that organization? What arguments could be made against the development of such a program?
6. Create a list of the major stressors in your life. Which of these could you change on your own? Which could be changed by others? Why haven't they been changed? Should they be changed?

7. Create a list of the major stress reactions which you currently are experiencing or recently have experienced. What steps could you take to change these stress reactions? What steps could be taken by others to change these reactions? Are all of these reactions negative?

NOTES

1. Most popular definitions of stress are discussed by **Cox, T.** (1978). *Stress*. Baltimore, MD: University Park Press.
2. This discussion is based heavily on the ideas of Selye, H. (1956). *The stress of life*. New York: McGraw-Hill, and the excellent overviews of **Ivancevich, J. M., & Matteson, M. T.** (1980). *Stress and work: A managerial perspective*. Glenview, IL: Scott, Foresman; and **Cox, T.** (1978). *Stress*. Baltimore MD: University Park Press.
3. **Cox, T.,** 1978, pp. 61–65; **Warburton, D. M.** (1979). Physiological aspects of information processing and stress. In V. Hamilton and D. M. Warburton (Eds.) *Human stress and cognition: An information processing approach*. Chichester, England: Wiley, 33–65.
4. Documentation and discussion of these stressors is provided by **Beehr, T. A., & Newman, J. E.** (1978). Job stress, employee health, and organizational effectiveness: A facet analysis, model, and literature review. *Personnel Psychology, 31*, 665–699.
5. See **Frankenhaeuser, M., Nordheden, B., Myrsten, A. L., & Post, B.** (1971). Psychophysiological reactions to understimulation and overstimulation. *Acta Psychological, 35*, 298.
6. **Ivancevich & Matteson,** 1980, provide a summary of representative research on these issues.
7. **Shaw, J. B., & Riskind, J. H.** (1983) Predicting job stress, using data from the position analysis questionnaire. *Journal of Applied Psychology, 68*, 253–261.
8. **McNeill, J., & Snavely, W.** (1983). *Job-related stressors: A scale analysis*. Paper presented at the Midwest Academy of Management Convention.
9. See **V. Hamilton & D. M. Warburton** (Eds.). (1979). *Human stress and cognition: An information processing approach*. Chichester, England: Wiley; **Brief, A. P., Schuler, R. S., & VanSell, M.** (1981). *Managing job stress*. Boston: Little, Brown; and **Ivancevich & Matteson,** 1980.
10. See **Balu, B.** (1978). Understanding mid-career stress. *Management Review, 67*, 57–62.
11. **Timio, M., & Gentili, S.** (1976). Adrenosympathetic overactivity under conditions of work stress. *British Journal of Preventative Social Medicine, 30*, 262–265.

12. **French, J. R. P., Jr., & Caplan, R. D.** (1973). Organizational stress and individual strain. In A. J. Marrow (Ed.), *The failure of success.* New York: AMACOM, 30–66.

13. **Beehr & Newman,** 1978.

14. Representative evidence is summarized by **Beehr & Newman,** 1978.

15. **Beehr, T. A.** (1976). Perceived situational moderators of the relationship between subjective role ambiguity and role strain. *Journal of Applied Psychology, 61,* 35–40; **Coburn, D.** (1975). Job-worker incongruence: Consequences for health. *Journal of Health and Social Behavior, 16,* 198–212; **House, R. J., & Rizzo, J. R.** Role conflict and ambiguity as critical variables in the model of organizational behavior. *Organizational Behavior and Human Performance, 7,* 467–505; **Lyons, T. F.** (1971). Role clarity, need for clarity, satisfaction, tension, and withdrawal. *Organizational Behavior and Human Performance, 6,* 99–110.

16. See **Beehr & Newman,** 1978, for illustrations.

17. See **French & Caplan,** 1973; **Ivancevich & Matteson,** 1980; and **Beehr & Newman,** 1978.

18. **Bammer, K., & Newberry, B. H.** (Eds.). (1982). *Stress and cancer.* Toronto: C. J. Hogrefe.

19. See **Friedman, M., & Rosenman, R.** (1974). *Type A behavior and your heart.* New York: Alfred A. Knopf; **Matteson, M. T., & Ivancevich, J. M.** (1979). Organizational stressors and heart disease: A research model. *Academy of Management Review, 4,* 347–357.

20. **Ikard, F. F., & Tomkins, S.** (1973). The experience of affect as a determinant of smoking behavior. *Journal of Abnormal Psychology, 81,* 172–181; **French & Caplan,** 1973; **Margolis, B. K., Kroes, W. H., & Quinn, R. P.** (1974). Job stress: An unlisted occupational hazard. *Journal of Occupational Medicine, 16,* 659–661.

21. **Beehr & Newman,** 1978.

22. **Korman, A. K.** (1974). *The psychology of motivation.* Englewood Cliffs, NJ: Prentice-Hall.

23. Originally proposed by **Yerkes, R. M., & Dodson, J. D.** (1908). The relation of strength of stimulus to rapidity of habit formation. *Journal of Comparative and Neurological Psychology, 18,* 459–482. Somewhat more recent research on this issue has been conducted by **Broadhurst, P. L.** (1959). The interaction of task difficulty and motivation: The Yerkes-Dodson law revived. *Acta Psychologica, 16,* 321–338. A contemporary examination of the phenomenon with somewhat of an alternative conceptualization is provided by **McGrath, J. E.** (1976). Stress and behavior in organizations. In M. D. Dunnette (Ed.), *Handbook of industrial and organizational psychology.* Chicago: Rand McNally, 1351–1395.

24. **Meglino, B. M.** (1977, Autumn). The stress-performance controversy. *MSU Business Topics,* 53–59.

25. **Janis, I.** (1974). Vigilance and decision making in personal crises. In

D. A. Hamburg, C. V. Coelho, & J. E. Adams (Eds.), *Coping and adaptation*. New York: Basic Books.

26. **Folkman, S., Schaefer, C., & Lazarus, R. S.** (1979). Cognitive processes as mediators of stress and coping. In V. Hamilton & D. M. Warburton (Eds.), *Human stress and cognition: An information processing approach*. Chichester, England: Wiley.
27. **Ivancevich & Matteson,** 1980, p. 175–176.
28. **Kahn, R. L., Wolfe, D. M., Quinn, R. R., Snoek, J. D., & Rosenthal, R. A.** (1964). *Organizational stress: Studies in role conflict and ambiguity*. New York: Wiley.
29. Ibid., 1964.
30. **Pitman, N. L., & Pittman, T. S.** (1979). Effects of amount of helplessness training and internal–external locus of control on mood and performance. *Journal of Personality and Social Psychology, 37,* 39–47.
31. **Lyons, T.** (1971). Role clarity, need for clarity, satisfaction, tension, and withdrawal. *Organizational Behavior and Human Performance, 6,* 99–110.
32. **Rosenman, R., Brand, R., Jenkins, C., Friedman, M., Straus, R., & Wurm, M.** (1975). Coronary heart disease in the western collaborative group study: Final follow-up experience of 8½ years. *Journal of the American Medical Association, 233,* 872–877.
33. A particularly useful reference for this section was **Newman, J. E., & Beehr, T. A.** (1979). Personal and organizational strategies for handling job stress: A review of research and opinion. *Personnel Psychology, 32,* 1–43.

Part

17 ■ The Management of Change

■ Epilogue: Ethics

The Management of Change and Ethics

Part VII contains just one chapter. It is, however, probably the most important chapter in this book. No matter how good the ideas you derive from Chapters 1 through 16, none of them will realize their potential unless they are effectively implemented. There is no question but that good ideas often fail. The purpose of Chapter 17 is to help you make good ideas work well through the effective management of the change process.

Chapter 17 begins by identifying the major forces to change which cause organizations to be as dynamic as they are. It is noted that the manager is placed in the center of these forces, having to respond to a wide range of changes.

A major reason why the implementation of change is often ineffective relates to the resistance to change on the part of persons involved in the change. This chapter systematically identifies the major reasons for the resistance to change. It may surprise you to find that virtually all of these reasons are quite logical and grounded in rational reactions. This is contrary to the common belief that when people resist change they always do so because they are just inflexible people (as will be noted, in comparison to others, inflexibility is actually a relatively minor cause of resistance).

After identifying reasons why people resist change, Chapter 17 examines a variety of useful techniques for preventing resistance from occurring and/or reducing resistance once it occurs. The focus here is on the creation of support for change. By providing a step-by-step overview of the change process, guidance is developed for the choice of a general change strategy and the selection of specific techniques for avoiding resistance and creating support.

In concluding, Chapter 17 provides a flowchart to guide you in coordinating the change process. Following this flowchart can enhance your effectiveness as a manager of change. Today, more than ever, "the good manager manages change."

The Epilogue focuses on the issue of ethics, which is relevant throughout this book. This Epilogue is not intended to teach you how to be ethical. It is intended, however, to alert you to many of the ethical considerations you will have to make on a regular basis. Several key factors which contribute to the making of ethical or unethical decisions are also identified. Finally, some basic actions an organization can take to encourage ethical behavior are briefly explored.

---

17 The Management of Change

OVERVIEW
FORCES TO CHANGE
Why Change?
Technological Forces
Human Needs and Values
The Social Environment
The Business and Economic Environment
The Organization
RESISTANCE TO CHANGE
Fear of Loss of Something of Value
Misunderstanding and Lack of Trust
Disagreement on Advisability of Change
Low Personal Tolerance for Change
DEALING WITH RESISTANCE TO CHANGE
Education and Communication
Participation and Involvement
Support
Incentives
Manipulation and Co-optation
Coercion
SELECTING A CHANGE STRATEGY
The Change Process
Selecting a General Change Strategy
COORDINATING THE CHANGE PROCESS
Identifying the Focus of the Change
Planning the Implementation Strategy
Implementation
Evaluation
SUMMARY

All is flux, nothing stays still . . . Nothing endures but change.

Heraclitus

OVERVIEW

The day of the static or slowly changing organization appears to be gone forever. Today's organization survives because of its ability to cope with change, develops through the evolutionary process created by change, and excels because of its adoption of new and better ideas. In short, the effectiveness of organizations is, in large part, a function of change.

For change to benefit an organization, it obviously must involve the introduction of good ideas. Yet, change created by a good idea can produce dysfunctional results for an organization if the introduction of the change is managed poorly. Similarly, the positive effects of a well-designed change can be enhanced by effective management of the change process.

Although the decision to implement a change in an organization often is made at the highest executive levels, by independent committee, or even by an external group (a governmental body, for example), it is usually the manager who assumes responsibility for implementing the change. Today, more than ever, an effective manager must learn to manage change. The primary objective of this chapter, therefore, is to prepare you to be an effective manager of change in your organization, regardless of the types of changes you are to manage. The same basic principles apply when introducing a new accounting system or a new piece of technology as when introducing a new leadership program or a behavior modification plan. Because this is true, give your utmost attention to this topic. Even if you discard other lessons from this book and your OB course, use the ideas in this chapter on how to make a good change work well.

This chapter explores the management of change by:

1. Identifying the major categories of "forces to change."
2. Exploring reasons why people resist change.
3. Examining techniques for dealing with resistance to change.
4. Giving an overview of the complete change process.
5. Providing a guide for selecting change strategies.

FORCES TO CHANGE

There are at least five major categories of factors motivating change in organizations (see Exhibit 17–1). Although the pressures provided by these **forces to change** do not always move the organization in the same direction, together they make some sort of organizational change inevitable. As can be seen in Exhibit 17–1, when

Exhibit 17–1 Forces to Change

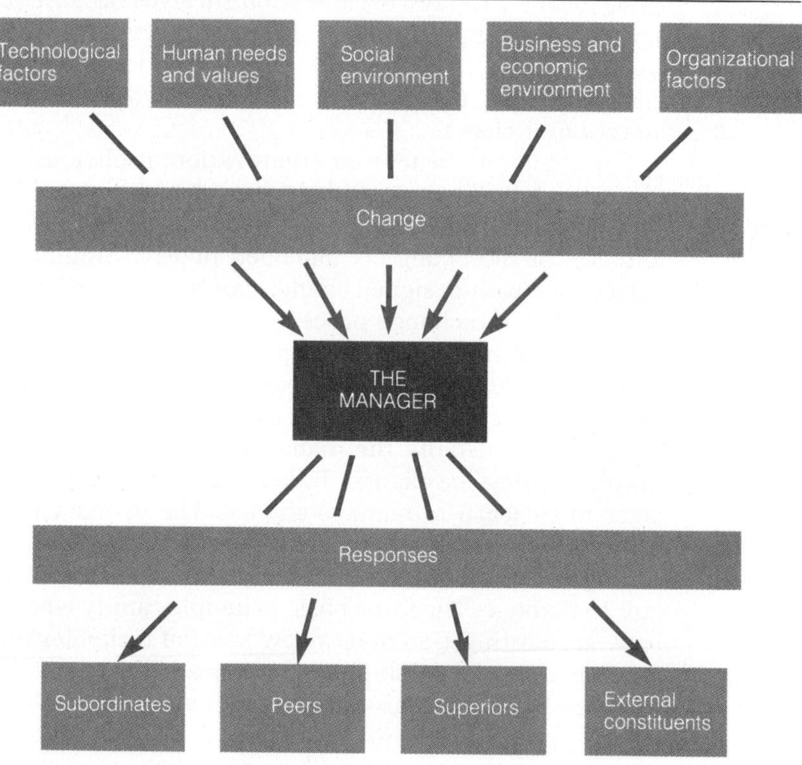

change does occur, the manager tends to be on the "hot spot." As a manager, you must respond to change with a wide range of "constituents" both within (e.g., subordinates, peers, superiors) and outside (e.g., customers, clients, contractors) the organization. At the same time, you must deal with your personal reactions to change.

Why Change?

Proactive change occurs when one of the forces to change leads an organization to conclude that a particular change would be desirable. **Reactive change** occurs when one of the forces to change makes it necessary for a change to be implemented. One example of proactive change is the acquisition of a new and better machine, even though existing machines are still functioning. Acquisition of the new machine would be a reactive change, however, if it were acquired because existing machines no longer worked. Another example of proactive change is the introduction of a new employee benefit plan because an organization believes it will enhance satisfaction and motivation. This same change would be reactive, however, if the new benefit plan was introduced because of employee demands.

Exhibit 17–2 Rate of Technological Change

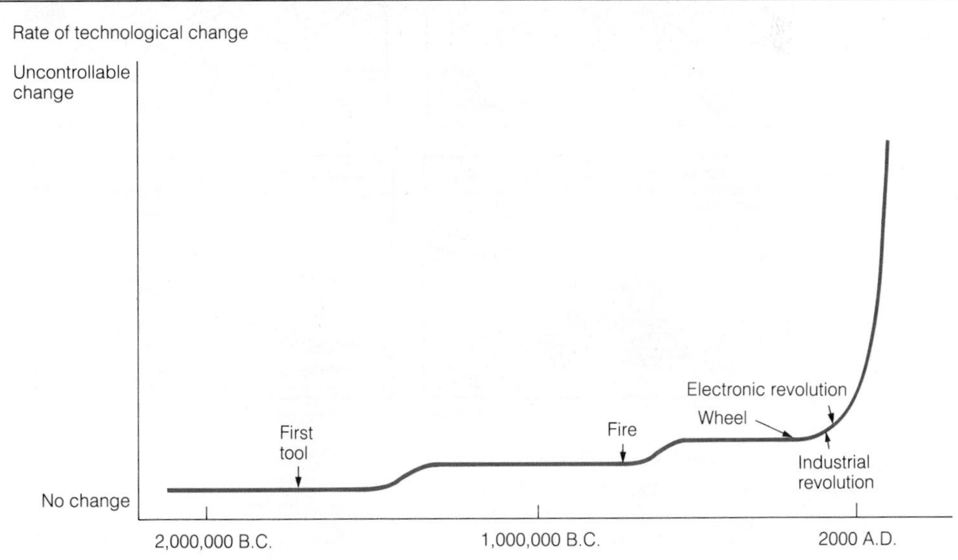

HÄGAR The Horrible
by DIK BROWNE
LOOK! UTZ HAS ONE OF THOSE NEW DOOR KNOCKERS
ISN'T IT KIND OF BIG FOR HIS DOOR?
IT'S FOR OTHER PEOPLE'S DOORS
ANOTHER LEAP FORWARD!
THE WORLD IS CHANGING SO FAST I CAN'T KEEP UP WITH IT!
I KNOW! I KNOW!
JUST THINK OF WHAT WE'VE SEEN IN THE LAST TEN YEARS... THE INVENTION OF THE CROSSBOW... THE TWO-HANDED SWORD...
THE MODERN CATAPULT, THE RACK, THE DUNGEON, THE BATTERING RAM...
NOT TO MENTION THE DISCOVERY OF WITCHCRAFT, ALCHEMY, AND THE TWO-HEADED AXE!
I KNOW
DIK BROWNE 4-3
AND YET... I WONDER... ARE PEOPLE ANY HAPPIER?

Technological Forces

Technological forces to change are extremely visible and often unpredictable. The rate of technological change is accelerating (see Exhibit 17–2), however, and you must learn to plan for it.

Consider some of the technological changes of the relatively recent past. Changes in transportation alternatives have made routine long-distance travel feasible (but the coordination of organizational members more difficult). Sophisticated communication capabilities have increased "telemarketing" (but decreased personal contact between a sales force and its customer). The photocopy machine, which you probably can't remember living without, was not readily available to college students until the 1960s.

Today, computer-based advances enable organizations to handle volumes of data which would have been physically impossible just 10 years ago. As a manager, many of your decisions will be computer-aided, or perhaps even made by computer. In the late 1970s, debates raged at many college campuses over the in-class use of calculators, which were thought to prevent a student from learning necessary quantitative skills. Today, many universities are beginning to *require* students to own a personal *computer* for class assignments.

The future undoubtedly holds even more rapid technological change than has been witnessed in recent years. Technological advances put tremendous pressure on organizations to change. As a manager, you will see robotics taking over some jobs currently performed by humans and employees working in their homes using electronic connections to the "office." Technology will provide much of the structure needed for performing the job and, at the same time, physically separate managers and subordinates. A manager's job will be very different than it is today.

Human Needs and Values

Human needs and values of organizational members change over time (see Chapter 5), causing both proactive and reactive changes in organizations. A proactive change occurs, for example, when an organization redesigns jobs voluntarily to give employees greater responsibility. A reactive change occurs when employees demand a new work schedule to meet their needs for leisure time.

At the beginning of the 20th century, basic needs such as survival and security appeared to be dominant in the American work force.[1] As a result, employees focused on organizational changes which would satisfy those needs. Changes made in organizations at that time included new safety standards, job security clauses in union contracts, shorter work days, and expanded employee pension plans.*

In the 1920s, social needs gained importance in the work force, and sweeping organizational changes were introduced to address these needs. Human relations programs were created; social opportunities were built into jobs; leaders were told to become people-oriented as well as task-oriented.

Today, ego needs are added to the list of human values driving change in organizations. Employees want to be challenged (given greater responsibility and career development opportunities). In response, organizations are redesigning jobs, introducing new training programs, decentralizing decision making, and developing new recognition programs for employees.

Social and ego needs will continue to drive organizational change in the future. In addition, self-actualization needs are likely to expand in importance. Workers will gain more control over their jobs and greater freedom from organizational interference with personal activities. Employees will want and receive more organizational rewards focusing on recognition and achievement.

The Social Environment

The social environment outside an organization frequently leads to change. A company may make a proactive change, such as altering a product line or advertising strategy to match changing social interests (e.g., caffeine-free soft drinks). Reactive changes occur due to legislation (e.g., new safety programs because of OSHA regulations, or new work and pay schedules because of Labor Department regulations), and general social protests or demands (e.g., environmental cleanliness standards, crashworthiness standards for automobiles).†

Even more dramatic social pressure in the next decade will encourage or even force organizations to provide a meaningful work experience for employees. Workers will participate in decision making; comparable pay may be required for comparable work. (Should this social pressure produce results, virtually every compensation system in every U.S. organization will need substantial revision.) A growing demand for permanent part-time jobs could lead to mandatory job-sharing programs. Should organizations accept responsibility for the results of stress induced by jobs? These issues and

---

*It is interesting to note that this pattern of changes in human needs and values corresponds very closely to that proposed by Maslow (see Chapter 5).

†Although many organizations have made changes such as these because of genuine concern for the issues involved, social pressure has led to greater, more rapid changes.

others stemming from the social environment will encourage or demand a wide range of organizational changes.

The Business and Economic Environment

Much of the pressure to change experienced by an organization comes from the general business and economic environment (or from other individual organizations). A significant difference in a competitor's marketing strategy, or revisions by suppliers in pricing and shipping, encourage change. The steel industry, for example, discovered changes were necessary when the auto industry increased its use of plastics (and decreased steel consumption).

> The 1980s recession introduced changes directly contrary to existing business practices. Many organizations *reduced* production levels, decreased compensation, laid off long-tenured employees, and encouraged early retirement. New finance and marketing strategies were adopted. Now that the economy is beginning to show signs of recovery, organizations are developing plans for growth, but without the "fat" often found in the past. "Productivity program" is a major buzzword of the mid-1980s, as organizations implement programs aimed at improving production efficiency.

A dynamic, diverse business environment requires an organizational structure which is highly differentiated yet highly integrated.[2] Less differentiation, on the other hand, is desirable as the business environment becomes more stable. Thus, organizations must change their very structure to remain effective. Uncertainty about the business environment leads to changes such as significant increases in marketing research.[3] These and other events in the business and economic environment produce frequent, often unpredictable pressure to change within organizations.

The Organization

Whereas many changes are influenced by one or more of the other forces to change, the organization itself appears to be the primary source of the change to the manager. At least, this is how you'll feel when you find a notice on your desk announcing that a new accounting system is to be implemented "to better meet the needs of the organization." Implementation of a management by objectives program, a leadership training program, or a conflict resolution program, for example, are decisions not necessarily driven by any of the other forces to change. Organizational activities such as those discussed in this book as well as those resulting from organizational strategy decisions to diversify, divest, or expand, drive a wide range of changes in the organization.

RESISTANCE TO CHANGE*

One of the major factors which determines how well a good idea will work is the degree to which employees support or resist it. Since member support for a change can range anywhere from very active resistance through passive resistance, to very active support, you need to encourage organizational members to position themselves toward the right side of the continuum shown in Exhibit 17–3.

Exhibit 17–3 Degree of Support/Resistance to Change

Very active resistance	Passive resistance	Very active support

Resistance to change does not always produce negative effects. Although it can lead to stagnation and reduced effectiveness, reasonable amounts of resistance to change can help stabilize the organization enough to allow effective management. Resistance also encourages advocates of change to examine carefully the merits of their proposed changes and to evaluate probable effects of change on organizational members prior to implementation.

People resist change for four primary reasons: *fear of loss of something of value, misunderstanding and lack of trust, disagreement on the advisability of change,* and *low personal tolerance for change* (see Exhibit 17–4). Furthermore, two or more of these factors may combine to compound the amount of resistance which occurs.

You can use your knowledge of these four categories in two ways. First, if you anticipate possible sources and reasons for resistance when planning a change, you may *prevent* active (and sometimes passive) resistance and move potential resisters toward the direction of support. Secondly, if you are aware of common sources of resistance, you will recognize signs of resistance as they occur so that you can deal with emerging resistance quickly. Unfortunately,

---

* Credit is due to John P. Kotter and Leonard A. Schlesinger of Harvard University for many of the ideas contained in much of the remainder of this chapter. The author must take responsibility, however, for any distortions of their thoughts, since a considerable number of modifications, additions, and expansions have been made. An excellent brief presentation of Kotter and Schlesinger's ideas is contained in their article, Choosing strategies for change (March–April 1979). *Harvard Business Review,* 106–113.

Exhibit 17–4 Common Sources of Resistance to Change

- Fear of loss of something of value
- Misunderstanding of change and lack of trust
- Disagreement on advisability of change
- Low personal tolerance for change

few managers take full advantage of either of these approaches, because they are so busy planning and implementing the change. In short, they spend a great deal of time making the idea better and too little time making the better idea work.

Fear of Loss of Something of Value

If you believe that the introduction of a change will cause you to lose something of value, you probably will resist the change. The greater the expected loss, the greater the resistance. Because this resistance is based on an employee's *perceptions* of what will happen (see Chapter 10), resistance is likely whether or not those beliefs are accurate. Common fears include the loss of: status, promotional opportunities, control over the work, the job itself, compensation, social opportunities, and the status quo.

Misunderstanding and Lack of Trust

Misunderstanding and lack of trust are often the cause of resistance to change. Sometimes an employee feels that a change was designed to take advantage of him/her. Even when a state of trust exists, a worker may be concerned about the unknown details and implications of the change and, thus, resist. Under conditions of mistrust, employees may fear that if they let an acceptable change go through, it will set a precedent for unacceptable changes to follow. This source of resistance is somewhat unique in that the reasons for resistance often have very little to do with the specific change in question.

Similar problems can emerge whenever employees do not understand fully the details of a change and/or when management is not trusted. Resistance of this type frequently combines with one or more other categories of resistance to produce particularly powerful effects.

A large marketing organization recently developed an organizational change designed to streamline administration and provide sales personnel with greater sales and earnings potential.* The planned change involved the creation of multi-salesperson "sales centers" to replace single salesperson offices. Each sales center was to be composed of three Account Executives (a title which would replace the previous title of Regional Manager). Each center was to be assigned a market share with five times the potential sales allocated to single salesperson offices. Commission schedules were not changed so the potential for increasing earnings was substantial.

The organization proudly announced the plan at a national meeting of salespersons. Although a very positive reaction was expected, the change was met with intense active resistance.

The major reasons for resistance focused on three areas in which the salespersons believed they would lose something of value. First, the title of regional manager was perceived to carry much more status than the title of account executive. Secondly, excellent sales previously could be attributed directly to the one salesperson in that office. Under the new plan, it was believed that it would be difficult to separate the relative effectiveness of the three salespersons, and they feared the loss of recognition. Finally, it was believed that the three Account Executives would be placed in direct competition with one another. They feared this direct competition would damage the positive social relationships which had developed between many of them, threaten the earnings of one center member to benefit another, and weaken the company's market share in comparison to other organizations.

Company executives were caught completely off guard by the intense resistance and said that the salespeople were acting like "spoiled babies." The salespeople responded that the company didn't care about the employees, or they would not have proposed such a plan. The dialogue went downhill from there. The plan was hastily withdrawn, and the national sales meeting ended without even finalizing an annual sales plan (which was the primary purpose for the meeting).

*This example is based on an actual incident which occurred in 1982. Some of the facts have been changed to protect the organization's identity.

Disagreement on Advisability of Change

Resistance to change may occur when two parties disagree on the advisability of change, usually because an individual or group believes the change would not be in the best interests of the organization.

Disagreement on the advisability of change can occur in two distinct ways, and different strategies are necessary for each. The first disagreement concerns a genuine difference of opinion between two persons or groups using the same information to assess the merits of

In early 1982, a small (100-person) manufacturing organization hired a consultant to design a performance appraisal system for use with all nonsupervisory employees.* Prior to beginning the development project, a high-level executive mentioned that "a lot of our problems are going to be solved as soon as we get our new performance appraisal system in place and supervisors become tough on poor performers."

The company's grapevine passed the word, and by the time the consultant arrived to begin the project, a fair amount of resistance to the idea had developed among supervisors. Research revealed that supervisors feared they would have to give up friendly relationships with subordinates; performance feedback from supervisors to subordinates would have to focus on negative factors; and supervisors would be used to "get rid of" employees who were not liked by management.

Fortunately, the level of resistance had not advanced to crisis stage. Furthermore, appropriate steps were taken as soon as the project began to avoid the development of further resistance. The result was that sensitivity to resistance helped identify a problem before it became critical. An effective performance appraisal plan was developed and successfully implemented.

*This example is also based on an actual incident which has been altered to conceal the identity of the company involved.

the change. The second type of disagreement occurs when the two parties use different sets of information. In the first situation, the same facts are interpreted differently by the two. The second situation is more common and often occurs when the two parties are at different levels and/or functional areas of the organization. For example, the director of marketing and the director of quality assurance may differ on the advisability of introducing a new product: one person is making an assessment based primarily on production and quality control issues while the other person's focus is on whether or not consumers would purchase the new product.

Kotter and Schlesinger made the following additional comments about this source of resistance to change:

> Managers who initiate change often assume both that they have all the relevant information required to conduct an adequate organization analysis and that those who will be affected by the change have the same facts, when neither assumption is correct.
>
> Moreover, if the analysis made by those not initiating the change is more accurate than that derived by the initiators, resistance is obviously "good" for the organization.[4]

Low Personal Tolerance for Change

People frequently resist change because of low personal tolerance for change. Indeed, a resister may agree that a change would be good for the organization, yet still resist. Although this appears irrational, there are several perfectly reasonable causes for such resistance.

Perhaps the most common cause is a fear by an employee that s/he will not be able to develop new skills required after the change is made. If you know how to operate an old machine effectively, you may resist its replacement, even though a new machine would be faster, cleaner, and more reliable. You may be guaranteed a continuing job; you may agree that replacement of the machine is a smart move. Even so, you still fear that it is too sophisticated to operate and that you will not be able to master the new operational techniques. This type of fear may be based on any type of skill, not just physical skills. A very common concern, for example, is the need for maintaining interpersonal relationships subsequent to a change.

Attitudes can be difficult to change once they have been learned (see Chapter 3). This stability of attitudes can also be a personal source of resistance to a change. A number of marketing directors, for example, are resisting the use of "telemarketing." The technique can be cost effective and beneficial to customer relations, but the attitude that sales should be made in person leads to resistance to the change. This type of resistance is probably a major reason why so many male managers resist the promotion of women into managerial positions.

Sometimes a person resists a change in an attempt to "save face." This is particularly true if the resister developed or supported the policy or practice being changed. To accept the change implies an admission that the policy or practice was faulty.

Group pressure can encourage you to resist a change, even if you personally favor it (see Chapter 12). In an actual situation, a set of proposed job changes was presented to a group of 15 workers during a unit meeting. After one influential member of the group expressed some negative feelings about the changes, the group voted not to make them. Shortly thereafter, an anonymous survey was given to each group member. *Eleven* workers stated on the survey that they personally would have liked to make the changes!

Personality characteristics influence the likelihood of resistance (see Chapter 9). Dogmatic (closed-minded) individuals tend to reject a new idea unless it is consistent with their personal view of the world. Persons with an internal locus of control resist a change unless they have participated in the decision to make the change. Authoritarian people support a change if it comes from a recognized source of power; otherwise it will be resisted strongly. Every individual has a certain need for *homeostasis*, both in mind and body. The need for regulation that exists for the body (relatively constant levels of oxygen, blood sugar, etc.), holds true for behavioral factors as well. Those persons with an extremely strong homeostasis need tend to resist any change to the status quo.

John P. Kotter and **Leonard A. Schlesinger** of Harvard University have written extensively on the management of change in organizations.

What are some of the most common reasons why good ideas work poorly? KOTTER: Most ideas inside organizations, in order to work, require the cooperation or at least the compliance of any number of other people. All too often, good ideas crash because the people who are trying to implement those ideas simply are not sensitive enough to their dependence on those other key actors. Because of this, they don't take the actions needed to properly manage that dependence.

How often do managers actually manage change as systematically as you suggest in your writings? SCHLESINGER: It is important not to confuse my call for a systematic approach to change management with a mechanical approach to change. To be systematic implies a thorough diagnosis of the situation, of the stakeholders in the change effort, and consideration of the magnitude of the change effort in the development of a change strategy. It does not imply a fixed, formula approach resistant to environmental feedback.

How do you respond to the manager who says, "If an idea is good enough it will work"? SCHLESINGER: The manager attempting to introduce change under such conditions is often dumbfounded by the resistance and ill prepared to respond to it. One must recognize that one's ability to successfully introduce change is a function not only of the quality of the change idea but also of the existing levels of dissatisfaction and the process of implementation. These three elements act as the three legs of a stool: without all of them the stool will fall.

Most managers, as a matter of style, use just one or two of the techniques you have identified for dealing with resistance to change. How much more effective could a manager be by matching the technique to the situation? KOTTER: I think that a lot of managers could be much more effective by expanding their repertoire of techniques and by more carefully matching the technique to the situation. The reality is that one of the reasons that some people—very capable people—are only mediocre managers is because of this limited repertoire in an environment which has more variety and demands more variety in responses.

DEALING WITH RESISTANCE TO CHANGE

Most people develop a personal style for dealing with resistance. This style usually involves a preference for *when* to deal with resistance (either before or after it emerges), and *how* to deal with resistance (which technique to use). A truly effective manager assesses the situation and selects the appropriate time and technique(s) to match the situation. Six of the most common of these techniques are: *education and communication, participation and involvement, support, incentives, manipulation and co-optation,* and *coercion* (see Exhibit 17–5).

Education and Communication

It is usually preferable to use education and communication prior to the emergence of resistance (typically, before a change is implemented). However, it can be used even after resistance has occurred. This technique includes an explanation of: *what* the change is; *when* it is to be introduced; *how* it will be implemented; *why* the change is needed; the *logic* which supports the change; and the *objectives* of the change.

Education and communication can diminish fear of loss by explaining why loss need not occur. Misunderstanding can be resolved by explaining exactly what is to happen. Some resistance due to personal intolerance for change can be resolved by helping the potential resister to deal with personal concerns. This technique is probably most effective, however, for dealing with disagreement on the advisability of change.

There are certain drawbacks to this approach. It may require a significant amount of time, effort, and money. It is even possible that, once organizational members fully understand a change, they will genuinely dislike it. Finally, education and communication usually work only when a reasonable state of trust exists. Otherwise, the method may appear to be a manipulative device.

Exhibit 17–5 Techniques for Dealing with Resistance to Change

- Education and communication
- Participation and involvement
- Support
- Incentives
- Manipulation and co-optation
- Coercion

Participation and Involvement

Participation and involvement are so popular that many managers behave as though they were the only technique necessary. Participation and involvement can be used at the planning stage of a change and/or at the time of implementation. All potential resisters or their representatives can be involved at one of these stages.

Potential payoffs from participation and involvement are very high. It is possible that the design of the change can be improved, and the effectiveness of the implementation plan enhanced. Furthermore, the likelihood of employee acceptance of the change and commitment to it increases. What will you do, on the other hand, if your employees develop a poor design? If you agree to it, you will implement a change you feel is inadequate. If you reject the idea, you risk creating resentment. When using this approach, therefore, it is best to define carefully the ground rules before participation begins.

This approach works best when the initiator of change does not have all the information needed to design and/or implement a change. It is also very useful when a high level of commitment is needed. Even when this technique works, however, it requires a fairly large investment of time and energy.

Support

Two types of support deal with resistance to change: facilitative and emotional. *Facilitative support* is assistance offered by the organization (appropriate tools, material, advice, training) to help make the change work effectively. Other facilitative support could involve the removal of organizational barriers which might hamper the change (an incompatible accounting system, an inadequate supply system), or the implementation of organizational policies to facilitate the change.

Emotional support directly addresses personal (as opposed to technical) concerns about the change. Frequently, this is provided by an understanding supervisor or co-worker. Sometimes, however, it may be necessary to use a professional counselor to deal with intense concerns.

This approach can be particularly useful when a worker fears, for example, that new skills may not be acquired quickly enough (by providing a training program). Similarly, you can assist employees experiencing anxiety induced by the change through compassionate listening and helping them work out their concerns. Realistically, though, both types of support can be expensive and time-consuming without any guarantee of success. This is especially true when emotional support deals with particularly strong feelings.

Incentives

Incentives can be used either before or after resistance emerges, but usually are more effective in preventing resistance. Incentives can be offered to encourage acceptance of the change itself or to encourage participation in the implementation of the change. The most effective incentives are long term and continuing, so that the employee sees it is in his/her best interest to support the change initially and over time.

There is a distinction between incentives which are a part of the change and those which exist independent of the change. If a change, for example, creates a more challenging job, greater promotional opportunities, or enhanced earning potential for you, and you positively value these outcomes, these incentives are part of the change. Factors such as a pay raise promised if you support the change, or time off for you to recover from stress induced by the change, are incentives independent of the change itself. "Built-in" incentives tend to be more effective.

Fear of loss of a valued outcome can be relieved by compensatory incentives (simple attempts to recover lost ground). While compensatory incentives may reduce the frequency of active resistance, only incremental incentives (those which add to the total set of positive outcomes) are likely to produce active support.

Incentives can be quite effective; they are also usually quite expensive and risky. If you provide incentives primarily for those who resist change, you actually may be encouraging others to show signs of resistance in the future (see the discussion of "rewarding A while hoping for B" in Chapter 6, p. 147).

Manipulation and Co-optation

Of all of the techniques for dealing with resistance, manipulation and co-optation are the only ones which are by nature deceitful and often unethical. In effect, these are ways to trick someone into accepting a change. Manipulation is the control or distortion of information so that a person receives only information encouraging acceptance of the change. The manager who tells subordinates that other companies using robotics increased productivity and raised employee pay is using manipulation if s/he is withholding information which shows that layoffs also followed introduction of robotics. Obviously, the use of false information to encourage support of a change is also manipulation.

Co-optation is a special and frequently used form of manipulation. On the surface, it resembles participation, because it gives someone a desirable, but figurehead, role in the design and/or implementation of a change. It also is possible to co-opt an entire group by providing a figurehead position for one member of the group. The primary difference between true participation and co-optation is that the person co-opting you is interested in your compliance, but not in your ideas.

Co-optation in China

At 78, strongman Deng Xiaoping does not have forever to shape China's future. Last week, he arranged for some help. The National People's Congress elected Li Xianian, also 78, to be China's president—the first chief of state since Mao purged Liu Shao-chi in the 1960s. One of the party's old guard, Li has been lukewarm toward Deng's economic reforms; his election to the *largely ceremonial* presidency placated conservatives—but neatly limited his chances to make trouble for Deng and Deng's chosen heirs.[5] [Emphasis added.]

At times, manipulation and co-optation are easy and inexpensive ways to gain support for a change. There are, of course, numerous drawbacks to this technique. In providing a person with a figurehead position, you also create the possibility that the position will be used to influence others who perceive that position as real. You may lose the ability to use other, more honest techniques for dealing with resistance. Furthermore, if organizational members see through a blatant attempt at manipulation or co-optation, they probably will increase their resistance. Unfortunately, since people react to what they perceive is real (see Chapter 10), honest attempts to provide information or to invite participation may also be perceived as manipulation or co-optation!

Coercion

The most forceful technique for dealing with resistance is coercion, or the use of power to force a person to go along with a change (see Chapter 13). Coercion can be either implicit or explicit. Thus, both implied and verbalized threats can be effective. Common threats involve potential loss of job, promotion, pay, or recognition.

For coercion to work, the potential resister must perceive that attempts to resist would lead to punishment. Learning theories (Chapter 6) and expectancy theory (Chapter 8) demonstrate that, if this perception is formed, active resistance is less likely. On the other hand, there may be unpredictable side effects. The change in question may not be resisted, but dysfunctional behavior may result in other areas.

The use of coercion can be expected to decrease satisfaction, increase resentment, and reduce the effectiveness of other techniques for dealing with change. However, in situations where change must occur quickly and other techniques would not be effective in such a short time period, a manager may have to choose between using coercion and seeing a change fail.

SELECTING A CHANGE STRATEGY

The Change Process

According to psychologist Kurt Lewin, the status quo is maintained when a balance exists between two sets of forces acting upon an individual, group, or organization.[6] *Restraining forces* act to prevent change; *driving forces* attempt to produce change. Because the overall strength of the two types of forces can vary, change occurs from time to time as the equilibrium is upset. To manage change effectively, you need to manage these two sets of forces. Lewin's widely known, three-phase model of **the change process** (see Exhibit 17–6) may help you develop this ability.

Unfreezing. The controlled upsetting of equilibrium between the two sets of forces is called unfreezing. If you want to place a cherry in an ice cube, you first should melt it. Your attempts to force a cherry into a frozen ice cube will lead to lots of resistance (and a real mess!). The same is true when introducing change in an organization. Unfreezing is an important first step: a phase at which a felt need for change should be created and steps taken to minimize resistance. Unfreezing can be accomplished by increasing the forces to change, by decreasing restraining forces, or through a combination of the two.[7] The best approach is usually to decrease restraining forces while increasing forces to change.

Changing. Once the situation has been unfrozen, you should work on changing the people, tasks, structures, etc., which are the focus of

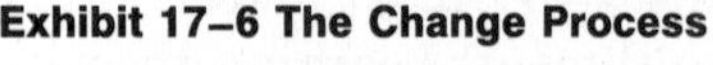

Exhibit 17–6 The Change Process

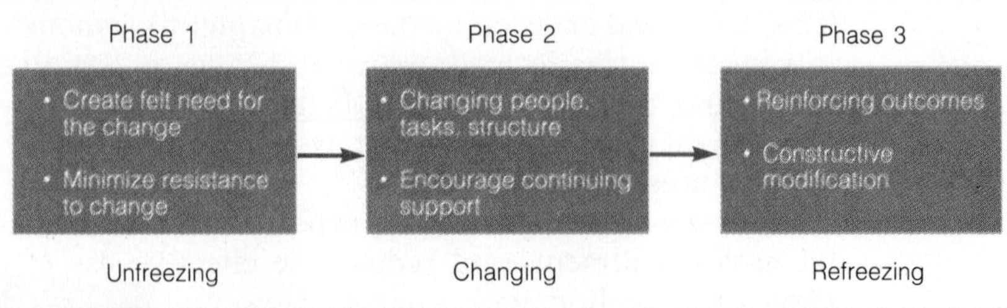

your plan. At this stage, you must continue to encourage support for the change and provide the necessary support to make it work. Implementation of the change should not be attempted until unfreezing has occurred.

Refreezing. Once a change is made, the forces which encouraged it initially will maintain it temporarily. Permanent stabilizing of the situation, or refreezing, requires your continued management of the change process well beyond the immediate time and place of implementation. You have implemented a desired change, produced a temporary state of balance, and you now desire to solidify the situation (put the unfrozen ice cube containing the cherry into the freezer). This critical last step is particularly important for persons affected by the change; they must experience positive consequences to strengthen their continuing commitment to the change. At this time, you also may consider constructive modification of the change. It might produce a "better change" and can enhance commitment by responding to concerns of workers affected by the change.

Selecting a General Change Strategy

Kotter and Schlesinger provided the guide shown in Exhibit 17–7 to aid in the selection of a general strategy for a change. According to this guide, the general change strategies available to a manager range from very fast to very slow implementation. Effective fast implementation usually is associated with a clear plan, little involvement of others in the change process, and an overpowering of any resistance which occurs. Effective slow implementation uses a plan which evolves during the change process, involves others considerably, and attempts to minimize resistance before it occurs.

As the amount of anticipated resistance to change increases, the change strategy should be shifted toward the right side of the continuum. As the amount of power possessed by the initiator of change relative to potential resisters increases, the change strategy *can* (but does not have to) be moved toward the left of the continuum. If the initiator of change possesses all of the information and knowledge needed to implement the change, the change strategy *can* move toward the left. When information or knowledge is needed from others, however, the strategy *must* move toward the right. Finally, when short-term risks to the organization are great if change is not made, the strategy must move toward the left.

After you have chosen a general change strategy, you must decide on specific techniques for minimizing or overcoming resistance. A review of the six major techniques for dealing with resistance to

Exhibit 17–7 Selecting a General Change Strategy

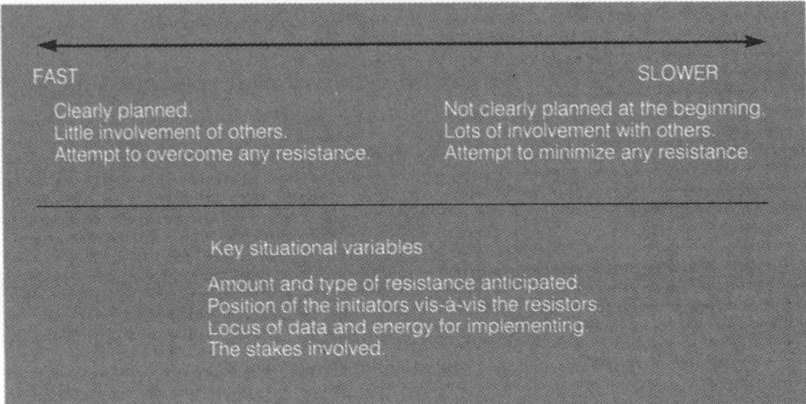

change is shown in Exhibit 17–8. This table briefly identifies situations in which each approach is commonly used and some advantages and disadvantages of each. Choose specific techniques consistent with your overall change strategy (e.g., don't use participation if a change is to be implemented very quickly; do use participation if a slower strategy is involved and input is needed from members).

Strategic continuum
FAST
SLOWER
Clearly planned.
Little involvement of others.
Attempt to overcome any resistance.
Not clearly planned at the beginning.
Lots of involvement with others.
Attempt to minimize any resistance.
Key situational variables
Amount and type of resistance anticipated.
Position of the initiators vis-à-vis the resistors.
Locus of data and energy for implementing.
The stakes involved.

COORDINATING THE CHANGE PROCESS

There is no question but that the effective manager manages change! You may find it difficult, however, to coordinate the entire change process while you are concentrating on the content of the change itself. The flowchart in Exhibit 17–9 is designed as a kind of checklist to guide your coordination activities. The steps involved are divided into four major subsets: *identifying the focus of the change, planning the implementation, implementation,* and *evaluation.*

Identifying the Focus of the Change

The first stage in managing the change process involves identifying the focus of the change. Presumably, the change is a reaction to

Exhibit 17–8 Evaluation of Techniques for Dealing with Resistance to Change

Approach	Commonly Used in Situations Where:	Advantages	Drawbacks
Education + Communication	Information is inaccurate or incomplete	Once persuaded, people will often help with implementation	Can be very time-consuming
Participation + Involvement	Initiators do not have all the information they need and others have considerable power to resist	People who participate will be committed, and information they have will be integrated into the change plan	Can be very time-consuming if participators design an inappropriate change
Support	People are resisting because of adjustment problems	No other approach works as well with adjustment problems	Can be time-consuming, expensive, and still fail
Incentives	Someone will lose out in a change, and that group has considerable power	Sometimes it is a relatively easy way to avoid major resistance	Can be too expensive if it alerts others to negotiate for compliance
Manipulation + Co-optation	Other tactics will not work or are too expensive	Can be relatively quick and inexpensive	Can lead to future problems if people feel manipulated
Coercion	Speed is essential and the initiators possess considerable power	Speedy, and can overcome any kind of resistance	Can be risky if it leaves people mad at the initiators

Source: Adapted from J. P. Kotter, and L. A. Schlesinger, Choosing strategies for change, *Harvard Business Review*, March–April 1979, p. 11.

Exhibit 17–9 A Systematic Procedure for the Management of Change

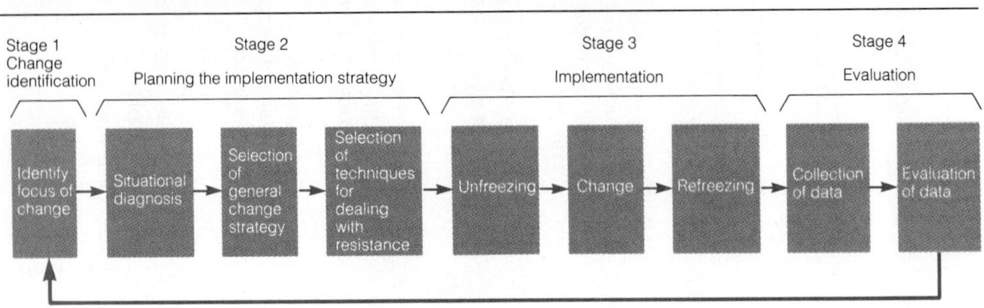

one or more of the forces to change. The details of the plan may or may not be developed at this point in time, depending on the nature of the problem. For example, you need to purchase a specific new machine before the end of the fiscal year (the change is completely defined). Or, you might decide to "take steps to reduce turnover among clerical employees" (a very general change decision). In this case, the details of the change will be worked out during the planning of the implementation strategy. It is important for you to identify objectives of the proposed change and the criteria to be used for evaluating whether or not the objectives are met. You will use these objectives upon completion of the change to evaluate its successes and failures.

Planning the Implementation Strategy

Three steps are involved in planning the implementation strategy. The first step is a situational diagnosis. Here is where you ascertain potential resistance, assess relative centers of power, identify sources of knowledge needed to implement the change, and explore the risks and benefits of making the change. Following this, you select the general change strategy based on the continuum shown in Exhibit 17–7. Finally, you evaluate and select specific techniques to develop support for the change, reduce resistance, and deal with resistance if it occurs.

Implementation

The implementation of a change is the stage at which you apply the three-step process discussed earlier. Unfreeze the situation (create a felt need for the change; use techniques to develop support for the change; try to prevent emergence of resistance to the change). Implement the change itself (provide lots of support for the change; be sensitive to any resistance which might emerge so you can treat it promptly). Finally, refreeze the situation (reinforce outcomes of the change; detect and treat any continuing or new resistance; make any constructive modification of the change that is necessary).

Evaluation

One of the most frequently overlooked steps of managing change is evaluation of the effectiveness of the change. (Perhaps most managers have exhausted their energy by the time they reach this stage!) This evaluation is essential, however, if you wish to acquire a great deal of potential knowledge about the organization. To do this, you must first collect information, usually starting in the implementation stage. The data you collect for evaluation should address the criteria identified at the planning stage of the change. Then, evaluate the information you collect. The general question to ask at this point is: "To what extent were the objectives of the change met? Not met?" (See the "sources of knowledge" section in Chapter 2 and the research techniques described in the Appendix for further requirements of data.)

In Exhibit 17–9 a feedback loop is shown connecting the final step of the change process to the first. This indicates that the evaluation of a change often acts as a catalyst for further change. Whether the additional change is corrective or progressive in nature, the dynamics of organizational environments make it unlikely that any change will be the last change. Because of this, the knowledge you obtain from the change experience can be very useful. The more thorough and careful your evaluation, the more useful this knowledge will be.

SUMMARY

Five major forces drive change in organizations: technological, human (organizational members), social, business/economic, and organizational. Together, these forces provide pressures which lead to the need for organizational change. The probability of a change being effective increases if support for it exists. It is possible to anticipate most of the major sources of resistance to change: fear of loss, misunderstanding and lack of trust, disagreement, and low personal tolerance. There are techniques for managing resistance to change: education/communication, participation/involvement, support, incentives, manipulation/co-optation, and coercion. Three distinct phases of the change process (unfreezing, changing, and refreezing) can aid the development of a change strategy. A "strategic continuum" will help you direct change activity in a manner consistent with key situational variables: resistance expected, the balance of power, sources of information and knowledge, and risks involved if change is not made.

In short, if you follow the flowchart presented in Exhibit 17–9, implement each change using the most effective technique possible, and evaluate carefully each change after it has been "up and running" for some time, you will be a valuable manager in today's fast-paced, rapidly changing organizations.

GLOSSARY

Forces to Change Factors which motivate change in organizations, including technological factors, human needs and values, the social environment, the business and economic environment, and organizational factors.

Proactive Change Change initiated by an organization because it is identified as desirable (i.e., the change is not "forced" on the organization).

Reactive Change Change implemented in an organization because it is made necessary by outside forces.

Resistance to Change The degree to which a change is resisted (either actively or passively) due to fear of loss of something of value, misunderstanding or lack of trust, disagreement on the advisability of change, low personal tolerance for change, or other factors.

Dealing with Resistance to Change Techniques for discouraging resistance and encouraging support for change, including education and communication, participation and involvement, support, incentives, manipulation and co-optation, and coercion.

The Change Process The sequence of events involved in unfreezing, changing, and refreezing.

STUDY QUESTIONS

1. Identify a significant organizational change made by an organization you belong to (or belonged to in the past). What were the major forces which caused this change to occur?
2. Consider the change discussed in Question 1. Who resisted the change? For what reasons?
3. What steps could have been taken by the organization to encourage greater support for the change discussed in Question 1?
4. Six types of techniques for dealing with resistance to change are discussed in this chapter. Identify a situation in which each of these techniques have been used. How effective were they? Why or why not?
5. Discuss reasons why organizations often implement change without giving adequate attention to the management of the change process.
6. Identify a change which you would like to implement in an organization which you currently belong to (or with which you are very familiar). Discuss the steps which should be taken in the management of this change.

NOTES

1. **Dunham, R. B., & Smith, F. J.** (1979). *Organizational surveys: An internal assessment of organizational health*. Glenview, IL: Scott, Foresman, 20–22.
2. **Lawrence, P. R., & Lorsch, J. W.** (1967). Differentiation and integration in complex organizations. *Administrative Science Quarterly, 12,* 1–47.
3. **Miles, R. E., & Snow, C. C.** (1978). *Organizational strategy, structure, and process*. New York: McGraw-Hill.
4. **Kotter, J. P., & Schlesinger, L. A.** (1979, March–April). Choosing strategies for change. *Harvard Business Review,* 106–113.
5. Filling a gap at the top (1983, June 27). *Newsweek,* p. 50.
6. **Lewin, K.** Frontiers in group dynamics. *Human Relations, 1,* 5–41; **Lewin, K.** (1951). *Field theory in social science*. New York: Harper & Row.
7. **Wieland, G. F., & Ullrich, R. A.** (1976). *Organizations: Behavior design and change*. Homewood, IL: Irwin.

Epilogue: Ethics

OVERVIEW
ETHICAL RESPONSIBILITIES
INFLUENCES ON UNETHICAL BEHAVIOR
Personality
Rewards/Punishment
Competition
Organizational Statements/Policies
CONCLUSION

The ill-fated Corvair was launched in the fall of 1959. The results were disastrous. I don't think any one car before or since produced as gruesome a record on the highway as the Corvair. . . . Young Corvair owners were . . . killing themselves in alarming numbers.

When Knudsen took over the reins of Chevrolet in 1961, he insisted that he be given corporate authorization to install a stabilizing bar in the rear to counteract the natural tendencies of the Corvair to flip off the road. The cost of the change would be about $15 a car. But his request was refused . . . as "too expensive."*

OVERVIEW

An *ethic* is a system of standards for moral judgment.[1] Group, organizational, and cultural ethics all exist. Each of these attempts to define acceptable behaviors. Together, they influence the personal set of values you adopt to define your own code of ethics.

Your personal code of ethics can exert a major influence on your behavior in organizations. As the author of a text which has just described techniques you can use to help or hurt others in an organization, I am very concerned about ethics. Because ethics are so very personal, I cannot teach you to "be ethical." Nevertheless, because there are potentially serious consequences of unethical behavior, this Epilogue reminds you of some of your ethical responsibilities and examines factors in organizations which encourage or discourage ethical behavior. I freely admit that the statements contained in this Epilogue are influenced heavily by my own personal ethics. They are not intended as "law," but only to get you thinking about your own ethics.

ETHICAL RESPONSIBILITIES

You are responsible for your own actions. You are equally responsible for actions you initiate and undertake at the direction of another. Convincing yourself that "you are only following orders" does

*John Z. DeLorean as quoted by J. Patrick Wright. From the book *On a clear day you can see General Motors* by J. Patrick Wright, p. 159. Copyright © 1979 by J. Patrick Wright. Published by Wright Enterprises. Reprinted with permission of Multimedia Product Development, Inc.

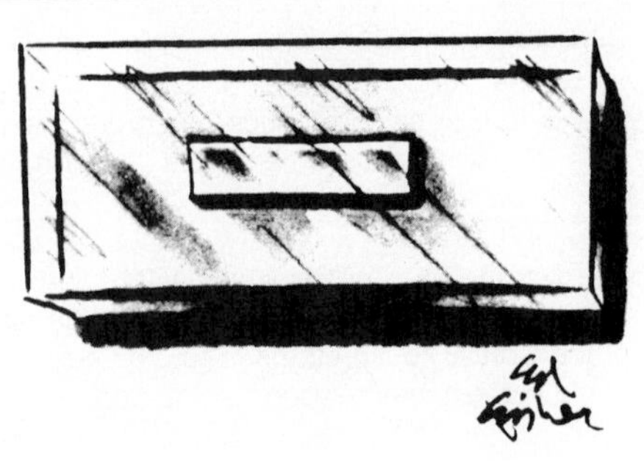

THE SINGLE STANDARD OF MORALITY (IN ITS HERMETICALLY SEALED CASE AT THE NATIONAL BUREAU OF STANDARDS)

not relieve you of full ethical responsibility for your actions (as evidenced by the Nuremberg War Tribunal or the Watergate convictions). The same holds true for behavior influenced by peer pressure. Unless you are forced beyond your physical and mental ability to resist, you cannot shed your responsibility by attributing blame to another.

You are also responsible for your actions as a part of a group. Chapter 12 discussed the Groupthink phenomenon which often leads to behaviors you would not consider as an individual. Social psychologists have explored carefully the phenomenon known as "group shift." With surprising frequency, groups make decisions and engage in behaviors which are much more extreme than would be undertaken by individual members of the group. This "shift" is in part due to a diffusion of responsibility by group members (each member denies personal responsibility because the decision or behavior was a group product). Diffusion of responsibility occurs on a regular basis and usually without conscious intent. This does not relieve you of your individual ethical responsibility. If you participate in a group decision which you personally would have considered unethical, you have behaved unethically.

You are responsible for the actions of your subordinates, peers, and even superiors if you encourage them to behave in a manner you would personally consider unethical. This encompasses a broad base of behavior. Dropping a hint to a subordinate which s/he reasonably interprets as encouraging unethical behavior makes you just as responsible as if you had ordered the unethical behavior.

Inaction also can constitute unethical behavior. Allowing the production of a product which you believe is unsafe is just as unethical as ordering the direct consequences of the unsafe product. Allowing a subordinate to behave in an unethical fashion is just as unethical as requiring the unethical behavior.

INFLUENCES ON UNETHICAL BEHAVIOR

My concern here is not whether your personal code of ethics matches mine. Nor is it whether your code of ethics is consistent with those of your peers, professional colleagues, or neighbors. Your ethical standards are deeply rooted in your personal values and have been learned over a number of years. It is true that anything learned can be relearned (including ethics), but it is unlikely that such major changes will be caused by a brief epilogue from an OB book.

The important thing is whether your behavior matches your internalized code of ethics. Even if you have a strong sense of ethics, you may engage in behavior you consider unethical. This has been referred to as the difference between a person's "ideological" and "operational" ethical standards.[2] Although there is still much to be learned about the factors which cause operational standards to be weaker than ideological standards, some interesting things have been learned about the determinants of unethical behavior.

Harvey Hegarty and Henry Sims conducted a series of studies focusing on the determinants of unethical decision behavior.[3] In these studies, participants played the role of Regional Sales Manager for a large wholesaling firm. These "managers" were faced with the decision of whether or not to pay kickbacks to purchasing agents. Since it was agreed that paying kickbacks was unethical, it can be assumed that the ideological ethic of participants was against the payment of kickbacks. Therefore, the provision of kickbacks would illustrate the departure of operational ethics from ideological ones. Four sets of factors were shown to influence unethical behavior: *personality, rewards/punishment, competition,* and *organizational statements/policies* concerning ethics.

Personality

The results of these studies indicated that unethical behavior (the payment of kickbacks) occurred more frequently for persons with certain *personality* characteristics. Specifically, Machiavellianism, an external locus of control, an economic value orientation, and a political value orientation were associated with unethical behavior.

Rewards/Punishment

One of the most powerful findings concerned the presence of rewards for unethical behavior. When participants believed that unethical behavior would increase their profits and personal compensation, the frequency of unethical behavior increased. Threats of public exposure and a financial fine, however, increased ethical behavior to a level higher than existed when no *reward* or *punishment* was likely. The effect of punishment was so strong that it overpowered the unethical impact of rewards for unethical behavior. Exhibit E–1 illustrates the strong magnitude of these effects.

Competition

Participants in the study were placed in differing levels of *competition*. It was found that competition increased unethical behavior even when competition consisted only of knowing about other sales managers' performance levels.

Exhibit E–1 The Impact of Reward and Punishment on Unethical Behavior

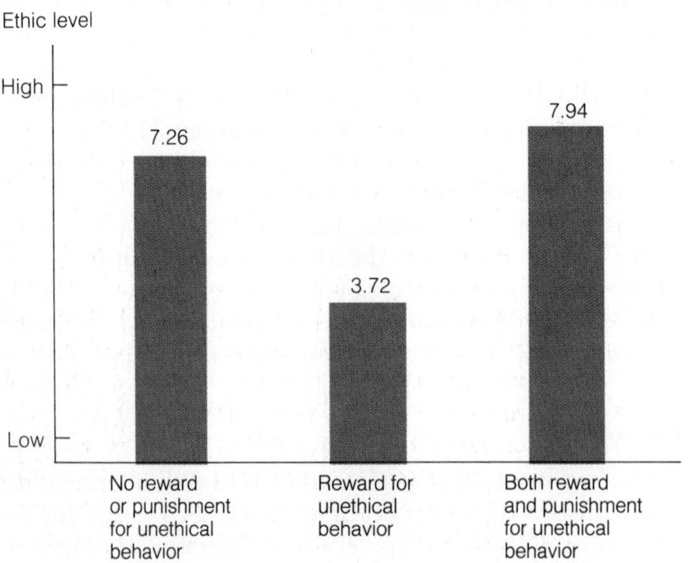

Source: Derived from W. H. Hegarty, and H. P. Sims, Jr., Organizational philosophy, policies, and objectives related to unethical decision behavior: A laboratory experiment. *Journal of Applied Psychology, 64*, 331–338, copyright 1979 by the American Psychological Association. Adapted by permission of the publisher and authors.

Organizational Statements/Policies

Ethical behavior increased when a person of authority in the organization (the president) provided a statement supporting ethical behavior. Similar effects occurred if an ethics objective was assigned by the organization.

CONCLUSION

Earlier I argued that you have a broad responsibility, not only for your own behavior but also for that of others over whom you exert influence in the organization. Furthermore, inaction can be as unethical as action if your inaction results in unethical behavior. It now appears that organizations can influence ethics in two ways: through the long-term learning and relearning of personal values; and through the immediate impact of organizational policies.

You can encourage ethical behavior in your organization to the extent that you contribute to the following:

1. Consider the personality characteristics of candidates for organizational membership. Either avoid personalities which would be likely to lead to unethical behavior or implement policies to stop the unethical tendencies.
2. Make public statements stating that ethical behavior is important and expected.
3. Develop organizational policies specifying ethics objectives.
4. Provide rewards for ethical behavior and avoid providing rewards for unethical behavior.
5. Provide punishment for unethical behavior and avoid punishing ethical behavior.
6. When placing members into competitive situations, be sensitive to the potential for unethical behavior and take appropriate steps to avoid it.

In closing, I ask you to consider the implications of the following statement made by William G. Scott of the University of Washington.

> Americans have drifted into the last quarter of the 20th century with just the slightest awareness that administrative systems, with their accouterments of organizational power and control, have become the dominant moral force in our lives—shaping and changing American values to suit their entailments. Modern organizations have influenced us profoundly, but so quietly and so benevolently that we are scarcely aware that they are the major agencies of value change in our country. Therefore, the serious *moral* issues presented by modern organization simply are not matters of interest to most Americans.[4]

Moral issues and organizations may not be of interest to many Americans, but they should be. It is possible to be both an effective and responsible organizational member.

NOTES

1. **Zenisek, T. J.** (1979). Corporate social responsibility: A conceptualization based on organizational literature. *Academy of Management Review, 4,* 362.
2. **Petit, T. A.** (1967). *The moral crisis in management.* New York: McGraw-Hill; **Zenisek,** 1979, p. 362.
3. **Hegarty, W. H., & Sims, H. P., Jr.** (1978). Some determinants of unethical decision behavior: An experiment. *Journal of Applied Psychology, 63,* 451–457; **Hegarty, W. H., & Sims, H. P., Jr.** (1979). Organizational philosophy, policies, and objectives related to unethical decision behavior: A laboratory experiment. *Journal of Applied Psychology, 64,* 331–338.
4. **Scott, W. G.** (1979). Organicism: The moral anesthetic of management. *Academy of Management Review, 4,* 21.

Appendix

The Sources of Knowledge

OVERVIEW
PERSONAL EXPERIENCE
- Potential Advantages of Personal Experience
- Potential Disadvantages of Personal Experience

CASE STUDIES
- Nonparticipant Case Studies
- Participant Case Studies

FIELD SURVEYS: INTERVIEWS AND QUESTIONNAIRES
- Some Potential Advantages of Surveys
- Some Potential Disadvantages of Surveys

CROSS-SECTIONAL STUDIES
- Some Potential Advantages of Cross-Sectional Studies
- Some Potential Disadvantages of Cross-Sectional Studies

LONGITUDINAL STUDIES
- Some Potential Advantages of Longitudinal Studies
- Some Potential Disadvantages of Longitudinal Studies

EXPERIMENTAL STUDIES
- Laboratory Experiments
- Simulation Experiments
- Planned Field Experiments
- Natural Field Experiments

SUMMARY

> Wise men profit more from fools than fools from wise men; for the wise men shun the mistakes of fools, but fools do not imitate the successes of the wise.
>
> *Marcus Porcius Cato, the Elder*

OVERVIEW

There are a wide variety of ways to obtain OB knowledge, but there is no one best approach. Each source or technique discussed here has advantages and disadvantages relative to the other methods. The approaches differ in a variety of ways including:

1. Time requirements.
2. Cost.
3. Reliability.
4. Ability to measure the issues of interest (construct validity).
5. Ability to establish cause-effect relationships (internal validity).
6. Generalizability of results (external validity).
7. Ethical considerations.

Being aware of the various sources of knowledge and their strengths and weaknesses will help you to evaluate information you receive in organizations. It will alert you to the wide range of information available; it will aid you in maximizing the usability of the information obtained. You will find that, in most cases, the best approach to the acquisition of useful knowledge is to combine several complementary approaches so that the weaknesses of each are at least partially overcome by the strengths of others.

PERSONAL EXPERIENCE

The personal experience (or naturalistic observation) approach is by far the most commonly used technique for acquiring knowledge

"He's cute, but everything he knows comes from books."

about the behaviors and attitudes of people in organizations. For many organizational members, it is almost the exclusive way information is obtained about what is happening and why. In fact, it has often been argued that "you can't beat personal experience." This argument is true in many ways but quite untrue in others. One fact is certain: by augmenting personal experience with information from other sources of knowledge you not only add new valuable information, you also increase the value of your personal experience knowledge.

Potential Advantages of Personal Experience

Much information we receive in organizations has been distorted—intentionally or not—by other people. Each person who handles information is likely to distort it somewhat. And the more people who have handled the information before you receive it the more distorted it becomes. The inaccuracies of rumors testify to the distortion which can occur without the knowledge of the person who is transmitting the information. Information we receive firsthand through personal experience is not subject to the distortion of other people. This can be a major advantage of this approach of obtaining knowledge.

Information you experience firsthand is "real" to you ("I'll believe it when I see it"). Thus, it is believable and much more likely to be accepted as true than is information received secondhand (as is the case with all of the other sources of knowledge).

Personal experience as a source of knowledge can allow great attention to detail and a focus on the critical issues of interest. It can help filter out unnecessary information. The alternative is to hope that someone else has obtained the appropriate information and recorded it so that it is readily accessible.

Potential Disadvantages of Personal Experience

The information you obtain directly through personal experience is not distorted by others—but it is definitely subject to distortion by *you*. Your own beliefs, expectations, and prior experiences all have the potential to influence the information you collect. And, you are much less likely to detect distortions from your own perceptual and evaluative processes than you are to detect distorted information from others. Just as the "realness" of personal experience information is a potential advantage (because you will believe accurate information), that "realness" can be a disadvantage (because you will believe the inaccurate information you collect as well). Training in observation techniques improves the quality of information obtained through personal experience. But even with training, many inaccuracies are often present, especially when the observer is overloaded, stressed, or rushed (as very often happens in organizations).

The information you can obtain through the personal experience approach is greatly limited because your experiences are greatly limited. Your position, the amount of observational time available, and many other factors severely limit the amount and type of information you can collect.

In collecting information through personal experience, you tend to focus on the dramatic or unusual—often at the expense of the more mundane but equally important information. Some things just catch your attention more than others—and you are more likely to notice and remember these factors. (The discussion of perception in Chapter 10 explores some factors which catch your attention and thus influence the information you notice and how you evaluate it.)

As noted earlier, information from the personal experience method seems very real and therefore is believable. This realness, however, often leads to overgeneralization. When you see something work in one situation, you tend to believe that it will also work in another situation.

These potential disadvantages of the personal experience method can be partially overcome by being aware of them and taking steps to minimize their effects. Even if all of the disadvantages could be completely eliminated, one major limitation to this approach remains: most people do not always learn by the trial-and-error method. To learn about an event through the personal experience approach, you must experience it. Aside from the fact that time constraints only allow the direct experiencing of a limited number of events, it would be undesirable to learn about many events firsthand. Most managers, for instance, would prefer to learn about the causes of organizational failure secondhand rather than by experiencing failure.

It should be obvious that, although the personal experience method has several potential advantages, it has a significant number of potentially serious disadvantages and limitations. A wise approach might be to:

1. Continue to use personal experience as one source of information about behaviors and attitudes in organizations.
2. Take steps to reduce the negative effects of the potential disadvantages discussed.
3. Use information obtained by this technique in conjunction with other sources of knowledge with complementary strengths.

Think about the following situation which describes the use of information obtained almost exclusively from personal experience.

The Hanover Radio Company

The Hanover Radio Company employs 375 workers to assemble portable transistor radios. The company had been suffering high costs due to returns and warranty repair work. In an attempt to decrease the number of defective radios being manufactured, the president of the company sent a letter to all workers informing them that the work of Hanover Radio Company employees was well below the industry standard and that such poor performance would no longer be tolerated. According to the letter, if the work did not improve, 10 percent of the workers would be laid off. Soon after this letter was sent to employees, the average work-team productivity level dropped from 50 radios per hour to 40. The president of the company responded to this drop in productivity by sending another letter to all employees. In this letter he informed the employees that he would not tolerate a work slowdown in protest to his pressure for improved work quality. He imposed an immediate wage reduction of 10 percent on the workers until productivity returned to its former level. In the two weeks following the president's second letter, productivity dropped even further, 42 workers quit their jobs, and 75 percent of the remaining employees signed election-authorization cards in an attempt to introduce a union to the company.[1]

The president of Hanover Radio made a number of critical decisions based on information he had acquired mainly through personal experience (observation). Some of his information was accurate: there was a high number of warranty returns and there was a decrease in productivity after this first letter was sent. But what about the president's information that the drop in productivity was in protest to his letter? Could the personal experience method provide the accurate information the president needed to make his critical decisions? Read the following composite interview conducted with a sample of workers; then make your own judgment about the adequacy of personal experience as the only source of information.

> When I received the first letter from the president, I was surprised and hurt. I had never been told that there was any serious quality problem with our radios and I had always been proud of my work. Anyhow, during lunch breaks that next week most of us talked a lot about how we could improve our quality. We decided that the best thing to do would be to slow down a little and make sure each and every radio was put together exactly right. We agreed that we would show our president that we could do things right. After all, Hanover Radio had always taken pretty good care of us and this was the first time the president had really acted like a. . . .
>
> When that second letter came, things changed right away. Here we were breaking our backs trying to help the company and that old guy rewards us by cutting our pay. Some of the guys got so mad that they took a couple of sick days and went job hunting—quite a few of them even took other jobs. The rest of us decided that, if we were going to be paid less, we would work less. We also decided that it was time to listen to the people who had been talking about forming a union so that this kind of thing couldn't happen again.

CASE STUDIES

The case method involves the presentation of a detailed, in-depth description of a sequence of organizational events. There are two major variations of the case study approach to obtaining information about behaviors and attitudes in organizations. The major difference between the two is the role played by the person collecting the case study information. In the first situation, the observer is present but does not participate directly in those events. This is called nonparticipant observation. In the second, the person not only observes events but also participates as a member of the group. This second approach is referred to as participant observation.

Nonparticipant Case Studies

In the **nonparticipant case** approach, the researcher is present in the organization specifically to observe the sequence of events of interest. Relevant events that are directly observed are recorded for later use in writing the case. Additional case information is often obtained by examining existing written documents, by interviews, or through other techniques. Cases typically focus on relatively narrow specific issues. The written case always consists of a description of the sequence of events observed. In addition, a case often presents the observer's evaluation of the reasons the events occurred, the perceived relationships between two or more observed events, and the importance and meaning of the events. Note that the primary function of a case is to collect relevant information and present a summary of it. Any evaluations added by the observer should be treated as separate information. In evaluating the reliability and validity of the case information, it is important to first evaluate the quality of the descriptive information about organizational events. If you are satisfied that this information is acceptable, then assess the appropriateness of the evaluations. Often readers of cases accept the adequacy of the description of the organizational events but disagree with the author of the case on their meaning.

Potential Advantages of Nonparticipant Case Studies. A well-prepared case study has the potential to provide a detailed and complete description of critical organizational occurrences in a concise form which can be processed quickly by the reader. In effect, the reader of a case can "experience" the events through the eyes of the observer. Because well-written cases are often enjoyable to read and are written in a journalistic style, the events described seem almost real. This makes the information believable. (A case is not as believable as firsthand experience, but more so than an informal report by an observer; and it is more real than information from more formal sources of knowledge.)

A major advantage of the case study is that it identifies good starting points for more systematic research. Thus, the reader of the case is encouraged to think about a wider range of relevant issues.

Another potential advantage of the case approach over more systematic formal sources of knowledge is that the collection of case information can be sensitive to unexpected events. With most formal approaches, unexpected events are often not measured because the formal design has no way to measure the unexpected occurrence. Use of the case approach does not guarantee that every relevant event will be detected. But it does allow the possibility of detecting a wide range of events, expected or not.

Potential Disadvantages of Nonparticipant Case Studies. Information used in the creation of a case study is obtained by one or more persons observing a sequence of events in an organization. This information is subject to distortion by the observer(s). This does not suggest that observers would purposely manipulate information. A more common problem is for their personal biases or expectations to distort their perceptions and, thus, the information obtained.

Even when the observer's information is not distorted, it may not be representative of all of the information available. Events which are expected by the observer or which are consistent with the observer's previous experience are likely to be noticed. Events which do not fit neatly into the observer's way of viewing the organization may not be.

Once an observer has collected a set of information about events in an organization, the case must be written describing them. Written cases tend to focus on dramatic or unusual events, often at the expense of routine but important ones.

It is usually very difficult to assess the reliability of case information. Unless the case author provides the information needed to evaluate reliability, the reader's judgment is greatly limited about the quality of the information.

It is also difficult to infer cause→effect relationships from case studies. A case will tell you that Event A occurred and later Event B occurred; but it provides insufficient information to prove that A led to B. There is, in fact, a tendency to jump to conclusions about cause→effect relationships in case studies. Before we can conclude that A caused B, all other reasonable explanations should be ruled out. (Did C cause B?) Case studies seldom contain comparison groups that show what happened in a similar situation where Event A did *not* occur. Thus, the internal validity of cause→effect claims from case studies must be carefully considered.

It is common to overgeneralize from the results of a case study. The sequence of events in one case is often used to justify action in another organization without adequate consideration of issues relating to external validity. As with any other source of information, the degree to which it is appropriate to generalize from one situation to another should be carefully considered.

Note that most of the disadvantages identified with the nonparticipant case method are *potential* disadvantages. They can be minimized by using appropriate information collection procedures, by carefully evaluating each piece of information, and by using the information appropriately. Continue to use the nonparticipant case method as one source of information about behaviors and attitudes in organizations; take steps to reduce the negative effects of its potential disadvantages; and use the information from it with that from other sources of knowledge with complementary strengths.

The following is a fictionalized example of a case study.

The Reliable Mortgage Insurance Company

Two observers obtained their information through observation of a series of meetings of key officers of Reliable, by examining a series of formal organizational memos, through interviews with organizational members, and from examination of formal company records.

The Reliable Mortgage Insurance Company insures mortgages issued by savings and loan organizations. If the mortgage holder defaults on an insured loan, Reliable is responsible for covering any losses incurred by the savings and loan. The table below shows the total premiums collected for insurance policies issued from 1969 through 1983. This table also shows the overall losses paid by Reliable in each of these years, the loss ratio (the ratio of claims paid to premiums received), and the premium retained (i.e., the money left for the company after paying claims).

Year	**Premiums**	**Losses**	**Loss Ratio**	**Premium Retained**
1969	$ 50,000,000	$ 10,000,000	20%	$ 40,000,000
1970	55,000,000	11,000,000	20	44,000,000
1971	75,000,000	18,750,000	25	56,250,000
1972	95,000,000	26,600,000	28	68,400,000
1973	100,000,000	32,000,000	32	68,000,000
1974	110,000,000	38,500,000	38	68,200,000
1975	125,000,000	50,000,000	40	75,000,000
1976	130,000,000	55,900,000	43	74,100,000
1977	155,000,000	71,300,000	46	83,700,000
1978	180,000,000	86,400,000	48	93,600,000
1979	190,000,000	95,000,000	50	95,000,000
1980	210,000,000	109,200,000	52	100,000,000
1981	180,000,000	86,400,000	48	93,600,000
1982	160,000,000	73,600,000	46	86,400,000
1983	150,000,000	66,000,000	44	84,000,000

On October 6, 1980, the president of Reliable called a meeting of the company executive committee (the president, the executive vice president, and the five vice presidents). At this meeting the president reviewed with alarm the steadily increasing loss ratio Reliable had been experiencing. He argued it was imperative that this trend be reversed and announced a three-pronged "Underwriter Development Program" he hoped would improve the quality of underwriting decisions being made by Reliable underwriters and therefore reduce the high loss ratio being experienced. His new program consisted of the following:

1. A series of training sessions would be held for underwriters to increase underwriting skills.
2. A new job was created and staffed by a highly competent individual who would be available as a resource person to all underwriters to help them make better underwriting decisions.
3. A new bonus compensation plan was implemented for all underwriters. Underwriters who experienced worse than average loss ratios

* The name of the company has been changed to preserve the anonymity of the company.

(continued)

> would receive no bonus. Those who had loss ratios near the average would receive a bonus of one half of one percent of the premium underwritten. Underwriters with loss ratios much smaller than average would receive a bonus of one percent of the premium underwritten.
>
> As can be observed from the figures for 1981, 1982, and 1983, loss ratios dropped after implementation of the "Underwriter Development Program." Unfortunately, the amount of premiums underwritten also dropped, resulting in a substantial decrease in the number of premium dollars retained. In fact, the trend indicated that the number of premium dollars was decreasing each year after the implementation of the new program. An increase in underwriter complaints about company policies suggested that underwriters were dissatisfied with the new program.

After reading this case, place yourself in the position of a manager who is trying to decide whether to implement an underwriter development program. Ask yourself the following questions and evaluate the strengths and weaknesses of this approach:

1. Did the case provide a lot of information in a small amount of space and did it require much time for you to read the information?
2. Did the case help you identify specific issues to pursue further?
3. Did the case identify some unexpected effects of the introduction of the underwriter development program?
4. Did the observers accurately perceive the attitudes of underwriters toward the program or could their biases have distorted this information?
5. Was the information obtained by the observers representative of all the important information available? For example, what happened to turnover among underwriters? How did the savings and loans react to the new program which caused underwriters to reject a larger number of requests for mortgage insurance?
6. Was too much attention paid to the dramatic changes in loss ratios and premiums retained? Should more attention have been paid to the more mundane issues of payroll costs, reputation of Reliable, etc.?
7. How reliable was the information about Reliable? For example, was information about the number of underwriter complaints reliable or would different information have been obtained if complaints had been recorded more precisely or by someone else? Do you have any way of knowing how reliable the information is?
8. Did the underwriter development program *cause* the changes in loss ratios, in premiums written, in premiums retained? Or could there have been some other factor involved (such as a downturn in the economy) which accounted for part or all of the effects?

What would have happened to loss ratios, etc., if the new program had not been introduced? Would they have changed anyhow? Did the case compare what happened at Reliable to what was happening at any other mortgage insurers?

9. Even if you decide that the underwriter development program did cause subsequent changes in the organization, can you assume that your organization would experience similar effects?

Participant Case Studies

In **participant case studies,** the observer also participates in the situation being observed. The participant observer can be an obtrusive observer; here, the other organizational members participating in the situation are aware of the observer's role. Or, the participant observer can be an unobtrusive observer; here, his/her role as an observer is concealed from the other organizational members. (The observer pretends to be just another member of the organization.)

The *potential advantages and disadvantages of nonparticipant case studies* also apply for the most part to participant studies. One additional advantage is that access to data not available to the nonparticipant observer is often possible. It is difficult, for example, for a nonparticipant observer to obtain comprehensive information about co-worker interrelationships without being involved in the situation. A second potential advantage to the participant approach is that nonparticipant observers often influence the behaviors and attitudes of organizational members due to their "poking around." When people know they are being observed by a researcher, they often alter their behavior (often to put their best foot forward). When conducted properly, participant observation approaches can reduce much of this effect.

The participant observer approach has some significant potential drawbacks beyond those of the nonparticipant method. The presence of the observer may influence organizational events even more than that of a nonparticipant observer. The participant observer must be careful not to exert undue influence. The participant observer may also lose objectivity after developing personal relationships with organizational members and becoming involved in daily organizational events. Thus, it is possible for the participant observation approach to provide access to events not otherwise accessible—but also to influence those events by being present and to perceive the events nonobjectively.

A special issue must be considered when participant observation is nonobtrusive. Here, the participant's presence is less likely to influence organizational events than when other participants know that an observer is present. It must be asked though, *whether it is ethical* to place an observer in an organization without telling organizational members that they are being observed.

Consider the following example of unobtrusive participant observation and ask yourself how you would feel if you were being observed in this manner.

A large manufacturing company was receiving a fairly high number of complaints from assembly line workers about the behavior of supervisors. When supervisors were asked about their behavior, they denied any wrongdoing, arguing that the line workers were unhappy with other factors and taking their frustration out on their supervisors.

To try to determine what was really happening, the Personnel Director decided to place unobtrusive participant observers onto several assembly lines. "New employees" (the observers) took jobs on the line and worked side by side with the regular workers. Their primary task, however, was to obtain information about the supervisor/subordinate problem which existed.

Consider the following:

1. Could the company have obtained this information any other way?
2. Would other approaches to obtaining this information have changed the way people behaved?
3. How would you feel if you were a regular worker on one of these assembly lines and discovered that the new worker next to you was an observer for management?
4. How would you feel if you were a supervisor and discovered that one of your new subordinates was an observer for management?

FIELD SURVEYS: INTERVIEWS AND QUESTIONNAIRES

The field survey is a systematic procedure (usually involving interviews and/or questionnaires) designed to obtain descriptive information about the current state of attitudes, motivation level, opinions, and self-reported behaviors of organizational members. In a field survey, all information is collected at just one point in time and no attempt is made to establish cause→effect relationships. The field survey is primarily a monitoring device.[2] The survey is analogous to a monitoring gauge on a machine which tells you the current status of the machine but does not necessarily tell you *why* the machine is in that condition. Although surveys do not provide cause→effect explanations, they can be very useful for tracking attitudes.

The techniques for acquiring information about the behaviors and attitudes of organizational members discussed to this point (personal experience and case studies) provide information about the behaviors and attitudes through observation only. The survey approach taps these factors more directly by going to organizational members and asking them to report this information about themselves.

The two common survey approaches are the *interview* and the *questionnaire*. The interview is a conversation with an organizational member designed to obtain specific information about that person. Interviews can be *structured* so that the organizational member responds by choosing from a set of possible answers provided by the interviewer:

> Think about your company as a place to work. Is it a better place to work today than it was when you started working here? Please answer yes or no.

Interviews can also be *unstructured* and, therefore, more open-ended and probing:

> How do you feel about your company as a place to work compared to what it was like when you started working here?

The more structured approach to interviewing provides information which can be easily tabulated, summarized, and compared across groups. The unstructured approach provides information which is more difficult to process, but which is of greater depth. Answers to the structured question above could be only "yes" or "no," while answers to the unstructured question could specify various aspects of working for the company which are better and others which are not as good now as they were. The response to the unstructured question might also provide information about the impact these changes have had on the employee's personal life and job performance.

The questionnaire survey approach differs from the interview approach primarily in that it takes the form of a "paper and pencil" request for information rather than a verbal request. In fact, sociologist H. W. Smith has called the questionnaire "a self-administered interview."[3]

The questionnaire can be structured or unstructured, as is true for interviews. The questionnaire approach to acquiring survey information is considerably less expensive than the interview approach and can be conducted more quickly with more participants than the survey method. The interview approach, however, allows flexibility which is not possible with questionnaires. A well-trained interviewer is capable of probing issues raised by the interviewee, of asking for clarification, expansion, etc. The paper on which questionnaires are printed is generally not very sensitive to the respondent. All questions to be asked by the questionnaire must be prepared prior to interaction with the respondent, but the interview approach allows the possibility of formulating questions based on preceding answers.

Some Potential Advantages of Surveys

Surveys provide access to the reactions of organizational members concerning events which occurred in the past. It is possible to ask "How did you feel about the pay freeze which went into effect last year?" or, "How did you react to the training program you experienced?" With the direct observation methods discussed previously, observers have to be present at the time the event occurred to obtain information. If information is to be obtained about many significant events, it is necessary to obtain this information from organizational members after the fact.

Surveys can provide information which is very reliable and valid if certain key factors are considered in the design and implementation of the survey. It is necessary, for example, to carefully assess the breadth and limits of the vocabulary of the respondents and make sure that all questions (whether verbal or written) fall within their skill level. Questions must be very specific so that respondents understand the issue being raised. Ambiguity must be absent from questions so that all respondents will interpret the questions in the same fashion. Questions must be simple and address only one issue at a time. Questions must not be leading so as to influence responses. If these and related factors are given sufficient attention, surveys can produce very good quality information.

The generalizability of information obtained from surveys can be assessed relatively easily by sampling from a variety of types of employees, jobs, etc., to explore the degree to which the information applies across situations.

A structure can be built into the survey approach to provide standardized data so that comparisons can be made across employees, organizations, etc. This structure also allows for appropriate statistical analyses to facilitate understanding of the meaning of the information.

Finally, the survey approach (particularly the questionnaire survey approach) allows for very efficient collection of information from a large number of organizational members. This can usually be done in a very cost-efficient manner as well.

Some Potential Disadvantages of Surveys

The information obtained from surveys is subject to distortion by the respondent. This often occurs due to memory inadequacies, biases, and a desire to answer in a socially acceptable fashion. The information also can be influenced by the interviewer or the person administering the questionnaire. The behaviors or apparent attitudes of the researcher often lead to distortions in the way organizational members respond to surveys.

If the interviewee is not motivated to respond to the survey, the reliability and validity of the information received can suffer badly. The respondent must devote time and energy to providing thoughtful, honest answers to the survey.

The survey approach is not designed for the purpose of establishing cause→effect relationships and does not provide information about *why* the behaviors and attitudes of respondents are as they are.

With the exception of the inability of surveys to provide cause→effect relationships, the other disadvantages can usually be overcome sufficiently. This requires careful consideration of the design and careful attention to the administration of the survey.

The following is an example of a questionnaire field survey conducted by the author of this book for a large pharmaceutical firm.

The Diversified Pharmaceutical Corporation *

The Diversified Pharmaceutical Corporation develops, manufactures, and markets a wide range of pharmaceutical products. The Solutions Division of the corporation has a marketing division responsible for the marketing of all intravenous solutions and related products. Because the marketing branch is extremely important to the organization, the company decided to conduct a survey of the Field Sales Force in each of three sales regions. The company wished to explore several aspects of the job satisfaction levels of employees: pay, promotions, co-workers, supervision, and the work itself.

The company decided to use the Job Descriptive Index (JDI),[4] which is a reliable, valid, and frequently used questionnaire for measuring the five aspects (facets) of satisfaction. The questionnaire containing these items was given to each field salesperson. The respondents completed the questionnaires in about 15 minutes and returned them to the researcher through the U.S. mail. Responses were anonymous. Questionnaires were returned from 139 employees (about 95 percent of all who were asked to participate).

Exhibit A–1 shows the results of this survey, broken down by region and compared to national norms (average levels of satisfaction for a representative group of employees from across the country). A score at the 50th percentile indicated that the satisfaction level for that group of employees was comparable to the average satisfaction level in the normative group. Therefore, examination of Exhibit A–1 allowed Diversified

*The name of the company has been changed to preserve the anonymity of the company.

(continued)

Exhibit A–1 Diversified Pharmaceutical Job Satisfaction Survey Results: Field Sales Force

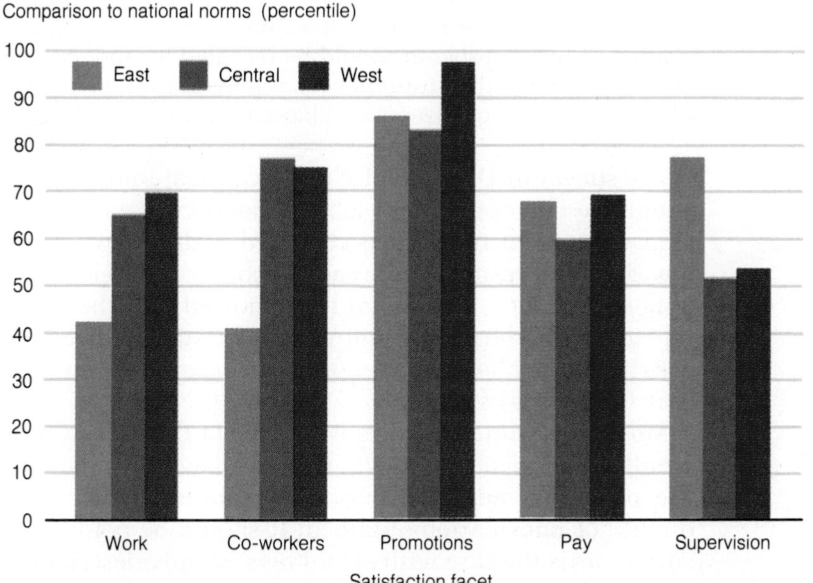

From *Organizational surveys* by Randall B. Dunham and Frank J. Smith, pp. 11–13. Copyright © 1979 by Scott, Foresman and Co. Reprinted by permission.

Pharmaceutical Corporation to determine which regions had higher or lower satisfaction levels (for each facet) than the other regions and to ascertain whether satisfaction levels for Diversified employees were above or below the national average.

Examination of Exhibit A–1 reveals that the satisfaction levels for this group of employees is relatively high compared to the national norm. The manager of the East Region noticed that his employees had the highest satisfaction of all three regions in the area of supervision satisfaction. His region also compared favorably with other regions for satisfaction with promotions and pay. He noted, however, that in the areas of satisfaction with the work itself and co-workers, his employees were not only substantially lower than the other two regions, but also below the national norm. The manager of the Central Region observed that her employees showed "healthy" satisfaction levels in all areas in comparison to national norms. She also observed that attitudes were near or above the other regions for four of the five satisfaction facets. For satisfaction with supervision, although her region was near the national average, it was well below the favorable level present for the East Region.

(continued)

The manager of the West Region saw that his employees' results were similar to those of the Central Region.

Based on the findings of this survey, the corporate office ordered the three regional managers to work together to explore ways to raise satisfaction with work, co-workers, and supervision in those regions where these were found to be relatively low. Management also announced that the attitude survey program would be repeated for the regions in one year. Furthermore, the attitudes survey program would be expanded to include other parts of Diversified Pharmaceutical.

The survey at Diversified Pharmaceutical told management a lot about the current state of job satisfaction in each of the three regions. This information was collected within a two-day period, at a low cost, and results were ready within four weeks from the beginning of the study. Statistical tests showed that the information obtained was both reliable and valid. The standardized format of the questionnaire allowed easy comparison across regions and to a normative national sample.

Most of the potential disadvantages of the survey approach were handled adequately through careful selection of the questionnaire, use of careful administration procedures, and evaluation of the quality of information obtained. It should be pointed out that this survey, as is the case with all surveys, simply described the existing level of the attitudes assessed. No attempt was made to identify the determinants of these attitudes. Other sources of knowledge would be required to identify the determinants of these attitudes. As such, the survey approach could be considered a diagnostic tool, but not a treatment tool.

CROSS-SECTIONAL STUDIES

Cross-sectional studies build upon the field survey approach. As with a field survey, all information is collected at one point in time (i.e., no attempt is made to assess dynamic relationships). As with field surveys, questionnaires and interviews are often used to obtain information (although more objective measures are also used quite frequently—absenteeism rates might be measured from company records, for example). As with field surveys, cross-sectional studies yield descriptive information about the current state of behaviors and attitudes. The primary distinguishing factor of the cross-sectional study is that it examines the *relationship* between two or more variables. Thus, a cross-sectional study which examines satisfaction and absenteeism level could demonstrate whether or not these two variables are related, and how strongly.

It must be emphasized that a cross-sectional study does not attempt to prove that A caused B. It merely determines the strength of the relationship between the two. If the Diversified Pharmaceutical Corporation field study described in the previous section had also measured attendance for each employee and examined the relationship between absenteeism and each of the five facets of satisfaction, that study would have become a cross-sectional study. The results of such a cross-sectional study might have shown that satisfaction with pay and promotional opportunities had the strongest relationships with absenteeism. Although this would not have proven that low satisfaction with these factors caused the absenteeism levels, it would have suggested that these two factors should have been explored more carefully as possible determinants of absenteeism. Furthermore, the degree of these relationships would have helped Diversified decide whether other factors must be explored as possible determinants of absenteeism (i.e., a relatively weak relationship would suggest that other factors are probably also important).

The cross-sectional study cannot prove that A caused B because it is equally possible that B caused A. Furthermore, since cross-sectional studies do not control other factors, it is possible that some third factor(s) is influencing both A and B, making it appear that the two variables might be influencing one another.

Some Potential Advantages of Cross-Sectional Studies

Cross-sectional studies share the following strengths common to the survey approach:

1. Information about past events can be recalled.
2. Information obtained can be very reliable and valid.
3. Generalizability of information obtained can be assessed.
4. The structured approach can allow comparisons to other studies.
5. Collection of information can be very efficient and can involve a large number of organizational members.

The major strength of the cross-sectional approach beyond that of the survey is that relationships between variables can be explored.

Some Potential Disadvantages of Cross-Sectional Studies

Cross-sectional studies share the following weaknesses or limitations with the survey method:

1. Information may be distorted by respondents.
2. The presence and behavior of the researcher can influence the information obtained.

3. Reliability and validity can suffer if respondents are not motivated.

Relative to sources of knowledge to be discussed in the remainder of this appendix, the cross-sectional approach provides weak evidence of cause→effect relationships. Specifically, a cross-sectional study can show that two variables are related and, therefore, one *might* actually "cause" the other. It cannot *prove* that this is true, however.

The following presents some of the results of a cross-sectional study done by Richard Hackman of Yale University and Greg Oldham of the University of Illinois.[5] This study was designed to examine the relationship between certain job characteristics and worker behaviors and attitudes.

A Study of Job Design and Worker Responses

Hackman and Oldham developed a theory which specified the expected relationships between the design of jobs and worker reactions to these jobs (see Chapter 15 on job design). To allow a preliminary examination of the appropriateness of this theory, they designed and conducted a cross-sectional study. In this study, 658 employees representing 62 different jobs and 7 organizations were administered a questionnaire to obtain measures of certain job characteristics (i.e., how much variety, autonomy, identity, significance, and feedback the job provides). These measures were combined to form a measure called the "motivating potential score" which, according to the theory, would determine the degree to which the job should produce favorable worker reactions. A questionnaire was also used to measure the motivation level of these employees and job satisfaction. Performance of each employee was rated by his/her supervisor.

Statistical correlations between the motivating potential score and the behaviors and attitudes indicated that there was a significant (albeit moderate) relationship between the motivating potential score and each of the behaviors and attitudes. This means that workers whose jobs were described as being high in the motivating potential score (variety, autonomy, identity, significance, and feedback) were more satisfied, were more highly motivated by their work, and were rated as being better performers.

The results obtained by this cross-sectional study are *supportive* of the theory being examined. That is, the predicted relationships were found to exist. Because of the limitations of cross-sectional studies, however, this study does not prove that the job characteristics *caused* the levels of behaviors and attitudes which were observed. A great many other factors might explain, in part, the causes of these behaviors and attitudes. The results clearly indicated, however, that the theory was worth pursuing with studies which could provide stronger cause→effect information. The results of this study, therefore, served to guide future research on the theory.

LONGITUDINAL STUDIES

The primary distinction between the cross-sectional approach and the longitudinal study is that, in the **longitudinal study,** one or more of the variables being studied is measured at two or more points in time. Measurements are made sufficiently far apart so that changes can occur in the variables. It is this measurement across time which permits stronger inferences about cause→effect relationships than were possible using the cross-sectional approach (the strength of these inferences, however, will not be nearly as strong as with the experimental designs discussed later in this appendix).

The basic objective of a longitudinal study is to identify changes which occur for one variable and determine if subsequent changes occur for another variable. If this happens, the researcher has evidence that changes in A are followed by changes in B. Although this still does not *prove* a cause→effect relationship, the evidence supports the likelihood of such a relationship existing. Although sophisticated statistical tools are available to demonstrate that it is more likely that A is influencing B as opposed to vice-versa, it is still possible that some third variable(s) is responsible for the changes which occurred for both A and B. If the researcher has the foresight also to measure the other variable(s) which might be explaining the observed effect (changes in B which follow changes in A), it is possible to determine whether or not the other variable(s) is responsible. Unfortunately, it is very unusual (actually, it is almost impossible) for a researcher to anticipate and measure all other variables which might provide reasonable alternative explanations for the observed effect. Nonetheless, the longitudinal approach allows stronger causal inferences than the cross-sectional approach (but, to repeat, not as strong as those made possible by experimental designs).

Some Potential Advantages of Longitudinal Studies

Longitudinal studies have the following strengths common to cross-sectional studies:

1. Information about past events can be recalled.
2. Information obtained can be very reliable and valid.
3. Generalizability of information obtained can be assessed.
4. The structured approach can allow comparisons to other studies.
5. Collection of information can be relatively efficient and involve a large number of organizational members. Generally, although

Worker Control and Turnover

Recent research and theory suggest that workers want to have a reasonable amount of control over what happens to them, both on and off the job. This research also has suggested that people who feel that they have insufficient control take steps to "regain control over their lives." If an organizational member feels that it is not possible to regain control over what is happening to him/her at the workplace, quitting the job is one "ultimate" way of regaining a sense of controlling one's life. David Greenberger of The Ohio State University wished to test the following hypothesis:

> *Workers who experience a decrease in the amount of control they have over their jobs will search for and find an alternative job more quickly than will workers who experience no decrease in control.*

To test this hypothesis, Greenberger used a questionnaire to measure the amount of control experienced by each of several hundred clerical workers at the insurance company. This measure was repeated four times over an 18-month period. This allowed examination of the amount of control being experienced and changes in control. Greenberger also measured the length of time employees worked for the company before leaving to accept another job (over 30 percent of the employees left during the study.)

Results of the study showed that those employees who experienced lower levels of control (particularly those for whom control was decreasing) worked for the company for a shorter period of time before quitting to take another job than did those employees who experienced higher levels of control (especially those for whom control was staying the same or increasing).

efficiency is relatively high, both the time required to conduct the study and the cost of the study are higher than for cross-sectional studies.

The major strength of the longitudinal approach beyond that of cross-sectional studies is the greater power for inferring cause→effect relationships.

Some Potential Disadvantages of Longitudinal Studies

Longitudinal studies have the following potential weaknesses in common with the cross-sectional approach:

1. Information may be distorted by respondents.
2. The presence and behavior of the researcher can influence the information obtained.
3. Reliability and validity can suffer if respondents are not motivated to participate.

In addition, the longitudinal approach requires that the researcher study each organizational member at each point in time. If a person is not available at any one of the points in time, data for that person is not useful. The impact of this constraint can be very minor if only a few organizational members are unavailable. On the other hand, this can be a major problem if a large number of people become unavailable, particularly if those who are not available differ from those who are available (e.g., if people with low satisfaction levels refuse to participate in the second stage of the study).

The following example of a longitudinal study was conducted in a moderately large insurance company. The study was designed to examine the relationship between the amount of control over job activities experienced by workers and the length of time workers kept their jobs with the company before taking other jobs elsewhere.*

The results of this longitudinal study are supportive of the hypothesis being examined. Low levels of control at work were followed by relatively quick resignations from the company. Because of the longitudinal design of the study, it is possible to draw relatively strong cause→effect conclusions about the likelihood that control levels influenced the turnover behavior. The results showed that control alone did not explain all turnover which occurred (and, therefore, other factors are probably also important), but it is very likely that control had some effect on the turnover. Because some third variable(s) possibly could have influenced both the amount of control experienced and turnover, it is not possible to say that the cause→effect relationship was proven, but it would be reasonable to say that there is a good probability that the cause→effect relationship was present.

EXPERIMENTAL STUDIES

There are three major characteristics of experimental studies which distinguish them from all of the other approaches discussed in this book. These are described below.

Manipulation of Variables. In all experimental designs one or more variables are "manipulated" and the researcher observes subsequent changes in behaviors and/or attitudes. Some experiments manipulate a variable by changing the variable from its existing

---

*I would like to thank the Office of Naval Research for funding this research entitled "Job Design and Redesign," R. B. Dunham and L. L. Cummings, co-principal investigators. Development of the measures of control, development of the hypothesis that control and turnover would be related, and analyses of the data were done by David W. Greenberger of The Ohio State University.

condition to a new condition. Thus, a researcher could experimentally manipulate the type of compensation system used in an organization by changing some employees from an hourly pay system to a piece-rate system (where employees are paid based on how much they produce). Many experiments do not "change" an existing condition but instead create a variety of conditions. To do this a researcher might hire new workers, open a new plant, and put some workers on an hourly pay system but others on a piece-rate pay system. Both of these approaches are said to "manipulate" the variable of interest (pay system). Both are designed to study the effect of a piece-rate versus an hourly pay system. The difference between these two approaches may appear subtle but often the process of changing can have an effect above and beyond the effect of the difference in the two conditions. In short, "*changing* from an hourly to a piece-rate pay system" could produce different effects than those of "beginning to work on a piece-rate system" as compared to "beginning work on an hourly basis."

Control of Variables. In all experimental studies, attempts are made to control (i.e., prevent from changing) other variables which might influence the behaviors and attitudes of interest. Thus, if an experiment manipulated the type of pay system to examine the subsequent effect on performance, the researcher would need to control other factors which might also influence performance. This is done to eliminate other possible explanations of any changes in performance which occur after the manipulation of the pay system. If new machinery was provided for workers on the piece-rate system but not for those on the hourly system, subsequent changes in performance could be due to either the pay system, the new machinery, or both. It would be impossible to separate the effects of the pay system and the machinery. To deal with this type of problem, when an experimental study is designed the researcher attempts to anticipate and control all other factors which might influence the behaviors and attitudes which the experimental manipulation are expected to influence.

Comparison Groups. All experimental studies use comparison groups (often referred to as control groups). A comparison group is studied by the researcher (i.e., relevant behaviors and attitudes are measured) but not manipulated. Thus, the comparison group addresses the question "What would have happened to the behaviors and attitudes of a group of people for whom the variable of interest was not manipulated?" This is very important for two reasons. The passage of time which occurred during the experimental study might have led to changes in behaviors and attitudes even if the experimental variable had not been manipulated. Consider a study designed to study the effects of vitamins on the growth rate of children. To conduct this study, the researcher has 100 5-year-old children take a vitamin tablet every morning. The researcher then measures changes in height and weight over the subsequent two-year period and finds that both height and weight increase. Was this effect due to the taking of vitamins? This cannot be known unless there is a comparison group of similar children who do not take the vitamins. If the comparison group shows a 10 percent increase in height and the group which took vitamins shows a 15 percent increase, it can be concluded that the use of daily vitamins led to a greater increase in height than would have occurred otherwise (assuming all other variables have been controlled and that the two groups of children really were similar except for the fact that one group took a vitamin each day and the other group did not).

A second important reason for using comparison groups comes into play if it is not possible to control all other variables which might influence the behaviors and attitudes of interest. Try as you might, there are almost always important changes that occur which you were either not able to anticipate or, despite anticipating them, you were not able to control. Consider a study in which a researcher wishes to determine the effect that changing to a piece-rate system has on turnover. During the course of the study, the economy takes a downturn, unemployment rises, and jobs become scarce. The researcher observes that turnover dropped from 30 percent per year to 20 percent per year after the introduction of the piece-rate pay system. Was this due to the pay system change or the unavailability of alternative jobs due to change in the economy? Even though the researcher anticipated the possibility of a downturn in the economy, it was not possible for the researcher to prevent the economy from changing. A comparison group which stayed on an hourly pay system could have been used to determine what would have happened to turnover for a similar group of employees who were not placed on the piece-rate system. If the comparison group showed a decrease in turnover from 30 percent to 10 percent during the course of the study, the researcher could observe that turnover dropped for employees who were placed on a piece rate system but that turnover would have been expected to drop even more if the employees had been kept on an hourly pay system. Thus, the effect of the piece-rate system is negative, not positive as was first believed.

Of all of the methods for obtaining knowledge, the experimental approach allows the strongest cause→effect inferences (i.e., internal validity). The reason for this is that the experimental method is able to remove most alternative reasonable explanations for the results of a study. This is accomplished through the manipulation of the variable(s) of interest, the control of extraneous variables, and the use of comparison groups. A well-designed experiment will capitalize on these strengths of the experimental method.

Four general types of experimental studies are examined here (*laboratory, simulation, planned field,* and *natural field*). To varying degrees, each of these types of experiments take advantage of the strengths discussed above.

One last point remains before examining the four types of experiments. In a true experiment, participants are randomly assigned to be in treatment or comparison groups to assure that there are not systematic differences in the types of people in each group (which could bias the results). Sometimes it is not possible to randomly assign participants to groups. This is often the case where a department of workers is assigned to be a comparison or treatment group rather than breaking up departments and randomly assigning individuals to groups. When this is done, the researcher compares the characteristics of the people involved to see if differences exist. This is often a satisfactory approach. It does, however, run the risk of decreasing internal validity since subtle differences in the people involved could be influencing the results. Thus, this type of study is called *quasi-experimental.* Note that although internal validity may be slightly lower in a quasi-experiment, external validity is often higher since those situations we wish to generalize to would seldom involve the random assignment of participants to groups (a company changing to a piece-rate pay system would probably be making this change with departments kept intact).

Laboratory Experiments

Laboratory experiments are conducted by a researcher in a situation created by the researcher specifically for the purpose of conducting the study. Furthermore, participants typically know that they are participating in an experiment and that the situation was created for this purpose. In a laboratory experiment, the researcher assigns participants to treatment and comparison groups, manipulates the variable(s) of interest, and studies the subsequent behaviors and attitudes.

Laboratory Experiment Strengths. The primary strengths of the laboratory experiment all contribute to internal validity (i.e., the ability to conclude that there is a cause→effect relationship). These potential advantages include the following:

1. Random assignment of participants to groups makes it possible to rule out extraneous effects due to characteristics of participants.
2. The tight control over the manipulation of the variable(s) of interest makes it possible to describe the *specific* conditions under which the observed effects occurred.
3. The tight control over extraneous variables makes it possible to rule out most alternative explanations for the observed effects.

Laboratory Experiment Limitations. There are three major limitations to laboratory experiments. As you will see, they concern very different issues:

1. Because of the very highly controlled, almost "sterile" conditions under which laboratory experiments are conducted, external validity is limited. Even when it is possible to say "This manipulation led to this effect," it must also be said that the effect occurred "in a highly artificial environment." It is therefore difficult to generalize the findings to real ongoing situations.

2. Laboratory experiments often have a tendency to cause participants to react to the fact that they are the subject of an experiment. This can produce a reaction to the "demand" characteristics of the experiment and cause participants to behave the way they think the experimenter wants them to behave. Or, participants might react in defiance by behaving differently than they believe the experimenter desires. These reactions can be reduced by masking the purpose of the experiment from the participants, but guesses will still be made about the purpose and any reaction to these guesses distorts the study's results. Reactions of this type threaten the internal validity of the study since the reactions are due not only to the manipulation but also to reactions to the experimental process itself.

3. The ethics of the experimenter should place major limitations on the design and conduct of experiments. For ethical reasons, many important organizational issues cannot be studied in the laboratory without violating the rights of participants. One example should suffice. A major concern to organizations is the effect of work demands on the stress levels of employees and the subsequent effects of this stress. The effects of varying levels of work demands on stress could be easily studied in a laboratory experiment by creating conditions which range from very low levels of demand to extremely high levels. It would be unethical, however, to subject participants to such high demands that potentially harmful stress levels would be produced. Thus, some much needed knowledge about the cause→effect relationship between work demands and stress cannot be obtained for ethical reasons (or can you justify causing negative effects for a few people for the potential of helping many?).

The following presents parts of a laboratory experiment conducted by Howard Garland of the University of Texas at Arlington.[6] One of the purposes of this study was to determine the impact of differences in goal difficulty.

A Study of Goal Difficulty and Task Performance

Eighty-six students from a course on human behavior in business at the University of Texas at Arlington were brought into an experimental laboratory, performed a "creativity test" (look at this adjective and give as many objects as possible that could be described by the adjective in one minute), and had the number of objects they identified counted as a measure of creativity performance. Subjects were then randomly assigned to one of three treatment groups. The difficulty of an assigned goal for future repetitions of the "creativity test" was manipulated by the experimenter by randomly assigning the participants to one of three goal-difficulty treatment conditions (easy, medium, and hard). The experimenter's objective was to determine if goal difficulty level influenced subsequent performance levels. After being assigned an easy, medium, or difficult goal by the experimenter, the participants repeated the "creativity test" 15 times and performance was measured each time (i.e., the number of objects successfully identified). Exhibit A–2 shows the results of this laboratory experiment. As can be seen, performance decreased for participants given an easy goal, increased moderately for participants with medium difficulty goals, and increased substantially for participants with hard goals.

In this well-designed and well-executed study, the researcher successfully supported his hypothesis concerning the effects of goal difficulty on performance level. Specifically, he showed that changing from no specified goal to difficult goals led to subsequently greater performance than when change was made from no specified goal to easy or medium difficulty goals. Note two limitations to this experiment. The first limitation is due to the fact that the experimenter chose to not use a comparison group for which no change in goal condition occurred (i.e., in which participants continued to work with no specified goal). Thus, the following question cannot be answered: "What would have happened to performance over time with no specified goal?" The second limitation to this laboratory experiment is a characteristic limitation of laboratory experiments. Specifically, the external validity of the results of this study are limited. We cannot know if the effects of goal difficulty obtained for a "creativity test" with a group of college students would also occur for a group of workers engaged in a realistic job task. We can state, however, that for the conditions under which this study was conducted, goal difficulty had a powerful effect on performance and that there are no apparent alternative explanations of the findings

Exhibit A–2 Laboratory Experiment Results: Goal Difficulty and Performance

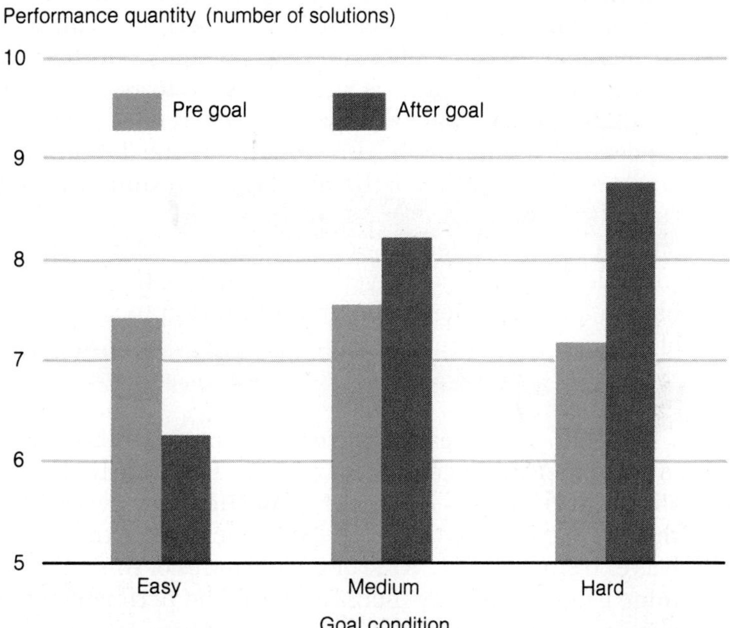

Source: Derived from H. Garland, Goal levels and task performance: A compelling replication of some compelling results, *Journal of Applied Psychology, 67,* 245–248, copyright 1982 by the American Psychological Association. Adapted by permission of the publisher and author.

(except that we don't know what would have happened if participants had continued to work without a specified goal).

Simulation Experiments

As was the case for laboratory experiments, simulation experiments are conducted by a researcher in a situation created specifically for the purpose of conducting the study. The simulation experiment, however, attempts to make the situation somewhat real (i.e., an attempt is made to *simulate* a real organizational setting). Depending on the specific design of the simulation experiment, the "realness" can range from participants feeling that they are in a realistic experiment (which presumably leads to more realistic behaviors and attitudes) to participants actually believing that they are involved in a real organization and not knowing that they are participating in an experiment. The simulation of a real organizational setting is intended to increase external validity beyond that which is possible in a typical laboratory experiment. Thus, the simulation experiment has the same strengths as the laboratory experiment plus the added advantage of increased external validity (which was the major limitation of the laboratory experiment).

Reaction to the idea of being in an experiment can occur for simulations as well as for laboratory experiments but this usually occurs to a lesser degree (and is very unlikely to occur at all when the simulation is so "real" that participants do not know they are in an experiment). One of the limitations of the laboratory approach, however, is magnified in the simulation. In simulations, ethical considerations become even more important as participants are not only being subjected to possible adverse effects but they are, to some degree, being deceived into believing that they are not taking part in an experiment. The final limitation to the simulation is one of resources. It typically requires more time, effort, and money to create and conduct a lifelike simulation as compared to a laboratory experiment.

The following presents parts of an unusually sophisticated simulation experiment conducted by Kim Boal (currently at Utah State University). In this experiment, participants were not aware that they were participating in an experiment since the situation created was extremely "real." One of the purposes of this study was to determine if providing pay increases based on performance would cause people to feel "controlled." A second purpose was to determine if redesigning a job produced greater satisfaction with the job. Due to the complexity of this study, not all of the questions addressed by the study are discussed. Because the results were analyzed with very sophisticated statistical procedures, these will not be presented in detail (the report of the results was over 100 pages long).

A Study of Compensation and Job Design

A temporary employment agency was used to advertise for "part-time help" to work on a limited-term basis. The researcher arranged for the employment agency to interview, hire, and pay about 100 "employees" hired in this fashion. The "employees" were told to report to the City Assessor's Office to do clerical work. The researcher arranged with the City Assessor for work space and for a real-looking task using documents from the Assessor's office. The participants were not aware that they were involved in an experiment. The complexity of the job was manipulated by the experimenter by creating two levels of complexity with random assignment to one of these conditions. After working for a period of time, employees were given a pay raise which was either "because of good performance" or "because of the cost of living." Thus, the researcher manipulated the type of pay raise provided. The experimenter measured the degree to which participants felt they were being con-

(continued)

trolled and measured job satisfaction before and after the changes were made. Comparison of the control group to the performance-based and cost-of-living groups allowed an examination of the effects of the two types of pay raises on experienced control (by examining control levels before and after the pay raises were received). Comparison of the simple and complex job groups allowed examination of the effects of the complexity of the job on satisfaction.

This simulation experiment permitted an evaluation of each of the researcher's hypotheses supporting the expectation that pay raises contingent on performance cause people to feel "controlled" and that complex jobs cause people to feel more satisfied with their work. Note that this was a very expensive study to address an issue which could have been explored much more efficiently through a laboratory study. However, due to the "realness" of the situation in which the experiment occurred, the external validity was much greater than would have been possible with a laboratory study. Note that, although external validity was relatively high, there are still limits to the generalizability of the results. The "employees" were temporary workers, the work was clerical, etc. Remember that it is most appropriate to generalize to similar groups of people, on similar jobs, in similar organizations, etc.

Planned Field Experiments

The primary distinction between field experiments and other experiments is that field experiments are conducted in *real* ongoing organizations (i.e., in the field), not in situations created specifically for the purpose of conducting the study. Conducting experimental research in real organizations creates some advantages, some limitations, and typically, many headaches. Planned field experiments have the potential for all of the strengths of any experiment. External validity increases because the experiments are done in the "real world" as opposed to an artificially created world (caution is still merited, however, as results should only be generalized to other organizations to the degree that they represent somewhat similar situations). The gain in external validity obtained with the planned field experiment is usually not realized without a very high price. Most do not allow for the random assignment of participants to treatment or comparison groups. Thus, most "experiments" done in the field are actually quasi-experiments and are not fully able to avoid possible effects which might be caused by differences in the characteristics of participants in the treatment and comparison groups. These experiments also typically have substantially less control over extraneous factors which might also influence the behaviors and attitudes of interest. This lack of control reduces the internal validity of the findings. Planned field experiments are rare (few organizations are willing to approve them, devote the necessary resources, and bear with the disruptions associated with an experiment).

Planned field experiments risk participant reaction particularly when the purpose of the experiment is obvious. In these experiments, participants might alter their behavior not only in reaction to what they think the experimenter expects but also to be consistent with their own best interests. Since the results of the experiments often influence future organizational practices, participants may attempt to generate a particular pattern of results supporting their own desires. Finally, ethical considerations are again important. Often an organizational member has little choice but to participate in an experiment if s/he wishes to continue as a member of the organization. This raises the question of whether it is acceptable to coerce participation in the experiment. Furthermore, it is necessary to design experimental treatments so that participants are not treated equally. (Would it be fair for your professor to conduct an experimental investigation of the effects of a specific review for exams by holding a specific review for half of the students in your class but not for the other half and then grade all students using the same curve for the exam?)

The following presents a planned field experiment conducted by the author of this book in conjunction with Jon L. Pierce of the University of Minnesota in Duluth. One purpose of this study was to document the positive and negative effects of the introduction of a flex-time work schedule (a schedule whereby each worker has some discretion in deciding what hours to work each day).*

A Study of Flex-Time and Worker Responses

Approximately 120 employees from a Midwestern utility firm participated in this experiment. All were working a traditional 5-day, 40-hour fixed-time schedule prior to the study. It was predicted that introduction of a flex-time schedule would favorably influence worker attitudes. Measures were obtained using a questionnaire with a variety of attitudes toward the work schedule (satisfaction with the schedule, satisfaction with family and friend interactions, work coordination under the schedule, customer service under the schedule, etc.). Half of the participants were then assigned to a treatment group which was placed on a flex-time schedule while the other half served as a comparison group (staying on the old work schedule). The attitudes of both groups of em-

(continued)

*I would like to thank the Department of Labor, The National Council on Employment Policy, and the University of Wisconsin Graduate School for supporting portions of this research.

ployees were measured again five weeks, three months, and six months after the introduction of the new work schedule. Exhibit A–3 shows some of the results of this planned field experiment. As can be seen, few changes occurred for the comparison group but major favorable effects were found for the treatment group.

The researchers supported their general hypothesis concerning the effects of a flex-time work schedule. The limitations of this study must be considered, however. First, the study was quasi-experimental in nature (subjects were assigned to treatment or comparison groups by departments rather than randomly by individual). If there were critical differences between the workers in the treatment and comparison groups on personal characteristics, these could at least in part explain the results. Secondly, because the study was done in a real organization there were a lot of factors which could not be totally controlled and which could have influenced the results. Presumably, these uncontrolled factors would have equally

Exhibit A–3 Planned Field Experiment: The Effects of Flex-Time on Satisfaction with Schedule

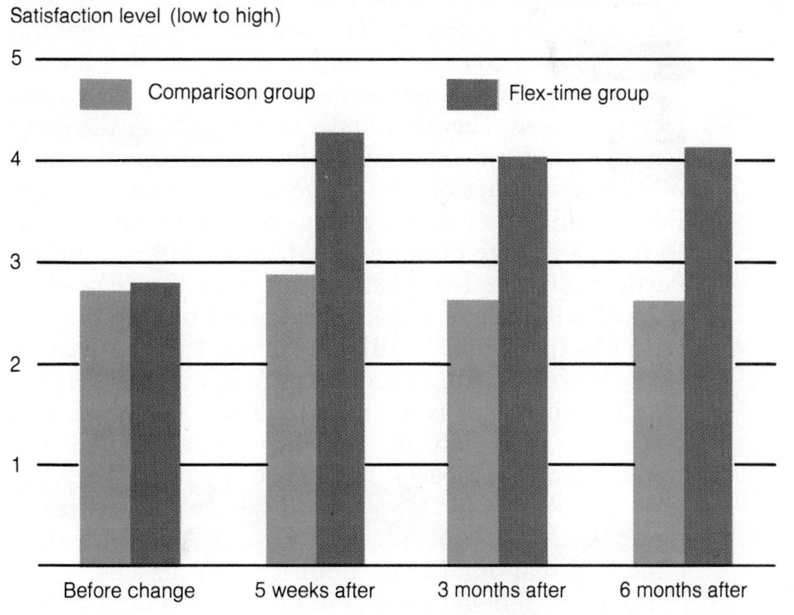

Based on data from a planned field experiment conducted by Jon L. Pierce (currently at the University of Minnesota in Duluth) and the author.

influenced the treatment and comparison groups, but you can never be certain. Finally, the workers had a vested interest in the results. Most wanted to be kept on flex-time on a permanent basis. This could have led to an intentional or unintentional distortion of the information provided by the participants. Steps were taken to prevent this from happening, but the danger is still present. Also note that, although external validity was relatively high for this study, the results are most representative only for similar situations. Thus, it would be safer to generalize to another group of utility workers with similar demographic characteristics than to a group of demographically different employees in a different industry.

Natural Field Experiments

Natural field experiments differ from planned field experiments primarily on the basis of the reason for the manipulation of the variable of interest. In the natural field experiment, the manipulation is not planned by the experimenter for the purpose of research. Rather, the manipulation involves an organizational change which would have been made by the organization whether or not the researcher was going to study the effects of the change. The researcher simply learns of the change and studies the effects which the change produces.

The natural field experiment has some advantages over the planned field experiment. The first advantage is that the cost is relatively low since the change will be made whether it is studied or not. The primary costs involve those associated with assessing the effects produced. There is usually much less resistance from organizations to a natural experiment than to a planned experiment which introduces disruption into the organization for the purpose of study. Despite this, some organizations will resist formal study of the effects of a change because they fear documentation of the results. Participants are less likely to react to the idea of being experimented with since no changes were introduced purely for research purposes (participants still might react to the idea of the change itself, however). Ethics are not as major a consideration for the researcher since s/he is not manipulating participants (although the researcher must consider whether it is ethical to study organizational members, especially if it is done without their consent and/or knowledge). Finally, external validity is typically as high or often higher than for planned field experiments since the study is not only done in a real organization but for real reasons.

The natural field experiment has the potential to suffer from several weaknesses beyond those of the planned field experiment. In natural experiments, the researcher has no control over the assignment of participants to treatment or comparison groups. Consequently, assignment is often nonrepresentative (organizations have a tendency, for example, to place more cooperative employees in treatment groups and "troublemakers" in comparison groups). This can reduce the internal validity of the study. In natural experiments, the researcher has almost no control over extraneous factors which might influence the results. If too many exist, the internal validity is reduced so much that the study is not worth doing. It should be emphasized that the potential weaknesses of the natural experiment compared to those of the planned experiment are only *potential* weaknesses. The researcher could be fortunate and find a natural experiment in which subjects are randomly assigned to treatment and comparison groups and in which most external factors are held constant other than the variable of interest.

The following example describes part of a natural field experiment conducted at a large multiline insurance company. The purpose of the study was to examine the effects of the introduction of a computerized microfiche system for record-keeping. It was hoped that the new system would increase efficiency without reducing job satisfaction.*

A Study of Technological Change

A total of 118 clerical and semitechnical employees from a large insurance company participated in this experiment. The company was planning the introduction of a computerized microfiche record-keeping system to replace the old paper-and-pencil system. One of the researchers learned of this planned change and obtained permission to study the effects of the change. A treatment group of 75 employees was provided with the new system while a comparison group of 43 continued to work using the old procedures. The researchers obtained measures of work efficiency and job satisfaction from all 118 employees one week before the introduction of the new system and again three months after the change. The results indicated that employees who obtained the new system became more efficient and effective while maintaining their job satisfaction levels. Employees in the comparison group showed no change in effectiveness, efficiency, or satisfaction.

Although the researchers appear to have supported at least some of their expectations, several limitations should be considered. This study was quasi-experimental in nature since employees were assigned to be in the treatment or comparison group based on office location rather than on an individual random basis. Thus, all em-

* This study was conducted by John E. Newman (with State Farm Mutual Automobile Insurance Co. at the time of the study), Richard S. Blackburn (now at the University of North Carolina at Chapel Hill), and Randall B. Dunham.

ployees from the office in one city experienced the change while all employees from the office in another city served as the comparison group. This allows the possibility that the people in the two groups may have been different, thus influencing the results. It is possible, for example, that the two groups of employees had different educational levels, thus leading to a greater or lesser acceptance of the computer-based change on the part of one group. Furthermore, although the jobs at the two offices were basically the same and policies and practices were basically the same, there may have been other factors which were different. Supervision might have been different, the communities might have varied, etc. In short, there were many factors which might have influenced the results in addition to the introduction of the new equipment.

SUMMARY

The study of existing literature in the organizational behavior area gives you "free use" of past work and a big head start in understanding and managing behaviors and attitudes in organizations. The discussion in this appendix of the various sources of knowledge and their strengths and limitations was designed to help you become aware of the various sources of information and to prepare you for evaluating the quality and usefulness of this information. It should be very obvious by now that there is no one best way to obtain knowledge about behaviors and attitudes. Rather, there are many possible approaches, each with particular strengths and weaknesses. The best strategy available to you for the assimilation of information is to utilize more than one approach for the collection of knowledge, carefully evaluate each piece of information obtained, and capitalize on the strengths of one method to overcome the weaknesses of another. Creative use of a variety of sources of information can produce a synergistic effect (the whole is greater than the sum of the parts) on the total knowledge you possess.

NOTES

1. **Dunham, R. B., & Smith, F. J.** (1979). *Organizational surveys*. Glenview, IL: Scott, Foresman, pp. 11–13.
2. For a complete discussion of the functions of organizational surveys, see **Dunham & Smith,** 1979.
3. **Smith, H. W.** (1975). *Strategies of social research: The methodological imagination*, Englewood Cliffs, NJ: Prentice-Hall, p. 170.
4. For a complete description of the JDI, see **Smith, P. C., Kendall, L. M., & Hulin, C. L.** (1969). *The measurement of satisfaction in work and retirement*. Chicago: Rand McNally.
5. **Hackman, J. R., & Oldham, G.** (1976). Motivation through the design of work: Test of a theory. *Organizational Behavior and Human Performance, 16*, 250-279.
6. **Garland, H.** (1982). Goal levels and task performance: A compelling replication of some compelling results. *Journal of Applied Psychology, 67*, 245–248.

Author Index

A

Adams, J. S., 165–172, 196
Adorno, T. W., 237
Aiken, M., 281
Aldag, R. J., 422–423
Alderfer, C. P., 110–112, 120, 125–126
Anderson, C., 237
Andrews, I. R., 196
Armstrong, S., 309, 329
Arnold, H. J., 66 n, 67
Atkinson, J., 113, 125

B

Bacharach, S. B., 281, 332 n, 336, 337
Back, K. W., 329
Baetz, M. L., 385–387
Baldes, J. J., 197
Balu, B., 454
Bammer, K., 455
Bass, B. M., 370 n
Beehr, T. A., 454–456
Beer, M., 95
Berthold, H., Jr., 154–155, 161
Bhagat, R. S., 73, 94
Birch, D., 126
Blackburn, R. S., 61, 407, 409, 423, 521 n
Blake, R. R., 372–373, 386–387
Blood, M. R., 422
Boal, K., 526
Bortner, R. W., 227
Bowers, D. G., 95
Brand, R., 456
Braunstrin, D. N., 126
Brayfield, A. H., 93–94
Brett, J., 69, 73, 94
Bridell, L. G., 125
Brief, A. P., 227, 422–423, 454
Broadhurst, P. L., 455
Brown, C. A., 93
Brummet, R., 95
Bruner, J. S., 265
Burdick, J., 309, 329
Burnam, M. A., 238
Burns, T., 407–408, 423
Burroughs, W. A., 143, 148–150, 160
Burtt, H. E., 94
Bryan, J. F., 191
Byars, L., 283, 296

C

Cabrero, A., 180, 198
Campbell, D. T., 24 n
Caplan, R. D., 455
Caplow, T., 357
Cartwright, D., 333
Cashman, J. F., 385
Chadwick-Jones, J. K., 93
Chemers, M. M., 366–37, 386
Chertkoff, J., 357
Christie, R., 222, 235, 237
Clark, R. A., 125
Coburn, D., 455
Cook, T. D., 24 n
Coon, D., 251
Cooper, C. L., 431
Costello, T. W., 266
Covaleski, M. A., 193, 198
Cox, T., 454
Crockett, W. H., 93–94
Cummings, L. L., 209, 217, 387, 518 n

D

Dalkey, N., 325
Dalton, M., 302, 328
Davis, K., 296–297
Davis, W. N., 126
Dawis, R. V., 44, 60
DeCharms, R. C., 126
Deci, E., 146, 160
Delbecq, A., 325
DeLorian, J. Z., 491 n
Dembo, T., 197
DeSwann, A., 357
Deutsch, M., 358
Dickinson, A. M., 151, 160–161
Dipboye, R., 255–256, 265

Dirsmith, M. W., 193, 198
Dodd, W. E., 296
Dodson, J. D., 455
Dorfman, P. W., 387
Dossett, D. L., 151, 160
Driscoll, J. W., 95
Drucker, P., 177, 192, 197–198
Dubin, R., 12, 15
Duncan, P. K., 160
Dunham, R. B., 43, 60–61, 95, 197, 235, 387, 407, 409, 432, 488, 513, 518 n, 528–529, 531 n, 533
Dunnette, M. D., 24 n, 94
Dyer, L., 95, 238

E

Ekman, P., 296
England, G. W., 44 n, 60
Evans, M., 374
Ewen, R. B., 73, 94

F

Feeney, E. J., 150–151, 160
Feldman, D. C., 66 n, 67
Festinger, L., 197
Fiedler, F. E., 364–370, 386
Filley, A. C., 357, 387
Finn, R. H., 173, 197
Flamholtz, E., 95
Fleishman, E., 94, 230–231, 238, 370
Folkman, S., 456
Forster, E. M., 60
Fossum, J. A., 238
Fowler, P. C., 198
Frankenhaeuser, M., 454
French, J. R. P., Jr., 332–333, 336, 337, 455
French, W. L., 197
Frenkel-Brunswich, E., 237
Friedman, A., 196
Friedman, M., 456
Friesen, W. V., 296

G

Galbraith, J., 217
Gamson, W. A., 357
Garland, H., 183–184, 198, 524–525, 533
Geis, F. L., 222, 235, 237
Gentili, S., 454
Getman, J. G., 94
Gilbreth, F. B., 395, 422
Glass, D. C., 238
Goldberg, S. B., 94
Golembiewski, R. T., 422
Goodman, P. S., 196
Graen, G., 362, 385
Green, C. N., 94
Greenberger, D. W., 518 n, 519
Greiner, L., 6, 15
Griffeth, R. W., 93
Griffin, R. W., 405, 410, 413, 422–423
Grunes, W. F., 265
Guetzkow, H., 295–296
Guilford, J. P., 229–230

H

Hackman, J. R., 95, 311, 329, 400–404, 406–407, 415, 416 n, 422–424, 516, 533
Hagarty, W. H., 494
Haire, M., 252, 265
Hall, C. S., 115
Hamilton, V., 454
Hamner, E. P., 160
Hamner, W. C., 75, 95, 160
Hamstra, B. W., 260
Hand, H. H., 93
Harper, R. G., 296
Harris, E. F., 94
Harrison, R., 296
Hawkins, B. L., 279–281, 296
Hegarty, H., 493, 496
Heider, F., 258, 265
Hellriegel, D., 237, 280
Hemphill, J., 370
Heneman, H. G., III, 66 n, 67–68, 93, 238
Herman, J. B., 43, 60, 94
Herzberg, F., 93–94, 117–123, 126, 178, 397–400, 422
Hodgson, J. S., 192, 198
Hogan, J. C., 238
Hohenfeld, J. A., 174–175
Hollis, J., 238
Holmes, T. H., 437
Homans, G. C., 164–165, 167, 197
Hosek, J., 49 n, 61
House, R. J., 122, 126, 304, 374, 385–387, 434, 455
Houston, B. K., 238
Howell, J. P., 387
Hulin, C. L., 45, 60, 65, 93, 422, 533
Hunt, J. G., 387

I

Ikard, F. F., 455
Inkson, J. H. K., 73, 94
Ivancevich, J. M., 183, 198, 429, 433, 435, 441 n, 454–456

J

Jackson, S. E., 185–186, 198
Jacobs, T. O., 385
Jacobsen, L., 265
Jacobsen, P. R., 196
Jago, A., 361–364, 376, 385–387
Janis, I. L., 319–322, 329, 455–456
Janson, R., 415, 424
Jenkins, C., 237, 456
Jermier, J. M., 381, 387
Jewell, L., 313–315, 329
Johnson, S., 309, 329
Jones, D. L., 155, 160
Jones, E. E., 266

K

Kahn, R. L., 456
Kalin, R., 126
Kanungo, R. N., 61
Kaplan, R. E., 125
Karmel, B. M., 224
Kejner, M., 61
Keller, R. T., 403
Kelly, H. H., 266
Kendall, L. M., 45, 60, 93, 533
Kerr, S., 147, 160, 381, 387
Kessler, J. J., 196
Kilbridge, M. D., 422
Killeen, E., 7
Kilmann, R. H., 352
King, N., 126
Kirchner, W. K., 94
Knowlton, W., Jr., 257–258, 266
Kochan, T. A., 95
Komorita, S. S., 357

Kondrasuk, J. N., 193, 198
Korman, A. K., 455
Kotter, J. P., 470 n, 473, 475, 481–483, 488
Kroes, B. K., 455
Kruglanski, A. W., 357
Kunin, T., 43, 60

L

Larson, L. L., 387
Larson, W. H., 7
Latham, G. P., 151–152, 160, 177, 179, 184, 187–188, 191, 197
Lawler, E. E., III, 78–79, 81–90, 95, 125, 201, 211, 216, 332 n, 357, 400, 402, 422–423
Lawrence, E. C., 198
Lawrence, P. R., 398–400, 422, 488
Lawton, B., 477
Lazarus, R. S., 456
Leavitt, H. J., 296
Lee, S. M., 173, 197
Levine, E. L., 423
Levinson, D. J., 237
Lewin, K., 177, 197, 480, 488
Likert, R., 93, 95, 386
Lindskold, S., 357
Lindzey, G., 115
Lipsky, D. B., 95
Listzman, S. I., 304, 434
Lloyd, E. E., 160
Locke, E. A., 61, 177–182, 183–184, 187–188, 191, 197–198, 213, 217, 386, 394, 407
Lodahl, T. M., 61
Lofquist, L. H., 44, 60
Lopez, E. M., 94
Lord, R. G., 174, 197, 253–254, 265
Lorsch, J. W., 488
Lott, A. J., 329
Lott, B. E., 329
Lowell, E. L., 125
Luther, D., 186, 189–191, 198
Lyons, T. F., 455–456

M

McClelland, D., 113–117, 125–126
McConkie, M. L., 198
McGrath, J. E., 455
McGregor, D., 104–105, 125, 177, 197
Machiavelli, N., 225, 237
Machungway, P. D., 126
McMahon, J. T., 183, 198
McNeill, J., 432–434, 454
Macy, B. A., 80, 95
Mahar, L., 386
March, J. G., 66 n, 67, 93, 296
Margolis, B. K., 455
Marshall, J., 431
Maslow, A., 103–112, 125, 178
Mastenbrook, M., 309, 329
Matarzzo, J. D., 296
Matteson, M. T., 429, 433, 435, 441 n, 454–456
Mausner, B., 93, 126
Meglino, B. M., 93, 455
Mehrabian, A., 296
Michaels, C. E., 68, 93
Michela, J. L., 266
Middlemist, R. D., 186, 189–191, 198
Migliore, R. H., 296
Miles, R. E., 488
Miner, J. B., 12, 15, 172, 179, 196–197, 210, 217
Mintzberg, H., 295
Mirvis, P. H., 78–79, 81–90, 95
Mitchell, T., 237, 257–258, 266, 276, 295, 387, 423
Mobley, W. H., 66 n, 93
Moon, T. H., 237
Moran, G., 329
Mouton, J. S., 372–373, 386–387
Mowen, J. C., 186, 189–191, 198
Muchinsky, P. M., 93
Mueller, R. A. H., 296
Murnighan, J. K., 323–324, 329
Murray, H., 112–117, 125
Myrsten, A. L., 454

N

Nathan, B., 253–254, 265
Newberry, B. H., 455
Newman, J. E., 454–456, 531 n
Nicholson, N., 93
Nisbett, R. E., 266
Nordheden, B., 454

O

O'Brien, R. M., 151, 160–161
Odiorne, G. S., 198
Oldham, G. R., 401, 404, 406, 415, 422–424, 516, 533
Osborn, R. N., 387

P

Pavlov, I., 130, 160
Payne, R., 431
Pennebaker, J. W., 238
Pesei, M. L., 296
Peterson, R. O., 93
Petit, T. A., 496
Pfeffer, J., 357, 424
Pierce, J. L., 387, 407, 409, 423, 528–529
Pinder, C., 100
Piore, M., 95
Pitman, N. L., 456
Pitman, T. S., 456
Pittner, M. S., 238
Pondy, L., 357
Porter, L. W., 93, 95, 201, 211, 216, 407, 423
Post, B., 454
Postman, L., 265
Preston, P., 279–281, 296
Price, J., 93
Purdy, K., 415, 424
Pyle, W., 95

Q

Quinn, R. P., 455, 456

R

Rabinowitz, S., 61
Rafalko, E. A., 422
Rahe, R. H., 437
Raphelson, A. C., 126
Raven, B., 332–333, 357
Read, W. H., 296
Reichers, A. E., 423
Reitz, H. J., 302, 313–315, 329
Rhodes, S. R., 71–72, 93–94
Riggs, C. J., 349, 351, 357
Riskind, J. H., 454
Rizzo, J. R., 304, 434, 455
Robbins, S. P., 357

Rosenbaum, W. B., 196
Rosenman, R., 456
Rosenthal, R., 254–255, 265, 456
Rotter, J. B., 222–223, 237
Rousseau, D. M., 409, 423
Ruble, T., 347, 358
Rue, L. W., 283, 296
Ryan, T., 177, 197

S

Saari, L. M., 151–152, 160, 179, 197
Salancik, G., 424
Saleh, S. D., 94 n, 61
Sanford, R. N., 237
Schaefer, C., 456
Schienle, J., 7
Schlesinger, L. A., 470 n, 473, 475, 481–483, 488
Schmidt, E. E., 386
Schmidt, W. H., 357
Schmitt, N., 126
Schneider, B., 423
Schriescheim, C. A., 18, 75, 95
Schuler, R. S., 227, 454
Schwab, D. P., 66 n, 67–68, 93, 238
Schweiger, D. M., 386
Scott, W. G., 197, 276, 295, 495–496
Sears, P. S., 197
Seashore, S. E., 329
Selye, H., 454
Shaw, J. B., 454
Shaw, K. N., 179, 197
Shaw, M. E., 295, 312, 329
Simmel, G., 358
Simon, H. A., 66 n, 67, 93, 295–296
Simpson, R., 296
Sims, H. P., 403, 493–494, 496
Skinner, B. F., 133, 160
Skrzypek, G. J., 386
Slocum, J., 237, 280
Smith, F. J., 46, 48, 60–61, 69–70, 75, 94, 488, 513, 533
Smith, H. W., 510, 533
Smith, K. A., 125
Smith, P. C., 45, 60, 93, 533
Smyser, C., 237
Snavely, W., 432–434, 454
Snoek, J. D., 456
Snow, C. C., 488
Snyder, M. L., 238
Snyderman, B., 126
Spector, P. E., 68, 93
Staelin, J. R., 151, 160
Staines, G. L., 47, 61
Stalker, G. M., 407–408, 423
Steers, R. M., 71–72, 93–95, 126
Stephens, T. A., 143, 148–150, 160
Stogdill, R. M., 329, 370, 372, 385–386
Stone, E. F., 249, 265, 423
Strang, J. R., 183, 198
Straus, R., 456
Strauss, G., 95
Suttle, J. L., 95, 125
Sweeney, B., 329
Szilagyi, A. D., Jr., 109, 403

T

Tannenbaum, A. S., 340
Taylor, F. W., 177, 393–394, 422
Tedeschi, J. T., 357
Telly, C. S., 197
Thomas, K. W., 345–347, 352, 354, 357
Thompson, J. D., 423
Thorndike, E., 135, 160
Thurstone, L. L., 229–230, 238
Timio, M., 454
Tomkins, S., 455
Triandis, H. C., 73
Turner, A. N., 398–400, 422

U–V

Ullrich, R. A., 488

Van de Ven, A., 325
Van Sell, M., 227, 454
Varela, J., 13–14, 15
Vecchio, R. P., 152, 174, 197, 386
Veroff, J., 126
Vroom, V. H., 93, 96, 122, 126, 216–217, 377, 379, 387

W

Wahba, M. A., 125
Wallace, M. J., Jr., 109
Wanner, E., 126
Wanous, J. P., 125
Warburton, D. M., 454
Ware, J. E., 289
Waters, C. W., 126
Waters, L. K., 126
Weber, M., 357
Weed, S., 237
Weiss, D. J., 44, 60
Wheeler, H., 156, 160
Whitsett, D. A., 126
Wickesberg, A., 296
Wieland, G. F., 488
Wiener, Y., 196
Wiens, A. N., 296
Wigdor, L. A., 122, 126
Winslow, E. K., 126
Woodman, R. W., 280
Wright, J. P., 491 n
Wurm, M., 456

Y

Yerkes, R. M., 455
Yetton, P. W., 377, 379, 387
Yoder, D., 66 n
Yukl, G. A., 381

Z

Zajonc, R. B., 305, 329
Zalkind, S. S., 266
Zander, A., 312–315, 329
Zedeck, S., 185–186, 198
Zenisek, T. J., 496
Ziller, R. C., 328–329
Zwany, A. A., 125

Subject Index

A

Ability; *see also* Skills
  and attribution, 257–258
  concept of, 219, 221, 228, 236
  individual level of, and goal setting, 182–183, 186
  intellective, 228, 230–231, 236
  interindividual versus intraindividual, 231–232, 236
  and job design, 411–413
  management of, 232–234
  physical, 228–231, 236
  and stress reactions, 443–444
Absenteeism; *see also* Attendance
  avoidable/unavoidable, 51, 68–69
  and disillusion stage, 317
  and perceived equity, 170, 173
  and productivity, 51–53, 56
  reduction of, and organizational behavior modification, 148–149
  and satisfaction, 68–70, 81, 83–92, 514–515
  statistics on, 51–53
  and stress, 441
Acceptance stage, 318–319
Accommodating strategy, 348–349, 354
Accountability, 397
Achievement
  need for, 113–117, 172, 186, 445–446
  opportunity for, 397
Action initiators, 448, 453
Action strategies, 448, 453
Adrenocorticotrophic (ACTH), and stress, 428
Affective component of attitudes, 34–36, 59
Affective stress reactions, 438
Affiliation, need for, 113–114, 116–117
Alderfer's ERG theory, 110–112, 124
Alternate forms agreement reliability, 21–22, 29
Ambiguity, tolerance for, 445
American Society for Personnel Administration, 46
Assembly line work, and stress, 434
Assertiveness, 347–348, 356
Association
  and attitude formation, 37–39
  and classical conditioning, 130–132
Attendance; *see also* Absenteeism
  and affiliation need, 116
Attendance—*Cont.*
  concept of, 51–53, 59
  and job design, 410–412, 414–416
Attitudes; *see also* Job involvement; Job satisfaction; *and* Work involvement
  changing, 39, 59
  components of, 34–37
  defined, 34, 39
  experimental studies of, 519–521
  financial impact of, 77–91
  formation of, 37–39, 59
  job attributes influencing, 398–399
  and resistance to change, 474
  surveys of, 509–510
  union, 74–76
Attribution, 251, 257–259, 263
Audience effect, 305
Authoritarianism
  in discipline, 153
  in personality, 223, 236, 312, 474
Authority
  and leadership, 362
  and power, 331, 336
Autonomy
  and job design, 398–400, 402, 409
  need for, 114

Avoidance learning, 136, 145–146, 158
Avoiding strategy, 348–349, 354

B

Basic fitness test, 229
Behavior
and conflict, 345, 347–349
ethical/unethical, 491–495
experimental studies of, 519–521
and involvement, 47
job attributes influencing, 398–399
and job satisfaction, 63–64
leadership; *see* Leadership
major types of, 50–56
and stress, 441–442
surveys of, 509–510
Behavior modification; *see* Organizational behavior modification
Behavioral accounting
caution in using, 89–90
concept of, 78–79, 92
and national attitudes, 90–91
steps in, 79–89
Behavioral shaping, 137–139, 146, 148, 154, 158
Behavioral tendency component of attitudes, 34, 36–37, 59
Bilateral channels of communication, 286, 294
Bluffs, 334
Body language, 287–288
Bonus basis, 189–191
Brainstorming, 324, 327
Bureau of National Affairs, 51, 80
Business environment, and change, 469

C

Career stressors, 430–431, 434
Case studies
nonparticipant, 503–508
participant, 503, 508–509
Cause→effect relationship, 24–25, 27; *see also* Internal validity
Central life interest, and work/job involvement, 49–50
Chains, in communication, 278
Change
dealing with resistance to, 476–480, 487
forces to, 464–469, 487
overview of, 463–464
and perception, 246, 263
personal, 451
proactive, 413, 465, 467–468, 487
process of, 480, 487
reactive, 413, 465, 467–468, 487
resistance to, 470–475, 487
selecting strategy of, 416, 480–482
steps in coordinating, 416, 482–485
of stress reaction, 449–450
of stressor, 446, 448–449
Classical conditioning, 129–132, 158
Cliques, 300–302
Closed groups, 302–303, 327
Closure, 248–250, 263
Coalitions, 342, 356
Coercion, and resistance to change, 476, 479–480, 483
Coercive power, 334–337, 339–341, 356
Cognitive component of attitudes, 34–35, 59
Cognitive learning models, 100, 202
Collaborating strategy, 348–349, 353–354
Collective bargaining, 342
Com-con network, 278–279
Communication
channels of; *see* Communication channels
concept of, 273–274, 294
distortions in process of, 275, 281–283
effective management of, 290–292
functions of, 276
group, 308, 318
model of, 274–275
networks of, 278, 294
patterns of, 278–285
and power, 342
and resistance to change, 476–477, 483
Communication channels
appropriateness of, 287–288, 294
capacity of, 285, 294
concept of, 274, 294
downward, 278–283, 294
duplication of, 286, 294
evaluating and choosing, 291
horizontal, 278–279, 283–284, 294
human/mechanical, 284, 294
immediacy of, 286, 294
inadequate, 275
informal (grapevine), 288–290, 295
modifiability of, 285–286, 294
nonverbal, 287, 295
number of linkages in, 287, 294
one-way, 284–285, 294
two-way (bilateral), 284–286, 294
upward, 278–279, 283, 294
Comparison groups, 520–521, 527, 530–531
Competition
and goal setting, 191–192
as strategy, 348–349, 354
and unethical behavior, 493–495
Complex groups, 302, 327
Compromising strategy, 348–349, 354
Computers, 465
Conceptualization stage of conflict, 345–347
Conditioned stimulus/response, 130–132, 158
Conditioning; *see* Classical conditioning *and* Operant conditioning
Conflict
aftermath of, 345, 350, 356
causes of, 345
concept of, 331, 343, 356
general orientation to, 351–352
group, 303–304, 312–313, 315–316
intraperson, 303, 327
intrarole, 304, 327
positive effects of, 343–344, 350
process of, 345–350, 356

Conflict—*Cont.*
  resolution strategy for, 350–353, 356
  and stress, 436
Conscious information processing, 259–261, 263
Consequence, operant, 133, 158
Consideration, 370–373, 375–377, 384
Construct validity, 24–26, 29, 365, 499
Content theories, 99, 103
Contingency theory of Fiedler, 364–370, 384
Continuous reinforcement schedule, 139–142, 146, 152, 159
Contrast, and perception, 244–245, 247, 251, 263
Control
  as function of information, 276
  and power, 331
  of variables, 520
  worker, 397, 518–519
Cooperativeness, and conflict, 347, 352, 356
Co-optation, and resistance to change, 476, 478–479, 483
Corrective discipline, 153
Cost items, 80–81, 83
Critical incidents, 122, 199–200
Critical psychological states, 402–403, 405
Cross-sectional studies, 514–517

D

Decision making
  ethical/unethical, 493–495
  and management by objectives, 192
  and stress, 443
  Vroom and Yetton rational model of, 493–495
Decision tree, 378–380
Decoding, in communication, 274
Deficiency needs, 107
Delphi technique, 325, 328
Delusion stage, 317
Depression, and stress, 438–439, 444
Discipline systems, 155–156
Disillusion stage, 317–318
Distributive justice
  concept of, 164–165, 195
  ratio of, 167, 175–176
Dogmatism, 225, 236, 445, 474
Downward communication, 278–283, 294
Driving forces, 480

E

Economic environment, as source of change, 469
Education, and resistance to change, 476–477, 483
Effect, Law of, 135
Effort
  and attribution, 257–258
  goal-directed, 182–183, 195
  as organization-related behavior, 50, 54, 59
Ego and esteem needs, 105, 107, 109, 124, 307, 468
Emotional support, 477
Emotive function of information, 276
Encoding, in communication, 274–275, 292, 294
Equity theory; *see also* Perceived equity
  concept of, 99, 163, 187
  integrated with expectancy theory, 213
  outlined, 165–172
  research on, 172–176
ERG Theory, 110–112, 124
Esteem needs; *see* Ego and esteem needs
Ethics
  and behavior, 491–495
  of case studies, 508–509
  defined, 491
  of experimental studies, 523, 526, 528, 530
  of organizational behavior modification, 153–155
  and power, 342–343
Existence, Relatedness, and Growth (ERG) Theory, 110–112, 124
Existence needs, 110, 112, 124
Expectancy; *see* Perceptual readiness
Expectancy perceptions, 202–204, 216
Expectancy theory
  applications of, 214–215
  and attendance motivation, 412
  basic model of, 202–210
  concept of, 99, 201–202
  and coercion, 479
  expanded model of, 211–214
  and goal setting, 177–178
  and locus of control, 223
  research on, 210
Experimental studies
  characteristics of, 519–522
  laboratory, 522–527
  natural field, 530–532
  planned field, 527–530
  simulation, 525–527
Expert power, 338–339, 341, 356
External attributions, 257–259
External locus of control, 222–223, 445, 474, 495
External validity
  of case studies, 505
  concept of, 25, 27–29, 499
  of cross-sectional studies, 515
  of experimental studies, 522–523, 525–526, 530
  of longitudinal studies, 517
  of surveys, 511
Extinction, 138–143, 158
Extraorganizational stressors, 430–431, 437
Extrinsic outcomes, 145, 185–186, 191, 412

F

Faces technique, 43–44
Facilitative support, 477
Feedback
  and achievement need, 113
  and change process, 485
  in communication, 284, 286, 291–292
  and goal setting, 177, 183, 394
  and job design, 394, 397, 399–400, 402
  and stress, 446
Fiedler's contingency theory, 364–370, 384

Field independence, 249
Field surveys, 509–514
Figure-ground differentiation, 248–249, 263
Fixed interval reinforcement schedule, 141–142, 159
Fixed ratio reinforcement schedule, 141–142, 159
Flex-time, 528–530
Flowchart, for change management, 482
Force, in expectancy theory, 202, 208, 216
Formal groups, 300–301, 306, 327
Frequency of sensory stimuli, 245, 247, 263
Frustration, and conflict, 345–346
Frustration regression, 112
Functional groups, 301, 327

G

Generalizability; *see* External validity
Goal acceptance, 184–186, 188–189, 193, 195
Goal commitment, 184–186, 188–189, 193, 195, 213
Goal difficulty, 180, 189–191, 193, 195, 213, 524–525
Goal-directed effort, 182–184, 195
Goal specificity, 178–179, 181–182, 189, 193, 195
Goal theory; *see also* Management by objectives
  application of, 186–191
  basic model of, 178–182
  concept of, 99, 163–164, 171, 177–178
  expanded model of, 182–186
  importance of, 177–178
  integrated with expectancy theory, 213–214
  and scientific management, 394
Goals
  and conflict, 343, 345, 349–350
  group, 299, 300–301, 307–308
  in path-goal leadership theory, 374–377
Grapevine, 288–290, 295
Group shift, 492
Groups
  closed/open, 302–303, 327
  comparison, 520–521, 527, 530–531
  complex, 302, 327
  defined, 299, 327
  developmental stages of, 312–319
  formal/informal, 300–301, 306, 327
  formation and cohesion of, 306–310, 316–317, 327
  functional, 301, 327
  horizontal/vertical, 301–302, 327
  norms and standards of, 308–312, 316, 327
  presence of, and behavior, 304–306
  problem solving by, 323–326, 377–380
  project, 301, 327
  and resistance to change, 474
  roles in, 303, 327
  unethical behavior in, 492
Groupthink, 317, 319–322, 492
Growth Need Strength Scale, 401–402
Growth needs
  in needs theory, 107, 110, 112, 117
  strength of, 401, 402–405, 407–409, 411, 415

H

Halo effect, 251, 253–254, 259, 263
Heart disease, and stress, 227, 440–441, 445–446
Herzberg's motivation-hygiene theory, 117–124, 178, 397
Homeostasis, and change, 474
Horizontal communication, 278–279, 283–284, 294
Horizontal groups, 301–302, 327
Human channels of communication, 285, 294
Human resource accounting, 78, 92
Hygiene factors, 117–122,124

I

I_o, 166–167, 195
I_p, 166–167, 195
Incentives
  in goal setting, 189–190
  and resistance to change, 476, 478, 483
  in scientific management, 394
Index of Organizational Reactions (IOR), 45–46, 71
Informal communication, 288–290, 295
Informal groups, 300–301, 306, 327
Information function of communication, 276
Information power, 338–339, 341, 356
Initiating structure, 370–373, 375–377, 384
Inputs, in equity theory, 164–167
Instrumentality perceptions, 202, 204–205, 216, 333
Intellective abilities, 229–230, 236
Intended message, 274, 294
Intensity of stimuli, 246–247, 251, 263
Interaction
  group, 299–300
  optional/required, 398–399
Interdependence level, 351–353
Intermittent reinforcement schedule, 139, 141, 159
Internal attributions, 257–259
Internal locus of control, 222–223, 445, 474
Internal validity
  of case studies, 505
  concept of, 24–25, 27, 29, 440
  of cross-sectional studies, 514–516
  of experimental studies, 521–522, 531
  of longitudinal studies, 517
Interpersonal relations stressors, 430–431, 436, 445
Inter-rater reliability, 21–22, 29
Interrole conflict, 304, 327

Interviews
in cross-sectional studies, 514
in field surveys, 510–512
Intraperson conflict, 303, 327
Intrarole conflict, 304, 327
Intrinsic motivation, 79, 81–83
Intrinsic outcomes, 144–145, 152, 185, 191, 412
Introversion, 445
Involvement
job/work; *see* Job involvement *and* Work involvement
and resistance to change, 476–477, 483

J

Job analysis, 233–234
Job Descriptive Index (JDI), 44–46, 64, 512
Job design; *see also* Job redesign
cross-sectional study of, 516–517
current issues in, 405–410
defined, 391, 421
early theories of, 393–398
examples of, 391–393, 396, 398
integrative model of, 410–413
job characteristics approach to, 398–405, 421
simulation study of, 528–529
Job Diagnostic Survey, 401–402, 414
Job enlargement, 395–396, 398–399, 405, 414–415, 421
Job enrichment, 396–399, 405, 414–415, 421
Job Improvement Teams (JITs), 417–418
Job involvement, 47–50, 59
Job performance; *see* Performance
Job redesign, 377, 413–417
Job-related stressors, 432–433
Job satisfaction; *see also* Satisfaction
and absenteeism, 68–70, 81, 83–91, 92, 514–515
and behavior, 63–64
Job satisfaction—*Cont.*
defined, 40
facets of, 38–39
and job characteristics theory, 405
and job design, 391, 410, 412–413
and job enlargement, 395
and job redesign, 414–416, 418–419, 526–527
and leadership, 372, 375–376
measurement of, 21–23, 25–27, 42–47, 512–514
in motivation-hygiene theory, 117–123
overall, 41–42
and performance, 72–74, 92
and turnover, 64–69, 83–92
and union activity, 74–77, 92
Job scope, 410–413, 415 418–419
Job variety, 398–400, 409

L

Laboratory experiments, 522–527
Leader Match program, 369–370
Leadership
behavioral approaches to, 362, 370–380, 384
contingency theories of, 362, 364–370, 374–380, 384
defined, 361–362, 384
and job design, 405, 410–411
neutralizers of, 380–382
substitutes for, 380–382, 384
supplements to, 381–382
trait approaches to, 362–370, 384
universal theories of, 362–364, 370–374, 384
Leadership Group, 370
Learning
of affiliation needs, 116
of attitudes, 37–39
avoidance, 136, 145–146, 158
and groups, 304–305
speed of, and organizational behavior modification, 148
Learning theory; *see also* Classical conditioning; Operant conditioning; *and* Organizational behavior modification
approaches to, 129
and coercion, 479
integrated with expectancy theory, 212–213
Least-preferred co-worker (LPC) scale, 365–370
Legitimate power, 335–337, 339–341, 356
Locus of control, 222–223, 236, 445, 474, 495
Longitudinal studies, 517–519

M

Machiavellianism, 225–226, 236, 495
Management by objectives (MBO), 177, 192–193, 195
Managerial Grid®, 371, 373
Manifest need theories, 112–117, 124
Manipulation
organizational behavior modification as, 156
and resistance to change, 476, 478–479, 483
of variables, 519–520
Maslow's need hierarchy theory, 103–112, 124, 178
Maytag Co., and job enlargement, 395–396
Mechanical channels of communication, 285, 294
Mechanistic organizations, 407
Minnesota Satisfaction Questionnaire, 44, 46
Misunderstanding, and resistance to change, 471
Motivation; *see also* Needs
and ability, 227, 231, 235
attendance, 70–72, 410–412, 414–415
and equity theory, 167
and job design, 391, 393, 410–412, 414–415
and performance, 72–74, 410, 412, 414–415
Motivation-hygiene theory, 117–124, 397

Motivator factors, 117–124
Motives, and perception, 244, 263

N

Natural field experiments, 530–532
Needs; *see also* Motivation
  achievement, 113–117, 172, 186, 445–446
  affiliation and social interaction, 113–114, 116–117, 306–307
  ego and esteem, 105, 107, 109, 124, 307, 468
  existence, 110, 112, 124
  and group formation, 306–308
  growth, 107, 110, 112, 117
  physiological and survival, 105–107, 109–110, 124
  power, 113, 116–117, 307
  relatedness, 110, 112, 124
  safety and security, 105–107, 109–110, 124, 306, 445, 467–468
  self-actualization, 105, 107, 109–110, 124, 318
  as source of change, 467–468
  and stress, 433, 445–446
Needs theory
  Alderfer's ERG, 110–112
  concept of, 99, 103
  Herzberg's motivation-hygiene, 117–123
  integrated with expectancy theory, 212
  Maslow's, 103–112, 124
  Murray's content, 112–117
  value of outcomes in, 166
Negative reinforcement, 135–136, 144, 146, 158
Noise, and communication, 276
Nominal group technique, 325–326, 328
Nonparticipant case studies, 503–508
Nonreinforcement, 138, 158
Nonverbal communication, 287, 295
Norms, group, 308, 310–312, 316, 327
Novelty, and perception, 246–247, 263
Number of stimuli, 246, 263

O

O_o, 166–167, 195
O_p, 165–167, 195
One-way communication, 284–285, 294
Open groups, 302–303, 327
Operant conditioning
  basic model of, 132–133
  concept of, 99, 129, 132, 158
  and organizational behavior modification, 143–145
  reinforcement schedules in, 139–143
  strengthening stimulus-response relationship in, 133–138
  weakening stimulus-response relationship in, 138–139
Operant stimulus, response, and consequence, 133, 158
Optional interaction, 398–399
Ordinary group interaction, 323–324, 327
Organic organizations, 407
Organization
  as change source, 467–468
  design of, and job design, 405, 407–409, 411
  role in, as stressor, 430–431, 433
  statements and policies of, and unethical behavior, 493, 495
  structure/climate of, as stressor, 430–431, 434
  support by, 182–184, 412
Organization, perceptual, 241, 247–250, 261, 263, 275
Organizational behavior (OB)
  caution in using, 13–14
  concept of, 6–8
  role of theories and research in, 10–13
Organizational behavior modification (OBM)
  concept of, 129, 143–144
  and discipline systems, 155–156
  and ethical issues, 153–155
  exemplified, 146–152
  and locus of control, 223
  outcomes in, 144–146
Organization behavior modification (OBM)—*Cont.*
  recommendations for using, 153
Organizational involvement, 79, 83
Organizational surveys, 48
Orientation stage, 314–315
Outcomes
  in equity theory, 164–167
  in expectancy theory, 203–208, 210
  extrinsic, 145, 185, 191, 412
  intrinsic, 144–145, 152, 185, 191, 412
Over-reward, 167–169, 172–173

P

Parsimony, 12, 177
Participant case studies, 503, 508–509
Participation
  in goal setting, 188–189, 193
  as organization-related behavior, 50–51, 59
  and resistance to change, 476–479, 483
Path-goal theory, 374–377, 384
Pay
  and attitudes, 40, 41, 526–527
  as extrinsic outcome, 185
  and perceived equity, 166, 168, 173–176
  piece-rate, 173, 189–191, 434, 520
  and reward power, 333
Perceived equity; *see also* Equity theory
  concept of, 166–168, 195
  desire to alter, 170–172
  ways of altering, 168–170
Perception
  and communication, 274–276
  components of, 241–259
  concept of, 219, 241, 263
  expectancy, 202–204, 216
  instrumentality, 202, 204–205, 216, 333
  of job characteristics, 405–406, 410–411
  of power, 332–334, 342
  reducing errors in, 259–261

Perception—*Cont.*
and resistance to change, 471–472
of stress, 438
valence, 202, 206, 216
Perceptual defense, 251, 257, 263
Perceptual readiness, 251, 254–255, 263
Performance; *see also* Productivity
and abilities, 227, 235
and achievement need, 113
and affiliation need, 116
and attribution, 257–258
in expectancy theory, 203–208, 211–212
and goal setting, 178–186, 188–191, 524–525
and groups, 305, 310
and job design, 391, 393, 410, 412–413, 414–416, 418–419, 526–527
and job enlargement, 395–396
and leadership, 372, 376
and management by objectives, 192–193
as organization-related behavior, 50, 54–55, 59
and perceived equity, 167–168, 172–175
and personality, 225–227
and satisfaction, 72–74, 92
and scientific management, 394–395
and stress, 441–442
Personal characteristics
of leaders, 362–370, 384
and stress, 427, 443–446, 453
Personal experience
and attitude formation, 37–39
as knowledge source, 499–503
Personality
authoritarian, 223, 236, 312, 474
concept of, 219, 221–222, 236
dogmatic, 224, 236, 445, 474
and goal setting, 186
and group norm conformance, 312
and leadership, 370
locus of control in, 222–223, 236, 445, 474, 495
Personality—*Cont.*
Machiavellian, 224–225, 236, 495
and perception, 244, 251, 263
and resistance to change, 474
and stress, 433, 445
Type A/Type B, 225–227, 236, 445
and unethical behavior, 493–495
Personalized power seekers, 117
Physical abilities, 228, 230–231, 236
Physical condition, and stress, 443–444
Physical reactions to stress, 440–441
Physiological and survival needs, 105–107, 109–110, 124
Piece-rate pay, 173, 189–191, 434, 520
Placement, 233, 236
Planned field experiments, 527–530
Policies and Practices Guide, 80
Positive reinforcement, 135, 144, 146, 158
Power
acquisition of, 341–342
bases of, 332–339
and coalitions, 342
defined, 331–332, 356
and ethics, 342–343
need for, 113, 116–117, 307
organizational control over, 339–341
Pressure to attend, 71–72
Primacy, 251, 255–256, 263
Primary reinforcers, 136
Proactive behavior, 348
Proactive change, 413, 465, 467–468, 487
Process theories, 99–100
Productivity; *see also* Performance
and absenteeism, 51–53, 56
as organization-related behavior, 50, 55–56, 59
and scientific management, 395
Project groups, 301, 327
Projection, 251, 254–255, 263
Proximity in space/time, 248, 263
Psychological condition, and stress, 443–444
Psychological health reactions to stress, 438–439
Punishment
and learning theory, 135, 138–139, 144, 146, 153–154, 159
and unethical behavior, 493–495

Q

Quasi-experimental studies, 522, 527, 529, 531
Questionnaires
in cross-sectional studies, 514
in field studies, 510–514
job satisfaction, 42–46, 81–82
in longitudinal studies, 519

R

Random assignment, 522, 527
Rational decision-making theory, 374, 377–380, 384
Reactive behavior, 348
Reactive change, 413, 465, 467–468, 487
Reality testing, 261, 263
Recency, 251, 256, 263
Referent power, 337–338, 341, 356
Refreezing, 416, 481, 485
Regression, group, 319
Regression analysis, 83–89
Reinforcement
defined, 135
positive/negative, 135–136, 144, 146, 158
schedules of, 139–143
Reinforcement theories, 99–100
Reinforcers
defined, 133–135, 158
primary/secondary, 136
Relatedness needs, 110, 112, 124
Relationship-oriented leadership, 365–370, 384

Reliability; *see also* Alternate forms agreement reliability; Inter-rater reliability; *and* Test-retest reliability
of case studies, 505
concept of, 19, 28–29, 499
of cross-sectional studies, 515–516
forms of, 19–24
of job satisfaction measures, 43, 45
of longitudinal studies, 517–518
of surveys, 511–512
and validity, relationship between, 28
Required interaction, 398–399
Required job duties, 410–411
Research, and organizational behavior, 10–13
Response
conditioned/unconditioned, 130–132, 158
extinction of, 138–139, 140–143, 158
operant, 133, 158
Responsibility
ethical, 491–493, 495
and job design, 398–399, 402
Restraining forces, 480
Retention, 51, 53, 59; *see also* Turnover
Reward power, 332–334, 336–337, 339, 341, 356
Reward systems
and group cohesiveness, 308
and power, 340–341
Rewards for unethical behavior, 493–495
Role, defined, 303, 327
Role ambiguity, 303, 327, 433, 448
Role conflict, 433
Role overload, 449
Role set, 303, 327

S

Safety programs, 148, 156
Safety and security needs
concept of, 105–107, 109–110, 124
and group membership, 306
Safety and security needs—*Cont.*
and organizational change, 467–468
and stress, 445
Satisfaction; *see also* Job satisfaction
and coercion, 479
and goal setting, 185–186, 188–189, 191
group, 309
pay, 175–176
Satisfaction progress, 110
Scattergram, 85
Scientific management, 393–395, 421
Secondary reinforcers, 136
Security needs; *see* safety and security needs
Selection
as component of perception, 241, 243–247, 259–261, 263, 275
personnel, 233–234, 236, 255
Self-acceptance, 259, 263
Self-actualization, 105, 107, 109–110, 124, 318
Self-concept
and perceptual changes, 170
and work/job involvement, 49–50
Self-esteem
and goal setting, 186
as need, 105, 107, 109, 124
and stress, 438–439, 444
Self-fulfilling prophecy, 255
Self-understanding, 259, 263
Sensation, 241, 243, 263, 275
Similarity, and perception, 248, 263
Simulation experiments, 525–527
Situational favorableness, 365–367, 384
Skills; *see also* Ability
and job design, 398–399, 402
and resistance to change, 474, 477
and stress reactions, 443–444
Skinner Box, 133, 135–139 passim
Social environment, as force to change, 468–469
Social learning, 37–39, 144, 253
Social needs
and needs theory, 105, 107, 109–110, 116, 124
as source of change, 468
and stress, 445
Socialized power seekers, 117
Spontaneous recovery, 139
Star, in communication, 278
Statistical aggregation, 324–326, 328
Status, need for, 307
Stereotypes, 251–253, 257, 259, 263
Stimulus
conditioned/unconditioned, 130–132, 158
discrimination, 136–137
generalization, 136–137, 156
operant, 133, 158
Stress
changes due to, 446
concept of, 427–430, 453
management of, 428, 448–452
perception of, 438
and personal characteristics, 427, 443–446, 453
Stress reactions
affective, 438
behavioral, 441–442
concept of, 427–430, 437–438, 453
physical, 440–441
psychological health, 438–439
treating, 449–450
and Type A/Type B personality, 227, 445
Stressors
career, 430–431, 434
changes in, 446, 448–449
concept of, 427, 429–431, 453
extraorganizational, 430–431, 437
interpersonal relations, 430–431, 436, 445
job-related, 432–433
organization role, 430–431, 433
organization structure/climate, 430–431, 434
Supervision, compared with leadership, 362
Support
organizational, 182–184, 412

Support—*Cont.*
  and resistance to change, 476–477, 483
Surveys, 509–514
Survival needs, 105–107, 109

T

Tardiness, 51, 59, 317, 441
Task identity, 399–400, 402, 409
Task significance, 402, 409
Technology
  as force to change, 467, 531–532
  and job design, 405, 409, 411
Telemarketing, 474
Termination, 53
Test-retest reliability, 21–23, 29
Theories, in organizational behavior, 10–13
Time and motion studies, 188, 393
Timeliness, 51, 59
Training, 233–234, 236
Translation, 241, 250–259, 261, 263, 275
Trust, lack of, 471–473
Turnover
  data on, 53
  defined, 51, 53
  and pay system, 521
  and perceived equity, 173
  and productivity, 56
  and satisfaction, 64–69, 83–92
  and stress, 441
Turnover—*Cont.*
  and worker control, 518–519
Two-way communication, 284–286, 294
Type A/Type B personality, 226–228, 236, 445

U

Unconditioned stimulus/response, 130–132, 158
Under-reward, 167–169, 173
Unfreezing, 416, 480, 484
Unions
  activity of, and job satisfaction, 74–77, 92
  as coalitions, 342
  and safety needs, 306, 467–468
United General Insurance Co., and Job design, 392–393, 395, 417–419
Universal leadership theories, 362–364, 370–374, 384
Upward communication, 278–279, 283, 294

V

Valence perceptions, 202, 206, 216
Validity; *see also* Construct validity; External validity; *and* Internal validity
Validity—*Cont.*
  concept of, 24, 29
  of cross-sectional studies, 515–516
  forms of, 24–28
  of job satisfaction measures, 43, 45
  of longitudinal studies, 517–518
  and reliability, relationship between, 28
  of surveys, 511–512
Values
  as source of change, 467–468
  and task attributes, 399
Variable-interval reinforcement schedule, 142, 159
Variable-ratio reinforcement schedule, 141–142, 149, 152, 159
Variables
  control of, 520
  manipulation of, 519–520
Variety, 398–400, 409
Vertical groups, 301–302, 327
Vertical job loading, 396–397
Vroom and Yetton model, 374, 377–380, 384

W

Wheel of communication, 278
Work involvement, 47–50, 59
Work pace, 398

This book has been set Linotron 202 in 10 and 9 point Aster leaded 2 points. Part titles are 24 point Helvetica, and part numbers are 24 point Helvetica Medium. Chapter titles are 18 point Helvetica. The size of the type page is 31 by 48 picas.